Effective Police Supervision

Effective Police Supervision

Seventh Edition

Harry W. More PhD,
Professor Emeritus
San Jose State University

Larry S. Miller PhD,
Professor
East Tennessee State University

AMSTERDAM • BOSTON • HEIDELBERG • LONDON • NEW YORK
OXFORD • PARIS • SAN DIEGO • SAN FRANCISCO
SINGAPORE • SYDNEY • TOKYO

Anderson Publishing is an imprint of Elsevier

Acquiring Editor: *Shirley Decker-Lucke*
Development Editor: *Ellen S. Boyne*
Project Manager: *Julia Haynes*
Designer: *Tin Box Studio, Inc.*

Anderson Publishing is an imprint of Elsevier
225 Wyman Street, Waltham, MA 02451, USA

Seventh Edition: 2015
Sixth Edition: 2011
Fifth Edition: 2007

Library of Congress Cataloging-in-Publication Data
A catalog record for this book is available from the Library of Congress

British Library Cataloguing-in-Publication Data
A catalogue record for this book is available from the British Library

ISBN: 978-1-4557-7760-0

For information on all Anderson publications
visit our website at http://store.elsevier.com

Typeset by MPS Limited, Chennai, India
www.adi-mps.com

Printed in the United States of America

15 16 17 18 19   10 9 8 7 6 5 4 3 2 1

www.elsevier.com • www.bookaid.org

Working together
to grow libraries in
developing countries

Contents

Online Resources

Thank you for selecting Anderson Publishing's *Effective Police Supervision*, 7th edition. To complement the learning experience, we have provided online tools to accompany this edition.

Please consult your local sales representative with any additional questions. You may also e-mail the Academic Sales Team at textbook@elsevier.com.

Qualified adopters and instructors can access valuable material for free by registering at: http://textbooks.elsevier.com/web/manuals.aspx?isbn=9781455777600

Students and other readers can access additional resources at: http://booksite.elsevier.com/9781455777600

Preface

When a police organization is identified as successful, it is because management/supervision is exceptional. Managerial experts acknowledge that the fulcrum of managerial effectiveness is at the level of the first-line supervisor. The best law enforcement agencies view the supervisor as an integral part of the managerial process.

In the preeminent police departments, the position of sergeant has merged into management slowly but surely and it is anticipated that this trend will continue. The early assumption that the sergeant was really an extension of line personnel has been soundly rejected. The outstanding law enforcement agency is one in which the first-line supervisor performs essential managerial activities.

When supervisors are engaged in activities that are best described as knowledge, human, conceptual, tactical, and affective based, they are applying skills that can only be described as integral parts of the management process. While it is acknowledged that supervisors apply the skills differently from police managers of higher rank, the fact remains that effective police organization integrates supervisors into the management team.

Police supervisors must develop behavioral and social skills in order to deal effectively with a rapidly changing society. Diversity is becoming an integral term in the police lexicon and offers a new challenge for the first-line supervisor. When police executives integrate the position of supervisor into the managerial process, the organization can improve both its internal and its external adaptive capabilities.

The primary aim of this text has been to help current or potential supervisors understand the differing beliefs and assumptions they hold about themselves, other officers, the organization, and society at large. The result is that the focus is on accountability and effectiveness as well as proficiency, and on how a supervisor can participate in the creation of a dynamic organization.

Each chapter has been updated to reflect current research and knowledge in areas that supervisors must understand if they are to make a significant contribution to the law enforcement agency and function as positive supervisors. This text addresses the supervisory process in community policing, which is a unique undertaking, and the extent and degree to which this becomes a realistic part of the American policing system is occurring at a rapid pace.

Effective community policing demands significant change in an organization; in particular, the operating style of each supervisor must change radically. Risk taking, originality, creativity, and problem solving must become part of the optimal operating style.

This text combines state-of-the-art behavioral theory with numerous cases that allow the reader to identify and resolve personal and organizational problems. Each chapter contains a case that translates theory into practice. The cases serve as a basis for classroom discussion and bring reality into the learning process. Additionally, they provide the reader with a means of interpreting the behavioral theory discussed in each chapter. Tables and figures augment and strengthen important elements presented in each chapter. As a means of facilitating learning, each chapter contains an extensive list of references.

The design of the text is such that it is user-friendly, pragmatic, realistic, and, at the same time, transcends the difficult problem that many texts in this area have of describing current behavioral theory and demonstrating how it relates to an operating entity. The primary goal of this text has been to address vital topics of interest to every manager by questioning the traditional means of supervision.

Effective Police Supervision has become a vital tool in the preparation of officers for promotion and is on the recommended reading list of numerous police departments. Users of the last edition have provided important feedback, and numerous suggestions have been incorporated into the current edition.

Harry W. More, PhD
Larry S. Miller, PhD

1

Supervision
The Management Task

CASE STUDY

Sergeant Willa Dawson

DEPARTMENT

The city manager has been appointed recently and is still becoming acquainted with the city council, department heads, business leaders, union officials, residents, and interest groups. The former chief, Ralph Turner, retired after 18 years at the helm of the department, and during his tenure he has taken a **laissez-faire** approach to management. He took the position that many of the things used in other departments were faddish and would pass. The new chief, Ralph Kruger, had previously worked in a department, where he attained the rank of assistant chief, that had successfully implemented community policing and was in the process of evaluating information-led policing, one of the latest police innovations. Kruger has only been in office for six months and he moved slowly because he anticipated resistance to any change that altered the status quo. He privately expressed the opinion that many of the older patrol officers felt that change was not needed and they should continue to do what they had always done. There are 158 sworn personnel who are full time and 16 auxiliary officers. Seven percent of the officers are female, 3 percent of the officers are African-American, and 26 percent are Hispanic. There are three major divisions—investigations, patrol, and administrative services. The patrol division has the majority of the sworn officers in the department. Officers conduct the preliminary investigation, and the investigative division conducts follow-up investigations.

The organization is traditional in nature, and very few of the officers will be eligible to retire in the foreseeable future. Officers, upon graduation from the academy, are assigned to either the swing shift or the midnight shift, and transfers are based upon seniority. There is a police union within the department, but they have taken few stands on important issues of concern to the line officers or the department.

CRIME

During the last year the crime index for the city exceeded that of cities of comparable population. There were 13 murders that were mostly gang-related occurrences. There were 37 forcible rapes, 211 robberies, 345 aggravated assaults, 622 burglaries, 1678 larceny/thefts, and 571 auto thefts. Overall crime has trended down slightly for the last three years, with the exception of gang homicides, which continue to plague the community. In arrests of burglary suspects, two-thirds of them were found to be non-residents. The vast majority of the burglaries are committed in areas readily accessible from thoroughfares, and the majority of such offenses are residential rather than commercial in nature. Many residents are indifferent about protecting their property because they are reasonably well insured. In numerous instances perpetrators enter residences through unlocked doors and windows. About one-quarter of the residents commute to a metropolitan city about 48 miles to the west, and many of the residents feel that they live in a safe area of the city and do not view gang activity as a real problem. Very few of the homes have a security system, and there are only three neighborhood watch programs in the city.

COMMUNITY

The Sierra Police Department serves a community that has a population of 136,665 and is located in a county in the eastern part of the state. There are 78,241 residents in the county area surrounding the community, and the city of Sierra is the county seat. The sheriff's office in the county has 228 sworn personnel. Most of them work in the jail or for the court system and 43 officers are assigned to field operations. The city has a high concentration of small businesses, although there seems to be a trend toward the creation of numerous strip malls. There is little vacant land for expansion, and property taxes are lower than those found in the nearby metropolitan city. Sierra has a cultural/entertainment center for the area that attracts many families to sponsored events. It has long been a bedroom community for those who commute to major nearby cities. A major north/south highway which is adjacent to the city provides easy access to other areas. Its population is 43 percent Caucasian, 31 percent Hispanic, 23 percent African-American, 15.6 percent Asian, 0.5 percent American Indian, and 0.2 percent of the members of the community are Native Hawaiian or other Pacific Islanders. Additionally, more and more residents are describing themselves as belonging to two or more races. The community has a city manager and an elected city council. It is a weak mayor system and council members are elected at large. The city has considerable transportation that includes a bus service and a major airport 54 miles west of the city.

OFFICER

Sergeant Willa Dawson is 29, married, and lives in the county south of the city. She has been married to Harry for five years and they have one child. She and her husband have an understanding that the best arrangement is to have two children. She completed a four-year degree in sociology and she minored in Spanish. She has returned to school, and has successfully finished 12 units toward a master's degree in management that is totally conducted online. The demands placed upon her by the job have limited her ability to attend regularly scheduled classes on campus.

After serving in the patrol division for five years on the midnight shift, Dawson took the sergeant's examination for the first time. There was no doubt in her mind that she would easily pass the examination. After completing the assessment center that was part of the promotional process, she thought that she had done an exceptional job. On the written examination, she came out first. Her total score for the examination process resulted in her being placed number one on the promotion list. She was so elated that she and her husband took a week's vacation and toured the Grand Canyon and other national parks.

Upon receiving her coveted stripes she was assigned to the day shift where she supervises four veteran officers. With guidance from her lieutenant and the departmental records, she interviewed the potential 12 candidates. She selected four out of the 12 officers that were approved by the chain of command. Two of the officers were from patrol and the other two were veteran detectives from the burglary and auto details. This special team was given three months to arrive at a recommendation for problem resolution. She explained the situation and the mandate she had received from the chief, and at the initial team meeting the ground rules were established in order to meet the deadline. In this new assignment she has been directed to address the burglary and automobile theft problems in high-frequency areas. She has been given free rein to deal with the problem, and departmental executives want her to utilize the research and statistical skills she has learned in her college classes. As the first woman to attain the rank of sergeant in the department, she anticipated that she could receive some resistance from line officers, especially with reference to any potential recommendation(s). She was happy to find that the selected officers were ready and willing to work within a positive problem-solving frame of reference to deal with the problem and utilize all available departmental resources. The planning unit was preparing documents that could be utilized by the team.

PROBLEM

Sergeant Dawson received the assignment from the new chief of police with the understanding that it was a temporary detail and that she would in all probability return to the field as a first-line supervisor. It was to be a test unit to see if interested community members and selected officers could address the problem. This was the first time such a team had been directed to deal with the burglary and auto theft problems. Sergeant Dawson, with the assistance of the team, created a research design for dealing with the charge.

Officers working with Sergeant Dawson attended a special three-day research class given by the local college and a planning unit civilian was assigned to the team as a resource person. Each member of the team had a minimum of two years' college education, and everyone had completed a problem-solving seminar.

WHAT WOULD YOU DO?

If you were Sergeant Dawson, what would be the first thing you would do after the initial planning meeting when you got together with your team? Why? What information would you want from the resource person? Why? What information would you want from other city departments? How would you integrate the investigators into the team? Why? Would you utilize human skills when addressing the problem? Explain. How important are conceptual skills in this situation? Explain. How would you use tactical skills?

The changeable nature of our police agencies demands a viable and doable response to the dynamism of public and managerial transformation. In a law enforcement organization, the first-line supervisor is the crucial managerial point where policy is transmitted into action. All levels of police administration from the top down must acknowledge the challenge of making the first-line supervisory position a key managerial part of the agency. Crime, disorder, and the desire of members of the community to reside in neighborhoods that truly represent the best aspects of our democratic society call for an enduring mandate to serve the public and enhance the quality of life. This requires accepting the dynamics of continuing and constant change and developing an organizational capability to take action that fulfills the mandate of every professional law enforcement agency. The position of first-line supervisor must evolve into a position where decisions are made in the best interests of the organization and community members through the attainment of goals and objectives. Supervisors must be given the training and skills needed to create a working milieu that energizes each member and that allows for a multi-skilled response. A common denominator present in police departments that do extremely well, throughout our nation, is the creation of a work environment that fosters the development of good supervisors. In exemplary agencies, the first-line supervisor is not apart from but is a viable component of management, and is directly responsible for augmenting the positive attributes of working life. Human resources are at a premium in every part of a police organization and the task of a supervisor is to assist employees to become productive members of the organization. It is a truism that an effectively performing supervisor makes things happen through the efforts of those supervised. Moreover, departmental and personal goals become achievable through the interaction between an emphatic supervisor and subordinates. As a result, the community is better served and officers find themselves working in a viable organization that emphasizes the enhancement of the working quality of life. An agency committed to excellence is one that challenges each member of the organization to grow daily and contribute to the realization of departmental objectives/goals.

Police work is without question an intricate undertaking. Current demands and the consequences of responding to them in new and innovative ways intensify the critical role played by the police in American society. It involves the use of an enormous amount of discretion and the use of criminal and civil law and the needs of citizens to sort out a myriad of problems. Today's police supervisor deals with problems and challenges totally unheard of several years ago and it is anticipated that the complexity of enforcement will occur at a rapid pace. This is evident in the fact that law enforcement in recent years has used the concepts and processes of intelligence-led policing and predictive policing in their efforts to improve the quality of life in communities and facilitate crime reduction, disruption, and prevention (Ratcliffe, 2008; National Institute of Justice, 2012).

External forces have a strong influence on every aspect of a contemporary police agency. The rapid proliferation of computer systems, telecommunications networks, and other related technologies presents concomitant widespread vulnerabilities compelling law enforcement to respond with highly trained and qualified officers (Stambaugh et al., 2000). The new millennium requires police personnel to be better prepared than ever before. Line officers and first-line supervisors of the future must be primed to confront and deal with a variety of diverse issues. For example, officers are increasingly expressing a desire to become more involved in the decision-making process and the creation of operational procedures. At the same time some recruits into the police service have a lesser degree of commitment, and set goals for themselves that in some instances transcend their commitment to the organization, but with appropriate supervision this can be changed.

Additionally, police departments have become increasingly urbane, and more reflective of the ethnic composition of the community. Diversity is apparent when one realizes that three states and the nation's capital have seen non-whites gain majority status. This is illustrated by the state of California where white non-Hispanics make up 43 percent of the population (Bureau of the Census, 2007). The United States population is one-third non-white and those groups accounted for 83 percent of national population growth from 2000 to 2008. Now nearly one-quarter of American children have at least one immigrant parent (Frey, 2010). Demography has become increasingly significant as new minorities alter almost every aspect of our life, ranging from geographical regions to exurbs (Frey, 2008). This diversity plays an increasingly important part, not only in enforcement activities but in the internal aspects of a department in terms of recruitment, selection, and operational implementation. It also involves the need for supervisors to respond to officers who retain vestiges of another culture with differing values and norms as they become members of the department. Population distribution and change during a 10-year period are of special interest, as the 10 most populous states contain 54 percent of the United States population, with one-quarter of the United States population living in three states: California, Texas, and New York (Mackun & Wilson, 2011).

There are also intensifying demands for police services, along with the public's dissatisfaction with police service, especially with the use of deadly force, and, more recently, the police use of racial profiling. Race and policing continue to be a lightning rod, and bias-free policing is a goal for which everyone is striving. Currently, officers are prohibited from discriminating on the basis of race, ethnicity, national origin, religion, gender, disability, or sexual orientation (Jerome, 2006). Racial profiling has become the object of increasing concern and civil rights activists have urged the collection of data on subjects stopped for traffic infractions. Almost every state has taken some steps to address the problem of racial profiling and it has become a political issue with extensive legislation introduced in the halls of Congress.

In the past a large number of local law enforcement agencies did not have a written policy regarding the progressive use of force, but this has changed dramatically as the police have responded to public and political pressure. Today, nearly all larger law enforcement agencies have a written policy pertaining to the use of deadly force (Reaves & Hickman, 2004). It is anticipated that these policies will become more conditional over the years and the search will go on to find less than lethal alternatives. Policies should focus on prevention and ensure that the use of force is used only to protect the officer and the public (Webb, 2011). Other less-lethal weapons have become increasingly popular, and more than 15,000 law enforcement and military agencies have adopted Tasers—conducted energy devices (CEDs)—and the use of pepper spray has provided a way to reduce injuries (Alpert et al., 2011).

The selection base for potential law enforcement officers has narrowed as more and more individuals have experimented with or in the past were part of the drug culture. Screening of applicants for past and current drug use has become the norm. This includes a consideration of such things as the time that has elapsed since drug use and the exact nature of the involvement. Assuming a candidate has been hired, a police supervisor must respond to the use of drugs by officers after they are on the job. In one department approximately one-quarter of all suspensions and dismissals of police officers were for drug use. Consequently, a supervisor must be alert to signs of drug use on the part of police personnel and under no circumstances should it be tolerated.

Many police tasks, in many instances, must be performed in a very violent environment where increasing numbers of officers have been injured on the job. Hostages are being taken more frequently, altering the way officers respond to this type of conflict. Barricaded suspects are becoming increasingly common, and many departments utilize SWAT teams to make arrests and serve search warrants. Gangs have become a major problem in many cities and are starting to emerge in rural communities. Overall violent crimes are too prevalent throughout the nation. This is especially true for child and spousal abuse, and it remains a perennial law enforcement problem in many communities. Even though the homicide rate has declined over the last three decades it has risen in the last reported statistical year. For years violent crime has represented an intolerable level in terms of the loss of human life and injuries sustained during a criminal offense, whether we like it not in our civilized society—in the eyes of some life has become cheap. One cannot ignore the fact that violence is a fundamental component of our culture, but an alert supervisor should work diligently at ensuring that it does not dominate an officer's perspective. Cynicism can be a by-product of enforcement activities and is something that should be anticipated and not allowed to spread like a virus (Henchey, 2005).

Civil disturbance can also be a factor, as indicated by the May Day melee that took place in 2007 in MacArthur Park, in which the Los Angeles Police Department allegedly used excessive force during an immigration gathering and march. Batons and rubber bullets were used to disperse the gathering, and the police action was recorded by photographers and television crews in the park. The incident received considerable media attention throughout the nation. Two years later, Los Angeles City Council approved a settlement that resulted in a $12.85 million payment and the police department submitted to court oversight (Reston & Rubin, 2009).

A first-line manager must communicate constantly with each officer supervised by allaying rumors, interpreting policy, coaching, mentoring, or utilizing persuasion when the situation dictates. A viable supervisor must work closely with each officer to ensure that they are aware of departmental policy involving personal conduct and ensure their adherence to that policy. Ethical behavior must be the standard that governs every public contact. All employees must know what is expected of them, and they must be held accountable for their actions (Martin & Matthews, 2000). Continuing contact with people who have criminal inclinations makes it essential that each supervisor cultivate a working environment that acknowledges and reinforces the fact that the vast majority of the members of our society are law abiding—not "gutter punks" or "scumbags."

In other instances, the failure to train officers can lead to civil liability. Like it or not a first-line supervisor is a trainer, a mentor, a guide, and the one in the best position to identify individual weaknesses and needs. Supervisors should be ever watchful and strive to identify areas of weakness where training can be improved and where closer control is essential. It is a never-ending process and calls for initiative, imagination, and resourcefulness. In most instances, the first-line supervisors are the initial ones to observe training inadequacies and top management should recognize them as a vital resource.

Our culture presents new challenges to the first-line supervisor, and it seems reasonable to assume that problems will not only increase in number, but that they will become more diverse. This means, then, that the supervisor must respond to these critical issues as they arise, and address them with a great deal of imagination and innovation, as well as anticipating problems. The supervisor is at the organizational focal point between officers and other managerial levels and supervisorial duties must be performed with absolute confidence and situational adaptation. If the police organization is to become more effective, the first-line supervisor must play a major role in responding to change that affects the organization. Isolation must be rejected and organizational rigidity must be refuted. Supervisors are the most transparent in the organization and have greater contact with the public than any other police managerial position.

If supervisors are successful in the performance of their duties, it follows that the organization will become more effective and the potentiality of attaining goals will be enhanced. Good supervision does not just happen: it has to be cultivated. Until recently, newly appointed supervisors were left to fend for themselves, but supervisory training courses are becoming more prevalent and an essential component of career development. In some states, improved performance has resulted because each newly appointed supervisor must complete a training program within a specified period after being promoted. Supervisory performance can be improved by establishing a mentoring relationship with others in the organization, conducting online research on leadership skills and other related topics, reading supervisory periodicals, taking courses at local colleges, and consulting with other supervisors. This is a long way from the time when newly promoted individuals had to fend for themselves. "Sink or swim" used to be the cliché of the day.

In the future, the new supervisor will have to work in a viable and dynamic police organization that is ever changing and is constantly creating new demands on everyone in the organization. The new supervisor will have to be more accommodating and open to change. Figure 1.1 sets forth an array of attributes that describe a viable police organization of the future.

Transformation

The conversion from a line position to first-line supervisor brings numerous rewards, but it also exacts a price. These factors are set forth in Figure 1.2. However, in addition to an increase in pay, the supervisory position is marked by prestige both within and outside the department, as well as the recognition that one has attained a supervisory rank, a new title, and added responsibilities. Administratively, the supervisor usually heads a given unit or operation, is more involved in the decision-making process, and at the same time becomes a part of management. If there is any issue that causes a new supervisor a great deal of difficulty, it usually

Organizational Attributes that are

Viable and

Dynamic

- Accountability applies to every level of the organization
- Acerbity of the police culture is the antithesis of modern law enforcment
- A proactive response to police problems is clearly the most acceptable standard operating procedure
- Moral and constitutional values need to control every aspect of officer comportment
- Organizational leaders have positive character and presence
- Organizational rigidity impedes change and must be dealt with accordingly
- Acts of corruption and officer misconduct are rejected
- Crime fighting is viewed as only one of several priorities
- Development of guidelines and their evaluation must occur continually
- Discretion is recognized and accepted as an inevitable component of police work
- Effective officers will typically make many decisions outside the purview of supervisors
- Empowerment is a viable managerial component
- Every effort is made to integrate every member into the organization
- Improving the quality of the working environment is an organizational mandate
- Integrity and ethical conduct must circumscribe officer behavior
- Supervisors are an integral part of the management team
- Recruitment and retention practices need to emphasize a search for quality
- Moral and constitutional values need to control every aspect of officer behavior
- Locus of decision-making varies but is concentrated at the lowest level
- Leader achieves by utilizing every component area as needed

FIGURE 1.1 Attributes of a viable and dynamic organization—a place where officers want to work.

is learning how to be an effective disciplinarian, especially when having to discipline a former fellow line officer. Does one maintain social relationships built up over the years or does one discontinue this type of interaction? There is not an easy answer to these dilemmas and each situation must govern the dictated reaction.

Further adaptation may be required as the new supervisor finds it necessary to attain objectives through the efforts of subordinates, while being held responsible for their success or failure. Accountability is fast becoming the byword of the day. The transition from being responsible primarily for oneself to slowly becoming a more integral part of administration requires a greater degree of commitment to the managerial process and furthering the success of the organization. This is an especially difficult transformation requiring the balancing of goal attainment and the development of personnel. It is normally not acceptable to take the time-honored position that "I would rather do it myself."

The conversion to the position of first-line supervisor may be fraught with difficulty, depending on the individual, but most agree it presents a challenge and demands the ability to accept and adapt to change. Historically, police executives have taken the position that prospective supervisors would intuitively know how to manage people, but such is usually not the case. A new supervisor may be placed in a situation that demands an expertise that has not been acquired from experience or training and if either of these conditions have not been fulfilled the new supervisor becomes a member of the "sink-or-swim" school of management (Frazier & Reintzell, 1997). In some instances, old ways and habits have to be overcome if one is to succeed in a new position. Traditional coping mechanisms can prove to be ineffective as one begins to work in new territory. It might be that a feeling of helplessness arises and if that happens one should seek out counsel from other supervisors, a mentor, or other managers. Above all a new supervisor should realize that it takes time to learn how to cope with new challenges. A new supervisor should realize the importance of immediately acknowledging the importance of the ecology of the organization and the fact that the department is a dynamic social system.

Officers have personal needs and objectives that the supervisor should help to fulfill while simultaneously ensuring they do not conflict with the attainment of organizational objectives. Interaction with employees is what most first-line supervisors deal with in the workplace. The greater the supervisor's knowledge in this area, the greater the likelihood that both individual and organizational goals will be attained. Based on their experience of conflict between

---

Advantages:
1. Additional training.
2. Broader perspective of the department's overall operation.
3. Commitment to success.
4. Develop rapport with peers, managers/subordinates.
5. Different assignments.
6. Feeling of accomplishment.
7. Gained reputation within and outside the department.
8. Greater chance of providing input into the decision-making process.
9. Increase in pay.
10. Interpreter of policy.
11. More control over the type of police service provided to the community.
12. Obligation to be more integrative.
13. Opportunity to be in charge of an operation.
14. Opportunity to influence and develop personnel.
15. Part of management.
16. Prestige of rank.
17. Required to foster innovation.
18. Step up in the organization.
19. Training/mentoring of personnel.
20. Work constructively under stress.

FIGURE 1.2 Transformation from a line officer to first-line supervisor.

Disadvantages:
1. Accountable for work (or lack thereof) performed by subordinates.
2. Acting like a boss rather than a close friend.
3. At the bottom of the seniority level in shift and work assignments.
4. Difficult or impossible to return to former position if being a supervisor is unwanted.
5. Increasingly vulnerable to criticism.
6. Less freedom of action.
7. Lesser commitment to the police union (in some instances).
8. Must function as a disciplinarian.
9. Must have a greater degree of commitment to management.
10. Must implement policy not personally supported.
11. Must make decisions every day.
12. Must make decisions that can have an adverse impact on subordinates' careers.
13. No longer just "one of the boys."
14. Objectives must be achieved through others.
15. One step removed from line operations.
16. Positioned in the middle, between the line and top management.
17. Risk taking is part of the game.
18. The need to be effective rather than trying to be liked.
19. The need to work through conflict.
20. Work in isolation part of the time.

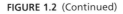

FIGURE 1.2 (Continued)

officers they will be able to notice such situations faster and intervene sooner. Being aware of the rewards that their former supervisor could have given them will make them more sensitive to officers' needs for recognition. On the other hand, the transition will prove to be difficult if they do not accept the responsibility of correcting and/or disciplining officers when warranted.

A supervisor soon becomes aware of the need to develop a range of skills if officers are to be highly productive and achieve the goals and objectives of the department. One study pointed out that in eight departments supervisors made important contributions to the capacity of an organization to achieve its goals through specific activities (Mastrofski et al., 2011). Good supervision is the result of the serious application of one's knowledge about human behavior to the work situation. In fact, the good supervisor develops the ability to obtain results through others. This means that a supervisor must learn to value people as organizational assets.

The Need for Accountability Management

Police executives have been conscious of the essentiality of accountability, but its application throughout a department has been a missing managerial element in many communities. While not a new concept, police managers are just starting to realize that it is a viable concept and must be incorporated into the law enforcement lexicon. Public safety budgets for many years have been sacrosanct in many communities, and as resources become increasingly short some in the public sphere have begun to question whether or not public agencies are in actuality well managed. For many years law enforcement has, along with fire departments, been almost exempt from budgetary pruning, but that is no longer a maxim. Reductions in force are becoming quite common and programs have shrunk and positions been eliminated. There is a feeling on the part of some that various government operations are accountable only to themselves. True or not this growing conviction is becoming more vocal as budgetary decision makers have been forced to moderate budgets. This is a realism that has been with us for some years and it is anticipated that it will not abate in the years ahead. Managing with a reduced funding amount is fast becoming an actuality. Hence, focusing on results is becoming increasingly demanded. Programs have to show that they are viable and worthy of budgetary support. Historically, police chief executives have been held accountable especially from the political sphere and the average tenure as the "top cop" has seldom proven to be excessive. "Achieve or out" has been the axiom and many of these positions have been filled with advocates who have performed as situational rectors and proponents of the status quo. Under such circumstances accountability has seen little application and its obligatory aspects have been ignored and permeated every level of a department to include first-line supervisor. This approach was aptly described by W. Artley as an operational attitude of "out of sight out of mind" (Artley, 2001).

Accountability becomes a viable concept when performance expectations are planned, defined, and negotiated between concerned parties. Performance is evaluated and adjustment implemented as needed and the responsible individuals are party to the total decision-making process. This is best done when emphasis is placed on performance improvement, not having to explain a lack of it (Artley, 2001). Throughout a positive managerial process responsibilities must be acknowledged and obligations assumed and it is necessary to accept the fact that there is a liability involved in such a working relationship. It is generally known that there can be both negative and positive sanctions involved in this joint process. For this reason accountability occurs because consequences are involved in the working relationships and this should be spelled out from the "get-go."

As accountability is applied throughout a police agency, and if it is mandated and eventually succeeds, it will move law enforcement to a higher and more rewarding operational entity. A caveat is that it remains to be seen if higher organizational levels will give up the power needed to ensure its viability at the operational level.

Accountability is viewed by some as a multidimensional concept and has become increasingly accepted by supervisors and managers. Experts have wrestled with this concept in an effort to make others aware of the concept of accountability. At times, the term responsibility comes into play when considering the term accountability, and for the most part some view these terms as synonymous. On the other hand, others make a distinction between the two terms and suggest that "responsibility" is the obligation to perform and "accountability" is the liability one assumes for ensuring that an obligation to perform (a responsibility) is fulfilled.

Definition of Accountability

Accountability refers to the obligation a person, group, or organization assumes for the execution of authority and/or fulfillment of responsibility (Artley, 2001). This obligation includes several features:

- Answering—providing an explanation or justification—for the execution of that authority and/or fulfillment of responsibility,
- Reporting on the results of execution and/or fulfillment, and
- Assuming liability for those results.

An effective organization is one where the above definition is taken to heart and circumscribes organization behavior. When fully accepted the definition is all-encompassing and it relates to personal as well as managerial accountability. Accountability is meaningless unless organizational members are liable for results. If there is a central element to this working definition it is the essentiality of assumption of "liability." As accountability permeates an organization it can result in a written or unwritten contract. It is founded on assigned authority that defines the relationship between an individual, a team, or elements of an organization. The result is a reciprocal working relationship. At the same time it has to be acknowledged that the initiating authority is responsible for providing resources and guidance.

The certainty of accountability is such that while individual and organizational inputs and outputs matter, the important thing that can address success is "outcomes," with an emphasis on results attainment. It necessarily follows that the part that documentation plays is imperative. An excellent reporting system eliminates guess work and brings reality to the fore, resulting in a more valid and reliable decision-making process. And first-line supervisors play an important part in this process.

Vital Characteristics of Accountability

All together there are a number of key aspects that relate to the concept of accountability which when followed improve the potential for a successful achievement.

It is a bond that can only be viewed as a two-way street, and is viewed by many as a contract.

Reporting is mandated and in fact is the "mainstay" of the process. Deficient reporting is detrimental to accountability unless it is coupled with criteria for improvement. Therefore, accountability is meaningless unless coupled with consequences that mean there is liability as well as obligation. The goal is to enhance performance, not to look for someone that can be held responsible and punished (Artley, 2001).

An interesting concept related to accountability is "obligation." The true acceptance of accountability, in actuality, demands the successful fulfillment of a contract and the achievement of assigned undertakings. No vacillating, just a serious effort to effectively accomplish a task(s). It is not a question of whether the process includes sanctions or rewards, but there has to be some type of consequence to make it a practicable process (More et al., 2013).

Accountability is operative and proactive when it is used to actually improve the operational performance of a team, taskforce, group, or the totality of the department. Additionally, there is a working relationship between internal and external stockholders (Connors et al., 1994; Connors & Smith, 2009). Inasmuch as the term accountability represents a challenge, it is at the same time an opportunity to accomplish tasks and attain objectives. The crucial aspect of this term is the concept that it is obligation fulfillment that comes into existence when there is a provision that provides consequences. In sum, when taken all together the real goal of the accountability process is maximizing achievement through goal attainment.

Five Levels of Accountability

The complexity of accountability is such that there are five levels: personal, individual, team, organizational, and stakeholders, as depicted in Figure 1.3. In this pyramid the foundation is "personal." This level involves a wide range of variables such as trustworthiness, honor, principled conduct, scruples, and reliability. Fulfillment of these traits calls for a great deal of introspection and the need to engage in self-examination, and the obligation of acknowledging the necessity of becoming aware of the need to look within one's self for answers, rather than engaging in rationalization or looking for someone or mitigating factors to blame. When a team, group, taskforce, or other organizational body is positive and attainment oriented it can be described as a healthy and skilled organizational entity.

The next level is "individual" accountability that occurs within a working configuration and can be labeled as a taskforce, team, group or other organizational entity. At this level it is a relationship that applies to an officer (one or more) and a supervisor. This is a different type of relationship inasmuch as it is a joint effort where everyone works together and strives for the highest possible achievement.

FIGURE 1.3 Five levels of accountability. *Source: Modified from Will Artley (September 2001)* Establish Accountability for Performance, *Volume 3. Washington, DC: U.S. Department of Energy, September 2001.*

It is a manager/supervisor (vested authority) and a delegatee (officer or civilian) functioning in a genuine working association. In this instance, the authority figure provides guidance, direction, and resources needed to fulfill an employee's mandate. In turn the employee is responsible for satisfying allocated responsibilities. In actuality, it is a reciprocal responsibility and each is accountable to the other. The focus is on mutual interaction that involves consulting on organizational intent followed by actual accomplishment.

In police departments, teams, groups, or taskforces obtain results because officers work under supervisors who function as a cohesive unit. Shared responsibility brings everything together and accountability becomes a certainty. Definite ownership comes into existence as a result of agreed-upon measured performance. Organizational accountability is both an internal and external relationship. Internal refers to the upward, downward, and lateral flow of information between management and officers and/or teams, groups, or taskforces. External accountability answers to or reports to its stakeholders with regard to the performance of the organization as well as organizational conduct.

At the very highest part of the accountability pyramid are the "stakeholders." In American law enforcement it is the political supervisory body and the public followed by the internal stakeholders. None can be left out whether they are unions, pressure entities, interests groups, assemblages, the legal system, other agencies, sworn officers, or civilians. Most of these are not involved in the everyday operation of the department but they are a source of counsel, information, assistance, or direction and the operational entity works at achieving positive outcomes.

Accountability does not just happen as the result of a spur-of-the-moment event; it is the result of encouraging and creating a positive environment within a working accountability framework. Accountability has to be embraced, as an integral element, of each individual, group, team, taskforce, and all other agency entities. An environment is positive when it can energize, and invigorates all of those involved in an effort to transform a traditional police bureaucracy that exemplifies control-control-control into a results-oriented agency that fosters positive relationships within the organization, the political entity, and the broader community. A positive police environment is a condition wherein individuals, teams groups, and organizational managers/supervisors are motivated to execute their authority and/or carry out their responsibility. In accountability, environment officers and civilian employees are encouraged to work toward achieving attainable results. It is also an environment where employees share results and accept a commitment of liability (Artley, 2001).

If there is a single most important element of the accountability environment, it is leadership. (Leadership is discussed in detail in Chapter 5.) It has to start from the chief executive officer and is supported by the positional authority needed to direct control and energize organization members. Leadership also cascades through the environment impacting every level of the organization. Reciprocation enables an environment that is clearly "two-way." It has been suggested that this process comes into existence when an assigned authority (individual or group) delegates responsibility and a "quid pro quo" relationship results. Also, the authority must provide direction, guidance, and resources. Additionally, it creates a guarantee of fairness and promotes the elements of clearness and transparency.

If there is a cornerstone to this process, it is equity. The organizational leadership that includes the first-line supervisor must totally support fairness. Inequity can create organizational imbalance, splinter the organization, and inhibit the institution of a positive accountability environment. Trust is the bonding agent of the accountability process. With trust transparency is apparent to all of those involved. To sum up, trust is mandatory if there is to be an accountability environment.

When individuals and groups feel a sense of ownership they can relate to "outcomes" and they fulfill their responsibilities and become positive performers. As pointed out by one researcher, ownership increases responsible behavior and a concerned attitude. Ownership can become a reality by the support of the first-line supervisor in the implementation of the accountability process.

Accountability comes with liability that has consequences and these can be either sanctions or rewards. Consequences enhance execution, fulfill responsibilities, and improve performance. But it should be kept in mind that consequences only have meaning when followed up by first-line supervisors and managers. It is necessary to recognize achievements as well as shortcomings. Rewards should be given when so indicated and corrective action taken when necessary (Artley, 2001).

Supervisory Skills Areas (Hu-TACK)

Once an individual assumes the position of supervisor, the role changes to such an extent that there is limited comparison to the tasks performed as a patrol officer. The supervisor is a manager and must perform managerial-type activities. Certainly one technique of motivating employees is for a supervisor to show officers how something can be done by actually performing the activity, such as making a number of DUI (driving while under the influence) arrests, conducting a number of field interviews, or backing up an officer. While such activity might accomplish an immediate objective, it represents only a small part of the things a supervisor does to be effective.

The selection of the best worker for the position of supervisor is a common agency practice that can prove to be disastrous. The temptation to improve one's salary, to enhance one's position, and to achieve a rank attained by few is seldom rejected by a highly competent patrol officer. In many instances, however, this practice results in a feeling of having divided loyalties. A supervisor cannot forget that they are part of management and no longer a line officer.

In some instances, the newly appointed supervisor performs so poorly that it becomes necessary to seek employment elsewhere or be demoted. Some play the supervisory game well enough to get by, but they become marginal supervisors and, in the end, are of limited value to the organization. Some newly appointed supervisors program themselves for failure because they impose rigid, process-oriented rules and regulations rather than strive to achieve results. Additionally, they will usually refuse to admit mistakes, fail to delegate, and manage in an ad hoc manner. Generally, the inadequate supervisor feels that a laissez faire managerial style is the "best way to go." In addition, the feelings of inadequacy foster an approach that emphasizes, "If I leave it alone it will go away," or "Why should I bother?" or "Why not let someone

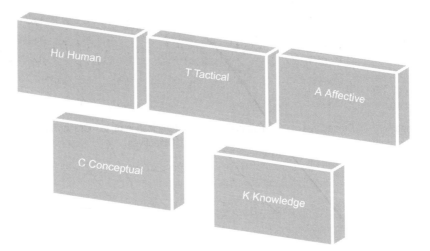

FIGURE 1.4 Supervisory skill areas (Hu-TACK).

else do it?" A supervisory position is not for everyone. It is a demanding job and can create an abundance of personal stress. The increase in salary and positional prestige can never compensate for the psychological discord that can occur if one is inadequately prepared, lacking in self-esteem, or just does not have the skills needed to perform effectively.

Supervisors should emphasize the development of the skills of their subordinates, rather than try to do everything themselves. Needless to say, the supervisor could probably accomplish the task in half the time in many instances. The timeworn axiom, "I would rather do it myself," must be rejected when one becomes a supervisor. As a means of maximizing effectiveness, a supervisor must work to attain objectives through the efforts of others, preferably by becoming operationally effective in one or more of the skill areas set forth in Figure 1.4. This acronym is known as Hu-TACK.

The skill areas are closely interrelated and overlap in their application. Knowledge-based skills are more important at the supervisory level than they would be to the chief of police, whereas human skills are vitally important at every managerial level. At the same time, managers at all levels must be concerned with applying some degree of conceptual affective and tactical skills. There is a continuing need for the integration of knowledge, human, and conceptual skills as modified by the emotionally based or affective characteristics that are constantly conditioning the managerial process. Figure 1.5 lists the supervisory functions.

In some instances, respect is earned by a supervisor because of their knowledge skills, which can have nothing to do with one's actual position or title. If a line officer is more competent and knowledgeable than his or her supervisor, it can lead to disenchantment and a lessening of organizational support. If an officer always has to turn to someone other than their immediate supervisor for such things as the amplification of a technical skill or policy interpretation, the supervisor will be viewed as working beyond their capacity. The same thing can occur if a supervisor does not keep abreast of technological change or state-of-the-art

Human	Tactical	Affective	Conceptual	Knowledge
Coaching	Capabilities	Attitudes	Analysis	Critically Review Reports
Communicating	Control	Empathy	Assessment	Directing
Counseling	Expertise	Equality	Decision-Making	Evaluating
Mentoring	Procedures	Fairness	Identification of Objectives	Organizing Work
Delegating	Task Orientation	Integrity	Prioritizing Problems	Scheduling Training
Integrating	Techniques	Interrelations	Solving Problems	Provides Administrative Credibility
Leading		Values	Interpreting	Policy Implementation
Resolving Conflict		Loyalty		

FIGURE 1.5 Supervisory functions by skill areas. *Adapted from Robert L. Katz (1974). "Skills of an Effective Administrator."* Harvard Business Review, *September–October: Volume 52, No. 5; Don L. Costley & Carmen Santana-Melgoza (1993).* Human Relations in Organizations. *St. Paul MN: West; and U.S. Department of the Army (2006).* Army Leadership. *Washington, DC: U.S. Department of the Army.*

equipment. Additionally, if a situation occurs where a supervisor has to perform line functions in an emergency and the performance is marginal or inadequate, the speed with which this occurrence spreads, via the grapevine, throughout the organization clearly demonstrates the viability of the informal organization. When ambiguity prevails, it can affect operations negatively.

Human Skills (Hu)

At the core of successful police supervision is a consideration of human skills. Employees have to be motivated, appraised, and counseled. Standards must be established, tasks analyzed, and expectations communicated. Officers must be trained, developed, and (even though distasteful) occasionally disciplined. All those tasks are an effort to meet organizational objectives (see Figure 1.6). These activities demand the application of human skills predicated on the absolute belief that employees will work hard and diligently if incentives are such that they become highly motivated.

A first-line supervisor must become personally acquainted with each employee and treat each one as an individual. Every member of a team should be expected to perform the kind

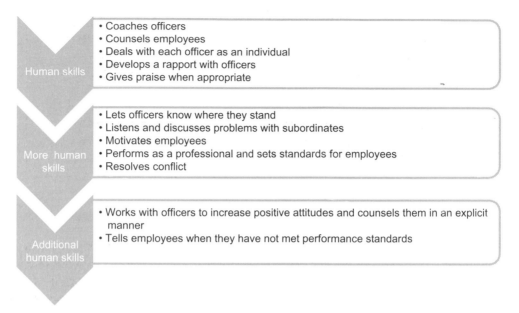

FIGURE 1.6 Supervisor's human skills.

of work that is vital to the success of the organization. It is imperative for work to be accomplished through people; this can only be done when the supervisor is thoroughly acquainted with the capabilities and limitations of each employee. The supervisor should set high standards for those supervised, and the standards should be applied to each and every employee.

In studying supervisor/subordinate relationships, officers have an entirely different view of how they are treated by supervisors as compared to how supervisors view the needs of subordinates. Supervisors feel that they clearly understand the problems that subordinates are faced with, but on the other hand, subordinates feel exactly the opposite. This is a gap that has to be addressed. It cannot be ignored. Such a disparity clearly reflects the importance of human skills and the need to understand the dynamics of human relationships if employees are to be successfully integrated into the organization. An emphasis on human skills addresses employee needs to include personal development, self-esteem, proficiency, and independence.

Tactical Skills (T)

Tactics, used by supervisors, come into play when it is necessary to apply leadership that enables one to control a situation and accomplish a mission in a field situation. It is a time when everything is brought into focus by providing purpose, direction, and motivation to an unusual occurrence. Field supervisors need to combine knowledge, human, conceptual, and affective skills when the time comes to apply tactical skills in an operational situation. It is one

1. Acquires skills needed to enhance the capability of mission attainment.
2. Applies appropriate techniques tailored to the problem at hand.
3. Develops the technical expertise needed to use appropriate equipment.
4. Establishes a system of control.
5. Establishes operational priorities.
6. Implements procedures in conformance with departmental policy.
7. Ensures that every officer is aware of the task and is oriented to its attainment.

FIGURE 1.7 Supervisor's tactical skills.

of the few times that mission accomplishment overrides other factors and becomes an inviolable imperative. Knowledge skills are used to organize for task accomplishment and conform to departmental operational policy. Human skills come into play in a tactical situation that requires the supervisor to communicate and lead officers. An additional human element is the delegation and assignment of officers in order to enhance goal accomplishment. Supervisors apply their conceptual skills by identifying, assessing, and prioritizing the problem and rendering decisions that lead to problem resolution when tactical skills are executed. Lastly, affective skills interact with other skill areas as the supervisor performs with integrity, a positive attitude, and a pattern of interactive relatedness with officers under his/her supervision. A truly effective supervisor will do everything needed to acquire the knowledge and experience needed to respond adequately to extraordinary situations and critical incidents. All of the acquired skills in each area come into focus when the supervisor controls a situation in such a manner that the tactical situation, whether it be a lost child, a disturbance, or a hostage situation, is appropriately resolved (U.S. Department of the Army, 2006). See Figure 1.7.

Affective Skills (A)

One other set of managerial characteristics are emotion based. They interact with and modify all the other characteristics (see Figure 1.8). The supervisor (by actions) modifies the attitudes, emotions, and values of employees. At the same time, the interaction modifies the supervisor's personal view of the managerial process and his or her own self-concept.

The emotion-based skills of the supervisor have to be utilized to the maximum. The first-line supervisor has to accept responsibility for errors and should never allow subordinates to be criticized for a mistake outside their control.

It does not take an alert supervisor long to realize that they are not knowledgeable in every area, and that they have weaknesses as well as strengths. Weaknesses can be numerous including a lack of sensitivity, emotional immaturity, a lack of drive, or the clashing of personalities. Effective supervisors apply numerous skills and perform several functions. An important duty is to perform with fairness and equity. If an organizational value based on fairness and equity

1. Accepts responsibility.
2. Creates an environment based on a belief in equality and the opportunity for all to succeed.
3. Deals fairly with subordinates.
4. Develops relationships based on equal treatment.
5. Demonstrates loyalty to the organization and subordinates.
6. Demonstrates the quality of integrity.
7. Integration of organizational and community value systems.
8. Knows personal strengths as well as limitations.
9. Performs as a role model.
10. Values employees and their potential contribution to the organization.

FIGURE 1.8 Supervisor's affective skills.

is to be communicated, it has to be on a continuous basis, demonstrated to each employee by ensuring that everyone is treated as an equal, with absolute fairness. In most situations, subordinates feel that supervisors are more concerned with mistakes than anything else. Subordinates feel that their supervisor seldom responds to what is done correctly because of an excessive emphasis on factors other than evenhandedness and fairness.

Obviously, this demonstrates the difference in line officers and supervisors' perception of fair treatment. Further indication of this difference in how the supervisory process is viewed is evident in that the vast majority of supervisors sense that subordinates feel comfortable when they are discussing work situations. Again, exactly the opposite is true. Subordinates, in general, are uncomfortable when dealing with a supervisor. Thus, there is apparently a barrier possibly precluding the successful communication of organizational values and their integration into the organizational value structure.

If employees perceive that managers refuse to acknowledge weaknesses and are always looking for a scapegoat, then the supervisors' affective skills will be muted and achievement of organizational goals can be jeopardized. One can apply knowledge-based human relations and cognitive skills, but the affective variable serves as a modifier and allows a manager to become aware of personal limitations as well as strengths. This activity allows the supervisor to recognize and accept responsibility to make necessary decisions and to be able to acknowledge the needs of peers and employees. The supervision of line employees is readily acknowledged as complicated and (in the view of many) demands the selection of supervisory techniques that transcend traditional responses.

Conceptual Skills (C)

Conceptual skills consume the least amount of the first-line supervisor's time. However, these skills are essential ingredients of the managerial process. The newly appointed supervisor,

1. Assesses performancc.
2. Conceptualizes the technical and human aspects of the work environment.
3. Demonstrates the ability to analyze data.
4. Develops and shares information.
5. Enhances and improves proficiency.
6. Identifies emerging problems and works for their resolution.
7. Identifies objectives.
8. Makes decisions.
9. Utilizes all sources in an effort to deal with the positive interpretation of information.
10. Works to eliminate errors.

FIGURE 1.9 Supervisor's conceptual skills.

whether assigned to patrol or investigations, must integrate their individual activities into the total organizational plan so agency goals can be attained. This can be accomplished when the supervisor is thoroughly aware of the department's mission, vision, and organizational culture.

The relationship of patrol to other specialized units (such as support services or investigation) can be tenuous; therefore, it is necessary for the first-line supervisor to be capable of understanding the complexities of the interrelationship of specialized units to the total organization (see Figure 1.9). A supervisor must respond to organizational conflict with seasoned judgment and visionary thinking.

To "conceptualize" is to form new ideas or concepts. The first-line supervisor is in the best position to identify and resolve conflict between specialized police units by employing conceptualization techniques and utilizing mediation skills (Umbreit & Coates, 2000). Key ambient factors of conceptualization involve the identification, prioritizing, and solving of problems. The supervisor also must develop and execute solutions by evaluating new responsibilities and re-examine assignments in an effort to achieve definitive managerial goals.

Knowledge and human skills will sometimes dominate the day-to-day duties performed by a first-line supervisor. Each of these areas helps to define working relationships within a variety of settings. At times, task accomplishment is seen as paramount and informality is encouraged as emphasis is placed on problem solving. The organization and the chain of command are utilized to facilitate communications and direct activities to the task. In this instance, achievement dominates and such things as position, power, rank, and status become subordinate factors.

Sometimes knowledge skills dominate the working environment, and in other instances it will be human skills. A healthy relationship between the two is needed, and it demands a supervisory response that acknowledges the need for the application of both types of skills. At times, it can foster a supervisory approach that is truly participative and the essence of sharing responsibilities. It is the opposite of the "we/they" style of supervision that utilizes "top-down" management. In other words, it can be a one-way street. The key for this approach is to tell officers not only what to do but how to do it. The other side of the coin gives serious consideration to the personal needs of officers. Employees are seen as a viable and vital part of the operational equation. There is a total awareness of the need for "people skills" if things are to be accomplished. When human skills falter, it is readily apparent that supervisors are not utilizing those supervised to accomplish tasks. Supervisors should determine the interrelationship of the technical and human aspects of the work environment and utilize this information to improve their supervisory style. Conceptually the supervisor can demonstrate the ability to analyze data and share information in order to attain organizational objectives. Also, he or she can work to eliminate errors and utilize every available source in order to deal positively with emerging problems. It then becomes apparent that conceptual application can lead to better decision-making and enhanced problem solving. Additionally, a supervisor can assess performance that will result in improved proficiency.

Knowledge-Based Skills (K)

At the time of appointment, the supervisor is usually endowed with all kinds of knowledge-based skills because of extended duty as a patrol officer (see Figure 1.10). In most instances, promotion to the initial managerial level has been predicated on success as a patrol officer or investigator. Unfortunately, the skillful application of operational techniques can seldom ensure successful performance as a first-line supervisor. The skills are different and the situation can become somewhat tenuous if, during the transition period to this newly acquired position, the new sergeant fails to adopt a managerial perspective. A manager can only succeed if results are obtained through the efforts of others. The supervisor must realize the necessity of training employees because they are an organization's most valued assets.

---

1. Demonstrates a real interest in seeing that officers do a *good* job and complete their assignments.
2. Fairly implements departmental policies, rules, and regulations.
3. Interprets departmental policy.
4. Is capable of doing all tasks an officer must perform.
5. Knows each officer's workload.
6. Organizes work in such a way as to effectively and efficiently achieve objectives and goals.
7. Provides officers with appropriate administrative and technical support.
8. Reviews officers' reports for accuracy, thoroughness, and quality.
9. Schedules officers according to organizational priorities.
10. Trains and develops officers.

FIGURE 1.10 Supervisor's knowledge-based skills.

Self-Appraisal

The initial and highly significant dilemma in becoming a truly competent supervisor is sorting through all the different supervisory techniques to select the approaches compatible with one's own temperament and personality. It is necessary to ask such questions as: "What is an acceptable level of conflict between employees? Can personal needs be made compatible with organizational needs? What managerial style will officers find most acceptable? How does one become an effective disciplinarian? Should one go by the book when enforcing rules and regulations? Can officer discretion be accepted as an integral part of the job?" Can errors be viewed as part of a learning process?

It is vital, for several reasons, for supervisors to have a clear idea of what they are doing and what is expected of them. First, it allows them to operate as professionals, above any potential conflict. Second, they are less apt, in hectic day-to-day operation, to delude themselves into believing there is only one potential solution to every problem, and that all officers can be treated the same.

Each officer is a distinct human being with varying skills, abilities, and personality, and is entitled to be treated as an individual. By accepting everyone as an individual and dealing with them on that basis, supervisors can reduce the potential for making errors and arrive at decisions suitable for both the individual and the organization.

The pivotal factor is to understand the real attitudes toward line officers and their capacity to work. Are they viewed as having the potential to become producers, or are they regarded as "drones?" The real issue, then, becomes crystal clear: the way employees are treated by their supervisor is strongly influenced by the way the supervisor views the officers. Most assuredly, the best supervisors adopt a managerial style acknowledging individual differences and they work diligently to tailor the style to the situation and the individual.

If the supervisor is better at conceptualizing than motivating, it becomes readily apparent that his or her approach to a supervisory problem will be entirely different than when the individual excels at motivating.

The two skill areas can be combined by emphasizing conceptual skills, carefully setting forth a plan to resolve a problem and then utilizing motivational skills to implement the program. For example, a plan can be devised, focusing on improving the working relationship between the line officers and other agencies dealing with the homeless in an effort to improve quality of life. Working with citizens and business owners, one patrol unit created a program to identify the extent and nature of vandalism, panhandling, loitering, thefts, and general deterioration of property. These problems were tracked and maximum use was made of emergency shelters for homeless people and action plans that included counseling, casework review, housing placement, and job training. Line officers were instrumental in referring the homeless to the comprehensive treatment program (Klein, 2000).

If the supervisor's anxiety threshold is high, it may be more comfortable to resolve a problem with a knowledge skill base rather than a human skill approach. In other words, one can view an issue as a simple rule or regulation violation or it can be approached as a conflict-resolution problem with a goal of maximizing human relations skills. In application, it can become an integration of the two approaches, but it actually is a matter of fitting the style to the situation.

No supervisory philosophy works all the time. It is important to use a flexible approach. Accomplished supervisors combine different approaches. This is what has become known as "network management."

Managerial networking at the supervisory level is concerned with the integration of each officer into the organization. Efforts are directed toward true communication and the sharing of ideas, information, and resources. It is the focus on decision-making that improves work life and productivity. Networks exist to foster self-help, exchange information, and share resources. The problem is focused upon, and networking enhances the ability of each individual to respond to that problem. In fact, the individual is the most important element of the network. The value of networking is rooted in informality, equality, and true acceptance. It is the fait accompli of effective supervision.

Management Expectations of the Supervisor

Supervisors serve as a communication link between line and higher management. They are responsible for turning the concepts and visions of those in higher positions into the "nuts-and-bolts" reality of police work. Sergeants must translate the intentions of management into actuality. Management expects results (not excuses), so it is the responsibility of the first-line supervisor to respond to this challenge. The key is for the supervisor to work diligently at developing the skills that cause employees to become energized and emphasize effective task completion. Vocational duties must be subordinate to getting work done through employees. One expert suggests asking the question, "What kind of employee would I like to have working for me?" The response to that question provides the first-line supervisor with a standard by which to work and live (Broadwell & Dietrich, 1998). It is a process that ensures success because it reinforces and focuses supervisory efforts.

Positive Attitude

Everyone likes to be around people who are positive. It can be contagious. It will have a strong influence on working relationships. Think of how much better it is to be involved with people who obviously enjoy work and the challenges it presents.

When a new general order or policy is promulgated, the best way to react to it is positively. Response should be based on a precise evaluation of ways that will ensure the policy is workable. Everyone, especially the supervisor, must refrain from finding reasons why it will not work (Dobbs & Field, 1993).

Supervisors should train themselves to think about the positive side of an idea or suggestion rather than the bad aspects. When addressing a problem there is no room for tentativeness. Problems should be addressed without circumspection. It is not a question of being unrealistic but looking for ways things can be done rather than why something will not work. When a supervisor focuses on achievement rather than failure, confidence becomes an integral component of success. It is fundamental to human nature that the boss will respond to recommendations suggesting, "This is what it will take to make this work" rather than "This is why this cannot be done" (Broadwell & Dietrich, 1998). Amazingly this works. Viewing things in a positive frame of reference focuses energies where they are needed to enhance policy implementation successfully. One can present negatives but should not dwell on them. Stressing the positive is a contagious supervisory process that works. Without question, enthusiasm is an intrinsic state of being. It is natural for one to be positive, creative, and challenged by the work being performed (Carlson, 1998).

The boss's ideas may still be questioned, but at the proper time and place. This simply means the idea should be carefully evaluated and constructively criticized, but not rejected simply because it has "never been done that way before." Individuals who think positively are "results oriented"—a characteristic management is actively seeking. The supervisor must view each obstacle as an opportunity and a challenge. It is like looking at a half-filled glass of water and trying to determine whether it is half-full or half-empty. It is obvious that the positive thinker views the glass as half-full.

Positive thinking is a way of dealing with obstacles in a constructive manner. It actually is a way of viewing life. The nature of circumstances, places, things, and attitudes toward people can always be affirmative if one wants to view them as such. Because desirable attitudes can be cultivated, the new supervisor should strive to identify means of finding workable solutions to conflict, starting with developing a positive attitude toward employees. A supervisor expresses positive thinking by noticeable enthusiasm, expressive body language, eye contact, and clarity of speech. It is also essential that the supervisor operates from a position that exudes confidence in such a manner that everyone knows where she/he stands.

Loyalty

The organization anticipates specific behavioral outcomes from first-line supervisors, and one of the outcomes is loyalty. It is of extreme importance. In should never be discounted. It should be an integral part of the police culture. Loyalty is the cornerstone of character. It is an indispensable characteristic of a positive working relationship between differing levels of management. Middle and top management want to feel that rules, regulations, policies, and decisions coming down through channels are supported by first-line supervisors. The supervisor should realize that policies set at one or two levels above them will in many instances lose some of their significance. In fact, their actual need for existence might be questioned by line personnel. A policy may be viewed as unreasonable when it is not fully explained. The first-line supervisor is seldom in a position to know all the facts and rationale for a new policy. The view from the top or middle of the organization is very seldom duplicated at the supervisory level. Only so much information can be sent down through channels. Most managers do not have the time to explain in depth the rationale for each policy. Normally, managers are making decisions based upon more factual material, possibly unavailable at the operational level.

If some information is needed before a new policy can be explained to subordinates, then the supervisor must ask for clarifying information. When one accepts the position of supervisor, they accept the obligation of being part of the team, not apart from it. This is not an easy task to accomplish but it must be done if the supervisor is to be successful.

Supervisors translate and implement policy and procedures within the organization. The supportive supervisors should ask themselves, "How can this policy be implemented in the shortest period of time with assurance of actual compliance?" The important factor in this situation is to find the solution that is best for the department. In addition, middle and top managers dislike being referred to as the "they" who take those unreasonable stands and demand non-achievable performance. Managers at higher levels have a need for personal loyalty from supervisors, and this should be reciprocated. Loyalty works both ways. First-line supervisors want to feel they have the support and backing of their immediate supervisor and others in the chain of command.

Integrity

Management must convey to every member of the department the ethical standards that govern each and every action taken when performing law enforcement duties. Without question, it is essential to convey a tradition of excellence, professionalism, and commitment to the protection of the constitutional rights of everyone (Hiester, 1996). The equal administration of justice is the cornerstone of the integrity required of every member of a police department. People cannot be left to speculate as to the values of the organization. Clear and explicit signals must be given both within and without the organization that integrity cannot be compromised.

Management must expect every supervisor to be a role model when it comes to integrity both on and off the job. A commitment to integrity cannot be just an abstract value; it must be reflected in the day-to-day conduct of every supervisor. It can never be compromised. Every word and every deed must reflect an adherence to a standard that is clearly above reproach. A supervisor is in a position to shape the attitudes and conduct of line officers by setting an example of personal conduct that exemplifies an adherence to a strong code of ethics (see the code of ethics in Chapter 11).

Setting an example is a leadership task that must be provided by a first-line supervisor. Integrity can never be compromised and every action must reflect a commitment to a principle of ethical policing. A supervisor must realize that once one's reputation is tarnished it is next to impossible to recover. The competent supervisor will never be placed in such a position that their personal integrity can be questioned. The significance of integrity at the supervisory level cannot be questioned. It is the administrative level where values can be reinforced and aberrant behavior controlled. An excellent example of the importance of integrity to an organization is the mission statement utilized by the Baltimore Police Department that expresses in no uncertain terms that the department must maintain the highest level of integrity in all of its actions.

Performance

Managers expect (and indeed have a right to demand) the thorough completion of tasks on time. Supervisors should do everything asked of them. If an assignment cannot be completed on time, the next manager up the line needs to be consulted with an explanation. Perhaps more time is needed or help is required in understanding the problem or completing the task.

There are very few managers who will not accept a request for help if assistance is necessary in completing an assigned project. Asking for help is not an admission of incompetence; it is an acknowledgment that the manager has an expertise as yet not acquired by subordinates. Every manager expects personnel to be on time and to take appropriate coffee or meal breaks. Supervisors should set the standard not only for their officers, but also for everyone else in the department.

First-line supervisors have to accept being at the fulcrum between management and line operations. If problems occur, first-line supervisors are usually the first to know. Supervisors also have a responsibility to identify problems and respond to subordinate complaints; thus they can serve as part of an early warning system. They are privy to the interaction between officers, they know what is being said on the radio and in emails, they read messages on mobile terminals, review reports, and they observe officers on a continuing basis. They know when things are going wrong and can act accordingly (McCarthy, 2000).

Functioning as go-between is a supervisory responsibility. No one else can effectively accomplish the tasks of interpreting rules, regulations, policies, and translating organizational demands for the cooperative attainment of agency goals. It is also essential that the supervisor be involved in the continual review of rules to ensure that they are practical (Solar, 2001).

Responding to Management

Because management is continually in need of information, supervisors must submit a wide range of requested reports in order to reflect adequately the tasks being accomplished by subordinates. Reports must be completed on time and must be comprehensive. There is nothing worse, in the view of most managers, than a poorly prepared or late report. The nature of police work is such that most supervisors are assessed largely on the basis of reports submitted. While supervisors might have continuing contact with their immediate manager, other management superiors might use the written work submitted by a supervisor as the only source for evaluating performance. In fact, in many medium- or large-sized agencies, supervisors have little or no contact with the "brass." Therefore, it behooves them to do everything possible to ensure completeness and accuracy of all reports. Special care should be taken whenever a report is to be submitted to other city departments, the prosecuting attorney's office, or other law enforcement agencies so these reports reflect favorably on the department. Figure 1.11 reflects what managers want from first-line supervisors.

If there is any doubt as to when a report is due, supervisors should ask their immediate superior for clarification. If the manager wants reports done in a certain way, compliance with the requirement is essential. In order to work well with a next level manager, an effort should be made to determine what is expected. This requires a great deal of judgment on the part of the supervisor. In general, routine matters are handled at the operational level and other matters of consequence should be referred to the next managerial level pursuant to departmental protocol (Garner, 1997).

1. Communicate subordinates' concerns, desires, and suggestions to management.
2. Complete assigned investigations.
3. Comply with procedures and policy.
4. Create a positive working environment.
5. Demonstrate commitment to integrity.
6. Meet with management, as needed, in order to resolve specific problems or concerns.
7. Prepare and submit budget requests.
8. Prepare written employee evaluations.
9. Render testimony at disciplinary hearings.
10. Respond in writing to various management requests.
11. Transmit the organizational value system to members.
12. Take action contributing to organizational improvement.

FIGURE 1.11 What management wants from first-line supervisors.

Supervisors must refrain from stereotyping their manager, and learn to look upon the person as a unique individual. This is especially imperative when it comes to determining the type of report the immediate supervisor wants in particular situations. Some managers are listeners and prefer, whenever possible, to have certain reports given orally. Others react best to written reports, allowing them time to assess and evaluate the information presented. The preference of one method over the other depends upon the nature of the problem or the type of information being reported. With this in mind, supervisors should determine their managers' strengths and weaknesses, work habits, and needs before responding accordingly.

When establishing and maintaining a good working relationship with the boss, never modify a report so it appears more favorable than it should. If something is wrong, state this. Be frank, open, and honest with reporting. To do less is to court disaster. Law enforcement is a process of responding to and resolving conflict. Naturally, mistakes will be made and in some instances supervisory judgment, or that of subordinate(s), may not be what it should be. A boss is human also. Most bosses are dedicated, have a definite sense of responsibility toward their work, and challenge not only themselves but also all personnel (Dobbs & Field, 1993). A supervisor should work with, not against, a boss. If it is obviously a situation that will be controversial, be sure to provide information leaving the individual in a position to resolve the situation. Prior field experience will (in all probability) tell supervisors when management will be forced to respond to higher authorities or the press.

Most departments have a policy requiring a written report to be submitted when any unusual occurrence happens. It is at this time that the supervisor can extend a helping hand to management by submitting a detailed report taking into consideration every possible question that might arise from the incident. The methodical application of this technique in a non-manipulative fashion produces a supervisor who accepts what may be a management problem as a personal one. When this has been accomplished, management will start to see its supervisors not only as valuable resources, but also as helpful colleagues and trustworthy professionals who are part of the management team.

Subordinates' Expectations of the Supervisor

If every subordinate worked to maximum capacity, if errors were never made, if all goals were achieved on time, and if organizations were perfect there would not be a need for first-line supervisors. Obviously, such is not the case. Law enforcement agencies are composed of human beings who deal with human problems in an imperfect environment. It logically follows that supervisors will continue to be an integral part of the managerial process in the years ahead.

Supervisors have to deal with numerous demands from varying sources from both within and outside the department. One that can be the most demanding is the subordinate. In fact, if there were no line personnel to be supervised, the position of supervisor would, in all probability, never have come into existence. Hence, the question has to be asked—"What should subordinates expect from a supervisor?"

The answer is not simple because of the human equation involved. Supervisors and subordinates are all different. While they are all members of the human race, they are still distinct and unique as individuals with varying needs. The primary reason for the existence of the supervisory position is the need for work to be effectively accomplished. If goals are not achieved, then there seems to be little reason for the continued existence of the organization.

The important consideration then is to maximize the talents of each subordinate. "What could be worse than a supervisor ignoring the skills possessed by subordinates?" A supervisor certainly must utilize every skill and every bit of knowledge a subordinate possesses. This is not a simple task. It is one demanding a continual appraisal and reappraisal of each employee's capabilities. Those abilities must then be directed toward the accomplishment of tasks essential to the attainment of organizational goals.

Subordinates have needs that, organizationally, must be met and satisfied (Broadwell & Dietrich, 1998). From an optimistic point of view, all those needs can be handled within the working environment, but usually this is not possible. If needs are met by the job, then the job is readily identified as an excellent source of motivation. If needs are not being met on the job then the question arises as to why the job is inadequately responding to employee needs.

Under no circumstance does this mean the supervisor has to accept a person's actions or inactions as an excuse for poor performance. A failure to perform at acceptable levels must always be addressed and resolved in favor of the organization. Generally speaking, it can be assumed that 85 percent of employees will respond to positive efforts by the supervisor. This is the group with which the supervisor should expend extra time and energy. Unfortunately, the remaining 15 percent of the subordinates (who for whatever reason are *poor* employees) will generally consume most of the supervisor's time. Eventually, that time will be nonproductive (except that employees who should never have been employed will be eliminated, or employees will receive aid to such an extent they will become productive employees).

1. Accessibility.
2. A role model.
3. Assistance in attaining individual and organizational needs.
4. Assistance in integrating the individual into the organization.
5. Creation of a work environment that provides for job satisfaction.
6. Fair appraisal.
7. Help in developing new skills.
8. Identification and maximization of talents that result in growth.
9. Providing information needed to accomplish tasks.
10. Support in becoming a productive employee.

FIGURE 1.12 What subordinates want from first-line supervisors.

Officers expect the supervisor to be a fair appraiser and to share with them in terms of skills and expertise. Accessibility and approachability are also something that subordinates feel is important when relating to a first-line supervisor. Other qualities that are looked for are calmness, trust, and a positive role model (see Chapter 9 for a discussion of role model). Additionally, there is an expectation that a "good" supervisor will create a working environment that will allow for job and individual satisfaction.

It is important for a supervisor to realize that people, time, and places have changed. Things are not the way they used to be. The authoritarian management approach should have been dispensed with long ago, but is still in limited use and is definitely not as viable of a managerial approach as it once was. The old assumptions about employees' lack of desire and inability to work no longer apply. As a group, officers cannot be classified as lazy, indifferent, or indolent. In fact, the constituency to be supervised is generally willing and capable of working (see Figure 1.12), but for different reasons and with different expectations than their predecessors.

A large problem facing police organizations today is that many officers do not feel they are a part of the organization. Officers want job satisfaction and this can only be provided by allowing officers to achieve individual needs while organizational needs are satisfied.

When the working environment limits the opportunity for satisfying personal goals, officers can become alienated from the organization. When an officer rejects the work situation, it can result in a lowering of work standards, general apathy, and a lessening of interest in the job.

Discontent with the job has traditionally resulted in absenteeism, tardiness, stoicism, and low-quality work. Now, however, officers have expressed this discontent by becoming more active in unions, engaging in work slowdowns, using alcohol and other drugs to a greater extent, filtering information for personal reasons, and, lastly, leaving the police field in increasing numbers (Scarano & Jones, 2000; Sullivan, 2004). See Figure 1.13.

Many younger officers have rising expectations and are not willing to accept the demands of a traditionally managed police organization. The bureaucratic model of management is

The Past Century	The 21st Century
acceptance of external direction	commitment
acquiescence	internalized response
autocracy	democratic workplace
closed communication	open communication
conforming	non-conforming
conventionality	spontaneity
dependent	independent
don't rock the boat	risk-taker
indifference	empathy
lack of trust	mutual trust
ordered	self-directed
passive	involved
personal goals ignored	personal goals attained
pessimistic	optimistic
quantity	quality
rules dominate	goal attainment dominates
subordinate	equal
value neutral	value oriented

FIGURE 1.13 Officer behavior.

the antithesis of everything they want from an organization. The rational aspects of work are rejected for those that are more "people oriented." In the past, officers sought job and financial security and the job took precedence over outside interests. Today, however, officers express a need for:

- Acquisition of new skills.
- Attainment of individual goals.
- Fulfilling and consequential work.
- Involvement in decision-making.
- Opportunity to excel.
- Opportunity to use their skills and expertise.
- Recognition.
- Responsibility.
- Self-management.
- Vision.

Those changing attitudes toward work suggest that younger officers want a better-rounded lifestyle. They will work and give their best efforts for a certain number of hours if they have a positive working environment. The successful police organization of the future will integrate the individual into the organization, and individual as well as organizational goals will be attained.

It is apparent that the composition of most law enforcement agencies will change dramatically (if it has not occurred already). Affirmative action mandates have changed hiring practices and "diversity" is the buzzword of the day. In the years ahead, more minorities and women will enter the law enforcement ranks, in part because of demographics. Additionally, continuing affirmative action programs serve to correct any imbalance between the proportion of ethnic minorities, those of unique sexual orientations, different religious affiliations, and women in a community as compared to the proportion of sworn officers. In sum, the goal is to create police departments that are more representative of the community at large (Commission on Accreditation for Law Enforcement Agencies Inc, 2006). These new employees and their white male counterparts will become a new breed of individuals with a different attitude toward work and a changing personal need structure.

Participation

A new set of values has entered the organizational setting, and it strikes right at the heart of the supervisor–subordinate relationship. In the past, employees have been "acted upon" rather than "reacted to." Except for a few instances, police employees have been passive rather than reactive. Today things are different. Many police officers want a part of the action. Progressive police organizations open the decision-making process to employees, and supervisors should train and critique officers in the process of decision-making (Oldham, 2007). That is not to say every employee is involved in every policy decision, but participation is allowed at all levels where employees are in a position to have first-hand information and are given an opportunity to study problems that come to the attention of the organization.

The idea of worker participation and involvement requires a redefinition of work and working relationships. It requires a fundamental change in one's view of employees and what they can contribute to the department. It demands that the supervisor work toward the creation of a working environment that gives officers an opportunity for involvement and growth.

Supervisors must learn that creating a real partnership means power must be shared, not hoarded. As the old authoritarian leadership style is discarded, it must be replaced by insight into, and a deeper understanding of, human needs and expectations. Participative management will not become operational overnight. In fact, it will undoubtedly be resisted by some in the years ahead and, in a few instances, never adopted. However, as individuals change, organizations must change. As everyone knows, change can be pleasant or it can be painful. Without a doubt, supervisors from the old school will be the recipients of high levels of stress as their work experience, training, and education are diametrically opposed to the demands of modern leadership.

The transformation of relationships between working employees and supervisors does not require an overhaul of human nature. Quite the contrary, it requires the elimination of distorted and outdated opinions of how human nature is viewed. When supervising the new breed, the task is that of facilitator, not power broker. The real by-product of participative supervision is the creation of a working environment in which the officers *want* to work. It is absolutely necessary for the supervisor to create a psychological ambiance projecting an air of caring for people and strive to do everything possible to make the department a pleasant place to work. This is accomplished by being constantly available for help or guidance, accepting and solving problems as they occur, making decisions based on knowledge, and exhibiting a genuine desire to empower employees to accomplish assigned tasks. An organization achieves a standard of excellence when a participative environment that is created by the first-line supervisor causes employees to excel and attain organizational goals.

Conflict Resolution

When first-line supervisors were asked to identify the most important functions they performed, it was found that the vast majority had to do with the resolution of conflict (see Figure 1.14). Subordinates constantly turn to supervisors as conflict resolvers.

Conflict cannot be ignored but has to be accepted as a certain consequence of human interaction. Subordinates expect and, in fact, demand that supervisors deal with and resolve conflict. Conflict is inevitable in police work. Line personnel are confronted with conflict daily and the first-line supervisor is not exempt from the realities of conflict.

---

1. Ameliorate conflict between subordinates.
2. Coach subordinates.
3. Conduct internal investigations in accordance with rules prescribed in the Officer's Bill of Rights.
4. Investigate incidents in which subordinates are involved (shootings or accidents).
5. Conduct investigations of observed or reported subordinate behavior that may have vicarious liability involvement.
6. Counsel subordinates with personal and job related problems.
7. Provide feedback to subordinates regarding job performance.
8. Personally conduct investigations of alleged subordinate misconduct.
9. Resolve citizen/officer conflicts.
10. Respond to subordinates' inquiries (policy, law, alternative courses of action, etc.).
11. Serve as an archetype of professionalism in all relationships with subordinates.
12. Train and develop subordinates.

FIGURE 1.14 Functions performed by supervisors when relating to subordinates.

Conflict must be resolved both internally and external to the department. Citizens file complaints that must be investigated. Conflict even occurs between officers, and likewise has to be met and resolved. Conflicts in this area range from a failure to respond rapidly when providing backup, or taking too much time for a meal break. In some situations, gripes about another employee can fester to such a point that the accomplishment of tasks is impeded. The supervisor must listen to such complaints and work toward their reduction or elimination.

The first-line supervisor must learn to distinguish between real employee complaints and petty bickering. A certain amount of griping can actually prove to be beneficial, but if it becomes excessive, it can be inimical to personal relationships and to organizational well-being. Furthermore, when officers are observed or reported to have engaged in activities creating a vicarious liability, they must be investigated.

Subordinates can become involved in shootings or accidents and the supervisor becomes a key factor in the investigation of such incidents. This is especially true when a firearm is discharged and someone is injured or killed. In agencies not having an internal affairs unit, the first-line supervisor is generally held responsible for conducting such an investigation.

Supervisors are the lead investigators in efforts to resolve conflicts as described above. It has been estimated that 73 percent of a supervisor's time is spent in resolving conflict. The supervisor's position is, without a doubt, primarily one of conflict identification and resolution.

Peer Expectations of the Supervisor

Successful accomplishment of tasks and goal attainment requires cooperation and coordination between supervisors. Supervision is a joint effort by numerous individuals and not the sole priority of any one first-line supervisor. Functions performed by one have a direct impact on every other supervisor in the department.

Getting along with and supporting fellow supervisors creates a more pleasant place to work. Occasionally someone will allow the desire to get ahead (or a strong drive to compete) get in the way of positive working relationships. Other supervisors may view their duties and responsibilities differently. If the differences are to be resolved, supervisors must make an effort to understand and get along with each other.

Supervisors have to recognize that peers have objectives to be met and commitments to be honored. They have problems that have to be dealt with and they may know best how to solve those problems. The first-line supervisor should always consider how their actions affect the duties of others.

If it is possible to make a helping decision rather than one that hinders, then it should be done. If it appears a decision will result in conflict for another supervisor, an attempt should be made to resolve the problem by direct communication. Fellow supervisors should talk over the differences and make a sincere effort to find a solution beneficial to both. See Figure 1.15.

Reciprocal, positive relationships between peers are those where experiences are shared. At the end of a shift, situations that occurred can jointly be discussed along with views on how they were resolved. Ideas and opinions should be thrown out on the table for discussion (and even debate) when needed.

1. Careful consideration of how their actions impact others.
2. Cooperation.
3. Coordination.
4. Focusing on work, not personalities.
5. Joint problem resolution.
6. Positive working relationships.
7. Sharing of information and ideas.

FIGURE 1.15 What peers want from other supervisors.

When the occasion demands, supervisors must meet with other supervisors to resolve problems, share information, and coordinate work activities. This might be especially pertinent when there is an ongoing investigation that cannot be completed on one shift.

A good supervisor does not wait for someone else to take action when a problem occurs, requiring consultation with peers. The offer to help should be extended and, if necessary, a meeting should be set up to discuss and resolve the problem. There are many instances when an end-of-shift briefing does not allow adequate time for dealing with the problem at hand.

This is best illustrated by the conflict arising when a new policy is implemented. Policies are open to interpretation and when one supervisor stringently enforces a new grooming policy and another ignores it, there will be an immediate reaction from line personnel. Such a situation is best handled by reviewing the policy in a conference setting and allowing adequate time for discussion in order to resolve differences in interpretation.

Positive relationships with peers can take many avenues, but those that have proven to be successful focus on the work to be accomplished rather than the personalities of those involved. It is not necessary to like someone in order to work with them. Personal feelings should be set aside and the need to get the job done should dominate peer relationships.

The ability to get along with people is the hallmark of the professional. It is a sign of maturity. Going out of your way to share credit and praise people when the situation dictates is vital. Everything possible should be done to develop positive working relationships and this usually involves communication. Peers need to explain actions, share information, let others know what is going on, send a memo, and make it a personal policy to maximize communication. In other words, take the extra step.

It should be expected that peer criticism will occur on occasion. Despite ultimate personal efforts, someone will find fault or be critical of the manner in which something is being done. Employees must try not only to accept criticism, but also to learn from it.

References

Alpert, G. P., Smith, M. R., Kaminski, R. J., Fridell, L. A., MacDonald, J., & Kubu, B. (2011). *Police use of force.* Washington, DC: National Institute of Justice.

Artley, W. (2001). *The performance-based management handbook, establishing accountability* (Vol. 3). Washington, DC: U.S. Department of Energy.

Broadwell, M. W., & Dietrich, C. B. (1998). *The new supervisor: How to thrive in your first year as a manager* (5th ed.). Reading, MA: Addison Wesley.

Bureau of the Census, (2007). *Annual population estimates by race, Hispanic or Latino— Origin and state.* Washington, DC: Department of Commerce.

Carlson, R. (1998). *Don't sweat the small stuff at work.* New York: Hyperion.

Commission on Accreditation for Law Enforcement Agencies Inc, (2006). *Standards for law enforcement agencies* (5th ed.). Fairfax, VA: Commission for Accreditation for Law Enforcement Agencies, Inc.

Connors, R., & Smith, T. (2009). *How did that happen: Holding people accountability for results the positive principled way.* New York, NY: Penguin Group.

Connors, R., Smith, T., & Hickman, C. (1994). *The QZ principle: Getting results through individual and organizational accountability.* Upper Saddle River, NJ: Prentice Hall.

Dobbs, C., & Field, M. W. (1993). Rational risk: Leadership success or failure? *The Police Chief, LX*(12).

Frazier, T. C., & Reintzell, J. F. (1997). Training sergeants: Today's leaders, tomorrow's executives. *The Police Chief, LXIV*(11).

Frey, W. H. (2008). *America's new demographics: Regions, metros, cities, suburbs and exurbs.* Washington, DC: Brookings Institute.

Frey, W. H. (2010). *"Race and ethnicity" cited in state of metropolitan America—On the front lines of demographic transformation.* Washington DC: Brookings Institute.

Garner, G. W. (2008). *Common sense police supervision: Practical tips for the first-line supervisor* (3rd ed.). Springfield, IL: Charles C Thomas.

Henchey, J. P. (2005). Ready or not here they come—The millennial generation enters the workforce. *The Police Chief, LXXII*(9).

Hiester, D. (1996). Guardians of the constitution. *Law and Order, 44*(5).

Jerome, R. (2006). *Police reform: A job half done.* Washington, DC: American Constitution Society for Law and Policy.

Klein, S. (2000). Dealing with homeless and improving quality of life. *The Police Chief, LXVII*(5).

Mackun, P., & Wilson, S. (2011). *Population distribution and change: 2000 to 2010.* Bureau of the Census, Washington, DC: Department of Commerce.

Martin, J. A., & Matthews, K. (2000). Measuring an agency's performance. *Law and Order, 48*(10).

Mastrofski, S. D., Rosenbaum, D. P., & Fridell, L. (2011). *Police supervision: A 360-degree view of eight police departments.* Washington, DC: National Institute of Justice.

McCarthy, R. (2000). Steps chiefs can take to prevent unethical behavior. *The Police Chief, LXVII*(10).

More, H. W., Vito, G. F., & Walsh, W. F. (2013). *Organizational behavior and management in law enforcement* (3rd ed.). Upper Saddle River, NJ: Pearson, Prentice Hall.

National Institute of Justice, (2012). *Predictive policing.* Washington, DC: National Institute of Justice.

Oldham, S. (2007). Supervisors at their best. *Law and Order, 55*(5).

Ratcliffe, J. (2008). *Intelligence-led policing.* Portland, OR: Willan Publishing.

Reaves, B. A., & Hickman, M. J. (2004). *Law enforcement management and administrative statistics, 2000: Data for individual state and local agencies with 100 or more officers.* Washington, DC: Bureau of Justice Statistics.

Reston, M., & Rubin, J. (2009). *Los Angeles to pay $13 million to Settle May Day melee lawsuits.* Los Angeles, CA: *Los Angeles Times.*

Scarano, S., & Jones, T. (2000). Following by example. *Law and Order, 48*(10).

Solar, P. J. (2001). The organizational context of effective policing. *The Police Chief, LXVIII*(2).

Stambaugh, H., Beaupre, D., Icove, D. J., Baker, R., & Cassaday, W. (2000). *State and local law enforcement needs to combat electronic crime*. Washington, DC: National Institute of Justice.

Sullivan, B. (2004). Can traditional work standards and the contemporary employee coexist? *The Police Chief, LXXI*(10).

Umbreit, M. S., & Coates, R. B. (2000). *Multicultural implications of restorative justice: Potential pitfalls and dangers*. Washington, DC: Office for Victims of Crime Resource Center.

U.S. Department of the Army, (2006). *Army leadership*. Washington, DC: U.S. Department of the Army.

Webb, H. (2011). *Managing the use of force incident for criminal justice officers, supervisors and administrators*. Springfield, IL: Charles C Thomas.

Further reading

Sharp, A. G. (1995). The 21st century cop—administrators predict law enforcement's evolving role in the future. *Law and Order, 43*(2).

Community-Oriented Policing and Problem Solving

Improving Neighborhood Quality of Life

KEY TERMS

actors	partnerships
analysis	problem solving
assessment	process facilitation
collaboration	quality supervision
community enhancement	response
empowerment	risk taking
environmental surveys	scanning
incidents	sequence of events
institutional	supervisory techniques
managing failure	third parties
offenders	victims

CASE STUDY

Sergeant Raul "Spike" Hernandez

DEPARTMENT

Raul Hernandez has been a member of the Range Police Department for seven years. The department has added a minimal number of officers and, in terms of sworn positions, the officers-per-thousand population is 1:12. This is the lowest ratio of the 17 cities in the county. Formerly, the department had 188 sworn positions and 39 civilian employees. Because of budgetary problems, the department currently has 165 sworn positions, and the coming fiscal year does not provide for additional positions. There are three major units in the department: field operations, investigation, and the administrative support services. Sergeant Hernandez works as a shift supervisor in field operations and reports to an area supervisor. He is assigned to the swing shift that works a regular 40-hour-week schedule. The division has 89 police officers and eight community service officers. There are also two school resource officers assigned to two local high schools. The division is headed by a deputy chief of police, and there are 13 sergeants. The division responds to the majority of calls for service received

---

by the department. During the last four fiscal years, on average, 78 officers were actually available, because of varying reasons including military, maternity, and sick leave as well as court appearances, vacations, and training. Sergeant Hernandez's commander works with him in setting priorities, deploying personnel, and responding to critical incidents. During the last three fiscal years, the vacancy rate was 10 percent. Currently the department is considering community-oriented policing (COP).

CRIME

There were 91,212 calls for service during the previous year, which was an increase of 3.6 percent. The department utilizes the county communications administration, and dispatchers inform the police department of all calls for service. In previous years the department had a service orientation and many members of the public turned to the police as a primary source for responding to a need or resolving non-criminal problems—many of which should have been handled by other city agencies. Hence, the calls for service have increased rapidly over the years. Several years previously, the county had instituted a non-emergency telephone system to handle non-criminal matters. As the new system became accepted by the public, the actual calls for police service dropped. Currently the calls for service provide dispatch service by placing calls into a four-category structure, with Part 1 allocated to emergencies where there is an immediate threat to life or an indication of grave personal injury. The department deals with seven Part 1 crimes, including homicide, aggravated assault, robbery, rape, burglary, motor vehicle theft, and arson. Under the Uniform Crime Report system, violent crimes include murder, assault, rape, and robbery. Other calls for police service cover a wide range, including prowler calls, abandoned vehicles, public drunkenness, traffic accidents, gang activity, suspicious persons, and other quality-of-life occurrences. Statistically, for the previous year the department reported a total of 961 violent crimes, which was fewer than those reported in the previous year. There were 19 homicides, 34 forcible rapes, 312 robberies, and 597 aggravated assaults. Additionally, there were 1701 burglaries, 2502 thefts, and 947 stolen vehicles. Forcible rapes are of increasing concern, and analysis reflected the fact that 28 percent were committed on business streets, 12 percent in residential areas, and the remainder in commercial establishments. The level of violent crime places the city in a category of the top 15 percent of communities with the greatest amount of violent crime.

COMMUNITY

The community has a council-manager type of local government and is the county seat. The current population is 146,322 and its growth for the past five years has been less than 1 percent annually. It used to be that many individuals retired to the community in order to live in a more suburban environment with a special desire to get away from city life and enjoy a more rewarding community life. As a consequence of current economics, the cost of living is less than that found in a metropolitan area and the prices of houses have dropped considerably. Numerous houses are in foreclosure and vacant, and this has started to cause the deterioration of some neighborhoods. The community has a very good public transit system, with buses, a light rail, and an interstate bus line. A state highway runs north and south and is east of the city. This allows for easy access to the metropolitan area some 42 miles north of the community. The population is 45.3 percent white, 45.2 percent Hispanic, and 3 percent African-American. The remaining residents are Islanders, Asian, and Native American.

The city has a community college, a private four-year liberal arts college, and two trade schools. The current unemployment rate is 12.3 percent, and one-third of the working residents are employed in service, 26 percent in the retail trade, and 14 percent work for government agencies.

OFFICER

Hernandez attended a local high school where he excelled in two sports—football and baseball. Academically he was clearly above average. He was a school leader and active in numerous activities. He joined the local National Guard unit after graduation from high school and he currently holds the rank of sergeant in an MP company. He is 28 years of age and joined the police department after completing one year of college. He has continued taking online classes and has been taking two classes each semester at the local private college. He anticipates graduating in business administration by striving to master upper-division classes. He has become a very good student and has a grade point average of 3.4. He is married and he and his wife are expecting their first child. Hernandez resides in the older section of the city that is convenient to shopping areas and close to numerous relatives. He is an Episcopalian and very active in a neighborhood church. He is best described as action oriented, and his supervisory assignment to the swing shift provides a wide range of experiences for himself and those that he supervises. He found it difficult to let others that he supervised do the work, and he had to work diligently "supervising" not "doing." As a supervisor he continues to complete assignments with zest and remains achievement oriented. Within the department he is viewed as a "comer." He obtained his supervisory position by scoring high on the written test and was ranked number one on the oral assessment. He enjoys police work and constantly strives to improve his field performance. He is an avid reader, subscribing to several police journals. Other than his devotion to his family and his religion, he lives and breathes law enforcement, and ever since middle school he has wanted to be a police officer. After three years of field experience, he was chosen to instruct field procedures in the departmental police academy. In all of his assignments he has worked well with other officers and has been accepted as competent by everyone he has worked with, including his supervisor. He is a police officer through and through.

PROBLEM

The chief of police informed line personnel of the continued difficulties with the budgetary crisis, the need to deal with the continuing gang problem, and his desire to move into COP. He was candid about the difficulties confronting the department and the need to analyze departmental operations and resource allocation. The chief felt it was important to create a viable strategic plan for the department. He stressed that the issues that had to be confronted were difficult ones, but that with careful scrutiny a number of potential solutions/remedies could come to light.

WHAT WOULD YOU DO?

As a member of management, if you were Hernandez, what would you do to see that the conversion to COP took place? Would you volunteer to be on the strategic planning committee? Why? Justify this position. Would you engage in process facilitation? Be specific and identify points that you want to emphasize. Would you create a plan for fostering open communication with those that you supervise? How would you build partnerships within the department? Justify. How would you identify stakeholders?

Community policing has been celebrated as the solution for the vast majority of problems faced by law enforcement. It arrived with a fanfare supported by many national police organizations and, to an ever-increasing degree, has taken the nation by storm. With financial backing of the federal government, it has been embraced by many police administrators and politicians. It has become the byword of the day, the elixir we have been waiting for, the dynamic phrase of the last 35 years. It is one of the hottest police topics of the last two decades and continues to be a mainstay for many departments. It grabs headlines in small as well as large police agencies. Over the years it has gained momentum as police and community leaders search for a means of providing better police services, and the public has become increasingly concerned about their quality of life. As community policing has evolved it has become an integral component of many police departments and reference to it can be found in mission statements, departmental websites, and annual reports (Reiss, 2006). As of 2009 it was estimated that 81 percent of the population of this country were policed by agencies that practiced community policing. In the last 15 years, the department of Community Oriented Policing Services has distributed more than $12 billion in the furtherance of expanding and enhancing community policing. Since 2009, 109,581 officers have been hired by law enforcement agencies (Diamond & Weiss, 2009).

Reformists have been adamant in their ardor for community policing and essentially absolutist in catapulting the new doctrine to the forefront. This was done without any consideration of skepticism in its epistemological assumptions. In some agencies the entire patrol division had adopted community policing, whereas in others a specialized unit has come into existence. It should be noted that the typical agency response has been to create a new unit to address community problems. All efforts have been a learning process as researchers have interviewed police officers and members of the community, analyzed crime trends, and monitored and evaluated programs. Community policing is viewed as an all-encompassing philosophy and managerial stratagem. It is a challenging process in which the public plays a new role. Citizen involvement is essential and requires the creation of new avenues where a true partnership is created between residents and the police. Working together it provides for identifying and prioritizing contemporary problems with the goal of resolving issues that are of concern. It includes the reduction or elimination of crime and the fear of crime. It also can address overall neighborhood decay and social problems. In addition, it is a process wherein consideration is given to addressing civil disobedience and it strives to improve the quality of life in neighborhoods.

Slowly but surely leaders of law enforcement agencies have begun to acknowledge that traditional approaches, such as neighborhood saturation with intensive patrol activities, have, in many instances, proven to be of limited and lasting value. Hence, a strong movement has evolved to include others in crime-fighting efforts and confronting issues raised by quality of life matters. This has called for the involvement of residents, other city departments, and other interested parties in addressing community problems. Accomplishment of this task calls for identifying community attitudes and values, dealing with the personalities of participants and key decision makers, addressing problems with an open mind, and dealing with varying preferences of all of those who are involved, from mayors and city managers down to the individual resident (Chapman & Scheider, 2006; Clarke, 2007).

The task of working with and actively embracing members of the community into decision making and problem solving varies considerably from neighborhood to neighborhood. Some residents will cooperate with enthusiasm, whereas others will take a path of least resistance because of their opposition to the police. Another problem is that in some instances it has been difficult to sustain participation over a period of time. Evidence shows that local organizations have proven to be effective in developing a viable and continuing partnership. Time is especially important, and there is a genuine need to have a continuing and constant face-to-face relationship among officers, merchants, representatives of other municipal or county agencies, and residents. In addition, everyone has to be trained in the nuances of community policing and problem solving. The goal in one community was to maintain beat integrity and keep team members on their beat, which proved to be difficult because of dispatch volume that overloaded officers with work. This was especially true with the desire to have officers focus on problem solving, but only 30 percent of the officers found time to work with community members on prevention (Skogan et al., 2000).

There is no one way of organizing a community-policing response that is superior to another proposed remedy. Experience demonstrates that approaches are as diverse as the number of communities (National Institute of Justice, 2004). A problem that has occurred in some communities, and in all probability will occur in other cities, is that leadership transition will test the department's commitment to a community-policing program as new leaders come on board. The tenets of community policing can vary as new managers place their imprint on the organization. In other situations, political commitment may change with succeeding administrations and support may wane or grow (Skogan, Steiner, DuBois, Erik Gudell, & Fagan, 2002). When community policing becomes something more than a police program, there is a strong possibility that the program can evolve into a positive organizational response to the needs of the community. The civilian component of community policing is as problematic as the police side and support has to come from both sides if this new style of policing is to survive (Skogan et al., 2000). Through the years departments have dropped rudiments or radically changed aspects of their program and substituted remedial elements, some of which have worked, whereas others have had to be abandoned (Skogan et al., 2002).

The variability of community policing is readily apparent, and about two-thirds of larger municipal police departments and sheriff's departments have a full-time community-policing unit similar to those created when community relations and team policing were in vogue. Additionally, almost all large municipal agencies sheriffs' offices have sworn personnel who are designated as community police officers, and in both instances the number has grown steadily over the years. About three-quarters of local departments operated one or more community substations. Another encouraging sign is that more and more agencies train all new recruits in community-policing methods. Also, increasing numbers of law enforcement agencies encourage patrol officers to engage in problem-solving projects. One can also find that larger agencies meet regularly with neighborhood associations, school groups, domestic violence groups, other local public agencies, and advocacy groups. This is encouraging and indicates a continuing effort to involve different segments of the public and governmental entities regarding efforts to improve the quality of life in communities. Another encouraging feature is that police are turning more and more to surveying citizen satisfaction with their efforts and are moving to the evaluation of program effectiveness (Reaves & Hickman, 2004).

Definition

Regrettably, in the past, there has been a lack of consensus in defining community policing. It has turned out to be a fuzzy term because programs have been tailored to local needs and resources. Some view it as the need to emphasize a traffic program, gun tip program, working with the aged, a gang control program, citizens on patrol, citizen police academy, or business survey projects. Other programs include cooperative truancy programs, foot and bicycle patrols, citizen surveys, and bringing probation officers into problem-solving situations. Any one of these programs can be part of a community-policing effort but this is true only if it is the result of direct participation and support of the community. In many instances, problem-solving partnerships were found to be something in name only or simply standard, temporary working arrangements. Partnerships involving short-term crackdowns are not in the spirit of problem solving nor are partnerships with citizens and businesses in which their involvement is limited to merely being *involved.*

In the past, the community relations unit was a status symbol. It was an indicator that the agency was responding to the needs of the community and was perceived as part of the vanguard of professional law enforcement. One can only wonder if community policing in some cities is a hollow effort to keep up with what is a momentous shift in policing. Others view it as the ideology underpinning the agency, suggesting that it provides the reason for the existence of the department. Philosophically it can be a significant change from the traditional emphasis on law enforcement. At the least it is semantical gamesmanship and at most it requires radical change, wherein some personnel work with the community in determining the delivery system for police services (Kappeler & Gaines, 2005; Reaves & Hickman, 2004).

Community policing is not a quick fix. If it is to be successful, it demands a long-term commitment. It should not be sold as a panacea and there must be realistic expectations as to its potential to improve the quality of life in neighborhoods. At the same time, research shows that 52 percent of municipal police departments formed problem-solving partnerships through written agreement. In reality, the majority of line personnel continue to perform traditional police services (Reaves & Hickman, 2004). Only time will tell if community policing becomes more dominant within police circles (Parks et al., 1999).

If community policing is to become a reality, it has to be done by something other than executive fiat. Some of the factors that reinforce the possibility for successful implementation of a community-policing program are set forth in Figure 2.1. There are many rocks in the roadway when an organization makes an effort to implement any new program, which is especially true of community policing. When implemented, it can threaten the traditionalists who will do everything to thwart the development of a program that dilutes their power and authority. Status is important and must be acknowledged when change is perceived as threatening autonomy or authority. Resistance has the potential of coming from any level within the department, starting with a patrol officer and moving on up within the organization, especially

1. Accept mistakes as part of the learning process.
2. Allow all participants to act outside of the chain of command without fear of reprisal.
3. Confront all efforts to undermine the program.
4. Create flexible policies that maximize independent decision-making.
5. Create a positive working environment.
6. Create organizational adaptability.
7. Endorse and get the most out of officer discretion.
8. Enhance and support community input.
9. Foster a positive working environment.
10. Include every management level in all aspects of community policing.
11. Involve all levels in planning.
12. Maximize two-way communications.
13. Measure qualitative and quantitative impacts.
14. Reward nontraditional duties, such as problem solving, application of evaluation techniques, and the creation and development of community groups.
15. Share power with line personnel.
16. Develop personnel evaluation procedures that measure the application of community-policing skills.

FIGURE 2.1 How to ensure that community policing will have a reasonable chance to succeed. *Adapted from V.A. Leonard and Harry W. More (2000).* Police Organization and Management, *Ninth Edition. New York: Foundation Press.*

from differing managerial levels as they perceive an intrusion into their administrative prerogatives. Officers are often creatures of habit and they have invested time, energy, and experience into their job—so why change? Most change, especially a dramatic one like a new style of policing, can be threatening and, at the least, inconvenient. Change, unless planned and implemented carefully, introduces uncertainty and ambiguity and should be accepted as part of the change process. Training, coaching, and counseling should be applied liberally throughout any change process as a means of enhancing the implementation of community-oriented policing. One successful technique is to implement change on a small scale and evaluate its effectiveness prior to full-scale implementation (More et al., 2010).

At this point it is appropriate to suggest a working definition of community policing as shown in Figure 2.2. The definition has not been poured in concrete and is general enough so that agencies can modify it in order to address the varying needs of a specific community. Over the last two decades the definition has evolved. Key elements of this generic definition include (1) development of a dynamic relationship with community partnerships (individuals and organizations); (2) consideration of the most urgent needs of the community, ranging from

Community policing is viewed as a philosophy that promotes organizational strategies, which support the systematic use of partnerships and problem-solving techniques, to proactively address the immediate conditions that give rise to public safety issues such as crime, social disorder, and fear of crime.

FIGURE 2.2 Definition of community policing. *Source: U.S. Department of Justice (2009).* Community Policing Defined. *Washington, DC: Department of Community Oriented Policing Services.*

criminal acts to the fear of crime; (3) utilization of community resources; and (4) application of the problem-solving process.

If this working definition is to have true meaning, it has to serve as a philosophical base for the officers involved. Each officer must accept the fact that the department needs assistance in order to maximize the public safety effort. Community policing is a mindset wherein the department believes that the public is a vital component of the operation and the public supports and understands the mission values and role of the police department. Community policing provides officers with an opportunity to move closer to the community. It is a procedure wherein the police organize members of the community, coordinate activities, and communicate with every concerned individual and organization.

A more recent definition of community policing, if it is to be successful, demands radical change over time if there is to be a significant alteration in the way the organization attains goals. If change is to occur, it has to be leader centered and engendered. The historical nature of police work, with its quasi-military orientation, mandates the need for change to emanate from the top down. It is a transitional process wherein the chief executive officer removes barriers that impede change, fostering the development of a culture in which actions contrary to traditional working methods are stimulated (Oliver, 1998). In community policing, top management must articulate the values of community policing and communicate them to every level and everyone in the organization. The police become an integral part of the community culture and members of the community help in defining future priorities and distributing resources. It is democracy in action. Active participation is required of everyone who has an interest in the welfare of the community. It differs substantially from traditional models of policing and places considerable power and authority at the lowest level of the organization. Line officers and supervisors are the recipients of this significant shift of power and authority.

Community policing initially consisted of three complementary core components, "community partnerships, organizational transformation, and problem solving" (Diamond & Weiss, 2009). Over time, this process has moved from one-way communication to a significant two-way communication process. Involvement with the total community has become a collaborative partnership between the law enforcement entity and those served. Positive relationships with the community have evolved in the quest to improve the quality of life, improve crime control, and engage in preventive activities. Resources are pooled with those of the community (individual and groups), private businesses, the media, nonprofit/service providers, and other government agencies to address the most urgent concerns of community members. The second modifier is proactive problem solving wherein the specific concerns of a community are identified and through which the most appropriate remedies to abate these problems are found and evaluated rigorously. The thing that really binds community policing together is that it is not just another way to police a community but a philosophy of policing that calls for real organizational transformation.

Empowerment

The characteristics of officers and supervisors operating in a community-policing program cover a broad range of traits, including integrity, risk taking, originality, creativity, individuality, and problem solving. Every aspect of the organization must foster the development of these skills in its officers. The operational atmosphere must be such that traditional ways are challenged and new and innovative approaches are the rule rather than the exception. This is the only way the organization can respond to the need to promote public safety and enhance the quality of life in neighborhoods. Responding to changing crime problems requires a type of response that demands flexibility and critical reasoning not only from the police organization, but also from each officer (Bureau of Justice Assistance, 2001).

Empowerment of line personnel and first-line supervisors is an essential ingredient of community policing. If it is missing, it is not really community policing even though it might involve some degree of citizen participation. It allows personnel to arrive at decisions based on delegated power and authority. Empowerment is the deliberate decision of police executives to create organizational change that allows officers to operate within a frame of reference of self-direction. It is the placing of authority and responsibility at the lowest levels of the organization. With supervisory support and the backing of top management, there is an absolute necessity for empowering line officers so that initiative can be exercised when deciding when operating within the philosophy of community policing (Parks et al., 1999). It is a question of giving community-policing officers the operational freedom needed to accomplish their assigned tasks. Achieving this is not for the faint of heart—authority and power, normally the prerogative of the supervisor, must be relinquished and line officers must be trained and assisted in the acquisition and application of new powers (see Figure 2.3). It is a question of challenging officers to balance the need to immediately and effectively respond to calls for service work and develop innovative and proactive responses to community problems. Officers must be responsible for working with residents in a viable partnership in an effort to make the neighborhood safer and a better place to live (Fort Lee Police Department, 2008).

The exercise of judgment by the first-line supervisor calls for the development of superior skills when working to identify community resources that can be used to deal with a problem or assisting an officer to develop a solution for a problem. Accessing other community resources is an added dimension of supervision and calls for a differing capacity than that found under more traditional approaches to policing. It is a skill that a supervisor should acquire.

1. Creation of an atmosphere that supports the assumption of additional responsibilities.
2. Decision-making is an operational part of the empowerment process.
3. Maximization of officer discretion.
4. Officers are allowed to function independently.
5. Placing of authority and power to the lowest level.
6. Risk taking is an acceptable component of the process.
7. Trust governs the relationship between officers and the supervisor.

FIGURE 2.3 Components of empowerment.

Instead of making decisions, the supervisor coaches, supports, mediates, and helps officers in identifying, planning, analyzing, and solving community problems. Using such a process, supervisors foster a working environment that increases officer discretion. The goal is to get line personnel to function independently. This makes for a fluid and dynamic procedure wherein there is an ongoing process of adjustment and readjustment between officers and the supervisor. As this process evolves each line officer becomes more independent and becomes aware of what information the supervisor needs to make proper decisions regarding such things as the allocation of resources. As officers gain experience they can become responsible decision-makers, and supervisors should support this evolutionary process that fosters the acquisition of abilities and skills that officers need to work effectively.

Community policing envisions the empowerment of officers (Diamond & Weiss, 2009). It is a process wherein officers are given the opportunity to take independent action to solve problems, work with members of the community, and strive to improve the social ecology of the neighborhoods. Of critical importance is the necessity for officers to become sensitive to the needs of members of the community. Empowerment is the opposite of a supervisor encouraging officers to "just do what I tell you," "stay out of trouble," or "don't bother me." Challenged with problems not responsive to routine solutions, officers can be empowered by sergeants to search for creative solutions to problems rather than a traditional response.

Trust is the sum and substance of leadership in an empowered organization. Officers become managers of their own destiny, and it is acknowledged that line officers have the capacity and ability to make operational decisions (Reiter, 1999). Additionally, the supervisor functions as a mentor, motivator, and facilitator. Obviously all of this calls for a significant change in attitudes and methods of supervision. Constant and close supervision and the restriction of discretion are no longer the parameters of effective police supervision. Officers operating under the concept of community policing have their discretionary power increased as they strive to achieve long-term problem reduction. The community police officer does not just take reports and pass on information so others in the chain of command can make decisions. Instead, the officer becomes a decision-maker, solves the problem if possible, or at least participates in decisions leading to problem resolution.

When empowerment occurs, community policing will flourish. Significant decision-making becomes the responsibility of line personnel and first line supervisors rather than the sole property of police bureaucrats. Freedom is the essence. Unduly burdensome regulations, the hallmark of many police agencies, must be rejected if community policing is to have an even chance of succeeding. Superimposing community policing on a traditional organization is fraught with difficulty and presupposed failure. With the eradication of red tape and the elimination of delays, those who are really familiar with community problems have the power of real input based on their knowledge of the local environment. Under community policing the first-line supervisor, in some instances, is confronted with the dilemma that not every officer wants to become involved to the extent required in order to function effectively in this collaborative approach to policing. Empowerment is rejected by some officers because with it comes the assumption of additional responsibility and the concomitant risk. The added accountability and the demands of becoming innovative can be unsettling to some. Other officers will embrace the concept of empowerment and find it rewarding even though it might involve the need to take risks.

In another instance, the importance of the first-line supervisor can be limited if the organization does not provide for an evaluation process that concerns itself with areas that are used to evaluate officer performance that relates specifically to community policing. For example, if officers are evaluated by their supervisor for completing field interrogations, the number of businesses visited when on patrol, or the number of *Terry* stops, and they are not evaluated or rewarded for problem-solving efforts or successfully creating partnership efforts such as working with a neighborhood association or other community-policing activities, community-policing efforts will be negated. Traditional policing will overwhelm community-policing efforts. Evaluations have to reflect current community-policing efforts, not the time-honored and traditional policing techniques. One effort to deal with this problem was the creation of an achievement medal by the Metropolitan Police Department in the District of Columbia (Ramsey, 2001).

Metropolitan police department-sworn or civilian personnel performing an outstanding act that results in improved administration or operation, applies unique problem-solving skills, provides substantial savings in labor or operational costs, enhances the mission of the department greatly, furthers the goals of policing for prevention, enhances the lifestyle of community stakeholders, or who brings great credit to the department, are eligible to receive the achievement medal. The act(s) must be representative of performance beyond the requirements of the normal work assignment.

Supervisors should work with reluctant employees in an effort to balance the interests of the organization and the officer. Every effort must be made to adequately retrain employees and help them develop needed skills so that they can feel comfortable with the demands of the newly acquired delegation of power. In some instances, it is a process of changing the culture and the structure of the organization. All of this takes time. Intensive training can turn a skeptic into a proponent. Training has to be consistent with what the department asks them to do. The goal is to create a working environment wherein what is taught in training permeates every aspect of day-to-day operations and the process becomes a win–win–win proposition (Cunningham, 1994; Diamond & Weiss, 2009).

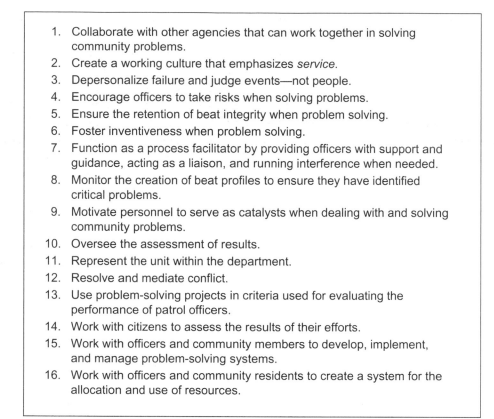

1. Collaborate with other agencies that can work together in solving community problems.
2. Create a working culture that emphasizes *service*.
3. Depersonalize failure and judge events—not people.
4. Encourage officers to take risks when solving problems.
5. Ensure the retention of beat integrity when problem solving.
6. Foster inventiveness when problem solving.
7. Function as a process facilitator by providing officers with support and guidance, acting as a liaison, and running interference when needed.
8. Monitor the creation of beat profiles to ensure they have identified critical problems.
9. Motivate personnel to serve as catalysts when dealing with and solving community problems.
10. Oversee the assessment of results.
11. Represent the unit within the department.
12. Resolve and mediate conflict.
13. Use problem-solving projects in criteria used for evaluating the performance of patrol officers.
14. Work with citizens to assess the results of their efforts.
15. Work with officers and community members to develop, implement, and manage problem-solving systems.
16. Work with officers and community residents to create a system for the allocation and use of resources.

FIGURE 2.4 Responsibilities of a first-line supervisor in community policing.

Quality Supervision

The necessity to work smarter becomes a reality when police departments are confronted with implementation of a community-policing program (Swope, 2000). The first-line supervisor takes center stage with the introduction of community policing into a department. Expectations are varied and include those set forth in Chapter 1. To these we must add the expectations of members of the public as they join forces with the police in an effort to recognize and resolve community problems. Above all, first-line supervisors must work at understanding the needs and perceptions of the public. This demands a constant interaction with members of the public to determine the services that need augmentation and the possibility that there is a need for innovative services.

Figure 2.4 lists several activities a supervisor must engage in when working within the parameters of community policing. Quality supervision envisions shared decision-making, teamwork, creativity, and innovation. It involves absolute commitment to the philosophy of community policing. The supervisor must personify the attributes of a facilitator, coach, counselor, mentor, role model, communicator, and coordinator if community policing is to succeed.

Beyond this, every action that a supervisor performs must be taken within the context of complete honesty and integrity (Scarano & Jones, 2000).

Quality supervision occurs when first-line supervisors decipher management's intentions and translate them into reality. Under community policing, getting officers involved in this new approach is an exceptional challenge and takes skills not needed under more traditional approaches to managing people. This supervisory process demands that the sergeant receives the training needed to adequately evaluate each officer's needs, goals, abilities, and motivational level. Having accomplished this, the supervisor can delegate responsibility and authority accordingly. If the supervisor is to accomplish his or her job, higher management must give that individual a great deal of authority and autonomy. This will allow the sergeant to exercise necessary discretion when determining the degree to which officers should be involved in the decision-making process and the extent to which they are held responsible for their actions. Additionally, it is important for the first-line supervisor to hold officers accountable for their community-policing efforts and activities. At the same time, each supervisor must be held accountable by higherups. The supervisor is key to the implementation and operation of a positive community-policing program (More, 2008). They are in a position to lead in the transformation that supports the philosophy of community policing.

Process Facilitation

The supervisor must convey the importance of community policing, especially in convincing police officers that community engagement and problem solving are *real* police work. If community policing is to succeed, the supervisor must genuinely support organizational changes. In some instances the change might include organizational structure and, at the very least, include new service policies and procedures. It is essential to articulate and reinforce the philosophy of community policing. Supervisors must become knowledgeable about the duties expected of them, and in this instance the applicable elements of Hu-TACK come into play. Initially, a supervisor might be unfamiliar with the working implications of the new service style. They must therefore make an effort to perform the role as expected. In this respect, the goal is for the supervisor to become comfortable in the new role. As the supervisor loses power to subordinates, an effort must be made to assume more managerial responsibility. A first-line supervisor is a manager, and operationally it is essential that the focus be shifted from the traditional role of being in charge to the role of facilitator. The operational motto is *facilitate–facilitate–facilitate.*

As a supervisor becomes more skillful in functioning as a process facilitator, he or she will find that considerable time is spent in educating, informing, and assisting officers in understanding, prioritizing, and resolving issues. A supervisor should accept the reality that some officers may resist the change to community policing. This must be expected, and the sergeant should work with these employees throughout the transition. Supervisors should keep in mind that community policing is a systematic view and what might seem as resistance might just be part of the process of adaptation. Radical change raises many questions, and a supervisor should be patient and deal with each objection as they arise. Officers who do not understand or object to aspects of a proposed change can become obstructionists if they do not see how they fit into a new program and what will be required of them. A partnership must be entered into with the officers by allowing them to take part in identifying needs and objectives. The supervisor has to work hard at communicating, advising, responding, and supporting officers that are having difficulty adjusting to this new style of policing. Finally, as a process facilitator, a supervisor must communicate openly. Additionally, they must become a team member and encourage officers to participate actively in problem solving. In community policing, beat officers are a positive resource and every effort should be made to tap their skills. A supervisor should identify those officers who have the knowledge, desire, and ability to carry out viable programs utilizing the resources inside and outside the department.

Building Partnerships Within the Police Department

The vital responsibility of building partnerships has several dimensions, including serving as a conduit—relaying information up the chain of command, explaining problems, and finding the means for resolving them. Additionally, efforts to build partnerships within the department, as a task, provide the supervisor with an opportunity to explain how community policing works cooperatively with other units, as well as requesting assets needed to resolve problems. This includes resources such as traffic officers, detectives, patrol officers, juvenile investigators, or a narcotics unit. It also involves relaying information to other unit supervisors about criminal activities that would be of interest to them, mediating conflict between units, and integrating unit activities with others. This activity involves not only sharing information but also a form of salesmanship wherein the supervisor tries to secure the commitment of resources to implement effective problem-solving strategies. These efforts are needed to encourage a spirit of cooperation throughout the ranks and foster the commitment of every officer to the community-policing process.

Of special importance is the working relationship between patrol officers and detectives. Under community policing it is necessary to reduce the isolation between the two units. To accomplish this, some departments (approximately one-half of larger police departments) have assigned detectives to cases based on geographic areas/beats. This clearly fosters and supports a working environment that allows for greater cooperation between the two entities. Officers can use neighborhood-based information for follow-up investigations, including the arrest of offenders. Information that was not available before will become available because of the continuing and constant contact between community police officers and members of the community. A supervisor should strive to draw upon the experience of successful officers and detectives and utilize their proven expertise when initiating programs that involve cooperative efforts. The supervisor should ensure that detectives give feedback to the officers when information results in the successful conclusion of an investigation. This reinforces the relationship between the two groups and motivates officers to continue to provide information. When one looks at municipal and county police departments, nearly all had sworn personnel designated as community-policing officers (Reaves & Hickman, 2004). For example, in Birmingham, 25 officers have been appointed as community-policing specialists. This means that the preponderance of the officers serve as generalists who concentrate heavily on 911 calls. It is this area where the supervisor can work at coordinating activities and advising other supervisors about what is being done and relaying information between the two entities (Parks et al., 1999). When possible, generalist officers can support the problem-solving activities of specialists.

The line officer remains the key to community policing and all other units should support problem-solving efforts. Institutionalization of this model is essential to success and it can flourish with unified responses to underlying factors that characterize true problem-oriented policing.

Collaboration

The basic doctrine of community policing is to work with other government and community-based organizations with a wide variety of resources needed to resolve identifiable community problems (Correia, 2000). Employing external resources may range from making a referral to another agency to asking an agency to participate in a cooperative effort. The identification of available and pertinent resources is a major phase in the development of a positive problem-solving program. If a department is fortunate enough, it will have a resource manual listing agencies, contact persons, and brief synopses of the services offered by the agencies. First-line supervisors should begin by contacting government and private agencies to collect information and develop responses to identifiable problems. Alternatively, if required, they should ask a commanding officer to make official contact. This allows supervisors to screen and identify viable agencies and it reduces the number of individuals who are contacting other agencies. In fact, in some communities, agencies encourage contact by appointed individuals.

Liaison and follow-up activities are essential if collaboration is to be effective. This is true for units within both the police organization and other city departments. Monitoring of follow-up requests is mandatory, and if the problems are not addressed within a reasonable time, the first-line supervisor should stimulate the needed response and provide feedback to line officers on accomplishments or progress made toward addressing crime and disorder problems (Community Policing Consortium, 2000). This function is critical to community policing because it proves that something can happen when citizens complain. It also directly affects the credibility of the line officer, as well as that of the police department. Other city agencies have been especially effective at removing abandoned vehicles, enforcing parking regulations, enforcing building codes, and demolishing vacant buildings. They can also control vendors and eliminate hazardous conditions on private property. One police department obtained the permission of owners of abandoned buildings (by working with the department of building and safety) to enter each building and evict trespassers prior to demolition of the buildings. In another instance, a city housing department actively helped apartment owners obtain loans to rehabilitate property, thus improving the quality of housing and setting a new standard for the community. The landlord-training program emphasizes cooperation among property owners, tenants, and law enforcement agencies to help neighborhoods fight drug-related crime. The landlord program involves a commitment to substantive problem solving and to building and sustaining effective community partnerships (Bureau of Justice Assistance, 2000).

Supervisors can reinforce the collaboration process of problem solving by monitoring the efforts of officers. Members of other agencies can be contacted to determine how well subordinates have performed in a collaborative effort. If the supervisor finds that the officer has functioned poorly, effort should be expended to provide the officer with assistance and guidance to resolve the problem. If the feedback is positive, this information should be relayed to the involved officers.

Working in partnership with community members and organizations is an effective and productive way to address neighborhood problems and needs. A partnership involves law enforcement agencies working with various groups based on equality. This means breaking new ground and developing skills in collaboration. For some the community represents *naysayers, police bashers, busybodies, vigilantes,* or *police wannabes.* If community policing is to work, these clichés must be rejected and members of the community must be allowed to become involved in the problem identification procedure. Potential partners come from groups who are directly affected by a problem, those who must deal with the problem, and those who would benefit if the problem did not exist. This can mean a wide range of groups ranging from service organizations, tenants' groups, and parent–teacher associations. A partnership is not something that happens automatically. It can take time and sometimes a great deal of effort to overcome the opposition of those who are skeptical and certainly those who are hostile. Possibly the only way to overcome this is a combination of time, example, and word of mouth.

Community-policing partnership requires residents who are active at the community level to select problems and to develop and implement strategies. Nevertheless, partnerships also require that the community have a say at the jurisdictional level where conditions of the partnership are set. A feeling of community can be generated by allowing citizens of an area to actually define what constitutes their neighborhood (Mittleman, 2000). Without give and take when establishing the guidelines of collaboration, partnerships will reflect the needs and concerns of police departments and not those of the neighborhood partners. Figure 2.5 is an example of a community enhancement request form that an officer can use to request specific services from city agencies to handle conditions that may result in crime or community decay.

The police should be working very consciously in partnership with those who are affected by the problems and who are working or will work with their neighbors to solve them. In one study, it was found that nearly all agencies met with various community groups during the year. The largest percentages met with neighborhood associations (89%) and school groups (79%), followed by business groups (69%), other local public agencies (62%), senior citizen groups (59%), advocacy groups (54%), and youth service organizations (57%) (Reaves & Hickman, 2004). There are two reasons for focusing on those who are organized. First, a collective community is more likely to be sustained and successful in solving a problem than individuals. Second, an organized effort is more likely to continue to exist after the problem is solved. The emphasis on working with residents who are organized does not mean that law enforcement agencies should stop responding to individual calls or refuse to work with individuals. It does mean that for community policing to be an effective crime-fighting strategy, there must be an emphasis on partners who can help produce long-term crime reduction. It does mean that where these partnerships do not exist or are weak, there must be an investment in creating or

RESOURCE

    Individual
    Officer
    Resident or Visitor
    Business
    City/County Departments
    Other Justice Entities
    Other Governmental Agencies

COMMUNITY ENHANCEMENT SERVICE

False alarms	Abandoned vehicles
Drug operations	Vacant buildings
Cruising	Vendors
Disorderly conduct	Lighting
Graffiti	Repair of roads and sidewalks
Identity theft	Gang activity
Loud vehicles	Enforcement of curfew
Aggressive panhandling	Fights
Shoplifting	Enforcement of parking
Drunkenness in public	Attractive nuisance
Stalking	Gun violence
Street prostitution	Financial crimes
Under aged drinking	Drug labs
Runaways	Acquaintance rape
Lighting	Check fraud
Breaking and entering	Prescription fraud
Burglary of residents	Rave parties
Theft from vehicles	Vandalism
Burglary of businesses	Trash collection

FIGURE 2.5 Quality of life in the community.

strengthening them. Partnerships are clearly something other than name only or simply routine, temporary working arrangements. True community partnerships, involving sharing power and decision-making, are rare at this time, found in only a few of the flagship departments. Other jurisdictions have begun to lay foundations for true partnerships and the trust needed for power sharing and joint decision-making should emerge (Roth & Ryan, 2000).

Problem Solving

A key characteristic of the modern approach to policing is a positive orientation to problem solving. It involves more than responding to 911. It is a matter of viewing incidents from a community perspective to resolve the problem, not just simply *handling* an incident. Problem-oriented policing shifts police efforts from a reactive to a proactive response to crime wherein officers work with residents to prevent crime (Police Executive Research Forum, 1996).

Citizens, police departments, and other agencies work together to identify problems and apply appropriate problem-solving strategies (Rabkin, 1995). This approach emerged in the late 1970s and was initially described by Herman Goldstein. It was his position that the police should be concerned with problems that were of concern to residents of a community (Goldstein, 1990). The central thesis of problem-oriented policing is that underlying incidents that police respond to are more general problems that, in order to be resolved, require a different type of response than incidents that are indicative of the problems. Problem solution requires analysis of the incidents by persons knowledgeable of the framework in which they are occurring, followed by imaginative brainstorming about and experimentation with promising responses. While problem-oriented policing theoretically can be conducted in the absence of community-oriented policing, it is an excellent method of achieving the goals of community-oriented policing. This is why the model that is proposed in this chapter is best described as *problem-oriented policing/community-oriented policing*.

This process is a proactive philosophy that promotes the concept that incidents consuming patrol and investigative time can best be dealt with more effectively when consideration is given to underlying problems. It also assumes that the expertise and creativity of line officers are reliable sources when developing solutions to problems. Finally, if problem solving in the community is to be successful, the police must work with the public to ensure that they are addressing the real needs of citizens.

Detectives and line officers are the ones who can use the problem-solving approach. It allows them to identify, analyze, and respond continuously to the underlying causes prompting citizens to request police services. It is not a one-shot project or program, but a comprehensive process for identifying, addressing, and resolving problems. The SARA model is not the only way to approach problem solving, but many police officers and supervisors have found it to be a very useful research device. It is a strategy consisting of four stages (Bynum, 2001; Spelman & Eck, 1987; Wolfer et al., 1999):

> **SCANNING**—Identifying the problem, where problems are defined as a group of related or recurring incidents or a particular concern of the community.
> **ANALYSIS**—An in-depth exploration of the problem and its underlying causes.
> **RESPONSE**—Implementing an analysis-driven strategy to address the problem, focusing on factors identified in the analysis phase.
> **ASSESSMENT**—Ongoing review and monitoring of the progress of the response in achieving its objectives.

It was determined that 58 percent of agencies surveyed that had more than 100 officers actively encouraged patrol officers to engage in problem solving, and that about one in three local agencies and one in five state agencies included problem-solving projects in criteria used for evaluating the performance of patrol officers (Reaves & Hickman, 2004).

On identification of a problem, actions can be taken to collect information about the problem. This in turn leads to a detailed analysis of the information. The final stage shows whether the actions had the desired effect on the problems.

Scanning

Instead of relying on legal terms such as robbery, burglary, or petty theft to guide a response, officers analyze specific offenses in a broader context and address them as problems. Then these problems are dealt with according to their impact on the neighborhood or the community. For example, a police incident such as auto theft might be a part of a "chop" operation (cutting up an automobile into saleable or usable parts). A series of house burglaries might in reality be a school truancy problem.

Scanning initiates the problem-solving process. In a genuinely problem-oriented police department, every member scans for problems and brings the problem to the attention of a supervisor. Some three decades ago the police working with members of the community and researchers clearly demonstrated that crime and disorder problems were amenable to the findings of comprehensive problem analysis. In Newport News, Virginia, burglaries were reduced in an apartment complex by 34 percent, prostitution-related robberies in the district were reduced by 39 percent, and thefts from two downtown areas by more than 50 percent. This led to the efficacy of the problem-solving process that was incorporated into the philosophy of community policing (U.S. Department of Justice, 2002).

With everyone involved, one can assume that it is someone else's responsibility. In other words, shifting the responsibility becomes somewhat limited. Some officers are better than others at identifying problems. Some accept the new process as a challenge, whereas others find that it is extra work to be avoided at all costs. Other officers are reluctant to identify problems because they might be stuck with working on the problem (Eck & Spelman, 1987). Overtime objections, such as those mentioned earlier, can be overcome as officers become more accustomed to the problem-solving process. The objectives of the scanning process include:

- Looking for problems.
- Initial identification of possible problems.
- Initial analysis to determine if the problem exists and whether a detailed analysis is needed.
- Prioritizing of problems and assignment of personnel.

Agency personnel have numerous sources that can be used to identify problems, but in many instances officers will initially rely upon their own experience to identify problems. The way that problems may come to your attention includes engaging in activities listed in Figure 2.6, which include a wide range of methods that can be used to identify problems. A problem can be defined as:

1. A cluster of similar, related, or recurring incidents, rather than a single incident.
2. A component of police business.
3. A place a person(s) (a repeat perpetrator of child abuse).

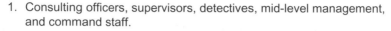

1. Consulting officers, supervisors, detectives, mid-level management, and command staff.
2. Consulting social services and governmental agencies.
3. Following media coverage and editorials.
4. Mapping specific crimes according to time of day, proximity to certain locations, and other similar factors.
5. Participating in community meetings.
6. Reviewing police reports.
7. Reviewing citizen complaints and letters.
8. Reviewing information from neighborhood associations and nonprofit organizations (local and national).
9. Routinely analyzing calls for service, crime incident data, and other agency records for patterns and trends involving repeat locations, victims, and offenders (police agencies may need to look at calls going back six months to a year to get an accurate picture of repeat calls for some types of problems).
10. Surveying community residents, business owners, elected officials, and students.

FIGURE 2.6 Methods of identifying problems. *Source: U.S. Department of Justice (2002).* Problem-Solving Tips—A Guide to Reduce Crime and Disorder Through Problem-Solving Partnerships. *Washington, DC: Office of Community Oriented Policing Services.*

4. A special event or time (a yearly parade, an annual festival).
5. A substantive community concern.
6. A type of behavior (such as panhandling, theft of bicycles) (Goldstein, 1990; U.S. Department of Justice, 2002).

Informally, a problem can be thought of as two or more incidents similar in one or more ways that are of concern to the police and a problem for the community. The key is the fact that both entities perceive the situation as a problem. Some problem solvers look at the link among the victim, the offender, and the place. This has become known as the crime triangle and allows the police to focus on factors that can be dealt with and the impact that one has on the other (Boba, 2003; U.S. Department of Justice, 2009).

Identifying Stakeholders

An officer should identify as many stakeholders as possible after the problem has been selected. This is important because each stakeholder may bring differing degrees of expertise and unique leverage that can affect the problem. Stakeholders are not created equal and as much time as possible should be spent identifying potentially competent and capable individuals and organizations during this selection process. In many instances, the greater the number of stakeholders allowed for the application, the greater the potential for dealing positively with a problem. Stakeholders include private and public organizations and groups of individuals such as youths, seniors, homeowners, renters, or merchants. The goal is to identify groups that will benefit if a problem is addressed. Stakeholders may include:

- Agencies or individuals who have some control over offenders such as parents, relatives, friends, school officials, probation and parole, landlords, or building managers.
- Business establishments affected unfavorably by the crime or disorder problem.
- Local social and governmental agencies with jurisdiction over the problem or an interest in a facet of the problem.
- National organizations or trade associations with an interest in the problem such as Mothers Against Drunk Drivers (MADD).
- Neighbors, co-workers, friends, and relatives of victims or anyone else who has been affected by the problem.
- Victims of the problem, including organizations that represent victims (U.S. Department of Justice, 2002).

In some instances, the police have found that the problem-solving effort is more effective if only two or three of the stakeholders—a nucleus group—work throughout the process and other stakeholders are brought into the process at varying stages, as needed, in order to have their input. In many instances, stakeholders are not in a position for a high level of participation, which should be kept in mind during each and every problem-solving effort.

Many officers are cautious about announcing the identification of a problem until they truly feel that a problem actually exists. This usually means that problems have been rejected before bringing the problem to the attention of others, which is where stakeholders come in and then can be used to apply their expertise to the problem. One thing an officer should consider is the use of crime prevention surveys, which provide information on criminal behavior, such as the exact times and kinds of offenses committed, the offender's method of operation, the targets of attack, crime generators, and hot spot locations. Follow-up crime surveys can identify some of the causes of crime and aid in the elimination of crime opportunities (Wolfer et al., 1999). Environmental surveys can also be used effectively by assessing the overall physical environment of an area as systematically and objectively as possible. The physical environment is composed of the buildings, parks, streets, transportation facilities, and overall landscaping of an area, as well as the functions and conditions of these entities. With these data, an officer can focus on determining how the physical environment affects the social environment. In other words, an officer might want to find out how features of the physical environment contribute to crime and disorder by facilitating offenders and inhibiting nonoffenders.

Analysis

After identification of the problem, the officers assigned should collect information from every conceivable source related to the problem. This includes private as well as public sources. For example, it can include information from neighborhood associations and neighborhood watch groups. Other sources include elected officials or the news media, as well as information from other law enforcement or governmental agencies. More recently, officers have turned to active offenders who can provide a wealth of information about crimes, motives, and techniques. Research with active offenders has focused on five categories (Decker, 2005):

- Drug dealers and users.
- Residential burglars.
- Armed robbers.
- Gang members.
- Gun offenders.

Additionally, officers can use a checklist to ensure that all needed information is collected (Figure 2.7). The three areas of concern include:

- Actors involved in the problem, including victims and offenders.
- Specific incidents, including the sequence of events and physical contact involved in the incidents.
- Responses by the community and institutional entities.

All the information gathered serves as a foundation for developing a thorough understanding of what is finally determined to be the real problem. This serves as a base for identifying causes and developing options for its resolution. The checklist reminds officers of areas and topics open to consideration. Implicit in the list are potential sources of information that might not have been covered under the scanning part of the assessment process. During analysis, emphasis is given to external information sources, such as consulting with citizens, business leaders, community associations, and other community groups. Another source in the analysis stage is the environmental survey that, along with other information, can lead to an understanding of conditions contributing to a problem. By measuring the physical environment of a drug-ridden area, for example, a survey may illustrate a connection between low lighting and overgrown bushes and an inability of local residents to keep watch over the area.

One of the best sources developed in recent years is Community Oriented Policing Services (COPS), which can be accessed via their website: www.communitypolicing.org. The mission of this office is to advance the practice of community policing as an effective strategy in improving public safety. This allows an officer to determine what is being done in other agencies by going to the Resource Information Center (RIC). The RIC offers publications, DVDs, CDs, and training material on a wide range of law enforcement concerns and community-policing topics. When utilizing the RIC, officers will not normally collect information from all of the sources listed, only from those related directly to the problem under consideration. Another qualifier is the time the officer has available to search for an appropriate response to the problem under consideration (Eck & Spelman, 1987). There is a tendency for officers to identify the response to the problem before completing the analysis; when this occurs, options might be eliminated from consideration. There are no hard and fast rules regarding the analysis process. The order of analysis activities depends on specific aspects of the problem, data needed to address it, and data initially available (Bynum, 2001). What is critical is early formulation of a plan to govern the order of analysis.

ACTORS

Victims' lifestyle	Security measures taken Victimization history This victimization
Offenders	Identity and physical description Lifestyle, education, employment history, medical history Criminal history
Third parties	Personal data Connection to victimization Nature of involvement Expectations for police action

INCIDENTS

Sequence of events	Target of act Type of tools used by offenders Events preceding act Event itself Events following criminal act
Physical contact	Chronology Location Access control Surveillance

Social context	Likelihood and probable actions of
	   witnesses
	Attitude of residents toward
	   neighborhood

RESPONSES

Community	Neighborhood affected by problem City as a whole People outside the city Groups
Institutional	Criminal justice agencies Other public agencies Mass media Business sector

FIGURE 2.7 Checklist for analysis of a problem. *Source: William Spelman and John E. Eck (1987).* Problem Oriented Policing. *Washington, DC: National Institute of Justice.*

A useful framework for developing analysis questions that may reveal the nature of the problem is the "crime triangle," which demonstrates the relationship among three elements of a crime: victims, offenders, and locations. Each of these elements is amenable to the time-honored and traditional who, where, why, when, and how questions as a starting point for eliciting pertinent details about a problem. In some incidents, victim-oriented analysis questions can produce relevant findings as to the relationship between the two entities: victimization rates and crime prevention action the victim may or may not have taken. Data about an offender can show the number, type, and location of prior offenses. In some situations it may show that an offender has specialized in certain offenses or locations.

For the location element of the crime triangle, it must go beyond a simple description of the crime location. One needs to know how characteristics of the problem location relate to occurrence of the problem. By grouping or mapping incidents coupled with environmental surveys it may be possible to understand how the lighting or access patterns and other aspects of the location both contribute to the problem. For example, it might lead to a pattern of access for the theft of automobiles and where the vehicles are taken, such as a chop shop (Bynum, 2001).

Before transition into response there should be a meeting of the analysis team to discuss the findings. This involves a presentation of the most significant findings, whether or not there are contradictory findings, and the most salient factors that have been discovered through the analysis. At this point and time the problem team is in a position to discuss appropriate responses.

Response

This stage requires initiative by the officer as different solutions are identified and the best solution is selected and implemented. Involving outside agencies that have needed resources and expertise that are seldom available within a police agency increases the number of potential solutions to a problem. This stage involves working with individuals, businesses, and private agencies. It also requires the officer to work with public agencies, such as the probation department, health department, public works, and the social service department. All of these sources are important because other agencies and entities can come up with responses that fall outside of the normal expertise possessed by law enforcement agencies. Combined resources can prove to be the most effective response to the problem being studied. Officers striving to find a solution to a problem should have free rein for discovering the answer. In one city the only restriction was that the solution had to be legally, financially, administratively, and politically possible (Spelman & Eck, 1987). It should also be pointed out that an environmental survey could guide responses to crime problems. A survey may shed light on activities within an open-air market where drugs are sold by drawing attention to the market's street design. In this instance, the response could be to work with city planners on redesigning the street to change traffic flow and accessibility.

Solutions to problems can be organized into six potential responses (Figure 2.8). The most desirable, but sometimes not attainable, solution is to totally eradicate a problem (Group 1). This generally occurs when the problem is relatively small, is something that has occurred recently, and affects a limited number of people. This could be as simple as congestion caused by the removal of a stop sign or having too few trash receptacles in a recently renovated neighborhood park.

In the second group of solutions, action taken by the police and members of the community can materially reduce a problem. These are generally found to be neighborhood crimes

---

1. Better handling of the problem and an improved response to the problem.
2. Fewer incidents.
3. Less serious or harmful incidents.
4. People and institutions affected by the problem are left better equipped to handle a similar problem in the future.
5. Remove the problem from police consideration.
6. Total problem elimination.

FIGURE 2.8 Possible solutions to problems. *Source: U.S. Department of Justice (2002).* Problem-Solving Tips—A Guide to Reducing Crime and Disorder Through Problem-Solving Partnerships. *Washington, DC: Office of Community Oriented Policing Services.*

and disorder problems. Such a solution usually involves persistent problems. The fact that they have been around for some time is evidence that they are unlikely to be eliminated. Examples include such problems as robbery, burglary, vandalism, drug dealing, and prostitution.

Group 3 solutions can most often be applied to problems where it is almost impossible to reduce the number of incidents they create, but it is possible to alter the characteristic of these incidents. These may be problems created by behavior that has unintended harmful effects. For example, officers may look for ways to reduce killings and injuries resulting from gambling among residents—the gambling is not stopped or reduced but some of the harm is reduced. These solutions can also be used in combination with other types of solutions. For example, Group 3 solutions may be used as part of attempts to deal with commercial robberies or rapes by showing potential victims how to act to minimize the chances of being killed or injured during an incident.

Group 4 solutions are generally applied to problems that are jurisdiction-wide and involve larger social concerns. For these problems, improving the way difficulties are handled may be the best solution in the short run. Over a much longer period, the solution, combined with other social changes, may reduce the problem. Examples include such problems as runaway juveniles, drug addiction and abuse, drunk driving, and elder abuse.

Group 5 solutions probably will be applied to problems that have been created by specific businesses or groups as a "by-product" of their ways of operating. Examples might include stores that arrest shoplifters but consistently fail to prosecute (Eck & Spelman, 1987). As a result, the problem is no longer of concern to the police.

Finally (Group 6), a solution occurs when people and institutions affected by the problem are left better equipped to handle a similar problem in the future. When a solution becomes apparent, implementation should occur immediately or incrementally depending on the circumstances. Some problems are subject to immediate solution because they are minor in nature or involve a few people. Other solutions might involve broad social issues that require a complex response.

An essential element of the response phase is to approach problems without any preconceived notion as to how the problem should be handled. An open mind is an essential element in problem response. In some instances, stakeholders are tempted to implement programs because they have been used successfully in other communities—this should be resisted. In many situations, off-the-shelf solutions will not work unless the situation is strikingly similar. Also, experience has shown that an officer can tend to revert to a traditional response, but the key is to develop a tailored response that is focused and linked directly to the findings in the analysis phase of the problem-solving effort (U.S. Department of Justice, 2002).

Assessment

Assessment is the final stage and involves measuring how well the program performed. Was it effective? The agency and the community can work together to answer this question. Possibly the initial analysis was flawed or the wrong response was selected. The process of assessment can provide an officer with the information needed to determine success. For some situations, assessment is quite simple and the results are obvious (Eck, 2002). In other situations, it is intricate and may involve the collection of complex data. Surveys are becoming increasingly common and among the possible objectives of a police department are the following:

- Analysis of crime and disorder problems.
- Comparison of a jurisdiction's community-policing efforts—and impact on victimization—with those of other jurisdictions.
- Comparison of local victimization rates with those of other jurisdictions.
- Evaluation of victimization—differences between reported offenses and actual victimization by individual characteristic such as race, gender, age, and income.
- Indicators of citizen fearfulness.
- Measures of citizen willingness to report crime.
- Measures of police performance—the survey can measure citizen knowledge and attitudes; satisfaction reflects how well the police are doing their job from the citizens' perspective.
- Measures of public information efforts (Weisel, 1999).

Community surveys can be designed to provide the police with reliable feedback from citizens about police performance. The COPS office and the Bureau of Justice Statistics have developed a software package that includes a standardized community survey that can be administered by telephone. The entire questionnaire can be obtained at no cost and addresses the following basic but critical issues:

- Why are we doing a survey and what do we want to know?
- What kind of resources and commitment do we have for this effort?
- Who should be surveyed and how?
- How many people should be surveyed?
- What do we do with the responses to the survey?

The guide comes with not only the software, but also a technical how-to manual. It provides an overview of key issues involved in conducting survey research. It includes some basic dos and don'ts for conducting surveys that can withstand close scrutiny. The Justice

Survey Software (JSS), web-based version 2.0, includes the following (Bureau of Justice Statistics, 2006):

- A built-in reporting module.
- A library of turnkey surveys that can be used as a starting point.
- A user-friendly interface for designing surveys.
- Easy data export in various industry standard formats.
- Real-time tools for monitoring progress during data collection.

Surveys can be used for a variety of purposes. For example, they are useful in gathering data on specific problems in target neighborhoods or among special populations. In Newport News, Virginia, a survey of residents in an apartment complex revealed concerns about the maintenance and physical structure of the complex. In Maryland, Baltimore County officers routinely use surveys to diagnose community problems confronted by special problem-solving units. In Los Angeles, a survey instrument was used to measure the effectiveness of a Model Neighborhood Program (Kerstein, 2001). In another community, a contractor conducted an annual citizen satisfaction survey to assess service delivery, which was accomplished by a telephone survey that queried approximately 400 citizens through a random digit-dialing approach (Weisel, 1999).

In other communities, surveys have been used to help define community concerns about drug problems. Special populations—the elderly, schoolchildren, women, minority groups, and others—can also be surveyed to learn their special concerns. When evaluating a problem-solving program, multiple surveys can prove to be most effective. For example, before-and-after surveys can be used to determine changes in citizens' fear of crime because of police intervention. Another area where surveys are very useful is recording and analyzing environmental characteristics of a problem area. They help an officer analyze the nature of a problem by identifying what factors contribute to the crime and pointing to incivilities in the problem area. Used before and after implementing a problem-solving effort, environmental surveys enable the officer to measure the effectiveness of the effort. During a 12-month period, nearly half of the departments studied (with 100 or more sworn personnel) surveyed citizens regarding their satisfaction with police services (50%), and two-fifths conducted a survey of citizen perceptions of crime-related problems (Reaves & Hickman, 2004).

There are, of course, other means of measuring the impact of a problem-solving effort, such as reduced instances of repeat victimization, decreases in related crimes or incidents, or other neighborhood indicators such as less loitering, fewer abandoned automobiles, and less truancy. The measures that are selected for accessing a problem will vary considerably because of the nature of the problem, preferences of the police and the community, and the ability of the jurisdiction to collect necessary data (U.S. Department of Justice, 2002).

The values of community policing are different from those practiced under the traditional response to crime. Expressed organizational values can serve as the basis for citizens understanding the police function in a democracy. The problem-solving process can be utilized to reinforce the values of the police department and the community and have proven to be an effective tool for law enforcement. Community policing involves giving officers greater control over their working conditions and empowerment. This requires a new style of supervision.

The authoritarian supervision style is unacceptable. No longer is it permissible to give an order and expect an officer to respond with absolute obedience.

Supervising Community Police Officers

There are many intrinsic rewards to officers who work in a problem-solving police department. An officer has greater control over the work performed, coupled with increased responsibility and a higher degree of autonomy. The most significant feature is the involvement of line officers in the decision-making process because of increased participation in the problem-solving process. All of these lead to improved job satisfaction. Supervisors can provide expertise needed to identify and solve neighborhood problems or help residents. A supervisor can also help officers manage their available time so that they may handle problems adequately. Some agencies authorize first-line supervisors to schedule flextime, permitting officers to amend their work hours as necessary and balance demands between calls for service and problem solving. Some departments allow officers to consult with other officers and a supervisor to work cooperatively by altering days off or changing schedules if the situation warrants.

Computer software is available that materially helps a supervisor by forecasting officer and vehicle needs by beat and neighborhood, generating alternative officer schedules that optimize services, and redesigning beats to optimally balance workloads and communities. Additionally, this software can automatically detect and rank problems by geographical areas and tie them to demographics, crime reports, patterns, and known offenders.

Supervisors will normally meet with officers at daily briefings to discuss scheduling, personnel problems, problem-solving techniques, resources, and other matters of mutual interest. Sergeants should spend most of their time working with officers in the neighborhoods. This allows them to become familiar with not only the neighborhoods but also the problems facing the officers so help can be provided as needed.

Successful community policing requires the supervisor to relay information up the chain of command about problem-solving efforts, as well as requests for needed resources. It is also an excellent time to reinforce the importance of community policing by indicating its contributions to the attainment of departmental goals. It should be kept in mind that praising good work is a must. It is amazing how far an accolade can go in improving morale and energizing an officer when engaged in a problem-solving process. Praise is a stimulus that can result in a continuing pattern of goal attainment.

Managing Failure

The first-line supervisor must manage in a casual manner. Community policing is new ground and problem solving is a new technique. It is not uncommon for mistakes to precede innovative results. In the struggle to resolve problems, officers will make mistakes and proposed solutions will fail. When risks occur and innovative solutions are sought, the margin for error increases dramatically as officers proceed through the learning curve. Managing and controlling failure can result in positive outcomes. Supervisors have to develop an attitude of acceptance of failure. Management of the total department begins with the attitude that positive failures can become the power that propels the organization toward the attainment of goals.

Looking for a "fall guy" has to be rejected out of hand. When failure occurs, the supervisor should work with the officer and document the reasons for failure. Circulation of this information to all interested parties is an essential part of the learning process. This critique process will undoubtedly identify training needs or other errors subject to correction. The supervisor should arrange for additional training or provide feedback in order to reduce future errors. A teamwork philosophy should replace power-oriented supervision emphasizing an atmosphere of risk taking, creativity, and the acceptance of errors in decision-making. When managing failure you must engage in a course of depersonalizing the failure and judging the actual event rather than the involved individual. When this is done, failure can be turned into a positive occurrence. Failure should lead to growth, not recriminations or discipline. It should be a learning process wherein a search can begin for identifying the reasons for failure, sharing that information with others, and searching for a solution that benefits the department and the community. This approach to dealing with failure can serve as the catalyst needed for actual professional development (Diamond & Weiss, 2009).

References

Boba, R. (2003). *Problem analysis in policing.* Washington, DC: Police Foundation.

Bureau of Justice Assistance, (2000). *Keeping illegal activity out of rental property: A police guide for establishing landlord training programs.* Washington, DC: Department of Justice.

Bureau of Justice Assistance, (2001). *The role of local government in community safety.* Washington, DC: Department of Justice.

Bureau of Justice Statistics, (2006). *Justice Survey Software (JSS).* Washington, DC: Office of Justice Programs.

Bynum, T. S. (2001). *Using analysis for problem-solving: A guide book for law enforcement.* Washington, DC: Office of Community Oriented Policing Services.

Chapman, R., & Scheider, M. (2006). *Community policing for mayors: A municipal service model for policing and beyond.* Washington, DC: Office of Community Oriented Policing Services.

Clarke, R. V. (2007). *Closing streets and alleys to reduce crime: Should you go down the road.* Washington, DC: Office of Community Oriented Policing.

Community Policing Consortium, (2000). Creating partnerships for the common good. *Links* Ph *VII*(2), Issue II.

Correia, M. E. (2000). *Citizen involvement—How community factors affect progressive policing.* Washington, DC: Police Executive Research Forum.

Cunningham, S. A. (1994). The empowering leader and organizational change. *The Police Chief, LXI*(8).

Decker, S. H. (2005). *Using offender interviews to inform police problem solving.* Washington, DC: Office of Community Oriented Policing Services.

Diamond, D., & Weiss, D. M. (2009). *Community policing: Looking to tomorrow.* Washington, DC: Police Executive Research Forum and Department of Community Oriented Policing Services.

Eck, J. C., & Spelman, W. (1987). *Problem solving: Problem-oriented policing in Newport News.* Washington, DC: Department of Justice and Police Executive Research Forum.

Eck, J. E. (2002). *Assessing responses to problems: An introductory guide for police problem-solvers.* Washington, DC: Office of Community Oriented Policing Services.

Fort Lee Police Department, (2008). *Community policing.* Fort Lee, NJ: Fort Lee Police Department.

Goldstein, H. (1990). *Problem-oriented policing.* New York: McGraw-Hill.

Kappeler, V. E., & Gaines, L. R. (2005). *Community policing: A contemporary perspective* (4th ed.). Cincinnati: Anderson.

Kerstein, A. (2001). Model neighborhood program offers effective complement to community policing efforts. *The Police Chief, LXVIII*(2).

Mittleman, P. (2000). Community policing: Building community trust thinking outside of the box. *The Police Chief, LXVII*(3).

More, H. W. (2008). *Current issues in American law enforcement: Controversies and solutions.* Springfield, IL: Charles C Thomas.

More, H. W., Vito, G. F., & Walsh, W. F. (2010). *Organizational behavior and management in law enforcement* (2nd ed.). Upper Saddle River, NJ: Pearson Prentice Hall.

National Institute of Justice, (2004). *Community policing beyond the big cities.* Washington, DC: Department of Justice.

Oliver, W. M. (1998). *Community-oriented policing: A systematic approach to policing.* Upper Saddle River, NJ: Prentice Hall.

Parks, R. B., Mastrofski, S. D., DeJong, C., & Gray, M. K. (1999). How officers spend their time with the community. *Justice Quarterly, 16*(3).

Police Executive Research Forum, (1996). *Themes and variations in community policing.* Washington, DC: Police Executive Research Forum.

Rabkin, N. J. (1995). *Community policing: Information on the "Cops on the Beat" Grant Program.* Washington, DC: USGPO.

Ramsey, C. H. (2001). *General order—Awards police, GO-ADM-201.05.* Washington, DC: Metropolitan Police Department.

Reaves, B. A., & Hickman, M. J. (2004). *Law enforcement management and administrative statistics, 2000: Data for individual state and local agencies with 100 or more officers.* Washington, DC: Office of Justice Programs.

Reiss, J. (2006). Community governance—An organized approach to fighting crime. *FBI Law Enforcement Bulletin, 75*(5).

Reiter, M. S. (1999). Empowerment policing. *FBI Law Enforcement Bulletin, 68*(2).

Roth, J. A., & Ryan, J. F. (2000). *COPS Program: Title 1 of the 1944 Crime Act, Research Report.* Washington, DC: National Institute of Justice.

Scarano, S., & Jones, T. (2000). Following by example. *Law and Order, 48*(10).

Skogan, W. G., Hartnett, S. M., DuBois, J., Comey, J. T., Twedt-Ball, K., & Erik Gudell, J. (2000). *Public involvement: Community policing in Chicago.* Chicago: Northwestern University.

Skogan, W. G., Steiner, L., DuBois, J., Erik Gudell, J., & Fagan, A. (2002). *Taking stock: Community policing in Chicago.* Chicago: Northwestern University.

Spelman, W., & Eck, J. E. (1987). *Problem oriented policing. Research in brief.* Washington, DC: National Institute of Justice.

Swope, R. E. (2000). Measuring success. *The Police Chief, LXVII*(3).

U.S. Department of Justice, (2002). *Problem solving tips—A guide to reducing crime and disorder through problem-solving partnerships.* Washington, DC: Office of Community Oriented Policing Services.

U.S. Department of Justice, (2009). *Community policing defined.* Washington, DC: Department of Community Oriented Policing Services.

Weisel, D. (1999). *Conducting community surveys—A practical guide for law enforcement agencies.* Washington, DC: Bureau of Justice Statistics and Office of Community Oriented Policing Services.

Wolfer, L., Baker, T. E., & Zezza, R. (1999). Problem-solving policing—Eliminating hot spots. *FBI Enforcement Bulletin, 68*(11).

3

Interpersonal Communications
Striving for Effectiveness

CASE STUDY

Sergeant Roger Cooper

DEPARTMENT

The Transaction County sheriff's department is organized into three major bureaus. These are: Administration, Enforcement, and Custody. The human resource complement for the department is 412 positions, and this breaks down into 74.5 percent sworn officers and 25.4 percent civilian positions. This is a rather large sheriff's department. Within the United States about three-fifths of the sheriffs' offices employ fewer than 25 sworn personnel. As is the norm, the position of sheriff is elected, and patrol responsibilities occur in unincorporated areas of the county except for a few agencies that provide contract enforcement to municipalities. The latest available national statistics indicate that there are approximately 183,000 sworn officers in the United States that work in a sheriff's department.

The Enforcement Bureau is comprised of three units—Patrol, Special Operations, and Investigation—and this is where the preponderance of the sworn officers are assigned. Patrol handled calls for service that totaled just fewer than 90,000 last year, and they provide a full range of law enforcement and emergency responses to a population of approximately 108,000. The Custody Bureau consists of a Detention Division and the Court Services Division. Detention is responsible for the intake, housing, and release of all inmates. Some 981 inmates are housed in 29 separate housing units, and sentenced inmates are assigned to facility work groups. The Administrative Bureau provides support for the other bureaus and handles fiscal matters, forensic services, and records. This latter entity has a civil unit that serves legal documents on individuals and businesses. The department has a search and rescue team comprised of deputies and volunteers. Another specialization is the mounted unit that assists search and rescue and participates in parade and ceremonial functions. Deputies are also assigned to a county-wide gang suppression team. After being hired and graduating from the academy, the new deputies are assigned to the jail for one year during their probationary period. Eleven percent of the deputies are female. Fifty-one percent of the deputies are white, 18 percent Hispanic, and the remainder are Asian and African-American. Beyond field supervision of approximately 400 hours after completing the academy, each deputy receives 24 hours of annual training.

CRIME

The sheriff's department offers an interactive map on their website that includes crime statistics by neighborhood. All one needs to do is enter an address on the site and it will show offenses such as vehicle break-in/theft, vandalism, or drug/alcohol offenses over a specified period of time. In one period checked for a week's time, the map reflected 48 offenses. For the previous year the crime statistics were 3 percent lower than the prior year for a total of 3359 serious (Part 1) crimes. Part 1 crimes include murder, sexual assault, robbery, aggravated assault, burglary, theft, and automobile theft. The categories of sexual assault, aggravated assault, and robbery decreased while the other categories increased. The number of murders increased by five. Priority 1 calls for assistance had a response time of 5.12 minutes, while Priority 2 calls took 11.54 minutes. Informational calls took 17.5 minutes. The overall number of the informational calls decreased by 16 percent. Traffic violations continue to be of major concern and while the number of injury accidents has leveled off, fatal accidents rose to 11 compared to the previous year of five.

COMMUNITY

The county has about 120 square miles of land that range from rolling foothills, with the highest peak occurring at 2444 feet, to a series of lakes adjacent to a large state park. The county has a variety of recreational areas, and it includes parts that are agricultural, industrial, and residential, as well as a large area of undeveloped land. Agriculture is a big industry and major employer for the county and provides a wide range of products such as apples, walnuts, and considerable truck farming. Another major industry is tourism, which is seasonal. Tourists come to camp and engage in water sports at the lakes. Within the state park there are numerous trails for hikers and for those who just enjoy getting out of urban areas. There is a private four-year college in the county that offers a broad range of classes, from wildlife conservation to business administration. This college has an enrollment of 9562, and students are attracted from many regions in the state. A majority of the students are housed on the campus. The county has a moderate climate with an average rainfall of 26 inches. Transaction County is governed by an elected board of five supervisors. All of the members of the board have served for more than two four-year terms, and there is no limit as to how long they can stay in office. The county has a 9.8 percent unemployment rate and a good number of the unemployed formerly worked in agriculture.

The county has a large number of retired residents (6.9%) and many younger people migrate to urban areas looking for employment. A total of 41.8 percent of the residents are Caucasian, 26.9 percent are Hispanic, 3.2 percent are African-American, and Asians comprise 11.3 percent. Hispanics are the fastest growing racial/ethnic group followed by Asians, and the Caucasian population is declining at a rate of 2.3 percent a year. During the last five years, the Arab/Muslim category has steadily increased. There are more women than men in the county, and just fewer than 40 percent of the residents have some college education.

OFFICER

Roger Cooper has been in the sheriff's department for six years and was promoted to sergeant two years ago. He has completed two years of college, which he attended part time, and has every intention of achieving a four-year degree. He is taking liberal arts classes and has not declared a major, but he has an inclination to major in business. He served in the military for four years and served two tours of duty in Iraq. In his overseas assignment he became conversant in Arabic and learned a great deal about the Muslim culture. He met and married his wife, Kaena, in Iraq and brought her to the United States after complying with a great deal of red tape. The couple have no children and Kaena is employed as a secretary in a local school district. They live in a condominium, which they are purchasing, and both of them have become involved in the Arab/Muslim community both religiously and socially. Kaena has a bachelor's degree and is enrolled in a master's program in sociology at the local private college. Sergeant Cooper was raised in a metropolitan city about 82 miles from their current place of employment. The couple thrives in the smaller community atmosphere. Cooper's original assignment was to patrol, and then he was assigned to a station as a crime prevention specialist where he spent the majority of his time working with residents, neighborhood watch programs, and commercial burglary prevention. He interacts well with others and has no difficulty in taking a leadership position. When assigned to patrol, he was viewed as competent and his team officers respected him for his knowledge and ability to solve problems.

PROBLEM

Within the local Arabic/Muslim community there is general disdain and lack of respect for law enforcement officers. This has led to a considerable gap in communications between the two groups, and the sheriff has assigned Sergeant Cooper the task of developing positive relationships with this group of residents. These residents live for the most part in the same neighborhood, and they limit their contact with other ethnic groups. Many of them express that they have a limited English capability and as a consequence feel that they are outsiders. Deputies have stated that they get little cooperation from the group and constantly find that they cannot communicate with victims or witnesses. Cooper is the only one who has some language capability in Arabic, and even though he is somewhat knowledgeable about the Muslim culture, there are some languages and cultural aspects of the Middle East that escape him. There is every reason to believe that this group will grow over the years and, if left alone, the communication problems will in all probability be exacerbated.

WHAT WOULD YOU DO?

The task confronting Cooper is considerable and the sheriff has given him free rein to determine how to deal with the cultural and language problem, with the understanding that he will be kept abreast of developments. What would be the initial thing you would do? Why? Would you consider developing a training program for deputies in the department? If so, how long should the program take? How would you justify the cost? What specifically would you do to improve relationships with the Arab/Muslim residents? If you decide to create a session that would explain the role of law enforcement in the community to this group, what would be its content? Explain. What translation resources are available that can be used, local, state, or federal, and how could they contribute to solving the communications problem? What do you see that you could do to improve the relationship? Describe in detail.

When discussing management with police executive officers, it is typical for them to identify one characteristic that "excellent" supervisors have in common—the ability to communicate. Outstanding supervisors have a significant attribute that distinguishes them from others in that they have the facility to communicate effectively. It can be said without question that it has proven to be the key to success. Communication is the foundation of interpersonal relations. When ideas and thoughts are communicated successfully, it fosters a positive working environment. In law enforcement agencies, the first-line supervisor engages in a number of activities, the first of which includes interpretation of the organization's culture, managerial values, vision, mission, goals, objectives, and operational policies into day-to-day decisions and operational activities. In addition, a supervisor uses communication to train, coach, counsel, mentor, and motivate each officer in an effort to improve performance and provide an improved quality of life within the community and the organization. Finally, the supervisor plans, organizes work, gives directions, teaches, coaches, mentors, issues orders, and monitors employee performance, all in an effort to improve the effectiveness of the organization. There is an unmistakable organizational need for supervisors who understand the intricate nature of the communication process and vigorously foster a working atmosphere that encourages open communication (Gaines & Worral, 2011).

The Importance of Communication Skills

As tasks performed within law enforcement agencies have become more complex and demanding, the need for good communications skills has become increasingly important. It is difficult to imagine a professional law enforcement agency without advanced communications, computer-aided dispatching, cellular phones, and laptops for the analysis of data and the preparation of reports. In fact, law enforcement has readily adopted hardware, but there is a clear-cut need for improved interpersonal and organizational communication.

Interpersonal communication exists at every level of any organization, but is most prevalent at the operational level, where, of necessity, there is continual interaction between supervisors and line personnel. When there is good communication, it is a result of effective supervision. Communication is an integral part of our everyday life and it is difficult to imagine an organization not fostering and encouraging strong communication skills. Communication is the lifeblood of an organization. It is the process that ties the whole organization together. When a mishap occurs, the immediate reaction is to blame it on an inability to communicate effectively—"why did you not tell me sooner or really let me know what you wanted?"

A breakdown in communication is an inevitable consequence of our inability to interpret what is said. It is easier to blame failures on poor or inadequate communication than deal with the problem directly. It is like treating the symptom rather than the disease. When one becomes a first-line supervisor, it does not confer upon one the ability to be an effective communicator. It takes considerable time to develop good communication skills, but they can be learned.

If communication is to be effective, it must be nurtured by all levels of management, from the top down. As stated previously, first-line supervisors are managers and are an integral part of the management team. They are in constant contact with operational personnel. Without question, their position is the lynchpin of the organization and the strategic position in any law enforcement agency.

Supervisors spend a large part of their working hours engaged in tasks that can be identified as communicating. Experience shows that first-line supervisors in municipal law enforcement agencies spend approximately 55 percent of their communication time performing tasks related to subordinates, 26 percent related to superiors, 15 percent related to the public, and 4 percent relating to other supervisors. These percentages are set forth in Figure 3.1.

Additional support that delineates the importance of communications for supervisors is reflected in a task analysis study of the first-line supervisor's position. When considering 53 specific tasks, 51 percent involved communication. These tasks, rated in terms of their importance, are set forth in Figure 3.2 and include a wide range of activities.

It can readily be seen that the first-line supervisor spends the preponderance of time communicating in various ways with subordinates. Officers need information and guidance in operational activities. In addition, when conflict occurs between subordinates, the supervisor must resolve the dispute in the interest of operational effectiveness. It is essential that the supervisor listen to every side of an issue and be sensitive to the needs of all individuals

Level	Percentage
Subordinates	55
Superiors	26
Citizens	15
Other supervisors	4
	100

FIGURE 3.1 Supervisor's communication tasks by level.

1. Conferencing with and providing direction to subordinates regarding particular events, incidents, or investigations.
2. Meeting with and resolving disputes among subordinates.
3. Meeting with managers to resolve specific problems or concerns.
4. Meeting with other supervisors to resolve problems and coordinate activities.
5. Providing feedback to subordinates regarding job performance.
6. Resolving citizen/officer conflicts.
7. Responding to subordinates' inquiries.

FIGURE 3.2 Communication tasks performed by supervisors.

involved in a conflict. Partiality or favoritism must be rejected out of hand. These activities can dominate the supervisory workload, and it is still necessary to meet with supervisory personnel as needed, as well as interact with citizens to resolve the inevitable conflict that occurs between officers and citizens.

It is amazing, when one stops to think of it, that so much of a human's waking time is spent communicating (Hargie, Dickson, & Gibbons, 2004). This is noticed especially in the work environment, and law enforcement is no exception. The first-line supervisor must understand the importance of verbal/nonverbal communication, the art of listening, and information processing. The interaction between sergeants and subordinates succeeds or fails as a direct result of their ability or inability to communicate.

Effective communication means *getting the meaning across*. In many instances, this can prove to be a difficult barrier to overcome. When analyzing why one supervisor is a better communicator than another, one characteristic stands out: an awareness of the need to communicate well. Successful communicators are not concerned about personal self-esteem. When communication falters, they do not look for someone to blame—they work to resolve the problem. If they know they have done a poor job in explaining something, good communicators will admit that they have erred and start over. It boils down to wanting to communicate well.

A good communicator avoids meaningless or imprecise words. Today, much of our communication is impaired by wordiness and verbosity prevails in many instances. Often the erroneous assumption is made that many words will clarify a situation and the problem will be resolved. The poor communicator fails to realize that, more often than not, words can confuse, confound, or mislead. Supervisors who have a reputation of being good communicators are known as individuals who have something to say. When it is necessary to communicate, they respond accordingly, whether it is on a one-on-one basis or in a group. A good communicator is a respected and valuable member of the law enforcement community.

The Communication Process

Defining communications might seem to be an easy and straightforward task, but it has confounded experts for years. In fact, one study reviewed managerial literature and found 94

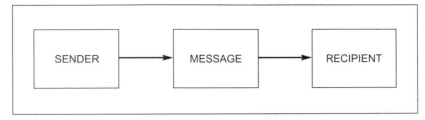

FIGURE 3.3 Simplistic communication process.

different definitions of the word *communication.* This demonstrates the complexity of the actual communication process. Communication can be defined as a process by which information is exchanged between individuals through a common system of symbols, signs, or behavior. If communication is to be effective, however, there is a need to have something more than just the exchange of information.

The sender of a message must make a sincere effort to affect the behavior of the recipient. Effective person-to-person communication involves more than just sending a message—it has to be decoded so that it can be interpreted and a true understanding occurs between the sender and the recipient.

On the surface, the process seems quite simple, but a careful analysis of the components indicates a number of places where the message can become misconstrued, garbled, or even ignored. It is somewhat similar to talking with someone from another country who has a limited knowledge of English (Boyd, 2003). One study showed that about 9 percent of residents in the United States have a limited ability to read, write, speak, or understand English and the individuals can be described as limited English proficient (LEP) (Shan & Estrada, 2009).

The recipient of the message may nod his or her head, look one straight in the eye, and seemingly absorb every word and respond to every nuance. However, if one asks the listener even the simplest question, it is readily apparent that while the message was transmitted, it was definitely not decoded. Therefore, it is recommended that when confronted with one who can be characterized as someone who can be described as LEP, several questions should be asked regarding message interpretation. Keep in mind that the same thing can also occur between two individuals who are fluent in the same language (see Figure 3.3).

The communication process is exceedingly complex, especially when one takes into consideration the fact that both the sender and the recipient of a message are affected by attitudes, skills, knowledge, opinions, and other forces existing before, during, and after the message is transmitted.

Interpersonal communication involves two or more people. Participants in a conversation send messages by verbal as well as nonverbal channels. The characteristics of senders and recipients can substantially influence the communication process—a continually changing one. For example, the sender may want to change the opinion, perception, or behavior of the recipient and will send a message in an effort to accomplish a specific goal. A problem can occur when the goals of the two individuals involved are in conflict. When this happens, there is a strong possibility of distortion and misunderstandings occurring. When goals are well matched, there is a greater possibility that a message will be interpreted accurately.

The sender of a message determines the relevancy of each message. This is generally known as *gate keeping*, inasmuch as the sender determines the importance of information. The sender, therefore, exercises complete control over the flow of information. This is especially apparent when supervisors, by virtue of their position in a police organization, operate as the primary communication point between upper management and line personnel. Operational autonomy, with primary guidance coming from departmental policy, places the first-line supervisor in the position of controlling the amount and nature of information entering the information system. Decisions are made constantly as to the need for passing information into the system. At the same time, the supervisor is in a position to control the amount of information subordinates will receive.

This is pertinent when the supervisor presides at the roll-call session preceding each shift. It can be a learning experience for the officers or it can be conducted in a perfunctory manner with a limited exchange of information. Many first-line supervisors believe that proper communication has occurred when they have simply told a shift of officers what to do. It is difficult to believe that no one who has been in an organization for a year or more has heard either, "I told you what the new policy was" or "Why didn't you tell me?" It seems that the message transmission could be accomplished without difficulty, but it is soon obvious that encoding the message can, and will, in all probability become complex.

Communication is an exchange of information involving two or more parties and all must participate. It is a process modified or constrained by such features as those listed here:

1. Insufficient information will seldom produce a preferred result.
2. The acceptor of the message determines the accuracy of the communication through decoding.
3. The recipient of the message, because of attitudes, experiences, and motivations, determines whether the message is decoded in the way intended by the sender.

Each person involved in a communication situation both encodes and decodes messages simultaneously. It is a continuous process, and as information is received, it is decoded. From the standpoint of the first-line supervisor, answers should be sought to the following types of questions:

- Can the message be misinterpreted?
- Does the message imply anything?
- Are data supporting the message's proposal?
- What is the actual communication to be encoded?
- What type of reaction will result from the message?
- Will the message yield results?

Each supervisor should make a conscious effort to deal with the practical problems readily identifiable from the aforementioned questions. With practice, a supervisor can soon develop messages that are clear, meaningful, and will obtain results (see Figure 3.4).

Another element of the communication process is the channel through which the message travels from the sender to the recipient. The term channel usually refers to one or more of the human senses. This obviously involves both verbal and nonverbal aspects of communication, although the first-line supervisor usually deals with oral communication.

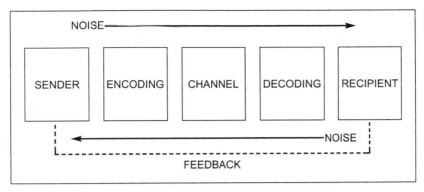

FIGURE 3.4 Realistic communication process.

Failure to acknowledge the importance of nonverbal communication and its impact on the recipient(s) will often cause problems. This was especially apparent in one agency when top management instituted a new policy prohibiting officers from carrying second weapons. At roll call, when the new policy was discussed, one of the senior sergeants made light of the new policy, leading everyone in attendance to believe that the policy would never be enforced and officers could continue the practice of carrying second weapons.

After an unfortunate shooting incident in which an officer used a second weapon, an internal investigation concluded that the shooting was justified and conformed with the departmental use of deadly force, but the officer was suspended for two weeks for carrying a second weapon. The investigation also recommended that the sergeant who had failed to explain and support departmental policy be suspended for two weeks. The chief of police, after an appropriate hearing, demoted the sergeant.

The distorted message sent by the sergeant in this situation proved disastrous for the officer as well as the supervisor. The content of the sergeant's presentation to the officers was clear and concise, but the context in which it was delivered proved to be the most persuasive part of the message. The context of any message cannot be ignored because it can prove to be more meaningful than content.

Once the message has been sent, it is up to the recipient to decode the message and attach significant meaning. There are six aspects to consider at this point:

- What the sender **MEANT** to say
- What the recipient **HEARD**
- What the recipient **SAID**
- What the recipient **THINKS** he or she heard
- What the sender **THINKS** the recipient said
- What was **IN FACT** said

These six aspects of the communication process are involved in every message, and the recipient reacts based on personal experiences, viewpoints, knowledge, and frame of reference. It is apparent that a failure in communication can occur at numerous points. With feedback, the cycle becomes a viable two-way process. Feedback (because of its type) can vary greatly. It can be as simple as a nod of the head or as complex as a multiple-page report. For

1. Carefully screen all information and ensure the inclusion of essential information.
2. During a presentation, move from generalities to specifics.
3. If the topic is new, lay a foundation to bring the recipient up to the same level of understanding.
4. Never assume that recipients are as knowledgeable about a subject as the presenter.
5. Start all discussions at a level that ensures an absolute certainty of mutual understanding.
6. Summarize salient features of the presentation before accepting questions.
7. The greater the complexity of data being presented, the greater the need to present the information step by step in a logical manner.
8. Videotape lectures and review them in order to improve the method of presentation.

FIGURE 3.5 Techniques for assessing one's verbal capacity. *Adapted from Karl Albrecht (1979). Stress and the Manager: Making It Work for You. Englewood Cliffs, NJ: Prentice Hall, Inc.*

example, the recipient could respond with a request for clarification: "As I understand it, you want me to notify every grocery and liquor store on my beat about the two-armed robbers. Is that correct?" Such a technique can leave no doubt as to what was meant by the sender and whether the message was understood.

Noise is the last feature of the communication process. Noise is anything that reduces the accuracy of a communication. An awareness of how noise affects communication will allow one to take steps to reduce it, thereby improving the accuracy of each communication. Noise can be present at any point in the communication process, but the greatest problem area is with the use of language.

Some people seem to have the ability to explain things clearly and with a great deal of simplicity. At the same time, another individual never seems to be able to find the correct expressive words and even a simple thought becomes entangled with complicated details. In a police department, written and verbal skills play an important part in one's success. Those who develop these skills are identified easily. Articulate individuals are generally at ease when discussing issues, seem to influence others easily, and get their way more often than not.

Individuals should assess their own verbal capacity and evaluate their ability to organize information and present it clearly to others. Some things one might want to consider are set forth in Figure 3.5.

These factors delineate how to improve communication and how a supervisor can (by following these general guidelines) convey thoughts, ideas, and decisions more effectively when engaged in the managerial activities of controlling and directing.

1. Provide feedback to subordinates regarding their job performance. This should include such things as identifying strengths, weaknesses, and exceptional or inadequate performance. Brief subordinates on new or revised policies and procedures.
2. Prepare written employee performance evaluations.
3. Respond to subordinates' inquiries regarding departmental policy, legal questions, and the application of discretionary decision-making.
4. Meet with and provide direction to subordinates regarding particular violations, investigative techniques, and case processing.
5. Brief subordinates on new or revised policies and procedures.
6. Communicate subordinates' concerns, desires, and suggestions to management.

FIGURE 3.6 Communications tasks in order of importance.

First-line supervisors in law enforcement agencies are task oriented: results are what count. Because line officers work within operating procedures (with limited supervision), they have considerable decision-making discretion. In fact, the application of discretion consumes a large part of the average officer's time, and when difficulties occur, officers consult their first-line supervisor. As pointed out earlier, supervisors spend 55 percent of their communication time communicating with the officers they supervise.

The realistic supervisor works with subordinates in an effort to develop them to the point where they can become committed and motivated to such an extent that they are *self-supervised*. Within this context, one study showed that when ranking communication tasks, first-line supervisors listed the items in Figure 3.6 in terms of importance.

Each of these items emphasizes the importance of the superior–subordinate relationship and alludes to the complexity of the communication process. A supervisor must be continually aware of the need to develop and maintain communication skills because it is the most important managerial tool. When demands are excessive and time is of the essence, a supervisor should emphasize feedback regarding job performance inasmuch as this provides immediate results. Other tasks can be responded to in descending order of importance. None can be overlooked, but some can be delayed. It is also essential that the supervisor serves as a conduit by communicating concerns, desires, and suggestions to management. If the supervisor does not perform this function, it will probably not be accomplished.

Communication Patterns

Communication is defined as the exchange of information between individuals, implying that it can be either one-way or two-way. Traditionally, one-way communication has dominated supervisory relationships with subordinates. The sender, in this situation, communicates without expecting or receiving feedback from the recipient. Typical of this type of communication activity is when a sergeant tells officers what will be done and how to do it, without any feedback.

Two-way communication occurs when the recipient provides feedback to the sender. An example would be when, during roll call, the sergeant discusses a new policy and then asks for feedback. Another example would be creation of a taskforce consisting of line officers assigned to develop a new grooming policy for officers and prepare a report for management.

Each of these methods has its advantages. One-way communication is preferable when:

- Compliance is imperative.
- Feedback is not wanted.
- Orderliness is significant.
- Speed is important.

When one-way communication is selected as the appropriate means to be used, the sender must spend a great deal of time preparing what will be said because there is no feedback to clarify issues or correct errors. It protects the sender's authority and power because mistakes are never acknowledged. Line officers might criticize the sergeant, but with one-way communication, potential criticism by subordinates is not allowed.

When a sergeant utilizes one-way communication, the assumption is that one's responsibility ends there and it is the responsibility of the listener to receive and decode the message. It is a simple one-way street and blame can be placed on the recipient for failure to understand the message. The sergeant can say, "I explained it to you and there is no reason for you not to understand the message." The problem is obvious. A message can be transmitted, but there is no actual communication unless the message is understood by the recipient. The sender is responsible for seeing that a message is understood, which can only be done if the message is received and there is an opportunity for feedback.

This is where two-way communication becomes useful. It is apparent that when one engages in two-way communication, there is not only a message sent, but there is also feedback allowing for modification and correction of the initial message. This is the exact opposite of the classic one-way communication process.

The drawback of two-way communication is that one must accept some risk and share power and authority. The sender's position may be subject to scrutiny by subordinates, and awareness that the sender is not completely knowledgeable in the subject area may develop. Two-way communication requires less planning because of the built-in opportunity for feedback and the subsequent correction of errors or the clarification of issues. For this to work it is imperative for the sender to listen and understand the feedback provided by the recipient; otherwise, there is just the façade of two-way communication.

The success of two-way communication depends on mutual understanding as an integral part of the communication process. The desire is to communicate, not to find fault or place blame. If there is a lack of understanding, everyone works to correct errors and clarify issues.

It is apparent from the aforementioned discussion that advantages of two-way communication include:

- Acknowledgment of the importance of communicating.
- Greater understanding.
- Improved accuracy.
- Recognition of subordinates' need to know what is expected of them.
- Sharing of authority and responsibility.

Barriers to Communication

An officer never reacts to a message in isolation. There is always a reaction to the relationship of the actual situation, the content of the message, and the recipient. An officer must feel free to discuss issues with superiors. Unfortunately, this is not always the case. If an officer is concerned about a negative reaction from a superior, then the officer is less likely to bring up the issue for discussion.

Barriers to communication are numerous, but generally include a concern about one's knowledge of a subject, the probability of being looked upon with displeasure, jeopardizing one's status, environmental influences, personal expectations, and semantics.

Some officers will assume that asking for clarification on any issue will make them appear unknowledgeable. There is concern that one might be viewed as less than a *real* officer who is aware and streetwise. Survival in the organization suggests that under no circumstances should officers leave themselves in a position in which their ability is called into question, especially if it might jeopardize favorable consideration when assignments are handed out.

Subordinates hesitate to discuss personal goals and aspirations if there is any question in their mind that the supervisor might not be receptive. They often believe that expressing concerns about the job or the need to learn something new can be taken as a sign of weakness and used against them. With inadequate two-way communication, actions taken by a supervisor are viewed as detrimental and the subordinates will, in all probability, grudgingly accept and implement them with a complete lack of enthusiasm. These actions may even be sabotaged (Bradford & Cohen, 1997).

"Physical barriers" in any given situation may block or lead to garbled transmission of messages. These barriers might be the result of a poor radio transmission, a poorly written note, or even incorrect use of the "Ten Code." It can even be something like noise created by automotive noises or other elements of the environment that make hearing difficult. Whatever the barrier, it should be identified. Steps should then be taken to ensure that blocks or distortions to effective communication are eliminated.

Psychological barriers include an individual's beliefs, judgments, values, needs, life experiences, education, training, and goals. In addition, the emotional state (hostility, apprehension, assurance) of either the sender or the recipient can impede communications. Neither can one forget personal attitudes of stereotyping, biases, and prejudice (Salmon, 1998). All of these combine to form a frame of reference for both the sender and the recipient of any message. Inasmuch as everyone has distinctive combinations of the aforementioned characteristics, it should be apparent that everyone has the potential to see and hear the same situation from different perspectives.

Personal barriers can be "physiological" in nature. Fatigue is especially important in law enforcement. Rotating shifts, working shifts out of sync with normal society, or sitting in court after a regular shift can negatively affect one's attention span, decision-making capacity, and ability to communicate (Vita, 2000). In some instances, physical fatigue, illness, discomfort, or other distractions such as work, family, or financial problems can also impede effective listening (Air Force Headquarters, 2004).

Another obstruction to effective communication is *semantics.* Some words are simply misunderstood or subject to misunderstanding (Salmon, 1998). There are many words or phrases that have multiple meanings and these can vary with each situation. For example, to *take a person into custody* can have a number of meanings, ranging from an actual arrest to protective custody. Slang, jargon, or organizational acronyms can also interfere with the communications process. Effective communication can only take place when the actual symbolic meaning of words is shared. Telling a subordinate "to hit the bricks and get with it" communicates little or perhaps nothing. Is it a meaningless instruction or does it mean there is a need to be more productive in terms of issuing more citations or conducting more field interviews? How will it affect the behavior of each officer? Figure 3.7 lists major barriers to communication.

A word is an incomplete representation of reality. It is a symbol that can be manipulated without regard to what is factual. Language can be used to distort facts or used according to the whim of the sender.

Another semantics problem occurs when a supervisor uses jargon or esoteric language known as *argot.* A supervisor (when dealing with subordinates) will sometimes assume that everyone is familiar with legal terms. Consequently, the process of communication may become clouded, if not completely distorted. At other times, jargon of the trade may be used to either impress someone or exclude him or her from a discussion.

Because words will often have strong symbolic significance, using them as labels should be done with a great deal of caution. For example, using terms such as *punks, pukes,* or *dirt bags* should be avoided, because such labeling can give officers the impression that these

---

1.	Concern about jeopardizing one's status.
2.	Fear of being looked down upon.
3.	Fear of being viewed as having a limited knowledge about a subject.
4.	Physical influences.
5.	Psychological factors.
6.	Physiological obstacles.
7.	Semantics.

FIGURE 3.7 Barriers that impede effective communication.

uniquely identified individuals can be treated differently and not accorded their complete constitutional rights.

Overcoming Communication Barriers

Many officers have had supervisors who have said, "Come into the office and let's talk it over." However, they have had a voice message—"see me." Messages like these can evoke all types of reactions, ranging from an open and honest discussion to the subordinate simply not expressing thoughts and feelings at all (see Figure 3.8).

Some officers will withdraw and turn the discussion into a one-way communication process in which the sergeant does all the talking or the officers will say things they believe the sergeant wants to hear. In either case, feedback does not occur, so the sergeant is limited in appraising or evaluating the situation accurately.

A supervisor can only obtain sound feedback when there is reason for officers to dispel fears and concerns impeding or impairing valid two-way communication. A superior must, due to the position of power, deal with the fears or misgivings of subordinates and work diligently to dispel them. This must be accomplished not only by words, but also by actions.

---

1. Use face-to-face communication continually. Strive to meet with each officer as often as possible in order to enhance the communication process. Personalize each contact and avoid written communications as much as possible.

2. Create a supportive relationship. Show a genuine concern for each officer and his or her welfare (personal and professional).

3. Develop an atmosphere of mutual trust. This can be done by demonstrating a real interest in all officers, accepting their input, respecting their judgment, drawing upon their strengths, and assisting them in overcoming their weaknesses. Get them involved in the decision-making process.

4. Develop an awareness of each subordinate's needs. Learn everything you can about all officers, especially their expectations.

5. Maximize the use of feedback. Clarify essential information and tell each officer about his or her job performance, strengths, and weaknesses.

6. Repeat communication when needed. Use the time-honored process of telling officers what you intend to tell them, then tell them, and then summarize what you have told them.

7. Strive to be acutely aware of semantical differences. If there is any doubt, define terms. Always be as explicit as the situation and topic allow.

8. Use direct and simple language. Move from generalities to specifics and screen all information that is passed on.

FIGURE 3.8 Techniques for overcoming communication barriers.

A supportive relationship, if it is also to be a viable and a positive working relationship, is one in which the subordinate is allowed to influence the supervisor. The foundation for real two-way communication occurs when subordinates accept a supervisor as someone who assists and supports rather than one who forces, demands, or orders. It cannot be a relationship in which communication is limited to such one-way positioning as "Do it now" or "I said 'do it' and that is the way it's going to be."

Subordinate involvement is a real working relationship in which true commitment requires some degree of power sharing. If subordinates have little or no power or if they cannot disagree or vigorously support an opposing position, there clearly is not a viable supportive relationship. An effective relationship can occur only when there is a genuine acceptance of one another, a concern for the needs of others, and a feeling of absolute trust and mutual respect (Bradford & Cohen, 1997).

Supervisors' lives would be very simple if they did not have to work diligently to listen to subordinates' ideas and thoughts, strive to share power, create a base for compromise and conciliation, and give feedback that leads to solving interpersonal problems. Supervision is hard work. Positive supervision maximizes the use of human resources—it does not waste them. A supervisory style that not only allows for individual differences but also views them as valuable assets contributing to the success of the organization must be adopted.

A supervisor can take many steps to ensure that individual differences do not affect superior/subordinate relationships negatively. Many times success is a combination of what the supervisor does and the way he or she does it. When a supervisor views each officer as a potential member of the team, there is the beginning of a positive working relationship. A supervisor must focus on bringing each officer into a working relationship, avoid making negative personality judgments, and stress strengths rather than weaknesses.

It is best to focus on resolving problems rather than employing criticism for the sake of criticism. Emphasis should be placed on reaching out to each employee to better understand his or her situation. The goal is to build a working relationship, allowing for a continual exchange of opinions and information. Placing emphasis on tasks performed by subordinates rather than their personalities can enhance this process. Effective leadership involves viewing personnel in a positive light.

Employees have a right to know where supervisors are coming from. A supervisor will be judged by the nature and quality of communications. If a supervisor treats every officer as fairly as possible and does not show favoritism, these actions will support the creation of a positive working relationship. A supervisor will probably feel more comfortable with some officers than with others, but it will be incumbent upon the supervisor to perform in such a way that individuals are not singled out for preferential treatment. Fairness is the leadership attribute to be followed.

A supervisor should also vary the assignments of the officers so that their performance can be improved and boredom reduced. In a police department, the third watch is normally less active, so the supervisor should distribute assignments to enhance working conditions and demonstrate equitable treatment.

Whenever possible, the supervisor should recommend additional training. Most employees like to be placed in a learning environment to give them additional skills. It will also make the officer more valuable to the organization. It is equally imperative for supervisors to keep abreast of changes in order to improve subordinate training.

If one of the officers does an excellent job, a direct compliment should be given and it should be done as soon as possible. In addition, the supervisor should send a note to higher management levels, pointing out the significance of the contribution to the organization. It carries more weight when recognition of a job well done is made part of the subordinate's personnel file. A sincere word of appreciation for excellent work can go a long way in building a supportive working relationship with subordinates.

Successful supervisors give serious consideration to creating a working environment in which there is mutual respect and trust between themselves and subordinates. It is not a matter of blindly trusting every officer and having faith that the task to be accomplished will be completed because there will always be a time and place where an officer will fail to follow instructions or complete a task as required by departmental policy. A supervisor must be willing to accept a certain degree of risk because positive results will generally exceed the errors or mistakes that inevitably occur.

Trust and respect are prerequisites to any working relationship. These qualities must come before there can be candid and open communication. Every officer must have the right to openly approach and resolve all interpersonal and task problems as they occur. They should be allowed to express true feelings and expect that they will be heard by the supervisor. Officers should always be able to anticipate an impartial and fair consideration of the issues.

A good supervisor's actions let every officer know that he or she is being treated fairly and equitably. Every action taken must convey that supervisors always keep their word, are concerned about employee welfare, and are willing to work with their officers to resolve problems. In a working relationship in which trust and mutual respect are part and parcel of everyday activities, officers will have no need to be guarded or suspicious of each other or their supervisor and energies can be directed to task achievement (Bradford & Cohen, 1997).

If there is but one supervisory principle a sergeant should follow, it is to communicate. This is an essential aspect of any leadership style and must be instituted at every opportunity, even to the point of overcommunicating. Officers are more secure when they know what is going on and have the feeling of being in control.

In many situations, it is necessary to communicate by memorandum, but face-to-face communication is strongly recommended whenever possible. Feedback can be immediate and more accurate, resulting in the reduction of conflict. Most people are more accustomed to expressing themselves with a greater degree of freedom when talking as opposed to writing. The spoken word, in contrast to the written word, reinforces supportive relationships and helps create an atmosphere of mutual trust and confidence.

Feedback

In any working relationship, it is essential for a sergeant to develop skills and techniques to provide officers with feedback regarding their performance. This can range from praising someone's work to telling an officer what he or she has done wrong.

The utility of feedback is limited unless it is viewed as a process intended to help the recipient understand the communication. The best communication is that which is supportive and in which the recipient of the message has a feeling of personal worth and comfort. When a message is delivered, it should be in such a way that it is not perceived as negative. When time allows, it is up to the supervisor to take the time to analyze the message. This can be done by asking the question, "Will what I am going to say really help the officer or will it confuse the issue?" Self-examination is clearly needed so that emotions, feelings, and values will not interfere with transmission of the message. Careful consideration should be given as to how to approach an officer with feedback, keeping in mind that part of the role of a supervisor is to be a trainer. Feedback influences behavior because it allows subordinates to become knowledgeable about their performance. As such, it can prove to be a motivational factor, generating an interest in and enthusiasm for the accomplishment of tasks and contributing to the attainment of organizational goals. Additionally, feedback can be looked upon as a means of increasing the frequency of desirable behavior (Dickson, Saunders, & Stringer, 1993).

Feedback that acknowledges subordinates' importance can build a foundation of trust between the supervisor and officers. However, if one resorts to an extremely critical assessment of every subordinate activity, engaging in only one-way communication, or constantly pulling rank, then feedback will soon be nonexistent because the foundation of trust will be eroded (see Figure 3.9).

Another feature of feedback is that it should be *specific*. Specific and detailed discussion of the issue under consideration is needed. For example, if a supervisor believes that one of the officers should respond more quickly when providing backup for another officer during traffic stops, it is best to recall definite instances when the officer was late in responding to the scene. It is entirely possible that a valid reason for the delay (of which others were not aware) will be given. At the same time, by recalling the date, time, and place of the officer's tardiness, it helps focus on the problem and not on personality. Feedback should be provided as soon as possible after the occurrence, while it is still fresh in everyone's mind.

In the situation just given, the aspect of validity was pointed out. It should be emphasized that it is important to be sure of one's facts before providing feedback. It can be embarrassing, if not harmful, to a working relationship with a subordinate if the facts of a situation have not been verified before bringing up an issue.

When feedback is provided, it should be descriptive and nonjudgmental. Most people find it difficult to accept negative feedback concerning their performance; therefore, when an incident is described (putting it into a context of time and place), there is a greater possibility of dialogue occurring rather than one-way communication.

A great deal of a supervisor's time is spent evaluating the conduct and actions of subordinates. Therefore, a good part of feedback is either instructive or corrective. This places an extra burden on the supervisor to ensure that when feedback is given, the officer is in a position to accept it. If the officer is mentally or emotionally unable to receive the transmission, then there is little gained in giving negative feedback at that time. This does not mean that negative feedback is inappropriate, but that there is a time and place for everything. Many things occur in police work that may temporarily leave an officer angry, confused, distraught, or defensive.

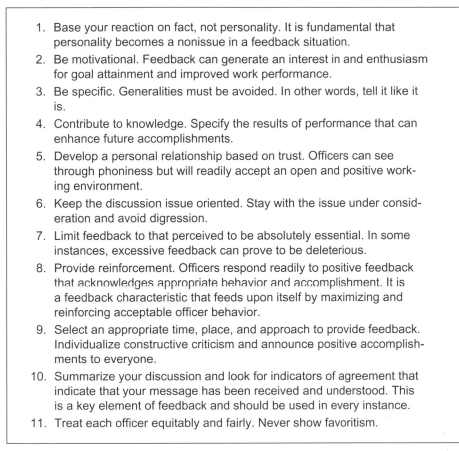

1. Base your reaction on fact, not personality. It is fundamental that personality becomes a nonissue in a feedback situation.
2. Be motivational. Feedback can generate an interest in and enthusiasm for goal attainment and improved work performance.
3. Be specific. Generalities must be avoided. In other words, tell it like it is.
4. Contribute to knowledge. Specify the results of performance that can enhance future accomplishments.
5. Develop a personal relationship based on trust. Officers can see through phoniness but will readily accept an open and positive working environment.
6. Keep the discussion issue oriented. Stay with the issue under consideration and avoid digression.
7. Limit feedback to that perceived to be absolutely essential. In some instances, excessive feedback can prove to be deleterious.
8. Provide reinforcement. Officers respond readily to positive feedback that acknowledges appropriate behavior and accomplishment. It is a feedback characteristic that feeds upon itself by maximizing and reinforcing acceptable officer behavior.
9. Select an appropriate time, place, and approach to provide feedback. Individualize constructive criticism and announce positive accomplishments to everyone.
10. Summarize your discussion and look for indicators of agreement that indicate that your message has been received and understood. This is a key element of feedback and should be used in every instance.
11. Treat each officer equitably and fairly. Never show favoritism.

FIGURE 3.9 Positive feedback techniques.

These feelings can be the result of a situation involving an abused child, an injury at an accident, or an abusive drunk. Any of these or similar situations could call for a delay in providing negative feedback.

Feedback should be selective and limited to the issue at hand. It should never be a situation in which every past omission or commission is brought to light and the supervisor "dumps" on the officer. At the very best, constructive criticism is difficult to accept, so it is essential to give it at an appropriate time and place. The ultimate goal is an improvement in performance.

The Art of Listening

Good supervisors generally practice a skill that is very difficult to learn: the art of listening. It is a primary qualification for the position of a first-line supervisor. Books are written on the subject, but few have read them. The value of developing the ability to listen should never be underestimated. If there is one pet peeve in interpersonal relationships, it is that one party does not listen. This is why some of the most successful supervisors are also the best listeners. Research suggests that most people listen at an efficiency level of approximately 25 percent (Sokolosky, 2003). Additionally, it is generally accepted that thought operates much faster than speech. The average person speaks two or three words a second—120 to 180 words a minute. However, most listeners can process up to 500 words per minute, depending on the incident under consideration. What occurs is that the differential between speech and thought can promote concentrating on something other than what is being said. Consequently, this should be taken into consideration during the supervisory process (Kline, 1996).

Becoming a good listener requires work; there is no single path to success. See Chapter 9 for a discussion of effective listening keys. Merely hearing what someone has said does not mean the real message has been received properly. Listening is an active process that requires one's intellectual capacities of comprehension and evaluation.

A good listener makes a sincere effort to understand the message. It might involve taking notes to ensure accuracy, asking the speaker to repeat him or herself, asking for clarification, or restating what the person said. Whatever the method or technique, the focus is on the message, ensuring that correct information has been received.

The first tenet of the art of listening is to pay attention to the speaker. As simple as this seems, the precept is often violated. When an officer wants to talk with his or her supervisor, the officer should be made to feel that no one else would be allowed to interfere with the discussion. Giving someone undivided attention can only be accomplished by shutting out all extraneous matters. An easy way to do this is to look directly at the person with whom you are conversing. Another is not to attempt to formulate a response until you have listened to the complete explanation from the individual to whom you are listening. In other words, be alert to what is being said and how it is being delivered. How often has a supervisor tried to tell something to another person and it was obvious that the other person was not listening? In other instances, the supervisor may not listen to a subordinate.

Listening is as much a persuasive art as speaking, but it must be developed. A successful listener should strive to keep an open mind and be fully cognizant of his or her own biases and preconceptions. An emotional block cannot be allowed to impede communication. If the officer being dealt with is someone who is personally disliked or has certain annoying mannerisms, the effect of these things can be minimized by analyzing the reasons for the negative emotional block. A good supervisor does not allow personal feelings to prevent communication, but addresses the situation intellectually so that the officer's ideas can be heard and understood.

One way to respond intellectually rather than emotionally is to concentrate on the conversation and to look for value and meaning in what is being said. Listen and wait. Take time to understand what is being said and then evaluate the content of the message. Use the time to listen for what the officer might really be trying to say. Another useful technique is to try to listen for what is *not* being said. Are pertinent points being avoided or glossed over (Salmon, 1998)? Look for implications or inferences that tell what the person really wants to say. A good listener waits until the sender completes a message before responding. This suspends

1. Adjust to the sender's message
   a. Reflect upon the content
   b. Search for the meaning the sender does not express
   c. Review and weigh what has been heard
   d. Minimize distractions
   e. Minimize or eliminate criticism
   f. Ask questions
   g. Repeat major points of the message
2. Attempt to listen unemotionally
   a. Do not respond to emotion-laden words
   b. Withhold judgment
   c. Be patient
   d. Do not interrupt
3. Give undivided attention to the speaker
   a. Maintain eye contact
   b. Show attentiveness through body language
   c. Nod approval when it is appropriate
   d. Be expressive when appropriate
   e. Make use of conversation enablers

FIGURE 3.10 Techniques that can be used for improving listening effectiveness.

judgment, reduces errors in interpretation, and allows the listener to concentrate on the entire message rather than jumping to a conclusion. A supervisor can work to improve listening effectiveness by following the recommendations listed in Figure 3.10. In recent years, greater attention has been given to implicit biases, and supervisory personnel should pay attention to any practices of discriminatory treatment of individuals and take appropriate action to remedy the situation (Gove, 2011). All of these combine to form a frame of reference for both the sender and the recipient of any message. Inasmuch as everyone has distinctive combinations of the aforementioned characteristics, it should be apparent that everyone has the potential to see and hear the same situation from different perspectives.

Greater accuracy in communication can be gained if one works diligently at developing good listening habits. Probably the first and most important action to be taken is to stop talking. One cannot listen if one is talking (Verderber & Verderber, 2007).

The art of listening requires one to expend considerable energy in order to understand and utilize the information transmitted by others. The opportunities to listen when functioning as a supervisor are considerable and it is one of the best ways to receive information from subordinates. Good listeners can easily expand their knowledge about a subject about which they have limited awareness. It is the responsibility of an effective supervisor to develop good listening skills to the highest point possible.

Nonverbal Communications

Communication involves more than sending, receiving, and assessing a message. It is a complex process that extends beyond the actual message to a consideration of nonverbal aspects of communication (Knapp, 2009). Feelings and emotions are important aspects of any message. Some experts have observed that it is more important to be competent in nonverbal communication than in actual verbal skills. There are three components of a message that contribute to the communication process. In terms of impact, only 7 percent can be accredited to the actual words, 38 percent to the way it was said, and 55 percent to nonverbal facets of communication (Mehrabian, 1981).

This means that the stance, gestures used, the facial expression, and other nonverbal aspects of communication all have a serious impact on the communication process. Body language (kinesics) is the study of nonverbal communication and concerns itself with understanding nonverbal signals (Beattie, 2004). It has been suggested that it actually reveals one's innermost thoughts and feelings (Mann, 2000). Body language needs to be accepted as an important element of the communication process if one is to be an effective supervisor. It must be remembered that many important things that are nonverbal transpire as part of the communication process.

One expert pointed out that one's state of mind can be acted out with nonverbal body language: an eyebrow can be lifted to convey disbelief; a nose rubbed to indicate puzzlement; folded arms indicate refusal or, in some instances, self-protection; a shrug of a shoulder might indicate indifference; a wink may convey intimacy; and a tap of the finger or a foot may reflect impatience (Fast, 1991).

Body language extends beyond these items by including a wide range of indicators such as posture, facial expression, body movement, positioning, eye contact, and body tension. All of these contribute to the communication process (Copland & Gwyn, 2003). Be aware of the image you project and realize that body language cues can be picked up. Keep in mind that any single nonverbal cue might not be especially significant but, when taken in conjunction with others, might have a great deal of significance. For example, stroking the chin accompanied by a relaxed smile will, in all probability, indicate that the listener's mind has been made up about the issue under discussion. One must develop an awareness of the fact that the body may not be conveying the message intended (Warfield, 2001).

An individual sends messages not only through language and words but also by tone of voice, pitch, and inflection. This form of communication is called *paralanguage.* Similar to body language, it is another means by which one can express emotion. Active emotions, such as anger and fear, tend to be expressed by a fast rate of speech, loud volume, high pitch, and "blaring" tone. However, passive emotions, such as sadness, are communicated by a slower rate of speech, lower volume, lower pitch, and a more unyielding feature.

Nonverbal communication is used primarily to convey emotions, desires, and preferences. Generally, nonverbal cues reinforce or contradict feelings that are communicated verbally. Feelings can be expressed through various types of nonverbal behavior, including facial expressions—in particular, eye contact, posture, and gestures (Dimitrius & Mazzarella, 2008).

Eye contact can be used effectively in controlling communication. It can be used to solicit or to actually suppress the transmission of a message. It can be used to support communication or to reinforce feedback. A supervisor can convey to a subordinate, through appropriate eye contact, a specific interest in him or her and the problem. Eye contact reinforces talking with a subordinate because they are given undivided attention. The failure to maintain sufficient eye contact can display aloofness, indirectness, a lack of confidence, or anxiety. The face is the primary communicator of emotions. One expert believes that there are 250,000 different facial expressions. Nonverbal messages, such as the following, can be conveyed by easily recognizable facial expressions:

- acceptance
- an expression of anger
- boredom with the problem or the topic
- concern
- disapproval of one's conduct or the action taken
- interest in the individual or topic

The supervisor, once aware of the importance of facial expressions, can utilize cues that support and reinforce communication, thereby reducing the probability that the recipient will misinterpret the sender's message.

Even one's posture serves as a cue to the communication process. When conversing with a subordinate, the supervisor can convey the importance of the topic and a definite interest in the matter simply by leaning forward. Other positive body language indicators are nodding, maintaining eye contact, or smiling (Dimitrius & Mazzarella, 2008). One should avoid slouching and always assume an erect but relaxed position (Verderber, Verderber, & Sellnowe, 2013). The supervisor's posture can be used to reinforce other nonverbal cues and reduce the potential for contradiction between an individual's verbal and nonverbal communication.

Gestures are the voluntary movement of a part of the body to explain, emphasize, or reinforce the verbal component of a message. It is an important part of what has been called the *silent language.* One expert has identified 5000 distinct hand gestures that have verbal equivalents (Axtell, 1997). For the most part, gestures are made with the hands and arms to clarify a point or to indicate a transition point in the conversation. Because there is less awareness of the gestures used, in contrast to eye contact or facial expressions, it is essential to become familiar with these gestures. A supervisor must use good timing in the use of gestures, realizing that they must be coordinated with the verbal message. Care also must be taken to control gestures possibly detracting from the message being transmitted. For instance, stroking the chin, folding the arms, or rubbing the nose can either reinforce or detract from the message. A simple technique for determining the extent and nature of gestures is to videotape a five-minute presentation and then review it, identifying specific gestures and determining their relationship to specific verbal points.

One should immediately be able to determine whether a conflicting message is being sent. When this is done, it can confuse others. Because the nonverbal message communicates emotion, it is essential to accurately reflect the intent of your message. Supervisors can ask themselves such questions as: "Does my body language support and reinforce my verbal message?" "Are conflicting messages being sent?" "Do my actions convey a genuine and sincere interest in my subordinates?" It is important to respond to these questions and do everything possible to ensure that effective communication occurs.

Communicating with Limited English Proficiency Individuals

The communication process becomes increasingly complex and difficult when an officer deals with witnesses, victims, or individuals seeking help who do not speak English or have limited English proficiency. Traditionally, this problem was dealt with by obtaining the assistance of a neighbor, friend, or relative of the individual being interviewed who could act as a translator (Herbst & Walker, 2001). Many officers have utilized the talents of younger individuals as interpreters because, in many instances, they, in contrast to older family members, are bilingual.

Executive Order 13166, entitled "Improving Access to Services for Persons with Limited English Proficiency," requires that the federal government and grant recipients take reasonable steps to ensure that people with LEP have meaningful access to the programs, services, and information they provide (Office of Justice Programs and Office of Weed and Seed, 2005). An example of a plan to implement a policy in accordance with the mandate states (Interagency Working Group on LEP, 2009):

> The police department is to take reasonable steps to provide timely, meaningful access to LEP persons to the services and benefits the police department provides in all programs and activities.
>
> All personnel shall provide free language assistance services to LEP individuals whom they encounter or whenever an LEP individual requests language assistance services. Police personnel will inform members of the public that language assistance services are available free of charge to LEP persons and police personnel will provide these services to them.

It is essential that first-line supervisors be fully conversant with the executive order and its impact on duties performed by those whom they supervise, such as:

1. Receiving citizen complaints.
2. Interrogating witnesses.
3. Arresting, booking, and holding suspects.
4. Operating telephone (911) emergency centers.
5. Providing emergency medical services.
6. Enforcing laws and ordinances.
7. Other duties.

In some departments, officers who are bilingual serve as translators when the occasion arises. In fact, it is becoming increasingly common for police departments to hire bilingual officers; in some instances, they are paid a bonus for the additional skill. Many departments across the nation make use of an interpreter service that offers interpreters for 144 languages and can locate speakers of many less common languages, given some extra time. Laminated cards list the languages for which interpreters are available and are issued to each officer. The federal government has an excellent language identification guide entitled "I Speak." It is a laminated guide that can be handed to an individual; it contains languages that range from Arabic to Zulu and the individual can point to their language. It serves not only to obtain interpretive services but to ensure consistent and effective interaction with LEP persons (Office of Justice Programs, 2006). Additionally, a number of departments are utilizing handheld translation devices such as the SpeedGuard and the Voxtec Phraselator, and it is anticipated that as these devices are refined, they will be utilized by more and more law enforcement agencies (Clossey, 2008; Manson, 2008).

One national commission recommended that the department under review complete a language needs assessment of the areas served and develop a plan to meet those needs. As part of the assessment it was recommended that the department take into account the number of persons arrested and the number of victims and witnesses in each area who speak little or no English (U.S. Commission on Civil Rights, 1999). As language diversity in the nation increases, there is a need to respond correctly and effectively. Needless to say, these issues are complex but there are numerous valuable resources on how to determine need, how to develop a language assistance program, how to identify resources, and how to work effectively with residents (Office of Justice Programs, 2007). A significant source is the federal Planning Tools for Creation of a Language Assistance Policy, which can be used to guide law enforcement agencies. When an agency has a policy in this area it is essential for a first-line supervisor to become conversant with that policy. A supervisor can ask those he or she supervises whether they have adequate access to language assistance services. Additionally, when operating in a community-policing mode, supervisors can ask residents if they know about the police department's language efforts. Finally, if it appears necessary, a request can be put through channels requesting that a community survey be conducted to evaluate the effectiveness of the department's language assistance program (Shah, Rahman, & Khashu, 2007).

In one police department with approximately 1000 sworn officers, the federal court ordered the department to give preference during hiring to candidates who were fluent in Spanish. Thus, the availability of Spanish-speaking officers increased dramatically. In many areas, community colleges have responded positively to police department needs and have developed special foreign language courses for officers. Other sources include Spanish on Patrol (http://SpanishOnPatrol.com), which contains 17 units with more than 100 online lessons, and Workplace Spanish (http://workplacespanish.com), which was created by a private company that worked with the Las Vegas Metropolitan Police Department (Shan & Estrada, 2009). Another effort in this area is online Spanish language training entitled *Español for Law Enforcement: An Interactive Training Tool*, which is available to the public free of charge. It helps the user obtain a working knowledge of the Spanish language and applies that knowledge to scenarios that involve law enforcement. The training tool provides English translations, phonetic spelling, and pronunciations of Spanish words in situations involving interviews,

1. Basic Knowledge
    Fundamentals
    Descriptors
    Interrogatives
    Arrest Commands
    Grammar
2. Interviews
    Interview 1: Traffic Accident
    Interview 2: Missing Child
    Interview 3: Drug Use
3. Crime Scene
    Crime Scene 1: Noise Complaint
    Crime Scene 2: Burglary
4. Motor Vehicles
    Motor Vehicles 1: Routine Traffic Stop
    Motor Vehicles 2: DUI Traffic Stop
    Motor Vehicles 3: Felony Traffic Stop
5. Domestic Violence
    Domestic Violence 1: Protective Order
    Domestic Violence 2: Violent Disturbance
    Domestic Violence 3: Domestic Violence Cross Complaint
6. Course Examinations and Final End-of-Course Test
    Examination 1
    Examination 2
    Final End-of-Course Test

FIGURE 3.11 Español for law enforcement: an interactive training tool. *Source: Office of Justice Programs (2008).* Español for Law Enforcement: An Interactive Training Tool. *Washington, DC: National Institute of Justice.*

crime scenes, motor vehicles, and domestic violence. The tool can be ordered from http://espanolforlawenforcement.gov. Figure 3.11 lists the course content.

If the police department serves a Spanish-speaking community, it is imperative for a supervisor to complete this course so that she or he might be better prepared to serve the residents and the community. The rapid growth of the Spanish-speaking population in the United States necessitates police officers becoming conversant in Spanish. It is estimated that by the middle of this century the Hispanic population will nearly triple, from 46.6 million to 132.8 million. Thus nearly one in three United States residents will be Hispanic (U.S. Census Bureau News, 2008).

An additional innovative approach, which illustrates what can be done to obtain expert assistance when language is a barrier, is the arrangement made by one department, in which foreign language instructors at a government agency are available as interpreters. Their expertise ranges from Arabic to Swahili.

In the event that a first-line supervisor encounters a foreign language barrier and an interpreter is not available within the department, consideration should be given to identifying interpreters who are employees of other city or county agencies. For example, in one library system, individuals who spoke 20 different languages were identified, and a memorandum of understanding was agreed upon in order for officers to utilize their expertise. The opportunities for such arrangements are extensive and departments should not overlook the language expertise to be found in high schools, colleges, or business establishments.

Intercultural Communications

Law enforcement officers are, in many instances, initial responders to critical incidents and, in many instances, are increasingly confronted by a diverse range of cultures; more critically, officers are confronted with a communications dilemma (Bonvillain, 2009). The last major national census found that 20 percent of our nation's residents spoke a language other than English at home (Grieco, 2003). Furthermore, 8 percent of the residents had LEP. Police officers cannot perform their duties when they are unable to communicate. Crimes cannot be reported and offenders cannot be described—consequently, it becomes difficult to provide a service or protect those in need. Moreover, officers can be placed in danger when language barriers are present (Shah et al., 2007).

Some LEP residents come from cultures where the police are viewed as the "enemy," and a barrier between the two elements exists that seems insurmountable in many instances. This is a carryover from their attitudes toward the police in their former country. Hence police are viewed negatively, and this animosity carries over to the relationship between immigrants and American law enforcement officers. Many immigrants are genuinely afraid of the police and do everything possible to avoid contact with all authorities. This is especially true for immigrants who have limited English language capability (Shah et al., 2007).

In response to this growing issue, police departments are beginning to train officers in diversity as our nation becomes more multicultural (Palmiotto, 2005). The heterogeneity of our country, in many areas, has become such that communication between police officers and immigrants has become increasingly difficult. Immigrants have concentrated in selected cities and in selected areas within communities. Recently, more and more immigrants are settling in suburbs, small towns, and rural areas where more jobs are available and the cost of living is lower (Shah et al., 2007). The ethnicity of neighborhoods has changed rapidly with the influx of varying nationalities, including Cubans, Puerto Ricans, Vietnamese, Cambodians, Mexicans, Koreans, Chinese, or Russians. As international travel has increased, tourists from other nations frequent many cities in the United States, further complicating the communication process (Lustig, 2003). The communication process, while different for each culture, is composed of essentially three components—language, culture, and ethnicity.

During the last 15 years the Arab/Muslim community has increased precipitously in many places in the United States. This places an additional demand upon law enforcement, calling for officers to become more knowledgeable about this culture (Navarro, 2002). In response to the "Arab world," the Los Angeles County Sheriff's Department has created a Muslim Community Affairs Unit that works with this group and trains officers about the Islamic culture, customs, and beliefs (Leggiere, 2012).

Consequently, it has become increasingly important for supervisors, as well as officers, to develop an intercultural competence (Lusting, 2009) and develop methods of communicating with people of other nations. A rudimentary knowledge of cultural variations and values can help a supervisor deal with the culturally diverse public. Another program that is proving to be valuable was developed by the Lexington (KY) Police Department. It utilizes an immersion program to increase officers' cultural competency—their understanding of Mexican culture and norms. Officers spend five weeks becoming culturally aware and working on their language kills. Upon finishing training, officers have a better understanding of Mexican immigrants' expectations when dealing with law enforcement (Shan & Estrada, 2009). One should learn the pronunciation of certain names so as not to offend.

Some Spanish-speaking cultures use double surnames, the Chinese place the family name first (Wu Ling Li, where Wu is the family name and Ling is the given name), and Filipinos place the given name first, followed by the surname. People of Russian and Ukrainian extraction construct their names in a manner similar to that of English names. Their middle name, however, is a patronymic (comes from the father's given name) and the surname is the family name (Dees, 2003). Supervisors can use the Name Reference Library to provide information on names that may be unfamiliar in structure, order, or origin.

Some cultures will tell you what you want to hear rather than what is the truth. Nonverbal behavior is culturally specific. Different cultures have differing norms for both verbal and nonverbal behavior. The uniqueness of different cultures is that they each have different rules for speaking and listening. Some cultures converse with a great deal of emotion, whereas others use extensive hand gestures. In some Asian cultures, eye contact is considered disrespectful, while Americans prefer eye contact. Space is another nonverbal cultural feature. Supervisors need to understand and respect the importance of proxemics, or personal and social space. Arabs, southern Mediterraneans, and Latin Americans stand close when they converse and touch while conversing—in sharp contrast to Americans, who generally reject someone who violates their personal space (Berryman-Fink & Fink, 2007). In contact cultures, physical closeness, occasional touching, and frequent gesturing are important and desired components of the communication process. A supervisor must be willing to become knowledgeable about intercultural communications. Above all, there should be an open-minded and flexible response to the demands of an increasingly diverse society.

Communicating with Hearing-Impaired Individuals

In the United States it is estimated that 21 million people have some degree of hearing impairment, and a large number of these individuals are completely deaf. This can be a serious problem for law enforcement officers when faced with someone whose communication is limited because of such an affliction. Supervisors who take the time to learn sign language can become

1. A person moving fingers and hands in repetitive patterns could be using sign language, hoping to be understood.
2. The individual appears unusually alert and follows every move with his or her eyes.
3. The person appears alert but fails to respond to any sounds, such as surrounding noises or spoken language.
4. The person gestures in a manner that suggests a desire to write something.
5. The person moves his or her lips without making any sound.
6. The person points to the ears or to the ears and mouth with an index finger.
7. The person speaks in a flat, harsh, or unintelligible monotone.
8. Repeating a sequence of body movements or gestures may be an attempt to communicate an unspoken thought or idea.

FIGURE 3.12 Recognizing hearing-impaired individuals. *Source: U.S. Department of Health and Human Services (1981). Emergency Medical Services (EMS) and the Hearing Impaired. Rockville, MD: USGPO; Office for Civil Rights (2001). Communicating with Hearing-Impaired Individuals. Washington, DC: DHHS; and Office on Disability—Emergency Preparedness (2006). Model Policy for Law Enforcement on Communication with People Who Are Deaf or Hard of Hearing. Washington, DC: DHHS.*

a valuable departmental resource and assist other officers. One sheriff's department has a 24-hour sign language course for emergency personnel which covers basic skills, as well as aspects of field patrol contacts and arrest considerations. The hearing impaired can usually be identified by careful and sensitive observation of an individual (see Figure 3.12).

Some deaf persons express themselves orally or may combine the use of speech with signing. The latter technique is described as a form of manual communication in which the individual uses movements of the body, hands, and face to convey messages. It is estimated that there are at least 500,000 deaf people who communicate by utilizing American Sign Language as their primary method of communication (Fant & Fant, 2008; National Association of the Deaf, 2008; Valli, 2006).

Lip-reading (speech reading) is another technique used by the hearing impaired. This is the process of recognizing spoken words by watching the speaker's facial expressions, lip movements, and/or body language. A deaf person must have a number of skills, including good visual acuity, knowledge of the language, and the ability to distinguish between words that look similar when they are spoken. Unfortunately, the speaker who has a beard or moustache or speaks with an accent can complicate the task of reading someone's lips effectively. When communicating with a deaf person, the supervisor should take into consideration the items listed in Figure 3.13.

Interpreters

Interpreters facilitate communication between hearing and deaf persons. The length, importance, or complexity of the communication will help determine whether an interpreter is

1. Family members and friends may not be effective or reliable as interpreters. They may lack objectivity and may misinterpret pertinent information. Such individuals should not be relied upon to provide sign language interpreting except in limited circumstances.

2. Lip-reading is often slow and requires a high degree of concentration. Keep in mind that lip-reading (or speech-reading) presumes that the hearing-impaired person speaks English. Lip-reading does not facilitate two-way communication.

3. Persons who are deaf and who communicate in sign language cannot communicate when they are handcuffed. Handcuffs of booked deaf individuals should be removed if removal does not result in a direct threat to the health and safety of any person in jail.

4. Qualified sign language interpreters can ensure effective communications. These are persons who have received specialized formal education and experience.

5. The judgment of the hearing-impaired person should be given primary consideration when determining the preferred form of communication, which is best accomplished by asking the person whether auxiliary aids and services are necessary to ensure effective communication.

6. Writing notes and finger spelling are both ineffective methods of communication for the majority of deaf persons. These methods are very slow and many deaf persons are unfamiliar with law enforcement jargon. Additionally, these methods presume that deaf persons are functionally literate in English.

7. When communicating orally, speak slowly and distinctly. Use gestures and facial expressions to reinforce what you say.

8. Before speaking, get the person's attention with a wave of the hand or a gentle tap on the shoulder.

9. Face the person and do not turn away while speaking.

10. Try to converse in a well-lit area.

11. Do not cover your mouth, smoke, or chew gum.

12. Remember that only about one-third of spoken words can be understood by speech-reading.

FIGURE 3.13 Considerations when communicating with hearing-impaired individuals. *Adapted from National Association for the Deaf Law Center (2000a).* Legal Rights: The Guide for Deaf and Hard of Hearing People, *Fifth Edition, Revised. Washington, DC: Gallaudet University; National Association for the Deaf Law Center, 2000b.* Police and Law Enforcement Responsibilities to Deaf Individuals. *Silver Spring, MD: National Association of the Deaf. Communicating with People Who Are Deaf or Hard of Hearing—ADA Guideline for Law Enforcement Officers. Washington, DC: U.S. Department of Justice.*

necessary for effective communication. In a simple encounter, such as checking a driver's license, a notepad and pencil normally will be sufficient. During interrogations and arrests, a sign language interpreter will often be necessary to communicate effectively with an individual who uses sign language (U.S. Department of Justice, 1998). Operationally, there are two types of interpreters. The first is a sign language interpreter, who listens to the speaking person and informs the deaf person of the content of the message by using sign language. The second is an oral interpreter, who repeats another's word without using voice. The words are mouthed and the deaf person speech-reads the interpreter.

"State and local law enforcement agencies have a federal mandate to ensure adequate and appropriate communication with deaf and hard of hearing individuals. Without effective communication serious violations of constitutional and civil rights can occur" (National Association for the Deaf Law Center, 2000b). This mandate is found in two federal laws protecting the rights of individuals with disabilities (National Association for the Deaf Law Center, 2001). An important settlement agreement between the United States of America, two complainants, and the city of Houston, Texas, was the result of police officers, jail officials, and court officials not communicating effectively with hearing-impaired persons. The city agreed that individuals with disabilities, including but not limited to crime victims, witnesses to crimes, and people under arrest, are entitled to effective communications (U.S. Department of Justice, 1998).

Additionally, U.S. Department of Justice regulation 28 C.F.R. Part 42 (July 26, 1991) requires law enforcement agencies to ensure that hearing-impaired individuals can be communicated with effectively. They are also encouraged to use qualified interpreters who are registered with a local or state chapter of the Registry of Interpreters of the Deaf founded in 1964. This organization has the responsibility of certifying individuals as qualified interpreters and, more recently, has worked with the National Association of the Deaf on a new testing procedure.

When working with an interpreter, a supervisor or officer should be aware of the following items:

- When asked to provide a sign language interpreter it is essential to ask which language the person uses—American Sign Language (ASL) and Signed English are the most common.
- Provide for an interpreter when interviewing a witness or a suspect or when engaging in any complex conversation.
- When using an interpreter, look at and speak directly to the hearing-impaired person, not the interpreter.
- Talk at a normal rate or slightly slower if you normally speak fast.
- Use short sentences and simple words.

A police officer must give primary consideration to providing the aid or service requested by the person with a hearing disability. The goal is to treat the hearing impaired the same way that other citizens are treated.

It is essential to have an interpreter present when a hearing-impaired individual is informed of his or her rights, when he or she is being questioned, and when a statement is taken. When a hearing-impaired individual is arrested, he or she should be provided with a printed form of the *Miranda* warning (which includes offering an interpreter to the arrestee without cost) and the form should point out that the interrogation will be delayed until an interpreter is present. The U.S. Department of Justice in 45 Fed Reg. 37630 sets forth this requirement (June 3, 1980).

References

Air Force Headquarters, (2004). *The tongue and quill, AFH 33-337.* Montgomery, AL: Maxwell-Gunter Air Force Base.

Albrecht, K. (1979). *Stress and the manager: Making it work for you.* Englewood Cliffs, NJ: Prentice Hall.

Axtell, R. E. (1997). *Gestures—The do's and taboos of body language around the world* (3rd ed.). New York: John Wiley and Sons.

Beattie, G. (2004). *Visible thought: The new psychology of body language.* New York: Routledge.

Berryman-Fink, C., & Fink, C. B. (2007). *The manager's desk reference* (3rd ed.). New York: AMACOM.

Bonvillain, N. (2009). *Language, culture and communications: The meaning of messages* (5th ed.). Englewood Cliffs, NJ: Prentice Hall.

Boyd, R. F., Jr. (2003). Improving access to services for persons with limited English proficiency. *The Police Chief, LXX*(4).

Bradford, D. L., & Cohen, A. R. (1997). *Managing for excellence: The guide to developing high performance in contemporary organizations* (2nd ed.). New York: John Wiley and Sons.

Civil Rights Commission, (2006). *Planning tool: Considerations for creation of a language assistance police and implementation plan for addressing limited proficiency in a law enforcement agency.* Washington, DC: Department of Justice.

Clossey, D. (2008). Voxtec 'Phraselator. *Law and Order, 56*(8).

Copland, J., & Gwyn, R. (Eds.). (2003). *Discourse, the body and identity.* New York: Palgrave Macmillan.

Dees, T. (2003). The name game. *Law and Order, 51*(5).

Dickson, D., Saunders, C., & Stringer, M. (1993). *Rewarding people: The skill of responding positively.* New York: Routledge.

Dimitrius, J. -E., & Mazzarella, M. (2008). *Reading people—How to understand people and predict their behavior anytime anyplace.* New York: Random House.

Fant, B. B., & Fant, L. (2008). *The American sign language phrase book.* New York: McGraw Hill.

Fast, J. (1991). *Making body language work in the workplace.* New York: Viking.

Gaines, L. K., & Worral, J. L. (2011). *Police administration* (3rd ed.). New York: McGraw-Hill Book Company.

Gove, T. G. (2011). Implicit bias and law enforcement. *The Police Chief, LXXVIII*(10).

Grieco, E. (2003). *English abilities of the US foreign-born population.* Washington, DC: Migration Police Institute.

Hargie, O., Dickson, D., & Gibbons, B. J. (2004). *Skilled interpersonal communication: Research, theory and practice.* Brisbane, Australia: Psychology Press.

Herbst, L., & Walker, S. (2001). *Language barriers in the delivery of police services: A study of police and Hispanics in a midwestern city.* Washington, DC: National Criminal Justice Reference Service. pp. 1–12.

Interagency Working Group on LEP, (2009). *LEP resources.* Washington, DC: Limited English Proficiency Interagency.

Kline, J. A. (1996). *Listening effectively.* Maxwell AF Base, Montgomery, AL: Air University Press.

Knapp, M. L. (2009). *Nonverbal communication in human interaction* (7th ed.). Australia: Wadsworth/Thompson Learning.

Leggiere, P. (2012). Outreach and results: *Homeland security today.* Washington, DC: Homeland Security.

Lusting, M. W. (2009). *Intercultural competence: Interpersonal communication across cultures* (6th ed.). Boston: Allyn & Bacon.

Mann, S. (2000). Body talk: The non-verbal language that reveals our innermost thoughts and feelings. *Professional Manager, 9*(6).

Manson, T. M. (2008). Speedguard handheld language translation. *Law and Order, 56*(6).

Mehrabian, A. (1981). *Silent messages: Implicit communications of emotions and attitudes.* Belmont, CA: Wadsworth.

National Association of the Deaf, (2008). *Position statement on American sign language.* Silver Spring, MD: NAD.

National Association for the Deaf Law Center, (2000a). *Legal rights: The guide for deaf and hard of hearing people* (Revised 5th ed.). Washington, DC: Gallaudet University.

National Association for the Deaf Law Center, (2000b). *NAD position statement on communication access by law enforcement personnel with deaf and hard of hearing individuals.* Silver Spring, MD: National Association of the Deaf Law Center.

National Association for the Deaf Law Center, (2001). *Police and law enforcement agency responsibilities to deaf individuals.* Silver Spring, MD: National Association for the Deaf Law Center.

Navarro, J. (2002). Interacting with Arabs and Muslims. *FBI Law Enforcement Bulletin, 71*(9).

Office for Civil Rights, (2001). Communicating with hearing-impaired individuals: *Washington, DC.* US DHHS.

Office of Justice Programs, (2006). *I speak, language identification guide* (2nd ed.). Washington, DC: State of Ohio and U.S. Department of Justice.

Office of Justice Programs, (2007). *Supporting limited English communities.* Washington, DC: U.S. Department of Justice.

Office of Justice Programs and Office of Weed and Seed, (2005). *Supporting limited English communities.* Washington, DC: U.S. Department of Justice.

Office on Disability—Emergency Preparedness, (2006). *Model policy for law enforcement on communication with people who are deaf or hard of hearing.* Washington, DC: DHHS.

Palmiotto, M. J. (2005). *Policing: Concepts, strategies, and current issues* (2nd ed.). Durham, NC: Carolina Academic Press.

Salmon, W. A. (1998). *The new supervisor's survival manual.* New York: AMACOM.

Shah, S., Rahman, I., & Khashu, A. (2007). *Overcoming language barriers: Solutions for law enforcement.* Washington, DC: COPS and Vera Institute of Justice.

Shah, S., & Estrada, R. (2009). *Bridging the language divide. Promising practices for law enforcement.* Vera Institute of Justice and Department of Community Oriented Policing Services.

Sokolosky, V. (2003). Listen up: *Southwest airline spirit.* Dallas: Southwest.

U.S. Census Bureau News, (2008). *An older and more diverse nation by midcentury.* Washington, DC: U.S. Census Bureau.

U.S. Commission on Civil Rights, (1999). *Racial and ethnic tensions in American communities: Poverty, inequality and discrimination, Vol. 5: The Los Angeles Report.* Washington, DC: U.S. Commission on Civil Rights.

U.S. Department of Health and Human Services, (1981). *Emergency medical services (EMS) and the hearing impaired.* Rockville, MD: USGPO.

U.S. Department of Justice (June 3, 1980). 45 Fed. Reg. 37630.

U.S. Department of Justice (July 26, 1991). 28 C.F.R. Part 42.

U.S. Department of Justice, (1998). *Settlement agreement between the United States of America, Rashad Gordon, Michael Edwards, and the City of Houston, Texas.* Washington, DC: Department of Justice.

Valli, C. (Ed.). (2006). *The Gallaudet dictionary of American sign language.* Washington, DC: Gallaudet University Press.

Verderber, R. F., & Verderber, K. S. (2007). *Communicate!* (12th ed.). Belmont, CA: Wadsworth.

Verderber, R. F., Verderber, K. S., & Sellnowe, D. D. (2013). *Communicate!* (13th ed.). Belmont, CA: Wadsworth.

Vita, B. (2000). *Tired cops: The importance of managing police fatigue.* Washington, DC: Police Executive Research Forum.

Warfield, A. (2001). Do you speak body language? *Training and Development, 55*(4).

4

Motivation
A Prerequisite for Success

CASE STUDY
Sergeant Louis "Lou" Maynard

DEPARTMENT

The Craigview Police Department bears a striking resemblance to many smaller police departments that are found in the United States, and it has a rich history in a unique area of the state. Early law enforcement activities were provided by the army and later the first marshal was appointed as the community grew as a result of new residents coming in to work in agriculture, timber, and mining. With the influx of new residents a police force was created and charged with the enforcement of laws and protecting the community. Currently the police department has two major divisions: Field Operations and Field Support. Operations provides 24-hour protection to residents and their property. The primary objective of patrol is dual in nature—providing for security and rendering services to residents and visitors. Operations is also responsible for traffic control, and parking on city streets overnight requires an annual parking permit. It also issues overnight parking stickers for residents and visitors. This unit works four 10-hour shifts, and each patrol officer is assigned to a team that is supervised by a sergeant. The staff includes six sergeants and 24 sworn officers who work within the city limits, encompassing approximately 22 square miles. Each patrol vehicle is equipped with a mobile data computer, in-car digital video, and E-citation equipment. The head of patrol is constantly evaluating new technology that will aid and assist field officers. Downtown is a tourist attraction. One officer is assigned to foot or bike patrol of that area on the swing shift. Two other officers work at the local high school and a middle school as school resource officers. During the last fiscal year the patrol unit responded to 39,831 calls for service that resulted in approximately 4254 arrests, 9989 crime reports, and 9981 collision reports.

The Field Support Division encompasses a number of functions including training, criminal investigation, volunteers, and a property section. This division, which has sworn and civilian personnel, is headed by a lieutenant and has primary responsibility for preparing the departmental budget. It also compiles traffic criminal statistics. In this type of organizational arrangement, support is the key word. Everything is done to provide patrol with the tools and information it needs in order to perform effectively.

CRIME

Craigview's violent crime has gone up slightly in several categories, and aggravated assault has increased the most. There were 120 assaults last year, as compared to the previous year when there were 109 such offenses reported.

The preponderance of this increase seems to be caused by transients and visitors. What has alarmed segments of the community is an increase in forcible rapes from three occurrences to a total of 21, as well as robberies that have increased from 61 to 77. For both types of incidents it is a new high going back more than 10 years. It is not known for sure, but it seems to be the action of a gang that has been organized recently, and this is a new phenomenon for the community. Considerable consideration is being given to how these occurrences can be better policed.

Property crime is relatively high for a community of this size, with 1589 offenses reported. Larceny/theft incidents occurred 771 times and burglaries occurred 564 times during the last year, which is a slight increase. Burglaries have been relatively stable over the last five years. Motor vehicle thefts occurred 164 times, compared to the previous year when there were 154 occurrences. Many of these offenses in the latter category were committed by youthful offenders, and joyriding occurred more often than not. There was no reason to believe that auto theft was an organized event.

COMMUNITY

Craigview is a rather small community with a population of 26,312 and it is the largest city in the county. There are six other smaller communities, and the greater part of the county is unincorporated. Geographically it is a coastal city. It is viewed as a special place to live, and it thrives on its small-town atmosphere. Numerous residents have lived in the city for several generations, which provides considerable city and neighborhood stability. Many houses are situated on tree-lined streets, and there are few fences that separate the houses. This has proven to be a major attraction for those who are interested in a small community atmosphere. During the last decade, retirees in particular have found the community to be a great place to live. There are numerous small neighborhood parks, a large community hall for cultural and educational programs, as well as a senior center. Additionally, there is a year round family swimming center that is used by many residents. There is a new high school that is centrally located. It provides academic classes as well as trade courses such as automobile repair, and has a strong orientation to the computer and communications world. There is exceptional support for fine arts. The teachers enjoy their work, and the community strongly supports their efforts.

In the downtown area there is a small center for artists where they can exhibit their work. The city has a shopping mall with numerous small stores that cater to the tourist trade, and a youth center near the mall has numerous programs for youths. The community has a varied tax base, with shopping and numerous small manufacturing companies. There is a weak mayor, five members of the city council who represent specific geographical wards, and also a city manager. At council meetings residents are allowed to present their views. There is a free exchange of ideas and opinions at the meetings, and the members of the city council work diligently at problem resolution. The local television station broadcasts the meetings.

OFFICER

Louis "Lou" Maynard entered law enforcement after returning from Iraq, where he served a nine-month tour and, though he was in combat areas, he returned physically unscathed. He remained in his National Guard unit as a sergeant in an engineer company. He has five years remaining to complete his military obligation. Prior to being on active duty with the military, he had worked as a truck driver and a bartender. After release from active duty, he applied for a position in the Craigview Police Department, was accepted, and placed as number three on the candidate list. He was hired and completed the academy, where he graduated fourth in his class. After his field training, he was placed on a team on the 4/10 swing shift—the busiest shift in the department. Maynard is 27 years old, married, and has one child who is three years old. His family lives in a house that he inherited from his mother. Additionally, they both have numerous relatives who live in the region. Lou and his wife went to the same schools in the community. Lou is low key and fits well into the policing environment. He gets along with peers, subordinates, and those of higher rank. His military service helped him to adjust to the department. After four years he took the sergeant examination and had no difficulty on the written exam or the orals. He was placed second on the promotion list and was appointed within six months in view of the fact that two sergeants retired. He was assigned to a team on the evening shift.

PROBLEM

After being on the team for six months, Maynard believes that the majority of the team responded positively to the demands of the job except for two officers. Both were close to retirement and seemed bored, as if they were just putting in time until they would become eligible to "hang it up" in one year. All of the other members of the team feel very strongly that the two potential retirees are not carrying their weight. The reports they submit are of marginal quality and lacking in content when arrests are anticipated to lead to prosecution. Maynard feels that their performance has become problematic but not poor enough to warrant sanctions such as a letter of reprimand. The two officers, who have worked together for many years, distance themselves from other team members socially and have stopped attending a coffee session at a local restaurant prior to going on shift. Each of the officers has functioned positively over the years and participated professionally and socially with other team members. It is as if they have grown tired of police work and just want to coast until they retire.

WHAT WOULD YOU DO?

As the immediate supervisor of the two officers, what would you do about this motivational problem? Why? Would just waiting out be a solution to the problem? Explain why or why not. What part does Theory X play in this type of situation? What effort to modify their behavior would you make? Are there negative consequences that might work in such a situation? Explain. What type of feedback would you engage in to let the two officers know that their behavior is unacceptable? Why? What would be your position in terms of advising the lieutenant about what is occurring? Explain.

A supervisor must take a multitude of factors into consideration when trying to understand the process of motivation. Central to that understanding is the human equation. A motive energizes one to take action and concerns itself with the choices one makes about goal-directed behavior. A motive causes one to act in a specific way as opposed to other options. Motives are the *why* of human behavior (Berryman-Fink & Fink, 2007). The preponderance of problems confronting an organization is unmistakably those identified as phenomena involving human conduct. Advances in physical and biological technology have not even identified what constitutes human behavior, much less presented a solution to understanding this complex area. There is a need for a technology of behavior, but this has not evolved and we seem to know little more about human behavior today than we did a century ago. Notwithstanding, supervisors must deal constantly with both acceptable and unacceptable behavior.

Behavioral sciences trace behavior by utilizing such terms as *attitudes*, *feelings*, and *state of mind*. These concepts can be interpreted differently; consequently, problems have arisen as the field has evolved. There is a continuous struggle as efforts are made to identify and measure behavior and, while a comprehensive theory of behavior has yet to be set forth, the quest goes on. At the same time, current research would suggest that we are aware of four qualities of motivation that give a supervisor a frame of reference for making officers more effective and productive (Berryman-Fink & Fink, 2007):

- **Motives are hierarchical in nature.** Some motives are perceived as more important than others, and in some instances a motive can prove to be very strong and achieve importance as compared to other motives. At times, for example, the work itself might be more important than working conditions, but at the same time there appears to be a rank order of motives that stimulate officers; this is a condition that continually affects a supervisor's motivational efforts.
- **Motives may be unconsciousness.** All of us have heard "I do not know what made me do that." This is not unusual because many of us are unaware of how or why certain behavior occurred. In fact, some officers can provide a whole litany of reasons as to why something occurred, but in the end accept the fact that they are not really aware of the inner needs and drives that resulted in a specific behavior.
- **Inference.** When it comes down to it, a supervisor can actually observe a specific action or behavior, but the motive underlying that behavior can only be inferred. What this really means is that truly understanding motivation resulting in a certain behavior is still an

unknown element in the motivation equation. Consequently, the actual determination of one's motives, with our present knowledge, is to observe and attempt to draw a conclusion based on one's best judgment.

- **Variability.** It is readily apparent that motives are changeable and have a limited stability. Time has a serious impact on motives and what works today might not work tomorrow. Motives are dynamic and leave us with the need to deal with the relationship of officers to the organization, the personal needs of officers, and the relationship that employees have with each other. It is a tall order, but achievable.

In the meantime, supervisors must deal with the behavior of subordinates and use all the knowledge at their disposal to motivate each employee so that organizational goals can be achieved. Successful supervisors know that a great deal of effort must be expended in order to motivate employees. Motivation is not just something to be turned off and on at one's leisure. It is a full-time, demanding process and can be all consuming. Employees will soon learn that a motivational speech at roll call asking them to "go out and make those streets safe" only serves to make the supervisor feel better. Rhetoric means little if it is not accompanied by positive and recurring reinforcements.

Why Officers Work

Behavioral scientists generally accept the proposition that behavior does not happen spontaneously—it is caused. Human behavior can be explained largely by determining basic human needs. Needs are fundamental to our basic existence and they cause things to happen. Needs cause one to act in a certain way, and goal attainment can result in need satisfaction. For example, before acquiring the rank of sergeant, an officer's behavior was directed toward passing examinations successfully, allowing for goal attainment.

It seems the more humankind is studied, the more we realize the complexity of human behavior. In the past, it was believed that reason was capable of solving all problems. Aristotle believed that reason held sway over all human capacities (Nirenberg, 1986). Our current knowledge goes well beyond this. Our intricacy demands that a systematic procedure be followed in attempting to understand the internal and external factors that motivate individuals to act the way they do. In general, behavior will follow a pattern showing that:

- A need will activate the energy to attain an acceptable goal.
- As the need increases in intensity, goal attainment is emphasized by the individual.
- As the need increases, behavior follows, hopefully resulting in the attainment of goals and resulting satisfaction.

From these patterns, the characteristics of human behavior become more apparent. A need arises and one's perception mobilizes the energy needed for reaching a goal. If the goal is not attained, the person tries again, mobilizing additional energy. Additional attention is paid to excluding factors that do not foster goal attainment. The motivation cycle is a vehicle that aids in understanding human behavior. This cycle will allow you to gain an appreciation of the

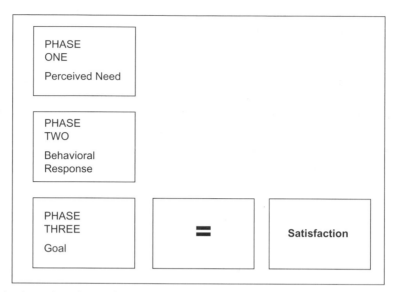

FIGURE 4.1 Motivation cycle. *Adapted from Associates of the Office of Military Leadership, USMA (eds.) (1976). A Study of Organizational Leadership. Harrisburg, PA: Stackpole Books.*

interacting forces and the resulting motivated behavior. Figure 4.1 depicts motivation as a continuous process consisting of three specific phases. The initial stage occurs when an individual experiences a need caused by external or internal forces, and there is a mobilization of these forces. In the next phase, a responsive behavior occurs, and there is an increase in energy. The last stage results in goal attainment and satisfaction results. The completion of one stage is not necessarily the end of the process. It can repeat itself or another need can arise.

An individual's motivation to act depends on two factors: the strength of the need and believing a certain action will lead to need satisfaction. For example, a patrol officer thought of becoming a sergeant and developed the desire to strive for the rank. The intensity of this person's motivation and the satisfaction of the need depend on the perception of the real value of the goal. If his or her desire to become a sergeant is more than a transient wish and he or she wants the extra pay, the status, involvement in the decision-making process, and the power that goes with the position, the individual's motivation will undoubtedly be high (Brown, 1992). Positional power should not be underestimated. When applied with caution and understanding, it can create trust and true understanding. Above all, favoritism cannot be justified as a supervisory technique and can prove to be highly disruptive (More, Vito, & Walsh, 2013; More & More, 2012).

This simple example fulfills the requirement of motivation inasmuch as the need was strong and the individual pursued a course to satisfy that need. A manager has a responsibility to motivate employees. In fact, most agencies have a written directive stating that supervisory personnel are accountable for the performance of employees under their immediate supervision (CALEA, 2006). Supervisors must create conditions that maximize the productivity of the officers. Their efforts must be coordinated to achieve departmental goals. A first-line supervisor will soon acknowledge every officer as a unique individual and each individual is generally stimulated by different needs.

Officers can be motivated by one need today, and tomorrow the need may reappear or a new need may become evident. In other words, as the situation changes, the individual's wants and desires can change. It is clear that subjective and objective features affect job satisfaction (Fincham & Rhodes, 2006). Fear, values, beliefs, interests, habits, culture, peer influence, love, moral standards, or other factors can motivate officers. It is evident that some of these factors are internal to the officer, while others are external. The combination of external and internal factors determines what motivates an officer to act in a certain way in a certain situation.

Motivational experts point out that the whole person is hired, not just a part. This means motivating the totality of a person's drives. Motivation is as complex as human behavior. Therefore, a supervisor should keep an open mind about motivating individuals and not fall victim to the desire to find the panacea to the motivational problem (White, 2001).

At one time in the police service, the primary motivational force was based on power. If the order was to jump, the required response was "How high?" A supervisor might have the power, but the work environment is different and employees, for the most part, will respond better to different motivational factors. It is a supervisor's responsibility to develop officers' needs and, when appropriate, make organizational needs overcome personal needs.

Effort must be directed toward attaining organizational goals through the work of individuals and groups. In order to accomplish this immense task, a supervisor should strive to create an atmosphere in the organizational working life in which most officers become self-motivated (Leonard & More, 2000).

The police supervisor who ignores the ecology of the organization will seldom be successful. A motivated employee is the product of interaction with the organization and the attitudes generated. Thus, the key to motivation is not just the individual, but also the department. There should be an organizational norm of supervisory activities that stimulate the development and growth of every officer. Above all, this calls for a supervisor to demonstrate consistency in the performance of supervisory duties. Extremes of supervisory style, such as authoritarian or laissez-faire supervision, should be avoided.

The whole individual must be motivated. If an officer can be placed in a well-structured organization with identifiable goals, where the culture is such that one can readily identify with it, where tasks are challenging, and where accomplished individuals are rewarded, then the organization is really motivating its employees.

Historically, a number of police agencies have exhibited characteristics definitely incompatible with the aforementioned description. These agencies personify the authoritarian mandate leadership style reminiscent of the time when a manager gave an order and the only acceptable reply was "When, where, and how much?" Fortunately, this type of supervision is outdated in most agencies (Charrier, 2000).

In our society, work is fundamental and a natural aspect of one's daily life. In fact, work performs an exceedingly strong role in the economic, social, and psychological aspects of one's life. Work is defined as effort directed to accomplish something. This definition is compatible with the concept of goals being attained through the efforts of individuals and groups.

Often an individual's sense of identity is obtained from work, as evidenced by most people describing themselves as a member of a department or agency. While this means that most people identify work as having great importance in their lives, it has to be acknowledged that there are some individuals who view work as unavoidable.

Work provides officers with a sense of accomplishment, as well as something with which to identify. Police work especially challenges one's skill and ingenuity. For many employees, the attainment of work-related goals has proven to be as important as material rewards. Most officers usually find police work challenging and demanding. In fact, everything else can become subordinate to work. Police work provides a sense of belonging, a sharing of duties, and a unique social bond.

A legitimate supervisory role is to create a work environment resulting in officer satisfaction. Two types of feelings come into play when one considers work. The first is *global* and describes an officer's expressed feelings about the total job. The second is *facet* and reveals an officer's feelings about one specific job element (Fincham & Rhodes, 2006). An example would be where an officer believes all promotions are based on "juice" (connections) and the support of a "rabbi" (mentor). Even with this as a dissatisfier, the officer expresses a positive global view of the job and believes that other job factors, such as importance of the work, feeling of accomplishing something, compensation, supervision, and equipment, are factors supporting a good working environment. In fact, a healthy place to work has five characteristics (see Figure 4.2).

Within a good workplace, the relationship between each employee and the organization is one of *trust*. The major finding of this unique book is that trust between managers and employees is the primary defining characteristic of the very best workplaces. When trust is present, officers get real satisfaction from the job. When managers and supervisors view employees as an important organizational component, it results in a realistic engagement resulting in participation that increases productivity and effectiveness (Brun & Cooper, 2009). Pride is another component of a good workplace relationship. The organization instills pride in each employee; in return, all employees feel pride in what they do. Officers enjoy working in an organization described as one in which trust is present and pride dominates the style of work. Thus, the workplace becomes a place where relationships are friendly, politicking is not present, and each employee is challenged to grow personally and professionally (Levering, 2000).

1. A pleasant place to work.
2. Politics are minimal.
3. Everyone is treated fairly.
4. It is more than just a job.
5. You really feel like it is your family.

FIGURE 4.2 Phrases that describe a good workplace. *Adapted from Robert Levering (2000). A Great Place to Work: What Makes Some Employees So Good—and Most So Bad? Republished. San Francisco, CA: Great Place to Work Institute, Inc.*

Motivation

If there is one word that seems to be overworked in the managerial lexicon, it is *motivation*. We apparently have an insatiable appetite for keeping up with the latest motivational techniques. It has reached the point where some businesses use motivational seminars extensively as a means of boosting morale. Some have even used the fire walk technique, in which participants walk across 12 feet of glowing embers. The response of one participant was, "It was a great feeling to do something that I did not think could be done, and after doing it I felt that I could accomplish anything" (Roman, 1986). Whether this type of training produces a more productive employee cannot be answered at this time, but it does illustrate the extent to which some agencies will go in an effort to motivate employees.

Why is motivation so elusive? Why have we heard so much about it? Why is it accepted as a means of achieving goals or increasing productivity? Is it something magical? A basic assumption of this chapter is that managerial skills to stimulate and motivate employees can be learned. They are skills that are not tenuous, but real, and demonstrate (without a doubt) that motivation can be managed.

Motives for each member of the department are highly individualistic. Every person has their own motivational hierarchy based on needs, rewards, and values. Another important aspect of motivation is that it is not unvarying. Motivating factors can change over time. What causes someone to respond today might not be true tomorrow or the day after that (Haasen, 1997). Motives are not static, but dynamic. Consequently, while a supervisor can observe behavior, the motive for that behavior can only be inferred. Motives are generally considered insentient, and for the most part one is unaware of what motivates one's behavior. Optimally, the best one can do is to work at changing behavior by using a variety of motivational techniques (Berryman-Fink & Fink, 2007).

Motivation is a mental process that produces an attitude resulting in an action leading to a result. Why do officers respond to a motivational factor? The primary reason is they derive a benefit from the result. Each person interprets and defines the reward differently. For one person it might be one thing, whereas for another the reward may be something entirely different.

The key to motivation is not only the individual, but also the organization. In practice, nearly every organization has its own approach to motivation, which is usually a difference of style, taste, or emphasis rather than one of substance (Gellerman, 1993). When an individual is placed in a department where the goals and values are easily identifiable, where there is room for growth, where one is allowed to be creative and accept a challenge, and where the officer feels secure and appreciated, as well as properly rewarded, then one finds an agency where the conditions are maximized for positive motivation. Police departments, however, have their own norms, and there are clearly those in which motivation plays a very important part and those in which it does not.

Where the dull are leading the dull, all the management experts in the world could not possibly improve the performance of employees. When a healthy culture evolves, it includes values, beliefs, and behavior built on a sound organizational base that develops and fosters the creation of truly committed and highly motivated employees. When the major motivational influence in the workforce is one's internal drive to achieve, supported by and developed by the organization, then morale is high, which in turn enhances performance (Aragon, 1993). When that occurs, the organization can be described as performing successfully. In its simplest explanation, employees need to be empowered, involved, and true participants in the decision-making process. Every supervisor must work with employees in developing their abilities, skills, and knowledge, and every employee needs the technical knowledge and skill to perform assigned tasks. The supervisor must also provide conceptual skill training (Hu-TACK). This is an ongoing process of developing employees who can relate their own performance to the mission and value structure of the organization. Each employee has an understanding of the organization's relationship to the community and how change in one part can affect the rest of the organization (Grant, 1990).

In order to become an excellent supervisor, a person must develop a plan that identifies obligations to both the officers being supervised and the immediate superiors. Some of the more specific responsibilities are listed in Figure 4.3. In reviewing the techniques listed in

1. Constantly work at improving the communication process.
2. Correct a situation immediately when something goes wrong.
3. Create a work environment where officers can grow and work toward self-fulfillment.
4. Decide what each officer should be doing.
5. Demand high performance of everyone supervised, including yourself.
6. Establish a supervisory style that precludes micromanagement.
7. Give prompt and explicit feedback.
8. Listen to officers' ideas and opinions.
9. Make sure that every officer knows what is expected of him or her.
10. Maximize the use of everyone's skills.
11. Monitor your performance and that of supervised officers.
12. Promote the highest ethical and professional standards.
13. Provide for a democratic workplace.
14. Recognize achievements and successes.
15. Solicit officer participation in the decision-making process.
16. Strive to become a positive role model.
17. Specify a time for the completion of assigned tasks.
18. Turn the workplace into a learning environment through appropriate coaching.
19. When appropriate, allow officers to assume new responsibilities and duties.
20. When appropriate, *praise–praise–praise*.
21. Work diligently at making everyone a part of a viable and positive organization.

FIGURE 4.3 Techniques supervisors can use to motivate officers.

the figure note that they are all part of what can be identified as an achievement–motivation program. The bottom line is that everybody works with greater intensity when there is something in it for him or her. A significant element of this process is that it demonstrates a caring supervisor who is concerned about those being supervised. Motivation is a complicated process and a number of theories are discussed later. Each theory is a foundation for supervisory techniques that can be used in work situations. Each theory is highly individualistic, and no single theory applies to all situations. Taken as a totality, the various motivational theories can provide you with a different way to look at behavior. The theories should be used by supervisors when working with line personnel, and experience shows that it will bring viable and positive results. A key is to avoid what a leading authority called the KITP (kick in the pants) approach to motivation as a process that was believed to be results oriented. Unfortunately, with this approach, short-term results could be positive but they never had a lasting impact on the behavior of an individual within an organization. This position was set forth 40 years ago and it is as viable today as it was then (Herzberg, 2008). Motivational theories are numerous and a supervisor should consider all of them, keeping in mind that an eclectic approach, at this time, based on our current knowledge of the motivational process, is the best path to take.

Needs-Based Motivation

Probably the most widespread motivational theory in use is that developed by Abraham H. Maslow. He postulated that people's needs were exceedingly complex and were arranged in a hierarchy. His studies were based on a positive concept of mental health, and his research cohorts were the very best individuals he could identify (Globe, 1970). These individuals were described as being self-actualized (S-A) and constituted less than 1 percent of the population. The self-actualized individual's personality was found to be more harmonious, and his or her perceptions were less distorted by fears, desires, hopes, false optimism, or pessimism (Maslow, 1987).

Interestingly enough, Maslow's superior individual was found to be 60 years of age or older, and the most universal characteristic was the ability to see life clearly. The self-actualized person was creative, risk prone, and possessed a low threshold for self-conflict. Additionally, the S-A individual possessed a healthy attitude toward work, finding it enjoyable to the point of actually being play. The ultimate key for a supervisor is to help employees actualize in other words, let them become all they can be (Dessler, 1993).

Based on the S-A personality, Maslow created a theory of motivation showing that a number of basic needs that are clearly identifiable as species-wide, unchanged, and instinctual motivate human beings. This theory identified five need categories: physiological, security, social, esteem, and self-actualization (Figure 4.4).

Physiological Needs

The strongest and most fundamental needs are physiological needs (survival needs). These life-sustaining needs include food, shelter, sex, air, water, and sleep. Maslow showed that

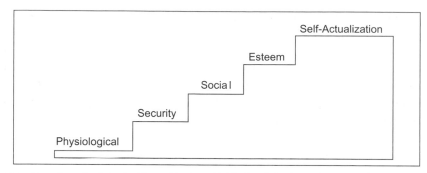

FIGURE 4.4 Hierarchy of needs. *Adapted from Abraham H. Maslow (1987).* Motivation and Personality, *Second Edition. Upper Saddle River, NJ: Pearson Education.*

throughout life the human being constantly desires something. Man is a wanting animal, and complete satisfaction is achieved for only a short time. As soon as one desire is satisfied, another takes its place. Imagine what it would be like to be hungry, to the point of almost being starved. This could not only cause physical discomfort, but could also lead to impairment or illness. It can readily be seen that such a state of need will be dominant. In most areas of the United States, police officers' salaries place them beyond the point of minimum subsistence so their basic physiological needs are generally fulfilled.

From a supervisory perspective, it becomes necessary to understand the degree to which officers are motivated by physiological needs. If these needs are not fulfilled, it becomes apparent that the work they are involved in has no meaning to them. When management concentrates on physiological needs as a means of motivating officers, they have assumed that people work foremost for financial rewards. Emphasis is placed on wage increases, better working conditions, longer breaks, and enhanced fringe benefits as means of motivating officers.

Security Needs

Security needs emerge once a person's basic needs are fulfilled. The dominant security needs are primarily the need for reasonable order and stability, and freedom from being anxious and insecure. Some officers have entered the police service because government agencies provide a secure and stable job. With security as a dominant need, officers will want stability and predictability above all else.

The managerial response should stress rules and regulations. Emphasis should be placed on traditional union demands such as pay and fringe benefits. In addition, management that meets security needs would limit efforts to encourage individual initiative, complex problem-solving situations, or any type of risk taking.

Security-minded officers want everything in black and white. The known is stressed over the unknown. Some officers never get beyond the level of satisfying security needs. Change is rejected and every aspect of their working life has to be geared to absolute safety. This creates difficulties for some officers who want things to be stable and predictable, as when courts change the time-honored practices revolving around procedures such as advising suspects of their rights or search-and-seizure techniques.

When a supervisor seeks security above all, it is obvious that everything is played close to the vest. Rules and procedures dominate, and absolute adherence to time schedules is demanded. Such a supervisor is organized to the point of rigidity. One's boss is not only omnipotent, but also omniscient. Everything possible is done to please and placate individuals who are higher in the chain of command. The supervisor fixated with security needs ignores the needs of subordinate officers, uses manipulation when necessary, and the need to develop feelings of growth is rejected. Officers are viewed as having no need to control their own lives and the key to success is close supervision.

It would seem realistic to examine one's own security needs. How far should you go to cover up personal mistakes? Would you cover up mistakes made by your superiors? Would you do anything just to be promoted? Do you always agree with the boss just because that person is the boss? Whatever the answers, one should know more about oneself after answering these questions.

Social Needs

This level is a clear departure from the two basic needs just discussed. With the fulfillment of physiological and security needs, social needs emerge. Maslow pointed out that human beings will hunger for affiliation with others, for a place in a group, and will attempt to achieve this goal with a great deal of intensity (Globe, 1970).

When this need is not fulfilled by the organization, the officer can respond by an excessive use of sick leave and inadequate productivity. It can lead to loneliness, boredom, and a poor self-image—affecting mental health. Most individuals want to be accepted by peers and supervisors. In fact, everyone has a strong tendency to identify with groups, and some people will modify their behavior to meet the group's criteria for membership. Central to this is acceptance and almost everyone strives for it.

When a supervisor becomes aware that social needs are motivating officers, then every effort should be made to promote social interaction. This can be difficult to do in a patrol unit that utilizes one-person patrol vehicles, but the supervisor can provide backup units whenever possible. In addition, the supervisor can act in a supportive manner whenever possible. A physical conditioning room, parties, or organized sports events can all provide a means for meeting social needs.

The socially motivated supervisor emphasizes officers' needs and will ignore organizational needs. If options are available, the decision is always made on the side of the employee. Everything is done to ensure that the supervisor is part of the group. The approval of everyone is sought: subordinates, peers, and bosses. Supervisors must accomplish tasks through the efforts of others; thus, a good supervisor must help by supporting the efforts of those who are working to achieve departmental objectives. It is important that realistic objectives be attainable and when this is true it has proven to be a positive motivational factor. A realistic objective should be one that inspires and motivates achievement (U.S. Department of Energy, 1996).

What about your own social needs? When you become a supervisor, can you change roles and lead? How strong is your need to be socially accepted? When you are promoted, can you accept being a part of management? These are not easy questions to answer and demand real soul searching to determine where you stand in relation to your needs.

Esteem Needs

Maslow described two categories of esteem needs. The first was self-esteem, including such factors as a need for independence, freedom, confidence, and achievement. The second area was identified as respect from others and includes the concepts of recognition, prestige, acceptance, status, and reputation (Globe, 1970). It is difficult to imagine one who has attained a supervisory rank not fulfilling these two categories of self-esteem.

Officers who do not feel their esteem needs are being fulfilled through the job can become discouraged (if not disgruntled) employees. Officers want to be recognized for their accomplishments. This has been done in part by such things as commendations, medals, and longevity stripes. In some agencies, the rank of corporal is awarded for achievement; in some cases an unusual act of bravery or a politically sensitive arrest can result in a promotion to an investigative status. The key is to acknowledge achievement that is above and beyond the fulfillment of normal duties.

The aforementioned external indicators of status can fulfill an officer's esteem needs, leading to feelings of worthiness, adequacy, and self-confidence. Supervisors who recognize the importance of esteem need to do everything possible to ensure that officers demonstrate self-confidence and have few self-doubts and a positive self-image.

The supervisor whose primary drive is esteem will, in all probability, be a successful manager. Such an individual will expend a great deal of energy in order to achieve recognition (Chandler, 2004). In the final analysis, the supervisor should take the time and expend the effort to convey to every officer that he or she is an important person, doing essential work and occupying an important place. Nothing less can be expected.

Self-Actualization Needs

Maslow points out that when most of the esteem needs are fulfilled, then what man *can* be, he *must* be. This is the stage of self-actualization, which is characterized by the need to develop feelings of growth and maturity, become increasingly competent, and gains a mastery over situations. At this level, the individual reaches the point where all talents and potential are put to use. Motivation is very internalized and external stimulation is unnecessary. Efforts of an S-A individual focus on applying creative and constructive skills to work situations, and such individuals are never bothered by feelings of futility, alienation, or bitterness.

Supervisors who manage S-A officers should do everything possible to make work meaningful. Participation should be maximized so that officers can use their unique skills. Special assignments should be made when possible in order to capitalize on an officer's talents. When taskforces are organized to deal with unique police problems, the S-A officer should be assigned. The self-actualized individual has a need to demonstrate the ability to assume responsibility and involvement at the highest possible level.

Maslow did not view the hierarchy of needs as a series of levels that are very independent of one another. In fact, the categories overlap and are not entirely precise. He suggests that it is unsatisfied needs that influence behavior. Once a need is satisfied, it has a limited effect on motivation. Maslow estimated that the average person is 85 percent satisfied in physiological

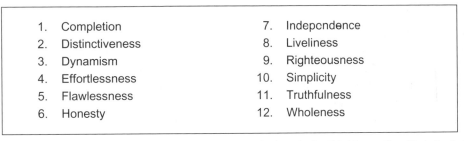

1.	Completion	7.	Independence
2.	Distinctiveness	8.	Liveliness
3.	Dynamism	9.	Righteousness
4.	Effortlessness	10.	Simplicity
5.	Flawlessness	11.	Truthfulness
6.	Honesty	12.	Wholeness

FIGURE 4.5 Higher or growth needs. *Adapted from Frank G. Globe (1970).* The Third Force. *New York: Pocket Books.*

Need	Behavior
1. Physiological	Uneasiness, anguish, possible injury, nervousness, or sickness
2. Security	Anxiety, apprehensiveness, tentativeness, dismay, or alarm
3. Social	Feelings of loneliness, distant, abandoned, dejected, or unloved
4. Self-Esteem	Unsteady, lack of a firm belief in one's own power, or a lack of confidence
5. Self-Actualization	Estranged, acerbic, controlled, exploited, or a feeling of worthlessness

FIGURE 4.6 Behaviors when needs are not fulfilled. *Adapted from Abraham H. Maslow (1962).* Toward a Psychology of Being. *New York: Van Nostrand.*

needs, 70 percent satisfied in safety needs, 50 percent in social needs, 40 percent in esteem needs, and 10 percent in self-actualization needs. Since the initial research, Maslow developed a new list of needs identified as growth needs (social, self-esteem, and self-actualization) as compared to basic needs (physiological and safety). He believed higher needs use basic needs as a foundation. Higher or growth needs are set forth in Figure 4.5.

Maslow pointed out that growth needs are interrelated, and when defining one value it is necessary to use the others. These values cannot be separated, and all values reflect the highest need category (see Figure 4.6). Maslow cautioned that we should not make the mistake of thinking that good working conditions will automatically transform all employees into growing, self-actualized individuals.

Motivation–Hygiene Theory

The hierarchy of needs motivational theory has numerous supporters, but the motivation–hygiene theory, while somewhat more controversial, has received increasing attention. Frederick Herzberg and colleagues developed this theory, based on semi-structured interviews

Motivators	Hygiene
Achievement	Interpersonal Relations
Advancement	Policies and Administration
Recognition	Salary and Benefits
Responsibility	Security
Work Itself	Working Conditions

FIGURE 4.7 Motivation–hygiene theory. *Source: Frederick Herzberg, Bernard Mausner, & Barbara Snyderman (1993).* Motivation to Work. *Copyright © Frederick Herzberg, School of Business, University of Utah. Reprinted with permission of the senior author; Frederick Herzberg (2008).* One More Time: How Do You Motivate Employees? *Cambridge, MA: Harvard Business School Press.*

with 200 accountants and engineers. Job satisfaction and its relationship were examined, and the central question of the investigation was "What do people want from their job?"

In this landmark study, researchers found 155 studies addressing this vital question. They found that different results were achieved when the research design was concerned with elements making employees happy with their jobs, as opposed to studies stressing factors leading to job dissatisfaction. In the Herzberg study, workers who were found to be happiest with their jobs identified factors relating to the performance of tasks, work events reflecting successful performance, and factors identified as growth.

The other aspect of the two-factor study related to feelings of unhappiness, and they were found to be totally unrelated to the actual accomplishment of work. These factors, identified as hygiene because they acted in a manner similar to medical hygiene, include supervision, interpersonal relations, physical working conditions, salary, company policies, administrative practices, benefits, and job security. Figure 4.7 sets forth this theory.

Motivational factors are readily identifiable because either they relate to the work itself or they revolve around such things as advancement, responsibility, or recognition. The hygiene factors are either determined by the organization or occur because of a memorandum of understanding negotiated by a police union. They are generally restricted to working conditions and policies, in contrast to the motivational factors that stimulate the individual. It is easy to see an immediate parallel between Maslow's concepts of self-actualization and esteem needs. What the employee wants is either growth or recognition (Bergland, 1993).

The factors that address the needs of employees that result in job satisfaction tend to satisfy an officer's needs over an extended period, in contrast to hygiene factors, which are more short-lived. A unique characteristic of Herzberg's theory is that motivators can result in a positive feeling toward work, while at the same time, some individuals respond negatively.

Both motivators and hygiene factors meet employee needs, but it is primarily motivators that result in job satisfaction. Workers studied by Herzberg and collaborators found, for example, that achievement was present in more than 40 percent of what were identified as satisfying situations and in less than 10 percent of dissatisfying situations. In terms of recognition, more than 30 percent of the situations were satisfying and less than 20 percent were dissatisfying.

Herzberg viewed satisfiers and dissatisfiers as separate and distinct entities. One can be satisfied and dissatisfied simultaneously. This means that hygiene factors cannot increase job satisfaction, but only affect the amount of job dissatisfaction.

There are definite differences between the theories of Maslow and Herzberg, as well as similarities noted by the fact that both theories identify motivational factors; in some aspects, the theories overlap. Herzberg created a category not discussed by Maslow, and he identified these hygiene factors (non-motivators) as generally reflective of the components of a bureaucratic police organization. The Maslow theory differs because it views human beings as social individuals who can be viewed as multidimensional and suggests that individuals have the capacity to prioritize needs hierarchically. Supervisors should search for motivational opportunities and strive to turn negative experiences into positives so that officers can consistently contribute their best (Silverstein, 2007).

Theory X–Theory Y

Douglas McGregor developed one of the best-known motivational theories. It is a straightforward theory based on the belief that managers conduct themselves according to the assumptions, generalizations, and hypotheses they have about human behavior (McGregor, 1960). McGregor views employees' attitudes and behavior as being in response to management's perspective of their own job and their basic mindset about human behavior.

The traditional view of direction and control, identified as Theory X, is set forth in Figure 4.8.

This view of human behavior is still somewhat prevalent in the policing field and is reminiscent of autocratic leadership. What are the consequences of such assumptions about human behavior? What roles are supervisors and officers forced to take? Human behavior is very complex, and it seems appropriate to suggest that Theory X can explain the behavior of a few employees, but certainly not the majority.

Closely paralleling Theory X is another motivational theory called "carrot and stick." Both theories seem viable when meeting an employee's basic needs at physiological and safety levels. The job itself, working conditions, and fringe benefits can be very strong control features

---

1. The ordinary employee has an aversion to work and will strive to do everything possible to steer clear of it.
2. Most people, because of their dislike for work, will have to be coerced, forced, directed, or told that punishment may be in order so that organizational goals can be achieved.
3. The chief concerns of employees are job security and survival. Consequently, because of their lack of ambition and a desire to avoid responsibility, employees need constant supervision. In other words, tell them what to do!

FIGURE 4.8 Theory X. *Adapted from Douglas McGregor (1960). The Human Side of Enterprise. New York: McGraw-Hill.*

when officers are struggling to get by, but when basic need levels are reasonably satisfied and officers become motivated by higher needs, the theories leave much to be desired.

If managers view employees as a necessary evil, they actually view themselves as the chosen ones possessing special abilities. They view the majority of individuals as having limited abilities. Thus, employees are viewed as fundamentally lazy, preferring to have decisions made for them, and readily accepting (and actually wanting) forceful leadership. Employees will continually take advantage of the work situation and have no concept of the factors constituting a fair day's work. If supervisors hold to Theory X, it will be reflected in every contact with those supervised.

Theory X places a strong emphasis on control and direction (Von der Embse, 1987). Procedures are devised for providing officers with close supervision (determining whether the task has been accomplished) and the creation of a means for providing rewards and punishments.

With increasing emphasis on the professionalization of law enforcement and an improved standard of living, fundamental needs (physiological and safety) have become less of a managerial issue. Thus, control becomes fundamentally inadequate as a means of motivating employees when they have developed a social, esteem, or self-actualization need.

This means a supervisor should consider a new generalization about the management of human resources, namely, the assumptions outlined by Theory Y, which is set forth in Figure 4.9.

A careful analysis of the factors clearly suggests that management should respond to the employees with an enlightened strategy. The managerial perspective will have to be creative, discover new organizational principles, and develop new means of directing employees. It

1. The average individual does not have a natural dislike for work. To the contrary, most employees will respond positively to work as they do to aspects of their personal life.

2. Employees will exercise self-control and self-direction when they are committed to an objective.

3. Individuals have the capacity to develop, to assume responsibility, and to direct their behavior toward goal realization.

4. Commitment to goals is a function of rewards associated with their attainment. Avoidance of responsibility, an emphasis on security, and limited drive are, for the most part, the result of experience, not an innate personal characteristic.

5. Management should create an organizational atmosphere that allows individual goal attainment while directing their efforts toward organizational objectives. The manager should provide guidance that fosters opportunities and personal growth, keeping in mind that many employees are capable of solving organizational problems.

6. The real potential of the average employee is underutilized.

FIGURE 4.9 Theory Y. *Adapted from Douglas McGregor (1960). The Human Side of Enterprise. New York: McGraw-Hill.*

should be acknowledged that while the perfect organization might not be attainable, there is certainly room for improvement.

McGregor pointed out that the complete integration of individual and organizational goals was not realistic. The ultimate goal for which we strive should be a degree of integration whereby workers can attain their own goals by directing their efforts toward the success of the organization. Workers must be encouraged to develop to their highest capacity by acquiring knowledge and skills to make the organization successful.

Interestingly enough, when a supervisor accepts Theory Y, it does not imply the abdication of his or her responsibilities of what has become known as "soft management." Theory Y assumes employees will exercise self-direction and self-control if they are committed to departmental objectives. If commitment is slight or nonexistent, then self-direction and self-control will be slight or nonexistent. External influences will have to be exerted in order to achieve goals. If the commitment is great, then external influences should be minimal or, better yet, nonexistent.

An appropriate application of Theory Y reduces the need for external control and relies on other managerial techniques for reaching organizational goals successfully. Generally, authority will prove to be an inappropriate technique for obtaining departmental goals, but authority is something that has to be used when an organization cannot get a genuine commitment to departmental objectives. Theory Y assumes that authority is not appropriate for all situations.

It can be seen readily that when a supervisor applies the concepts predicated by Theory Y, each employee is viewed as a real asset. Officers have a definite capacity for growth and development. Employees can be highly creative and willing to accept responsibility. It is the supervisor's job to create a working environment in which the potential of every officer can be tapped. Employees are usually not indolent, stupid, irresponsible, or hostile. The supervisor accepts that there will always be a few such officers, but they are the exception, not the rule.

Such an orientation requires the supervisor to be concerned primarily with the quality of interpersonal relationships. One's effort is directed toward developing an organizational atmosphere that fosters a commitment to departmental goals. Each employee is given an opportunity to become self-directing, innovative, and growth oriented.

There are contrasting sets of attitudes when one compares Theory X and Theory Y. What, then, is the answer? What theory should a supervisor follow? Not surprisingly, neither theory can be applied in every situation. A supervisor probably functions at some point between the two extremes. When an officer is on probation and new to the job, a Theory X approach may be more appropriate until the officer is capable of functioning alone. During a narcotics raid is not the proper time for officers to question what is being done or take it upon themselves to deviate from the prescribed procedures. Safety is imperative and officers must follow orders.

However, as an officer grows and develops, control can be reduced and the officer can be given a greater opportunity for self-direction and self-control. The assumptions a supervisor makes about what theory to use depends on a detailed evaluation of each officer's abilities and qualifications. The more knowledgeable and competent officers can be extended a great deal of freedom in their work environment. When these conditions are not met, the supervisor must emphasize control and dependent subordinate behavior.

Expectancy Theory

Predicting behavior in organizations has always challenged behaviorists. A model predictor holding promise is one developed by Victor H. Vroom. This model is predicated on the concept that it is the internal state as well as external forces impinging on individuals that will cause them to act in a specific manner. In the final analysis, a worker will be motivated to put forth the necessary effort when it will result in the attainment of desired goals.

There are four basic assumptions about human behavior that serve as the foundation of the expectancy theory. They demonstrate the complexity of not only human behavior, but also of motivation. The first assumption is that behavior is not determined exclusively by the individual. It is a product of the vitality of an individual and the environment, and within this context, each individual will develop a preference for available objectives. When the preference is high, the acceptance will be greater. However, the employee will avoid undesirable consequences. If an individual values promotion over everything else, behavior will be adjusted in order to meet that need.

Second, employees have expectancies about outcomes. To put it another way, each person anticipates what will occur. If results are not compatible with efforts, then the activity is ignored or avoided. Expectations vary from individual to individual. What one police officer feels is important might be unimportant to another officer. Some individuals feel that job security is important above all else, whereas others want to perform demanding and challenging tasks.

One aspect of expectancy is called effort–performance (E-P), which refers to an individual's motivation to choose a specific performance objective and the relationship of effort to that objective. Factors affecting an individual's expectancy perception include such things as self-esteem, previous experience in similar situations, one's capability, and the style of supervision. This list is not meant to be comprehensive, but it does illustrate the range of such factors. It is believed that each individual seeks to increase self-esteem by searching for psychological success. One experiences psychological success when (Handy, 2005):

- A personal, challenging goal is set.
- Methods of achieving that goal are set.
- The goal is relevant to one's self-concept.

When an officer experiences psychological success, he or she feels more competent. The more competent one feels, the more apt that person is to take risks in perceived areas of importance. However, when one is not successful psychologically, it can lead to the lowering of personal goals as the person strives to protect his or her self-concept (Handy, 2005). While the importance of self-esteem is evident, the whole process should be approached with some degree of caution, especially if there are other influencing factors, such as limited manpower or inadequate equipment. Not all the desire in the world can achieve the impossible.

Another aspect of expectancy is performance–outcome (P-O), which deals with an officer's anticipation of performing at a specified level and the outcome of those efforts. This can best be illustrated by a situation in which an officer may feel that a superior effort will result in different outcomes. Such efforts can undoubtedly result in unintended consequences. While a merit increase might be forthcoming, it might also foster resentment from peers and cause difficulties at home because of excessive absence from the family. It is clear, then, that any single outcome might be positive in some ways and negative in others.

Needless to say, one way of analyzing motivation is to view the consequences resulting from expectancies and valences. Then motivation can be viewed as:

$$\text{Motivation} = \text{E}(\text{Expectancy} \times \text{Valence})$$

Valence is defined as the strength of an individual's desire for a particular outcome. Synonyms for valence include *drive*, *incentive*, or *desire*. Valences range from −1.0 to 1.0, and when the valence is in the negative range, the officer does not want to reach or attain the objective. When the valence is positive, the outcome is highly desirable. When the valence is zero, the officer is indifferent to the outcome (Luthans, 2010). It is important to realize that what really matters is the employee's perception of what will occur.

Supervisors seem to underrate the factors necessary for motivating employees. They forget it is the *officer's perception* that matters most—not the supervisor's perception. The expectancy motivational model combines the previously discussed need theory with the concept of perceived outcomes. Officers are motivated, for example, by satisfying their esteem needs, such as receiving a promotion or obtaining a preferred assignment to a special unit (such as a SWAT team). They can be motivated by the successful completion of the probationary period because of the security it will provide. The interplay occurring between officers who are involved in team policing can fulfill the need for socialization.

Another study revealed that when studying three levels of employees (low, middle, and upper) there was hardly any difference among the levels when they rated the importance of needs (security, social, esteem, autonomy, and self-actualization). The real difference came when the three levels rated the degree to which needs were satisfied. Lower level employees were much less satisfied with the number of higher order needs being met on the job (Hawkins, 1981). The most successful supervisors will concentrate on helping officers to clarify their needs and on becoming aware of how officers perceive those needs. Once this is accomplished, the expectancies of outcomes can be dealt with through such techniques as training, delegation, and acknowledgment of a job well done or the granting of greater autonomy.

Equity Theory

Fairness is the keystone of equity theory and is viewed as one of the process theories of motivation. Law enforcement executives are paying increasing attention to this theory as they struggle with how to reward officers and civilian employees for their work. When viewed from a motivational perspective, equity occurs when specific rewards are looked upon as fair and foundational to the total reward system (Cole, 2003). John Stacey Adams, a behavioral psychologist and a student of workplace behavior, created this theory of motivation, which has had considerable acceptance in business and public administration (Adams, 1963). It calls for rational stability between an officer's inputs and outputs. Inputs are listed in Figure 4.10.

Inputs	Outputs
Expending of effort	Pay
Dedication	Health benefits
Fidelity	Retirement
Knowledge	Sick leave
Dependable	Bereavement leave

FIGURE 4.10 Equity theory.

Adams postulates that when there is a feeling of inequity it is, in reality, a state of mind. Thus, when employees have a feeling of inequity in the manner in which they are treated, they will respond to eliminate the discomfort and restore a sense of equity to the situation (More et al., 2013).

It is readily apparent that when inequities are perceived there is a true imbalance in what officers see as incentives received for their output when compared to others within the organization who are expending an equal effort. This definitely violates the widely accepted norm that officers should be treated equitably. Under the concept of equity one expects acceptable job performance to be meaningfully rewarded. Within everyone there is a need to maintain a balance between inputs and outputs and maintain *distributive fairness* (Aldag & Kuzuhara, 2009). This occurs when each member of the organization believes that employees are getting what they deserve—not more, not less (Dessler, 1999).

What occurs is that officers compare an existing condition or state with what is perceived as a standard. It has been found that employees continually compare their work with others on their team. Unfortunately, what occurs in some agencies is that a patrol officer will compare what they do with the work being done by someone in a specialized unit. As departments have moved from a traditional focus on control to one of community policing, comparison of duties of the work being done during the changeover was primarily noncomparable, but comparisons were drawn anyway; in one department, community policing officers were called "plastic cops." As a consequence, during such a transition many officers were left in the lurch and there was a tendency for morale to become lower. In another instance, an inequity occurred when selected officers received all of the overtime they wanted while other officers were denied. Under such circumstances it becomes difficult for management to justify work allocation. Even though managers think that everything is fair, what is important to the officers is their perception of fairness. The truism is that some degree of inequity is inevitable. Inequities exist when unequals are treated as equals, as well as when equals are treated as unequals (More et al., 2013). What it boils down to is that perceived inequities are inevitable when officers interact in an organization. Inequities come into existence because of the following factors:

- Pay differential
- Diversity, racial, sexual orientation, and social discrimination (perceived or actual)
- Preferential assignments based on longevity
- Political promotions

- Favoritism
- Lack of resources

Equity theory assumes that all employees compare themselves to others in terms of what they get out of a job (outputs) versus what they put into the work (inputs). In application, a negative inequity exists when a police officer believes that she or he is receiving less of a valued outcome than other officers engaged in the same activities. When the input/output ratio is equal, a sense of equity is experienced (Stroh, Northcraft, Neale, Kern, & Langlands, 2001).

When the reward for work equals or exceeds the fairness standard, it results in repeated behavior. If the reward is less than the perceived equity, dissatisfaction will set in and motivation to continue the activity will lessen. Adams believed that when there is inequity, cognitive dissonance and disequilibrium would set in and behavior of the following kinds would possibly occur:

- When a positive inequity is perceived, performance, workload, and other kinds of input justify higher rewards.
- When a negative inequity is perceived, there will be a decrease in performance, workload, and other kinds of input.
- Change of output through personal persuasion, collective bargaining, legal action, or dysfunctional behavior such as misappropriation, employee theft, and outright corruption.
- Change of output by persuading low performers to increase their efforts and discouraging higher performers from being rate busters.

Two authorities suggest that managers can control equity in their work unit if they follow these rules (Aldag & Kuzuhara, 2009):

- Assess employee perceptions of equity.
- Identify those who perceive inequity.
- Determine the basis for employee perceptions on inequity.
- Evaluate management policies and practices to determine the validity of employee perceptions.
- Identify changes that can be made to address employee inequity.
- Implement changes and communicate them to employees.

It is thought that the rules just given will make the personnel process more objective. Research has demonstrated that the perception of inequity leads to reduced output, but there are detractors who tend to believe that it is a special-purpose theory rather than a general theory of motivation (Whisenand, 2010). The value of equity theory is that it gives police managers a framework for evaluating critical issues such as equity, fairness, and justice in the allocation of rewards.

Sensitivity Theory

Two researchers have suggested that the sensitivity theory can be used to identify individual differences reflecting basic motivational needs. Furthermore, they suggest that fundamental motives are the keys that in time will actually predict human behavior. This theory is a genetics–behavior–cognitive model of axiomatic motivation. It is the position of the two psychologists that human behavior can be separated into two categories based on the purposes of the behavior:

Means: This is indicated when someone performs an act for a useful purpose.
End: This occurs when an individual performs a behavior for no evident reason other than its own purpose.

When means are important to an officer, it might be indicated by the quest of a college degree solely to make one eligible to receive a monthly increase in salary for educational attainment. Another example is an officer who works additional shifts and enhances his or her income in order to purchase a sailboat. In both instances, money provides for goal attainment. The means allow one to attain a desired goal that has been identified and is believed to be reachable. At the same time, the goal is one that is personally beneficial and one for which an individual has no difficulty becoming motivated because of the reward that can be received at the end of the process.

This process differs from that involving the pursuit of an end. What is important is the nature of the involvement. In contrast, when someone walks or hikes for the sake of enjoyment or when an individual exercises for pleasure, the end is what is important. It does not really matter what has to be done as long as the anticipated result occurs. What occurs in this instance might serve a useful purpose, but it is something that was never intended.

Researchers postulate that human desire stems from 16 basic desires (see Figure 4.11). They range from abstracts, such as honor or social contact, to bodily wants, such as eating or romance, and to more intellectual ambient factors, such as idealism and order. Of special

---

1. Social interaction is the desire for social interaction.
2. Honor is the desire to behave with truthfulness.
3. Optimism is the desire for social justice.
4. Inquisitiveness is the desire to gain knowledge.
5. Freedom is the desire for self-reliance.
6. Orderliness is the desire to put in order.
7. Saving is the desire to accumulate.
8. Physical exercise is the desire for muscle movement.
9. Romance is the desire for sex and beauty.
10. Authority is the desire for power.
11. Acceptance is the desire for appreciation.
12. Eating is the desire for nourishment.
13. Family is the desire to raise one's children.
14. Revenge is the desire to get even with those who offend.
15. Position is the desire for self-importance.
16. Serenity is the desire to be free of worry, fear, and pain.

FIGURE 4.11 Fundamental motives—16 basic desires. *Adapted from Steven Reiss (2002). Who Am I? The 16 Basic Desires That Motivate Our Actions and Define Our Personalities. New York: Jeremy P. Tarcher/Putman. A copy of this list was provided by Steven Reiss.*

interest to the work situation are such fundamental motives as honor, power, curiosity, acceptance, status, and independence. A police manager can use these as a guideline for motivating officers. Some officers will strive for acceptance, whereas others will strive for independence. It is up to the supervisor to determine what "button" to push in order to achieve the meshing of personal and organizational goals.

Reflections of the fact that humans are social animals are such motives as social contact and social prestige. All of us are concerned with the 16 basic desires, but the intensity and the priority that one gives to them vary from individual to individual. If a supervisor finds that an officer focuses more on motives such as family, it presents an entirely different supervisory problem than an officer who is more concerned with order. When compared to other motivational theories, the list is extensive and encompasses a great deal of variance. It clearly demonstrates the complexity of human behavior. This theory goes well beyond those that stress the avoidance of pain and the maximization of pleasure (Reiss, 2002).

How to Motivate

The theories just discussed have their place, and supervisors have been successful in varying degrees in applying these theories to the work environment. If there is a drawback in this application, it is that they are somewhat subjective. This is readily apparent when one closely examines the theories and such related terms as *needs*, *satisfaction*, *psychological success*, *self-concept*, and *expectancies*.

In analyzing the behavior of officers, it is necessary to study what will happen if a certain action is taken. It is important to determine what the officer believes the consequence of the act will be—not what the supervisor thinks. A supervisor utilizing the concept of behavior modification shapes behavior based on the belief that when an activity results in a positive consequence, the activity is apt to be repeated. If the activity results in a negative consequence, the activity tends not to be repeated. Within the framework of behavior modification, the supervisor works to influence officer behavior in such a way that organizational objectives and goals are attained (Laird, Laird, & Fruehling, 1989). Officers generally take the position that when they expend efforts on behalf of the agency, they will be rewarded and, as a consequence, will pursue agency goals (Fitch, 2008). The advantage of this approach is that the supervisor does not need to become aware of such things as officer needs or motives, but can limit efforts to altering the behavior by altering some aspect of the reward system. This approach to people management has demonstrated over the years that not only can an officer's behavior be changed regardless of what their attitudes might be, but once the behavior has changed, the attitude usually follows (Fournies, 2000). Interestingly, it is not events or communications that generate behavior, but it is the interpretation an officer gives to the phenomenon that will lead to a positive reaction and explicit behavior (Flaherty, 1999).

If, in the judgment of the officers, the consequences are important, then behavior can be viewed as being based on the following two principles:

- When behavior results in a positive consequence, officers will sustain that behavior.
- Officers will suspend or curtail a specific behavior when the result is negative.

On the surface, behavior modification seems to be quite simple, but it becomes somewhat complex in application. Karen Brethower, who expanded the theory to the job situation, suggests:

- When a specific behavior is desired, but another behavior results and there is a positive event, then the second behavior intervenes and dominates.
- When officer behavior results in a positive outcome in one situation, but negative consequences occur in another situation, the positive behavior will always dominate.
- When the task to be performed does not require a specific type of behavior or is of no consequence, such behavior is inconsequential and will eventually come to an end.
- When the consequence of a certain behavior is far removed (in time) from the behavior, there will be a smaller impact on the behavior of the officer (Williams, DuBrin, & Sisk, 1985).

By utilizing the two principles and the four corollaries discussed earlier, a supervisor can respond to the tasks performed by officers and engage in reinforcing activities, including praise, a commendation, special assignment, or additional training. Officers usually have a good understanding of what management expects from them (in terms of job performance) so they act accordingly. A supervisor who utilizes this process selects techniques that are appropriate to the given situation after considering internal and external variables.

If behavior is to be modified, consequences must occur immediately after a behavior occurs, not days or months afterward. To delay responding leads to either officer indifference or refusal to engage in such activities. Positive behavior must always be rewarded, not ignored. Ignored negative behavior will, in all probability, harm either the supervisor or the department.

In other words, when reinforcement is used to modify behavior, it must be done continuously and consistently. Any given task performed by a police officer can be performed as management desires or in an unacceptable way. Supervisors actually want officers to perform their duties with reasonable dispatch and effectiveness. If reinforcement is to work, it must be response contingent. Any response to officer activity should be clearly and definitely related to performance or the effort to reinforce will be blunted or even meaningless.

Positive reinforcement works because there is a greater probability that desirable behavior will occur. It is direct, simple, clear, and practical. Above all, it is not encumbered by negative side effects. If there is a problem with managing with a reinforcement focus, it is that our society in general deals with most negative performance by punishment or criticism. If a supervisor has been reared in a family where punishment dominated, and schools as well as the job reinforce this negative approach, it becomes apparent that when this individual becomes a manager, his or her first instinct is to deal with all undesirable behavior by punishing.

Punishment is viewed by some as the quickest and most effective way of obtaining compliance, but in reality it is seldom long-lasting and, when used exclusively, is generally ineffective. Another problem is that unpredictable punishment can easily lead to more negative consequences, such as reinforcing the schism between the department and a police union or estrange officers.

Initially, punishment will eliminate or reduce undesirable behavior, but managing fear, coercion, or threats as a means of getting work done serves only to alienate officers from managers and from the department itself. Punishment is based on power, and the individual's task is to conform or punishment will occur (Handy, 2005). In many instances, officers actually feel they are not extended the common courtesy of being treated as human beings, let alone individuals. As one expert pointed out, some supervisors, wanting to improve the performance of officers they are supervising, are so effective at punishing that they actually reinforce alienation. Viewed realistically, the officer who is treated with contempt and disdain by an immediate supervisor can be expected to react negatively (Nirenberg, 1986).

At some point, some employees will have to be punished, but punishment should be as a last resort, not a supervisory style. Certainly, punishment will provide a lessening of undesirable behavior, but once the punishment is eliminated from the supervisory process, the employee can resume unacceptable behavior. A punishing style of leadership requires the supervisor to operate continuously from a negative managerial style and always be alert to correct unacceptable officer behavior. It actually means that the supervisor must watch employees so closely that, in many instances, the officers are forced to react defensively and production is reduced, not increased.

Punishment as a managerial style can, and most often will, lead to a negative emotional reaction in which an officer can react with anger, become hostile, act out aggressively, or withdraw. Any or all of these reactions can create a working environment in which it becomes uncomfortable to work, the personal satisfaction of doing a good job becomes unimportant, and the atmosphere is devoid of positive motivational factors.

In police work, an additional consequence of a punishing atmosphere can be one in which the officers respond by becoming very inflexible in their enforcement of the law and officer discretion becomes nonexistent. In this instance, the public loses, and in the end, the department loses. As one officer pointed out, "If they want conformity, that's what they are going to get—absolute conformity. Go by the book and toe the line because that's the only way to keep out of trouble."

A supervisor using reinforcement techniques is attempting to shape behavior. If the process is to be successful, it is necessary to use reinforcement thoughtfully and systematically. Initially, a supervisor must recognize that changing behavior is more difficult than sustaining and supporting the change once it has been put in place. This means that the supervisor should apply the greatest amount of reinforcement during the early stages, and the frequency of reinforcement should be greater during this period. If the initial employee efforts go unnoticed or are ignored by the supervisor, those efforts, in all probability, will not be sustained.

It is also important for a supervisor to respond to behavior *after* the fact, not before. If reinforcement is used before the desired behavior, it will not shape behavior. Reinforcement must be tied to a specific act by the employee and should occur immediately after the specific activity. This is one reason why annual or semiannual performance reviews generally prove ineffective in changing job behavior. Short-term behavior changes may occur because of a performance review, but the change in behavior seldom lasts more than two or three months. Lasting changes in behavior can be accomplished only by immediately responding to an act, not waiting until the next review, which might be one year away. A supervisor should reinforce every performance improvement, no matter how slight. When the desired behavior becomes an established pattern, reinforcement can then be used periodically or randomly. Behavior modification is used in counseling, applied behavioral analysis, self-protected skills training, and treatment of behavioral problem (Miltenberger 2011; Martin & Pear, 2010).

When instituting a behavior modification program, a supervisor should consider the following (Williams et al., 1985):

- All employees need to know what is expected of them.
- Feedback is essential. Officers need to know that what they are doing is right or wrong.
- If officers perform poorly because of a deficiency in knowledge, they should be coached, trained, or mentored.
- In most instances, punishment will have numerous harmful side effects.
- Positive reinforcement should be consistent and unbroken.
- Positive reinforcement will result in improved performance.
- Punishment should be used as a last resort.
- Reinforcement should be tied to positive behavior.

Reinforcement will modify behavior. It is a technique whereby officers can be motivated to work harder and with a great degree of effectiveness. This can result in an improvement in organizational pride, morale, and loyalty and give rise to a working environment that stimulates officers to achieve their potential. It can create a pleasant place to work with minimal organizational politics and leave officers with the feeling that it is a great place to work.

References

Adams, J. S. (1963). Inequity in social exchange. In L. (1963). Berkowicz (Ed.), *Advances in experimental social psychology* (Vol. 2). New York: Academic Press.

Aldag, R. J., & Kuzuhara, L. W. (2009). *Organizational behavior and management: A skills based approach.* Dubuque, IA: Kendall Hunt.

Aragon, R. (1993). Positive organizational culture. *FBI Law Enforcement Bulletin, 62*(12).

Associates of the Office of Military Leadership, & USMA (eds), (1993). *A study of organizational leadership.* Harrisburg, PA: Stackpole.

Bergland, S. (1993). Employment empowerment. *FBI Law Enforcement Bulletin, 62*(12).

Berryman-Fink, C., & Fink, C. B. (2007). *The manager's desk reference* (2nd ed.). New York: AMACOM.

Brown, M. F. (1992). The Sergeant's role in a modern law enforcement agency. *The Police Chief, LIX*(5).

Brun, J-P, & Cooper, C. (2009). *Missing pieces: 7 ways to improve employee well-being and organizational effectiveness.* New York: Palgrave Macmillan.

CALEA, (2006). *Standards for law enforcement agencies* (5th ed.). Fairfax, VA: Commission on Accreditation for Law Enforcement Agencies, Inc.

Chandler, S. (2004). *100 ways to motivate yourself: Change your life forever, revised edition.* Franklin Lakes, NJ: Career.

Charrier, K. (2000). Marketing strategies for attracting and retaining generation X police officers. *The Police Chief, LXII*(12).

Cole, G. A. (2003). *Management theory and practice* (6th ed.). Cengage Learning Business Press.

Dessler, G. (1993). *Winning commitment: How to build and keep a competitive workforce.* New York: McGraw-Hill.

Dessler, G. (1999). *Management, principles and practices for tomorrow's leaders.* Upper Saddle River, NJ: Prentice Hall.

Fincham, R., & Rhodes, P. S. (2006). *Organization behavior* (4th ed.). London: Oxford University.

Fitch, B. (2008). Motivation: Rethinking the supervisor's role. *Law and Order, 56*(3).

Flaherty, J. (1999). *Coaching—Evoking excellence in others.* Boston: Butterworth Heinemann.

Fournies, F. F. (2000). *Coaching for improved work performance* (3rd ed.). New York: McGraw-Hill.

Gellerman, S. W. (1993). *Motivation in the real world: The art of getting extra effort from everyone—Including yourself.* New York: Dutton.

Globe, F. G. (1970). *The third force.* New York: Pocket Books.

Grant, P. C. (1990). *The effort-net return model of employee motivation: Principles, propositions, and prescriptions.* Westport, CT: Greenwood Press.

Haasen, A. (1997). *A better place to work: How a new understanding, of motivation leads to higher productivity.* New York: AMACOM.

Handy, C. (2005). *Understanding organizations* (4th ed.). East Rutherford, NJ: Penguin Global.

Hawkins, B. L. (1981). *Managerial communication.* Santa Monica, CA: Goodyear.

Herzberg, F. (2008). *One more time: How do you motivate employees?.* Cambridge, MA: Harvard Business School Press.

Herzberg, F., Mausner, B., & Snyderman, B. (1993). *The motivation to work.* Somerset, NJ: Transaction Publishers.

Laird, D. A., Laird, E. C., & Fruehling, R. T. (1989). *Psychology: Human relations and work adjustment* (7th ed.). New York: McGraw-Hill.

Leonard, V. A., & More, H. W. (2000). *Police organization and management* (9th ed.). New York: Foundation.

Levering, R. A. (2000). *A great place to work: What makes some employees so good—and most so bad. Republished.* San Francisco: Great Place to Work Institute.

Luthans, F. (2010). *Organizational behavior* (5th ed.). New York: McGraw-Hill.

Martin, G. L., & Pear, J. (2010). *Behavior modification: What it is and how to do it* (9th ed.). Upper Saddle River, NJ: Prentice Hall.

Maslow, A. H. (1962). *Toward a psychology of being.* New York: Van Nostrand.

Maslow, A. H. (1987). *Motivation and personality* (3rd ed.). New York: Harper and Row.

McGregor, D. (1960). *The human side of enterprise.* New York: McGraw-Hill.

Miltenberger, R. G. (2011). *Behavior modification: Principles and procedures* (5th ed.). Belmont. CA: Wadsworth.

More, H. W., & More, T. L. (2012). *Effective police management—Striving for accountability and competence.* Springfield, IL: Charles C Thomas.

More, H. W., Vito, G. F., & Walsh, W. F. (2013). *Organizational behavior and management in law enforcement* (3rd ed.). Upper Saddle River, NJ: Pearson Prentice Hall.

Nirenberg, J. (1986). Motivation as if people matter. *Supervisory Management, 26*(3).

Reiss, S. (2002). *Who am I? The 16 basic desires that motivate our actions and define our personalities.* New York: Jeremy P. Tarcher/Putnam.

Roman, M. B. (1986). Beyond the carrot and the stick. *Success, 33*(8).

Silverstein, B. (2007). *Best practices: Motivating employees: Bring out the best in your people.* New York: Harper Paperbacks.

Stroh, L. K., Northcraft, G. B., Neale, M. A., Kern, M., & Langlands, C. (2001). *Organizational behavior: A management challenge* (3rd ed.). Mahwah, NJ: Lawrence Associates.

U.S. Department of Energy, (1996). *Guidelines for strategic planning*. Washington, DC: U.S. Department of Energy.

Von der Embse, T. J. (1987). *The essentials of supervision: Managerial leadership for a new era*. New York: Macmillan.

Whisenand, P. (2010). *Supervising police personnel: The fifteen responsibilities* (7th ed.). Upper Saddle River, NJ: Prentice Hall.

White, J. L. (2001). The work itself as a motivator. *FBI Enforcement Bulletin, 70*(2).

Williams, J. C., DuBrin, A. J., & Sisk, H. L. (1985). *Management and organization* (5th ed.). Cincinnati: South-Western.

Leadership
The Integrative Variable

CASE STUDY

Sergeant Donald Quest

DEPARTMENT

The Lakeview Police Department currently has 327 sworn police officers and civilians. Additions after the next academy graduation will allow for an increase of seven positions. The remainder of the class will replace retiring/resigning personnel. This will bring 27 new faces into the department, including two lateral transfer officers. This is the largest turnover of personnel in more than a decade. The department is large enough to support its own academy, and it provides classes to potential officers from nearby communities. It is normal to have two graduating classes annually and the academy has been rated highly by graduates and is affiliated with a nearby college. The latest departmental report indicates that the ethnic breakdown of personnel is 16.7 percent Asian/Pacific Islander, 49.1 percent Caucasian, 23.6 percent Hispanic or Latino, 9.3 percent African-American, and 1.3 percent classify themselves as being from two or more races. The most recent class of recruits represents greater diversity than ever before, and is more reflective of the demographic composition of the residential population.

The department is somewhat traditional in its organizational arrangement and has four deputy chiefs, who head the following major bureaus: Administrative, Community Services, Investigation, and Uniform. The latter organizational entity has the largest number of sworn officers and its subunits include airport, patrol, and traffic. It provides direct police service to members of the public, ranging from street patrol to responding to calls for service. The Investigation Bureau is responsible for investigating personal crimes, property crimes, and unusual occurrences. It also handles narcotics and vice investigations. The Community Service Bureau coordinates community policing for the department as well as team-oriented policing. Additionally, it oversees neighborhood watch as well as ordinance enforcement and licensing. The Bureau also has a section that supervises the D.A.R.E. (Drug Abuse Resistance Education) and G.R.E.A.T. (Gang Resistance Education and Training) programs as well as overall departmental recruiting. The Administrative Bureau handles, among other duties, the budget, inspections, training, human resources, and property.

CRIME

As found in numerous cities across the nation, crime was down in Lakeview for the last fiscal year. That is good news, but crime still includes an unwanted range of occurrences. Compared to two years ago, homicides have dropped by approximately 18 percent. The majority of these offenses were committed using a gun or a knife. Rapes were also down by 18 percent and, compared to a decade earlier, there were 20 more offenses in this category. Robberies still plague the community, but there was a 5 percent reduction compared to the previous fiscal year, and 101 fewer robberies compared to a decade earlier, as greater resources were devoted to this type of offense. Aggravated assaults increased slightly, with 832 reported offenses. Fewer burglaries occurred during the fiscal year and numbers have not changed a great deal as compared to a decade ago. The number of larceny/thefts remained about the same, with 3412 occurrences—many of these reported during the summer months. Stolen vehicle reports have dropped rather consistently during the last decade; for the most recent year, there were 345 reported. The Crime Analysis Unit provides management and officers with crime data in terms of Part 1 and Part 2 crimes and conducts analyses on offenses detected, including a current pilot study of shots fired in areas that have a camera compared to those in areas that do not have a camera. The unit limits camera usage and has a policy that covers video storage, length of storage, and freedom-of-information compliance, and has penalties for misuse.

COMMUNITY

The Lakeview Police Department serves a community that has a population of 145,391. It is 74 miles from a major metropolitan area. The community has an excellent transportation system, including buses and light rail, and a network of major thoroughfares and a freeway system that circles its perimeter and allows access to all parts of the city. It has an executive airport, and commuter aircraft transport residents to major airfields in the northern part of the state. It is the county seat and, as a consequence, has numerous governmental buildings in the downtown area that include a county jail and several court buildings. There is a judicial training center that provides classes for judges and court personnel.

The city was founded in 1864, as many people moved west. It has become a significant light industrial area and has a major mall that provides residents and those from the surrounding area with many services, including a variety of shops, three theaters, an ice skating rink, and numerous restaurants. It has several cultural locations within the city limits, including a Shakespearian summer festival center as well as opera. It has a large private university that has many cultural events and "town and gown" get along well. Many residents take courses at the university, which has an exceptional business program. Recreational opportunities are many. The city has numerous parks, as well as sports facilities ranging from soccer to lacrosse fields. A nearby dormant volcano offers many hiking trails and exceptional outdoor camping facilities.

Extensive urban renewal has taken place. The downtown area has been modernized and become a viable commercial and residential area. The city has a land area of 59,030 square miles, and there is a considerable commercial area set aside for light industry. Population-wise, those under 18 years constitute 21.9 percent and those over 65 years of age come in at 12.5 percent. Females outnumber males by 3 percent. The Caucasian population numbers 53 percent, African-Americans 12.7 percent, American Indian and Alaska natives 1.8 percent, and Hispanics/Latinos 23.5 percent. Foreign-born residents constitute 9.6 percent of the population of the city, and 21 percent have a language at home other than English. There are 54,897 housing units in the city, and the average number of persons per household is 2.43. The median household income is $59,783. The educational level is rather high, and 26 percent of those over age 25 have a bachelor's degree or higher.

OFFICER

Sergeant Donald Quest is a supervisor of Team Nine for patrol operations and has been in that position for three years. He came to the department as a lateral transfer after serving for two years in a smaller community in the northern part of the county. He felt that a larger department had more opportunities and a place where he could gain more experience and earn a higher wage. He was raised in an agricultural area of the state. His life changed considerably after graduation from a two-year college, after which he spent two years overseas as a missionary, as required by his religion, where he was fortunate to become conversant in Spanish. The different culture opened his eyes and he saw those of a different culture and race in a new light. It made him more tolerant of others so that he readily accepts differences. He had always thought of law enforcement as a career and after returning from overseas he applied for a police position in his home town. He had no difficulty in passing the entrance examination, the oral, and the physical, and he was assigned to work with an older officer until he learned the ropes. It was not until after nine months that he was able to attend a regional academy. Street time gave him a new appreciation of what was expected of him, and he adjusted readily to his new working environment. After two years he felt that he was capable of working in a more demanding law enforcement environment. Sergeant Quest is 31 years of age, 6 foot 2 inches in height, and weighs 198 pounds. He is in very good physical shape. He enjoys competitive running and is working diligently to enter his initial marathon in the coming year. Since coming to Lakeview he has been on the swing shift, and he enjoys it a great deal because of the variety of tasks and the action.

PROBLEM

Sergeant Quest has seven officers on his team and there has been a constant turnover of personnel because of training assignments, military duty for two weeks a year, maternity leave, or other assignments. He feels that as soon as things seem to settle and he can work at developing his team, one or more changes of personnel occur. With the anticipated graduation from the academy, he knows that he will have to work with two new officers who will require a great deal of supervision and coaching. From experience he knows that this will limit team development for some time. Working with the new officers and supervising others of the team stretches things rather thinly. At the same time he knows that he has to produce at a high level and demonstrate greater team effectiveness.

He feels that it is an increasingly difficult task but one that he must confront with confidence and do everything possible to perform at the highest possible level.

WHAT WOULD YOU DO?

If you were Sergeant Quest how would you approach dealing with this dilemma? Why? What would you expect from older members of the team? Explain. How would you go about integrating the newer members into a viable team? List several key considerations that would need to be confronted. Would you try a directive or consultative leadership style? Why? Assume the participative leadership style might be a good approach and list five potential people-oriented supervisory functions in order of priority. Be prepared to discuss the potential leadership mistakes that you might have to deal with. Explain in detail.

A well-managed police department is easily distinguishable because of its positive leadership. It is the catalyst that proves to be synergistic in nature. It gets things done. It is innovative and maximizes efforts to provide the services needed to improve the quality of community life and fulfill the conditions of the police mission and vision. A marginal or inept organization can be transformed into a successful one through effective leadership. It gives life and reinforces an organization in its efforts to achieve agency goals and objectives. A truly effective supervisor provides officers with a clear sense of purpose that can be translated as the vision provides guidance to the future, the mission describes the intent of the organization, and goals provide a framework for achievement (Gostick & Elton, 2009). It can be seen readily that good leadership, while an intangible quality, must be present if officers are to be galvanized into task accomplishment.

When leadership is truly inspirational, it can be extremely contagious and result in officers achieving high levels of quality production. Leadership is not just something that occurs. It must be cultivated and nurtured. It is a question of applying leadership principles in practice. It is a continuous process and not just something that can be turned on and then off. It is a process that results in efficiency as a result of ethical communications (Van Wart & Suino, 2012). Without a doubt, leadership is the indispensable component of a positive law enforcement agency (Haberfeld, 2006). If a person has ever worked for a good leader, it has undoubtedly proven to be an exhilarating experience. A true leader is one who is optimistic and confronts adversity with persistence and consistency. Above all, a leader acts to overcome obstacles and strives to establish a strong organizational culture (Wexler, Wycoff, & Fischer, 2007). Additionally, a leader networks with others; works at creating open, candid, trusting relationships; and uses moral and ethical values when confronting difficult issues (Porter, Neal, & Medina, 2000). To really excel as a leader, one must be able to convert past experiences into positive input, as well as possess the capacity to visualize a desired future. If one has hopes of becoming a supervisor or is currently at that level, it would behoove him or her to accept the challenge to work diligently at becoming a truly top performer who constantly looks forward and does not dwell on the past (Kouzes & Posner, 2010).

One thing a person does not want to be is an incompetent boss. Horror stories abound in the police field about supervisors who are ignorant, dictatorial, egomaniacal, domineering, manipulative, power happy, or simply unfit. Whatever the label attached, such supervisors can destroy or severely impede the effectiveness of line officers. In fact, officers can (and do) become the victims of exploitative leadership styles, and such a working environment has led to the resignation of many competent officers or the creation of a situation in which officers conform to meet their supervisors' low expectations and become minimally effective. Few officers work effectively when constantly under abusive stress. An incompetent supervisor can soon dampen enthusiasm and constrict even those who are highly motivated. Figure 5.1 depicts terms that describe styles of police supervision used in the past and the style of supervision of the future.

The key question then is, "Why is one supervisor competent and another incompetent?" This is an ageless question that still confounds the best of police thought. Taking on a leadership position rather than being a follower involves a shift in the way people view themselves and the way they operate (Griffin, 2006). A newly promoted supervisor generally has the experience of moving from being a highly proficient employee to one who is less sure of him- or herself. Operational skills are still important, but other skills must now be applied in order to be an effective supervisor. Reliance on knowledge, methods, and techniques that dominated

The Past	The Future
admonish	counsel
closed	open
command	coach
control	empower
coordinate	facilitate
decision-maker	shared decisions
decree	influence
dictate	enjoin
mandate	guide
passive	creative
pessimistic	optimistic
people orientation	task oriented
punish mistakes	error allowance
punish	exonerate
reactive	proactive
rigid	flexible
status quo	visionary
supporter of cohesiveness	acceptance of cultural conflict

FIGURE 5.1 Changing leadership attributes.

work in a line position and allowed performance of specific operational tasks must now be shifted to a greater consideration of human and conceptual skills.

Varying demands on a person in a supervisory position call for a different mix of supervisory skills (Hu-TACK). Instructing others on how to conduct a line-up or a field sobriety test will call for operational skills. Human and affective skills may dominate in a situation in which a supervisor combines directing with motivation in an effort to control the behavior of one or more officers. In tactical situations the accomplishment of the mission overrides other skills.

Finally, while it does not occur as often as operational or human situations calling for the application of differing skills, the supervisor will be required to handle situations involving the application of conceptual skills. The most common situation probably occurs where there is conflict between the goals of individual officers and the primary objective of the department. One's knowledge of the overall organization and awareness of how the unit fits into this organization will allow the supervisor to work toward the enhancement of organizational life and increased efficiency.

When one analyzes the first-line supervisory position in law enforcement, it is apparent that human skills dominate. An effective supervisor must develop the ability to understand why people behave as they do and work toward developing an effective means of changing, directing, and controlling behavior.

First-line supervisors in police agencies exceed the number of managers in all other administrative positions. In a nationwide survey, 111 police departments indicated that the median percentage of personnel in the rank of sergeant was 9.67, while there were only 6.23 percent of sworn personnel in the combined ranks of lieutenant, captain, and major. In a Florida study, it was found that in 33 municipal agencies, the percentage of personnel working in administrative positions ranged from 2 to 13 percent (Reaves & Smith, 1995). The number of managerial positions varies extensively from agency to agency. In the Metropolitan Police Department of Washington, DC, 2.6 percent of the officers assigned to patrol (2250) are in administrative positions. In Tucson, Arizona, there are 85 sergeants supervising officers assigned to field services (this is one sergeant for every 6.258 sworn officers); obviously the ratio has been quite static over the years (City of Tucson, 2005). This means that the organizational pyramid, as it becomes constricted, offers a limited number of opportunities for promotions. Hence, when a first-line supervisor envisions rising higher in the organization, the characteristics that will set him or her apart from contemporaries will be leadership skills (Hughes, Ginnett, & Curphy, 2005).

It is a stimulating experience when one meets or works for someone who exhibits genuine leadership skills. There is an increasing awareness of the importance of leadership. When leadership is missing or ineffectual, the organization is generally ineffective. Problems develop that are seldom resolved, and chaos is likely to occur. When there is positive leadership, operational tasks are completed and objectives are attained. Being a leader is a demanding role and forces a supervisor to make decisions, apply discipline, or control behavior, which arouses feelings as well as responses. Whether or not leadership is effective involves a complex interrelationship of leaders, followers, and circumstances.

Studies on leadership are numerous, extending over a considerable period, and cover every phase of leadership. In fact, there are so many studies that it is difficult to assimilate them.

It can easily be suggested that the more one studies leadership, the more it can be seen as an art and not a science. The key would seem to be to continuously strive to improve your leadership skills, and it has been suggested that there is a possibility that effective leaders may be those who constantly strive toward self-improvement (Schafer, 2008).

In recent years, total quality management (TQM) has emphasized the critical roles that leaders should assume in order to deal with the organizational environment and with the continuing and constantly changing demands of the community. It views trust as a by-product of integrity and ethical conduct that will build a cooperative working environment. This provides a base for empowerment and encourages commitment. TQM fosters openness, fairness, and sincerity and provides for involvement of everyone. This has resulted in the identification of four critical tasks that skilled leaders need to carry out in a high-performance organization (Harrison, 1996):

- permits decisions to be made at the appropriate organizational level
- builds trust and openness
- empowers others
- creates a vision and communicates it to everyone in the organization

These are demanding tasks, and a supervisor should accept this challenge. Decisions must be based on facts rather than on gut reaction. Instead of doing things the same old way, breakthrough thinking is advocated. Instead of a quick fix, stress is placed on long-term, continuous, and sustained improvement. Innovation and creativity will become increasingly common, and assuming risks becomes acceptable (Engelson, 1999). All of these factors focus on creating a high-quality organizational culture that focuses on problem-solving efforts where creative efforts are endorsed and supported. It is a question of staking out a claim on futuristic needs. Supervisors must be given the authority to motivate and manage those they supervise. This means that top administrators must delegate and, at the same time, hold first-line supervisors accountable. Trust and openness are vital by-products of positive interaction between the supervisor and line officers. When motivation is heightened, it will lead to positive trade-offs, such as openness and the enhancement of confidence of everyone involved. This is especially true when a supervisor challenges followers by empowering officers to become involved in the decision-making process and allows them to be engaged in a continuing learning process (Wuestewald & Steinheider, 2006). This eventually leads to a vision of excellence as values are shared and renewed energy is directed toward goal attainment. It is easy to accept the position that contemporary police officers want to work in a viable agency that exemplifies excellence and is guided by a vision that reflects integrity and professionalism (Haberfeld, 2006).

A good definition of leadership proves to be elusive. For purposes of this chapter, the most comprehensive definition is used. Leadership is defined as the process of influencing group activities toward the achievement of goals. There are a number of implications to this definition, and it must be recognized as a process of influencing that can include such activities as telling, selling, ordering, coaching, joining, or consulting. At the same time, influencing others must be directed toward the achievement of some objective or goal—otherwise it can be an exercise in futility. Whatever the objective, whether it is an arrest or assisting a lost child, the first-line supervisor is responsible for ensuring the attainment of the objective.

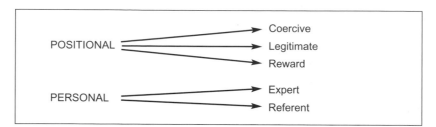

FIGURE 5.2 Supervisory power sources. *Source: Adapted from J. French and B. Raven (1959). "The Bases of Social Power." In D. Cartwright (ed.), Studies in Social Power. Ann Arbor, MI: Institute for Social Research. Reprinted with permission.*

Another aspect of the definition is that the first-line supervisor is no longer primarily a doer, but a coordinator of others' activities. Group members respond to and willingly accept direction from someone who has a leadership style that emphasizes the coordination of subordinates. This means a supervisor should comply with the "50-percent" rule. At a minimum, supervisors should spend half of their time managing others rather than being just another employee (Von der Embse, 1987).

Finally, the definition demonstrates that the leader operates from a position of power based on the authority delegated to the supervisor (Patterson, 2009). The position has numerous power sources, including reward, coercive, legitimate, referent, and expert (French & Raven, 1959). These sources are listed in Figure 5.2.

Power

Within a police agency, power plays a very important role. In fact, the national accreditation program specifically calls for directives addressing the position of supervisor. First, it is recommended that there be one written directive setting forth the need for supervisory personnel to be held accountable for the performance of employees under their immediate supervision. Another directive should point out that in order to permit effective supervision, direction, and control, employees should obey any lawful order of a superior promptly. Finally, a directive should address the necessity of having each officer be accountable to only one supervisor at any given time (CALEA, 2006). Figure 5.3 is an example of a policy statement suggesting partial authority for a first-line supervisor. Policies such as this should be reviewed annually to ensure compatibility with agency goal attainment (Carpenter, 2000).

Beyond formally derived power, the first-line supervisor can extend power by using a number of power tools when dealing with others (Covey, 1992). Persuasion is such a technique. It is imperative that the supervisor share his or her reasons and justifications when exerting influence over others (Cialdini, 2008). At the same time, the supervisor should genuinely demonstrate an interest in each officer's ideas and position. Officers should be told why as well as what needs to be done. Patience is another technique to be emphasized when relating to subordinates. Consideration must be given to the shortcomings and weaknesses of each employee, and these must be balanced against an immediate desire to attain objectives.

Compliance with Lawful Orders

The department is an organization with a clearly defined hierarchy of authority. This is necessary because unquestioned obedience of a superior's lawful command is essential for the safe and prompt performance of law enforcement operations. The most desirable means of obtaining compliance are recognition and reward of proper performance and the positive encouragement of a willingness to serve. However, negative discipline may be necessary where there is a willful disregard of lawful orders, commands, or directives.

FIGURE 5.3 Authority. *Source: Harry W. More and O.R. Shipley (1987). The Police Policy Manual—Personnel. Springfield, IL: Charles C Thomas. Reprinted with permission of Charles C Thomas.*

Short-term impediments, and in some instances actual opposition, must be dealt with, placed in proper perspective, and balanced with a realistic commitment to the achievement of objectives and goals. Another power tool is gentleness and its related tool of kindness (treat others with respect). It might best be described as catching more flies with honey than with vinegar.

Another technique is that of teachableness (to be enlightened). Supervisors seldom have the best answer to every problem or situation. One should accept and value the insights, discernment, and seasoning of those being supervised (obviously a two-way street).

The technique of openness serves as a vehicle for communicating with subordinates. Officers should be accepted not only for who they are now, but also for what they can become as growth occurs. If friction occurs, the process of compassionate confrontation should moderate it. A supervisor's perspective should be based on accurately acquired information about each officer, including an awareness of goals, values, desires, and intentions. In some instances, actual behavior can become secondary as the supervisor strives to increase power.

Consistency is another technique a supervisor should follow in order to increase power. This means doing what is expected of you so subordinates will always know where you are coming from and never have to feel like they are being manipulated. A leadership style reflecting consistency will then become a manifestation of one's true character, reflecting values and personal code.

Finally, integrity is a technique resulting in the extension of power. Officers know when they are working for someone who is honest and who demonstrates a real concern for others. A supervisor should constantly strive for control that can only be interpreted as fair, impartial, and nonmanipulative (Covey, 1992). A supervisor demonstrates integrity when his or her actions are consistent and are governed by established principles. It is the process of doing what is right because it is the right thing to do. In other words, every action is based on the highest moral standards and honesty guides every action (U.S. Department of the Army, 2006).

Coercive

Coercive power is based on fear and on the ability of the supervisor to administer some type of punishment. A first-line supervisor in law enforcement has coercive power, but usually much less than other managerial positions. This type of power is subject to review, depending on the nature and type of disciplinary action taken. As noted in Chapter 6, it can be construed as very negative and may not result in the desired behavior. Supervisors have power that should be used with care, ensuring adequate employee performance.

In some instances, coercive power can be applied without taking formal disciplinary action, such as giving an officer an undesirable work assignment or enacting a closer supervisory pattern. Reports written by officers can be reviewed with an emphasis on minutiae and returned to the officer for correction. These actions, as well as numerous others, are extensions of the formal coercive power that circumscribes the relationship between a superior and a subordinate. It is also an example of how a supervisor can extend personal power beyond that which is assigned to the position.

Expert

If the sergeant has had previous experience in either patrol or investigation and is currently supervising in that area, then there is a vast reservoir of special knowledge and expertise (expert power) to be called upon when supervising officers. Subordinates will respond to supervisors who possess this greater amount of knowledge, knowing that it ensures the successful completion of tasks. Expertise in law enforcement is coveted, and officers continually strive to improve their operational skills. A knowledgeable supervisor who demonstrates the ability to implement, analyze, evaluate, and control situations and to resolve problems is readily accepted.

Expert power is extremely narrow in scope. If it is to be a continuing source of influence, it is imperative for the possessor to stay abreast of new developments because one's expertise can rapidly become diluted in many areas. An example of this is in criminal law, where court decisions can alter criminal procedures in one term of the U.S. Supreme Court.

Legitimate

The reference given earlier to written directives provides a clear-cut example of what is known as legitimate power. The directives spell out not only the responsibility of the supervisor for subordinates' performance, but also the requirement that subordinates comply with lawful orders. This power is essential for the safe and prompt performance of law enforcement operation. Officers are well aware of the first-line supervisor's status in the organization and the support of other managerial positions. At the same time, the officers are fully aware that the incumbent of a supervisory position has the formal right to exercise influence.

Referent

An additional source of influence a supervisor can call upon is referent power. It is the only aspect of a potential power base that is not directly attributable to the position the supervisor holds. It is a type of power that is associated with the leader's personality. Some would identify it as charisma. Whatever the description of this quality, it is something that makes the supervisor likable, and subordinates respond by imitating the style of the leader or struggling to accomplish tasks in order to receive the leader's approbation.

An additional source of referent power for a supervisor is a good reputation, especially when it is based on effective police work. This power is evident when subordinates refer to a supervisor as a "cop's cop" and respond accordingly. Acts of heroism and bravery or outstanding performance, accompanied by departmental citations, go a long way in establishing a base of referent power.

Reward

Reward power is somewhat limited in law enforcement because promotions are usually based on service regulations; thus, the supervisor's role in the process is limited. It might also refer to annual raises (until an officer is at the top step) or cost-of-living raises, which are usually automatic.

Officers are more likely to respond to reward power when the authority of the supervisor affects operational working conditions. Officers will comply when the supervisor has the authority to give out preferential work assignments, influence the assignment of officers to special training programs, or support such actions as transfer requests. Compliance results in a reward and the officers respond accordingly.

To be useful to a supervisor, power should be viewed positively. It is something to cultivate, not ignore. Power is the base that legitimizes the supervisor's position. When the five power sources are analyzed, it is obvious that each has limitations, but they must be developed and used if a supervisor is to maintain an effective relationship with subordinates. There are, of course, other ways to view power, and Gene N. Landrum believes that there are developmental stages of power, including physical, financial, knowledge, titular, charismatic, and, finally, willpower. Of special interest is willpower, which is generated internally by one's mind and value system. It is of special importance because it makes each person unique and is foundational in nature (Landrum, 1997).

Theories of Leadership

Theories of leadership are as numerous as the number of individuals who have investigated the topic. The approaches to this important topic can be grouped into three categories: (1) behavioral theories, (2) contingency theories, and (3) trait theories.

Behavioral

A great deal of research has focused on the actual behavior of leaders rather than on the trait model. Under the direction of Carroll Shartle, studies at Ohio State University rejected the concept of leadership behavior occurring on a single continuum and, after having subordinates describe the behavior of superiors, concluded there were two basic types of leadership behavior.

The two factors are identified as initiating structure and consideration. The concept of initiating structure is defined as "the leader's behavior in delineating the relationship between him/her and members of the work group and in endeavoring to establish well-defined patterns of organization, channels of communication, and methods or procedures." Consideration is defined as "behavior indicative of friendship, mutual trust, respect and warmth in the relationship between the leader and all members" (Johns, 1996).

The Ohio State University leadership studies resulted in a model of four quadrants plotted on two separated axes that identify the two principal aspects of leadership behavior defined in the preceding paragraph (see Figure 5.4).

Studies at Ohio State University noted that leadership styles vary considerably from individual to individual. Some leaders are characterized as task oriented and rigidly structure subordinate activities. However, there are leaders who demonstrate (through their behavior) the capacity to build and maintain good personal relationships. Finally, other individuals exhibit leadership behavior that is a mixture of consideration and initiating structure.

A supervisor who feels comfortable emphasizing consideration as a leadership approach is more likely to use two-way communication (see Chapter 3), show respect for officers' ideas, and work best when there is a feeling of mutual trust. This style is especially applicable when officers are well trained and the goals and methods of performing tasks are clear-cut and unambiguous (Johns, 1996). Such a leader continually demonstrates a concern for the needs of each officer when there is a high degree of consideration. When there is a low degree of consideration, the supervisor is more impersonal and shows less concern for the needs of those supervised.

When a supervisor emphasizes initiating structure, objectives are attained by carefully structuring a subordinate's role. Activities are carefully planned and communicated. Deadlines are established, and giving instructions dominates the interpersonal relationship between the

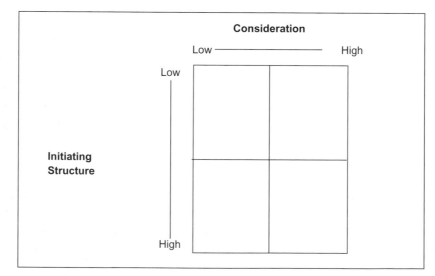

FIGURE 5.4 Leadership behavior.

sergeant and the officers. Tasks are scheduled, and rules and regulations are adhered to in an effort to ensure a high standard of performance. In fact, the task proves to be more important than the needs of the officers.

If there is a limitation to the Ohio State University studies, it is that they ignore the influence of the situation and concentrate on the relationship between the leader and the follower.

Contingency

Proponents of the contingency model of leadership hold that the leader's style (if it is to be effective) must match the demands of the specific situation. The situation causes the leader to use qualities that ensure success. The situations assume that the leader will emerge from the situation. This approach broadens the scope of leadership beyond the trait or behavioral approaches.

In landmark research, Fiedler and associates developed the first contingency model of leadership. This theory postulated three factors of major importance and identified them as (1) the leader's position power, (2) the structure of the task, and (3) the interpersonal relationship between the leader and members.

Position Power. This term is defined as the degree to which the position itself confers upon the leader the capacity to motivate officers to accept and comply with directions. Position power can be measured. Fiedler & Chemers (1984) developed an 18-item checklist that incorporates various indices of power, such as:

- Leader can recommend punishments and rewards.
- Leader has official rank and status.
- Leader is knowledgeable in terms of the position and work of subordinates.
- Leader's knowledge allows for a decision about how a task is to be done.

The value of position power for a supervisor is readily apparent. Rank and status provide the leader with the tools to get the officers to perform their tasks. While the sergeant does not have the position power that can be attributed to lieutenants or those of higher rank, power is enhanced because the first-line supervisor has more frequent and intense contact with line personnel (More, Vito, & Walsh, 2013).

Task Structure. Task structure is the extent to which a task is routine and structured as compared to an ambiguous and poorly defined task. When tasks are defined carefully, it is much easier for a supervisor to control operational duties and officers can be held responsible for their actions or inactions. In many law enforcement agencies, standard operating procedures abound and policy manuals can take up a substantial part of a bookshelf.

Routine police tasks are usually highly structured and circumscribed by numerous legal requirements. Consequently, there is little or no reason for an officer to question the right of a supervisor to give instructions supported by departmental policy. Fiedler states that the structured task is enforceable, whereas the unstructured, ambiguous task is difficult or impossible to enforce.

Personal Relationships. When the relationship between subordinates and a leader can be described as a good working relationship, the leader is in a favorable position to influence behavior (Johns, 1996). This is due to the trust that has developed between them.

In most instances, the newly appointed supervisor, because of position power, is acceptable to a certain degree, and his or her conduct is seldom questioned unless it is clearly inept. The interpersonal relationship developing between a leader and followers depends in part on the personality of the leader. Of the three factors, personality has been found to be the most important in terms of the leader's capacity to influence a group of officers.

When a sergeant is very acceptable from the officer's viewpoint, loyalty is inspired and compliance is generated from the interpersonal relationship, thus giving rank and position power a limited meaning. When a supervisor and the officers get along reluctantly, to the point where friction is readily apparent, compliance may be obtained, but in many instances, it is obtained with reservation. When there is such a strained relationship, it can cause a lessening of the leader's influence.

When followers reject the first-line supervisor and strife prevails, it comes down to basic survival from the leader's point of view. Considerable effort must be expended if even a margin of productivity is to be achieved. Control becomes the essential means to ensure attainment of goals, and ordering officers to do something usually gets immediate results.

Fiedler points out quite candidly that it is much easier to work with followers who are loyal and devoted than with those who are tolerant or antagonistic. The life of a leader supervising the latter group will prove to be most difficult.

If effective leadership is to prevail, it is necessary for the leader's guidance style to be congruent with the demands of the specific situation. Fiedler identified two basic styles of leadership. One style is task oriented, and the leader's satisfaction is generated by effective task accomplishment. The second leadership style is predicated on the desire to achieve personal acceptance and is identified as relationship oriented. By themselves, neither of these styles can be described as effective; they depend on the situation as modified by the three dimensions discussed earlier. When there is mutual trust and respect and the task is highly structured, the supervisor has high position power and the situation can then be considered favorable. However, if the leader is not respected and has limited support, the position power is weak and the task will be unstructured and vague, creating an unfavorable situation.

The effectiveness of a leadership style is highly variable (Yukl, 2005). In all probability you will find that in one situation, it might be most effective to be task oriented, while in another it might be effective if a relationship-oriented style is used. In other words, no one style is consistently successful all the time.

For the newly appointed supervisor whose influence is (in all probability) limited, the task-oriented leadership style will be most effective. When situations are moderately favorable in terms of influence, the best leadership style has been found to be relationship oriented. If a supervisor is a failure, it is probably due to an inability to adapt to the situation. A supervisor's position demands considerable flexibility when compared to a line officer's position. As pointed out in Chapter 1, a line officer's position is dominated by the need to achieve tasks, whereas the first-line supervisor's position requires a response to situations in which human relations become more important. The situation changes when it becomes necessary to accomplish objectives through the efforts of others.

There are times in a police organization when both relationship-oriented and task-oriented supervisors have been found to function effectively under certain conditions but are less than effective under other circumstances. If a supervisor fails to function effectively, it is usually not a question of intelligence or innate ability, but the development of a different situation where the leadership style proves to be inappropriate.

In some situations, the supervisor can change the leadership style by using positive features of the hierarchical organization and structuring the tasks more carefully. This will result in greater compliance with departmental policy. In addition, the supervisor can make more decisions, initiate a closer review process of certain calls for service, or let the officers know where they stand when faced with certain situations. For example, the supervisor can provide backup in certain types of situations, review all felony arrests, or carefully scrutinize reports submitted by the line officers.

A first-line supervisor may find that the work environment is tense and that the interpersonal relationships are less than adequate in some situations. It would seem that task-oriented leadership has contributed to this situation. The supervisor should then implement a relationship-oriented leadership style. Emphasis can be placed on reducing close supervision activities (allowing line officers more discretion in specific situations), involving subordinates in the decision-making process, or, in general, doing whatever is necessary to create a relaxed and viable working environment.

Trait

The trait theory of leadership identifies distinguishing qualities or characteristics a person possesses when functioning as an effective leader. It has been widely accepted because it is interesting, uncomplicated, and clear-cut. Clearly, the abilities, skills, and personality traits found in successful leaders are not present in poorly functioning leaders.

The number of traits manifested by successful leaders varies considerably—from a few to as many as 56. It is quite improbable that any one individual could possess every trait. The possession of specific traits creates an impossible ideal. There are numerous examples of supervisors who do not exhibit many qualities but have proven to be highly successful. Notwithstanding the criticisms of the trait approach, it is still accepted by many managers.

Numerous problems become apparent if one attempts to use traits as a means of identifying potential leaders. In many instances, it is difficult to determine whether the leadership position results in the development of the traits or If the individual had the traits before becoming a leader. In addition, trait theory studies do not weigh the relative importance of each characteristic. In other words, if being tolerant is believed to be an essential trait of a good police supervisor, one must determine how much tolerance is needed before an individual can become a good supervisor.

Finally, the trait approach does not acknowledge the complex interaction between the actions of the leader and the situation. It is clear that the situation modifies the interaction between the supervisor and the follower. In many instances, the environment modifies the leadership process. This is especially evident during police emergencies.

From the discussion of the supervisor's role in Chapter 1, it is apparent that supervisors deal with five types of skills (Hu-TACK): human, tactical, affective, conceptual, and knowledge. All are conditioned and reconditioned by the uniqueness of each situation. Acknowledging the limitations of studies of the trait approach to leadership qualities, one researcher has identified six groups of traits associated with leadership effectiveness. After analyzing thousands of articles and books, Ralph Stogdill found a relationship among leadership capacity, achievement, responsibility, participation, situational, and status, each of which is set forth in Figure 5.5.

These leadership traits clearly dominated the literature over the years and the need for the potential leader to become immersed in the variability of the leadership syndrome. At the same time it has to be acknowledged that the search for universal traits will go on, and it should be

	Traits
ABILITY	Brainpower Reasoning Mental alertness Creativeness Verbal ability
ACCOUNTABILITY	Reliability Desire to excel Resourcefulness Perseverance Self-control Assumes responsibility
ATTAINMENT	Capacity to present ideas Academic achievement Ability to work in a group Successful in sports
INVOLVEMENT	Flexibility Cooperativeness High activity level Friendliness
SITUATIONAL	Mental level Needs and interests of followers Objectives to be achieved Status Skill
STANDING	Economic position Popularity Social position

FIGURE 5.5 Leadership traits. *Source: Adapted from Ralph M. Stogdill (1990). Stogdill's Handbook of Leadership—A Survey of Theory and Research, Revised and Expanded Edition by Bernard M. Bass. New York: The Free Press. Reprinted with permission of The Free Press, a Division of Simon & Schuster Adult Publishing Group. Copyright 1990 by The Free Press.*

noted that many job descriptions continue to list traits. It is also supportive of our continuing search to determine traits that relate to truly effective leadership. It also has to be acknowledged that situational factors and pressures have a major place in our effort to determine what constitutes effective leadership; it is now essential to turn to another aspect of leadership.

Leadership Continuum

The success of a first-line supervisor depends on numerous factors. The relationship between a supervisor and subordinates is best described as existing along a leadership continuum. Some researchers have identified two basic types of leadership and identified them as autocratic and democratic. Another researcher's list expands on this and lists five styles: authoritarian, democratic, laissez-faire, bureaucratic, and charismatic.

Other experts have stressed sharing power in the decision-making process and described seven types of leadership behavior in which the style is increasingly subordinate centered. What can occur is for leaders to enter into a working relationship, wherein goals that can prove to be challenging, by working with followers, when initially establishing jointly agreed upon goals. This type of leadership exhibits confidence that followers can do the job and work efforts are supported fully. Effectiveness and accountability rule such a partnership (Howell & Costley, 2005). Whatever the number of leadership styles, it seems apparent that supervisors do not use any single leadership style consistently. Seldom is any style found in its pure form because the supervisor's behavior varies depending on the situation.

Most supervisors—in fact, most individuals—are not capable of being infinitely flexible in applying leadership styles, but they can employ styles that are consistent with their personality. Leadership is highly personal and projects one's innermost beliefs and feelings. For the purposes of this discussion, it is best to describe three types of leadership behavior that can be used when a supervisor wants to influence the behavior of line officers: consultative, directive, and participative.

Consultative

If everyone in a police organization worked at his or her maximum capacity, there would probably be a limited need for a supervisor. However, such is not the case. Problems must be resolved and conflict must be reduced, thus the need for supervisors. One style of leadership is consultative. It represents an additional description of leadership behavior. In recent years, it has become an increasingly popular approach to supervision.

It is, in reality, a leadership position adopted by a supervisor as a compromise position when it has become apparent that line officers have values and attitudes different from those held by older police officers. The supervisor decides that officers can no longer live in the past. It is then necessary to acknowledge the need for changes in working conditions and proceed to make these changes.

The supervisor cannot completely abandon the directive style of leadership, however, because it is the type that higher managers expect to see in operation. However, the supervisor may believe that another style of leadership will prove to be more productive while improving officer working conditions.

The consultative supervisor shows concern for officers and their needs as well as organizational needs. Subordinates are allowed to participate in the decision-making process and are accepted as part of the team. It is, thus, an acknowledgment that officers have something to offer and that they are knowledgeable and capable.

The consultative style of leadership works best when decisions deal with relatively simple tasks or issues. When issues are complex or there is not enough time to permit discussion and analysis, the supervisor should make the decision. This is especially true if the decision involves an emergency and directive leadership would be the most appropriate response.

If the decision involves the personal or work life of an officer, then input should be sought so that a mutually acceptable decision can be made. Input from subordinates should also be sought when a decision involves the behavior of one officer that affects other officers.

A supervisor should provide for officer input when it is felt that the process will result in a better decision. In addition, officers should be involved in the decision-making process when it is clear that group commitment and effort will be needed to implement a program or introduce a process. This will generally reduce resistance.

When there are two or more appropriate solutions for the same problem, the decision can generally be left to subordinates. In this way, an arbitrary decision is avoided and compliance is ensured. In addition, ideas and suggestions are sought on a regular basis and, on occasion, are accepted and implemented (see Figure 5.6). A consultative leadership style is a significant departure from the directive style, but is not fully participative.

Directive

Many supervisors feel most comfortable when exerting directive leadership behavior. In many instances the supervisor who practices this style of leadership was previously supervised by someone who relied on a directive leadership style. Other terms used to describe a directive

Advantages	• Improves the quality of decisions • Involves subordinates in the decision-making process • Reduces stressful situations • Shows concern for the welfare of subordinates • Utilizes subordinate ideas
Disadvantages	• Leaves personnel in the middle, never knowing what to expect • Limited effectiveness in solving problems • One never knows what impact a suggestion will have

FIGURE 5.6 Consultative leadership.

style include autocratic and dictatorial, indicating the variability of behavior; consequently, leadership styles are best represented on a continuum.

While some suggest that directive leadership is on the decline, this is certainly not the case in many law enforcement agencies. In fact, the work environments of some police departments are such that it is very difficult for a supervisor to use any leadership style other than directive.

The directive supervisor exhibits little concern for officers and allows little or no involvement in the decision-making process. The supervisor makes the decision and ensures it is implemented. If the situation dictates, this type of leader will listen to questions, but never for the purpose of altering the decision. Control dominates the situation, and "Do as I say" is the prevailing philosophy.

A first-line supervisor, by virtue of position power, is firmly entrenched in a position of unquestioned authority and will wield the power necessary to accomplish assigned tasks. To show weakness to subordinates is to give them an opportunity to undermine one's authority so this is never done. Many supervisors will want to move up the "food chain"; consequently, they will strive to comply with directives from on high.

Knowledge of the task to be performed is used to support position power and status. Whenever possible, assignments to special details and tasks can bolster a positive response to authority. The description of Theory X, as set forth in Chapter 4, holds that a directive supervisor perceives line officers as being lazy and untrustworthy. Consequently, officers should be told what to do, and their conduct and activities should be monitored closely.

A directive leadership style emphasizes a combination of elements, such as structuring the tasks in such a way as to control officers easily. A supervisor who uses this style uses the authority inherent in the position as the basis for subordinate obedience. If deviation from the desired behavior occurs, then the supervisor controls the subordinates by assigning blame. Control is maintained by relying on rules and regulations as a means of ensuring compliance.

Close attention is paid to adhering to schedules. Progress reports are required to be on time; late or inadequate reports constitute reasons for immediate discipline. Failure to comply with standard operating procedures results in closer supervision and will likely result in disciplinary action.

Because it is authoritarian, directive leadership relies on position power to reduce or suppress conflict. Authority should never be questioned, and absolute obedience is required. The supervisor makes decisions, and input is never allowed. The primary concern is to get the job done and ignore social interaction unless it enhances goal attainment. What this means is that personal needs are subordinate to departmental needs.

This type of task-oriented behavior for the supervisor certainly lets the officers know what is expected of them. It also ensures the use of uniform procedures and eliminates or substantially reduces officer discretion. The advantages and disadvantages set forth in Figure 5.7 make it apparent that the directive style of leadership has drawbacks. The style of leadership used by a supervisor must vary with the individual and the situation.

Participative

A participative leadership style can be used only when the supervisor has a genuine belief in and respect for subordinates. It is in sharp contrast to the Theory X view of worker and

Advantages	<ul><li>Decisions are made quickly</li><li>Decisions are not challenged</li><li>Enhances compliance with departmental rules and regulations</li><li>Focuses on goal attainment</li><li>Logical extension of position power</li><li>Maximizes control of subordinates</li><li>Subordinates know what has to be done</li></ul>
Disadvantages	<ul><li>Can be punitive and seldom rewarding</li><li>Isolates the supervisor</li><li>Limits two-way communication</li><li>May result in a lowering of morale</li><li>Minimal compliance</li><li>Negative feelings can be generated</li><li>Stifles creativity</li><li>Stressful for the supervisor</li></ul>

FIGURE 5.7 Directive leadership.

leadership behavior described as directive. The supervisor consults with subordinates and involves them in the decision-making process. Attitudes, values, and officers' feelings are viewed as important and are taken into consideration.

Group involvement is sought and power is shared. Every effort is made to create a work environment in which two-way communication is stressed, ideas are accepted, and creativity is fostered. Officers are encouraged to develop to their highest potential, and every effort is made to get officers to accept responsibility as well as handle delegated authority. The informal organization is accepted as an integral element of the formal organization, and each officer is encouraged to think critically.

A change from directive to participative leadership style can prove to be very difficult. It is usually because of an initial misunderstanding as to what participative supervision is or is not. It does not mean that officers have veto power over the decision-making process. Employees do have meaningful input, but in every instance the supervisor or someone higher makes the final decision. At the same time, the supervisor is always held responsible for the accomplishment of objectives.

Participative leadership is not permissiveness in which leadership skills are not exercised, but exists when the recommendations of subordinates influence the decision-making process (see Figure 5.8). A truly participative leader strives to create a work environment in which controls are minimized and officers develop to their highest potential. The goal is to have employees actively engaging in self-management (Grinder, 2003).

Participative leadership integrates each officer into the work unit. A work environment in which officers can achieve and master the tasks they have to perform is created. Traditions are

Advantages	• Better decisions • Committed employees • Employees are motivated • Improves working relationships • Totally acknowledges subordinates' skills and abilities
Disadvantages	• Raises officer expectations • Slows down the decision-making process • Takes a long time to evolve • Time-consuming

FIGURE 5.8 Participative leadership.

challenged continuously and, if circumstances warrant, modifications are introduced. When planning has to be accomplished, and circumstances permit, knowledgeable officers are consulted.

A participative manager never performs the task alone when it can be accomplished through the efforts of others. Subordinates' creativity in problem solving is encouraged, and shared leadership is axiomatic (Pearce & Conger, 2003). Motivating officers consumes a great deal of the supervisory working week, and emphasis is placed on recognition of good work. When appropriate, officers are given additional authority and responsibility. When officers do good work, it is praised, and when praise alone will not suffice, commendations are forwarded through channels.

A participative management style works best when the department has a positive orientation toward its human resources and subordinates have some discretion in performing assigned tasks. When tasks to be achieved are less structured and officers are given a considerable degree of freedom to perform, they are more apt to accomplish the task successfully and will do it with a greater degree of satisfaction.

A truly people-oriented supervisor functions best when serious efforts are expended to foster a work environment in which officers are viewed as an organizational asset. Within a truly positive organization, the focus is on the role of human capital. What really makes a difference is "people." A supervisor must recognize the need to manage human capital by acknowledging the importance of the key role that officers play when effectively pursuing organizational goals and the mission of the department. There is a constant and continuing demand to reduce conflict between the needs of the organization and the needs of human capital (More & More, 2012; U.S. General Accountability Office, 2003). The atmosphere is such that people enjoy coming to work. It is a friendly and supportive ambience where officers are listened to and are involved in the decision-making process. Problem solving is encouraged, and communication is open and above board. When people are supervised from the view that they are assets, they become a critical part of the organization, and their importance is never underestimated in the demand to achieve a unit's mission. Risks are minimized and management standards function

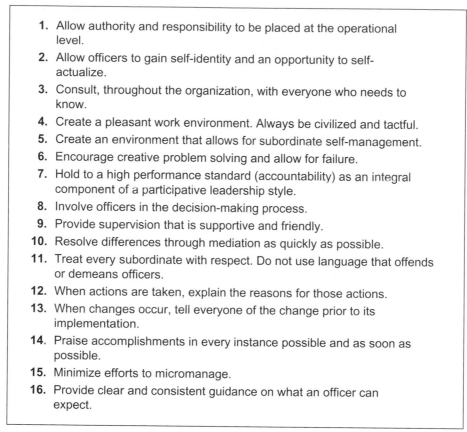

1. Allow authority and responsibility to be placed at the operational level.
2. Allow officers to gain self-identity and an opportunity to self-actualize.
3. Consult, throughout the organization, with everyone who needs to know.
4. Create a pleasant work environment. Always be civilized and tactful.
5. Create an environment that allows for subordinate self-management.
6. Encourage creative problem solving and allow for failure.
7. Hold to a high performance standard (accountability) as an integral component of a participative leadership style.
8. Involve officers in the decision-making process.
9. Provide supervision that is supportive and friendly.
10. Resolve differences through mediation as quickly as possible.
11. Treat every subordinate with respect. Do not use language that offends or demeans officers.
12. When actions are taken, explain the reasons for those actions.
13. When changes occur, tell everyone of the change prior to its implementation.
14. Praise accomplishments in every instance possible and as soon as possible.
15. Minimize efforts to micromanage.
16. Provide clear and consistent guidance on what an officer can expect.

FIGURE 5.9 Tasks for people-oriented supervision.

to achieve results (More & More, 2012). Additionally, officers are recognized for their achievement and rewarded accordingly. Teamwork is the operational mode, and supervisors are supportive. It is a good place to work (Figure 5.9).

Supervisory Styles

In all probability, an examination of a field supervisor's style can have an intense impact on patrol officer behavior. From a study of urban police departments, four supervisory styles were identified: traditional, innovative, supportive, and active; they are discussed next. Interestingly, none of the styles were found to be ideal. Each has benefits as well as drawbacks. Each of the styles is self-contained and mixed supervisory styles were not included (Engel, 2003).

Traditional Supervisors

This type of supervisor is highly task-oriented and expectations have been long established in law enforcement agencies throughout this nation. Aggressive enforcement is the *sine qua non* of why public safety agencies exist. Officers must produce something that can be measured such as field interrogations, arrests, or citations to include the necessary paperwork. This style of supervision downplays community-oriented activities. When providing backup for an officer, this type of supervisor is more likely to make independent decisions and tell the officer what to do. Relating to an officer is not considered, and specific instructions are the way the game is played. Rewards and acknowledgment of a job well done are given sparingly, and punishment or control prevails. More than 60 percent of traditional sergeants agreed strongly that "enforcing the law was the patrol officer's most important responsibility." In addition, what is important is the chain of command adherence to rules and regulations.

Supportive Supervisors

Supervisors in this category are less concerned with enforcing rules and regulations. They have a lesser concern for paperwork and ensuring that officers produce. They encourage officers through praise and acknowledgment, counsel officers as needed, and consistently demonstrate a concern for subordinates. In fact, they support officers through praise significantly more than the other supervisory styles. Just over two-thirds of these supervisors believed that it was their duty to protect officers from unfair censure or punishment. They believed that this was one of their most important functions. This style of supervision calls for serving as a buffer between officers and management, thus allowing officers an opportunity to function without constant worry of disciplinary action for honest mistakes. In some cases, supportive supervisors do not have strong ties or a positive relationship with management. Consequently, this type of working relationship results in the supervisor functioning as a "protector" rather than a "supporter."

Innovative Supervisors

These supervisors are labeled innovative because they generally encourage those supervised to embrace new philosophies and methods of policing. This type of supervisor is someone who is more likely to delegate decision-making, refrains from telling officers how to handle a situation, and seldom intercedes and takes over an incident. They are also found to spend more time per shift working with the public or other officers than supervisors functioning under a different style umbrella. Innovative supervisors are more apt to consider those supervised as friends and work at establishing a positive relationship with subordinates. Thus, they have a more positive view of followers. Ninety-six percent of these supervisors agreed strongly with the statement: "a good patrol officer will try to find out what residents think the neighborhood problems are." The response to this statement reflects the supervisor's expectations for community policing and problem solving.

Active Supervisors

Leading by example is the hallmark of active supervisors. They feel a need to be actively involved alongside those supervised, which provides them with an opportunity to control officer behavior while performing as a street officer and a supervisor. They are reluctant to become removed from active involvement. The preponderance of active supervisors went, on their own initiative, to incidents (95 percent of the time) when an officer they were supervising responded to a call for service. These supervisors also spend more time patrolling (on their own initiative) than supervisors who practice other supervisory styles. Supervisors with an active style are characterized by directive decision-making, a strong sense of supervisory power, and a relatively positive view of subordinates. However, they are less likely to encourage team building, coaching, or mentoring. It appears that this type of supervisor strives to create a balance between being active in the field and controlling subordinate behavior. There seems to be an effort to draw a fine line between positive supervision and micromanaging. In contrast with other supervisory styles, the active supervisor appears to wield a great deal of influence over patrol officer actions. This is especially true, regardless of the style, that when a supervisor is present at the scene of an incident, it is more likely an officer will make an arrest. The longer the supervisor is present, the more likely there is to be an arrest. Also, patrol officers with active supervisors spend more time in proactive activities. Interestingly enough, patrol officers with an active supervisor are more likely to use force against a suspect; however, the study found that the mere presence of a supervisor did not have a significant influence on the use of force (Engel, 2003).

The four supervisory styles reflect the wide range of supervisory activities that can affect officer behavior in the field. Each of these styles can cause a new supervisor to reflect on their own style in their search to determine a style that is appropriate to the situation in the changing environment of law enforcement. At the same time it should be kept in mind that research up to this point and time suggests that an active supervisory style that personifies leading by example may be the best way to influence officer behavior.

Leadership Mistakes

Functioning as a supervisor can prove to be very difficult. Often a supervisor will feel suspended somewhere between line officers and upper management. It is a difficult position to be in and one that occurs more often than one would like it to. It is imperative for a supervisor to accept being part of management, and the only way things are going to be accomplished with any degree of effectiveness is to see that assigned tasks are performed by line personnel. It is the officers who are doing the work, and it is a supervisor's job to work for and with them.

This means making certain that operational personnel are properly trained and equipped to perform their jobs. Supervisors work for both management and subordinates. Their task is not only to tell employees what to do, but also to coach them when the situation dictates, consult when necessary, and join with the employees to attain objectives. Do not make the mistake of trying to change human nature. Accept each employee as a unique individual. Certainly supervisors can use power to ensure compliance, but in the long run that may prove to be detrimental. Accept individual differences and work to develop employees by improving the contributions they make to the organization. One should assist officers by really trying to understand them. Determine their needs and work to improve their self-image. Furthermore, one should realize that supervision is not a popularity contest. Making difficult decisions can ruffle the feathers of some, and being unpopular at times goes with the territory (Townsend, 1998).

Most people find it very difficult to reprimand their subordinates for poor performance. Without question it is a most difficult task. Nearly all supervisors hope that it would never have to be done. Additionally, supervisors are reluctant to admonish an officer because of the impact on everyone supervised—not just the errant individual. Keys to instituting the process with the least amount of difficulty are to:

- allow an officer to save face by indicating how the dispute might be resolved
- allow the subordinate adequate time to respond
- discuss the problem with the subordinate without letting emotions enter the exchange
- discuss the facts, not the personality of the one being admonished
- have the subordinate repeat what you have said so that there is a clear understanding of the issues (McDevitt, 1999)

Supervisors who criticize employees in public make a serious mistake. The true mark of a competent supervisor is a strong sensitivity toward the feelings of others. When it is necessary to criticize someone, do it privately and in a sensitive manner. While it might be an unpleasant process, there are times when there is no other alternative.

Many problems facing a supervisor will stem from letting the acquisition of power become more important than the actual attainment of objectives and goals. Officers will make mistakes or errors, and by virtue of position power, you can criticize, discipline, or even become involved in the dismissal of an employee (Mendofik, 1994). Excessive or improper use of power is unacceptable. It might prove useful initially, but over time such abuse could lead to the downfall of a first-line supervisor.

Newer supervisors sometimes have trouble with subordinates and will do a task themselves rather than spending the time necessary to coach employees in the proper technique. This is a clear-cut failure to manage. As stated repeatedly throughout this text, as a supervisor you must accomplish goals through the efforts of others. The supervisor should ask himself or herself such questions as: "Is too much expected?" "Are requirements stated clearly?" "Are the officers properly trained to accomplish the task?"

A supervisor should never show favoritism to a subordinate. One will soon find out that employees have a built-in sense of what is right and wrong and will strongly object when preferential treatment is extended to a few and denied to others. When rewards can be extended (such as assignments), they should be based on merit, not likes or dislikes. It is essential for a supervisor to be perceived as fair and trustworthy. A good supervisor is one who accepts the challenge of leadership with all of its problems and rewards.

References

CALEA, (2006). *Standards for law enforcement agencies* (5th ed.). Fairfax, VA: Commission on Accreditation for Law Enforcement Agencies, Inc.

Carpenter, M. (2000). Put it in writing—The police policy manual. *FBI Law Enforcement Bulletin, 69*(10).

Cialdini, R. B. (2008). *Influence: Science and practice* (5th ed.). New York: Allyn & Bacon.

City of Tucson,   (2005). *Adopted budget operating detail—Fiscal year 2005-2006* (Vol. II). Tucson, AZ: City of Tucson.

Covey, S. R. (1992). *Principle-centered leadership*. New York: Summit.

Engel, R. S. (2003). *How police supervisory styles influence patrol officer behavior*. Washington, DC: National Institute of Justice.

Engelson, W. (1999). Leadership challenges in the information age. *The Police Chief, LXVI*(3).

Fiedler, F. E., & Chemers, M. M. (1984). *Improving leadership effectiveness: The leader match concept* (2nd ed.). New York: John Wiley & Sons.

French, J., & Raven, B. (1959). The bases of social power. In D. Cartwright (Ed.), *Studies in social power*. Ann Arbor, MI: Institute for Social Research.

Gostick, A., & Elton, C. (2009). *The carrot principle: How the best managers use recognition to engage their people, retain talent, and accelerate performance*. New York: The Free Press.

Grinder, D. (2003). People-oriented leadership. *The Police Chief, LXX*(10).

Griffin, R. W. (2006). *Management* (9th ed.). Boston: Houghton Mifflin.

Haberfeld, H. R. (2006). *Police leadership*. Upper Saddle River, NJ: Pearson Prentice Hall.

Harrison, S. J. (1996). Quality policing and the challenges for leadership. *The Police Chief, LXIII*(1).

Howell, J. P., & Costley, D. L. (2005). *Understanding behavior for effective leadership* (2nd ed.). Upper Saddle River, NJ: Prentice Hall.

Hughes, R., Ginnett, R., & Curphy, G. (2005). *Leadership: Enhancing the lessons of experience* (5th ed.). New York: McGraw-Hill/Irwin.

Johns, G. (1996). *Organizational behavior. New York: Harper Collins College Publisher*. Glenview, IL: Addison-Wesley Educational Publishers.

Kouzes, J. M., & Posner, B. Z. (2010). *A leader's legacy*. San Francisco, CA: Jossey-Bass.

Landrum, G. N. (1997). *Profile of power and success: Fourteen geniuses who broke the rules*. New York: Prometheus Books.

McDevitt, D. S. (1999). Common sense leadership. *Law and Order, 47*(8).

Mendofik, P. J. (1994). Reflections on leadership. *FBI Law Enforcement Bulletin, 63*(8).

More, H. W., & More, T. L. (2012). *Effective police management: Accountability and competence*. Springfield, IL: Charles C Thomas.

More, H. W., & Shipley, O. R. (1987). *The police policy manual—Personnel*. Springfield, IL: Charles C Thomas.

More, H. W., Vito, G., & Walsh, W. F. (2013). *Organizational behavior and management in law enforcement* (3rd ed.). Upper Saddle River, NJ: Pearson Prentice Hall.

Patterson, D. (2009). Be an effective leader. *FBI Law Enforcement Bulletin, 78*(6).

Pearce, C. L., & Conger, J. A. (Eds.). (2003). *Shared leadership: Reframing the hows and whys of leadership*. Thousand Oaks, CA: Sage Publications.

Porter, C., Neal, S., & Medina, A. (2000). Leadership development at the executive level. *The Police Chief, LXVII*(10).

Reaves, B. A., & Smith, P. Z. (1995). *Law enforcement management and administrative statistics, 1993: Data for individual state and local agencies with 100 or more officers*. Washington, DC: Bureau of Justice Statistics.

Schafer, J. A. (2008). Effective police leadership—Experiences and perspectives of law enforcement leaders. *FBI Law Enforcement Bulletin, 77*(7).

Stogdill, R. M., & Bass, B. M. (1990). *Stogdill's handbook of leadership—A survey of theory and research*, revised and expanded edition. New York: The Free Press.

Townsend, J. C. (1998). Mentors—The art of leadership. *Law and Order, 46*(5).

U.S. Department of the Army, (2006). *Army leadership—Competent, confident and agile, FM 6-22*. Washington, DC: Headquarters, U.S. Department of the Army.

U.S. General Accountability Office, (2003). *Results-oriented cultures: Creating a clear linkage between individual performance and organizational success*. Washington, DC: U.S. General Accountability Office.

Van Wart, M., & Suino, P. (2012). *Leadership in public organizations: An introduction* (2nd ed.). Aremonk New York: M.E. Sharpe.

Von der Embse, T. J. (1987). *Supervision: Managerial skills for a new era*. New York: Macmillan.

Wexler, C., Wycoff, M. A., & Fischer, C. (2007). *Good to great policing: Application of business management principles in the public sector*. Washington, DC: Police Executive Research Forum and the Office of Community Oriented Policing.

Wuestewald, T., & Steinheider, B. (2006). Shared leadership—Can empowerment work in police organizations? *The Police Chief, LXXIII*(1).

Yukl, G. A. (2005). *Leadership in organizations* (6th ed.). Upper Saddle River, NJ: Prentice Hall.

Team Building
Maximizing the Group Process

BLOW concept
building a winning team
cliques
conducting meetings
collaboration
conform
contribute
controversy and conflict
cooperation
deadly force
effective relationships
formal groups
group development
  process
group development
  stages
group norms
group performance
group problem solving
groupthink
horizontal cliques
individual
individual and the group

importance of the
  individual
informal groups
interactions
isolation
law enforcement
  norms
loyalty
performance
police culture
preparation
random cliques
resolution
role of the group
silence
size of the group
stages of group
  development
taskforce
team building
team goals
team meetings
vertical cliques

CASE STUDY
Sergeant Wade Craig

DEPARTMENT

Organizationally, the Landfall Police Department has two major bureaus: Field Operations and Administrative Operations, which provide police services to the residents of the community. It is the largest department in the county. Field Operations is headed by a captain and has the greatest number of personnel in order to perform its duties 24/7 annually. Its mission is to respond to calls for service and to maintain the quality of life for each and every resident or visitor. This bureau is comprised of the following elements:

- Patrol
- Traffic
- Special Weapons and Tactics
- K-9 Unit
- Crisis Negotiation
- Graffiti Abatement
- Special Shift Assignment
- School Resource Officers

Officers assigned to patrol operations are on a specific beat as part of the community-oriented policing (COP) philosophy. Every effort is made to keep officers on a beat so that they can become familiar with stakeholders.

The department services a population of 78,250 citizens and has 88 sworn officers and 47 civilians. The non-sworn personnel work in administrative positions, animal control, records, planning, crime prevention, and sex offender registry. Communications are provided by a county-wide unit that services seven departments. During the last calendar year, the calls for service numbered 52,987, which was a reduction over the previous year because non-emergency telephone calls are routed to a special telephone number wherein community service officers (part of Records) provide assistance to residents. There is a strong emphasis on crime prevention, and a wide range of programs are utilized, ranging from a computer-generated telephone calling procedure to check on resident welfare to a citizen police academy that familiarizes participants with the mission and role of law enforcement.

Administrative Operations provides for many of the housekeeping functions, including:

- Human Resources
- Training
- Budgeting
- Maintenance—Fleet and Buildings
- Records
- Planning
- Accreditation

Investigation, headed by a captain, is responsible for the follow-up of all felonies and handles both adult and juvenile cases, from securing complaints to conviction. It is responsible for the investigation of missing persons as well. It also houses several crime scene technicians who collect and preserve evidence.

Additionally, it supports crime analysis efforts directed toward the prevention of occurrences.

Records provides support for the department by tracking and logging reports, and serves the public by providing copies of crime and traffic reports.

CRIME

The Landfall Police Department reported 302 violent crimes for the last reporting year. This is a slight reduction for the third year in a row. There were 10 murders, and 61 percent of these cases were solved. Forcible rapes were up considerably and occurred 22 times. Over a five-year period, rapes tripled. This has alarmed many citizens. Several women's groups are up in arms, calling for action to reduce an unacceptable level for this offense. The department is creating a taskforce to deal with forcible sexual offenses. Other violent crimes included 69 robberies and 201 aggravated assaults. Property offenses occurred 3005 times, and the greatest frequency was larceny/thefts coming in at 2161 for the last reporting year. This was followed by burglaries with 701 occurrences; there were 139 motor vehicle thefts and four arsons. Property crimes have dropped by 9 percent over a three-year period, and efforts are being set forth to ensure a continued reduction in this category of offenses. With newly installed technology, dispatchers have reduced the average response time by two and one-half minutes for Part 1 offenses and further reduction in time is anticipated as dispatchers become more familiar with the new equipment.

COMMUNITY

The city of Landfall is governed by a city council of five elected members and the mayor's position is rotated annually. Each council member represents a ward and they are elected to a four-year term. The mayor holds what has been described as an almost powerless position. The city manager, Jim Wilson, held a similar position in a community with less than one-half the current population of Landfall. The city council appoints the city manager, who in turn appoints heads of departments like the chief of police. The city manager prepares annual budgets and the capital improvement plan and advises the council of the fiscal condition of the city. During the last three years, there has been a budgetary reduction. Overall personnel have seen a 9 percent reduction in positions, with each department required to leave positions vacant.

The community population has remained stable and males slightly outnumber females. The median resident age is 34, and the estimated median household income has been reported to be $48,521. The community is located at an elevation of 905 feet and the land area is 17.93 square miles. The nearest larger community (population: 234,790) is 845.2 miles to the east of Landfall. Resident Caucasians total 49.72 percent, African-Americans 12.4 percent, Hispanics 29.9 percent, Asians 6.4 percent, and other races combine at 1.58 percent.

Landfall is the shopping area for residents and those who live in surrounding non-incorporated areas or smaller communities. There is one large shopping mall and light manufacturing construction, and retail provides the majority of employment. There are three lakes nearby that provide recreation for residents and tourists, and the community has six parks that are used extensively within the city limits. There is one small college and a business trade school. There are four high schools (two private and two public). Additionally, there are 11 elementary and middle schools.

OFFICER

Wade Craig applied for a law enforcement position because he was personally acquainted with several officers of the local police department and he thought it would be a rewarding career. Even the thought of having to work varying shifts did not deter him, so he applied for the test and passed it without difficulty. He really enjoyed the preparation provided by the 16-week academy. He excelled in field training. His field training officer (FTO) rated him as exceptional. Craig worked at varying jobs, ranging from a taxi driver to sales, and on occasion he worked as a bouncer for a local club. Craig has been married for three years. He and his wife live in a condominium in a residential area on the north side of the city. He was elected to the board of directors of the condominium for a three-year term and was active in the maintenance of the structure and the grounds that contained 198 units. He continued his higher education and is currently taking two classes per semester, majoring in urban studies. He and his wife are avid bicyclists and find it an excellent means for exercising. They each have close relatives in the city and participate in many family outings. Craig took the promotional test as soon as he was eligible. He studied diligently for the test along with three other officers, and all of them passed the written as well as the oral examinations. The final hurdle was a polygraph examination, which they all passed easily. He assumed a position in the Patrol Division as a supervisor. He was assigned to the midnight shift, which had an allocated complement of six officers, although the number that were available for work varied considerably because of such things as special assignments, vacation, sick leave, and other reasons. After three years he was assigned to Investigation, where he handled forcible rape, spousal abuse, and other sexual offenses. He became very knowledgeable about these types of investigations and was the recipient of outstanding evaluations as an investigator. His most troubling cases involved sexual abuse of children, and the trauma they suffered caused him a great deal of anxiety.

PROBLEM

Community pressure was escalating and the news media was clamoring for action. The chief of police and the two bureau commanders selected a number of officers of varying ranks to serve on the Sexual Abuse Task Force. This group had representatives from: Patrol, Investigations, Planning, and Records within the department. Outside stakeholders included a representative of the city manager's office, a local women's organization, a victim's advocate group, and a member of the prosecuting attorney's office. The city manager and the council approved the composition of the taskforce and requested that a council member sit on the committee. This was approved by all involved members. Sergeant Craig was appointed to the taskforce because of his investigative experience in the field being studied. The taskforce was given a free rein, and the group was charged to come up with recommendations within five weeks. The taskforce commander asked Sergeant Craig to prepare an agenda for the initial meeting, which was to be a platform for defining the problem. Taskforce members were asked to prepare a short written document defining the problem and suggesting possible solutions. A civilian from Records was asked to identify available reports, and the representative from Planning was asked to identify external information sources. The latter two were asked to make short presentations at the initial meeting.

WHAT WOULD YOU DO?

What do you believe should be included in an initial agenda to ensure that the taskforce has focus and will consider the importance of the issue? Explain. What would you include in your presentation for the initial meeting? Why? How do you perceive your role in the taskforce? Explain. If conflict occurs, what would you do to get team members to work together? Do you think the taskforce is representative of the department and the community? If not, why? Is the taskforce large enough? Who else may have been included? Identify other sources, if appropriate. Can you defend the current taskforce composition? Explain in detail. Do you think there may be difficulty in sharing the decision-making power? Why or why not?

Extraordinary management on the part of first-line supervisors is the catalyst that causes a group of individuals to become an effective team. This is especially true because the first-line supervisor is at the focal point of translating departmental goals into reality. Group dynamics are an actuality in a police organization. They will not go away and must be dealt with if the organization is to function effectively. When dealing with human behavior as a supervisor in a police organization, it is of utmost importance to acquire an understanding and working knowledge of group dynamics. Generally speaking, everyone has been involved with different groups, such as family, church, or school, during the early years of their life, and later become involved in clubs, employment, associations, volunteer organizations, or the military, just to name a few. Some of these groups are highly structured, whereas others are informal and loosely organized. Some have had a substantial impact on the individual, whereas others have had a limited influence. Groups are a fabric of our society and exceptionally diverse. In some instances, groups can be dysfunctional, but in most instances they are functional and contribute to organizational goal attainment. Some groups accept change, whereas other groups resist change and prefer the status quo. Whatever their characteristics, they are the focal point for human interaction.

One of these groups is law enforcement, and potential members are those who have an interest in a police career and go through a screening process before acceptance. If entry is successful, the individual enters what has been described by some as a closed and formal group. It should be kept in mind that groups are the basic unit of social organization. Police organizations can be further identified as a primary group where special, friendly, and lasting relationships occur. At the same time there are numerous groups ranging from formal to informal.

An effective supervisor is one who has taken the time to become aware of group processes. It is impossible to ignore groups in a law enforcement agency. They are a meaningful and indispensable component of the organization. Interrelationships between groups within an organization can be exceedingly complex and can influence effectiveness.

A group consists of two or more people who interact with and influence each other for a common purpose. Two factors are important to the definition of a group: (1) interaction and (2) influence. The interaction of group members can be either extensive or limited. It can be based on a close interrelationship between two or more officers or it can be distant to the point where there is no face-to-face contact. Even if there is some degree of contact between members, it might turn out that body language will prove to be the most important variable in the group process.

The second component of our definition is influence, and its impact may range from limited to extensive. Such factors as position, power, rank, experience, reputation, or expertise generate influence. Individuals seldom exhibit behavior not influenced by the group to which they belong. It is normal for individuals to want to work together and accept the values of a social group that generates a commonality of beliefs, attitudes, and values and that is reasonably successful at doing what is best for the common good and reduces conflict. For many, individual success depends on one's ability to get along within the group and most individuals strive for acceptance.

The Individual

Socialization into the police agency is the means by which rookies are transformed from civilian status to productive members of an operating agency. It is the means by which the new employee is indoctrinated into (and acquires the values and norms of) the organization. The police culture or, in the case of police organizations, a subculture sets the norms that guide the behavior of police officers. They are the truths that officers feel in their bones—the touchstones that rule their attitudes and behavior (Gaffigan & McDonald, 1997). Furthermore, the police, for the most part, subscribe to specific values that clearly set them apart from the public at large. This is a normal process that occurs in many professional areas, and within the police there are many interlocking networks of groups that tie the total organization together. Groups and their interaction serve as the base for achieving the departmental mission, goals, and objectives.

For the majority of officers, the police occupation is not only demanding, but also requires a positive identification with the police task and fellow police officers. This can occur even to the point where there is a degree of mistrust and the job becomes one of "them or us." The police view themselves as the thin blue line against the world. The police are similar to other occupational groups that close ranks when confronted with adversity. It is a matter of survival, and there is a natural tendency to respond to what is perceived as a threat. The belief is that the occupation provides a positive normative influence that is not available from the general public. As a consequence there is a tendency to become increasingly committed to the department and fellow officers and collective trust becomes progressively more important.

The job itself socializes the officer because it is highly circumscribed by law. The law underpins the vast majority of action taken by officers. It serves as a foundation for interpreting citizen conduct and justifying police actions. The law is the focal point for police actions, and there is a powerful normative pull through the socialization process (Herbert, 1998). If that is not enough, there are always policies, rules, and regulations tending to influence beliefs, attitudes, values, and actual behavior. Additionally, the organizational structure designates a formal reporting relationship between groups and individuals and facilitates communications (Johnson, 1994).

The new candidate for a police position interacts with the police social system from the point of initial contact when applying for a position through the socialization occurring throughout one's career. In the traditional organization the new employee is expected to adjust to the organization—under no circumstances is the organization allowed to adjust to the individual. In many instances, it is ritualistic; this reinforces the customs and traditions of each department. The police have a distinctive job-related vocabulary that serves to set them apart. Officers are expected to remain unruffled and composed in highly stressful situations. Above all, they are to be in control at all times and limit reactions, leaving nothing to interpretation. They must be the arbiter of values and interpreter of the law. Violations of the folkways can result in negative reaction by other members of the department.

The officer adapts to the police value system, which is the only acceptable conduct allowed. In other words, this obedience is the price that must be paid in order to become a member of the organization. The agency will generally require officers to acquire norms, values, and specific behaviors that emerge from their inculcation into the organization. Officers within some agencies have been found to have a number of strong beliefs, which are set forth in Figure 6.1. Each of these items can have a significant impact on the group process.

A significant mindset of the police culture is that the police are the true crime fighters in our society and that members of the public do not support the police effort. In fact, many members

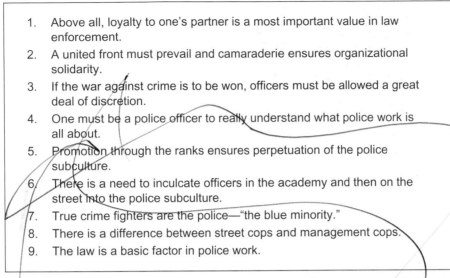

1. Above all, loyalty to one's partner is a most important value in law enforcement.
2. A united front must prevail and camaraderie ensures organizational solidarity.
3. If the war against crime is to be won, officers must be allowed a great deal of discretion.
4. One must be a police officer to really understand what police work is all about.
5. Promotion through the ranks ensures perpetuation of the police subculture.
6. There is a need to inculcate officers in the academy and then on the street into the police subculture.
7. True crime fighters are the police—"the blue minority."
8. There is a difference between street cops and management cops.
9. The law is a basic factor in police work.

FIGURE 6.1 Significant beliefs of the working police subculture. *Adapted from Steve Herbert (1998). "Police Subculture Reconsidered."* Criminology, *Vol. 36, No. 2, pp. 143–369; and Harry W. More, Gennaro F. Vito, & William F. Walsh (2013).* Organizational Behavior and Management in Law Enforcement, *Third Edition, Upper Saddle River, NJ: Pearson Prentice Hall, p. 199.*

of the public are viewed as being antagonistic. Additionally, many line officers express the belief that a police officer is the only one who can understand and appreciate the reality of working the street. In general, even police management is viewed as being divorced from the actuality of what is really going on when interpreting and applying the law to genuine situations. This is viewed as being especially true when police managers have been removed from operations for more than four years. Many line officers value discretion and believe they are in the best position to interpret the law and should be allowed to bend the rules in their view of what should be done to protect society. Finally, except for a few departments, specialized assignments such as investigations are highly sought after, and many officers think that patrol is the least desirable assignment.

The police academy is a significant point in the new officer's career socialization process, as this is where identity with the occupation is emphasized. In the academy, conformity is emphasized throughout the process, and new officers are molded in such a way as to become the visible expression of the ideal cop. It is somewhat of a cookie-cutter mentality in which the candidate is expected to dress appropriately, accept authority, never criticize the agency, and become a member of the team. Expression of individuality is rejected. There is usually one best way to do things—the way it is taught at the academy. Historically, police academy training was adopted from the military model that emphasized loyalty, discipline, and conformity. In recent years, some agencies have shifted to a more academic model of training, blending it with traditional paramilitary training (Weinblatt, 1999).

On completion of the academy, the officer may be supervised by a field-training officer (FTO) or at least by a senior officer. Field-training officers can either support organizational value systems or pass on their own cultural norms. This can bring into play the old adage

"Forget everything you learned in the academy, this is where reality becomes vividly apparent" (Johnson, 1993). Thus, the socialization process continues and norms of the agency are emphasized. At the same time, the peer value system comes into play. Peers are often the most relevant evaluators of other officers because they have a unique perspective of the performance of fellow officers and can play a key role when determining accountability (More & More, 2012). Peers as well as supervisors should remain vigilant about malfeasance and when an officer cannot be deterred from misconduct, it should be reported (Bills et al., 2010). In some instances, this is where new police officers are told "Now that you are in the real world, this is how we actually do things rather than the way you were taught in the academy." Identification with the department, rather than with the community, serves to isolate the officer and reinforce police solidarity.

In recent years there seems to have been less organizational effectiveness in promoting and reinforcing a strong and viable police identity. Several reasons have been suggested to explain why current recruits are not adjusting to the agency as they have in the past. First, it is seldom possible for every member to go along with all group norms. Next, the average recruit today is older and, in many instances, has more work experience and education. Third, because the standards for entry into the field have been modified by diversity programs, the ethnic mix of some departments has changed drastically. Finally, the recruitment of women is altering a previously male-dominated occupation (National Center for Women in Policing, 2002). One study shows that by 2007 nearly 4000 state police, 19,400 sheriffs, and 55,300 local police were women. During the 1990s and 2000s there was only a slight increase in the employment of women (Langton, 2010). Each factor contributes in varying degrees to the impact of the individual's socialization process and to the perceived weakening of the police identity, resulting in the potential for enhanced change in the socialization of members of police departments.

Even though there is an indication that the identity of the individual to the department is not as strong as in the past, it is still an important factor because it is a means of building commitment and creating a feeling of loyalty to the department. Esprit de corps and high morale are by-products of the socialization process. Thus, the more committed the individual becomes to the agency, the sooner the possibility that he or she will become a full-fledged member of the organization. Acceptance has proven to be of importance to police officers in the earlier part of their career and it is a plateau to which they strive.

The Individual and the Group

In the day-to-day work environment, the police officer will often work alone. However, police departments are becoming increasingly aware of the benefits to be obtained from the use of groups of officers formed to operate in a team, a taskforce, a quality control circle, or certain aspects of community policing. Healthy groups can satisfy officer needs in many ways, including association, friendship, recognition, and self-esteem.

A police department is a social organization, and by creating groups, a sense of belonging can develop, there is an attachment to the agency, and officers have a sense of stability. An individual can find that the group becomes a social anchor. Groups are not automatically more effective than individuals are when performing certain tasks. Everyone is aware of the cliché "too many cooks can spoil the broth." Thus, there are some situations in which the group approach to problem solving is best and other instances in which an individual effort will prove most effective. Certainly most of us are more comfortable working with friends and associates. In a group, some of the members become leaders and others become followers. These roles can change as expertise becomes operational and new situations occur. Groups can generate motivational energy that becomes synergistic in nature. As officers become involved in team efforts that result in positive experiences, self-esteem is reinforced.

Some police tasks are accomplished most effectively by a joint response to the situation. Barricaded individuals, an armed robbery in progress, or house-to-house searches for a lost child are examples. It would be difficult to accomplish such tasks in any way other than a coordinated group effort.

In this approach to management, it is the primary responsibility of a supervisor to achieve results through people. It is impossible for a good supervisor to perform all tasks without the assistance of others. Thus, interaction with others to obtain positive results is imperative. In this context the human being is important, and the supervisor can have a positive influence on the individual and their work effectiveness as part of a group. A positive leader excels in obtaining active individual involvement, bringing commitment to achieving both unit and departmental goals.

As the law enforcement function has become increasingly complex, the supervisor soon discovers a lack of knowledge in some areas; therefore, not every decision may be correct. Interaction with other units, such as tactical, traffic, or the investigative division, requires supervisors to depend on their information and knowledge if goals are to be attained (Hu-TACK). Interaction is essential (especially if the decision affects more than one unit of the organization), and both individual and group knowledge must be tapped if the best decision is to be made.

Unquestionably, some individuals have difficulty adapting to groups due to personality, the specific situation, or even variables unknown to the supervisor. Officers within a group perform a number of social roles. The exact role will vary from group to group, depending on the tasks being performed, the nature of the group, and the situation confronting the group. The most common social roles are set forth in Figure 6.2.

1. Devil's advocate
2. Enforcer
3. Expert
4. Facilitator
5. Follower
6. Leader
7. Scapegoat

FIGURE 6.2 Social roles within a group/team. *Source: Harry W. More, Gennaro F. Vito, & William F. Walsh (2013).* Organizational Behavioral and Management in Law Enforcement, *Third Edition. Copyright © 2010. Reprinted by permission of Pearson Prentice Hall, Upper Saddle River, NJ, p. 192.*

Not all of these roles will be played out in every group, but they recur enough to be of special interest to every supervisor. The facilitator can be especially useful in promoting compromise and consensus building. However, the devil's advocate will question every suggestion or management decision and, if left to run amok, will destroy the effectiveness of the group. The supervisor should work diligently to ensure that the failure of the group/team does not reflect on any particular member of the group/team, resulting in scapegoating. The expert should be allowed to bring his or her relevant skills to the decision-making process of the group/team. Finally, the enforcer can stabilize a group/team by seeing that group norms and values are understood. This typology allows the supervisor to analyze the dynamics of a group.

Nevertheless, a reduction in conflict between the individual and the organization must always be the goal. When considering the relationship between the individual and the group, the supervisor should consider the following (Cartwright & Lippitt, 1957):

- An understanding of group dynamics will enhance the achievement of goals.
- Groups, both formal and informal, will always exist within an organization.
- Groups can be both destructive and supportive.
- Groups can become power centers that will have an important impact on the agency.

The individual is a crucial part of the group. The more knowledge a supervisor accumulates about each member of the group, the greater the opportunities for effective work with the group (Hu-TACK). A supervisor should review personnel files and interview other supervisors and officers who have worked with potential candidates for a group effort. Emphasis should be placed on finding individuals who can contribute to the achievement of team goals. Additionally, consideration should be given to finding people who have a positive attitude and will mesh well with the rest of the team. The supervisor should also look for good communicators and those willing to share responsibilities. Time spent in the selection process will yield an abundance of rewards.

Role and Function of the Group

If a supervisor is to understand how an organization actually operates, it is essential to develop an acute awareness of how a group functions. This is especially critical for the first-line supervisor position. While a great deal of a sergeant's time is spent with individual officers, it must be kept in mind that those officers belong to one or more groups. When a supervisor understands the interaction between individuals and groups, it will (in all probability) lead to more effective problem solving, the potential for the development of group loyalty, and the creation of a foundation that will lead to improved morale. When considering organizational behavior, groups can usually be described as either formal or informal.

Formal Groups

Formal work groups are those created and supported by the organization for the express purpose of fulfilling specific organizational needs or performing special tasks. These groups can be either temporary or permanent, depending on the needs of the organization. A shift of officers under the supervision of a sergeant is an excellent example of a command group or team. Another example is a group created to function as a sting operation for purchasing stolen prop erty. This undercover operation culminates with the arrest and prosecution of the accused.

The assignment of officers to a special traffic detail—conducting a sobriety checkpoint in an effort to identify impaired drivers—is another example of a work group set up by the police and then dissolved after its task has been accomplished. Prior to its implementation, planning for such an effort can involve a great number of agencies in a systematic approach that includes highly visible and coordinated efforts by law enforcement, prosecutors, judicial officers, and traffic safety organizations. Such a task group can include community partners such as the media, the local chamber of commerce, and other interested community partners.

Another type of formal work group that is becoming increasingly common in law enforcement is the taskforce. It is usually a temporary group formed to achieve a specific objective or perform a specific task. In recent years, police departments have set up special taskforces to apprehend fugitives, investigate serial killings, catch sexual predators, or investigate a series of armed robberies. In some instances, taskforces have involved the coordinated efforts of more than one agency to include representatives from city, county, state, and federal agencies. More recently there has been a trend to use joint efforts to deal with terrorism and homeland security.

Narcotics taskforces are being used increasingly in joint efforts, normally within a county, and usually are formed on a permanent basis. It has been estimated that there are more than 1000 multijurisdictional antidrug taskforces in the United States. Temporary taskforces have been used to deal with a wide range of problems, including the development of policies or the creation of rules and regulations. In one instance, a lieutenant with the purpose of determining when an officer should or should not wear a hat while in uniform chaired a taskforce consisting of nine members from various units and levels of the organization.

Informal Groups

Formal work groups are obvious to any new employee, but it can take some time before one can identify informal groups. In many instances, these groups have never been sanctioned by the formal organization. It is also interesting to note that informal groups cut across organizational lines rank is usually not important when forming an informal group. For example, an informal group can be composed of individuals who have a common interest, such as pistol shooting, who get together for the pure enjoyment of the sport. The department does not sanction this group.

Informal groups form quite naturally and according to personal preferences. Officers will establish a variety of personal relationships as they search for a means of fulfilling their needs. Informal groups evolve because of an inability of the formal organization to meet all social or departmental officer requirements. Such groups can work to support or not to support the formal organization.

Workers become members of informal groups for various reasons, such as to improve working conditions or to obtain equipment to enhance job performance. In one department, a group of officers worked together in an effort to set up a shift rotation system rather than the current seniority-based system. Some might argue, then, that the majority of police unions evolved from informal groups.

Informal groups have also often proven to be the most supportive of the formal organization. This is particularly noticeable when officers assist each other in performing tasks that are supposed to be performed by another officer or when they have shown there is a better way of doing something. One observer pointed out that in many instances, if it were not for such activities, the organization would undoubtedly perform less effectively.

Another informal group can be based solely on social needs for friendship and interaction with others. Such a relationship can effectively support task accomplishment, reduce absenteeism, and elevate job satisfaction. However, the social interaction between members of a group can occur to such an extent that it distracts them from getting work done. One of the most common examples is the coffee or smoke break, suddenly extending from a 15-minute break to 20 minutes and then 30 minutes. In other instances, officers congregate at certain eating establishments for coffee or meal breaks and there are so many police vehicles in the parking lot that it almost looks like a police substation.

Some informal groups control the rate of production. This seems to occur most often in such areas as the number of field interrogations performed by an officer or the number of traffic citations issued. Take note of those who work too hard or whose production clearly exceeds the norm for a shift of officers constantly interacting. There is nothing wrong with competition, but one should never do anything to make another officer look bad. The group will bring pressure on anyone who does not abide by the accepted code of behavior. Punishment of nonconforming officers usually takes the form of excluding them from after-hours social events, athletics, and police-related clubs.

Informal groups can evolve into cliques—something a supervisor should be aware of. Cliques can easily lead to misunderstandings and, in some instances, hostility. Cliques generally fall into one of three categories: vertical, horizontal, or random.

Horizontal Cliques. This type of clique cuts across departmental lines and will normally include a number of first-line supervisors. This clique will function either defensively or offensively depending on the situation and the nature of the threat. If the threat is imminent, the clique will take an aggressive posture, but such groups prefer to work defensively because of the bureaucratic nature of most police departments. The horizontal clique functions effectively under most circumstances because of the experience its members have acquired from working within the bureaucracy.

This clique functions most effectively when it is dealing with problems perceived as weakening someone's authority or creating some type of change that is viewed as inimical to its members' welfare. New policies that erode operational authority are always suspect. This might include instituting new review procedures when making felony arrests and reducing the first-line supervisor's power. The expansion of controls from above is considered fair game in terms of the type of issue with which this clique concerns itself.

The horizontal clique generally assumes a defensive posture and functions only when the situation dictates that it must respond to ensure the status quo. It is generally more powerful than the vertical clique and can be used effectively by a first-line supervisor when the issue is of general interest. This is especially true when it involves such issues as a reduction in authority, an expansion of review procedures, a significant reorganization, or a reduction in force.

Random Cliques. This type of clique bears no similarity to the other two types of cliques. Rank, role, and unit assignments have no bearing in terms of its membership. Officers become members primarily to exchange information. There is no effort by its members to strive for a change in working conditions, just a basic desire to associate with other members of the department.

In most departments, members of this clique are not active members of either horizontal or vertical cliques. The random clique proves to be important to the first-line supervisor because it is usually the primary source of rumors. It can be used to pass on information or as an information source. It serves a highly important function by intensifying social relationships within the department. The officers who get together at the end of the shift for a beer or a meal are an excellent illustration of a random clique.

Vertical Cliques. This type of clique generally occurs in one unit of the police department, such as patrol or investigation. The relationship is generally between the first-line supervisor and subordinate officers. The supervisor in this type of clique does everything possible to assist and protect underlings. When it is necessary to demand something from an officer, the request is temporized as much as possible. When errors are made, they are disregarded or everything possible is done to minimize the problem. The goal is to humanize the organization and reduce friction between the department and the officers.

This clique is not a one-way street. The officers also look out for the welfare of the first-line supervisor. If there is a threatening situation, the supervisor is made aware of the incident immediately. For example, when a manager of higher rank appears unannounced, the word is instantly relayed back to the supervisor. Officers also apprise the sergeant of all situations that might cause trouble or generate waves, such as any type of occurrence to which the press will respond.

Group Development Process

As a newly organized group evolves, it passes through six stages: orientation, conflict and challenge, cohesion, delusion, disillusion, and acceptance (Jewell & Reitz, 1981). In some instances, the process can be rather fast, but in other situations the evolution from stage 1 to stage 6 might never occur. It all depends on a number of variables, including difficulty of the task, the maturity of the group, and the time and resources allocated to the group (see Figure 6.3).

The beginning stage, *orientation*, can be most crucial to the group's success. Thus, the supervisor should do everything possible to properly prepare for the first meeting to ensure that as many members as possible are aware of the ground rules. Questions such as "Who is the head of the group?" "What procedures are to be followed?" and "Why does this group exist?" need to be answered in order to clarify ground rules. New members of a group want to know what is going on and what is expected of them.

The *conflict and challenge* stage may occur almost immediately and is a result of the ambiguity arising in any group. Anxiety and uncertainty play a significant part as the group evolves. Especially in the introduction stage, things are not set in concrete and an effort must be made to get on the right track. Sometimes things fall into place quickly, whereas other times it takes time to work the kinks out and this exemplifies this stage. It is normal to anticipate that the leader of the group will be subjected to "confrontation" as procedures for conducting meetings

Number	Stage
1	Orientation
2	Conflict and challenge
3	Cohesion
4	Delusion
5	Disillusion
6	Acceptance

FIGURE 6.3 Group development stages. *Source: Adapted from Linda N. Jewell & H. Joseph Reitz (1981).* Group Effectiveness in Organizations. *Glenview, IL: Scott Foresman. Reprinted with permission of H. Joseph Reitz.*

are agreed upon, as potential decisions are discussed, and as resource allocation is considered. A supervisor should work diligently at handling conflict in a constructive manner. Conflict should not be swept under the table or ignored. Handling conflict takes time, and effort spent at this point can be highly beneficial.

Stage 3 is *cohesion* and occurs when each member of the group has received enough information to accept group objectives and leadership is legitimized. If the problem to be considered and resolved by a group is controversial or if the group is highly polarized, cohesion may never occur. Nevertheless, if a great deal of care is taken when composition of the group is decided, the potential for reaching the third stage will be enhanced. Creating a working relationship in which employees believe their values can enhance cohesiveness results in organizational alignment. Acknowledgment of input is essential, and praise and commendation should be used whenever appropriate as a means of fostering cohesion.

Stage 4, *delusion*, is the point at which uncertainty enters the picture. Members of the group become aware of the fact that not everything is moving smoothly and that, in fact, the group has numerous interpersonal problems. In some instances, members will go along with the group even though they disagree with the way things are being handled. Others will take the position that it is of no use to fight it because they cannot change anything anyway. This is a normal occurrence and should not be looked upon as being destructive but a challenging opportunity to deal with conflict.

Stage 5, *disillusion*, concerns a process by which members of the group fully accept that they are on a treadmill and are going nowhere. There is a polarization between members who want to confront issues and others who resist the process. It is at this point that strong leadership must exert itself—issues should be clarified and differences resolved. In many instances, progress seems to be a long way off and the supervisor should do everything possible to see that this stage is passed through with the least amount of disruption and divisive turmoil. Move the agenda by moving from trouble-free decisions to thorny decisions.

The last stage is *acceptance*. It is the point at which a newly organized group interacts positively as it strives to achieve its assigned goals. If the supervisor remains positive throughout the developmental process, the group will arrive at this stage more quickly and with fewer traumas. The supervisor should focus on the benefits of working as a group, such as how much more can be achieved through a team effort and the fact that every member can benefit from the expertise of other team members. A supervisor who is positively focused can generate the enthusiasm needed to ensure team success.

Group Norms

As a group evolves from the interaction of its members, group norms come into play. Norms are the techniques members of a group develop as a way of controlling the behavior of others. As members interact, initial norms are developed that specify the way members should conduct themselves. Members of a group soon learn the difference between acceptable and unacceptable behavior.

A supervisor constantly responds to group norms and must deal with the conduct they generate. Undeniably, norms exert a strong influence over an individual's conduct. If officers are to perform effectively, they must have some common areas of agreement on which to base their attitudes, values, and perceptions. In the absence of norms, the guidance necessary for success is nonexistent.

Norms are unwritten, but in many instances are more influential than organizational rules and regulations. Norms strongly influence conduct because they are backed by the power of the group in terms of some type of sanction when the situation calls for it. They not only set forth the type of acceptable behavior, but also include the group's value judgment as to what is permissible and whether something is right or wrong.

Norms come into existence because of social interaction of the members of the group. In most instances, any formal process does not establish norms, nor are they consciously decided. Norms provide continuity in the work environment—the predictability of behavior that leads to a feeling of well-being and the carrying out of routine procedures without disruption. A realistic evaluation of the importance of the group should lead to awareness by the supervisor of each member's importance and the fact that groups have a definite impact on the behavior of each member.

Law Enforcement Norms

Identification of the norms in any particular agency proves to be difficult because certain departments will have some of the operational norms listed in Figure 6.4, whereas other departments will have all these norms, as well as others not identified here.

Loyalty. Most police departments have a quasi-military structure, and the chain of command mentality is strongly entrenched (Johnson, 1994). Consequently, police departments exact a strong degree of loyalty from all members, including non-sworn personnel. Extensive rules and regulations serve to reinforce this norm, and specific sanctions apply to those who deviate from the expected behavior. Loyalty is demanded in terms of every action and reaction. Nonconformists are ostracized both formally and informally. Under most circumstances, loyalty applies to the police at large and is not restricted to the department to which an individual

<table>
<tr><td>Loyalty</td></tr>
<tr><td>Silence</td></tr>
<tr><td>Danger</td></tr>
<tr><td>Isolation</td></tr>
<tr><td>Performance</td></tr>
</table>

FIGURE 6.4 Significant law enforcement norms.

belongs. In other words, loyalty is to the profession first. This is apparent in instances in which the investigation of a fellow officer is mishandled in order to shield that officer and prevent untimely publicity. During the investigation of a driving under the influence case in which a captain was involved, it was determined that it was a one-vehicle accident. Because of the mishandling of the case, an assistant chief and a sergeant were demoted and three other officers were suspended. The chief took the position that the officers handled the investigation without regard to their training and experience. This is clearly a case of misplaced loyalty to a fellow officer.

In Oakland, California, a small group of officers known as the "Riders" enforced the law by planting evidence and beating suspects. All four of the officers involved were fired. One is currently a fugitive, and the other three were charged with 49 felonies. These officers have been tried twice and the last trial resulted in no convictions, a few not-guilty verdicts, and jury deadlock. Prosecutors have thrown out more than 60 cases handled by the "Riders." Rookie officers were pressured to sign reports indicating criminal activities they never witnessed. One of the "Riders" stated:

> "F—probable cause and everything you learned in the academy." "If you're a coward, I'll terminate you." "If you're a snitch, I'll beat you myself and if you're a criminal, I'll put you in handcuffs, and put you in the back of the car and put you in jail myself." (Read, 2001)

Upon completion of the second trial, the prosecutor decided that it would not be in the interest of justice to have a third trial. A lawsuit was filed by the officer who was found not guilty of all of the charges and he filed in federal court against the city charging fraud that resulted in a settlement for him of $1.5 million.

The Riders case led to a settlement agreement in United States District Court for the Northern District of California that had a significant impact on the practices of the police department, and many of these applied to supervisory reform:

- Frequent supervisory contacts with subordinates on calls for service to include review of arrest documentation to determine whether probable cause for the arrest or reasonable suspicion for the stop is articulated. Supervisors shall respond to the scene of arrest for felonies, narcotics-related possessory offenses, and where there is an investigative use of force.
- Each member of the department shall have a single, clearly identified supervisor.
- Sergeants should work the same schedule and have the same days off as the individuals they supervise.

- One primary sergeant will be assigned to each Area Command Field Team and, in general, the supervisory span of control shall not exceed eight members.
- Supervisors shall meet individually with officers at least twice per month for informal performance reviews. Supervisors shall maintain a record for identifying patterns of improper behavior. In particular sergeants shall scrutinize arrests and uses of force that have been historically associated with police misconduct. Failure to identify such patterns and instances of misconduct when the supervisor knew or reasonably should have known of the misconduct shall constitute grounds for discipline (Henderson, 2003).

Silence. The socialization process within a police department makes it abundantly clear that the code of silence is operational at all times and under no circumstances will officers discuss police procedures with outsiders or tell them how they cope with the demands of the occupation. While department policy may control conduct, the norm of secrecy, coupled with that of loyalty, dictates that one officer will never inform on another officer. This is true even though it might involve brutality by an officer. The secrecy norm even extends to all police incidents, and one officer never turns in another for sloppy work, sleeping on the job, delaying response to a call for service, or failing to perform his or her duties.

When the code of silence is operational, it forces officers to cover up crimes committed by other officers—even when the crime is an act they strongly disapprove of. In addition, officers will feel the need to falsify records and perjure themselves when the code is defended from the investigation of wrongdoing. What is also troubling about the code of silence is its pervasiveness when it comes to corruption. There are grave consequences for violating the code. Officers who report misconduct can be ostracized and harassed. They can become targets of complaints and even physical threats. Additionally, they can be left alone on the street in a time of crisis. A former New York City police officer testified:

Question: Were you ever afraid that one of your fellow officers might turn you in?
Answer: Never.
Question: Why not?
Answer: Because it was the Blue Wall of Silence. Cops do not tell on cops. Moreover, if they tell on them, just say if a cop decided to tell on me, his career is ruined. He is going to be labeled as a rat. Therefore, if he has 15 more years to go on the job, he is going to be miserable, because it follows you wherever you go. In addition, chances are if it comes down to it, they are going to let him get hurt. (Mollen, 1994)

This same conduct has been reported in the Los Angeles Police Department, where a former LAPD whistleblower pointed out:

When an officer finally is fed up and comes forward to speak the truth that will mark the end of his or her police career. The police profession will not tolerate it and civil authorities will close their eyes when the retaliatory machine comes down on the officer. (Chemerinsky et al., 2000)

Danger. From the first day at the academy through termination of supervision by an FTO, the dangers of police work are emphasized continually. This is done in order to combat complacency, but to such an extent that many officers perceive almost every situation as potentially dangerous. Officers can make numerous vehicle stops without incident, but the next stop might result in a violent confrontation. Danger is reinforced by the social interaction between officers and can reach the point where officers view the majority of the public with some degree of suspicion. This suspicion tends to strengthen the kinship felt between police officers. Policing occurs in a dangerous work environment wherein an officer can be killed or injured. Law enforcement can be a hazardous occupation, and even an arrest for an apparently minor infraction can result in a felonious assault against a police officer.

Despite efforts to improve officer safety, the number of officers killed or injured has varied, with 72 officers feloniously killed in 2011 and 47 in 2012, as reflected in preliminary data. Unfortunately, we are still in a quandary; although one possibility, as recommended by researchers, is to concentrate on the "deadly mix" that consists of three components: the officer, the offender, and the circumstances that brought them together. It is hoped that continued assessment of this mix will lead to an answer to the incomprehensible question: "When will we find an answer to the question of officer safety?" Violent encounters are inevitable and street officers will continue to mediate situations. Officers will continue to be exposed to hostility and aggression as they are called upon to defuse and deal with imponderable situations.

The overall concern with officer safety is a major characteristic of some police departments and determines how officers respond to specific calls in which danger can be anticipated. This is especially true when a community has areas that are perceived as antipolice. In these parts of the community, antennas go up immediately and safety becomes paramount. Officers become more cautious, more observant, and are more apt to wait for backup. Safety governs every move, with the goal of preserving the well-being and life of responding officers. Additionally, responding officers are especially concerned with obtaining all the information they can about the location and possible occupants so that they can make the best possible decision on how to approach and enter a dwelling or business. Of special concern is whether the subjects in question are armed or whether they have a police record. Other important information includes the frequency of response to a specific location and previous action taken by responding officers. All of these actions are taken to ensure officer and citizen safety (Herbert, 1998). Supervisors should monitor and scrutinize officer compliance with departmental safety policies and practices. In addition, they should intervene immediately when an officer engages in any type of risky behavior that places themselves, their fellow officers, or citizens in danger. All law enforcement managers, especially supervisors, should prepare those they supervise to be aware of the risks and guide them accordingly (Pinizzotto, Davis, & Miller, 2006).

Isolation. Law enforcement, as an occupation, leads to isolation from the community. Some view the police as a necessary evil. When you need them, they are never there, and when you commit a traffic infraction or violate a minor ordinance, they are always there. Officers soon conclude that their work usually is not appreciated and that the public they are supposed to protect is uncaring. This leads officers to turn inward for recognition and support. In time, many officers limit their socialization to other officers and their families. The more they are rejected by members of the community, the more they turn to their job and the police social system. Isolation reinforces clannishness and occupational solidarity. Additionally, the shifts that many officers work preclude them from interacting with non-police personnel, and much of their social life revolves around other officers and their families.

Insularity erects protective barriers between the police and the public and creates an "us versus them" mentality. Far too many officers see the public as a source of trouble rather than as the people they are sworn to serve. This mentality starts when impressionable recruits and rookies are led by veteran officers to believe that the ordinary citizen fails to appreciate the police and that their safety depends solely on their fellow officers. Consequently, officers learn early that they must protect themselves from the public (Mollen, 1994). In the Los Angeles Police Department, it has been reported that there is a siege mentality that justifies excluding those who are not a part of the department from evaluating or criticizing it (Chemerinsky et al., 2000).

Performance. The police are no different from other working groups in the sense that they have working norms that officers accept. In most instances, it is not a question of restricting productivity because the dispatcher usually dictates the workload. In large cities, the demand is such that calls for service of a nonemergency nature are stacked until an officer can respond. Within this context, officers can control the number of cases they handle by being exceedingly meticulous when completing reports. Officers know what other officers are doing, so norms affecting performance come into existence. It is generally a given that one never does anything that makes another officer look bad by any level of management. If one exceeds the performance norm it can lead to being ostracized or socially isolated. Every officer wants to be accepted, and the pressure to abide by performance norms can be exceedingly strong. This is especially true when backing up a fellow officer is required and there is a late response or departmental procedures are not followed. Such conduct is unacceptable because of the overriding concern for safety. If one seriously steps out of line the consequences can be considerable. The key is to carry your own weight, and a supervisor is normally immediately aware of deviations from the norm (Herbert, 1998).

At other times, officers on the midnight shift will find the workflow very slow; thus, patrol can become exceedingly monotonous. In this situation, officers will take long meal breaks, numerous coffee breaks, sleep if the opportunity presents itself, or leave their beat to socialize with other officers. In other instances, officers will violate department policy and congregate at certain eating establishments. The brotherhood of law enforcement dictates that one officer will advise another as to what is acceptable and what is not acceptable in terms of on-the-job conduct and work performance. It has been found that the more cohesive the group, the greater the possibility that productivity will be controlled by establishing tolerance levels. By listening, watching, reviewing reports, and supervising officers in action, an effective supervisor is soon aware of the norms that govern officer conduct.

The Group Process

A supervisor's attitude toward the group and its ability to perform is critical to its success and the attainment of departmental objectives. If working with a group is viewed as forcing one to conform and is a process by which one loses identity or is never allowed to excel, then it is a group doomed to failure.

There is no doubt that problems must be faced and dealt with before a group can become effective, but it should be accepted as a challenge (Lencioni, 2005). This is best accomplished by cultivating a positive attitude toward groups. They should be viewed as a tool for bringing collective judgment together for the purpose of solving problems.

Exceptional performance can occur when the group uses its resources effectively and each officer is motivated to achieve. Groups have the potential for greater productivity for several reasons, including allowing officers to specialize and use their own unique skills.

Groups serve as a vehicle for enhancing personal relationships because social needs are satisfied more easily. Furthermore, as a group develops and becomes more close-knit, members of the group will obtain status. As they become more productive, recognition will be received from the group.

Cohesiveness can be important to the group and is the result of the officer's desire to be a member of the group and the degree of commitment felt by group members. If individuals satisfy their needs in a group, the group becomes something the officers seek out so they can become members. A group generating a high degree of cohesiveness finds that its members are more loyal, identify with the group readily, accept group decisions, and are more apt to conform to group norms. Group cohesiveness becomes evident when everyone is aware of his or her team spirit (Rothaus, 2006). If a positive outcome is generated by cohesiveness, it is the development of a workplace that officers find more supportive, friendly, and pleasant.

When a group performs successfully by attaining its objectives, it becomes more cohesive. When there is a degree of positive participation and a great deal of communication, coupled with acquiescence to norms, the group will be more successful. There is a positive relationship between cohesiveness and performance. Successful task accomplishment by a team or group serves as a catalyst for cohesiveness, and it has been found that a highly cohesive group performs at higher levels of productivity (Ivancevich, Szilagyi, & Wallace, 1977).

For many reasons, cohesiveness is a positive factor for a supervisor to cultivate, but this is only true when the group's goals are compatible with organizational objectives (Maxwell, 2001). For example, if a group of officers violates the rights of defendants as a means of achieving an agreed-upon arrest standard, then cohesiveness can create a problem for a supervisor rather than serving as a factor that integrates and energizes a group.

Cohesive groups can also become a concern for first-line supervisors because they have more power than any one officer does. A group of managers in a medium-sized police department successfully destroyed the effectiveness of a team-policing program by resisting it in every way they could because they felt their power and authority were threatened. Notwithstanding the negative aspects of cohesiveness, positive aspects are such that the supervisor should work diligently to create a work environment that fosters cohesiveness. The more cohesive the group is, the more likely it is to be highly productive.

When analyzing the behavior of effective supervisors who have demonstrated the capacity to change a random collection of officers into a productive work unit, it is obvious that they perceive their role as being one in which they wear many different hats. This includes being a trainer, counselor, facilitator, mentor, developer, and team builder. It also includes an acceptance that the aggregated energies and inventiveness of a team are far greater than those of the individual. A positively focused supervisor works to develop a team that is best characterized as a cohesive entity (More & More, 2012). When cohesion occurs, the team members will value their participation in the group and will defend the group's purpose. Members will work to see that goals are attained. As cohesiveness increases, members will work to maintain open channels of communication, and position and status become secondary to the group process.

Effective team building involves more than learning a few interpersonal skills. Team building is a complex process that does not just happen—it takes a great deal of leadership and team effort. Real teamwork becomes a reality when responsibilities and decision-making are shared. Members of a team have to learn how to work together, and it is something that must be worked on constantly. Team members need direction, not explicit orders; they need to be coached, not ignored; they need to be trained, not left to fend for themselves. Above all, they need to be led, not supervised to the point of distraction (Leonard & More, 2000).

Effective group leaders generally exhibit a number of readily identifiable behaviors (Figure 6.5). These behaviors can result in the development of a winning team. One characteristic they have in common is goal attainment. This process is initiated by raising and resolving the real issues, consequently focusing on attaining results (LaFasto & Larson, 2001).

In addition, effective group leaders serve in a liaison capacity with other units, facilitate the participation of every member of the group, and participate actively in the group as needed.

Absence of the easily identifiable characteristics of successful teams can result in less-than-adequate performance. Above all, team members must have shared values. It creates the foundation on which a team leader can achieve the other characteristics of a successful team. Shared values are based on trust and confidence in the team. A group of officers begins the process of becoming a team when members value cooperation, commitment, competence, and positive collaboration. These are genuine, definitive values. Team members are committed when varying opinions are accepted readily, even when members obviously disagree. Another key element of teamwork is the willingness to take risks. Teams that are resoundingly effective have a crystal-clear understanding of team goals with an underlying belief that the goals are worthwhile, achievable,

---

1. Participates in the group actively, but does not dominate or thwart individual input.
2. Assumes responsibility for interrelating with groups and units and reporting results to group members.
3. Focuses constantly on the goal/objective as a means of achieving group effectiveness.
4. Serves as a coach and as a facilitator.
5. Supports group members in assuming leadership roles as the need arises. In fact, does everything to foster each member's growth.

FIGURE 6.5 Five characteristics that make a group leader effective.

and genuinely elevating. Values, a shared vision, goals, and commitment may never occur without principled leadership if a high-performance team is to come into existence (Gostick & Elton, 2010). Member effectiveness has been shown to improve dramatically when the work environment makes them feel like they belong and that they are making a significant contribution (Ray & Bronstein, 2001). The ethical and professional standards of the first-line supervisor should be of the highest order, and every action should be above reproach. Finally, and most critical, is positive and constructive feedback. Effective feedback is best described as a process that is exact, valid, and well timed.

An operationally effective group can be identified easily because authority emanates from knowledge rather than rank or position. The degree of participation is focused and based on enhanced knowledge and the skill of team members, resulting in the creation of a positive work environment. An observer of such a group can see that members are staunch supporters of the team and are committed to obtaining results. Members trust each other and genuinely believe they are on a winning team (Thompson, 2007). The energy of the group is synergistic, and group members are given an opportunity to achieve and grow. Their opinions are respected and contributions are acknowledged. Accolades are given to those who contribute to the unity of the group and to those who facilitate goal attainment (Leonard & More, 2000).

Numerous factors influence the effectiveness of the group, including the size of the group, its norms and goals, and the environment in which the group operates. In every instance, strong leadership can overcome limitations imposed by any of these factors. The goal of a supervisor should be to create a climate in which the officers supervised develop to the point at which they truly function as a team. Team building does not just occur—it is the result of hard work and a consideration of the behavior of both the members of the group and the leader.

It is the task of a supervisor to develop a truly winning team in which each officer accepts and promotes the **BLOW** concept of team membership (Figure 6.6). The first consideration is the willingness to "be part of the cause" and participate in the team process. Every member of the team needs to be self-reliant and perform within the parameters of the team concept. Commitment to the cause is essential and this can be accomplished by transmitting values into goals that each team member can accept. Dedication that is founded on a truly identifiable cause gives meaning to purpose. Each team member must pull his or her weight, and the supervisor must ensure conformity and bring recalcitrant members into line. At the extreme, this could mean replacement of a team member.

Be part of the cause
Lend a hand
Obey the rules
Work in partnership

FIGURE 6.6 Team membership—the BLOW concept *Source: Adapted from Ken W. White & Elwood N. Chapman (1999). Organizational Communications—An Introduction to Communications and Human Relations. Upper Saddle River, NJ: Prentice Hall..*

The second consideration is a willingness to "lend a hand" and assist other team members by setting the interests of the team above individual interests. In the beginning, this can be difficult for officers who have been used to working alone. Team members have to contribute skills to problem solving and not hold back for personal or selfish reasons. Additionally, there must be a desire to "obey the rules" and conform to cooperative guidelines when working with other members on a creative idea, regardless of who receives more recognition for success. "Working in partnership" can allow team members to feel that they belong and set the framework for truly understanding that their judgment is important and accepted by team members. Team vitality is important when each team member is allowed to achieve, grow, and advance within the team. When true partnership occurs it provides members with an opportunity to commit to each other. It is best if supervisors praise not only the accomplishments of the team, but also those of individual team members. This is a given and must be followed religiously. Above all, praise must be sincere and provided as soon as possible after occurrence. When partnership results are positive, loyalty and commitment become vital by-products. Once officers fulfill the criteria of BLOW, tasks will be accomplished with enthusiasm, self-discipline, and minimal supervision. This leads to the attainment of objectives that could not be achieved by the efforts of individuals working separately.

Controversy and Conflict

Controversy and conflict within a group are inevitable and should be handled openly. When a disagreement occurs, it should be discussed with all members of the team in a forthright manner. Keep in mind that disagreements are a normal consequence of the interaction between team members. This is especially true when a team is composed of individuals of differing ranks, skills, and knowledge. Above all, discuss issues, not personalities. This allows team members to deal with facts and reduces the nature and degree of emotional response. Members should work through issues and problems that will result in interdependence within the group.

A supervisor should endeavor to treat every team member's opinion respectfully. Favoritism toward any particular member's opinions over those of others should never be shown. In other words, a supervisor should be as impartial and fair as possible.

One should work diligently to spot potential problems and personality clashes before they occur by being aware of everything happening and by dealing with undercurrents. A good way to do this is to interact with every team member constantly and, above all, listen. There is a lot more to be learned this way than can ever be learned from communication that can easily become one-way rather than two-way.

If conflict has occurred, or is possible, deal with it immediately. Conflict can lead to the creation of factions within a team, as well as misunderstanding, a reduction in cooperation, and destruction of team morale. A supervisor should identify and attempt to eliminate conflict before it occurs. The best strategy is to encourage controversy and discourage discord.

It is helpful to deal with problems that result from a lack of cooperation on the part of team members by approaching each situation with a sincere effort of problem resolution (Figure 6.7). One's attitude is important, and a supervisor should take the position that resolution is possible. Team members can prove to be difficult to deal with when they have a difficult personality, have

1. Become thoroughly acquainted with every member of the team—their personal goals, attributes, and needs.
2. Be persistent without being offensive.
3. Call attention to the consequences of detrimental differences.
4. Evaluate the course of action continuously.
5. Involve team members in a comprehensive discussion of the topic under consideration.
6. Present a solution that stresses how the team can gain from implementing the task.
7. Recognize that team members can and will have other opinions.
8. Strive to ameliorate differing views and positions while striving for a recommended solution.
9. Underscore the need for cooperation.
10. When things are deadlocked, consider obtaining the assistance of a knowledgeable person to intercede.

FIGURE 6.7 A supervisor needs to develop an attitude of resolution. *Source: Adapted from Stewart Levine (2009). From Getting to Resolution—Turning Conflict into Collaboration. San Francisco, CA: Berrett-Koehler.*

power that other members do not have, or are obstinate and refuse to yield on any point. There is no easy solution for these situations—they can prove to be highly frustrating and formidable, but they are challenges that must be dealt with frequently as team members interact with each other. The goal is to create an environment that fosters trust. Listen to the ideas of others and strive to find common ground that leads to resolution. As a supervisor, you must sincerely believe that resolution is inevitable and develop an ongoing learning process in which team members are accepted and respected for their viewpoint, even when it is in conflict with team goals. Being open, fair, and sincere is difficult but essential if resolution is to occur (Levine, 2000).

Effective Relationships

In today's law enforcement agency, except in clearly identifiable situations, control is out and the development of dedicated and committed groups is the byword. The foundation for effective relationships is one in which guidance is provided, not micromanagement. It is one where officers are coached or mentored and not viewed as just insignificant individuals. In addition, officers need to be trained in group dynamics and not left to fend for themselves. They also need to be led and not supervised to the point of distraction. Research clearly shows that officers will be more effective when they are committed, feel that they are part of the group, and believe that they belong to a viable and vibrant organization (Leonard & More, 2000; Ray & Bronstein, 1995).

When supervising a group, it is best to develop a personal relationship with that group. At first, it may seem like a waste of time, but some members of the group do not view the supervisor the way supervisors view themselves. In fact, one might be surprised to find that some view the supervisor as highly competent, whereas others view the supervisor as mediocre. There may

1. Are meetings informative?
2. Are team goals clear?
3. Can meetings be more productive? How?
4. Does everyone feel like a member of the team?
5. Does the team have adequate resources to accomplish its task?
6. Does the team use all possible skills?
7. How can the performance of the team be improved?
8. Is there adequate sharing of information?
9. Is everyone allowed to participate in the decision-making process?
10. Is planning adequate?
11. Is everyone on the team treated with respect?

FIGURE 6.8 Questions for determining effective group relationships.

be others who either dislike or even despise a supervisor. Some may view the same supervisor as warm and understanding, whereas others may see him as cold and indifferent. Whatever the actual situation, the supervisor should determine an exact personal status of each of the team members and use this information in the work relationship.

A supervisor can do this by approaching those with whom there is a close relationship and asking for their opinion. This should give some idea as to the supervisor's standing with members of the group. Then the supervisor should sit down and talk with each member of the group, in the most relaxed environment possible.

The opening statement when talking with a member of the team might be something like "Your help is needed in solving a team problem." The initial reaction might not be everything anticipated, but it is an opening, and then numerous questions can be asked to enhance the personal working relationship with a team member (Figure 6.8).

It is important to ask questions that deal with problems rather than with personalities. Solutions are needed or, at the very least, the identification of problem areas. Once the concerns of other members of the team are determined, the supervisor should review his or her own opinion regarding the matter in an attempt to resolve a problem. This can be difficult, but it must be done, and every effort should be made to really understand everyone on the team.

Personal judgments about other officers should never be allowed to interfere with team efforts. As a supervisor, it is imperative to make every effort to see that team members see eye to eye about working together. A great deal of time and effort can be expended on resolving problems between members, but such efforts can be better spent on goal attainment. Intergroup conflict can be devastating. A supervisor who is thoroughly knowledgeable about the needs of each team member and who works to meet their needs and reduce conflict with organizational needs deals with it best.

Developing positive personal relationships takes time; it cannot be accomplished overnight. It can also be frustrating—one may never reach the stage needed to have a well-coordinated team. However, it is a goal worth striving for, and the rewards will usually outweigh the disappointments. Every effort should be made to develop a team that is self-managed (Straub, 1998).

Interaction

One of the most difficult tasks for a supervisor to do when assigned to patrol is to arrange for officer interaction. In many departments, this is limited to roll call and can become a one-way communication process unless the sergeant makes a sincere effort to create an atmosphere that fosters interaction.

When new policies are discussed, ample time should be allowed for determining their impact on operations or the conduct of employees. This necessitates follow-up by the sergeant on a one-on-one basis when officers are supervised in the field. If the policy proves to be ambiguous or subject to varying interpretations, it should be discussed not only at the next roll call, but also (if there is a need) at a special team meeting.

If adequate time cannot be found during working hours, the supervisor should hold meetings outside the job. This technique should be used sparingly and only when the situation dictates. The scheduling of officers' time should be such that there is adequate time for group interaction. If group interaction is not maximized, the officers will feel that it is a misuse of free time.

Interaction can be maximized if a first-line supervisor sets forth a sense of direction for the group. There should be no doubt concerning where they are going and how they will achieve objectives. Priorities should be established, and there should be no room for misinterpretation. Each member of the group should know what is expected of them specifically and what their responsibilities will be. Every goal should be truly meaningful, and every member should have a specific assignment with a designated deadline for an accomplishment of assigned tasks. All of this fosters the interaction process.

Team Size

The larger the team, the more difficult it is to create a positive work environment, leading to esprit de corps and a cohesive working entity. The smaller the size of the unit, the greater the potential for interaction between group members and the more rapidly cohesiveness will evolve. It is a process wherein walls are broken down, ideas are interchanged, encouragement is provided, and leadership evolves (Rothaus, 2006). In addition, group norms are developed more easily in a small group and have a greater impact on group activities.

There is no magic number where a group changes from small to large, but it seems to be in the area of 10 members. This is particularly evident in patrol, where officers usually function independently. In a selection of departments from a nationwide survey by the Police Foundation it was found that the number of officers supervised by a sergeant ranged from 4.5 to 16.6, and the average team consisted of slightly more than eight members.

The same study reflected that when departments had tactical units, the number of officers supervised by a sergeant ranged from 4.5 to 10.6, and the average team had slightly more than seven members. In the same study of 61 departments, it was found that a sergeant supervised 22 percent of the tactical units. The majority of departments serving cities with populations of less than 75,000 fell into this group. In another study, it was found that 81 percent of local agencies assigned full-time officers to multiagency drug taskforces (Reaves & Hickman, 2004). In this latter group, the size of the team can be larger.

Group identity and team spirit are a reflection of the size of a team; consequently, it is recommended that teams be kept under 10 members, whenever possible, as a means of fostering cohesiveness within the group. This number is ideal, but it should be kept in mind that the purpose for which the team was created will, in many instances, dictate team size. This is especially true for interagency teams.

Group Problem Solving

In recent years, the police field has turned to the group as one process to be used effectively in solving problems. The group is commonly known as a taskforce and is distinguished from other groups because it is usually temporary in nature and focuses its attention on one subject or problem. The taskforce has been especially useful in dealing with problems affecting the entire department, such as a policy for the use of roadblocks or selection of a new handgun.

It is widely accepted that groups can be highly productive when it is necessary to generate numerous ideas, recall information accurately, or assess doubtful situations. The role of the supervisor is to maximize the advantages inherent in group decision-making so that the best possible decision is reached.

Another advantage of a team is the greater likelihood of the final solution being implemented because of the involvement of a cross-section of the department. The involvement of individuals in the taskforce from various units throughout the department enhances the awareness of how others function. This leads to better coordination as the members work to achieve organizational goals (see Figure 6.9).

Team efforts can serve as vehicles for training employees as they learn how to work with others and arrive at a decision based on consensus. This process contrasts sharply with many police situations in which the officer makes a decision, usually independent of immediate supervision. The officer is expected to command the situation. Such group interaction forces its members to

1. Broader perspective on problems.
2. Collaborative problem solving.
3. Greater acceptance of the decision.
4. Greater access to information.
5. Greater unity of purpose.
6. Improved coordination.
7. Improved communications by member involvement.
8. Improved decision-making.
9. Increased job satisfaction.
10. Intrinsic legitimacy in the process.
11. Sense of self-fulfillment for members.
12. Shared power.

FIGURE 6.9 Advantages of a team effort.

think of broader issues and their implication to the whole agency. Finally, the team force serves as a vehicle for power sharing. Members have the opportunity to express their opinion and become part of the decision-making process. Just the establishment of the team reduces the power of the individual who has authorized it.

There are, of course, problems that may occur when a team is created. A supervisor should review these carefully and try to avoid them. An individual can come to a team assignment with a complaint and defend this position at all costs, never considering alternative solutions. Because such an individual can serve as a disrupting influence, the supervisor must demonstrate strong leadership skills by structuring meetings in such a way that all sides of an issue are discussed.

Another situation that works to a supervisor's disadvantage occurs when one individual exerts an exceptional amount of influence on the team to the point at which the total decision-making process is impaired or disrupted. In some instances, individuals who have a higher rank, or have a great deal of expertise in an area under consideration, tend to influence the process markedly.

From time to time, a team will have a member who dominates every meeting. This domination usually does not stem from rank, expertise, or bias, but from the personality of the individual. It can be due to the individual's charisma, but is more likely based on exceptional interpersonal skills. One technique that is useful to a supervisor who must deal with such an individual is to encourage others to express their opinions by directing specific questions to them and asking other members to summarize issues and positions. If this technique does not work, it will be necessary for the supervisor to meet privately with the disruptive member and firmly establish ground rules for subsequent meetings.

When a team makes a recommendation, it is based on the judgment of the group. Consequently, members usually take the position that they are not individually responsible for the final decision. There is little a supervisor can do about this particular disadvantage but accept it as an inherent disadvantage (see Figure 6.10).

Finally, it is necessary to consider the cost of including officers in the decision-making process. In one law enforcement agency, the cost per hour for a patrol officer, including all benefits, is $45. Just stop and think how quickly that can add up with a taskforce of nine officers plus the sergeant

---

1. Bias of members may be intensified.
2. Cost in terms of time and money.
3. Decision-making process limited by groupthink.
4. Domination by a member of the group.
5. Excessive influence of individuals with rank or expertise.
6. Interpersonal gamesmanship may dominate the proceedings.
7. Pressure to conform.
8. Responsibility may be diffused.
9. "Win at all costs" may interfere with the team process.

FIGURE 6.10 Disadvantages of a team effort.

in charge of the taskforce, whose cost is $65 per hour. The cost, then, for each hour of meeting will be $470. A team taking 10 hours to reach a decision will cost $4700. If the meetings are held during working hours, it is a loss of 100 person-hours of work that could have been devoted to other police tasks. Undoubtedly, teams can contribute to the effective management of an agency, but consideration should be given to the expenses involved each time they are established. The benefits should outweigh the costs. In most instances this has proven to be a justifiable expense.

Conducting Meetings

An important function with which a supervisor must immediately become acquainted is conducting effective meetings. Meetings are viewed by many as an exercise in futility and a total waste of time. Clearly, some meetings are unproductive and costly in terms of time and money. A supervisor should prepare for a meeting by setting aside adequate time to conduct the research needed to become familiar with the topic to be discussed. Preparation is the key to success. If you anticipate spending eight minutes for the initial team orientation, it can, in all probability, take several hours of preparation. This ensures that you have an introduction that gets everyone's attention. This should be followed up with the identification of key components of your proposal. Every point that you stress should be easily understandable. Above all, you should strive to obtain team member commitment to the program you are describing. This can be accomplished by providing several reasons for each of the components of the program. By following such a highly organized and structured procedure, one conveys the capacity of being organized, rational, and clear.

Supervisors can learn skills to utilize a team effort in such a way that problems can be resolved and solutions can be recommended. It is a team leader's function to perform as a facilitator. Every effort should be made to bring out the best in people and create a working environment that maximizes problem solving. A key to meetings is to make them productive. To maximize effectiveness and clarity, meetings should start on time and be limited in duration. There is little reason to hold a meeting any longer than 45 minutes. Meetings that go longer tend to be bogged down in trivia. When short meetings are held, there is a tendency for people to arrive on time, be better prepared, and to follow the agenda (Kriegel & Brandt, 1997).

A supervisor should start out on the right foot by clearly establishing ground rules at the first meeting. Information should be set forth as to how often meetings will be held. Subsequently, the nature of the problem should be identified and the authority set forth. It is also best to state the various subjects not included within the authority of the taskforce, such as grievances or personnel matters. If the group is merely to present a recommendation (rather than make a final decision), the facts should be presented so that misunderstandings about the reasons for forming the taskforce are eliminated.

After these issues have been clarified, it is necessary to outline specific rules to use in governing each session. The group should participate in this process by agreeing on such basic issues as (1) meetings will begin and end on time; (2) members will not be interrupted when they are presenting their views; (3) ideas will not be criticized; (4) agendas will be prepared and given to each member before the meeting; (5) members will be treated as equals regardless of rank or

1. Ask questions to stimulate discussion.
2. Close each meeting on a positive note.
3. Create and follow an agenda.
4. Encourage the presentation of all ideas.
5. Function as a facilitator, not a dictator, and move the agenda along.
6. Listen and learn from others' beliefs and ideas. Interchange on everyone's part is essential.
7. Never allow any person to dominate the meeting.
8. Never ask leading questions.
9. Never make specific recommendations, including a solution to the problem.
10. Provide all necessary data and information pertinent to the problem under consideration.
11. Refrain from criticizing individuals.
12. Set ground rules to include what is expected from each member and how conflict will be resolved.
13. Set the time and date for the next meeting.
14. State the problem in a straightforward manner without any indication of a solution.
15. Strive to not monopolize the discussion.
16. Summarize and clarify.
17. Start the meeting on time and end it on time.

FIGURE 6.11 Conducting a successful meeting.

seniority; (6) discussion time will be limited to that set on the agenda; and (7) the focus will be on issues, not personalities.

The extensiveness of these ground rules depends on the composition of the group and the nature of the problem under consideration. Some groups have proven to function effectively with a minimum of rules, whereas other groups need an extensive list of rules to govern their activities.

It cannot be emphasized too strongly that the group, not the leader, decides the rules. Consensus is important and facilitates the decision-making process greatly inasmuch as members have a greater commitment to rules when they have been involved in their development. While experts vary in their judgment about how to conduct the meeting, it would seem at the very least that a leader should consider the points set forth in Figure 6.11 (Watson, 1999).

One of the most difficult problems for a meeting leader is to deal fairly and justly with every member. The leader must control those attempting to dominate meetings (especially those who talk just for the sake of talking) and whose wordiness exceeds their knowledge. One way to do this is to set a time limit for each presentation or set up a rotation system for presentations.

A definite barrier to effective group communication can occur easily if members will not enter into the discussion because they are unwilling to oppose the opinion of someone of a higher rank or if they are uncertain whether their judgment will be accepted. The reason for non-communication is unimportant; however, the situation must be controlled, preferably by structuring every meeting to ensure maximum participation by everyone. When a group member seems reluctant to state opinions, specific questions can be asked to stimulate their participation. In other instances, in order to get the meeting started, you might want to ask one of the more vocal members of the team to share their ideas or experiences.

Those who might attempt to dominate the meeting can be scheduled as the last participants. The same might be done for those who have rank or seniority. It is essential for the overall group work environment to be positive and straightforward so that members feel free to express ideas even though they might conflict with the opinions of others. Some supervisors are very adept at dealing with disruptive behavior. Some have been successful at doing nothing and letting other team members take care of the problem. Another way to deal with disruptive behavior is for the supervisor to discuss the problem with an offender either before or after the meeting and spell out exactly what he or she expects from participants. Behavior that is sarcastic, cynical, or exceptionally competitive is not acceptable and must be confronted. As unpleasant as it may be, one-on-one feedback may be the only option.

Groupthink

Irving Janis coined the term "groupthink" and it has received a great deal of attention for more than a third of a century (Janis, 1972). Like many theoretical concepts, it has its supporters and its detractors (Turner & Pratkanis, 1998). Groupthink is a by-product of cohesiveness and it is more or less the glue that binds members of a group together. It is a blending of the characteristics of all members of a group. When members exhibit similar values, attitudes, and cultural background, a group is more likely to be cohesive (Egolf, 2001; Yukl, 2009). When a group has all of the attributes of cohesiveness, the greater is the possibility that the phenomenon of groupthink will come into existence. Unfortunately, it can be too much of a good thing. Every aspect of the norms of law enforcement can contribute negatively to the problem-solving process. A number of symptoms describe the concept of groupthink (Janis & Mann, 1977):

- The false notion of being invulnerable.
- Rationalization preempts conflicting ideas.
- The belief that decisions of the team/group are morally correct.
- Extreme stereotyping of those who oppose decisions.
- Insist that members be compliant and conform.
- Members do not oppose group consensus.
- Silence on the part of members is viewed as agreement.

Groupthink is a potentially inhibiting factor that the group leader must consider if the group is to accomplish assigned tasks and achieve organizational goals. Members can use a deliberating style when consensus is more important than arriving at the best solution. Generally, discussion is limited to reviewing a limited number of alternatives, while the consequences of the decision are ignored. In other words, do not let reality get in the way because (1) the process is more important than results, and (2) alternative solutions just get in the way so they are ignored

(Moorhead, Neck, & West, 1998). Another groupthink characteristic is the extensive amount of time spent justifying the decision. It can be an endless process, and it is seldom that the leader can justify the expenditure of such resources. When a group becomes increasingly isolated from the department, groupthink is more likely to occur. In addition, the group begins to believe that it has solutions to every problem and input from external sources only gets in the way.

Groupthink can be handled effectively by selecting someone in the group to be the "devil's advocate"—to seriously question the solution. The position of critical evaluator should be rotated within the membership. Asking the group to identify and review the weaknesses of the solution one by one might be helpful. Finally, the leader can bring in experts to present their position.

With imagination and resourcefulness, a group leader can maximize the positive aspects of group decision-making and negate the objectionable. Because groups can make excellent decisions, the leader should strive for consensus, as this provides a basis of support for a decision and helps ensure its implementation (Robbins & Finley, 2000).

References

Bills, J., Ching-Chung, K., Heringer, R., & Mankin, D. (2010). Peer-to peer accountability. *FBI Law Enforcement Bulletin, 79*(8).

Cartwright, D., & Lippitt, R. (1957). Group dynamics and the individual. *International Journal of Psychotherapy, 7*(1).

Chemerinsky, E., Hoffman, P., Levenson, L., Samuel Paz, R., Rice, C., & Sobel, C. (2000). *An independent analysis of the Los Angeles Police Department Board of Inquiry report of the Rampart Scandal.* Los Angeles, CA: University of Southern California.

Egolf, D. B. (2001). *Forming storming norming performing.* Lincoln, NE: i. Universe, Inc.

Gaffigan, S. J., & McDonald, P. P. (1997). *Police integrity—Public service with honor.* Washington, DC: Office of Community Oriented Policing Services, and National Institute of Justice.

Gostick, A., & Elton, C. (2010). *The orange revolution: How one great team can transform an entire organization.* New York: Free Press.

Henderson, T. D. (2003). *Settlement agreement. Delphine Allen, et al., Plaintiffs, v. City of Oakland, et al., Defendants,* Master Case No. C00-4599 TEH (JL), United States District Court, Northern District of California.

Herbert, S. (1998). Police subculture reconsidered. *Criminology, 36*(2), 343–346.

Ivancevich, J. M., Szilagyi, A. D., & Wallace, M. J. (1977). *Organizational behavior and performance.* Santa Monica, CA: Goodyear.

Janis, I. L. (1972). *Victims of groupthink.* Boston: Houghton Mifflin.

Janis, I. L., & Mann, L. (1977). *Decision making: Psychological making: A psychological analysis of conflict, choice and commitment.* New York: The Free Press.

Jewell, L. N., & Reitz, H. J. (1981). *Group effectiveness in organizations.* Glenview, IL: Scott Foresman.

Johnson, R. A. (1993). Culture, mission, and goal attainment. *FBI Law Enforcement Bulletin, 62*(1).

Johnson, R. A. (1994). Police organizational design and structure. *FBI Law Enforcement Bulletin, 63*(6).

Kriegel, R., & Brandt, D. (1997). *Sacred cows make the best burgers—Paradigm-busting strategies for developing change-ready people and organizations.* New York: Warner.

LaFasto, F., & Larson, C. E. (2001). *When teams work best: 6000 team members and leaders tell what it takes to succeed.* Thousand Oaks, CA: Sage Publications.

Langton, L. (2010). *Women in law enforcement, 1987–2008*. Washington, DC: Bureau of Justice Statistics.

Lencioni, P. M. (2005). *Overcoming the five dysfunctions of a team: A field guide for leaders, managers, and facilitators*. San Francisco, CA: Jossey-Bass.

Leonard, V. A., & More, H. W. (2000). *Police organization and management* (9th ed.). New York: Foundation.

Levine, S. (2000). *Getting to resolution: Turning conflict into collaboration*. San Francisco, CA: Berrett-Koehler.

Maxwell, J. C. (2001). *The 17 indisputable laws of teamwork: Embracing them and empower your team*. Nashville, TN: Thomas Nelson.

Mollen, M. (1994). *Commission to investigate allegations of police corruption and the anti-corruption procedures of the police department*. New York: City of New York.

Moorhead, G., Neck, C. P., & West, M. S. (1998). The tendency toward defective decision-making within self-managed teams: The prevalence of groupthink for the 21st century. *Behavior and Human Decision Processes*, *73*(2/3).

More, H. W., & More, T. L. (2012). *Effective police management—Striving for accountability and competence*. Springfield, IL: Charles C Thomas.

More, H. W., Vito, G. F., & Walsh, W. F. (2013). *Organizational behavior and management in law enforcement* (3rd ed.). Upper Saddle River, NJ: Pearson Prentice Hall.

National Center for Women in Policing, (2002). *Equality denied—The status of women in policing: 2000*. Los Angeles, CA: NCWP.

Pinizzotto, A. J., Davis, E. F. G., & Miller, C. E., III (2006). *Violent encounters—A study of felonious assaults on our nation's law enforcement officers*. Clarksburg, WV: Uniformed Crime Reports, Federal Bureau of Investigation.

Ray, D., & Bronstein, H. (1995). *Teaming up: Making the transition to a self-directed, team-based organization*. New York: McGraw-Hill.

Ray, D., & Bronstein, H. (2001). *The performance culture: Maximizing the power of teams*. New York: ICP.

Read, D. (2001). Accused cops get hearing today—Story of Riders corruption unfolds. *San Jose Mercury News*, *21*(1B), 5B.

Reaves, B. A., & Hickman, M. J. (2004). *Law enforcement management and administrative statistics, 2000: Data for individual state and local agencies with 100 or more officers*. Washington, DC: Bureau of Justice Statistics.

Robbins, H., & Finley, M. (2000). *Why teams don't work: What went wrong and how to make it right* (2nd ed.). San Francisco: Berrett-Koehler.

Rothaus, G. P. (2006). 6 strategies for successful team-building workshops. *The Police Chief, LXXIII*(6).

Straub, J. T. (1998). *The Agile manager's guide to building and leading teams*. Bristol, VT: Velocity Business Publications.

Thompson, L. (2007). *Making the team* (3rd ed.). Upper Saddle River, NJ: Prentice Hall.

Turner, M. E., & Pratkanis, A. R. (1998). Twenty-five years of groupthink theory and research: Lessons from the evaluation of a theory. *Organizational Behavior and Human Decision Processes*, *73*(2/3).

Watson, J. (1999). The minute taker's handbook. North Vancouver, BC: International Self-Counsel.

Weinblatt, R. B. (1999). The paramilitary vs. academic training. *Law and Order*, *47*(12).

White, K. W., & Chapman, E. N. (1999). *Organizational communication—An introduction to communication and human relations strategies*. Upper Saddle River, NJ: Prentice Hall.

Yukl, G. A. (2009). *Leadership in organizations* (7th ed.). Upper Saddle River, NJ: Prentice Hall.

Change
Coping with Organizational Life

CASE STUDY

Sergeant Eric Struthers

DEPARTMENT

The Dexter Police Department is a full-service police agency and the largest department in the county. It has been the epitome of a service orientation approach to law enforcement. The service orientation has been foundational to evolving neighborhood police sections and the concept of community-oriented policing. Saturday nights can get a little wild when bars are closing, and officers have done an excellent job of seeing that the party-goers do not drive when they have had too much to drink. A great deal of effort is directed to identifying designated drivers or even providing a ride home in a police vehicle or a designated cab program that has been worked out between bars, restaurants, and the major cab companies in the community. Old Town, a downtown section of the city, is the primary area for excessive behavior and seldom impacts the remainder of the community. The service orientation governs the activities of the department and is supported by the "city fathers" and the majority of community members.

The department has three major units: Uniform, Detective, and Administrative. The Uniform Division dominates, and the other two units are considered as supportive. The department performs many traditional duties, including a fingerprint specialization, property and evidence maintenance, training, and victim assistance. Quality of life has been a major focus for years, and noisy parties or outings are closely supervised and officers are expected to be proactive in their response.

Noise violation citations have increased by 87 percent during the last calendar year. Visibility and investigations are the hallmark of the patrol function. It also performs code enforcement for the community, and seven officers are assigned to this duty; these officers work in designated areas in the community. A captain heads the Uniform Division and the other two major units are supervised by lieutenants. The department serves a population of 56,341 and is staffed by 132 sworn officers and 32 civilians. There are four lieutenants and 18 sergeants. Patrol responds to calls for service, and investigators perform follow-up and support the patrol officers as needed. Sergeants perform backup duties, as do field training officers (FTOs), and officer safety is considered to be imperative.

CRIME

Crime has stabilized during the last three years and it is anticipated that it will be reduced marginally in the coming calendar year except for homicides. Most of these incidents are random acts or domestic disputes. All together there were 171 violent crimes that occurred within the city limits. Robbery has remained about the same, with 89 occurrences, and aggravated assaults increased to 65 from 59. The number of forcible rapes was 10, which is below the average for communities of similar populations. Property crimes occurred in 1754 incidents, and larceny/theft outpaced the other property crimes. There were 504 burglaries, 875 larceny/thefts, 370 motor vehicle thefts, and five incidents of arson. The department is reviewing the concept of predictive policing and, if adopted, it is hoped that it will increase the number of arrests. A community survey completed during the previous year (repeated every other year) indicates that a majority of the residents rate the performance of the police department as satisfactory or very satisfactory. The service model has paid off over the years. Knowledgeable citizens expressed the belief that community-oriented policing (COP) will make the department accountable and more effective.

COMMUNITY

The city of Dexter is governed by an appointed city manager and the mayor is elected for a four-year period, as are the five other members of the city council. Other elected positions include city treasurer and city controller. Council members represent geographic wards, and the agenda and council minutes are available to residents on a website as well as being broadcast by the media. The city has 27.54 square miles of land. It is located in the northern part of the state and has four distinct seasons. The economic development office of the community has a very positive program and strives diligently to attract major businesses and light industry. Its geographic location is such that it is readily accessible by a major highway, rail system, and a commuter airport. The community has a blend of residence and commerce, with some 60 percent of the land devoted to residential living. It has a growing retail trade, and 12 percent of the businesses are classified as light industry. It has just over 24,000 housing units, and there is a 61 percent homeownership rate. The residents are reasonably well educated, with 25.1 percent having attained a bachelor's degree. Major businesses include banking as well as medical, professional, and business services. There is a large mall and numerous shopping districts within the city limits. Old Town is an attractive entertainment area. Women outnumber males by 3.5 percent. Sixty-seven percent of the residents are Caucasian and the next largest race is Hispanic at 16.7 percent.

The city has a wide range of quality parks and recreational services; it sponsors special events and has numerous sports leagues. There is a zoo, a water sports center, a roadhouse theater, a dance academy, and a performing arts center. Winter skiing is available in a nearby range of mountains, and a state park is 15 minutes away. The K-12 school system is highly acclaimed. The university campus is 25 miles to the west, and additional college classes are taught at a downtown location.

OFFICER

Eric Struthers had difficulties in finding himself after graduating from high school. He was not sure what he wanted to do with his life. Some of his friends went into the military, but that was never attractive to him. He worked in construction for a while and then as an apprentice mechanic for a year, but that turned out to be unsatisfactory. His closest friend joined the metropolitan police department in the southwest part of the state and told Eric that it was a wise choice and that he found police work rewarding. As a result, Eric took the entrance test in his home town of Dexter and passed the written and oral components of the test, resulting in his placement as the third highest scorer. After six months he was selected and assigned to the 16-week police academy and entered the patrol unit under the tutelage of an FTO. He was convinced that police work was for him and that he had found his place in life. He found the work demanding and exceptionally interesting.

Assigned to the swing shift and working in Old Town was challenging. He started on a walking beat and worked hard to become familiar with his assigned area. He enjoyed resolving conflict and solving problems. He performed with a service mode as his primary means of dealing with problems, and many of those with whom he came into contact responded positively to this approach. He was well liked by those he worked with, and his outgoing personality proved to be a positive in his favor. He received outstanding performance evaluations and after three years he took the test for sergeant.

After promotion to a supervisory position he was assigned to the midnight shift, where he supervised six officers. He had no difficulty in relating to those he supervised, and enjoyed backing up officers and coaching them when needed. He was accepted by those he served, including the three offices who were senior to him. In a relatively short time they readily acknowledged that he was a supervisor and a capable officer. As a backup responder he always seemed to be there when needed and do the right thing. His introduction to those he supervised was: "See those three stripes? The first is G; the second is O; and the third is D. All together that means GOD!" With that he was readily accepted as a fellow officer and a supervisor. His cooperative and sharing supervisory approach paid off.

PROBLEM

The move to COP is somewhat of a tangent from the service philosophy of policing. Like any change, it can be fraught with "rocks in the roadway." The initial response from line personnel had mixed responses. Some immediately supported the new effort, others immediately rejected the proposed change, and quite a few were neutral. Much depended on how they felt the change would impact the tasks they had to perform. The initial meeting at roll call announcing the proposed change was short on details, which led to a lot of speculation as to what changes would have to be made. Detractors were not sure whether the change would be an improvement and were satisfied with the way things were already being done. Changes must be perceived as potentially beneficial to the officers and the organization. The department must inform officers in detail as to what the change actually does in an effort to resolve uncertainty and above all set forth all of the positive aspects of the proposed effort. Within a week this was done and officers were informed of upcoming training sessions that would explain the changes in policy and procedures. Even with the above efforts, however, there was some skepticism that occurred in the locker room and the hallways. Up to this point the union had not taken a position on COP.

It was immediately apparent to Sergeant Struthers that the future might be somewhat tenuous. He found that he had mixed feelings. He was desperately hoping that additional announcements would reduce the ambiguity and help to soften the scuttlebutt, that time would work to the department's benefit, and support would be forthcoming. It really boiled down to: Why change? One position of the opposition was that the department and officers would lose control as community stakeholders became involved in the decision-making process. Struthers felt he was walking a tight rope with no room for error. As a supervisor he knew that he was part of management, and would be the key to problem resolution as change came into existence. He knew that he had to have answers. The focus of ambiguity was the real meaning of the partnership with the community. Those he supervised felt that the department would lose and that community stakeholders would dominate to the detriment of residents of the community. In general, the line officers wanted input during the discussion process, as well as during the implementation process. They wanted to remain law enforcement officers and not become social workers. So far, the resistance had been emotional rather than rational because of what was perceived as a lack of information. Eric telephoned his friend in another police department and found that under the umbrella of COP there was considerable variety in its actual implementation.

WHAT WOULD YOU DO?

What information would you need from those higher up in the chain of command? Explain. How would you go about determining the working relationship of line officers to community stakeholders? Is there an ideal working relationship between the two? If so, what is it? Why? How would you handle emotional resistance to the implementation of COP? Explain. Discuss why the new style of policing is superior to the traditional service orientation, if it is.

Change is kaleidoscopic in nature and an inevitable consequence of our energetic social system and the reaction of our law enforcement agencies to its dynamic elements. Every aspect of our lives is impacted by change and the police environment is no exception. Organizations are forced to change at a faster pace and more radically than ever before (Kotter & Cohen, 2002).

Our bodies of knowledge, social trends, officer expectations, more active participation by citizens, community trust, and demographics have had a resounding impact on police agencies (More, 2008; Office of Community Oriented Policing Services, 2009). At the same time, all of these trends have had a significant impact on organizational life within police departments. It is impossible to ignore change. It is a process that can be simple or convoluted, unhurried or rapid, but it must be confronted and dealt with (Leonard, 1997). Furthermore, it is both exciting and challenging for those involved in the change process on a daily basis (Kriegel & Brandt, 1997). It is a reality of the working environment in which policing occurs. One does not have to work long in a department to realize that very little is static. The names and places may change, and the dynamics of the situation exemplify anything but the status quo. At the same time, there is a significant difference between superficial and profound change. Change may be simple window dressing, a political expediency, or may alter the working relationships within the organization dramatically.

While change may make one uncomfortable, it will occur and must be accepted as part of the price one pays to work in a law enforcement bureaucracy. In fact, it is vital to the growth of a law enforcement agency. As a bureaucratic institution, the police usually respond to change rather than initiate it. In fact, change in law enforcement agencies has never been looked upon as a positive event. The dislike for significant change in law enforcement is endemic, and the typical authoritarian managerial style has stifled efforts at innovation and creativity. Police innovation has always had to confront resistance from within. If an organization is to change, there must be a change in the behavior of department members. Officers join an organization with certain expectations, and when those are confirmed, they have an investment in the organization with the expectation that things will continue to function in the same way. Relationships and commitments are made that provide a sense of stability and continuity. When crucial changes are announced, it can create a range of responses from uncertainty to out-and-out opposition (Moore & Stephens, 1991). Sustained organizational change will not occur unless the police organization acknowledges the potential impact of change, confronts the reality of organizing the department in such a way as to respond to community needs, and develops new departmental norms (DeParis, 1997). The reality is that over the years a great deal of the change in police departments has occurred when forces external to the department have clamored for change. The demands range from a political cataclysm to a significant event (Greenberg & Flynn, 2009).

It is necessary to realize that while the police have seldom fostered change, they are certainly reactors to it. Change must not only be met and accepted, but anticipated whenever possible, and finally it must be managed (Farias & Johnson, 2000). In fact, police managers should always anticipate the potential for continuing and constant resistance to the change process. This is especially true at the operational level (Zhao, 1996). Police planners can disclose the need to change, but the process seldom affects them. It is more normal for them to function as change agents. At the same time, police managers at high levels are somewhat distant from the reality of operational change. They foster change and are only affected indirectly. It is the first-line supervisor who must deal with the reality of change on a day-to-day basis, and it is at that level of operation where management has its greatest influence on officer behavior (Jerome, 2006).

A careful observer of the functions performed by a line supervisor will immediately acknowledge that practically everything pertinent to everyday police operations is concerned with implementing change. This can range from breaking in a new officer to implementing a new procedure. For example, it was not too many years ago that a bag of white powder found at an intersection was just kicked over to the gutter. Now it is treated as a hazardous materials spill and the intersection is closed, pending the arrival of experts and identification of the unknown substance. Currently, training is available so that officers can identify the presence of hazardous materials and initiate protective actions to ensure the safety of persons in the area (Hanson, 2007).

At one time, high-speed police pursuits of dangerous suspects were standard policy, but currently many departments are rethinking and standardizing pursuit policy because of the potential danger to the public. There is no question that a supervisor plays a key role by assuming control of a pursuit and monitoring the situation in most agencies (Illinois Law Enforcement Training and Standards Board, 2004; More, 2008).

It also has to be acknowledged that *real* organizational change is effectuated by first-line supervisors, not middle or upper management (Charrier, 2000). The ability to deal with change requires the application of numerous skills discussed throughout this text, including interpersonal communication, motivation, team building, training, and leadership. For officers to change, it is necessary to challenge their long-held beliefs, which can only be done by reconsidering and revising those beliefs. Most of us find change disconcerting. Some find it unwelcome. Those who have conducted research on organizational change suggest that approximately 10 percent of employees will actively embrace change. Eighty percent will wait to be convinced or wait until the change is unavoidable. The remaining 10 percent will actively resist change. For these people, change is very upsetting. In some cases, this latter group may even seek to subvert or sabotage the process.

Dissenters, in many instances, will not openly oppose changes that disturb and disrupt the way things have always been done, but will passively resist the proposed change by doing things just the way they have always done them. It is usually easy for the first-line supervisor to use the 10:80:10 ratios as a frame of reference for managing change. Because of their knowledge of those they supervise, potential supporters or detractors can be identified and strategies developed in order to ensure the fulfillment of the intended change. By working for consensus, an organizational environment will be created in which priorities can be set, timetables created, and programs implemented (Community Policing Consortium, 1998). When challenging the process of change, a supervisor should enable others to act and should strive to foster collaboration by promoting cooperative goals and building trust (French & Stewart, 2001).

Factors that Foster Change

Time itself implies change, and time becomes a proxy for maturation, growth, and learning. It affects not only the individual but also the organization (Pennings, 1997). Change does not occur in a vacuum, nor is it static. Change is synergistic and cumulative, often being called for in one area because it has taken place in another. For example, in recent years, numerous county or city jails have become so overcrowded that convicted offenders have been released early because of a court order. Currently, states are going through a similar problem and are confronted with large budget shortfalls; one state is considering releasing roughly 1000 inmates 90 days early (it costs the state $120 per day for each inmate). Another state is considering reducing its inmate population by one-third, and the newly released inmates would become a problem for sheriffs, police, parole agents, and probation officers, severely affecting local jails because of the propensity to reoffend (Green, 2009). Another indirect impact has been the implementation of a new policy, in some departments, when minor offenders are cited rather than booked. While a supervisor might believe that, in a particular instance, the accused would (in all probability) benefit from incarceration and society would be protected, it cannot be done because of conditions that are beyond the control of any first-line supervisor or the department.

Change places many demands upon supervisors and includes factors that range from changing *work values* to the increasing power of police unions, technological change, and a constantly changing legal system (Figure 7.1).

1. Legal system
2. Work values
3. Technology
4. Unions

FIGURE 7.1 Factors that foster change.

Legal System

Without question, change has both rational and emotional aspects that a supervisor is expected to deal with, which is certainly true when dealing with the legal system (Leban, 2007). The law conditions and reconditions the functions performed by the police. "All you have to do is wait for the next session of the U.S. Supreme Court and you will have to change the way you enforce the law" is a common complaint of many officers. Other problems are the ambiguity and vagueness of the law. The language of some statutes is so unclear that the courts must interpret it, but this is usually done after the fact, not before. The officer on the street is continually faced with the problem of enforcing the law and then accepting the consequences if the decision is questioned.

Other laws are obsolete and outmoded but are still on the books. In practice, the police are expected to enforce all laws; however, many are unenforced and routinely disregarded. Occasionally police officers are criticized because they do not enforce a law. This usually occurs with sumptuary laws involving gambling. In one case, in which the police department was not enforcing the law, bingo games were being sponsored as a means of raising funds for charity by several churches and organizations such as the Elks. Before the issue receded from the front page of the newspaper, it was necessary to change the state statute on gambling to exempt bingo.

Actually, it would seem that the United States has become a society inundated by laws. The policy seems to be that if there is something we do not like, then we must pass a law against it. At the focal point of this landslide of laws, one finds the members of patrol units. Undoubtedly, there are too many criminal laws. There are too many purely personal activities involving law violations that should not be within the purview of the law (i.e., social gambling in a private residence).

This is obviously true in the area of victimless crimes where, in general, enforcement is limited, but the police must deal with it as a continuing issue when working the streets. Political pressure can alter enforcement of victimless crimes overnight as a specific crime becomes a headline and the mayor's office becomes unglued. It seems strange for an officer to ignore a minor drug violation or sexual offense one day and be expected to enforce the violation fully of the law the next day. It is the ambiguity of the whole process that is of concern to the officer, as the process is nonpredictable and such changes are not only frustrating, but also difficult to handle.

Work Values

There is rapid and constant change occurring in our social, political, and economic environments that affect organizations and individuals (Harigopal, 2006). In turn, these changes affect work values that are principles that guide individuals in their professional context. Not only are organizations changing, so are people within law enforcement agencies. In actuality, work values provide a frame of reference on how an officer relates to co-workers, supervisors, and consumers. Identifiable values include autonomy, competiveness, dedication, ethics, loyalty, professionalism, punctuality, remunerative worth, and team player. They provide the context within which a supervisor has to respond to those supervised and the intensity of each principle proves to be modified by other values, such as personal, social, and cultural. It is the milieu that confronts a supervisor that places demands that are new compared to those that operate when one is working as a street cop or a member of a team. It calls for a transformation from doing something yourself to accomplishing things through others—keeping in mind the governing work values of each officer (Career Services, 2009).

Change is a continual process that at times can be gradual, but sometimes is rapid. Within an organization, change can be supported or resisted. The more bureaucratic the department, the more it will resist change. The larger the department, the more likely that supervisors will be confronted by barriers that impede change.

The majority of first-line supervisors are selected from their own department—thus, they normally have a somewhat narrow view of the variety of ways in which a task can be accomplished. The manager's view is usually predicated on a maze of rules and regulations that they have been responsible for developing and implementing. Thus, management's view can easily become one that says, "This is the way that it will be done because it has always been done this way."

It is more than a marriage of convenience; it is a deep commitment to the status quo. Strict interpretation of rules and regulations is a must. First-line supervisors generally have a work value system that differs from line personnel. Generally, they are at least five to 15 years older, and their attitudes toward the organization are more set.

The image of a good police officer has changed because of necessity. No longer is the primary criterion for selection based on "give me someone with a lot of strength and muscle." Today's image is as diverse as the culture in many of our communities. Officers come in all shapes and sizes, not just those who are six feet tall and perceived as being able to handle themselves in a barroom brawl.

Today's officer is apt to be better educated, more intelligent, emotionally stable, and more compassionate than many of those in positions of higher authority. Rigorous selection criteria, based on an array of examinations and tests, ranging from psychiatric to polygraph, result in the selection of candidates who are highly qualified. With this changing nature of the workforce, it is no longer appropriate to treat every employee the same way. Increasing diversity—age, gender, race, and ethnicity—has important implications for how a supervisor should deal with the new breed of officer. Supervisors will have to find ways to support the desire of employees to use their skills and expertise. Officers must be given a variety of tasks and must be allowed to use them to find their job satisfying (DeSantis & Durst, 1998).

Younger officers are more likely to be dissatisfied with departmental policies that require them to "go by the book" at all times, regardless of circumstances. Many of these officers perceive absolute conformity as stifling initiative, but soon find that implementing discretion can only result in being written up by a supervisor or someone else in the chain of command.

Today's line officer is more apt to have been raised in a lenient family setting and is less likely to have spent time in the military. These two factors, coupled with less rigid schooling, have resulted in many officers never having experienced a no-nonsense leadership style that demands unquestioning obedience and absolute compliance with orders. It has been shocking and decidedly unsettling to many young officers to be treated as a mere cog in the wheel and to have their opinions ignored.

Today's line officer has needs and expectations that are not met in a police department that is extremely bureaucratic and structured along traditional paramilitary lines. The values and attitudes of line officers are different from those of earlier generations. Supervisors cannot live in the past or yearn for the "good old days" when those supervised were more pliable, willing to accept authority, and take orders without question.

Supervisors must adjust to situations that they find undesirable. When values differ greatly between those supervised and those supervising, conflict is inevitable. Line officers have demonstrated their frustration by defying management in different ways, including marching in front of city hall in opposition to working conditions.

One of the main targets of officers has been oppressive and exceedingly detailed departmental policies. These conditions often make officers feel as though they are "just a number" and powerless. When treated with such indifference they feel like nonentities. As political and social conditions affect an agency, departmental policies change and consistency becomes the exception rather than the rule (Leonard, 1997). Placed in this situation, the first-line supervisor again becomes the reactor to change and must serve as the mediator and implementer between those supervised and top management.

Technology

Law enforcement agencies have been strongly influenced by technological change. This has occurred to such an extent that it can be labeled as almost revolutionary in nature. New techniques and equipment abound, knowledge has exploded, and there are an increasing number of specialists working to police our nation. Information technology has the potential to become the most important global transformation since the industrial revolution (Youngs, 2003). Technological innovation includes such things as computerized records management software, automated fingerprint identification, DNA, patrol car video systems, evidentiary breath testers, biometric recognition, robots, voice mail, integrated ballistics identification, handheld computers, global positioning, wireless devices, COMPSTAT, intelligence policing, less lethal technologies, imaging, the auto arrestor system, checkpoint barrier strip, and crime data analysis, to name a few (National Law Enforcement and Corrections Technology Center, 1995). The mastery of technology as it applies to information, with its exponential growth, and its current delivery systems exacerbates the revolution that confronts law enforcement. The future is upon us and it will be necessary for the first-line supervisor to develop the skills needed to keep up with and manage the rapidly increasing change and recurrent change that technology is forcing upon us (Blair, Kamaby, & Zone, 2007).

Unions

Police unions are powerful organizations in most cities and exercise a great deal of power not only within the department, but also within communities. They have a great deal of influence over their members and within legislative chambers. In many instances, police unions have fostered the insularity that characterizes the police culture. Union representatives, over the years, have opposed commissions that were responsible for the investigation of police corruption. In New York City during the Mollen Commission investigation, such action created a negative attitude toward the investigative process and reinforced the public's cynicism toward members of the department, as well as enhancing departmental insularity. Just after the commission began its inquiries, the Captains Benevolent Association initiated a lawsuit to dissolve the commission (Mollen, 1994). However, there is a positive side to police unionization. When police management has proven to be capricious, incongruent, or antagonistic to agency personnel, the response nationwide has been to unionize. Unions have, in many instances, been responsible for departments developing positive personnel programs. Overall, police unions have done much to increase the pride and professionalization of police officers.

Consequently, line officers have shown increasing support for labor unions. It has been estimated that 73 percent of the nation's police officers are represented by some form of association or union (More, 1998). One major organization is the National Association of Police Organizations (NAPO), which is a coalition of law enforcement unions and associations and represents 2000 police unions and associations with an estimated membership of 241,000 sworn law enforcement officers, 11,000 retired officers, and 100,000 citizens who share a common dedication to fair and effective crime control and law enforcement (National Association of Police Organization, 2012). This group advances the interests of law enforcement through legislative and legal advocacy. It does not take a new officer long to realize that there is strength in numbers. A police union is viewed as a way to fight for improved working conditions, institute grievance procedures, or have a say in the management of the organization.

Police officers have willingly accepted union leadership when it has led to the opportunity to participate in decisions that affect their future, provide for some semblance of economic security, and challenge the autocratic power of police managers. Collective bargaining, a process by which the department and the union negotiate a formal written agreement about wages, hours, and working conditions, is legal in about one-half of the United States and has become a means of clarifying management rights. In one study, 51 percent of the law enforcement agencies worked under a formal contract negotiated under enabling state law, and 18 percent operated under a memorandum of understanding (DeLord & Sanders, 2006). Some of the primary interests of police employee organizations are to have a voice in policy making and to improve benefits, including salaries, overtime, compensation time, pensions, paid holidays, health insurance, life insurance, and court time and tuition reimbursement. In more recent years, it has become increasingly evident that cooperation between police executives and union representatives has become more frequent, but in a recent study, 60 percent of the union representatives stated that they had not been consulted regarding complaints filed by citizens, and 59 percent had not been consulted regarding the assignment of officers.

Police unions have viewed collective bargaining as the best means of checking or stalemating the abuse of power by police managers. Unions have been successful in altering rules and regulations, and it is quite common for unions to bargain for the right to review new policies before their implementation. Some 32 percent of union representatives said they did not confer with the administration regarding updating policy manuals. Of special interest is that, concerning supervisory issues, 39 percent of the chiefs indicated they did not confer with representatives of a union/association (DeLord & Sanders, 2006).

Active support of police unions increases daily because officers view administration as far apart from line officers and nonsupportive. In many instances, unions battle for control of the police department and influence the appointment of a new chief of police. There certainly are departments that do not fit this description, but enough exist to call into question the relationship between line officers and managers.

It does not take an officer long to learn that it is necessary to safely cover all personal actions. In many instances, bureaucratic restrictions protect top-level supervisors to the detriment of line officers. Another issue in collective bargaining involves first-line supervisors and whether they should be considered a part of management or labor. The answer is self-evident because a sergeant is a manager and an integral part of the management team. Most authorities agree that under no circumstances should a supervisor be a part of a line-bargaining unit.

Police unions cannot be ignored if organizational change is to occur. Police executives should explain their rationale and concerns to union leaders so that a collaborative effort can be directed toward implementation of the change process. Recommended changes, if not thought through carefully, can conflict with contractual issues, such as staffing requirements, shift assignments, disciplinary procedures, or promotional criteria. Unions must be involved in planned organizational change and should not have to find out about something after the fact. First-line supervisors should interact with union representatives, explaining the rationale for the change and stressing the need to work together (Glensor & Peak, 1996). In one police department, the police union was successful in eliminating implementation of an early warning system designed to monitor officer behavior. In this instance, the union was not involved in the planning and implementation of the system.

Positive Aspects of Change

The first-line supervisor deals with the reality of change from two perspectives. First, the sergeant is usually the person who interprets new policies, and is placed in the position of spokesperson for management. However, supervisors are concerned because the primary work group that deals with those new policies on a continuing basis is composed of line officers. Their concern must be dealt with if the squad of officers is to operate effectively. It surprises new officers to find out that the main person to consult for advice on these matters is the immediate supervisor, not top managers. Beyond an occasional roll-call session or a major emergency, higher-ranked officers in the department are seldom seen.

The sergeant whose supervisory style exemplifies objectivity, fairness, and concern for subordinate welfare will soon find that not all change is resisted. Not many organizations accept change as readily as law enforcement agencies. The police are subject to continual change from external agencies, and their greatest displeasure would seem to be with the failure of police managers to adapt to changing times.

The average police officer takes the position that the police department fails to provide an environment that satisfies important personnel needs. It is the quality of work life that takes priority in satisfying the need system of officers. The job is viewed as dominant and the positive feelings generated by the job lead to increased job satisfaction.

One study found that when examining the actual police job, the most important characteristic (as perceived by the employees) was the feeling that the job was important and yielded a feeling of accomplishment. Job satisfaction differs for each employee, but studies seem to confirm that essential elements include a wide range of ambient factors, such as relationships and the type of supervision. Several of these variables are listed in Figure 7.2.

In a recent study of police officers, it was found that more experienced officers, who were skilled in interacting with the community, had greater job satisfaction (Gorenak, 2004). In another study of an urban sheriff's department, a comparison of detectives with other officers revealed that detectives experienced more satisfaction with all aspects of their job, which was expected given their greater autonomy, greater task variety, and higher pay. In addition, involvement in COP was highly correlated with job satisfaction, although this varied by the amount of importance placed on COP by the department (Barnes, Sheley, Logsdon, & Sutherland, 2003). In another study of small police departments, the researchers concluded that there was an apparent connection between stress and overall job satisfaction. It was also determined that higher stress levels often affect those on rotating shifts, and officers' perceptions of departmental morale impacted the levels of overall job satisfaction (Julseth, Ruiz, & Hummer, 2011).

As it stands now, still much is unknown when one considers employee attitudes and job satisfaction, but some promising research suggests what is important is the perception of the

1.	Achievement	7.	Compensation
2.	Administration	8.	Interaction
3.	Advancement	9.	Management
4.	Answerability	10.	Resources
5.	Challenge	11.	Workload
6.	Comfort		

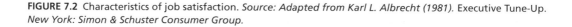

FIGURE 7.2 Characteristics of job satisfaction. *Source: Adapted from Karl L. Albrecht (1981). Executive Tune-Up. New York: Simon & Schuster Consumer Group.*

job itself, which is related to core self-evaluation traits—self-esteem, generalized self-efficacy, locus of control, and emotional stability—with job performance and job satisfaction (Judge & Bono, 2001). Further research in this area has identified two other personality traits—extraversion and conscientiousness—that affect job satisfaction directly (Judge, Heller, & Mount, 2002). There is also evidence that dissatisfaction resulting from one's job can spill over into one's life satisfaction (Wheaton, 1990). Hence, one possible conclusion is that organizations only have so much control over a person's job satisfaction (Sarri & Judge, 2004).

The supervisor must work with these variables and identify those that are important to each individual and then strive to achieve selected departmental goals by optimizing worker needs and reducing undesirable side effects.

Pending clarifying research, when the variables listed earlier are recognized and handled with dispatch, there is less likelihood of negative reaction to change. Unfortunately, this particular negativism will always overshadow the positive aspects because it seems that bad news is always of greater interest than good news. Officers are not, by nature, antichange in their approach to new situations, but they can become burned out to the point where they become negative in their outlook toward life and their job. If this is allowed to happen, police management has lost its chance to tap its most important resource: its employees.

Officers are certainly adaptable to change and will accept it more readily when involved in the decision-making process. If officers are informed, resistance will be less when they know that changes are being made and know the advantages of the changes (White & Chapman, 1996). If supervisors accept this premise, they can then proceed to determine reasons for resistance when it occurs and confront it objectively (Harvey, 1995).

Accepting Change

Reasons for acceding to change vary considerably and are listed in Figure 7.3 (Gray, 1984).

An important feature of change is the prospect of *alternatives*. If individuals are knowledgeable about the consequences of the change, a decision to accept is more apt to occur because it is something they want to do, not something they have been forced to accept. *Alternatives* imply the possibility of rejection, but providing adequate information and involving members in the decision-making process can foster a positive response to selection of an alternative.

Another reason for accepting change is that the event can create *enhancement*. This is especially true if a change improves working conditions; it becomes immediately acceptable to

1. Alternatives
2. Enhancement
3. Knowledgeable
4. Need is fulfilled
5. Planned

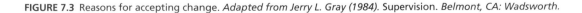

FIGURE 7.3 Reasons for accepting change. *Adapted from Jerry L. Gray (1984).* Supervision. *Belmont, CA: Wadsworth.*

most officers. For instance, after having driven a squad car for more than 100,000 miles, it is a great feeling to get behind the wheel of a new vehicle. The same concept applies to working conditions when, for example, a city adopts computer-aided dispatching, allowing the officer to respond more quickly.

When officers are to be impacted by change, acquiescence is more apt to occur when they are *knowledgeable*. It is reassuring to know all pertinent facts right from the start. It is disconcerting when a decision has been made that affects the way officers are required to operate, but which was discovered after the fact. With today's means of communicating, there is every reason for management to keep its employees fully informed. In fact, it can be suggested that in the majority of instances, too much information will prove to be helpful rather than detrimental. When one is aware of all operations, it reduces anxiety.

When a fundamental need is fulfilled, change becomes readily acceptable to those affected. If an officer has a need satisfied by a change, there is less reason to anticipate resistance to the change. Each person has needs that the job can fulfill. This can vary from providing greater self-esteem to improved job satisfaction. It is believed that when management meets the majority of officer needs, there will be a decrease in absenteeism and turnover. In addition, it is theorized that there will be increased productivity and fewer accidents. When events or situations are *planned* for, acceptability is enhanced.

When change becomes necessary, it is important to plan for it rather than to react to it. Planned change acknowledges that officers will be affected and any alteration of policy or procedure can have a positive or negative impact. When, for example, computers are introduced into patrol cars, they affect not only the officers, but the entire department, including records, dispatching, and even deployment of personnel.

With the changing composition of many police departments, it is essential to plan for social changes. The introduction of women into patrol units, preferential selection of employees who are bilingual, and promotion of officers to obtain racial balance are all programs that require careful planning for implementation. Such programs must be monitored carefully and adjusted when necessary. When fully aware of the reasons why officers accept change, the first-line supervisor is in a better position to deal with the variables that support, rather than impede, change.

Resistance to Change

Change can occur because of a wide range of contingencies. It can be from such things as confusion, denial, or even silence (Maurer, 2005). There is a great deal of speculation as to why people resist change. One author postulated that there were at least 33 reasons that individuals were resistant to change, ranging from homeostasis to human mindlessness (O'Toole, 1996). A clear understanding of the reasons officers resist change will allow a supervisor the opportunity to deal with *resistance*. When a change is viewed as threatening, most employees will resist it.

If the change is immaterial or of no consequence, it will, in all probability, not be resisted. If, in fact, the change proves to be supportive or helpful, everyone will most likely welcome it.

Resistance to change is viewed mainly as an effort to maintain the status quo. In part, resistance occurs because of the fear of the unknown. It may be thought that a new procedure may be more difficult to use than the current system. Acceptance of many change efforts can be thwarted unless it is totally supported by top management. It is also essential to communicate a change effort to all involved in the organization, especially when it is a major shift in policy or procedures that will affect the culture of the organization. Needless to say, officers must receive effective training concerning expected changes. Nothing can be left to chance. It will be necessary to hold meetings in order to orient personnel about the changes and to convince officers that the changes are beneficial and important not only to them, but also to the organization. Officers need to be told about their proposed responsibilities and duties. This is especially true when basic assumptions about the police function have to be changed and there is a transition from a traditional system to one that emphasizes newer concepts (Alpert, Kenney, & Oettemier, 1998).

When change is implemented operationally, it may require members of the organization to behave in an entirely different manner, require more effort, or require officers to learn new things. It might be associated with the creation of a new working environment and seem to contain a number of imponderables that affect how officers perceive things and, above all, how they affect their personal well-being. In other words, is there a loss, tangible or intangible (Mastrofski, 2007)?

Additionally, it might be a question of whether the change is *worth it*. The gain may not be worth the conflict created by the change (Tosi, Rizzo, & Carroll, 1994).

Resistance takes many forms and can range from just ignoring something to open resistance (De Meuse & McDaris, 1994). In one police agency involved in a pay dispute, most of the officers left the state so they would not be served a court order to require them to return to work. In another instance, officers enforced traffic regulations to the maximum, causing a public outcry when the resulting traffic jams created havoc in the downtown area. Figure 7.4 lists some of the reasons employees resist change.

Ambiguity

Because the effects of change are often unknown, officers are more apt to oppose it when there is doubt as to the possible consequences. When ambiguity is pervasive, the greater the

---

1. Ambiguity
2. Cultural reasons
3. Discretion is restricted or eliminated
4. Economic reasons
5. Habits are altered
6. Relationships are restricted
7. Unpopular decisions

FIGURE 7.4 Resistance to change.

possibility is for resistance. Most officers soon learn that one positive value of numerous rules and regulations is the tendency to create stability and to reduce uncertainty. When things are done *by the book*, each officer is provided with guidance, increasing the probability that the outcome is known and predictable. Change, especially when it is extensive, can disturb or disrupt established procedures and generate resistance (Ortiz, 1994).

If a specific change is looked upon as creating uncertainty (although there is no evidence to support this conclusion), it will make most officers anxious about the new change. If a proposed change is slight or viewed with indifference, officers will be more likely to accept it, especially if they perceive the change as being somewhat beneficial. Again, however, there is no evidence to support such a position. If positive management practices are to occur, ambiguity must be confronted and supportive *change maker* leadership internalized (Dale, 2000). Normally it is a question of resolving uncertainty and reinforcing the positive aspects of a proposed change.

Cultural Reasons

The police culture is unique, deep seated, and powerful. Through the years, a distinct social orientation has developed within police organizations. Values, attitudes, expectations, norms, and behavioral patterns are transmitted from one officer to the next and become operational reality. Figure 7.5 sets forth a number of characteristics of police subculture. The typical culture of a police organization develops certain values, and longtime members feel that the way their organization approaches problems is the only way it should be done. Attitudes and values support the customary way of doing things (Cohen & Fink, 2002). To conceive of other ways of doing something is usually perceived as wasteful, so it is resisted. Organizational culture reinforces the need to do something the way it has always been done—it has worked for many years, so why change?

Discretion is Restricted or Eliminated

In many instances, management will take steps to spell out authority, responsibility, and accountability in an effort to circumscribe and limit the power of line officers. In most instances, predictability becomes a means to an end, and discretion is viewed as inescapable and controlled in every instance. The bureaucracy must prevail and must never be subjected

1. Code of silence	8.	Organizational norms
2. Cohesiveness	9.	Protectors
3. Common values	10.	Secrecy
4. Conformity	11.	Shared attitudes
5. Group mores	12.	Social orientation
6. Insularity	13.	Solidarity
7. Loyalty	14.	Taboos

FIGURE 7.5 Attributes of the police subculture.

to criticism. Reporting procedures are spelled out carefully in minute detail, and rules and regulations abound. This can include how long your hair should be or whether or not you can have tattoos. The more discretion is controlled, the greater the amount of power that the line officer loses in the process. Street cops generally feel that excessive control limits their ability to perform effectively, especially when it involves such a thing as clearing every arrest with the immediate supervisor. Managers (especially those at the top) are perceived as bureaucrats who have lost touch with street reality and have forsaken line personnel (Chemerinsky et al., 2000). The freedom to act when confronted with uncertainty is viewed by many officers as paramount to providing the public with quality police services to enhance their safety.

Economic Reasons

Money (in terms of salaries and fringe benefits) is a key issue for most police officers. This is especially noticed when income is below what is considered par. If officers know that neighboring agencies have higher pay levels, they are more likely to engage in activities that are adverse to the department. This can involve income from the job or income earned when off duty (Young, 2006).

If the city moves to reduce or eliminate overtime pay, it can be a definite threat to an officer's welfare. In agencies that allow overtime to become an integral part of the payroll, an elimination or reduction will have an immediate and negative impact on the lifestyle of each officer. The same can occur when city councils reduce fringe benefits, such as dental, medical, or retirement benefits, which have become an integral part of a pay package. One California sheriff's office increased its retirement benefits from 2 to 3 percent annually. This means that an officer at age 65, after 25 years of service, can retire at 75 percent of his or her salary. This, along with a significant pay raise, occurred because so many deputies were transferring laterally to obtain a living wage.

Money weighs heavily in officers' decisions to resist change. If any part of a pay package is threatened, it is difficult to imagine that it would not be met with collective resistance. This has increasingly been done through associations or unions. Like other occupations, officers have found that a united response will generally produce results when compared with individual efforts to right a perceived monetary wrong.

Habits are Altered

Individual resistance to change can stem from something as simple as habit (Tichy & Devanna, 1997). Officers become comfortable doing something a certain way, prefer to keep things the way they are, and see no reason to change. This is especially true if the officers receive satisfaction from a habit that is firmly established.

If officers are required to learn new skills to perform their job, but it is not viewed as an improvement over the way they are currently doing it, resistance will occur. There is comfort in doing things in a familiar way. The greater the chances of change altering an established habit, the greater the possibility that it will be resisted. Change causes losses and people resist, in many instances because of the loss, not the actual change itself (Bridges & Bridges, 2009).

Relationships are Restricted

With the exception of certain shifts or areas of a community, it has become increasingly common for officers to work alone. The result is that social relationships between officers become very important. Generally, officers will go to great efforts to socialize with fellow officers by eating meals together, taking breaks at locations where other officers gather, getting together at the end of a shift, or engaging in off-duty activities together.

Most officers generally resist efforts by management to restrict or limit social interaction. Group norms determine behavior and can be the most difficult source of resistance for managers to control. Because patrol officers are usually isolated from the community, they turn to each other for support. The result is development of a police subculture in which common occupational values come into existence. Officers readily share job-coping techniques in an effort to deal with policies that affect social relationships negatively.

A change in organizational structure may be resisted if it revises or alters working relationships between officers. An example is a department in which officers have traditionally had the responsibility of coordinating certain types of investigations with neighboring beat officers when circumstances dictated. A new policy provided that investigators would now be responsible for coordinating such investigations. An immediate and vociferous resistance scuttled what management perceived as a needed reform.

Unpopular Decisions

All managers must, at some time, make an unpopular decision, which is certainly true of first-line supervisors. Certain decisions seem to be of more concern than others, and it is important to know which managerial decisions might cause dissent and how one might work to obtain compliance when it is known in advance that a decision will be unpopular. Top police managers readily realize that first-line supervisors are responsible for ensuring policy compliance (Charrier, 2004).

Just as important is the need to determine what action employees will take when an unpopular decision is first announced. One study identified the following three situations as unpopular managerial decisions: actions dealing with discipline, changes in work schedules, and changes affecting salaries (Malik & Wexley, 1986).

Compliance-gaining techniques vary depending on the situation, but the most effective technique is to give officers adequate justification for the decision. Next (in terms of reducing resistance) is the technique of obtaining input from officers before issuing what is known will be an unpopular decision.

It should be noted that, in general, the more highly educated the officers and the greater their career longevity, the more likely they are to want some justification of, or input into, the decision-making process. It is also important to note that the majority of officers will not take overt actions when responding to unpopular decisions. The decision is either accepted without dissent because management is perceived as having the authority to make it or the resistance increases in proportion to the unpopularity of the decision.

The police academy transmits attributes of the subculture. New officers are taught how to act, think, and feel as they are inculcated into the police subculture. When they hit the streets, on-the-job experience reinforces values of the formal organization, and new officers are introduced to influences of the informal organization. Officers share a common language and argot of the profession (More, Vito, & Walsh, 2013). They are loyal to each other, and the realities of police work reinforce their commitment to each other.

As proud members of the "thin blue line," they perceive themselves as the true protectors of society. Officers soon see the need for secrecy, and "the code of silence" further isolates the police from the community (Chemerinsky et al., 2000). Additionally, the isolation of the police, loyalty ethic, and esprit de corps serve as pillars of socializing officers into the police subculture (Mollen, 1994).

Law enforcement has traditionally demanded conformity, making the organizational culture unreceptive to change (Tichy & Devanna, 1997). Changing the culture of a police organization is not only difficult, but can be a long-range proposition. Management must be committed to change—it cannot be mere lip service, which can only be accomplished by a strong commitment at every level of management within the organization. If change is to occur, it is essential to build a foundation for the change by convincing others of the essentiality of the change efforts (Switzer, 2003). Above all, change will have a limited prospective for implementation unless it is supported by first-line supervisors (Ortiz, 1994). Features present in law enforcement agencies reinforce the need for the first-line supervisor to be aware of the uniqueness of the police social system and work within that system to foster change. In view of the individuality of cultural impact, a supervisor is advised to work with each officer before engaging in group discussions. The best results are obtained when significant change is phased in over time in order to allow for individual adjustment. Mandated change, catchy phrases, or buzzwords tend to hinder change rather than promote it (Mulder, 1994).

The Nature of Resistance

Resistance to change can, at times, be completely *rational* and have no emotional basis whatsoever. When first challenged with a proposed or actual change, officers have, in some instances, become immediately aware that a new procedure will create more problems than it will resolve. This form of resistance should be viewed as something to enhance the change process, as it results in an in-depth analysis of the problem. A first-line supervisor should analyze a change carefully to see if there might be a real basis for rational resistance. When identified as such, the resulting conflict can be utilized to alter the change so that line personnel as well as management can support it.

For example, officers in one agency resisted a new procedure for booking youthful offenders in juvenile hall. While it simplified the booking process for probation personnel, it doubled the time that police officers had to devote to their booking process. In this instance, the proposed procedures were altered to the satisfaction of both agencies and all personnel.

"Emotional" resistance to change presents the supervisor with an entirely different problem. In some instances, the problem seems to be with the first-line supervisor, who may view a proposed change as beneficial to everyone involved, but officers view it differently.

Because the perception of change is usually individual rather than collective, it is essential for a supervisor to try to understand how others view the change (Gray, 1984). In one department, a change in radio procedures received negative reactions because line personnel believed that dispatchers were given too much authority. An analysis of the resulting conflict determined that the resistance was emotionally based because officers felt that it limited their control of emergencies and was the first of multiple efforts to restrict their authority. It was the position of management, however, that the proposed change would enhance officer security.

Supervisors must distinguish between rational and emotional resistance if organizational change is to be accomplished. If a supervisor makes a serious effort to distinguish between the two types of resistance, it can then be handled to the benefit of all concerned. In some instances, providing officers with more information might serve to resolve the problem, whereas in other situations, the supervisor may need to deal directly with each officer in an effort to determine the reason for resistance.

In addition, a supervisor should keep in mind that what might be construed as line officer resistance might not be the actual case. Adapting to a new culture is difficult, and officers may just be making an effort to determine if a new program or policy is viable and what effect it will actually have on each of them. There should be a reasonable adjustment period during which line officers can be allowed to assess proposed changes and be allowed to obtain additional information that will assist them in the transition process. It is normal for people to want to *check things out* and really see how changes impact their daily working life (Haught, 1998).

It is essential that first-line supervisors remain focused on the fundamental issues of any change process. Under no circumstances should they take acts of resistance personally. Overreacting to backlash is an intolerable reaction. Conflict should be worked through, and it is essential that all issues are discussed openly. Some conflict is inevitable due to the competing demands within the organization and the competitive nature of human beings. Fortunately, most of the potentially damaging conflict that occurs is preventable. Managed conflict can reveal and clarify problems, improve problem solutions, and promote growth. Conflict can be positive when it helps the first-line supervisor ameliorate or eliminate negative attitudes and feelings, correct misunderstandings, and generate the commitment for change (Tracey, 1990).

Working for Change

Resistance must be identified before it can be handled properly. Solutions to the resistance problem may be as simple as providing those in opposition with more information or, at the other extreme, involving personnel in the decision-making process. It has become increasingly

1. Being knowledgeable
2. Communication
3. Involvement
4. Informal leaders
5. Mandated change

FIGURE 7.6 Working for change.

common to be almost constantly involved in some type of change process. In some instances, the consequences of change are identified as having the potential for limited impact. In other situations, it can be interpreted as being potentially harmful. Finally, there may be no way of determining what will happen when a change occurs.

If several changes occur at the same time, the problem of dealing with resistance can become quite complex. At this point, it becomes necessary for those who are working for change to use more than one strategy when making an effort to overcome resistance to change. If the supervisor is part of management (and not apart from it), there is a greater potential for being involved in the planning that precedes change. If not, the first-line supervisor will be at a definite disadvantage. Dealing with conflict occurs after the fact and limits the alternatives the supervisor can use.

Whatever the realities of the situation, there are techniques a supervisor can use when attempting to defuse situations that can develop into resistance to change. There are always forces that support the belief that no change is good change. However, change for the sake of changing is of questionable value. It is somewhat like managers who feel they have to be at the forefront, always involved in implementing the latest fad whether it works or not.

The first-line supervisor is not in a position to resolve every occurrence that creates resistance, nor will his or her use of a specific technique always be successful. In other words, there is no proven method that will sell change successfully, but some techniques have proven to be more successful than others. Some of these methods are discussed in Figure 7.6.

Being Knowledgeable

Ignorance might be bliss, but it is out of place when a supervisor is working to develop a strategy for selling change. Because change seldom occurs without stimulation from management, supervisors must take the view that change must be sold. Before a person can be convinced that a change should occur, it is necessary to gather and assimilate all the available facts regarding any proposal. It takes work to become knowledgeable about a proposed change, and it takes time to acquire information. This is especially pertinent when change drastically alters the current habits of officers or their social relationships.

Above all, officers must always be apprised of pending changes and given as much information as possible. To do less is to create an atmosphere of distrust, in which rumors will become rampant. Rumors can negatively affect the working environment and the general process of planned change. Supervisors must work diligently to keep channels of communication open and deal directly with rumors. When rumors are not confronted with accurate and complete information, they can cause irreparable damage to the change process (White & Chapman, 1996).

Human behavior is complex, so a supervisor should develop more than one strategy for fostering desired change, keeping in mind the critical elements of Hu-TACK. The advantages and disadvantages of each alternative should be reviewed, and the strategy with the greatest promise should be selected (Cameron & Green, 2004). In one instance, a sergeant (who had the complete support of management) considered several alternatives and finally decided that the greatest resistance would come from three informal leaders within the department. Meeting with them on an individual basis to explain the change before presenting the new proposal at roll call was felt to be the best strategy to enhance its implementation.

Communication

Without communication, a proposal to implement a new policy or any other type of change will, in all probability, have a limited chance of succeeding. In most instances, keeping channels of communication open will provide a supervisor with information to be utilized when working at change implementation (Farias & Johnson, 2000). In most instances, change generates an emotional response that can range from mild to extreme, depending on the extent of the impact that it will have on individuals and how much it will alter working relationships. As a means of dealing with this, the supervisor should listen actively to every officer and respond accordingly. The supervisor should encourage a free flow of information. Letting the officer tell you what he or she thinks does this best. At this point, careful listening is imperative and there is a need to demonstrate a real interest in what is being said. The supervisor should ask open-ended questions and phrase them in such a way that the officer cannot answer with a simple *yes* or *no*. An actual dialogue must occur. This serves as a ventilating process and provides for the exchange of particulars and the reduction of emotions.

Even over-communication will generally prove to be beneficial, although it can create unnecessary employee anxiety. This will be especially so if the information involves a change in working conditions. While it can be argued that waiting until more information can be obtained would upset a number of employees, it is still a judgment call. Evidence would seem to support the importance of communication as much as possible and as soon as possible (Gray, 1984).

When officers know that management has made every effort to maintain and foster open communication, it will reduce resistance and provide them with greater prospects of implementing change. Efforts to restrict the flow of information can only enhance resistance and reinforce the informal organization. In such a situation, the grapevine will soon prevail and rumors will abound.

As a supervisor, it is essential to make a compelling case for any proposed change. Everything possible should be done to communicate every aspect of the change to those supervised. Every technique should be utilized to convey information about the change, including team meetings, roll-call sessions, personal contacts, email, and memorandums. A key is to address not only what is being done, but also why it is being done. As a supervisor, you should never assume that the reasons for change are obvious—"communicate–communicate–communicate."

Involvement

The potential for creating a positive environment that will be more receptive to a proposed change is enhanced by involving those who will be most affected by it. This is not to suggest that this will always succeed, but experience has shown that the advantages of this technique outweigh the disadvantages. Those involved in the change process are in a position to use facts to combat rumors and erroneous information. Another important feature is the reduction or elimination of anxiety as officers become less concerned about pending change (Gray, 1984).

Involvement reduces resistance because the unknown becomes the known. It is important that those who will be affected become knowledgeable about why a specified change is needed and are made aware of the advantages of the change. Including employees in discussions about change does this best. When the decision is made to involve personnel in the change process, it is imperative for management to totally support the implementation of such a program. Open communications and involvement of line personnel can alert managers to potential problems that might arise when the change is implemented. Lip service or the tactic of manipulation will, in short order, weaken or destroy future efforts to involve personnel in the decision-making process. In many departments, street cops have been highly successful at thwarting change that has been forced upon them by management. In fact, the ingenuity of officers in opposing change has resulted in the failure of numerous programs as departments have instituted the "fads" of the day (Skolnick & Fyfe, 1995).

Because participation is time-consuming, the rewards should exceed the costs. This brings up the question of when, during the decision-making process, affected employees should be involved. There is no simple answer, but in general, it has been found that participation can be maximized if management has done its homework efficiently and gathered all data needed to initiate a positive participation process.

In many instances, it will be important to spell out that participation will be limited to the specific topic under consideration. This sets limits that allow for a freer exchange of ideas and keep the decision-making process on target. As involvement becomes a part of the leadership style, the supervisor may find that some subordinates feel most comfortable when they are not involved in the decision-making process. However, what is of utmost importance to many subordinates is being given an opportunity to be involved if they so desire and becoming knowledgeable about proposed changes. When employees are involved in deciding how to implement changes, those changes become their changes, and cooperation is more likely to follow. They tend to see the value of the change and how it affects their jobs, as well as the organization (Sewell, 2002).

Influence of Informal Leaders

As indicated previously, a normal by-product of groups is the development of *informal leaders*. Officers who fulfill this role can usually be identified easily. Normally, one officer in a group will be the social leader and another officer will be looked upon as the group leader. The more the supervisor knows about each of the informal leaders in terms of their concerns, objectives, and personal styles, the better the chance of influencing those individuals (Cohen & Bradford, 2005).

Informal leaders are a vital resource in the change process. In almost all instances, they should be integrated into the team or group as soon as possible so that they will be a part of the change process and not apart from it.

Circumstances will dictate whether a first-line supervisor should include formal leaders in the change process. When it is evident that informal leaders are influential, they should be involved; otherwise, supervisors may be totally unaware that individuals (or situations) are playing an important part in resistance to change.

Involved informal leaders who are committed to the proposed change can, in most instances, reduce employee resistance and facilitate implementation. Informal leaders can provide information to the decision-making process that might otherwise be unavailable, allowing those involved the opportunity to meet this resistance head on.

Informal leaders have influence that should be used—not ignored. It must be kept in mind that informal leaders should never be manipulated when being integrated into the decision-making process. First-line supervisors should maintain respect for the ideas of the rank and file and maximize their input when working for change.

Mandated Change

It is inevitable that a supervisor will eventually meet a situation in which every effort has been made to involve officers in the change process, but they are unsuccessful. Change may occur without consultation or involvement because of inadequate time to prepare for the change. This is a fact of managerial life, and there is no easy solution for this situation.

It is imperative for a supervisor to be open and candid with everyone and explain the reasons for the change carefully. Obviously, such a straightforward approach is an effort to deal with anticipated or actual resistance rationally. Such an appeal will be ignored if resistance is based on emotion.

At this point, the supervisor must make every effort to emphasize the positive aspects of the change, explaining the way it can help each officer. Everything the supervisor does will elicit a reaction of some sort from the officers, so the sergeant (supervisor) should strive to be a reliable source of information and a steadying influence during the initial stages of a change.

It is the supervisor's responsibility to shield subordinates, as much as possible, from the anxiety created by change. Showing genuine concern for the officer's welfare can do this. In other words, a supervisor must have a caring attitude. Officers generally will respond positively to their supervisor's efforts to stabilize a situation and show sound judgment. If officers respond even slightly to such efforts, the supervisor has begun to lay a foundation, hopefully leading to a reduction or elimination of resistance.

References

Albrecht, K. L. (1981). *Executive Tune-Up*. Englewood Cliffs, NJ: Prentice Hall.

Alpert, G., Kenney, D. R., & Oettemier, T. N. (1998). *Facilitating organizational change: Shaping action through individual and organizational evaluations*. Washington, DC: National Institute of Justice.

Barnes, C., Sheley, J., Logsdon, V., & Sutherland, S. (2003). *Stress and job satisfaction in an Urban Sheriff's Department: Contributions of work and family history, community oriented policing and job assignment*. Sacramento: Institute for Social Research, California State University, Sacramento.

Blair, B. G., Kamaby, J., & Zone, I. (2007). *All the moving parts: Organizing change management*. Los Angeles: Puzzles Press.

Bridges, W., & Bridges, S. (2009). *Managing transitions: Making the most of change* (3rd ed.). New York: NL De Capo.

Cameron, E., & Green, M. (2004). *Making sense of change management: A complete guide to the models, tools and techniques of organizational change*. Sterling, VA: Kogan Page.

Career Services, (2009). *What are values*. Toronto: Seneca College of Applied Arts and Technology.

Charrier, K. (2000). Marketing strategies for attracting and retaining Generation X police officers. *The Police Chief, LXII*(12).

Charrier, K. (2004). The role of the strategic manager. *The Police Chief, LXXI*(6).

Chemerinsky, E., Hoffman, P., Levenson, L., Paz, R. S., Rice, C., & Sobel, C. (2000). *An independent analysis of the Los Angeles Police Department's Board of Inquiry report on the Rampart Scandal*. Los Angeles: University of Southern California.

Cohen, A. R., & Bradford, D. L. (2005). *Influence without authority* (2nd ed.). New York: John Wiley & Sons.

Cohen, A. R., & Fink, S. L. (2002). *Effective behavior in organizations* (7th ed.). Boston, MA: McGraw-Hill/Irwin.

Community Policing Consortium, (1998). *Module four: managing organizational change*. Washington DC: Community Policing Consortium.

Dale, N. (2000). Turning around an agency—How the Fort Pierce Police Department did it. *Law and Order, 48*(11).

DeLord, R. D., & Sanders, J. (2006). Project coordinators, police labor-management relations *Perspectives and practical solutions for implementing change, making reform and handling crises for managers and union leaders* (Vol. 1). Washington, DC: Office of Community Oriented Policing Services.

De Meuse, K. P., & McDaris, K. K. (1994). An exercise in managing change. *Training and Development, 48*(2).

DeParis, R. J. (1997). Situational leadership: Problem-solving leadership for problem-solving policing. *The Police Chief, LXIV*(10).

DeSantis, V. S., & Durst, S. L. (1998). Job satisfaction among local government employees: Lessons for public managers: *The Municipal Yearbook—1997*. Washington, DC: International City/County Management Assoc.

Farias, G., & Johnson, H. (2000). Organizational development and change management: Setting the record straight. *Journal of Applied Behavioral Science, 36*(3).

French, B., & Stewart, J. (2001). Organizational development in a law enforcement environment. *FBI Law Enforcement Bulletin, 70*(9).

Glensor, R. D., & Peak, K. (1996). Implementing change community-oriented policing and problem solving. *FBI Law Enforcement Bulletin, 65*(7).

Gorenak, I. (2004). *Influence of communication with the society on the job satisfaction of police officers from policing in Central and Eastern Europe: Dilemmas of contemporary criminal justice*. Ljubljana, Slovenia: University of Maribor.

Gray, J. L. (1984). *Supervision*. Belmont, CA: Wadsworth.

Green, F. (2009). Early release proposal gets mixed response. *Richmond Times-Dispatch* Monday, July 20.

Greenberg, S., & Flynn, E. A. (2009). Leadership and managing change. In D. C. G. Sheriff Los Vegas Metropolitan Police Department (Eds.), *Strategic plan 2008–2010*. Las Vegas: Institute for Executive Development.

Hanson, D. (2007). Hazardous duty: Training officers to tackle Hazmat emergencies. *Law Enforcement Technology, 34*(4).

Harigopal, K. (2006). *Management of organizational change: Leveraging transformation* (2nd ed.). Thousand Oaks, CA: Sage.

Harvey, T. R. (1995). *Checklist for change: A pragmatic approach to creating and controlling change* (2nd ed.). Boston: Allyn & Bacon.

Haught, L. (1998). Meaning, resistance and sabotage—Elements of a police culture. *Community Policing Exchange, Phase V*(20).

Illinois Law Enforcement Training and Standards Board, (2004). *Police pursuit guidelines.* Springfield, IL: Illinois Law Enforcement Training and Standards Board.

Jerome, R. (2006). *Police reform: A job half done.* Washington, DC: American Constitution Society for Law and Policy.

Judge, T. A., & Bono, J. E. (2001). Relationship of core self-evaluation traits. *Journal of Applied Psychology, 86.*

Judge, T. A., Heller, D., & Mount, M. K. (2002). Five-factor model of personality and job satisfaction. *Journal of Applied Psychology, 87.*

Julseth, J., Ruiz, J., & Hummer, D. (2011). Municipal police officer job satisfaction in Pennsylvania: A study of organizational development in small police departments. *Police Science and Management, 13*(3).

Kotter, J. P., & Cohen, D. S. (2002). *The heart of change.* Boston: Harvard Business Review Press.

Kouzes, J. M., & Posner, B. Z. (2011). *Credibility: How leaders gain and lose it, why people demand it* (2nd ed.). San Francisco: Jossey-Bass.

Kriegel, R., & Brandt, D. (1997). *Sacred cows make the best burgers—Paradigm-busting strategies for developing change-ready people and organizations.* New York: Warner Books.

Leban, B. (2007). *Managing organizational change* (2nd ed.). New York: Wiley.

Leonard, K. S. (1997). Making change a positive experience. *Law and Order, 45*(5).

Malik, S. D., & Wexley, K. N. (1986). Improving the owner/manager's handling of subordinates resistance to unpopular decisions. *Journal of Small Business Management, 32*(4).

Mastrofski, S. D. (2007). *Police organization and management issues for the next decade.* Washington, DC: U.S. Department of Justice.

Maurer, R. (2005). *Beyond the wall of resistance: Unconventional strategies that build support for change* (2nd ed.). Austin, TX: Bard.

Mollen, M. (1994). *Commission report—Commission to investigate allegations of police corruption and the anti-corruption procedures of the police department.* New York: City of New York.

Moore, M. M., & Stephens, D. W. (1991). *Beyond command and control: The strategic management of police departments.* Washington, DC: Police Executive Research Forum.

More, H. W. (1998). *Special topics in policing* (2nd ed.). Cincinnati: Anderson.

More, H. W. (2008). *Current issues in law enforcement—Controversies and solutions.* Springfield, IL: Charles C Thomas.

More, H. W., Vito, G., & Walsh, W. (2013). *Organizational behavioral and management in law enforcement* (3rd ed.). Upper Saddle River, NJ: Pearson Prentice Hall.

Mulder, A. E. R. (1994). Resistance to change—A personal assessment. *Law and Order, 42*(2).

National Association of Police Organizations (NAPO), (2012). *What is NAPO?.* Washington, DC: NAPO.

National institute of Justice, (1995). *National law enforcement and corrections technology center.* Gaithersburg, MD: National institute of Justice.

National Law Enforcement and Corrections Technology Center, (2005). *New technologies demonstrated for law enforcement.* Rockville, MN: National Institute of Justice.

Office of Community Oriented Policing Services, (2009). *Building trust between the police and the citizens they serve—An internal affairs promising practices guide for local law enforcement.* Washington, DC: U.S. Department of Justice.

Ortiz, R. L. (1994). Police culture: A roadblock to change in law enforcement. *The Police Chief, LXI*(8).

O'Toole, J. (1996). *Leading change—The argument for value-based leadership. Overcoming the ideology of comfort and the tyranny of custom.* New York: Ballantine.

Pennings, J. M. (1997). Innovation and change. In A. Sorge & M. Warner (Eds.), *The IEBM handbook of organizational behavior.* London: International Thomas Business Press.

Sarri, L. M., & Judge, T. A. (2004). Employee attitudes and job satisfaction. *Human Resource Management, 43*(3).

Sewell, J. D. (2002). Managing the stress of change. *FBI Law Enforcement Bulletin, 71*(3).

Skolnick, J. H., & Fyfe, J. J. (1995). Community-oriented policing would prevent police brutality. In P. A. Winters (Ed.), *At issue: Policing the police.* San Diego: Greenhaven.

Sweeney, E. M. (1997). Vehicular pursuits—Balancing the risks. *The Police Chief, LXIV*(7).

Switzer, M. (2003). Five steps to building commitment for change. *The Police Chief, LXX*(10).

Tichy, N. M., & Devanna, M. A. (1997). *The transformational leader* (2nd ed.). New York: John Wiley & Sons.

Tosi, H. L., Rizzo, J. R., & Carroll, S. J. (1994). *Managing organizational behavior* (3rd ed.). New York: Harper and Row.

Tracey, W. R. (1990). *Leadership skills: Standout performance for human resource managers.* New York: AMACOM.

Wheaton, B. (1990). Life transitions, role histories and mental health. *American Sociological Review, 55*

White, K. W., & Chapman, E. N. (1996). *Organizational communication—An introduction to communication and human relations strategies.* Needham Heights, MA: Simon & Schuster.

Young, W. (2006). Effecting change—Avoiding the pitfalls. *The Police Chief, LXIII*(7).

Youngs, A. C. (2003). Law enforcement in 2003 and beyond. *Law and Order, 51*(4).

Zhao, J. (1996). *Why police organizations change: A study of community-oriented policing.* Washington, DC: Police Executive Research Forum.

8

Performance Appraisal
The Key to Police Personnel Development

CASE STUDY

Sergeant Gina Thompson

DEPARTMENT

The police department is composed of 272 sworn officers. The patrol division makes up the bulk of operations and is composed of four watches: watch 1, watch 2, watch 3, and the power unit. The power unit is a watch that overlaps the afternoon and evening shifts when calls are at peak levels. The criminal investigation division is the second largest operations function and has four main bureaus: crimes against persons, crimes against property, narcotics, and the juvenile bureau. The department is not presently accredited by the Commission on Accreditation of Law Enforcement Agencies (CALEA) but is planning for a preaccreditation site visit within the next year. The newly hired chief of police is a firm believer in accreditation and also believes in the community policing concept. The chief is progressive and has initiated a number of new programs designed to upgrade and professionalize the department. He initiated the officer education program, in which the city reimburses tuition for officers taking college classes. He also encourages officers to seek additional specialized training, such as in crime scene investigations, traffic crash reconstruction, foreign language, and counterterrorism instruction. He is well liked and respected by most members of the department. His open-door policy was praised by officers in the lower ranks but criticized by middle managers. Middle management said the open-door policy tended to thwart the chain of command.

CRIME

While crimes of violence have seen a slight decline over the past three years, property crimes have seen a significant increase. Burglaries and larcenies are up 12 percent over last year, motor vehicle theft is up 7 percent, and arson is up 3 percent. One of the largest increases has been in reported incidents of drug dealing. On the positive side, offenses cleared by arrest have increased substantially. This is especially true in narcotics. Arrests have increased 22 percent, and clearance rates for both personal and property crimes have increased to 53 percent.

COMMUNITY

The city has a population of 148,000 people. There is a wide diversity of ethnic and racial cultures but they are typically clannish and settle in pockets of the city. The city has two large shopping malls, located on the east and west sides of the city. Three interstate highways merge near the center of the city. The east side of the city houses most of the industrial plants and railways. The east side is where most of the lower income and federal housing projects are located. This is also the area where most crimes are reported. The city center and southern areas are composed of medical facilities, a university, numerous restaurants, and auto sales lots.

OFFICER

Sergeant Gina Thompson is a 12-year veteran of the police department. She was promoted to sergeant six years ago and had been assigned to the criminal investigation department. She requested a change of assignment primarily because she missed patrol duty. She enjoyed investigations but found it a little boring and less challenging than patrol work. At least that is what she told her superiors. The fact of the matter was she simply liked the excitement of patrol better than investigations. While a detective, she did not have any supervisory duties. Now that she is back in uniform, she has a platoon of officers that she will have to supervise and evaluate on an annual basis.

PROBLEM

Sergeant Thompson was assigned to Baker 3, a patrol zone in the east side of the city. Her zone is composed of predominantly low-income government housing units. Two years ago, the department initiated a community-policing program in Baker 3. Sergeant Thompson was instructed to increase the community-policing efforts there. Because Sergeant Thompson was unfamiliar with supervisory duties, she had to familiarize herself with the performance evaluation process that she would now have to use with her platoon. The evaluation process was a graphic rating scale form that had been in use for as long as she could remember. It was the same form she had been evaluated on when she was a patrol officer.

Sergeant Thompson is concerned that the officers under her supervision will not score well on the old form, even though they have been very productive within the community and effective in bringing about a number of community changes that will ultimately benefit the police. The community has a different feel about it now. Citizens are helping the police in their efforts rather than shying away from things they consider to be "police matters." The officers themselves seem to be enjoying their new relationship and partnership with the community, but the evaluation form does not measure these types of positive changes. In fact, the officers in Baker 3 may look worse because the crime rate has increased in the area. The increased crime rate is the result of more arrests and citizens coming forward with information on criminal activity—a true measure that the community is beginning to trust and have faith in the police.

WHAT WOULD YOU DO?

If you were Sergeant Thompson, how would you conduct the performance evaluations? What changes could you make that would reflect the true performance of these officers? What other types of evaluations might be a better measure of individual as well as group performance? How would you, as a sergeant, go about initiating a change in the way officers are evaluated?

People Power

Police work is a unique, multibillion dollar, labor-intensive industry built around order maintenance, law enforcement, and the provision of other essential government services. By the early 2000s, for example, more than 17,000 police agencies at all levels of government spent nearly 48 billion dollars to "protect and serve" their constituents. Most of these funds—80 to 90 percent—went to cover salaries and benefits for more than 850,000 full- and part-time law enforcement personnel. Municipal governments spend more than 20 percent of their total budgetary outlay on police services. The per capita expenditure for police service in cities and counties ranges anywhere from $131.00 to $848.00 per year, with a mean expenditure of $264.00. It is estimated that it now costs more than $300,000 per year to field a fully equipped and professionally trained police officer around the clock in urban high-crime areas (Hamblin, 1994; U.S. Department of Justice, 2009).

In light of these phenomenal costs, local governments are now beginning to realize that they have a vested interest in recruiting, hiring, and retaining only the most efficient, effective, and productive personnel. Police managers are becoming sensitive to the fact that numerical strength alone does not guarantee quality service. Quality is much more likely to be determined by the intelligence, ability, skill, experience, integrity, and dedication of the police department's human resources. Consequently, police managers are forced into being much more personnel conscious.

Many observers have come to the conclusion that personnel development may be the only truly viable solution to problems caused by an erosion of the tax base and dwindling resources in the public sector. According to the Office of Community Oriented Policing Services (2011), an estimated 10,000 to 12,000 local law enforcement officers were laid off and approximately

30,000 police positions unfilled in 2011 due to the poor economy. With personnel shortages, police agencies have had to make up the difference with more efficient and effective use of existing personnel. Personnel development focuses on the employee. It is a management strategy designed to improve both the quantity and the quality of each individual's output, while ensuring that employees work collaboratively (in groups) to achieve the organization's mission, goals, and objectives. Based on modern management theory, personnel development is an ongoing process that begins on the day the rookie police officer joins the police department and continues throughout his or her career.

Systematic performance appraisal is regarded as the key to employee development and is now viewed as the centerpiece of an effective police personnel system (Gul & O'Connell, 2012; Kramer, 1998; Travis & Brann, 1997).

Performance Appraisal

Evaluation of job performance is a managerial task that is normally delegated to first-line supervisors in healthy, work-based organizations. Formal (objective) performance appraisal has been emphasized in government and has become the standard by which the legitimacy of any public sector personnel system is judged.

Many police supervisors do not fully understand the purpose of, or need for, regular performance appraisal. They approach the evaluation of subordinates in a negative manner. Evaluation becomes an unpleasant and stressful chore that requires them to assume the awesome responsibility for honestly assessing the job-related strengths and weaknesses of their fellow police officers. Some police supervisors are simply not prepared to take on this very important role-related responsibility.

In a generic sense, seven common justifications are used by management for requiring first-line supervisors to evaluate their personnel. They are summarized here.

1. To determine whether subordinates are doing the job they were hired to do.
2. To measure the quantity of work and quality of performance and provide rewards for those who are doing well.
3. To correct specific problems and improve the employee's overall performance.
4. To estimate employee potential and prepare that employee for promotion within the organization.
5. To assess employee attitudes and strengthen each supervisor's understanding of subordinates.
6. To let employees know exactly how they are doing, where they stand, and what they can do to improve their own on-the-job performance.
7. To provide supervisors (and management) with sufficient objective data to make and, if necessary, defend decisions concerning personnel within the agency.

In addition to these specific objectives, many management theorists contend that an objective and fair performance appraisal tends to fortify and enrich supervisor–subordinate relationships in the workplace (Swanson, Territo, & Taylor, 2012).

A great deal of time, effort, and creative thought have gone into the search for a comprehensive, multipurpose performance-appraisal process designed to give police managers objective data that can be factored into administrative decisions concerning salary increases, promotions, transfers, discipline, or personnel development. While progress is being made, no such process presently exists, and it is doubtful that one will be perfected in the near future (Travis & Brann, 1997).

Many personnel specialists, or human resources managers, as they are now called, believe that the achievement of multiple objectives is not feasible and think that a performance-appraisal system should be limited to one (and only one) objective: to inform employees about the quality of their work so that they can strive to improve their own performance. This is commonly referred to as "developmental" as opposed to "judgmental" performance appraisal (Steinmetz & Todd, 1992).

According to Leonard (2013), the purpose of a formal merit rating, performance review, or employee appraisal is to synthesize, in objective terms, the performance, experience, and capabilities of individual employees and to compare them with the requirements of a particular job. This assessment is almost always based on observable criteria, such as cooperation, dependability, productivity, quality of output, follow-through, judgment, or safety. Regular performance appraisal provides rank-and-file police officers with some assurance that they are not being overlooked and that the supervisors, managers, and various superiors within the police organization know something about them as individuals.

The key to effective performance appraisal is knowing exactly who is responsible for doing what and how it (the job) is to be done. The essential components or elements of the total job must be carefully identified and communicated to the subordinate personnel. The most important elements of performance appraisal have the following characteristics:

1. They are job centered and focus on the specific task or tasks to be performed.
2. They are clear and simply stated.
3. They are observable as well as objective.
4. They target actual on-the-job performance.
5. They are measurable in terms of predetermined performance standards.

The second step in effective performance evaluation is applying a standard designed to specify the minimum level of acceptable performance for each particular job. This standard becomes critically important as a performance-measuring device (Jones, 1998). It clearly delineates what is expected from the police officer in terms of productivity, accuracy, completeness, timeliness, dependability, or safety. The first-line supervisor, normally a sergeant, is in the best position to utilize the information concerning elements of the job, performance standards, and objective appraisal criteria to forge a meaningful composite that reflects each subordinate's job performance accurately (Iannone & Iannone, 2013). The performance profile is an invaluable source of information for management decision-making.

There are literally thousands of different performance-appraisal instruments in use today. Virtually all of them incorporate elements of the job (based on a job description), some type of graduated performance measurement, and objective evaluative criteria. Needless to say, none of them is perfect.

The four universal aspects of performance appraisal are (1) a performance goal, standard, or plan; (2) measurement of job-related performance; (3) comparison of employee performance with the goal, standard, or plan; and (4) use of corrective action as required in a given situation (Walsh & Donovan, 1990). These represent the conceptual pillars on which the employee evaluation process is built.

The Employee Evaluation Process

While the actual mix may differ from one jurisdiction to another, there are nine basic steps in most formal employee evaluation systems. These steps have been summarized here:

1. Preparing a detailed job description and specifying minimum performance requirements. In other words, local management determines what is to be done and how well each employee is expected to do it.
2. Discussing the job, acceptable performance standards, and the formal evaluation process with the employees and making adjustments if necessary.
3. The employee does the work. How well it is done will be influenced by personal ability, training, adaptability, time, resources, and an error factor based on chance.
4. Observing and evaluating the employee's job performance by appropriate supervisory personnel. This will be influenced by the skill of the evaluator, frequency of the observation, predispositions of the supervisor, and random error.
5. Recording evaluative data derived from objective criteria on an appraisal form designed to measure the quantity, as well as the quality of an employee's work, using very specific performance standards.
6. Explaining the mechanics of the particular evaluation and discussing the contents of the evaluative report with each employee.
7. Forwarding the evaluative report to the central personnel unit or the appropriate manager, where it is interpreted from an organization-wide perspective.
8. Considering alternative responses and taking appropriate administrative action.
9. An appeals process is made available to ensure administrative due process and to safeguard the rights of the employee.

These steps have become institutionalized in public sector personnel administration. In police work, for example, they have become an integral component of all civil service systems, collective bargaining agreements, and municipal human resources management programs. From a management perspective, performance appraisal is necessary in order to (1) allocate resources, (2) reward competent employees, (3) provide valuable feedback to workers, and (4) maintain fair relationships and open communication (Fulmer, 1988).

Police officers, first-line supervisors, and managers play very distinct, yet interrelated, roles in performance appraisal. They are assigned specific responsibilities but must work cooperatively to ensure the success of the evaluative process (see Figure 8.1). Unity of purpose is a critical variable.

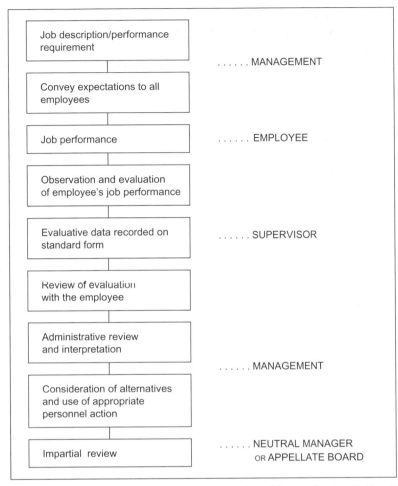

FIGURE 8.1 Roles and responsibilities in the evaluation process. *Adapted from Richard N. Holden (1994).* Modern Police Management, *Second Edition. Englewood Cliffs, NJ: Prentice Hall, Inc.*

While performance evaluation is always a major undertaking in complex criminal justice organizations, it is an absolutely essential component of managerial control. Job performance must be observed, compared with objective standards, and evaluated so that police supervisors and managers can implement effective strategies designed to mitigate performance problems or remove employees from the workforce who cannot or will not change their unacceptable job-related behavior.

Frequency of Evaluation

The National Advisory Commission on Criminal Justice Standards and Goals emphasized the importance of regular performance appraisal in law enforcement. According to Standard 17.1, every police agency should adopt a policy of retaining or promoting to higher ranks only those personnel who successfully demonstrate their ability to assume the responsibilities and perform the duties of the position to which they will be promoted or advanced. Personnel who have the potential to assume increased responsibilities should be identified and placed in a program that will lead to full development of that potential (National Advisory Commission on Criminal Justice Standards and Goals, 1973).

Thirty years later, the CALEA reiterated the importance of regular performance evaluations. According to Standard 35.1.2, "A written directive requires a performance evaluation of each employee to be conducted and documented at least annually" (CALEA, 2006). The key ingredient in this type of screening process is an accurate assessment of the employee's past performance, initiative in the area of self-development, and the person's potential for advancement within the organization. Standardized performance appraisal for both probationary and certified police personnel has become the norm in progressive police departments.

While conscientious supervisors evaluate the performance of their subordinates continuously, formal objective evaluations, such as those discussed earlier, are much less frequent. From a very practical point of view, formal evaluations should be performed on a predictable schedule. Sequencing is critical. If employees are evaluated too often, the supervisor is likely to place undue emphasis on and be swayed by normal day-to-day occurrences. If, however, they are infrequent, evaluators tend to forget critical incidents and much of the data that should be factored into the appraisal.

As a general rule and for CALEA standards, police departments evaluate their permanent personnel once a year. Due to the nature of the work and the value that is placed on proper performance of the police role, it would be a better and more reliable practice to evaluate certified police officers twice a year. This would provide management with a cumulative database upon which to make decisions concerning the individual employee.

No matter how careful a department has been in selecting its new personnel, there is a continuing need for quality control. Probably the most valuable technique for determining a rookie's suitability for police service is a trial period on the job. Police managers and seasoned first-line supervisors firmly believe (almost as an article of faith) that a probationary period is an essential element in the personnel screening process. It gives them the necessary time to judge the new employee in terms of ability and character. It also allows them to assess the recruit's capacity to cope with the demands of police work and to detect deficiencies that manifest themselves only under actual working conditions.

Probation, if it is to fulfill its role in quality control, must be predicated on a very careful, consistent, and objective evaluation of each new employee's on-the-job performance. The men and women who are truly unsuited for a career in law enforcement should be separated from police service as quickly as possible (Gaines, Southerland, & Angell, 2012). While it has been customary in many civil service systems to evaluate probationary employees once or twice before they are certified and given permanent status, most management theorists and many practitioners now recommend more frequent evaluation. CALEA Standard 35.1.3 recommends at least quarterly evaluations of all entry-level probationary employees (CALEA, 2006). Under ideal circumstances, police departments should require at least two years of probation with rookie police officers evaluated every six months. After four objective and very thorough evaluations by a competent first-line supervisor or group of supervisors, it is usually clear to supervisory personnel, management, and the employee whether the awarding of permanent status will be in the best interests of the police department. The department should be given the benefit of the doubt in all borderline cases (Leonard & More, 2000).

Objective, thorough, and frequent performance appraisals help ensure the quality of police service. They protect the public and promote professionalism within the ranks. When used regularly and in an appropriate manner, performance reviews foster professional growth and create a genuine esprit de corps.

The Sergeant's Role

As first-line supervisors, sergeants play a leading role in the employee evaluation process. Based on their strategic position in the management structure, they are responsible for appraising the on-the-job performance of almost all line personnel. For all practical purposes, they provide quality assurance within the police establishment. The assessment of human resources "goes with the turf."

As noted before, many sergeants do not fully understand or appreciate their unique role in the evaluative process. They perceive it as a difficult and distasteful part of their job. Consequently, they attempt to insulate themselves from the stress associated with performance appraisal. If they cannot avoid it altogether, they approach it as perfunctory and adopt a blasé attitude. This is very unfortunate because apathy is normally a precursor to deterioration in police service.

Due to insecurity, immaturity, poor training, or the inability to cope with criticism, many sergeants fear judging their subordinates and use all sorts of excuses to avoid it. They claim that it takes too much time away from their other duties, strains personal relationships, is ignored by management, and is almost always perceived by fellow employees as an unwarranted intrusion into their professional lives. These rationalizations are unacceptable. Sergeants must be prepared to accept responsibility for meaningful performance appraisal.

Accepting sergeants' stripes means more than merely an increase in pay. It represents an advancement in rank that thrusts the newly promoted noncommissioned officer into a different, very demanding role within the organization. Sergeants are expected to assume risks inherent in the evaluative function. They must honestly assess how well each employee is doing the job and articulate, in meaningful terms, what they think about that person's overall performance as a police officer. Once again, personnel evaluation goes with the territory.

Not everyone has the inclination or the talent to be a good evaluator. In fact, whether a particular first-line supervisor becomes a competent evaluator will, in the long run, depend on that person's:

1. Ability to be firm, fair, and impartial when dealing with others.
2. Orientation to and understanding of the personnel evaluation process.
3. Self-confidence in making judgments about the strengths and weaknesses of other people.

4. Human relations and communication skills.
5. Capacity to empathize with subordinates.
6. Knowledge of the assigned tasks performed by the employee.
7. Training as an evaluator.
8. Experience with performance appraisal.
9. Ego strength when it comes to dealing with disagreement or criticism expressed by significant others within the police organization.

Being a good evaluator requires natural talent, knowledge, and the acquisition of special skills. Personnel evaluation is one of the most difficult aspects of a very complex job.

Human factors alone cannot guarantee the success of a particular performance appraisal program. Institutional support is absolutely essential. First-line supervisors exhibit enthusiasm for and derive satisfaction from their role as evaluators when they are given adequate management support. Genuine support does not come from professional rhetoric; it comes from action.

To do their job effectively, sergeants need to have clear-cut authority based on department policies, procedures, rules, and regulations in order to perform a meaningful evaluation of subordinates. They must also believe that their assessment will be accepted and respected by their superiors as a professional judgment concerning the competence of the employee. Unless police sergeants are given time, training, and access to adequate institutional resources, performance appraisal becomes a sham. It is nothing more than window dressing. Ritualistic performance evaluations that lack relevance are an unwelcome burden that helps destroy the supervisor's morale and undermines the credibility of management (see Figure 8.2).

---

1. Role—A job description outlining the sergeant's role in performance appraisal.
2. Authority—Formal department policy granting first-line supervisors authority to evaluate immediate subordinates.
3. Procedure—Mutually acceptable procedures specified in department manuals, civil service regulations, or collective bargaining agreements.
4. Relevance—A clear-cut statement about how evaluative data will be factored into administrative decisions concerning personnel.
5. Resources—Supervisor training and career development opportunities.
6. Utility—Evaluative data factored into the actual decision-making process.
7. Stature—Sergeants accepted as members of the management team who make valuable contributions to the department through their quality control and personnel development functions.

FIGURE 8.2 Institutional support for performance appraisal.

First-line supervisors in healthy, work-based organizations take their job very seriously. Top-notch sergeants evaluate their employees frequently. They accept performance appraisal as a challenge and are willing to take the risks associated with it because it gives them an opportunity to provide both form and substance to the department's human resources. They help weed out incompetent personnel, identify employees who need assistance, and provide positive reinforcement for good workers. Police sergeants are in a key position to influence the efficiency, effectiveness, and productivity of the individual employee, as well as the police department as a whole.

While performance evaluation protocols differ in design, they have three common objectives:

1. To assess each employee's contribution to the organization.
2. To provide employees with valuable feedback concerning their on-the-job performance.
3. To develop a mutually acceptable plan for correcting performance-related problems.

The evaluation process itself consists of (1) assessment, (2) evaluation interview, and (3) remediation. The sergeant is a central figure in the evaluation process.

Methods of Appraisal

There is no consensus about the best way to approach performance appraisal in complex criminal justice organizations. In fact, there are several competing schools of thought. Some of the most important are outlined here.

Graphic Rating Scale. The graphic rating scale is probably the most frequently used performance assessment device. Each characteristic or trait that is to be evaluated is represented by a line (or scale) on which the evaluator indicates the degree (usually 0 to 100) to which it is believed the person possesses that particular trait or characteristic. Scales represent a graphic continuum that ranges from one extreme (negative) to another (positive). A space for rater comments is found on most graphic rating scales. This gives a supervisor the opportunity to support a rating with facts (see Figures 8.3, 8.4, and 8.5).

A number of advantages are associated with a graphic rating scale:

1. It is fairly simple to design and construct.
2. It is easy for supervisors to use.
3. Interpretation is not particularly difficult.
4. Employees can be compared based on a composite score.

There are disadvantages as well. Rigidity, rater error, and intentional manipulation can skew results. They undermine the credibility of the evaluation process and strain interpersonal relations within the organization.

The accuracy of a particular scale (in assessing an employee's performance) is almost always contingent on the selection of identifiable and measurable on-the-job traits, the design of the rating instrument, and the competence of the person doing the rating. The rater's knowledge, training, and inclination to take a risk are critical variables that actually may determine

INSTRUCTIONS
FOR USE OF THE PERFORMANCE EVALUATION REPORT FORM

GENERAL:

1. Using preliminary draft sheet and pencil, complete Section A first, then other appropriate sections. The rater should review the draft report with his or her own supervisor. Markings and comments should then be typed or inked in on the final form. Either the rater or the reviewer (or both) should then review the rating with the employee in a private interview. All signatures shall be in ink. Changes and corrections shall be initialed by the employee.

2. If space for comments is inadequate, dated and signed attachments may be made (either typewritten or in ink).

3. Due dates shall be observed and are particularly important for final probationary reports. Filing dates for these are flexible, and both the first and the final reports may be filed any time between the receipt and the printed due date.

4. All probationers (either entrance level or promotional) shall be evaluated at the end of each month of probationary service. Probationers may be separated at any time such action is deemed necessary by the township manager through use of either a scheduled or an unscheduled performance evaluation report.

5. All permanent employees and entrance level probationers in their second year shall be evaluated annually as of the printed due date.

6. The "Guide to Performance Evaluation" should be consulted for suggestions, definitions, interpretations, and further instructions.

7. The main purposes of this form are to inform the employee of his performance, to improve performance when possible, and to sustain superior performance.

SECTION A: Check one column for each factor. Column 5 may be checked when a factor is not considered applicable to a particular job. Additional spaces have been provided to write in any additional factors. Each check mark in Columns 1 and 2 requires specific explanation in Section E. In the absence of specific standards for a factor, use your own opinion as to what constitutes standard performance. Standard does not mean average; in fact, standard performance can often be higher than average performance.

Exceeds Standards: Total performance is well above standards for the position. This evaluation should be reflected by marks for critical factors in Section A, and superior or excellent performance should be noted in Section B. Only a few employees would normally qualify for this rating.

Effective—Meets Standards: Consistently competent performance meeting or exceeding standards in all critical factors for the position. If margin is narrow and standards are barely met, explain in Section E. Most employees would be rated in this category.

Some Improvement Needed: Total performance occasionally or periodically falls short of normal standards. Specific deficiencies should be noted in Section E. This evaluation indicates the supervisor's belief that the employee can and will make the necessary improvements.

Not Satisfactory: Performance clearly inadequate in one or more critical factors as explained or documented in Section E. Employee has demonstrated inability or unwillingness to improve or to meet standards. Performance not acceptable for position held.

SECTION B: Must be used to describe outstanding qualities or performances when check marks are placed in Column 4. Use this section to record other progress or improvements in performance resulting from employee's efforts to reach previously set goals.

SECTION C: Record agreed-upon or prescribed performance goals for the next evaluation period.

SECTION D: Use for describing standard performance.

SECTION E: Give specific reasons for check marks in Columns 1 and 2. Record here any other specific reasons why the employee should not be recommended for permanent status or—if the employee is already permanent—any specific reasons for required improvement.

SIGNATURES: Both the rater and the employee shall sign the report. The employee's signature indicates that the conference has been held and that he/she has had an opportunity to read the report. If he/she refuses to sign for any reason, explain that his/her signature does not necessarily imply or indicate agreement with the report and that space is provided for him/her to state any disagreement. Further refusal to sign shall be recorded in the report after which it shall be forwarded.

ROUTING: Keep the preliminary draft at the division level until the next rating period and then discard. Route the permanent copy through channels to the township manager's office.

FIGURE 8.3 Performance evaluation report.

PERFORMANCE EVALUATION REPORT

NON-SUPERVISORY

NAME	CLASS TITLE	DIVISION

PERIOD COVERED BY EVALUATION REPORT FROM: TO:	ASSIGNMENT

RATING INSTRUCTIONS:

1. Check each item box.
   - ◆ STRONG   ✓ STANDARD
   - − WEAK   N NOT OBSERVED
2. Rate each factor by circling the appropriate number.
3. Multiply the circled number by the weight for each factor and write the results in the "score" column.
4. Add the "score" column and record the sum.

Use spaces below for comments. Ratings other than competent should be substantiated in writing. Use reverse side for additional space.

PERFORMANCE FACTORS	1 = UNSATISFACTORY	2 = IMPROVEMENT NEEDED	3 = COMPETENT	4 = HIGH COMPETENT	5 = OUTSTANDING	WEIGHT	SCORE (RATING X WEIGHT)
QUANTITY ☐ AMOUNT OF WORK PERFORMED ☐ COMPLETION OF WORK ON SCHEDULE	1	2	3	4	5	25	
QUALITY ☐ ACCURACY ☐ NEATNESS ☐ THOROUGHNESS ☐ ORAL EXPRESSION ☐ WRITTEN EXPRESSION	1	2	3	4	5	25	
WORK HABITS ☐ PUNCTUALITY ☐ ATTENDANCE ☐ COMPLIANCE WITH ORDERS ☐ INTEREST ☐ INITIATIVE ☐ RESOURCEFULNESS ☐ AGGRESSIVENESS	1	2	3	4	5	15	
PERSONAL TRAITS ☐ EMOTIONAL STABILITY ☐ MATURITY ☐ ATTITUDE ☐ COMPATIBILITY WITH OTHERS ☐ PERSONAL APPEARANCE ☐ COMMAND PRESENCE ☐ LOYALTY	1	2	3	4	5	15	
ADAPTABILITY ☐ PERFORMANCE IN NEW SITUATIONS ☐ PERFORMANCE UNDER STRESS ☐ PERFORMANCE WITH MINIMUM INSTRUCTIONS ☐ ABILITY TO LEARN	1	2	3	4	5	10	
JOB KNOWLEDGE ☐ TECHNIQUES ☐ PROCEDURES ☐ SKILLS	1	2	3	4	5	10	
						100	
						SUM	SUM

1. Examples of work well done; Superior performance:

2. Performance deficiencies; Suggestions for improvement or continuing development:

3. General comments (e.g., overall performance, progress since last report, plans, goals; any other remarks):

This report represents my best judgment of the employee's performance based on my observations and knowledge.

RATING SUPERVISOR _____ DATE _____

I have read and approved this report.

DIVISION COMMANDER _____ DATE _____

This report has been discussed with me.

EMPLOYEE'S SIGNATURE_____ DATE _____

F 2021-54

FIGURE 8.4 Performance evaluation report.

the success or failure of the performance evaluation process. Unless sergeants take responsibility for performance appraisal and play their role as first-line supervisors very skillfully, the performance evaluation will become just another element in mutual admiration that perpetuates mediocrity. Sergeants should not forget that excellence is the by-product of selectivity and

PERFORMANCE APPRAISAL REPORT FOR POLICE OFFICER

EMPLOYEE _____ DATE OF EVALUATION _____

JOB TITLE _____ FROM _____ TO _____

DEPARTMENT _____ PURPOSE OF EVALUATION: Probationary _____ Annual _____ Special _____

Performance Measures and Evaluation

1. EMERGENCY CALLS FOR SERVICE	ALWAYS DOES IT	USUALLY DOES IT	SELDOM DOES IT	NOT APPLICABLE	COMMENTS
a. Responds quickly but safely when dispatched within established "Code 3" procedures					
b. Exercises reasonable caution in response to emergency calls for service					
c. Gains effective and prompt control of the situation and properly utilizes necessary supporting resources					
d. Exhibits calm, tactful, deliberate, organized and poised demeanor when handling emergency situations					
2. GENERAL ASSISTANCE CALLS	ALWAYS DOES IT	USUALLY DOES IT	SELDOM DOES IT	NOT APPLICABLE	COMMENTS
a. Responds within a reasonable time and safely when dispatched in conformance with established procedures					
b. Minimizes "out of service" time and completes the assignment within an acceptable time period					
c. Exhibits concern and interest in the call even when routine and maintains a highly professional manner					
3. COMMUNITY AND HUMAN RELATIONS	ALWAYS DOES IT	USUALLY DOES IT	SELDOM DOES IT	NOT APPLICABLE	COMMENTS
a. Projects a positive image to individuals and groups as a professional, competent and helpful police officer					
b. Communicates effectively and openly with all types of individuals and groups					
c. Relates well to people even in stressful situations					
d. Exhibits sincere interest in, and concern for, the problems and viewpoints of others					
e. Takes proper care of equipment and vehicles and pride in their appearance					
f. Maintains effective working relationships with co-workers and supervisors					
4. CASE INVESTIGATION	ALWAYS DOES IT	USUALLY DOES IT	SELDOM DOES IT	NOT APPLICABLE	COMMENTS
a. Uses productive techniques in case investigations Recognizes and carefully collects and preserves all evidence					
b. Prepares clear, concise, accurate and logical reports for departments and court use					
c. Exhibits a professional and poised demeanor in court and functions well as an objective witness					
d. Maintains acceptable clearance and complaint issuance level					
e. Works cooperatively and constructively with other organizations and resources					
5. ARREST PROCEDURES	ALWAYS DOES IT	USUALLY DOES IT	SELDOM DOES IT	NOT APPLICABLE	COMMENTS
a. Protects the safety of himself/herself and others in the apprehension process					
b. Utilizes only reasonable and legal levels of force and restraint in accordance with department policy in arrest situations					
c. Makes "quality" arrests which are compatible with departmental or team goals					
d. Respects the civil rights of persons placed in custody					
6. TRAFFIC CONTROL	ALWAYS DOES IT	USUALLY DOES IT	SELDOM DOES IT	NOT APPLICABLE	COMMENTS
a. Maintains acceptable enforcement levels and relates activities to the location, time and causes of serious accidents					
b. Gains effective and prompt control at an accident scene and properly utilizes necessary supporting resources					
c. Minimizes citizen friction and complaints in traffic law enforcement					
d. Maintains an acceptable record of judicial support of citations issued					
7. CRIME PREVENTION	ALWAYS DOES IT	USUALLY DOES IT	SELDOM DOES IT	NOT APPLICABLE	COMMENTS
a. Keeps abreast of crime problems, hazards, and prevention priorities in assigned patrol sector					
b. Maintains acceptable and productive levels of field activity–including "on-view" stops and arrests, which can actually impact crime levels					
c. Exercises initiative in finding and developing resources in the community to help in crime prevention					
d. Makes citizens aware of their crime prevention responsibilities and assists them in reducing hazards					

FIGURE 8.5 Performance evaluation report.

that they are in a position to mold the department's human resources into a more efficient, effective, and productive workforce.

Critical Incident Method. The critical incident method involves identifying, classifying, and recording significant employee behaviors. A critical incident can be favorable or unfavorable, but both must be recorded accurately. Events chosen by the supervisor for analysis must be concrete indicators of effective or ineffective on-the-job performance. The three basic steps in the critical incident approach to performance appraisal are:

1. Gather and record accurate information about critical incidents involving employees.
2. Abstract the information into a manageable number of categories describing significant job behaviors.
3. Provide the evaluator with a list of categories and a form on which to record an analysis of the employee's performance during various critical incidents.

The worksheet becomes an accurate record of actual behavior and gives management a profile of each employee in terms of that employee's performance-related strengths and weaknesses. The critical incident method has a number of distinct advantages. It deals with factual situations, zeroes in on positive and negative aspects of behavior, and is well suited for the employee–counseling aspects of performance assessment. However, the critical incident method also has several disadvantages. It takes a great deal of time, specialized training, and management oversight to do it correctly.

The critical incident approach to performance evaluation is much more subjective when compared to the use of graphic rating scales. It requires a great deal of interpretive skill and introspection on the part of the evaluator. The sergeant must know how the critical incident should have been handled, as well as have the expertise to judge the performance of subordinates in relation to that standard. This requires professional competence and confidence in the supervisor's ability to evaluate the on-the-job performance of working police officers. Critical incidents, if evaluated objectively, help alert supervisors to problems and raise "red flags" that tell a great deal about that employee's ability to function as a police officer. These red flags often indicate the type of remediation that may be necessary to correct a performance deficit. While the critical incident method has proven effective in certain situations, it has not been widely used in police work because it is too complex. However, as the police profession matures, we will undoubtedly see more enthusiasm for and interest in the critical incident approach to performance evaluation.

Behaviorally Anchored Rating Scales (BARS). These scales are gaining popularity as performance-measuring devices in police work. They focus on what employees should be doing rather than on their personal traits by relating specific performance to critical job responsibilities.

Each scale identifies specific on-the-job activities to be evaluated. There are sample statements describing (in behavioral terms) what is considered unacceptable, average, and excellent performance in representative incidents. Supervisors look for and rate definite, observable, and measurable job behavior related to these categories. They may choose

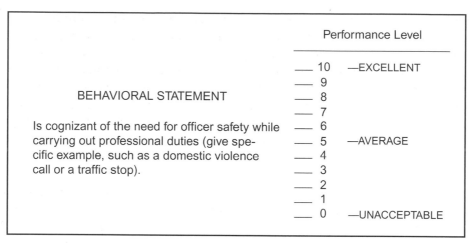

Performance Level

BEHAVIORAL STATEMENT

Is cognizant of the need for officer safety while
carrying out professional duties (give specific example, such as a domestic violence
call or a traffic stop).

—— 10   —EXCELLENT
—— 9
—— 8
—— 7
—— 6
—— 5   —AVERAGE
—— 4
—— 3
—— 2
—— 1
—— 0   —UNACCEPTABLE

FIGURE 8.6 Application of BARS to police work.

a numerical designation that best fits the performance level of the person being evaluated
(Holt, 1993).

Using a continuum of performance measurement ranging from 0 to 10, the behaviors (tasks
or activities) being evaluated are incorporated into a matrix configuration. The actual score is
assigned by raters based on their professional judgment. This produces a multidimensional
assessment of performance as that performance relates to critical tasks or activities.

BARS (see Figure 8.6) use a sufficient array of critical incidents and corresponding behaviors to determine the level of performance as displayed in a graphic rating scale format. In
order to work effectively, it is essential to have a participatory environment in which behavioral
statements are developed by consensus between police officers and managers who are thoroughly familiar with the actual behavior being evaluated.

While the BARS approach to performance evaluation is fairly complex, it elicits valuable
information for input into the self-development and managerial decision-making processes.
Complexity can be overcome through training of first-line supervisors and a cooperative spirit
on the part of rank-and-file police officers. The effective use of BARS produces a "win–win" situation for both police managers and rank-and-file officers because there is no confusion as to
what performance activities are being measured.

Paired Comparison. Paired comparison evaluations can be a formal process or an informal process. In the formal procedure, the supervisor is provided with a set of all possible pairs
of officers and is instructed to select the individual in each pair who is the "better" performer.
Eventually, the process can rank the entire group from best to worst. Some of the advantages of
this procedure are:

1. Does not require the use of standards.
2. Officers who perform similar duties are compared against each other.
3. Relatively simple and saves time.

However, the formal paired comparison procedure has several disadvantages. First, it forces supervisors to make tough choices. More importantly, there is no mechanism or process to provide a reason or explanation to support the supervisor's decision. Every individual has strengths and weaknesses, and making a forced choice comparison may prevent a supervisor from making a proper assessment. If used informally, however, the advantages of paired comparisons can be adopted to use with another form of performance evaluation. In the informal process, the supervisor selects the positive characteristics and abilities among all the subordinates and creates a model officer that can be compared with each individual officer. In this way, each individual officer is evaluated on duties and activities he or she specifically performs.

Management by Objectives (MBO). Management by objectives is viewed as a complete management and control system. It is a process designed to convert goals and objectives into specific programs. MBO identifies exactly who is to do what within a given time frame based on the allocation of existing resources. MBO is a novel approach to performance evaluation. Instead of focusing exclusively on past performance, the first-line supervisor and the employee get together to map out future goals and objectives (which are consistent with the organization's mission). They work together to develop goals and objectives, measures of achievement, and mutually acceptable time frames. The next regularly scheduled performance review, based on the concept of MBO, is held to evaluate how well the employee has done in accomplishing specified objectives. Plunkett (1992) has identified a series of distinct steps that he believes will make MBO work in just about any organizational setting. They are:

1. Setting mutually acceptable goals and objectives
2. Identifying resources and necessary actions
3. Prioritizing goals and objectives
4. Setting precise timetables
5. Evaluating the results

Clarity and specificity are essential components of MBO. While MBO produces a precise measurement of accomplishment, it requires time and a great deal of planning.

The accuracy of a performance evaluation protocol based on MBO will ultimately depend on the individual rater's judgment, knowledge, training, and ability to establish a positive, empathetic, collaborative, and goal-oriented relationship. Sergeants must have the desire, competence, and human relations skills to help working police officers formulate legitimate, realistic, and measurable job-related performance objectives. When used properly, MBO cuts through ambiguity and wishful thinking to establish concrete benchmarks with which to assess each employee's accomplishments. All successful MBO performance evaluation programs are built on a foundation of cooperation, collaboration, and trust. Whether an MBO performance evaluation protocol works in a particular police department will depend on the caliber of the supervisors who come up through the promotion process.

Many other forms of performance appraisal are currently being used or experimented with by police agencies. Self-evaluation, peer evaluation, group ratings, and rank-order methods have been used by several agencies with mixed results.

Regardless of the method selected, police sergeants are in a strategic position to determine the success or failure of the performance evaluation process. Through neglect or by design, they can sabotage everything. Success in achieving the goals and objectives of performance appraisal, however, depends almost entirely on their knowledge, maturity, specialized training, and human skills. Their decisions must reflect sound judgment, and their actions must be firm, yet fair.

The Human Factor

The integrity of the performance assessment process is inexorably linked to the ability and skill of those who have been promoted to the rank of sergeant. It is nurtured by experience and is reinforced through continuous training.

In order to become impartial evaluators, sergeants must first accept themselves as human beings who are fallible and susceptible to influences that can bias their judgment and skew their decisions. Acceptance of oneself as flawed is the first step on the road to objectivity.

In the jargon of personnel evaluation, influences that distort perceptions and interfere with an objective assessment are known as errors. While the chance of error cannot be eliminated altogether, supervisors can be trained to recognize common errors and to devise strategies designed to mitigate their effect on performance appraisal. Police departments with a desire to make the performance assessment process work train raters to recognize and deal with these errors so that supervisors can avoid some of the common pitfalls (Iannone & Iannone, 2013). Some of the most widespread rating errors are explored next.

The Error of Leniency

The error of leniency is probably the most common error in rating police personnel. It involves the human tendency to give people the benefit of the doubt and evaluate their on-the-job performance beyond what the circumstances warrant. Police sergeants succumb to exactly the same pressures that tempt all other supervisors to be lenient with subordinates: the desire to be popular, to avoid interpersonal conflicts, to shield one's ego from criticism, and to protect those who are less talented and more vulnerable. Some sergeants believe that by giving negative performance appraisals (even to officers who deserve them) they draw undue attention to themselves and showcase their own limitations as a first-line supervisor. To many, it is an unacceptable risk. In some cases, sergeants opt to be lenient in evaluating their immediate subordinates in a calculated effort to offset the leniency of other supervisors within the police department. This is their attempt to create balance and ensure that their employees have a fair shot when it comes to advancement.

Regardless of its cause, the error of leniency (if unchecked) acts to undermine the objectivity of the performance assessment process and almost always has a debilitating effect on the organization itself. Supervisors lose their credibility, morale suffers, and employees are placed in positions for which they are unprepared. Good first-line supervisors simply do not allow personal considerations to cloud their judgment. They strive to ensure the integrity of the performance evaluation process by being impartial and fair in their evaluation of each subordinate.

The Error of Central Tendency

In a normal distribution, more people will be rated closer to the mean than to any other point on the evaluative scale. This becomes an error of central tendency only when it fails to reflect a truly objective appraisal of on-the-job performance and forces many employees into an artificial category labeled "average." Whether supervisors lack sufficient data for valid assessments, fear there will be repercussions, or are merely lazy, central tendency is an escape. It offers them a way to avoid risks. Average evaluations are the safest and least controversial. Thus, supervisors are able to avoid justifying high and low evaluations. By taking the middle road, the sergeant avoids criticism from other supervisors and minimizes chances of a confrontation during the evaluation interview.

Central tendency is most likely to rear its ugly head in situations in which sergeants are unfamiliar with the person or persons being evaluated, there is a lack of verifiable performance data, or there is some ambiguity in terms of policies, procedures, rules, and regulations. Labeling everyone as average does a disservice to individual employees and the police organization. It penalizes competent, achievement-oriented subordinates and rewards marginal employees. Central tendency destroys the credibility of the evaluation process and plays havoc with employee morale. Sergeants must recognize the problem created by central tendency and be ready to deal with it. This knowledge and a commitment to regular, thorough, and objective performance appraisal will help safeguard the integrity of the evaluation process.

The Halo Effect

One of the most frequently committed errors is known as the halo effect. This means that the first-line supervisor permits just one outstanding (positive or negative) characteristic or critical incident to shape the overall rating given to the employee. Once the supervisor formulates a general impression that the subordinate's on-the-job performance is good or poor, all evaluative ratings are adjusted to reflect that particular judgment. In other words, the sergeant assigns similar values to all characteristics or traits irrespective of the police officer's actual on-the-job performance. In this situation, the evaluator uses selective perception to justify the initial assessment.

The halo effect is the MBO version of the self-fulfilling prophecy. The distortion caused by the halo effect is often compounded by the error of related traits and the error of overweighting (Iannone & Iannone, 2013). The error of related traits occurs when the evaluator assumes that an employee who exhibits one strength will automatically possess others. The error of overweighting (or recency) is the tendency of a supervisor to be unduly influenced by a critical incident, either good or bad, involving the evaluated officer near the end of the performance review period. Due to the dynamics involved, a recent critical incident can skew a performance evaluation to the point at which it becomes meaningless. Formal performance appraisals should profile the whole person. Better supervisors guard against letting isolated traits or critical incidents dominate performance analysis.

The Error of Bias

One of the most important and widespread errors involves personal bias. Many supervisors have a tendency to rate the employees they know and really like much higher than can reasonably be justified by an objective assessment of performance. Factors such as race, sex, sexual preference, color, creed, lifestyle, and physical appearance may be imbued in the evaluation either intentionally or unintentionally based on the first-line supervisor's norms, values, prejudices, and operational stereotypes. It is human nature for supervisors to write much more favorable performance evaluations for those with whom they are compatible and to view the people they dislike as being of little or no value to the organization. It is fairly easy for supervisors to fall into the trap of overrating subordinates they helped select or currently supervise in elite or highly specialized units. There is a certain egoism involved in stating that "employees are good because they work for me" or "if they work for me, they must be good." These supervisors have forgotten a basic principle in personnel management—they are rating the person instead of on-the-job performance. This type of "personal politics" destroys the morale of truly competent employees and induces other supervisors to become more lenient when they evaluate their own personnel. Unless a police officer's social background and personality interfere with personal performance, they should not be factored into the appraisal process. While the sergeant may not like a subordinate, the evaluation must be fair and based on the analysis of objective data. First-line supervisors simply cannot allow personal biases and prejudices to cloud their judgment about the performance of an employee. Supervisors need to recognize and deal with their biases in order to keep them from subverting the performance assessment process.

The Contrast Error

This particular rating error, according to Trojanowicz (1980), arises from the tendency of some first-line supervisors to judge subordinates in terms of their own expectations and aspirations. Police officers who vicariously fulfill the personal needs of the sergeant are generally rated higher than others, regardless of their actual performance on the job. They are valued by the supervisor for what they represent, not for what they accomplish or the skill required to accomplish it. This type of emotion-based evaluation is inherently subjective and self-serving. The contrast error forces the employee to guess what qualities or traits the supervisor is looking for and to curry favor (in the form of a positive appraisal) through gamesmanship or outright deception. First-line supervisors must learn to separate their own expectations and aspirations from those of the evaluation protocol. A valid and reliable performance assessment can be derived only from an analysis of what really exists rather than from what supervisors would like to see. Subjective personnel appraisals increase anxiety and threaten to undermine the credibility of the evaluation process itself.

Recency Error

A recency error occurs when too much weight is placed on the employee's behavior immediately prior to the rating evaluation. Most performance evaluations are designed to cover a specific time frame, such as one year. If the supervisor does not keep documentation on the subordinate's activities during the evaluation period, there may be a tendency to overemphasize easily recalled behavior, usually the most recent. If recent performance is not indicative of the entire evaluation period, the evaluation is subverted. Generally, a recency error results in a higher rating than that actually deserved by the subordinate. Most subordinates are aware of evaluation dates and are most likely to improve their performance in anticipation of evaluations.

Sergeants are the human ingredient in performance appraisal. If they are knowledgeable and competent, the performance evaluation process will work. They hold the key to efficiency, effectiveness, and productivity in police work.

The Validity and Reliability of Performance Appraisal

Performance assessments are a waste of time and energy unless appropriate steps are taken to make sure they are both valid and reliable. The objective is to develop a reasonably accurate profile that reflects the competency of personnel, their individual capabilities, and their overall value to the police organization. This is a complex process that involves the use of an objective measuring instrument and the exercise of mature judgment by the first-line supervisor. Validity and reliability are critical variables in the success or failure of the performance review process.

A valid performance appraisal is an accurate measurement of traits (graphic rating scale), applied problem solving (critical incident), or goal acquisition (management by objectives) the evaluation process purports to measure. It zeroes in on the essential elements of the job and a limited number of important job-related behaviors. The appraisal itself is an assessment of the degree to which a very specific accomplishment is related to a clearly stated performance standard. If the measuring device is sound, essentially the same results will be achieved by any rater who uses it.

The employee appraisal process is considered reliable when it measures appropriate job-related performance accurately and consistently each time it is used. A reliable performance appraisal is not biased by the idiosyncrasies (or errors) of the rater, manipulation by the person evaluated, flaws in the design of the measuring device, or the constraints of time or place. Reliability relates to the degree of confidence one has that the supervisor, with the tools available, developed a realistic profile of the subordinate's on-the-job behavior.

Due to the nature of performance appraisal in criminal justice organizations, reliability is often difficult to achieve. No evaluative protocol is perfect. Performance ratings are developed, administered, scored, and acted on by people who exhibit prejudices and who, at times, exercise poor judgment. While these problems are fairly serious, they are not insurmountable. The following actions may be needed:

1. Adoption of clear-cut policies, procedures, rules, and regulations designed to govern the performance evaluation process.
2. Selection of a relatively simple yet valid performance appraisal instrument.

3. Training for supervisors in gathering and analyzing objective evaluative data.
4. Active participation by those being evaluated in all aspects of performance assessment.
5. A commitment by management to base appropriate personnel decisions on data derived from formal performance appraisals.

These measures will add to the reliability of the process and should help allay the anxiety of police officers who are scheduled for a performance appraisal. A relevant, reliable, and fair evaluation protocol is the keystone of a sound police personnel system.

The Evaluation Interview

Once the formal performance rating has been compiled, it (along with all recommendations for remediation) should be communicated to the employee as soon as possible. This is almost always done in what is known as an evaluation or appraisal interview. Again, the sergeant is the lead actor in this drama.

If the evaluation interview is handled well, everyone benefits. The employee is molded into a more competent police officer, the sergeant gains self-confidence in the area of personnel development, and the police agency becomes more efficient, effective, and productive. Mature human beings are able to deal with and accept criticism they view as deserved, constructive, and fair. However, if the interview is handled poorly, no one benefits. What started out as a creative way to motivate subordinates degenerates quickly into misunderstanding, distrust, resentment, and open hostility. Under these circumstances, performance appraisal becomes a demotivating factor that can jeopardize the organizational health of the entire police department.

The performance appraisal interview is a forum for positive face-to-face interaction between first-line supervisors and their subordinates. It is designed to facilitate collaborative problem solving and mutual goal setting. Both parties share responsibility for making the process work. Sergeants need to be open, honest, helpful, and supportive in dealing with employees. Police officers, however, must be willing to cooperate with and take reasonable direction from their superiors. Sincerity, empathy, and mutual respect are essential.

Statistically speaking, one-half of all employees fall below the median in terms of performance. Nonetheless, research shows that average employees estimate their own performance level at around the 75th percentile. Consequently, appraising and reporting on another person's performance (especially when there is a conflict in perception) can become one of the most emotionally charged of all management activities (Robbins, 2009).

The purpose of the appraisal interview is to explore the employee's strengths and weaknesses in light of objective evaluative data. If the performance meets or exceeds reasonable expectations, positive reinforcement should be provided. Praise or a sincere "thank you" is appropriate. Other types of rewards may also be in order. If deficiencies or performance problems are identified, however, remedial action must be agreed upon and initiated. At this point, the appraisal interview is transformed into a vehicle for collaborative problem solving and mutual goal setting. The two parties must work cooperatively to formulate a strategy for improving the employee's on-the-job performance. The ultimate value of the interview will depend on a police officer's ability to recognize the need for self-improvement and the sergeant's ability to stimulate that subordinate's desire to change.

A constructive performance assessment interview is designed to focus the subordinate's attention on the future rather than belaboring the past. According to management theorists such as George Bohlander & Scott Snell (2013), first-line supervisors should:

1. Discuss actual performance in very specific terms and express their criticism in a helpful, tactful way.
2. Emphasize the strengths on which the employee can build, as opposed to stressing only the weaknesses to be overcome.
3. Avoid suggestions involving only a cosmetic change in traits by promoting conformity through acceptable on-the-job behavior.
4. Concentrate on the opportunities for both personal growth and professional development that exist within the framework of the person's present position.
5. Limit expectations and specific plans for substantive change to a few important items that can be achieved within a reasonable period based on the expenditure of available resources.

The performance appraisal interview is a supervisor–employee activity that involves evaluating, teaching, coaching, and counseling. Once again, this task is not nearly as simple as it might appear. In order to accomplish even these relatively modest objectives, the sergeant must be able to establish rapport, empathize, and communicate effectively with subordinates. Sergeants must also possess the leadership skills necessary to motivate their personnel. Without natural talent, specialized training, supervisory experience, and leadership ability, sergeants are bound to fail. Under these conditions, performance appraisal is nothing more than a ritualistic exercise in futility.

While there is no best way to handle the performance appraisal interview, a number of operational steps can add structure to the process and help ensure a positive outcome. These steps are discussed here:

Step 1. Exercise care in scheduling the formal performance appraisal interview. Choose a time and place that affords maximum privacy and is free of unwarranted interruption. Encourage meaningful interaction by allowing sufficient time for full exploration of evaluative data as well as the sergeant's report. Solicit input and relevant feedback from the officer. Defuse anxiety and reduce defensiveness by using techniques designed to put the officer at ease and to stimulate a dialogue about performance problems and possible solutions to those problems. The environment in which the interview takes place is a critical variable in determining the overall value of the performance appraisal.

Step 2. Adequate preparation is absolutely essential. Both parties (supervisor/subordinate) should be ready and willing to review documentation, compare notes, and reach a consensus concerning the employee's job-related performance. Thorough preparation and uninhibited participation are key elements in effective performance appraisal. Anything less tends to undermine the reliability of the subordinate's performance profile.

Step 3. Compare the police officer's accomplishments with specific objectives or targets. Use objective data derived from the appraisal instrument. Do not be vague or use generalizations. Be precise about what was expected and about how close the employee came to actually meeting the goal. Specificity is an essential element in the performance assessment process.

Step 4. Give adequate credit (in terms of recognition and other forms of positive reinforcement) for what the police officer has, in fact, accomplished. Do not succumb to the temptation to take for granted things that have been done and to zero in on the employee's deficiencies or problems. Give credit where credit is due; build on the employee's strengths. Use the appraisal interview as a vehicle for growth and development, not as a forum for punishment.

Step 5. Carefully review objectives or tasks that have not been accomplished by the subordinate during the review period. Emphasize exactly where improvement is required. Explore with the officer why on-the-job performance must be improved and just how it can be done. Encourage dialogue and develop a plan to ensure full participation. Mutual problem solving and collective goal setting represent other key elements in the performance evaluation process.

Step 6. Do not assume that the fault is all due to the subordinate. If both parties have contributed to the performance problem, admit it. Do not overemphasize the officer's mistakes, faults, or weaknesses. Judge the police officer's performance, not his or her personality. Never compare the subordinate to an ideal-type third person. Stick to a mutual examination of concrete data and facts in an effort to determine exactly what they mean to the police officer, the sergeant, and the police department as a whole.

Step 7. Formulate and agree on new objectives and goals to be achieved during the next evaluation period. Be very specific in terms of what and how much is to be accomplished in a particular period. Show how the new objectives and goals are directly related to what has or has not been accomplished during the current evaluation period. This sets the stage for an even more objective performance appraisal the next time around.

Step 8. Review what you, as a first-line supervisor, can do to help the officer achieve specific objectives and goals. Identify resources that are available and explain how to access them. Play the role of teacher, coach, and counselor. Improvement in job performance is almost always a mutually dependent activity. Sharing the responsibility for personal and professional development brings about mutual respect, a shared sense of confidence, and renewed enthusiasm, as well as a commitment to the job.

Step 9. Formulate (in conjunction with the employee) a plan to monitor remediation and reevaluate the situation as conditions change. The belief that there will be some type of follow-up is a powerful catalyst for change. It motivates police officers to improve their own on-the-job performance and places an affirmative responsibility on the sergeant to make sure that actual improvement takes place (Bittel, 1993).

The appraisal interview is critically important. From a human resource development perspective, it is the nexus between police department needs and improved employee performance. The goal of the sergeant should be to handle the interview in such a way that officers (with the exception of incompetents and malcontents) will return to their job with an enthusiastic attitude and a genuine desire to improve their own on-the-job performance.

Performance appraisals and evaluative interviews are meaningless exercises unless there is remediation and follow-up. Follow-up is the synergistic ingredient in the performance evaluation process.

Remediation

As noted previously, there are three basic elements in the formal performance evaluation process: (1) objective assessment, (2) appraisal interview, and (3) remediation. Remediation refers to using available resources to correct a personnel problem or remedy a deficiency. While sergeants are almost always responsible for the assessment and normally conduct the appraisal interview, their role in remediation is often less direct.

If a deficiency or performance problem is relatively minor or fairly easy to correct, the sergeant is almost always authorized to deal with it directly. Due to the rank structure used in police work, sergeants resolve most performance-related problems informally and at their level (in the organization) based on their appraisal, teaching, coaching, and counseling skills. They keep "noise" out of the system. As first-line supervisors, sergeants are also responsible for the maintenance/direction function. They continuously monitor each officer's job-related performance in an effort to keep it on an even keel and to make sure it is consistent with the police department's mission, goals, and objectives. Sergeants use the formal performance appraisal process to diagnose serious problems, communicate concern, plan for remediation, provide follow-up, and schedule more difficult cases for administrative intervention. The performance review process is built on a medical model that has been adapted to police management.

In the event that there is no improvement in the police officer's on-the-job performance or if it continues to deteriorate, the sergeant has an obligation to take further action. The sergeant may be forced into recommending remediation through retraining, increasingly severe disciplinary action, or total separation from police service.

Due to the nature of bureaucracy, more serious and persistent performance problems are handled in a much different manner. They are "kicked upstairs," so to speak, for remediation or resolution. Consequently, the sergeant's role shifts to that of a supporting actor. All major personnel decisions are made by superior officers and are based on an organization-wide perspective. The sergeant gathers information for and makes recommendations to decision-makers, but no longer controls the evaluation process. Under these circumstances, the administration assumes responsibility for quality assurance within the police department.

Many of the more progressive police departments in the United States have initiated comprehensive employee assistance programs (EAPs) designed to help deviant, maladjusted, or marginal personnel who still may be capable of making a contribution to the organization. They also provide a variety of positive support services, such as marital counseling, stress management programs, and financial as well as preretirement planning. Specialized employee assistance programs represent an investment in the department's human resources, and a tacit recognition that first-line supervisors are not miracle workers. Sergeants are simply not equipped to handle problems related to health, stress, alcoholism and other drug addiction, domestic conflict, and so forth. Sergeants can be trained (using a thorough performance evaluation) to formulate a preliminary diagnosis of the problem and to make an appropriate referral. According to CALEA Standard 35.1.15:

> *A written directive establishes a personal early warning system to identify agency employees who may require agency intervention efforts. The system should indicate procedures for:*
>
> **a.** Provisions to initiate a review based on current patterns of collected material.
> **b.** Agency reporting requirements of conduct and behaviors.
> **c.** Annual evaluations of the system.
> **d.** The role of first- and second-level supervision.
> **e.** Remedial action.
> **f.** Some type of employee assistance, such as a formal employee assistance program, peer counseling, etc. (CALEA, 2006).

The EAP movement is predicated on the assumption that it is often much more cost-effective to salvage employees through medical, psychological, and social intervention than it is to apply negative sanctions or to separate them from the service. Therefore, sergeants play a pivotal role in the development of a police department's human resources.

Follow-Up

Follow-up by the supervisor completes the evaluation cycle, sets the stage for subsequent appraisals, and provides momentum for the performance assessment process. Sergeants are expected to check on each subordinate's progress in meeting the mutually acceptable goals established during the performance appraisal interview. This role-related task requires surveillance and continuous examination of data derived from a variety of performance measurements. In order to fulfill this responsibility, the sergeant should:

1. Recognize and reward police officers who are doing a good job.
2. Provide positive reinforcement for police officers who are making a good faith effort to change their behavior and improve their on-the-job performance.
3. Assist (through training, coaching, counseling, and other referral services) police officers who need help improving their performance.
4. Recommend appropriate disciplinary action for individual police officers who will not change their behavior or work to improve their job-related performance.

Follow-up is a supervisory activity designed to motivate personnel and to serve as a springboard to professional growth and development. Without adequate follow-up, periodic performance appraisals become rather mundane, routine managerial tasks with little or no practical value. Police managers, sergeants, and their subordinates merely attempt to project

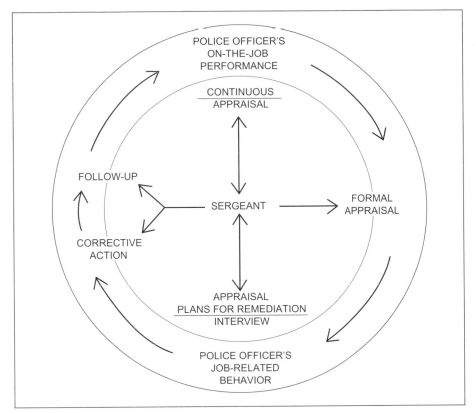

FIGURE 8.7 The Sergeant's role in performance appraisal.

the impression that they care about the efficiency, effectiveness, and productivity of human resources in police work. Perfunctory performance appraisal is used to disguise the discrepancy between the status quo and what could be; honest assessment motivates those in search of excellence. Appraisal should be a daily activity that is summarized periodically in a formal appraisal report and interview. All other things being equal, police officers who accept the inevitability of fair and continuous assessment will try to perform their best work at all times, not just during the formal evaluation period (see Figure 8.7).

Trends in Performance Appraisals

While total quality management guru W. Edwards Deming called performance appraisals "management by fear" (Behn, 1994), they are not headed for extinction in modern police work. On the contrary, they are becoming much more help oriented and far less punitive. Based on the realization that rank-and-file police officers are the primary source of all productive gain, the philosophy stressed throughout this chapter is that supervisors must lead their subordinates to higher levels of performance by using natural forces within the work group as opposed to the formal authority vested in them by virtue of their position in the organization (Kennish, 1994). This is a quantum leap from the days when negative discipline reigned supreme and humane concern was the exception rather than the rule (Coens & Jenkins, 2002).

Two new trends that will have an impact on first-line police supervision are now emerging. The first deals with evaluating police officer performance under community-oriented policing. The second relates to subordinates evaluating their supervisor's performance. Both of these trends are by-products of the new emphasis on participatory management in modern police work.

Performance Evaluation in Community-Oriented Policing

Community-oriented policing, regardless of its specific form, is essentially a program in which the police adopt organizational arrangements that focus on fear reduction and order-maintenance activities through the involvement of citizens, while using mutually acceptable problem-solving techniques (Gaines & Kappeler, 2011). It is an interactive process in which police officers and citizens work together collaboratively.

More and more municipal governments are experimenting with community-oriented policing. It is designed to elicit different kinds of resources for use in the battle against crime. First-line police supervisors are expected to achieve total quality results with human resources in the work group, coupled with those in the community at large.

Community-oriented policing is based on the assumption that delegation of authority plus meaningful participation in decision-making leads to empowerment. The empowerment of police personnel and members of the community is viewed as the bottom line in any effective law enforcement strategy (Whisenand & Rush, 2011).

Traditional performance evaluation methods are not, in and of themselves, sufficient to gauge the quality of officer performance in a community-oriented policing environment. Three other dimensions have been identified and must be integrated into the process. Performance evaluations are also used to:

1. Convey reasonable expectations to police personnel about both the content and the style of their behavior, while reinforcing commitment to the department's mission, values, goals, and objectives. This serves as a vehicle for socialization.
2. Document the types of problems and situations that officers encounter in the neighborhood and approaches they take in resolving them. This provides an analysis of the types of resources and other managerial supports needed to deal with problems. It gives police officers an opportunity to have their individual efforts recognized.
3. Identify organizational factors that hinder performance enhancement or the solicitation of ideas for dealing with changing conditions. This gives the people doing the work a meaningful role in reshaping that work in order to improve departmental as well as individual performance.

The Houston Police Department embraced community-oriented policing as its new policing style in 1986. Known as neighborhood-oriented policing, it provides managers with a philosophical foundation and conceptual framework to direct the organization in a manner that is consistent with community needs. From an operational point of view, it encourages police officers to assume responsibility for managing the delivery of essential services in the geographical areas to which they are assigned.

A taskforce composed of police officers and first-line supervisors spent a considerable amount of time gathering, manipulating, and collating information. A second group, consisting of police volunteers, took the information gathered by the taskforce and developed a new performance evaluation protocol. This process and the resulting instrumentation sought to bridge existing roles and responsibilities with emerging ones based on the neighborhood policing philosophy.

Performance evaluations of patrol officers and their respective sergeants used six newly developed forms designed to elicit data and feedback. Each of the forms is described:

1. Patrol Officer's Biannual Assessment Report. This form is used by sergeants to evaluate police officer performance based on 22 specific criteria. In addition, space is provided for written comments regarding work assignments, overall work progress, and special recognition. Criteria reflect the department's expectations concerning police officer performance when it comes to neighborhood-oriented policing.

2. Patrol Officer's Monthly Worksheet. The form is designed as a tool to guide each officer's actions during a designated tour of duty. Police officers are given direct input into their own appraisal. This allows officers to identify the different types of projects or programs they have worked on during the evaluation period and report on progress they have made.

3. Community Information Form. Citizen–police officer interaction is implicit in all neighborhood-oriented policing strategies. This particular form, if the officer chooses to submit it, elicits information from citizens who worked on projects with specific officers. The information requested is very specific and provides sergeants with additional insight into what the officer was trying to accomplish and how the officer is going about doing it.

4. Calls for Service—Citizen Feedback Form. Like almost all police departments, the most frequent source of officer–citizen interaction is the call for service. The Calls for Service—Citizen Feedback Form is designed to gather information on the quality as well as the nature of the contact. Citizens are asked a few questions by sergeants. The responses are made a matter of "record" and factored into the overall evaluation. Sergeants use the form at least once a month.

5. Investigator Questionnaire. All police officers are expected to conduct high-quality criminal investigations. Even though the information contained in an investigative report provides a critical database for case managers, this material was seldom reviewed by the officer's immediate supervisor. The function of the investigator questionnaire is to obtain information from investigative sergeants concerning an officer's knowledge and quality of performance as these factors relate to both preliminary and follow-up investigations. The police officer determines whether to submit the form.

6. Officer's Immediate Supervisor Assessment Form. Officers are given an opportunity to evaluate their immediate supervisors in relation to different dimensions of supervisory

work. While the feedback is fairly general in nature, the form must be completed and returned to the sergeant's superior. The information helps identify significant trends in the relationship between the sergeant and subordinate personnel (Wycoff & Oettmeier, 1996).

Needless to say, the performance evaluation protocol just described represents a radical departure from past practices in law enforcement.

Some police departments have experimented with team evaluations and entire department evaluations using citizen surveys. These types of evaluations focus on how well the entire agency is accomplishing its mission. While many departments use crime rates, arrest rates, ratios of police-to-citizen population, and timely response to calls as measures of effectiveness and efficiency, these measures do not truly reflect the effectiveness and efficiency of the police per se. Because of the increased emphasis on community policing, it is the community that can best evaluate how well the police are doing. Therefore, reduction of the fear of crime within a community is a better measure of the police than experiencing a lower crime rate. To assess how a community feels about the police, several departments have initiated citizen and community surveys that measure fear of crime and citizen concerns with their local police. This allows for feedback and prevents the police from losing touch with the community they serve.

A.J. McKee (2001) has developed and tested a community survey that addresses how well a police department's community-policing efforts measure up with the community. The evaluation survey was tested in Hattiesburg, Mississippi, and examined four scales: (1) quality of police contact, (2) perceptions of crime and disorder, (3) personal fear factor, and (4) community cohesion. Surveys such as McKee's allow smaller police departments to evaluate their community policing efforts without undue expense (see Figure 8.8).

New approaches to police work generate a need for new performance evaluation strategies. Houston's evaluation protocol is experimental and undergoing continuous revision. One thing is certain—it has changed the traditional role of the police sergeant in the performance evaluation process. It also subjects first-line supervisors to performance evaluation by their subordinates.

Evaluating the Performance of Supervisors and Managers

In a related development, management theorists are placing more emphasis on employees evaluating the performance of their own supervisors and managers. Theorists link this to the popular participatory management and worker empowerment movements sweeping the country today.

While some mainstream academic, industrial, and corporate entities see some value in having employees rate their supervisors (McGaney & Smith, 1993), the concept has been slow to develop in police work. In most police departments, performance evaluation is still considered the prerogative of management. The evolving participatory management and worker empowerment movements in law enforcement may alter the status quo, however.

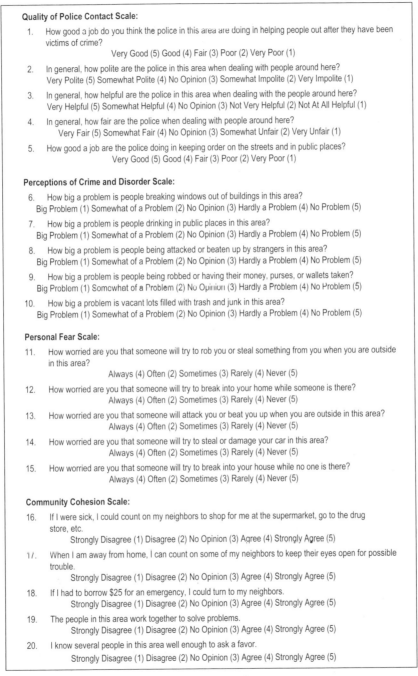

Quality of Police Contact Scale:

1. How good a job do you think the police in this area are doing in helping people out after they have been victims of crime?
   Very Good (5) Good (4) Fair (3) Poor (2) Very Poor (1)

2. In general, how polite are the police in this area when dealing with people around here?
   Very Polite (5) Somewhat Polite (4) No Opinion (3) Somewhat Impolite (2) Very Impolite (1)

3. In general, how helpful are the police in this area when dealing with the people around here?
   Very Helpful (5) Somewhat Helpful (4) No Opinion (3) Not Very Helpful (2) Not At All Helpful (1)

4. In general, how fair are the police when dealing with people around here?
   Very Fair (5) Somewhat Fair (4) No Opinion (3) Somewhat Unfair (2) Very Unfair (1)

5. How good a job are the police doing in keeping order on the streets and in public places?
   Very Good (5) Good (4) Fair (3) Poor (2) Very Poor (1)

Perceptions of Crime and Disorder Scale:

6. How big a problem is people breaking windows out of buildings in this area?
   Big Problem (1) Somewhat of a Problem (2) No Opinion (3) Hardly a Problem (4) No Problem (5)

7. How big a problem is people drinking in public places in this area?
   Big Problem (1) Somewhat of a Problem (2) No Opinion (3) Hardly a Problem (4) No Problem (5)

8. How big a problem is people being attacked or beaten up by strangers in this area?
   Big Problem (1) Somewhat of a Problem (2) No Opinion (3) Hardly a Problem (4) No Problem (5)

9. How big a problem is people being robbed or having their money, purses, or wallets taken?
   Big Problem (1) Somewhat of a Problem (2) No Opinion (3) Hardly a Problem (4) No Problem (5)

10. How big a problem is vacant lots filled with trash and junk in this area?
    Big Problem (1) Somewhat of a Problem (2) No Opinion (3) Hardly a Problem (4) No Problem (5)

Personal Fear Scale:

11. How worried are you that someone will try to rob you or steal something from you when you are outside in this area?
    Always (4) Often (2) Sometimes (3) Rarely (4) Never (5)

12. How worried are you that someone will try to break into your home while someone is there?
    Always (4) Often (2) Sometimes (3) Rarely (4) Never (5)

13. How worried are you that someone will attack you or beat you up when you are outside in this area?
    Always (4) Often (2) Sometimes (3) Rarely (4) Never (5)

14. How worried are you that someone will try to steal or damage your car in this area?
    Always (4) Often (2) Sometimes (3) Rarely (4) Never (5)

15. How worried are you that someone will try to break into your house while no one is there?
    Always (4) Often (2) Sometimes (3) Rarely (4) Never (5)

Community Cohesion Scale:

16. If I were sick, I could count on my neighbors to shop for me at the supermarket, go to the drug store, etc.
    Strongly Disagree (1) Disagree (2) No Opinion (3) Agree (4) Strongly Agree (5)

17. When I am away from home, I can count on some of my neighbors to keep their eyes open for possible trouble.
    Strongly Disagree (1) Disagree (2) No Opinion (3) Agree (4) Strongly Agree (5)

18. If I had to borrow $25 for an emergency, I could turn to my neighbors.
    Strongly Disagree (1) Disagree (2) No Opinion (3) Agree (4) Strongly Agree (5)

19. The people in this area work together to solve problems.
    Strongly Disagree (1) Disagree (2) No Opinion (3) Agree (4) Strongly Agree (5)

20. I know several people in this area well enough to ask a favor.
    Strongly Disagree (1) Disagree (2) No Opinion (3) Agree (4) Strongly Agree (5)

FIGURE 8.8 The community policing evaluation survey. *Adapted from A.J. McKee (2001). "The Community Policing Evaluation Survey: Reliability, Validity, and Structure."* American Journal of Criminal Justice, *Vol. 25, No. 2, pp. 199–209.*

Whetstone (1994) has outlined what should be evaluated in terms of beneficial supervisory traits, as well as pitfalls inherent in the evaluative process. Because much of a supervisor's or manager's work is not observed by subordinates, he argues that the appraisal of performance should focus primarily on leadership issues.

In order to provide superiors with meaningful feedback, police officers should have sufficient training to perform the evaluation. In Whetstone's opinion, officers should use a standard forced-choice instrument designed to provide structure and guide the rater in evaluating the attributes that the police department thinks are most important.

While there are several commercially available upward-feedback rating forms on the market, Whetstone believes that departments may be ahead of the game by creating their own. In doing so, they can target the traits that are most important to them.

The notion of supervisor evaluations sounds good, but some police officers are reluctant to support this concept for fear of some type of retaliation by those who receive negative appraisals. This fear, coupled with the "errors" discussed earlier in this chapter, could have an adverse effect on the objectivity of the evaluation and create morale problems. The success or failure of the upward-feedback program depends on management's commitment to the concept, as well as the safeguards built into the implementation process.

Whetstone argues that police officers doing the evaluation should sign the rating form. This gives top management the opportunity, when necessary, to check with the evaluator on specific incidents used as the basis for the evaluation. He also recommends that the completed rating forms be turned in to a neutral evaluation proctor. In one pilot program, it was found that officer confidence, candor, and security increased when they were allowed to have meaningful input in the proctor selection process. Individual evaluations are held in total confidentiality, with the contents integrated in such a way as to produce a composite profile.

Upward-feedback programs are designed to promote more positive interaction between employees, provide top management with a new source of information about individual on-the-job performance by all police personnel, and aid in the career development of those who are involved in the process. Armed with knowledge (concerning their strengths and weaknesses), supervisors and administrators are in a position to adjust their leadership style to benefit subordinates, the police department, and themselves. The ultimate goal is self-improvement.

Even though bureaucratic inertia is well entrenched in police work, changes are in the air. The emerging emphasis on meaningful employee participation, total quality management, total quality results, community-oriented policing, and empowerment makes it a truly exciting time to be in law enforcement.

References

Behn, R. D. (1994). Motivating without rewards: A challenge to public managers. *Governing*, 7(8).

Bittel, L. R. (1993). *What every supervisor should know* (7th ed.). New York: McGraw-Hill.

Bohlander, G. W., & Snell, S. A. (2013). *Managing human resources* (16th ed.). Cincinnati, OH: South-Western.

CALEA, (2006). *Standards for law enforcement agencies*. Fairfax, VA: Commission on Accreditation for Law Enforcement Agencies, Inc.

Coens, T., & Jenkins, M. (2002). *Abolishing performance appraisals: Why they backfire and what to do instead.* San Francisco, CA: Berrett-Koehler Publishers.

Fulmer, R. M. (1988). *The new management* (4th ed.). New York: Macmillan.

Gaines, L. K., & Kappeler, V. E. (2011). *Policing in America* (7th ed.). Boston: Elsevier (Anderson Publishing).

Gaines, L. K., Southerland, M. D., & Angell, J. E. (2012). *Police administration* (3rd ed.). New York: McGraw-Hill.

Gul, S. K., & O'Connell, P. E. (2012). *Police performance appraisals: A comparative perspective.* Boca Raton, FL: CRC Press.

Hamblin, K. (1994). Why the surprise at crime bill's catch-22? *Denver Post* Oct. 23: 3F.

Holden, R. N. (1994). *Modern police management* (2nd ed.). Englewood Cliffs, NJ: Prentice Hall.

Holt, D. H. (1993). *Management: Principles and practices* (3rd ed.). Englewood Cliffs, NJ: Prentice Hall.

Iannone, N. F., & Iannone, M. (2013). *Supervision of police personnel* (8th ed.). Englewood Cliffs, NJ: Prentice Hall.

Jones, T. L. (1998). Developing performance standards. *Law and Order, 40*(7).

Kennish, J. W. (1994). Managing: Motivating with a positive, participatory policy. *Security Management, 38*(8).

Kramer, M. (1998). Designing an individual performance evaluation system: A values-based process. *FBI Law Enforcement Bulletin, 67*(3).

Leonard, E. C. (2013). *Supervision: Concepts and practices of management* (12th ed.). Cincinnati, OH: South-Western.

Leonard, V. A., & More, H. W. (2000). *Police organization and management* (9th ed.). New York: The Foundation Press, Inc.

McGaney, R., & Smith, S. (1993). When workers rate the boss. *Training, 3*(1).

McKee, A. J. (2001). The community policing evaluation survey: Reliability, validity and structure. *American Journal of Criminal Justice, 25*(2).

National Advisory Commission on Criminal Justice Standards and Goals, (1973). *The police.* Washington, DC: U.S. Government Printing Office.

Office of Community Oriented Policing Services, (2011). *The impact of the economic downturn on American police agencies.* Washington, DC: U.S. Department of Justice, Office of Community Oriented Policing Services, October. Available at <http://www.cops.usdoj.gov/files/RIC/Publications/e101113406_Economic%20Impact.pdf>.

Plunkett, R. W. (1992). *Supervision: The direction of people at work* (6th ed.). Boston, MA: Allyn & Bacon.

Robbins, S. P. (2009). *Organizational behavior* (13th ed.). Englewood Cliffs, NJ: Prentice Hall.

Steinmetz, L. L., & Todd, H. R., Jr. (1992). *Supervision: First-line management* (5th ed.). Boston, MA: Richard D. Irwin.

Swanson, C. R., Territo, L., & Taylor, R. W. (2012). *Police administration* (8th ed.). Englewood Cliffs, NJ: Prentice Hall.

Travis, J., & Brann, J. (1997). Measuring what matters: Developing measures of what the police do: *National Institute of Justice Research in Action.* Washington, DC: U.S. Department of Justice.

Trojanowicz, R. G. (1980). *The environment of the first-line police supervisor.* Englewood Cliffs, NJ: Prentice Hall.

U.S. Department of Justice, (2009). *Justice expenditure and employment extracts.* Washington, DC: Bureau of Justice Statistics.

Walsh, W. F., & Donovan, E. J. (1990). *The supervision of police personnel: A performance-based approach.* Dubuque, IA: Kendall/Hunt.

Whetstone, T. S. (1994). Subordinates evaluate supervisory and administrative performance. *The Police Chief, LXI*(6).

Whisenand, P. M., & Rush, G. E. (2011). *Supervising police personnel* (7th ed.). Englewood Cliffs, NJ: Prentice Hall.

Wycoff, M. A., & Oettmeier, T. N. (1996). *Planning and Implementation issues for community oriented policing: The Houston experience.* Washington, DC: National Institute of Justice.

9

Training, Coaching, Counseling, and Mentoring
Helping Officers Grow and Develop

CASE STUDY
Sergeant Lara Whitehouse

DEPARTMENT

The Lawrence Police Department's history goes back to 1887, when three marshals were employed to keep order in the newly created town. Over the years it grew slowly as more and more people migrated west, and it was finally incorporated in 1902. A chief of police was appointed by the first elected mayor with the approval of the three-member city council. Departmental personnel grew with the increase of population, and recently there were 64 sworn officers that handled calls for service. In the last calendar year there were more than 48,000 emergency and informational calls. Organizationally the department has three bureaus: Investigative, Operations, and Administration. A majority of the sworn officers are assigned to Operations, which has a patrol unit and a traffic component. It also contains a K-9 program, a mounted component, and a communications center.

The patrol unit, which is a component of the Operations Division, and the assigned officers record and conduct a preliminary investigation, enforce ordinances and laws, perform routine and directed patrol, and are responsible for traffic control and regulation. Patrol is divided into three watches. The watch commander is a lieutenant and sergeants supervise assigned personnel. Field officers work four 10-hour shifts weekly. In more recent years, effort has been placed on improving the quality of life for residents, with an emphasis on such things as reducing graffiti, excessive noise, aggressive panhandling, and public drunkenness. The department has seven patrol beats that cover around the clock.

The Investigative bureau duties include a range of activities and auxiliary services such as: recruitment, crime prevention, youth services, media relations, and a citizen's academy. Its major components include a detective unit, special operations, and records. Traditionally, when vacancies are available, line officers are selected to become investigators, and they serve for a three-year period unless promoted to a higher rank. It is part of a rotation program that allows officers to vary the tasks they perform. There has always been excellent cooperation between investigation and patrol. The follow-up investigators pass a copy of the report back to the officers who conducted the preliminary investigation.

Administration is a smaller unit and is headed by a civilian. Its functions include the analysis of offenses, fingerprinting, and budget forecasting and preparation. It also supervises vehicular and facilities maintenance. The director of this unit presents the budget to the city manager for his or her consideration and approval.

The chief of police is the designated coordinator of emergency services and is responsible for preparing and maintaining programs that provide a means for the community to respond to normal, manmade, or technological catastrophes. There is a community response emergency team (CRET) that responds to various types of disasters. Part of this program is a completely automated alert notification service that allows for contact at home or work, or directed to a mobile phone (rapid notify).

CRIME

Lawrence, for a city its size, has a relatively low violent crime rate and a slightly high property crime rate. During the past calendar year for which statistics are available, 131 violent crimes were reported and 2210 property offenses occurred. There was only one murder and non-negligent manslaughter, and this proved to be the consequences of domestic violence. There were 16 forcible rapes. Most often these offenses were committed in the older part of town, which contains numerous bars and restaurants, as well as three party clubs. Additionally, there were 37 robberies and 77 aggravated assaults. The property crime index was down 2.5 percent compared to the previous year, with the exception of motor vehicle theft, which totaled 145 offenses (an increase by 10 occurrences). Burglaries occurred 388 times, and 91 percent of these occurrences were residential in nature. They occurred on every beat with no clear pattern as to why or where. Larceny/thefts were reported 1687 times and happened throughout the community. There were six reported cases of arson that were investigated by detectives and the fire marshal's office—none of which were cleared. The overall crime rate for the city reduced over the last seven years, and there is no real explanation for the reduction. A recent community survey suggested that the fear of crime, especially violent offenses, was of great concern to residents. In response to this, a city-wide taskforce was created to respond to the fear and is scheduled to have a preliminary report in six months. This information will be given to the city manager, and it is anticipated that there will be numerous open meetings to present the findings to political leaders and residents.

COMMUNITY

In its early years the city grew steadily, as water became more accessible from deep well drilling and the valley flourished with truck gardens, vineyards, orchards, and poultry products. Along with settlers some unsavory people arrived, and law enforcement became problematic. After many years, the population stabilized, and it exceeded the 100,000 mark at the beginning of the twenty-first century. Ethnic breakdown in the community reflects a small changing mix as more Hispanics move into the community. The last census numbered that population at 18.41 percent. Caucasians are the largest group at 72.39 percent, followed by Asians at 7.36 percent; the remainder include African-Americans, American Indians, Alaskan Natives, and Islanders. The population is 50.5 percent male and 49.5 percent female. The median age is 35.7 years, and those 19 and under are just under one-third of the population. Within the unified school district there are three high schools and three middle schools. Additionally, there is one continuation high school and an adult educational program. The climate is moderate, and the annual yearly rainfall is 23.2 inches. There are considerable recreational and cultural activities, including 23 parks, three golf courses, two city swimming pools, a performance arts center, and three major theaters. The city is blessed with a large interstate highway nearby as well as two state highways. The railroad provides a freight service as well as an Amtrak train service, and an airport is 19 miles north. There are 43,943 occupied dwellings; two-thirds of these are owner-occupied. Additionally, there are six mobile home parks.

OFFICER

Sergeant Lara Whitehouse had been a high school teacher for three years before applying for and being accepted by the police department. She had a cousin who was a training officer in the nearby metropolitan police department, and once she showed an interest in law enforcement, he encouraged her to apply for the test in the Lawrence Police Department because the department had an excellent reputation and was known to emphasize crime prevention and working with youths. She came to the department with a teaching credential and bachelor's degree in psychology. She continued her higher education in a master's program in counseling and had completed four courses with straight As while attending part-time. She is single, 31 years of age, and plans on law enforcement as her career. She chose a local department because she wanted to stay in the area, and she knew that "Feds" had to move around a great deal in most instances. In high school she played volleyball and softball, and as a senior she was on the county all-star softball team as a shortstop. After graduation she continued playing in an adult women's league and that, along with running, keeps her in good physical shape. Additionally, she joined Toastmasters, which helped her improve her speaking skills and gave her greater confidence when making presentations before groups. Her initial assignment was to the swing shift in patrol, and she was posted to beat three, which was a mixed area that was residential with two strip malls and a number of small businesses.

She was under the tutelage of a field training officer (FTO) and learned quickly how to deal with street situations. She received excellent ratings during the period she was being closely supervised and coached. After three years' experience on the swing shift, she took and passed the examination for sergeant and came out number two on the list. After selection she was switched to the midnight shift serving under the lieutenant, who was the watch commander, and on occasion she served as watch commander. After several years' service she was transferred to the day shift and served in a crime prevention assignment.

PROBLEM

The city was beginning to see the appearance of what appeared to be a youth gang. Graffiti was becoming increasingly common. Residential burglaries committed by juveniles also increased during the last three years, and there were indications that some of these offenses were committed by the same group of teenagers. School authorities and the county juvenile probation department were in the dark about these matters, as were departmental officers who worked in youth services.

Wanting an answer, the bureau operation commander created a taskforce to determine the extent and nature of the problem. The charge was relatively simple: "Let us nip this potential problem in the bud before it becomes a serious issue." The taskforce was to be given whatever resources were needed from within the department, and the bureau commander stated that he would arrange for external assistance as needed to include drawing upon the experience of all levels of government that have been confronted with similar problems. He was especially interested in the potential of applying video-text chat to a crime prevention program. A component of the taskforce was to determine what training was needed in the department for investigators and line officers. Sergeant Whitehouse was in the small group that was assigned this task, while other taskforce members addressed other issues. Currently the police academy has an eight-hour block of instruction on juvenile law and procedures.

WHAT WOULD YOU DO?

The initial step taken was to review the studies done by the National Institute of Justice and the data available through the National Criminal Justice Reference Service. Do you agree with this initial approach? Why or why not? What other sources would you go to? Identify. Put yourself in Sergeant Whitehouse's place. What would you do to prepare for the initial meeting? Why? Would a formal presentation by you be appropriate? Why or why not? Explain. Other departments have school resource officers assigned to selected schools. Is that an option? How would you apply the ROSE acronym about the assumptions of learning when designing a block of instruction? Justify. What part should the field training officers' play in the development of training in this area? How would the task analysis such as STAR help when creating a curriculum? Be prepared to discuss. Does a sergeant have a unique position in the proposed process? If so, what is it? Justify your position.

Training, coaching, counseling, and mentoring are all significant elements of today's modern law enforcement didactic process. Over the years, this practice has become highly formalized. Police academies and state standards for teaching law enforcement personnel the skills, knowledge, attitudes, and behavior needed to function successfully proliferate in every part of this nation. Moreover, in its many forms, training serves as the focal point for creating and maintaining the efficiency, effectiveness, and productivity of a department. Each component contributes to the professionalization of the field, and significant progress has been made overall from the time that an individual was given a badge and a weapon and sent out on the street by himself or herself or with an old-timer.

In recent years, it has become increasingly common for high-performance law enforcement organizations to design and implement training and developmental programs by:

1. Identifying the knowledge, skills, abilities, and behaviors (competencies) that employees need to support the organizational mission, vision, core values, and goals. Furthermore, it is essential to measure the extent to which employees actually possess those competencies.

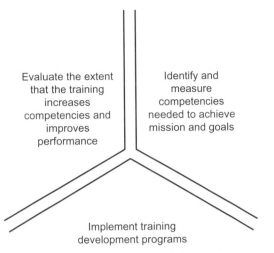

FIGURE 9.1 Key steps in developing training programs. *Source: U.S. General Accountability Office (2006). Human Capital—Design, Implementation, and Evaluation of Training at Selected Agencies. Washington, DC: GAO.*

2. Designing and implementing training programs to meet any identified gaps in those needs.
3. Evaluating the extent to which training programs actually increase employees' individual competencies and performance levels, as well as overall organizational performance.

There are certain key steps in developing viable training programs, which are set forth in Figure 9.1.

Law enforcement agencies may encounter certain challenges in their effort to identify and measure the human, tactical, affective, conceptual, and knowledge-based skills that officers need to possess to support the mission of the agency and achieve organizational goals. The tactical and knowledge-based skills are readily apparent, such as physical fitness, application of the law, and marksmanship, but greater difficulty is encountered when skills are affective or conceptual in nature. In progressive agencies, training programs are evaluated periodically to determine if the agency has provided the training and development opportunities needed to ensure that core skills were actually developed. Currently, many agencies utilize post-training tests to determine the extent to which employees actually possess identifiable core skills. A critical variable in the evaluation of training is the need for staff resources to accomplish this vital aspect of the training process. In actuality, what might occur is that some training is limited because of budgetary restraints and new police officers generally complete an academy that consists of basic training that is usually mandated by state law enforcement training entities and can include topics ranging from community policing to racial profiling.

Teaching Officers

Supervisors and trainers should work to realize the effectiveness of their most valuable resource—people. Consideration must be given to providing for affective outcomes such as attitudes and motivation that can include such variables as the desire to learn, safety considerations, and one's orientation to customer satisfaction (Della, 2004). Supervisors should especially be aware of the theory of andragogy, which addresses in particular the needs of adult learners. The key is that officers have to enter each learning activity with a persona that is best described as encompassing a positive self-image and as someone with the qualities of being self-directing, reliable, mature, and an independent learner. Adult learning should reflect the theory of andragogy, which emphasizes that adults are self-directed and are willing to take responsibility for their decisions. The proponent of this theory, Malcolm Knowles, stresses that instructors of adults need to focus primarily on the process rather than just the transmission of content. In other words, one should make every effort to function as a resource. The supervisor must endeavor to function as a facilitator, rather than the traditional focus on lecturing as a means of transmitting knowledge. Adults readily become goal oriented and will learn things needed to achieve a place in an organization. Supervisors can respond to this need by teaching a new officer how to write an acceptable incident report rather than emphasizing the principles of composition. Adults tend to focus on problem orientation and strive to acquire the skills and knowledge needed to deal with real-life situations. Adults have a real psychological need to be self-directing and positive participants. If the training process does not provide for this type of involvement, officers can, over time, become aggrieved and resistive. In addition, adults over the years have been involved in various learning situations that have allowed them to accumulate a considerable reservoir of experiences that can serve as a base for the evaluation of events in the current learning situation. In other words, tap that resource as a means of enhancing the learning process.

Essentially, andragogy is based on four assumptions about learning; this acronym is known as **ROSE** and is listed in Figure 9.2.

Officers respond best to being provided an opportunity to demonstrate how one applies new knowledge to an actual field situation under the tutelage of a supervisor. Experience shows that greater retention occurs when an officer is allowed to experience something personally followed by a supervisor discussing the specifics of a situation with an officer in terms of what was done and, if necessary, how the process can be improved. The supervisor should keep in mind that listening should preempt lecturing. In fact, lecturing should only be used in exceptional situations. It is best to discuss the issue and strive to let the officer solve the problem by telling you exactly how he or she might proceed. The old fallback is for the supervisor to

R	Readiness to learn
O	Orientation to learning
S	Self-concept
E	Experience

FIGURE 9.2 Assumptions about learning (ROSE). *Source: Adapted from Brian C. Della (2004). "Nontraditional Training Systems: Realizing the Effectiveness of an Agency's Most Valuable Resource." FBI Law Enforcement Bulletin, Vol. 73, No. 6: 2–39.*

listen, respond to questions, and engage the officer in a discussion of issues. An officer's retention increases according to the following guidelines:

1. Sixty percent of what we discuss with others.
2. Seventy percent of what we experience personally.
3. Eighty percent of what we discover and solve individually (Della, 2004).

These are in sharp contrast to the fact that an officer will only recall 20 percent of what is heard and only 40 percent of what is seen and heard. Thus, active participation in the learning process is the key to the professionalization of each officer.

When instructing, coaching, mentoring, or counseling, it is absolutely essential to treat each officer as a responsible adult. Above all, officers should not be passive participants. Each and every learning activity should focus on action and positive involvement. The relationship between an officer and the supervisor should be supportive, friendly, and informal, and every effort should be made to foster a sense of mutual respect. The philosophical underpinning is that each component of this equation has the capability of learning from each other. Under no circumstances should one being supervised be placed in the position of being a passive recipient (Kennedy, 2003). An early step in the training process is for the supervisor to base a positive involvement process on the previous experience of the officer. This is especially true for lateral transfer officers or for those who have gone through a field-training officer program, as well as those who are new academy graduates with limited or no supervision in the field. Whenever possible, officers should be given an opportunity to draw upon previous experience and share those experiences with the supervisor/trainer through positive interaction. A supervisor should make every effort to see that each learning activity has a direct application to a field situation. When officers determine that the content of a learning activity is relevant, it can serve as a catalyst for acquiring and retaining needed job knowledge and skills, resulting in goal and mission attainment.

Formal Training

In a recent year more than 50,000 recruits successfully completed academy training and 13 percent of the recruits who started an academy training program did not complete the course. It is apparent that the academy has become a strong element in the screening process for new employees. Many academies provide recruits with a basic level of training that exceeds state requirements. The median level of training was 720 hours. Nationwide there are 626 state and local law enforcement academies that offer basic law enforcement training. In addition, there are other basic training sources, such as regional academies, colleges, universities, and technical schools. Training is big business and academies employ 12,200 full-time instructors and twice as many part-time instructors. Additional types of training include:

1. In-service
2. Specialized
3. Supervision

4. Field training officer

5. Managerial

Eighty-four percent of state and local academies offer specialized training, such as K9 and SWAT, and more than two-thirds offer first-line or higher supervisory training. In addition, more than half offer training for FTOs (Hickman, 2005). Interestingly, more than 90 percent of the academies had access to an outdoor firing range, a vehicle operation range, a weight room, and a defensive tactics room. Also, academies were found to have laptop computers (65%), Internet/online classes (53%), or mobile data terminals or computers (50%). Figure 9.3 sets forth the various topics and the median number of hours of instruction for each topic. All states require some form of basic training for the newly hired, and the Commission on Accreditation for Enforcement Agencies has been at the forefront by creating standards for police training. In recent years, more law enforcement agencies have availed themselves of the accreditation process. Following are some standards that apply to training:

33.4.1 The agency requires all sworn officers to complete a recruit training program prior to assignment in any capacity in which the officer is allowed to carry a weapon or is in a position to make an arrest, except as part of a formal field training program required in standard 33.4.3.

33.4.2 A written directive requires the agency's recruit training program to include:

    a. A curriculum based on tasks of the most frequent assignment associated duties of officers who complete recruit training

    b. Use of evaluation techniques designed to measure competency in the required skills, knowledge, and abilities. (Commission on Accreditation for Law Enforcement Agencies, 2006)

All states require some form of basic training for police recruits. Determined by a federally funded research project, Figure 9.3 lists topics by percentage as well as the median number of hours of instruction for each element. Overall, there is an amazing commonality of topics with few exceptions.

Training in the topics listed in Figure 9.3 allows recruits to acquire and improve job-related skills. Trainers can provide the fundamentals needed to move officers to a higher level of intellectual thought and keep people motivated, hence improving the agency's ability to serve the community. It also serves as a base for an officer's career development. It has been shown that when officers learn in a purposeful environment they tend to become lifelong learners who seek further educational and training opportunities.

Once a curriculum is created through task analysis, police managers can determine whether a training course provides the knowledge and skills required to do the job. If the training is inadequate, police managers have an obligation to reexamine the training methods. One of the first major task analyses involving police officers was Project STAR (System Training and Analysis of Requirements). Project STAR focused on the roles, tasks, and training needs of police personnel. Research has determined that police officers performed 13 roles fulfilled by 33 unique tasks (Smith et al., 1974). After the individual tasks were identified, specific performance objectives

	Percentage of Academies Providing Training in Topic Areas	Median Number of Hours of Instruction Required
Training Topics		
Firearms skills	99%	60
Basic first-aid/CPR	99	24
Emergency vehicle operations	99	38
Self-defense	99	44
Criminal law	98	40
Domestic violence	98	12
Ethics and integrity	98	8
Investigations	98	45
Patrol procedures/ techniques	98	40
Juvenile law and procedures	98	8
Constitutional law	96	11
Cultural diversity	95	8
Health and fitness	95	50
Officer civil/criminal liability	93	6
Human relations	92	11
Use of nonlethal weapons	91	12
Community policing	90	8
Stress prevention/ management	86	6
Hate crimes/bias crimes	85	4
Mediation skills/conflict management	83	8
Domestic preparedness	78	8
Problem solving	64	6
Computer/information systems	59	8
Basic language (such as survival Spanish)	35	16

FIGURE 9.3 Basic Instruction on various topics and median number of hours of instruction. *Source: Matthew J. Hickman (2005). State and Local Law Enforcement Training Academies. Washington, DC: Bureau of Justice Statistics.*

and a curriculum were developed. Project STAR spawned other task analysis protocols for use in law enforcement. An extensive task analysis project was undertaken in the early 1980s. The project produced a database that led to a comprehensive curriculum revision. Based on results of the analysis, Miami-Dade Community College revised its basic law enforcement and FTO programs. It also factored job-relevant tasks (as standards against which to measure performance) into the entry-level assessment center process. The task analysis project has been credited with enhancing the efficiency, effectiveness, and overall productivity of municipal police personnel throughout the area. The job task analysis prototype developed in south Florida was under the direction of James D. Stinchcomb. Task analysis is action-oriented applied research keyed to law enforcement's mission, goals, and objectives. This analysis is job related and legally defensible. Researchers identified and grouped 102 specific knowledge areas, skills, and abilities required of entry-level police personnel. Based on analysis of data, researchers isolated eight traits or characteristics that applicants need in order to become successful law enforcement officers:

1. **Directing Others.** Police officers must be able to initiate action and assume control of the situation. They assist, guide, direct, and control others on a daily basis.
2. **Interpersonal Skills.** Police officers are expected to deal with the needs, feelings, and problems of people in a courteous and considerate way that is consistent with the use of discretion in exercising police authority. Demeanor is a critical variable in successful police work.
3. **Perception.** Police work takes place in an environment of ambiguity. Police officers must be observant and must be able to identify and understand critical elements in a situation, recognize circumstances that require immediate action, and comprehend the implications of that action.
4. **Decision-Making.** Police officers must use logic and sound judgment in making many important decisions. Their decisions must reflect an understanding of the facts, definition of the problem, consideration of alternatives, and formulation of solutions that are consistent with the department's policies, procedures, rules, and regulations.
5. **Decisiveness.** Police officers are required to make on-the-spot decisions and take decisive action based on the needs of the situation. They are expected to use judgment and must be able to defend their decisions or actions when confronted by others.
6. **Adaptability.** Police officers must be flexible in dealing with dynamic situations. They must be prepared to alter their course of action when there is a change in personal or environmental circumstances.
7. **Oral Communication.** Police officers must be able to communicate effectively with other people. Language skills, vocabulary, grammar, eye contact, and a strong voice are invaluable assets.
8. **Written Communication.** The ability to write clearly and effectively is absolutely essential. Much of the police officer's work will be in vain unless it is backed up by clear, concise, accurate, and well-written records that can withstand scrutiny in a confrontational system of law (Stinchcomb, 1996).

Performance objectives formulated as a result of a task analysis give direction to the training process and motivate trainees as long as they are relevant and achievable. Trainers must then specify the content of the curriculum and demonstrate exactly how the expected outcomes are related to the performance objectives. The next step is to select an appropriate training strategy or strategies (including a style and methodology) that will produce the desired outcome. Once training has been completed, various types of evaluative data should be analyzed to determine the overall effectiveness of the training in accomplishing its objectives. These data are factored into the training process so that necessary and appropriate adjustments can be made.

Civil Liability for Failure to Train Police Personnel

Police departments (and individual police officers) are no longer immune to civil litigation. They can be sued for civil rights violations under a federal law (42 U.S.C. § 1983) known as Section 1983. Police departments are held liable if their policies or procedures are responsible for any deprivation of rights enumerated in the U.S. Constitution. In many states, police departments can also be sued for negligence. The tort of negligence involves conduct (by an officer or a department) that presents an unreasonable risk of harm to others, which in turn is the proximate cause of the injury. State courts have extended liability to police departments when they have determined that there was a duty to perform according to a reasonable standard of care and that the failure to perform caused a loss or injury. Major areas of concern are as follows:

1. **Negligent Employment.** It must be shown that the officer who caused the injury was unfit for appointment and that the employer knew or should have known the person was not suited for the job.
2. **Negligent Supervision.** It must be shown that a police manager had an affirmative duty to supervise an employee and that the failure to do so led to the injury or loss.
3. **Negligent Training.** It must be shown that the employer had improperly trained or failed to train police personnel in conceptual issues (such as constitutional rights or minority relations) or skill areas (such as pursuit driving, use of deadly force, firearms, and first aid), and that the injury or loss was the result.

Some of the compensatory and punitive damages awarded by the courts have been truly mind-boggling. Some communities have been forced into bankruptcy. Others have reached into the "deep pockets" of the local taxpayers. The courts have been sending a forceful message to police administrators: hire the right people, train them, and provide appropriate on-the-job supervision. Anything less is unacceptable. Under these circumstances, training is no longer a luxury. It is a legally mandated necessity.

The Police Sergeant's Role as a Trainer

The sergeant's primary job is to obtain results through people. He or she is judged on the ability to motivate subordinates to help accomplish the department's vision, mission, and values in an efficient and effective manner. Training is one of several tools available to help sergeants achieve this end.

There is no doubt that training is a universal responsibility of all first-line supervisors. Sergeants will not get far unless they fulfill their training duties. Supervision and training are always interdependent. Everything a supervisor does in directing the workforce has some element of training in it; conversely, every training activity involves an element of supervision. Supervision and training are inherent in the sergeant's role. Sergeants who take an active interest in their subordinates and perceive counseling, mentoring, coaching, and teaching as parts of their role make an incalculable contribution to the growth and development of the department's human resources.

Sergeants interact with their subordinates on a daily basis and, in most cases, are trusted by other police officers as street-level compatriots. Consequently, they are in an ideal position to influence the job-related behavior of the men and women who work for them. Mature sergeants who possess good interpersonal skills have the most influence. They are able to perform their training function in a low-key and nonthreatening manner. At the most elementary level, training takes place when the sergeant guides or assists subordinates in doing their work. In a more formal sense, training consists of guided interaction, practice sessions, special seminars, planned courses, or any other type of organized activity designed to produce a particular learning experience.

Good first-line supervisors tend to have what the late Douglas McGregor has referred to as a Theory Y orientation (Holden, 1994). They make certain assumptions about human beings and allow those assumptions to guide their behavior regarding their subordinates. Theory Y supervisors believe that:

1. Management is responsible for organizing the elements of productive enterprise, such as money, material, equipment, and human resources, in order to achieve specified goals and objectives.
2. People are not, by their nature, passive or resistant to the organization's needs. They become that way as the result of negative on-the-job experiences.
3. The motivation, potential for development, capacity for taking responsibility, and readiness to direct behavior toward the organization's goals are all present in human beings. Supervisors do not put them there. In the final analysis, it is the sergeant's responsibility to make it possible for police officers to recognize and develop these characteristics for themselves.
4. The essential task of management and first-line police supervisors is to arrange the organization and methods of operation so that police officers can achieve their own goals by directing their efforts toward accomplishment of organizational objectives.

Modern police supervision is moving away from the view of individuals as static and toward seeing them as being in process. The supervisor's job is to create opportunities, release potential, remove obstacles, encourage growth, and provide guidance (Whisenand, 2008).

The Theory Y orientation, with its emphasis on developing employees beyond their present level, produces an empathetic supervisory style that treats police officers as professionals. Under these circumstances and based on a professional paradigm, they are often allowed to work out the details of their own job and to make many of the decisions concerning how it should be done. Because active learning is far more effective than passive learning, police officers benefit from resolving problems and making decisions for themselves. Training employees to govern themselves is an important concept in modern management.

In their capacity as developers of human resources, sergeants may be called upon to provide formal training to their subordinates. They normally conduct roll-call training and are often used to disseminate new department policies, procedures, rules, and regulations. Sergeants use the principles of learning, instructional methods, and teaching techniques to accomplish their objectives. However, much, if not most, of the training done by sergeants is informal. Sergeants train their subordinates by example. They serve as role models. In so doing, they set the ethical and professional tone for their colleagues. Sergeants spend a great deal of their time teaching and correcting police procedures and techniques. They also give advice on how to handle situations involving officer safety. In other words, sergeants function, in most instances, in a continuing training mode.

Good sergeants monitor the professional growth and development of their personnel. When they detect a problem or a deficiency, one research project proposed some form of counseling was found to be most common, and in some instances supervisors can take action to remedy the situation, by either taking over, or even doing nothing and letting the officer learn from experience (Fridell et al., 2011). It is a judgment call and varies from individual to individual. If they do not have the counseling skills or training expertise to handle the problem, it will be referred up the ladder for an appropriate disposition.

Being a good supervisor/trainer is not an easy task. It requires ability, a positive attitude, human relations skills, training, and a commitment to the concept of human resource development. While the job can be very frustrating, it has rewards. A few of the benefits are listed here.

1. **You get to know your subordinates.** The dual role helps you understand the needs, wants, and potential of those who work for you. This information can be factored into decisions concerning discipline, transfers, promotions, and pay raises.
2. **You promote good human relations.** Through training, police officers gain self-confidence, pride, and a sense of security. Your actions give them reasons to cooperate with their peers and the administration. Training helps establish unity of purpose, trust, and mutual respect.
3. **You feel good about your accomplishments.** Training subordinates to do a good job produces a good feeling and motivates the supervisor to put forth even more effort. For all practical purposes, "success is its own reward."
4. **You further your own career.** As your subordinates grow in ability, expertise, and reputation, so will you. As your people look better, feel better, and perform better, they enhance your reputation as a supervisor. Reputation is a product of positive training efforts.
5. **You gain more time.** Training helps make people more confident and self-sufficient. As their performance improves, you will spend less time on corrections. This time can be invested in other supervisory functions, such as planning, organizing, and coordinating. Coordinating is considered the essence of supervision if there is a well-trained workforce.

There is no doubt that sergeants should be totally involved in and held responsible for the professional development of all personnel in the work unit. Whether sergeants assume this responsibility will depend on their status within the police department and the training they themselves have been given in order to fulfill this role.

In an ideal working environment, officers always attain organizational goals and satisfy their own personal needs, concurrently. In such an environment, officer behavior is exemplary and complaints against officers become outdated. In a perfect situation, tasks would be performed without hesitation and internal and external discord would not exist. Would not such a perfect world be great? Such is not the case. Organizational and personal shortcoming reigns and a first-line supervisor must deal with both internal and external imperfection. Working in an imperfect world is a challenge that a first-line supervisor must accept, and everything must be done to foster a positive working environment. Subordinates expect and should receive positive leadership that emphasizes communications and provides for a balance between professional and personal life. First-line supervisors function as teachers, coaches, mentors, and counselors—a daunting and demanding position in a law enforcement agency (Moriarty, 2009). In any first-line supervisory training program there should be a unit of instruction on skills needed to coach line officers successfully. It is no longer acceptable to allow supervisors to "wing it" (Nowicki, 2008).

Coaching, Counseling, and Mentoring

First-line supervisors must learn to manage as a coach/counselor/mentor. The terms "coach" and "counselor" are interchangeable. Developmental counseling and mentoring are unique in their own right. These are not new concepts—they have been around for many years. In fact, field-training officers, in departments that have the luxury to provide such a service, have provided for the training and development of effective police officers for a specified period after graduation from an academy. When a first-line supervisor performs as a coach/counselor/ mentor, it complements and reinforces efforts expended by FTOs. When a supervisor engages in each of these activities it provides a base for building a constructive relationship with subordinates and creates a positive environment where members of the organization interact by talking and working together, creating a trusting working relationship (Peterson & Sancovich, 2003). As pointed out elsewhere in this text, a "good" supervisor acknowledges that knowledge-based skills are more important at the supervisory level when compared to higher levels of management. At the same time, human skills consume the greatest part of a supervisor's day. Affective skills have to be utilized to the utmost as they interplay with and modify the tasks that have to be performed at the supervisory level. Additionally, conceptual and tactical skills enter into the formula as the sergeant modifies the managerial process and interaction occurs with those supervised (Hu-TACK).

Coaching is best viewed as a process wherein officers are provided with the knowledge and skills needed to develop into professional police officers, thus allowing them to become more successful in their chosen profession and their personal life. Research has demonstrated that coaching, along with training, increases learning retention by up to four times as much as training alone (Rock, 2009). Coaching is a positive process that places a supervisor in a position to help officers perform more effectively, achieve at a higher level, and become increasingly self-sufficient. Coaching affirms positive results and helps officers become more confident as their competence is enhanced and positive performance is acknowledged (Duxbury, 2009). It involves challenging officers to assume responsibility rather than being told what to do and how to do it (Brounstein, 2000). When officers are coached correctly, they become committed to the mission of the agency and its goals. They willingly accept responsibility for their performance and readily become motivated to achieve at a higher level. When a supervisor continually communicates the vision and the principles of the department, officers become motivated and committed; as a consequence, the cohesiveness of the department is enhanced greatly (Duxbury, 2009). With coaching, officers become entirely aware of performance expectations. Individuals who are coached can make a real contribution to the department, become more fulfilled, and therefore react positively to work that has become meaningful.

It has become increasingly important for supervisors to realize that coaching is more important today than it ever has been. Today's officers have an enhanced expectation of their rights and expect more on-the-job privileges. Even if the expectations are in part unrealistic, they are still part of the "psyche" of current candidates. In today's working environment, coaching can be used to ensure that officers:

1. Accept responsibility more readily.
2. Are clear about performance expectations.
3. Are committed to the organization.
4. Are given an opportunity to use their skills and knowledge.
5. Become motivated.
6. Become oriented to the mission and goals of the department.
7. Follow the vision of the organization.
8. Have an opportunity to attain individual goals.
9. Practice the concept of service before self.
10. Receive recognition.
11. Strive to achieve at a higher level.
12. Understand organizational priorities (Stone, 2007).

These are not unreasonable expectations and are the benefits of coaching. It is a process wherein the supervisor can develop officer skills and abilities to their fullest, resulting in attaining improved work performance. What it tells the supervisors is that when officers being supervised do well, they succeed as supervisors, and in turn, the organization becomes more responsive—internally and externally. It also reinforces the humanistic mandate that a supervisor should obtain results through the efforts of others.

Coaching is at the opposite end of the continuum from bureaucratic rules and regulations and the domination of the individual by the organization. Progressive first-line supervisors who follow the tenets of motivational research (see Chapter 4) understand that most officers have a real interest in bettering themselves and achieving at an acceptable if not at an exceptional level (Stone, 2007). Demanding or ordering officers to do something (in most instances) is incongruent with modern managerial premises. Employees must be given an opportunity to achieve at the highest possible level. Supervisors who work with employees as coaches create a working environment that increases employee competence, provides for greater fulfillment, allows for a greater contribution to the organization, and exposes officers to what can really be meaningful work.

Characteristics of an Effective Coach

A number of characteristics come to mind when one considers the qualities possessed by those who can be described as performing effectively. Effective coaches have the aptitude to interact positively on a face-to-face basis with each person under their supervision. They set high standards and expect officers to perform to the best of their ability. Another key variable is that the supervisor trusts each person supervised. Additional characteristics include vision, self-confidence, and self-development (Federal Emergency Management Agency, 1994).

Vision

A needed and inherent quality found in those who perform successfully as a coach and a leader is vision. They have the ability to "tell the forest from the trees" and discern what might be possible. They look to the future and seldom dwell on the past. Trends in their chosen profession are readily identified as opportunities, and when things do not go the way they should, the lack of achievement is viewed as a learning situation—not a disaster. Enthusiasm is transmitted to those they supervise, and problems are viewed as a challenge and an opportunity to improve methods, techniques, and procedures. When concentrating on the "big picture," the coach acknowledges the importance of the role of the department in the community and works toward the accomplishment of the agency's mission. The importance of services provided by the department is reinforced constantly with special reference to the vision, mission, and core values of the agency. Within this frame of reference, the supervisor recognizes and utilizes the unique skills and abilities of each officer (Federal Emergency Management Agency, 1994).

Self-Confidence

Exemplarity is the hallmark of effective coaching. Great coaches have been found to have an exceptional and resilient sense of their value to the organization and to those that they supervise. They believe that they can make a difference in how the organizational members whom they supervise perform their duties. First-line supervisors, for the most part, are fully aware that they have earned their position because they have successfully passed a screening process that reflects the fact that they have assumed a position that is vested with authority and power, and the organization has acknowledged their potential. Rightfully so, they take pride in their promotion and self-confidence is high. As they adjust to the supervisory position, they realize they have to become increasingly effective and acknowledge that they will be held responsible for success or failure as a coach and leader. At this point, self-confidence becomes increasingly important as they realize that they are not just "one of the guys" and must focus on leading and coaching as a means of ensuring task accomplishment. Over time, even small accomplishments serve to enhance self-esteem and reinforce self-confidence, which serve as key components of the motivational process. Additionally, in order to enhance one's coaching skills, a supervisor must keep abreast of technical skills and knowledge and share newly acquired expertise with subordinates (Anthony, 2008; Federal Emergency Management Agency, 1994). When one is self-confident, others take note and you are viewed as a professional.

Self-Development

Attaining the rank of first-line supervisor and accepting the responsibilities of that position place a new and demanding dimension on the necessity for self-development. Success at this new level calls for the enhancement and expansion of previously acquired skills, knowledge, and experience. Without question, self-development is a continuing and constantly evolving process. It calls for the expansion of knowledge acquired from institutions of higher education and from institutional training, as well as previous operational assignments. What is called for is the establishment of a goal that calls for increasing your capacity for success in your new position and the growth needed to succeed in this position of greater responsibility (U.S. Department of the Army, 2006). There is an assumption that you had the competence and commitment needed to get where you are and you should acknowledge any weaknesses and possible inexperience. If you need direction this is the time to ask for it from your immediate manager. Your developmental level must be assessed and specific goals or tasks identified. Maybe you need specific feedback on outcomes and/or expectations. Maybe you need support that will encourage risk taking or how to provide positive feedback for improvement in task assignment. Not everyone is a self-starter who can take the ball and run with it. Possibly you need some coaching and your immediate supervisor should be turned to or you can ask another first-line supervisor for assistance. Overall, take action when it is needed. In fact, you have an obligation as a supervisor to develop your individual attributes, skills, and actions needed to become competent in every aspect of your job. In other words, challenge yourself and apply the initiative needed to become the best of the best. Internalize the vision, the mission, and the core values of your department and apply them in your day-to-day duties.

Coaches should work with officers in such a way that they become more competent and, at the same time, create a feeling of fulfillment and accomplishment. Consequently, officers are more likely to contribute to the organization while finding real meaning in their work (Brounstein, 2007). Over time, well-coached officers will know when they are performing well and if that is not the case, they will make adjustments. A true coach strives to create a working environment where coaching skills can be used to develop officer competence. It is a process wherein the officer becomes increasingly self-sufficient. Well-coached officers know this and will continually find ways, on their own, to improve (Flaherty, 2010).

Principles of Coaching/Counseling/Mentoring

Supervisors can fulfill their responsibilities by following several principles (Figure 9.4) whether dealing with an individual or a team. Supervisors who show willingness to following these principles will provide a frame of reference wherein officers will have the capacity to realize

1. Communicate by emphasizing listening.
2. Establish a positive working relationship.
3. Know the mission, goals, and values of the organization.
4. Provide feedback.
5. Teach technical skills and techniques.
6. Understand yourself.

FIGURE 9.4 Principles of coaching/counseling/mentoring. *Adapted from Florence M. Stone (2007). Coaching, Counseling, and Mentoring. How to Choose & Use the Right Technique to Boost Employee Performance. New York: AMACOM; James Flaherty (2005). Coaching Evoking: Excellence in Others. Boston: Butterworth-Heinemann; and Frances Hesselbein, Erick K. Shinseki, & Richard Cavanagh (2004). Be, Know, Do: Leadership the Army-Way. New York: Jossey-Bass.*

their full potential. A by-product of this process is increased employee loyalty and dedication to the organization.

Communicating by Emphasizing Listening

Communicating by emphasizing listening is an art and a skill that can be learned. It can be developed by you and put into practice. If a coach asks the right question, it means little if the response is not listened to (Stone, 2007). Unbelievably, the best coaches actually listen. One must listen at the same level as the sender of a message. Every effort has to be made to capture the real meaning of the message based on its content. Additionally, careful attention is paid to nonverbal cues, such as the body posture of the sender of the message and its possible implication. This is done in order to assess the true feeling behind the message and the veracity of its content. A coach should also pay attention to a message by utilizing body language to communicate interest in what a speaker is saying (Stone, 2007).

A truly effective coaching process involves two-way communications. The more a coach talks the greater the possibility that a two-way process evolves into one-way communication. When this occurs, it becomes obvious that officers are less involved in the process and interaction can either slow down or cease to exist. Alternatively, in other instances, officers can completely tune out a supervisor who does not let them engage in two-way communication. The best way to find out what officers need is for the supervisor to listen. Effective listeners can begin to understand and gain insight into the real interests of officers. A coach and a subordinate must communicate at the same level if the coach really wants to understand where officers come from. There is no one way to listen but experts suggest that active listening is the most effective way. To engage in this type of listening, a coach must show an understanding—"verbally"—when interacting with an officer and not be judgmental. It is a powerful tool—"active listening"—and can spark officers to speak up, set forth their ideas, and begin on the path of involvement (Brounstein, 2000).

Active listening involves the supervisor responding fully to a subordinate's message in terms of not only listening, but also observing the officer's mannerisms. This includes maintaining eye contact without being intrusive in order to show interest. The supervisor should exhibit a body posture that indicates a demonstrated concern in such a way that the officer is placed at ease and views the process as a relaxed atmosphere. It is also essential to keep one's facial expressions neutral, and occasionally nod to indicate your concern. Finally, the supervisor should let the officer engage in the preponderance of the conversation as long as it is within the parameters of the discussion (U.S. Department of the Army, 2006).

Establish a Positive Working Relationship

Relationship is the foundation of coaching. It is the process of influencing the actions of others in such a way that the outcomes are mutually satisfying to everyone concerned. This is done through communicating and listening. Creation of a positive relationship between the coach and those supervised reinforces organizational intent and purpose, as well as providing for an opportunity to assess and inspire officers. A first-line supervisor can review personnel files (in agencies where that is allowed) and evaluate them in terms of previous training and education. Such files are also an excellent source for determining personal information about each officer. Knowledge gained from such a review is vital to the creation of a positive relationship and is a fundamental element of successful leadership. Information gained from training files can be used to identify skill deficiencies and knowledge limitations that can lead to the identification of training/educational needs. It can also give some indications as to whether learning can occur by example or experience.

Additionally, a coach can, based on newly acquired information, interview each supervised officer and identify interests and aspirations. It is also a good time, if the officer is willing, to discuss personal items, such as family, outside social or sports interests, membership in community organizations, and participation in religious activities (Johnson, 2005). An officer might be active in organizational entities that will reflect his or her interests. Such organizations can range from union affiliation or sports groups to special interests in a variety of activities such as motorcycle clubs, pistol teams, or study groups for promotions.

Know the Vision, Mission, and Values of the Organization

An agency's mission, vision, and value system breathe life into an organization. They articulate the rationale for a department's existence. Coaches have to be conversant in organizational values. Values give breath and spirit to an organization. They are the reasons an organization exists. They are more abstract than rules and regulations. They set the organizational tone and are of a higher order—expressing a fundamental belief system. They convey meaning that serves as a guide to officer behavior. They are a belief system that has to permeate the total organization (Leonard & More, 2000). As a fundamental belief system, it must be shared with every employee, and the coaching process serves as an excellent means of reinforcing the value system.

Constant strengthening of a value system provides officers with a reason for an organization's existence and informs officers what they have to do and why. Values that guide individual behavior are apparent in statements such as "this is the way we do it around here." With value application permeating the total organization, there is an attitudinal change on the part of officers and members of the public. In the field, a coach proves to be a linchpin in the transmission of values. Through positive communications, coaches express a concern for the welfare of employees. A coach must constantly reinforce the validity and value of the department's value system when working with subordinates. A coach should work diligently at maintaining positive communications. Dialogue must be encouraged constantly, and a coach must listen intently to the opinions and ideas expressed by subordinates. Officers being supervised should be allowed to have a candid, open, and frank voice in the department without fear of harmful consequences. When a coach communicates honestly and reinforces agency values sincerely, a message of trust is conveyed to subordinates. A coach and subordinates can benefit from the creation of a working environment that encourages subordinates to set forth their ideas, participate in decision-making, allows officers to become an integral part of the department, and allows subordinates to work within the frame of reference of the agency's value system (U.S. Department of the Army, 1999). It should be kept in mind that a coach works with those supervised when making decisions, but it does not mean that decisions are always made by consensus. Certain decisions have to be made by a supervisor, but there are also decisions that are the responsibility of an officer. When an officer is allowed to make appropriate decisions, accountability follows and the supervisor is functioning as a coach (Brounstein, 2000).

Provide Feedback

When a supervisor functions in a noncoaching manner, work issues are discussed, but the officer is never told about how they are actually doing. Possibly the supervisor is satisfied with this process, but the officer is left in limbo and really does not know what he or she is expected to do. Feedback is a compelling coaching skill, which is especially true when it involves an evaluation of actual performance (Luthans, 2010). Officers should be told whether a particular job was accomplished successfully or whether there is a need for improvement—and if so what improvement is needed. Two-way communication comes into existence when a coach engages in the practice of realistic and tangible feedback. The actuality of feedback can be acknowledged by a nodding of the head, a hand gesture, or responding with a memorandum or a formal report. Feedback should be a constant process so that officers know whether a performed task is acceptable or not. It is not something you do several weeks before an evaluation report is due and then is ignored for the rest of the reporting period (Salmon, 1999).

Constructive feedback can be of two types—optimistic or corrective—when dealing in the realm of performance coaching. Constructive feedback is directed toward aspects of the job, and is non-accusatory, timely, and specific (see Chapter 3 for a detailed discussion of feedback techniques). A significant by-product of constructive feedback is the development of trust between a coach and employees. It also provides a foundation for improved morale and heightens the potentiality for fulfilling the mission of the department, as well as attaining goals. When optimistic feedback occurs on a continuous basis over an extended period, an operational climate exists where information can be shared freely and without restraint. Assumptions can be verified or corrected readily. Decision-making can be improved, and officers will feel free to express their opinions about work issues. Optimistic feedback calls for positive reinforcement and appropriate praise of achievements. Corrective feedback is tailored to tell officers that improvement is necessary. It should be provided in a positive manner. It should include specific instructions as to how something can be improved. It can either be a need for minor improvement or possibly a significant change in the procedure or a technique used by an officer. Constructive feedback should reject praise and criticism that focus on evaluations based on opinions, hunches, or feelings (Brounstein, 2000).

Teach Technical Skills

At the operational level, technical skills of the coach are highly significant if the supervisor is to understand the job performance of those supervised (Stone, 2003). If officers cannot learn from their immediate supervisor, there is a lessening of respect for the supervisor. A failure to concentrate on developing skills of subordinates results in unsound or unproductive supervision. At the same time it should be kept in mind that even the most skilled coach will diminish his or her impact if "people skills" are ignored. One managerial expert has pointed out that it is easy to disguise a deficiency of knowledge skills but impossible to disguise a lack of human skills (Frunzi & Savini, 1997).

In part, a supervisor who functions as a coach constantly makes important decisions that directly affect the effectiveness and quality of police operations—both the type of service provided to the community and the commitment and competence of officers who provide that service (More et al., 2012). First-line supervisors are an agency's primary quality-control agents, and in this arena, development of the skills and knowledge of subordinates take priority in order to cope with current and future challenges effectively (Frunzi & Savini, 1997).

A good coach has the ability to train officers either as a team or individually. After reviewing available training records, interviewing the officer, and conducting a performance evaluation, the coach should be in a position to identify gaps in knowledge (if there are any) that must be filled. A skillful coach realizes that learning by experience can take a long time and that officers may need individual instruction and/or advice to accomplish an objective by approaching a problem a different way or utilizing an entirely different technique. Alternatives can be presented that result in a shortening of the time needed to accomplish specific tasks. Providing needed skills enhances productivity and allows an officer an opportunity to select from alternatives. The coach who is in a position to identify alternatives not realized by the individual being coached can improve this process. This is especially true if the coach indicates the consequences of the alternatives (Fournies, 2000). Thus, the officer can respond more positively in a shorter period after mastering the actions needed to become competent.

Understand Yourself

Knowing oneself is an essential and important quality if a supervisor is to be successful as a coach. It places the coach into an entirely different relationship with a subordinate. A supervisor must assess himself or herself, realizing that there are weaknesses and strengths that must be addressed as they commit themselves to coaching. A supervisor must realize that there is a big difference between doing something yourself and coaching an officer successfully, whether it be imparting knowledge or leading by example. A supervisor must resist the temptation to do something themselves rather than equipping subordinates with the necessary tools that will ensure success.

A coach should never preempt an officer by making decisions that should be made by the officer. In order to achieve this, the coach must restrain himself or herself from reverting to the posture of "I will do it myself." It takes time to overcome one's past operational mode. A coach must work diligently at becoming aware of their own attitudes, beliefs, biases, frustrations, values, and opinions so they will not negatively influence his or her effectiveness. A supervisor should also be aware of the power of nonverbal communications. One has to be aware of personal mannerisms, behavioral quirks, and demeanor that reinforce or contradict a spoken message (see Chapter 3 regarding nonverbal communication).

A coach's value system is especially important, and old values are replaced by new values as a coach grows and develops the skills needed to become operationally sound. A value system helps one decide when there is internal conflict and facilitates the decision-making process. A value system motivates the coach to achieve and attain goals. It serves as an ethical and moral standard. Understanding oneself serves as a frame of reference for encouraging analytical thinking about objectives and the socially accepted means for attainment of those objectives (More et al., 2012). Without question, coaches really have to "know themselves."

The Supervisor as a Developmental Coach, Counselor, Mentor

Accomplishment of the police mission is dependent upon every member of the force performing up to organizational standards. An effective supervisor mentors subordinates utilizing training techniques, coaching, and counseling. These are not mutually exclusive and overlap each other. Sometimes it is difficult to determine where one process starts and the other ends. When coaching, the first-line supervisor functions much like a football coach by identifying weaknesses, setting objectives (goals), and developing a course of action that resolves a problem(s), resulting in motivated officers and improved performance. Such an accomplishment requires the supervisor to become aware of each subordinate's goals, strengths, and weaknesses and to consider those elements during the coaching process (U.S. Department of the Army, 1999).

A number of qualities are needed to be an effective counselor. These qualities range from building commitment, to creating an operational climate, to acting as a role model. Each of these is equally important, and an emphasis on such qualities in the coaching/counseling process serves to support subordinate development.

Building Commitment

An officer should never have to wonder about a supervisor's expectations. Officers need to know the mission goals and values of the department. A counselor should continually stress the need for inculcating the norms, values, and ethics of a department into the operational aspects of the agency. This is especially true for new recruits as they are taught to perform their duties in a certain manner. Senior officers must also be taken into consideration, and it is essential that a supervisor realize that this group will need to be approached differently. A coach must consider the necessity of transferring agency values in such a way that a specific mode of conduct occurs. In one situation, it may be necessary for a supervisor to encourage and support officers informally, whereas in other instances it may result in a formal training session. Alternatively, in another situation it might be a mentoring session with an officer as a means of strengthening skills and knowledge (Brounstein, 2000). When officers know the values of the organization, they are in a better position to understand the role of the agency in society and conform to group-shared expectations.

When focus is strong, officers know what they have to do and how to do it to accomplish their job. Priorities become clear, and when changes occur, a coach can reorient officers to ensure that everyone is aware of organizational direction, intent, and purpose. Officers should never be left in limbo. Knowledge must be shared, and a coach should strive for the maximization of communications whenever dramatic change affects the organization. A coach needs to be specific not only about tasks that have to be performed, but about priorities when assignments are given and then assessed.

Involvement is another important aspect of commitment, and a coach allows officers to become involved by allowing them to have authority over things that affect their daily work situation. Officers must feel involved. This means that they have input into decision-making, planning, and problem solving that influences their level of accountability when this is appropriate.

This can be a question of sharing power or empowering people that work in the organization and this is entirely different than managing people that in actuality turns out to be controlling people (Chandler, 2011). Officers need the authority to carry out plans and tasks and should be held responsible for producing high-standard results. Additionally, a coach should develop an attitude that allows for functional independence. Job involvement generates a feeling of importance, which in turn gives an individual a feeling of being a contributor to the department. When an officer is given a reasonably free rein it can serve as a mechanism that reduces work tension and allows an individual to respond in a professional manner (Leonard & More, 2000). One expert cited an old truism—"people support most what they help create" (Brounstein, 2000). When officers become strongly committed to organizational values that reward them for accomplishments, there is a greater likelihood that the individual will become progressively more committed to the department. A supervisor should acknowledge that employees have differing degrees of commitment to work, but it also should be recognized that every officer has the ability to change from a low to a higher level of commitment. A committed individual has no difficulty in identifying with the department and working toward goal achievement. When commitment is strong, the job becomes very important to the officer (O'Leary & Griffin, 1995).

Operational Climate

A counselor should strive to develop a working environment that is open, trusting, ethical, and built upon a foundation of integrity. Every effort must be made to maximize the effective use of people as a resource. Without question it is the duty of a supervisor, acting in the capacity of a coach, to invest the necessary time and energy that it takes to help every officer reach his or her fullest potential (Stroh et al., 2002).

A supervisor should develop the capability to relate to those supervised. One way is a matter of showing that you care about them as individuals. You should demonstrate a willingness to work with officers and listen to their concerns about work-related problems, as well as personal problems when the occasion arises. What might seem trivial to you as a supervisor can prove to be of great importance to an officer. When officers are treated fairly and with respect, it is normal for a trusting relationship to evolve. This process can be reinforced by demonstrating an honest interest in those supervised and allowing for constant and candid two-way communications (Stone, 2007). A supervisor can strengthen a trusting relationship by telling an officer what you are going to do, accomplishing exactly that, and then pointing back to the fact that you did what you said you were going to do (Flaherty, 2010).

Depending on the operational climate, a coach can adjust his or her operational style so that officers will be internally motivated to achieve mutually agreed-upon goals. One way of doing this is to create a working relationship that focuses on supporting officers in ways that respond to their individuality. Some officers need to be coaxed, others given suggestions, and still others possibly need to be prodded gently. Additionally, a coach can be confronted with a situation where a temporary solution might be a verbal equivalent of a kick in the pants. Treating people fairly does not mean treating them as if they were all cut from the same cloth. A coach who works diligently at his or her job soon finds that different people need different things as they grow and mature into professional officers. Above all, a supervisor must just be himself or herself, and in so doing, a base is established that can lead to trust and credibility; anything else comes across as phony and disingenuous (U.S. Department of the Army, 1999).

Role Model

A supervisor should be a role model for those supervised. He or she should constantly perform at the highest possible professional level. When officers see that the supervisor's performance is of the uppermost quality, it establishes a viable performance standard. It is the opposite of the old axiom "Do what I say, not what I do." All of the verbalization in the world will prove to be of no avail if you the supervisor does not act with integrity (Griffin, 1998). As a role model, you must be constantly learning and transmitting acquired knowledge to your subordinates. If you want those whom you supervise to take responsibility for their accomplishments, as well as risks that might result in failure, you must accept the challenge and become the best coach possible. As a role model, you need to accept responsibility for your actions and the actions of those that you supervise. You must never allow double standards. Everyone should be held to the same standard—"excellence." It is also essential that you function within the limits of your authority. If you exceed your positional authority, it will become immediately apparent to those you supervise. Additionally, when you promise something, you should be sure that you follow through with an appropriate action. In other words, only promise a subordinate something when you are sure that you can keep that promise. Be fair, credible, and maintain your professional integrity. Functioning in this manner will place you in the position of being a positive role model.

When there is a positive organizational environment, the values and attitudes of each officer can focus on the collective pursuit of organizational goals. Subordinates readily recognize such a milieu and they are always aware of the role played by the supervisor. A resonant role model energizes all employees, which is especially true when supervisors perform in an upbeat manner. A role model cross-trains whenever the opportunity occurs, continues to pursue more formal education, and keeps abreast of trends, technology, and current events. If time is available, a role model lectures in agency training academies and in regional or state training programs. Finally, a role model develops special expertise or skills in order to pass it on to those supervised.

Developmental Counseling

Developmental counseling is a subordinate-centered course of action that produces a plan outlining actions necessary for subordinates to achieve individual or organizational goals (U.S. Department of the Army, 1999). The development of personnel is one of the most important functions performed by a supervisor acting in the capacity of a counselor. If a supervisor is to function as a counselor, he or she must inaugurate a personal and intellectual transformation that will change his or her organizational outlook, idea of work, and relationship with those supervised. This is not an easy adjustment, as it takes time and effort. One should keep in mind that there could be differing expectations between what subordinates anticipate and what a supervisor anticipates. The differing expectations must be thought through carefully. If not understood and responded to by both sides, it can create conflict and role ambiguity (More et al., 2012). The supervisor's success depends on whether he or she works diligently at building a positive relationship upon mutual respect and trust (Cordner, 2013).

Supervisors must mentor their subordinates through imparting knowledge, through the process of coaching and counseling. Counseling is a means wherein a supervisor develops personnel by imparting skills and information so that officers can meet daily performance challenges. A counselor identifies weaknesses and creates jointly agreed-upon task objectives within the framework of an operational plan for subordinate professional growth. The key is to "know the people you supervise." A coach functioning in a developmental capacity has to become thoroughly familiar with each subordinate's weaknesses, strengths, and personal goals. Tasks that a subordinate must accomplish are identified, and consideration is given to creating a plan as to how an officer can achieve individual, team, and/or organizational goals (Hesselbein, Shinseki, & Cavanagh, 2004).

When counseling is developmental, it proves to be a long way from being adverse. It is non-punitive. Counseling is a helping process that can make officers operationally sound, better members of the team, improve their performance, and serve as a sound foundation for future growth. As is true for all managerial situations, there is no one best way for a supervisor to be an effective counselor, but what experience shows is that by utilizing the following features, a supervisor can develop a successful counseling style. These characteristics are set forth in Figure 9.5.

If there is one best-kept secret, it is that communication is the quintessence of successful counseling. When talking with an employee, it is essential that a counselor establish open,

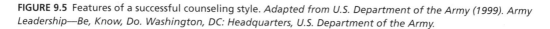

1. Communication
2. Flexibility
3. Intention
4. Support

FIGURE 9.5 Features of a successful counseling style. *Adapted from U.S. Department of the Army (1999). Army Leadership—Be, Know, Do. Washington, DC: Headquarters, U.S. Department of the Army.*

two-way communications. When a performance problem or standard is discussed, it is not the time to be ambivalent. If there is a problem, address it. It is not the time to discuss trivia or misdirect the discussion. The counselor should address the problem directly, providing timely and specific information. If one does less, it can be construed as an inconsequential discussion and of really no importance. If the officer perceives it that way, why should he or she consider changing behavior if they believe you are not serious about their conduct? Directness is not a fault, it is a virtue. Being direct rather than blunt are entirely different things. When a counselor is blunt about an issue, an officer will usually feel that they have been treated harshly (Brounstein, 2000). If that occurs, the counseling relationship is in jeopardy. An officer is more apt to listen and understand if told specifically that failure to follow a specific procedure when making a felony stop can lead to severe consequences, such as injury. If you "dance" around the topic, it can leave the officer confused or indifferent. As a counselor, you have an obligation to tell them like it is—"your performance is not acceptable and not up to departmental standard, but this is how you can deal with it." If there are deficiencies in performance, they should be spelled out, followed by a discussion as to how, by following a specific technique or procedure, future performance will be acceptable. The officer should be told that expectations have to be of the highest and minimal acquiescence is not acceptable. Expectations should be set forth based on specific criteria by which the officer's performance can be measured. Counseling is a helping process and before a discussion is ended, the subordinate should be required to respond as to how he or she will deal with the problem.

As noted previously in this chapter, an effective coach listens more than he or she speaks. You might want to consider practicing the 20/80 rule. You should speak only one-fifth of the time. Under no circumstances should a counselor dominate the conversation. One always learns a lot more from listening than talking. Taking such a stance during a counseling session greatly reduces the propensity for a session to become confrontational and allows the officer to recommend a solution to the problem.

Another feature of a successful counseling style is the necessity to be flexible when dealing with subordinates. This means that the counselor should provide some officers considerable support and advice, whereas other officers may need minimal support and advice. The counselor concerned about those supervised should be fully aware of each officer's needs and expectations. Some employees may lack initiative, whereas others may need to be reined in. An effective flexibility approach, in one-on-one counseling, is to ask probing open-ended questions about specific instances, such as the content of an arrest report or showing up late for roll call. This is done in order to assess problem causation as specifically as possible. In some situations, it might be necessary to answer a number of more specific questions. The desire is to get to a point where the real reason is determined and the employee acknowledges the difference between actual performance and expected performance (Stone, 2007).

A different characteristic of an effective counseling style is to make it clear that the intent of counseling is to assist officers in developing a plan to resolve some of the issues that can occur in the workplace, such as friction, frustration, or other problems such as poor performance. The intention of counseling is not punitive in nature. It is a shared effort to identify strengths and weaknesses and work together to develop a plan that will resolve a performance issue. It is not just a question of discussing an issue and then forgetting about it. Follow-up is an essential element of counseling with the intent of having the subordinate committed to improvement by accomplishing an agreed-upon goal and becoming candid in their assessment of the problem.

Finally, support is a key element of the performance developmental counseling process. It is essential that the total process focus on the future with a consideration of the subordinate's strengths, areas needing improvement, and, most important, their "potential." Positive performance counseling is an excellent time for a supervisor to establish and clarify expected values, attributes, skills, and actions. Performance counseling is not a distinctive, separate area and can be extended from a consideration of problem resolution to addressing duty performance. The counseling session can also be extended to discussing opportunities for professional growth if the situation warrants (U.S. Department of the Army, 1999).

Styles of Counseling

The competent supervisor must approach each subordinate as a unique individual with a distinct set of values, beliefs, norms, and attitudes that are brought to the workplace after exposure as a police recruit to the academy where they acquire new values, beliefs, norms, and attitudes that are incorporated and modified by the preexisting position (Caldero & Crank, 2011). The crucial aspect of the counseling style to be used is to consider the uniqueness and individuality of each officer. The myriad of diverse situations that confront an officer can require a differing counseling approach specifically tailored to the situation or event. The three styles of counseling are combined, directive, and nondirective.

Directive style. This approach is best used to correct uncomplicated problems, make a correction on the spot, or correct aspects of job performance. Using the directive approach, in these situations, the supervisor engages in primarily one-way communication. It is seldom a collaborative effort but more of just telling an officer what to do. In most instances the counselor makes no provision for give and take and just tells an officer how to perform something and when to do it.

A supervisor, acting in a counseling mode, is apt to choose this approach when time is of the essence, when an officer is in a quandary as to what should be done, or if the officer is new on the job and does not have the wherewithal to handle a field situation. Moreover, the directive approach can be used when a subordinate needs direction, is not fully informed, or is lacking confidence.

Nondirective style. This approach to counseling is preferential over other methods, in most situations. In this approach, a climate is created wherein each employee can grow, develop, and perform more effectively. Officers are viewed as wanting to do a good job and have a need to exercise self-direction and self-control as they evolve into a professional police officer (More et al., 2012). Furthermore, officers are encouraged to seek out and accept responsibility as they develop their professional skills. A counselor will draw upon his or her own experience, insight, and opinion to assist officers in developing solutions. Experience would suggest that it is best to initiate this type of counseling by describing the counseling process to the officer at the beginning of an interchange and then explaining what is expected of them. This technique provides a sound base for a two-way interchange. Then, as indicated earlier in this chapter, the counselor should listen more than talk.

The intent is that the officer will make a sound plan rather than the counselor making decisions and giving advice. When a counselor responds, it should be to clarify what has been said, thus causing the officer to respond to clarified points and better understand the situation. If the conversation is stymied, the counselor should summarize what has been discussed. It is also essential that the supervisor should avoid presenting solutions or rendering an opinion. What should be done is focusing on individual and department goals and making sure that the officer's plan of action supports the department's mission, goals, and objectives. In some situations, it might take several counseling sessions to create an acceptable action plan (Hesselbein et al., 2004).

Combined style. The effective counselor utilizes every possible technique to set the moral tone and perform activities that result in goal attainment. Depending on the developmental level of the officer, the counselor uses the combined counseling style by selecting techniques from each of the aforementioned approaches and adjusting them to what is best for the subordinate. The combined approach stresses that planning and decision-making are the responsibility of the subordinate. The counselor assists the officer when a plan of action is created. The supervisor listens, analyzes, recommends solutions, and suggests possible courses of action. He or she should also point out good and/or bad features of a solution.

Altogether, it is a process of helping an officer fully understand all possible aspects of an issue and encourage the subordinate to identify the best solution. Advantages and disadvantages of counseling styles are set forth in Figure 9.6.

The Counseling Process

Effective counseling takes into consideration a number of variables, such as timing, location, and preparation. In actuality, a supervisor can conduct a developmental counseling session at any time. It can occur in the field, at the station, when the supervisor is accompanying an officer on patrol, or when conducting an investigation. In some departments, the supervisor responds to a field event as backup or to observe an officer. A good supervisor takes advantage of naturally occurring events to provide officers with feedback (Hesselbein et al., 2004). If it is a matter of minor importance, it can be conducted on the spot such as telling an officer a better way to do something, such as a search technique, or how to improve interviewing skills when

	Advantages	Disadvantages
Combined	Moderately quick. Encourages maturity. Encourages open communications. Allows counselors to use their experience.	May take too much time for some situations.
Directive	Fastest method. Good for officers who need clear, concise directions. Allows counselors to use their experience.	Does not encourage subordinates to be part of the solution. Tends to treat symptoms, not problems. Tends to discourage subordinates from talking freely. Solution is the counselor's, not the subordinate's.
Nondirective	Encourages maturity. Encourages open communications. Develops personal responsibility.	More time-consuming. Requires greatest counselor skills.

FIGURE 9.6 Counseling styles. *Adapted from U.S. Department of the Army (2006). Army Leadership. Washington, DC: Headquarters, U.S. Department of the Army.*

dealing with a victim. This is especially true when working with rookie police officers. If it is a matter of an officer's safety, the supervisor should intervene, take action, and then tell the officer what occurred and why it was done in a particular way. Additionally, when a supervisor observes the conduct of an officer or receives information about a questionable event, he or she can initiate a counseling session as a means of improving a subordinate's skills or knowledge.

Atmosphere

Creating a positive atmosphere improves the potential for factual two-way communications. It is a helping process that allows an officer to relax, speak freely, and respond to feedback after discussing the issues and developing a plan of action. Advantages of an informal atmosphere clearly exceed the old process of commanding a subordinate to do something and expecting immediate compliance. It is also important for a supervisor, acting in the capacity of a counselor, to discuss an issue with a subordinate in an environment that is distraction free. If appropriate, the supervisor should sit in a chair facing the officer inasmuch as a desk can become a barrier, inhibiting the transmission of information. Furthermore, whenever possible, a counseling session should be held during duty hours. Counseling after duty hours can be viewed unfavorably and as an unnecessary intrusion into an officer's non-duty time.

Counseling Errors

A counselor should make every effort to make the counseling process error free. A counselor should never dominate a counseling session. Listening is definitely more productive for a supervisor than being loquacious. Competent leaders do not rush to judgment, refrain from losing emotional control, and do not project personal likes or dislikes (U.S. Department of the Army, 2006). Additionally, counseling errors include the failure to:

1. Admit to stereotyping.
2. Acknowledge and control personal bias.
3. Acknowledge the tendency to rush to judgment.
4. Be aware of personal concerns of subordinates.
5. Follow up.
6. Help the officer to help himself or herself.
7. Give the officer your full attention.
8. Keep oneself under emotional control.
9. Know what information to keep confidential.
10. Praise when appropriate.
11. Use flexible counseling techniques (Boyatzis & McKee, 2005; Fournies, 2000; Hesselbein et al., 2004; Johnson, 2005).

Counseling serves as a medium for creating an organizational environment that allows officers to grow, develop, mature, and work toward the goal of becoming a true law enforcement professional. In today's changing work milieu, counselors who address performance issues confronting officers prepare them for survival in the future, stressing changes in the workplace and the working environent (Leonard & Hilgert, 2004). Officers can meet these challenges when they receive needed counseling support. It is clear that the majority of police officers are ready, willing, and able to meet career demands, perform tasks with dispatch, and look forward to exercising self-direction and self-control (More et al., 2012).

Counseling Session

Above all, a counseling session should be void of rigidity. Flexibility is the byword of the day. A counselor should start a session by stating its purpose and creating a subordinate-centered environment. If appropriate, previous documentation should be reviewed prior to the session. Once this is done, the key is to let the subordinate speak and remember the adage *listen–listen–listen*. The goal is to help the officer understand the process of counseling. When performance is not up to standards the counselor should work with the officer, emphasizing the need to work together to clarify expectations, developing a plan of action that targets improvement, and providing support needed to ensure improvement (Brounstein, 2000).

Above all, counseling is a process, not just a single shot. It is a means of improving job performance. Every supervisor should strive to develop and improve counseling techniques, which are accomplished by following the guidelines listed in Figure 9.7.

1. Ask open-ended questions.
2. Avoid interrogating.
3. Avoid interrupting.
4. Be empathetic.
5. Be objective.
6. Demonstrate confidence in the officer's ability to turn a situation around.
7. Do not interrogate.
8. Do not make snap judgments.
9. Do not reprimand.
10. Encourage the officer to take the initiative when discussing a problem.
11. Establish an officer's role in the event.
12. Keep personal experiences out of counseling, unless you believe your experiences will really help.
13. Know what information to keep confidential.
14. Listen more than talk.
15. Listen to what the officer says and how it is said.
16. Paraphrase the remarks of the officer as a means of demonstrating that you are an active listener.
17. Use silence to get an officer to respond.
18. Make your expectations clear.

FIGURE 9.7 How to improve counseling. *Source: Adapted from U.S. Department of the Army (2006). Army Leadership. Washington, DC: Headquarters, U.S. Department of the Army; and Florence M. Stone (2007). Coaching, Counseling, & Mentoring: How to Choose and Use the Right Technique to Boost Employee Performance. New York: AMACOM.*

A counselor should become familiar with the problems that confront officers in the field and in their personal life and develop interpersonal skills to deal with the problems. Additionally, a counselor should work diligently at achieving credibility with officers by repeatedly showing a willingness to help and demonstrating consistency in word and action.

Documentation

Documentation provides a basis for providing feedback to a subordinate, as well as establishing a counseling record of accomplishments. Advanced notification to an officer places him or her on notice and the officer knows why the counseling session is needed. It also allows an officer the opportunity to prepare for the session. When an agreed-upon plan of action evolves from a joint discussion, it should be documented to include specifics of the plan, suggested improvements (in concrete terms), and main points of the counseling session. It is necessary to specify the means to be used in order to achieve a desired result and how the subordinate should modify behavior to accomplish a goal.

Documentation should be clear, concise, concrete, and direct. The total process should emphasize the continuous strengthening of an officer's skills, knowledge, and professional growth (Brounstein, 2000). Documentation can lead to recommendations for a range of things, from the need for further training to a suggestion that additional counseling is necessary.

Time

In a counseling session, contact with a subordinate can range from a brief encounter to an hour-long session. It should be noted that all counseling sessions should be an hour or less. The controlling factor is the complexity of the issue under consideration. If it is a matter of reporting late for duty three days in a row, the counselor should be able to clear such an issue up in a short period. However, if it is a significant violation of departmental policy, it might take one or more sessions. In any event, if there is need for a more formal session, the counselor should notify an officer in advance of the need for a counseling session, and above all the supervisor should prepare for a counseling session ahead of time. All pertinent information should be reviewed, including documenting events and circumstances leading up to the decision to schedule a counseling session. Another controlling factor is to schedule a counseling session as close to the occurrence under consideration as possible. That way everything is fresh in the minds of the counselor and the officer.

Mentoring

A relatively new concept in law enforcement is mentoring. It is interrelated to developmental counseling and coaching as set forth in the beginning of this chapter. Additionally, teaching is an important element of a first-line supervisor's responsibility in this complex and overlapping area. Teaching focuses primarily on the improvement of technical and tactical skills. Developmental counseling is best for improving human, affective, and conceptual skills (see Chapter 1), and coaching utilizes every skill area (Hu-TACK). It should be kept in mind that the development of subordinates is a significant first-line supervisory responsibility and that every tool possible should be utilized to assist officers in growing and developing their skills to the maximum (Swope, 2001).

Mentoring can be defined as the proactive development of each subordinate by observation, assessment, coaching, teaching, developmental counseling, and evaluation. It is an inclusive process. It is an essential leadership skill for managing and motivating officers (Mind Tools, 2009). Every officer under the immediate supervision of a sergeant could be a candidate for mentoring. One department created a mentoring program by using the field training officer (FTO) as the mentor. The training goal was to help officers identify and implement a formal mentoring program. This process was utilized primarily to help a lateral transfer to assimilate the new organizational culture (Cartwright, 2009). A mentor works in ways that exceed performing as simply a trainer. A mentor focuses on sharing expertise, experience, astuteness, and a practical understanding of the organization. A truly focused mentor promotes professional growth and serves as a motivator. Knowledge is passed on to less experienced officers so that they may develop their capabilities and amplify their potential (Crouch, 2005). In some police organizations, formal mentoring has been implemented as a means of reducing employee turnover. In other instances, informal mentoring serves as a vehicle for passing on the tradition and lore of the department and law enforcement in general (Crouch, 2005; Sprafka & Kranda, 2003). This is especially true for police departments that, in an effort to retain women, have created monitoring programs to cultivate one-on-one partnerships between new and veteran officers that will encourage employees to reach their fullest potential as law enforcement professionals (Bureau of Justice Assistance, 2001).

In other instances, a sergeant can work with a newly appointed supervisor to help them deal with rocks in the roadway, especially during the early transition stage. Mentoring provides for a faster learning curve and can put an officer into position to become a higher performer. It can also increase loyalty and improve one-on-one communication and a sense of team within the group supervised (Stone, 2007). Mentoring moves beyond coaching and counseling, although it will use many of the same techniques. Mentoring provides individuals (mentees) with a psychosocial reinforcement that includes acceptance, belongingness, a sense of identity, and, above all, encouragement. A mentor can give officers information that will allow them to interpret the meaning of organizational events and the organization's external environment—it gives them a sense of things beyond their control (Nelson & Quick, 2005).

Moreover, it includes a career facilitation function that includes support, challenging assignments, links, and increased organizational visibility. In addition, it can intensify subordinate job satisfaction, as well as organizational commitment. Every human being has the need to grow and develop toward the realization of his or her own unique potential, and the mentor can help fulfill this desire. Mentoring can also help a mentee develop realistic expectations. It is clearly more than training, coaching, or counseling. When the mentoring process is successful, a mentor has rewards, such as greater job satisfaction and the benefit of improving their own leadership and communications skills (Mind Tools, 2009). Moreover, the benefit of helping others grow and develop provides the mentor with the intrinsic reward of feeling better about a successful achievement. One's behavior as a supervisor should be a model to emulate, as pointed out earlier in this chapter. One study found that to best influence their patrol officers' behavior, field supervisors must lead by example. It suggests that an active supervisor functions by being actively involved in the field and at the same time controlling officer behavior (National Institute of Justice, 2003). If the mentor practices values that are of the highest order, an example is set for subordinates to imitate and follow (Swope, 2001). This is no small undertaking, and it should be noted that individual values and a value system are critically important variables inasmuch as they automatically filter the way people perceive their working environment. Most importantly, they serve as ethical as well as morale standards. Values facilitate the decision-making process and motivate officers to move toward the completion of important organizational goals and objectives (More et al., 2012). Values held by a police officer give substance to one's personal and professional self. Future values influence behavior somewhere down the line (Whisenand, 2008). This is the point where a mentor can demonstrate by his or her own conduct how a true professional applies judgment and skills to field situations and to interpersonal relationships.

Additionally, values are of critical importance to a mentor because they serve as a basis for resolving internal conflict that can result in a reduction of anxiety. A mentor can help an officer reach out, gain self-identity, grow as a person, and work toward self-actualization.

When a mentor with a positive value system believes that integrity, truthfulness, and frankness in human relationships are critical behavioral elements, then that mentor will do everything possible not to abuse positional or personal power. Manipulation of people or even the appearance of manipulation is out of the question (Leonard & More, 2000). A mentor practicing such a positive value system can, without hesitation or reservation, say, "do what I do—my integrity cannot be questioned" (Griffin, 1998).

A mentor is not afraid to share power and practices participative management as a means of enhancing employee satisfaction and improving performance. Acceptance of disagreement is inevitable and an essential element of problem solving. The successful mentor is able to resolve differences by mutual concessions and to facilitate continuing cooperation. A mentor learns the necessity of accepting others' imperfections. Being tolerant of others, their weaknesses and strengths, is essential if a mentoring relationship is to be functional. There has to be a basic assumption that the officer performing line duties has the capability of solving problems, and the mentor must provide the support needed to ensure a successful application of operational skills. The mentor knows that tasks have to be accomplished through others and that officers, being supervised, possess valuable ideas and knowledge needed to solve problems. A motivated officer, working with a mentor, will strive to improve their productivity and contribute to the attainment of organizational goals.

A mentor who wants to develop a positive working relationship with a mentee requires the acceptance of new ground rules for superior–subordinate relationships. This calls for adjustment and readjustment over time. At some point, a powerful synergistic relationship comes into existence as the mentor and mentee reinforce each other. Mentoring requires the rejection of the status quo and the mindset that says "don't rock the boat." Mentoring is not as time-consuming as many anticipate, but it should be kept in mind that there must be a serious commitment to the mentoring process if it is to be successful.

If a mentor can avoid the pitfalls given in Figure 9.8, it will make employees less dependent. It will encourage initiative and action, but, most importantly, it will serve to create an employee dedicated to his or her work. There are a wide range of determinants that make one dedicated to work, and the mentor can prove to be a vital component in creating professional officers. Once an officer becomes dedicated, there is an immediate identification with the organization and the officer can strive energetically to attain and sustain established goals. Officers that respond this way will find that they have greater job satisfaction.

Autonomy is another feature of dedication. When an officer is given a reasonable free rein, it reduces work tension and allows the officer to become more professional. Functional independence generates a feeling of importance, which in turn gives an individual a feeling of being a contributor to the organization. When expectations are met and the organization is viewed as dependable and looking out for employee interests, there is greater employee dedication.

It has to be acknowledged that there are modifiers to this process, and each officer will respond based on his or her own perception of the needs of the organization and individual

1. Advising more than giving feedback
2. Criticizing
3. Displaying a negative attitude
4. Failing to delegate
5. Failing to exhibit confidence in officers supervised
6. Failing to network with other supervisors
7. Ignoring input from supervised officers
8. Micromanaging
9. Not admitting your mistakes
10. Not keeping officers informed
11. Not giving praise and recognition
12. Not supporting mentees
13. Running a popularity contest

FIGURE 9.8 Mentoring pitfalls. *Adapted from Florence M. Stone (2007). Coaching, Counseling and Mentoring: How to Choose & Use the Right Technique to Boost Employee Performance. New York: AMACOM; and Marty Brounstein (2000). Coaching and Mentoring for Dummies. New York: Wiley.*

needs. A first-line supervisor, when functioning as a mentor, soon becomes aware of the uniqueness of each officer. Some officers develop slowly and others at a rapid pace. Some need a great deal of attention, whereas others can be off and running with limited supervision and guidance. The key is that when appropriate mentoring practices are applied and the pitfalls mentioned earlier are avoided, truly dedicated officers will emerge. A mentor has to become aware of differing degrees of capability and to respond accordingly. It is the task of a mentor to guide and assist officers so that they will become more dedicated.

References

Anthony, R. (2008). *The ultimate secrets of total self-confidence.* New York: Berkley Trade.

Boyatzis, R., & McKee, A. (2005). *Resonant leadership.* Boston: Harvard Business School Press

Brounstein, M. (2000). *Coaching and mentoring for dummies.* New York: Wiley.

Brounstein, M. (2007). *Coaching for dummies.* New York: Wiley.

Bureau of Justice Assistance, (2001). *Recruiting and retaining women: A self-assessment guide for law enforcement.* Washington, DC: Office of Justice Programs.

Caldero, M., & Crank, J. P. (2011). *Police ethics: The corruption of a noble cause* (3rd ed. (revised)). Boston: Elsevier (Anderson Publishing).

Cartwright, G. (2009). Mentoring for the transition. *Law and Order, 37*(4).

Chandler, S. (2011). *The life coaching connection—How coaching changes lives.* Bandon, OR: Robert D. Reed Publishers.

Commission on Accreditation for Law Enforcement Agencies, (2006). *Standards for law enforcement agency accreditation program* (5th ed.). Fairfax, VA: CALEA.

Cordner, G. W. (2013). *Police administration* (8th ed.). Boston: Elsevier (Anderson Publishing).

Crouch, R. (2005). Mentoring in the Auburn police department. *Law and Order, 53*(6).

Della, B. C. (2004). Nontraditional training systems—Realizing the effectiveness of an agency's most valuable resource. *FBI Law Enforcement Bulletin, 73*(6).

Duxbury, P. (2009). *The power of coaching.* Melbourne, Australia: Business Performance.

Federal Emergency Management Agency, (1994). *Leadership strategies for supervisory success.* Washington, DC: United States Fire Administration.

Flaherty, J. (2010). *Coaching: Evoking excellence in others* (3rd ed.). Boston: Butterworth-Heinemann.

Fournies, F. F. (2000). *Coaching for improved work performance* (3rd ed.). New York: McGraw-Hill.

Fridell, L., Maskaly, J., Cordner, G., Mastrofski, S., Rosenbaum, D., Banfield, G., et al. (2011). *The longitudinal study of first line supervisors.* Washington, DC: National Institute of Justice.

Frunzi, G. I., & Savini, P. E. (1997). *Supervision: The art of management* (5th ed.). Upper Saddle River, NJ: Prentice Hall.

Griffin, N. C. (1998). The five I's of police professionalism: A model for front-line supervisors. *The Police Chief, LXV*(11).

Hesselbein, F., Shinseki, E. K., & Cavanagh, R. (2004). *Be, know, do: Leadership the army-way.* New York: Jossey-Bass.

Hickman, M. J. (2005). *State and local law enforcement academies, 2002.* Washington, DC: Bureau of Justice Statistics.

Holden, R. N. (1994). *Modern Police Management* (2nd ed.). Englewood Cliffs, NJ: Prentice-Hall, Inc.

Johnson, R. R. (2005). Personal relationship with subordinates. *Law and Order, 53*(3).

Kennedy, R. C. (2003). Applying principles of adult learning: The key to more effective training programs. *FBI Law Enforcement Bulletin, 72*(4).

Leonard, E. C., & Hilgert, R. L. (2004). *Supervision: Concepts and practices of management* (9th ed.). Cincinnati: Thomson/South-Western.

Leonard, V. A., & More, H. W. (2000). *Police organization and management* (9th ed.). New York: Foundation.

Luthans, F. (2010). *Organizational behavior* (12th ed.). New York: McGraw-Hill.

Mind Tools, (2009). *Mentoring: An essential leadership skill.* London: Mind Tools.

More, H. W., Vito, G. F., & Walsh, W. (2012). *Organizational behavior and management in law enforcement* (3rd ed.). Upper Saddle River, NJ: Pearson Prentice Hall.

Moriarty, S. E. (2009). The Leadership in Police Organizations Program in the Delaware State Police: Recommendations for law enforcement leadership development. *The Police Chief, LXXVI*(5).

National Institute of Justice, (2003). *How police supervisory styles influence patrol officer behavior.* Washington, DC: Office of Justice Programs.

Nelson, D. L., & Quick, J. C. (2005). *Organizational behavior: Foundations, realities and challenges.* St. Paul, MN: West.

Nowicki, E. (2008). Training supervisors as coaches. *Law and Order, 56*(2).

O'Leary, A. M., & Griffin, R. W. (1995). Job satisfaction and organizational commitment. In N. Brester & C. Wilson (Eds.), *Psychology and policing.* Hillsdale, NJ: Lawrence Erlbaum Associates.

Peterson, R. S., & Sancovich, A. C. (2003). Emerging themes from a new paradigm. In S. P. Randall & E. A. Mannix (Eds.), *Leading and managing people in the dynamic organization.* Mahwah, NJ: Lawrence Erlbaum Associates.

Rock, D. (2009). *What is coaching?* Melbourne, Australia: Business Performance.

Salmon, W. A. (1999). *The new supervisor's survival manual.* New York: AMACOM.

Smith, C. P., Pehlke, D. E., & Weller, C. D. (1974). *Project STAR.* Cincinnati, OH: Anderson-Davis, Inc.

Sprafka, H., & Kranda, A. H. (2003). *Leadership.* Alexandria, VA: International Association of Chiefs of Police.

Stinchcomb, J. D. (1996). *Opportunities in law enforcement and criminal justice.* Lincolnwood, IL: VGM Career Horizons.

Stone, F. M. (2003). *The manager's question and answer book* (2nd ed.). New York: AMACOM.

Stone, F. M. (2007). *Coaching, counseling and mentoring: How to choose & use the right technique to boost employee performance.* New York: AMACOM.

Stroh, L. K., Northcraft, G. B., Neale, M. A., Kern, M., Langland, C., & Greenberg, J. (2002). *Organizational behavior: A management challenge* (3rd ed.). Florence, KY: Taylor and Francis.

Swope, R. (2001). Mentor the first line supervisor. *Law and Order, 48*(10).

U.S. Department of the Army, (1999). *Army leadership—Be, know, do.* Washington, DC: Headquarters, U.S. Department of the Army.

U.S. Department of the Army, (2006). *Army leadership—Competent, confident, and agile.* Washington, DC: Headquarters, U.S. Department of the Army.

Whisenand, P. (2008). *The managing of police organizations* (7th ed.). Upper Saddle River. NJ: Pearson Prentice Hall.

10

Discipline
An Essential Element of Police Supervision

KEY TERMS

constructive discharge
constructive discipline
disciplinary action
disciplinary action
   made to stick
firm, fair, equitable, and
   lawful
first-line supervisors as
   disciplinarians
Garrity protection
goal of discipline
"hot stove" concept
negative discipline

objectives of the
   discipline system
peace officer bill of
   rights
positive discipline
PRICE protocol
progressive discipline
property right
total quality
   management
types of discipline
vicarious liability

CASE STUDY

Public Safety Officer Jane Roberts

DEPARTMENT

The Astonville Police Department has 166 sworn officers who are also certified as firefighters. Twelve years ago, the Astonville city council adopted a proposal to combine traditional fire and police personnel into one public safety unit. The measure was intended to reduce costs and make more efficient use of manpower. As it turned out, neither traditional police officers nor traditional firefighters liked the idea. While it did save money during the first few years, costs associated with the public safety officer (PSO) program have continued to rise. For one thing, turnover is very high. The city is always trying to fill positions in the PSO program. New recruits obtain training as police officers and then obtain training as firefighters. Once certified, they can apply for traditional police or firefighting positions elsewhere in the state, often making considerably more money than with Astonville. In an effort to keep officers from taking other jobs in nearby cities, the administration encouraged supervisors to be "easy" on discipline and to give officers under their supervision some leeway. As a result, officers are "allowed" to take extra time on breaks, take classes at the local university during their shift, and even take time out of their shift to go to special functions at their children's schools and such. "As long as the calls are answered promptly, let them have a break if nothing is going on," supervisors were told by the managers.

CRIME

Astonville enjoys a low crime rate. It is located in a suburban area 20 miles from a metropolitan city. There were two homicides last year, both domestic in nature. Four rapes were reported, all involving juvenile girls with adult perpetrators. Fourteen felonious assaults and two robberies were the total of crimes against persons last year. Property crimes were up from the previous year, particularly residential burglary. Several new, high-income housing projects were developed in Astonville, which seems to have attracted burglars to the area.

COMMUNITY

Astonville had a population of 84,000 at the last census. However, the city has been growing steadily for the past several years. Due to its convenient location to the metropolitan area and its low property tax rates, Astonville has become popular with younger professionals working in the metropolitan area. The result has been an increase in the number of subdivisions with high-income housing.

Astonville has a shopping mall and several specialty shopping centers. The downtown area hosts specialty shops and restaurants that are popular with the younger professionals that have recently moved to the city. There are seven public schools and three Christian schools. The Christian schools are also popular with the younger professional residents. There is one hospital and also several private clinics. The largest and most visible institution in Astonville is the state university, which normally has about 12,000 students. The state university has a criminal justice program, and the city frequently tries to recruit new graduates from that program into the Astonville Public Safety Bureau.

OFFICER

Public Safety Officer Jane Roberts has just fulfilled her six-month probationary period with the Astonville PSO Bureau. She was in the top 10 percent of her graduating class from both the police academy and the fire training academy. She is attractive, single, and young. She is also a bit self-assured, not afraid to speak her mind, and can hold her own with some of the more flirtatious male officers with her no-nonsense demeanor. Roberts has a lot of common sense and is capable of doing the jobs of both policing and firefighting, as she has demonstrated over the past six months. She graduated with a baccalaureate degree in criminal justice from the state university. Although she was offered jobs with other substantially larger departments, she elected to take the job with Astonville. The cross-training in police and firefighting is what attracted her to the department.

PROBLEM

Roberts was assigned to a field training officer (FTO) for her six-month probationary period. Sergeant Williams, Roberts' supervisor, assigned her to FTO Andrew Tibbetts. Sergeant Williams had some doubts about assigning Roberts to Tibbetts. After all, Roberts was an attractive young woman and Tibbetts, although married with two children, is considered to be something of a "ladies man." Tibbetts is jokingly known as "Adonis" by other officers because of his extreme neatness and concern for his physical appearance. However, Roberts seemed to be able to handle these types of men and Tibbetts was the best FTO.

Roberts completed her field training and probationary period with high evaluations from both FTO Tibbetts and Sergeant Williams. And while Roberts is now on her own as a regular member of the shift, she still relies heavily on Tibbetts for advice and backup. Sergeant Williams also noticed a more than friendly "bond" between the two and has overheard other officers comment about seeing Tibbetts and Roberts kissing in the police parking garage on occasion. In fact, Sergeant Williams found the two having a heated argument in the parking garage last week. When the sergeant intervened to find out what was wrong, the two parted simply saying "nothing's wrong." The sergeant assumed it was a "lover's spat" and decided it was none of his business so long as they both did their jobs.

The next day after roll call, Roberts stopped Sergeant Williams, asking to meet with him. The sergeant escorted Roberts to the supervisor's office and asked her to sit down. Roberts refused to sit but wanted to explain what the argument was about in the parking garage between her and Tibbetts.

"Sergeant, I want you to know first. I'm pregnant. The baby belongs to Tibbetts. He won't leave his wife and won't have anything to do with me now."

"Oh, Jane, I'm sorry to hear about that. But you know our policy about pregnancy. You'll have to take a leave of absence and…"

"Damn your policies," Jane interrupts. "This happened because of you. It's your fault. You put me with that ladies' hound for over six months. You knew what kind of man he was and how vulnerable I was. You didn't supervise us at all, just turned us loose. And to top it off, I got pregnant on duty. I talked with a lawyer friend of mine last night, and she said I could claim workers' compensation since my condition occurred on duty, right under your nose."

WHAT WOULD YOU DO?

Who is at fault in this case? What recourse does Sergeant Williams have at this point? What mistakes were made from the beginning, and how can future situations like this be prevented? Do you think Roberts has a workers' compensation claim?

The Nature of Discipline

The goal of discipline is to produce desirable behavior. This function can be accomplished by encouraging appropriate behavior and punishing inappropriate or unacceptable behavior.

Discipline, as an operational concept, is closely related to other managerial aspects of first-line supervision in paramilitary-type police organizations. It should not be viewed as a derogatory term or dirty word. In fact, discipline is regarded as the essential element in work that ensures overall productivity and an orderly environment. Unfortunately, it is the word discipline, in and of itself, that causes the problem. It has a number of different (at times conflicting) meanings and must be used carefully in order to avoid confusion.

The term discipline is most often used to describe an adversarial process resulting in the application of various kinds of negative sanctions or punishments. It may also refer to the state of affairs within a given organization that produces order, a shared sense of purpose, and common goal-oriented behavior. In this particular context, discipline is considered positive and means teaching, instruction, training, and remediation. Its purpose is to facilitate collective action, the internalization of self-control based on the norms and values of the workforce, predictable behavior, and organizational efficiency. From this perspective, maintaining discipline is a management function that involves conditioning subordinates in order to promote (1) obedience, (2) internal self-control, and (3) acceptance of punishments designed to curb individual deviance or professional misconduct.

Discipline in the Ranks

Human resources provide the linchpin for delivery of all public safety services in a given community. Police work is, in itself, a labor-intensive government activity in which personnel costs consume the lion's share of the budget. Attempting to maximize the efficiency, effectiveness, and productivity of the police department, while holding the line on spending, is clearly a management function. It is the first-line supervisor, normally a sergeant, who has direct responsibility for accomplishing the organization's mission, goals, and objectives through the collaborative efforts of immediate subordinates. Consequently, each first-line supervisor must develop the skills necessary to influence the behavior of others, coordinate their activities, and lead or direct employees in such a way as to gain their respect, confidence, trust, and positive cooperation. Supervision, based on this model, is viewed as an art rather than a science.

As first-line supervisors charged with getting police work done through others, sergeants play two distinct, yet related, roles when it comes to on-the-job behavior of their subordinates. Sergeants are expected to nurture professionalism in the employee, yet are responsible for initiating disciplinary measures when formal action is required to deal with individual deviance. The trick is to find the appropriate balance between employee self-regulation and organizational control (Covey, 1992).

Like all other first-line supervisors, police sergeants find themselves sandwiched between upper management and operational personnel. While their authority is often ambiguous, sergeants are generally expected to use existing human resources in an effort to translate official department policy into both efficient and effective action on the street. In order to fulfill this awesome responsibility and to play a meaningful role in police personnel administration, sergeants use positive as well as negative discipline. No matter which form they choose, the objective is always the same. Sergeants try to encourage safe, reasonable, and predictable conduct in the workplace so as to create an environment in which competent, well-trained police officers "protect and serve" the community while satisfying their personal needs and achieving their professional goals. Needless to say, police sergeants play a pivotal leadership role in the administration of criminal justice. In the long run, it is the first-line supervisors who (based on their ability, training, and human relations skills) will determine the success or failure of the police department in achieving its mission, goals, and objectives. According to Dwight Eisenhower, "Leadership is the art of getting others to do something you want done because they want to do it."

Positive Discipline

The words "disciple" and "discipline" have the same root meaning: to teach or mold. Positive discipline involves a systematic approach designed to instruct or guide employees in such a way that they become loyal, dedicated, responsible, and productive members of the organization (Sherman & Lucia, 1992). From a practical point of view, discipline is considered positive or "good" when all police employees share a common sense of purpose, practice self-discipline, and voluntarily follow the policies, procedures, rules, and regulations established to promote order and to facilitate work within the department. Positive discipline is used to prevent deviation from group-shared expectations or to deal with difficult employees without resorting to punishments or other kinds of negative sanctions. This particular orientation to discipline (built on an esprit de corps) is not unique to police organizations and is based on the fundamental assumption that police personnel are no different from other employees. Police officers who have mastered their craft, who know what is expected of them as professionals, and who understand the rationale behind those expectations are much more likely to identify with the department in terms of its mission, goals, and objectives and to invest their time, energy, effort, and expertise in work-related activities. According to the legendary O.W. Wilson (sometimes referred to as the father of modern police administration), positive discipline manifests itself in the officer's willingness to conform and participate in self-restraint, based on professional dedication or a personal commitment to the ethos of the police department (Fyfe, Greene, Walsh, Wilson, & McLaren, 1997).

The most positive form of discipline is the self-discipline built on the human tendency to do what needs to be done, to do what is right in a given situation, and to comply voluntarily with the reasonable standards of performance and conduct that apply to all members of the workforce. Mature employees know that following instructions and obeying rules is part of the game. Responsible and cooperative behavior at work is a tacitly accepted condition of employment in virtually all organizations.

Every first-line supervisor should strive to create an environment in which self-discipline is rewarded and external or imposed discipline is held to an absolute minimum. In modern police work, the sergeant plays a crucial role in the employee development process. It is the sergeant's job to promote professional growth and to foster a sense of self-worth in each subordinate. The success or failure of this effort will depend, in the long run, on the supervisor's technical knowledge and human skills. All first-line supervisors in healthy police organizations are multidimensional players who act as technical advisors, role models, teachers, counselors, leaders, and, when all else fails, disciplinarians. They learn to accentuate the positive and to cultivate each employee's sense of competence, craftsmanship, and pride through constructive interpersonal relationships built on a bedrock of empathy and mutual respect. Effective supervision and good supervisors help keep subordinates interested in their job and satisfied with working conditions (see Figure 10.1).

Even though money and other material rewards are powerful incentives, recognition (based on sincere assessment of an employee's personal worth) can have an even more dramatic impact on job-related behavior. It costs little or nothing; however, as with money, almost everyone responds to it in one way or another. It is amazing how hard police officers will work when the psychological payoff is feeling appreciated and important. While she may have overstated the case somewhat, Mary Kay Ash, who created a $600 million-per-year cosmetics business, believed that there are two things people want more than sex or money—they covet both

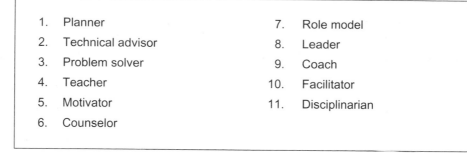

1.	Planner	7.	Role model
2.	Technical advisor	8.	Leader
3.	Problem solver	9.	Coach
4.	Teacher	10.	Facilitator
5.	Motivator	11.	Disciplinarian
6.	Counselor		

FIGURE 10.1 Basic supervisory roles.

recognition and praise from those in a position to judge their on-the-job performance and exert a positive influence on their career (LeBoeuf, 1985).

Good supervisors are enthusiastic team players who have the skills necessary to influence their subordinates in a positive way. They help create an environment in which police personnel buy into and make a willing contribution to the organization. According to Dale Carnegie (1992), there are nine ways in which a sergeant can change a person's attitude without giving offense or arousing resentment:

1. Begin with praise and honest appreciation.
2. Call attention to the other person's mistakes indirectly.
3. Discuss personal mistakes before criticizing others.
4. Ask thoughtful questions instead of giving direct orders.
5. Always try to let the other person save face.
6. Praise, whenever possible, even the slightest improvement.
7. Give the other person a fine reputation to live up to.
8. Use encouragement and make faults seem easy to correct.
9. Make the person happy about doing what has been suggested.

Effective supervisors have learned to criticize the work done by an employee rather than the employee himself or herself. They know what Michael LeBoeuf has called "The Greatest Management Principle": the things that get rewarded get done. Recognition and praise are rewards.

Police departments use commendations, citations, certificates, and plaques as physical indicators of a job well done. These psychological rewards are among the most powerful motivators at the disposal of the first-line supervisor. They are the key ingredient in morale and serve as the cornerstone of esprit de corps. According to the Commission on Accreditation for Law Enforcement Agencies Standard 26.1.2, "A written directive establishes procedures and criteria for recognizing and rewarding employees for good performance" (CALEA, 2006).

Camaraderie, unity of purpose, technical expertise, and effective supervision create natural parameters for accepted and expected behavior in a given organization. Once internalized and reinforced continuously with positive sanctions or rewards, these parameters form the basis for self-control. Self-control is an important trait of police professionalism. Once employees know their job and accept the standards by which their on-the-job performance will be judged, they gain a great deal of self-confidence and personal security. They feel more comfortable exercising discretion and accept the fact that there are limits beyond which they must not go. If a subordinate crosses over one of these boundaries, it must be understood that some type of legitimate disciplinary action will follow.

Total quality management (TQM) is a technique designed to assist in developing a positive performance-oriented culture, as well as employee commitment within the work environment. Through meaningful participation, TQM empowers employees to become partners in making the organization work more efficiently and effectively by removing the barriers that inhibit commitment, creativity, and high-quality service. First-line supervisors must become facilitators who elicit from their people their maximum effort to contribute ideas, creativity, innovative thinking, attention to detail, and analyses of process, products, and services in the workplace (Whisenand & Rush, 2011).

From a practical point of view, all police officers must be treated as adults if that is the behavior expected in return. Supervisors can almost guarantee improvement in employee performance through use of the PRICE protocol. PRICE is the acronym for pinpoint, record, involve, coach, and evaluate (Blanchard, 1989).

1. Pinpoint. Supervisors must scan the work environment continually in order to pinpoint performance problems that merit attention.
2. Record. Supervisors should record (and quantify) the current performance level of those who are having problems.
3. Involve. Supervisors must involve the employee(s) in determining the best way to deal with the problem, the coaching strategies to be used, how the supervisor will be monitoring progress, and the rewards or punishments to be associated with success or failure of the corrective process.
4. Coach. Supervisors should implement the agreed-upon coaching strategy by observing performance and providing timely advice, continuous encouragement, positive reinforcement, and retraining (if and when it is necessary).
5. Evaluate. Supervisors must evaluate and provide feedback on a continuous basis in order to determine whether the goals of the PRICE protocol have been achieved.

If employee performance does not reach the mutually agreed-upon level, the supervisor needs to determine the cause. There may be a need to redefine goals. However, there may be a need for further assistance (Aragon, 1993). Additional time or training might be required. Police officers who "cannot" or "will not" perform at an acceptable level should be disciplined and—if necessary—separated from the police service.

The Commission on Accreditation for Law Enforcement Agencies includes in its standards a section detailing the necessity for establishing a directive for a disciplinary system (Standard 26.1.4, CALEA, 2006). The disciplinary system is to include:

1. Procedures and criteria for using training as a function of discipline.
2. Procedures and criteria for using counseling as a function of discipline.
3. Procedures and criteria for taking punitive actions in the interest of discipline.

Negative Discipline

In ideal circumstances, employees are expected to be willing and capable of assuming responsibility for the quantity and quality of their productive output. Under these conditions, the employee's ego satisfaction, pride in achievement, professional competence, and job security become very powerful motivators and are key ingredients in a work-based reward system built on self-discipline. Unfortunately, this utopian view of on-the-job behavior is overly simplistic and, in many ways, a figment of the management theorist's imagination. As valuable as it is, self-discipline is insufficient, in itself, to regulate behavior in complex criminal justice organizations. Consequently, the police sergeant must be prepared, when circumstances warrant, to supplement employee self-discipline with external, and at times negative, imposed discipline.

Discipline that is based on the use of punishment rather than rewards is referred to as negative discipline. When used in this context, it is synonymous with the phrase "disciplinary action" and is imposed by those in authority when all positive approaches have failed to produce conformity with specific performance standards or behavioral expectations. Disciplinary action is adversarial in nature and is inherently punitive. It is designed to regulate work-related behavior and to safeguard the integrity of the organization. Negative discipline in the form of disciplinary action is considered a legitimate and necessary behavior-control mechanism in virtually all paramilitary-type police departments.

First-line supervisors in bureaucratic police organizations spend a great deal of time and energy trying to cope with marginal employees. A marginal employee is not a deviant per se. Some individuals (for a variety of idiosyncratic or cultural reasons) simply do not measure up to reasonable expectations. These employees do the minimum amount of work to get by. They lack or have lost interest in their job and have adapted their behavior to, and are comfortable with, their present level of incompetence. Many marginal employees freely admit that they are just "putting in time."

Sergeants are expected to deal with employee problems, motivate marginal employees, and increase the employee's productivity through effective supervision. Unfortunately, a sergeant may or may not have the diagnostic or human skills needed to accomplish this objective.

In large police departments, first-line supervisors may have access and be authorized to refer marginal employees to an employee assistance program designed to deal with mental health problems, alcoholism and other drug addiction, stress, domestic difficulties, and so on. In smaller departments, the sergeant serves as the employee assistance program. Problem solving and counseling come with the stripes. As a result, sergeants are expected to have a wide range of knowledge and a knapsack full of human relations skills.

When all else fails, sergeants are forced to rely on the imposition of negative discipline to deal with both deviant and marginal police personnel. This tends to overload the system and is not cost-effective. Discipline and morale begin to suffer when most of the sergeant's time is spent on a few deviant or marginal employees. From a practical point of view, formal disciplinary action should be the last resort in human resources management.

While it is clear that the vast majority of all American police personnel exercise a considerable degree of self-discipline, there are always a few (up to 15 percent) who will, for one reason or another, continue to violate departmental policies, procedures, rules, and regulations, even though they are aware of the potential consequences of their deviant behavior. They simply cannot or will not toe the line and accept responsibility for disciplining themselves. At this point, the sergeant is obligated to initiate appropriate disciplinary action. Under these conditions, negative discipline becomes a necessary, albeit time-consuming, aspect of effective supervision.

Sergeants as Disciplinarians

Because of their position in the department hierarchy and the legitimate authority vested in their rank, sergeants play a much more important and direct role in the disciplinary process than almost any other police manager. For all practical purposes, they are the departmental disciplinarians—with the power to discipline nearly every line officer engaged in the delivery of police services. Many of their subordinates are inexperienced, inadequately trained, or in need of some corrective remediation. When all else fails, it is the sergeant's responsibility to:

1. Identify weaknesses, deficiencies, failures, or overt behavior of subordinates that indicate the need for corrective action.
2. Analyze all relevant factors to determine the appropriate action to be taken.
3. Initiate and, in many cases, carry out the disciplinary action.
4. Document the case (in terms of "cause," "analysis," "action," and the "appropriateness of the discipline") for subsequent review by superiors (see Figure 10.2).

Sergeants, as responsible first-line supervisors, have a professional duty to act reasonably, decisively, and promptly in resolving disciplinary problems. They are expected to act in the best interests of the employee, the department, the law enforcement profession, and the community at large. Needless to say, all disciplinary actions should be "constructive" rather than "destructive," in the sense that they are administered in a firm, fair, and impartial manner. Constructive discipline is built on a foundation of sensitivity and good judgment. Its goal is the correction or remediation of deviant behavior as it occurs, as well as improvement in the overall behavior of the employee and other members of the police department in the future (Leonard, 2013).

---

1. Recognize disciplinary problems as they arise.
2. Gather pertinent data concerning the situation.
3. Analyze factors relevant to the problem.
4. Determine appropriate disciplinary measures.
5. Initiate disciplinary action.
6. Discipline subordinates when authorized.
7. Document the case for subsequent review.

FIGURE 10.2 The sergeant's role as disciplinarian.

Fair and Equitable Discipline

Disciplinary action in complex criminal justice organizations should not be an idiosyncratic or random exercise of power by those in authority. As noted earlier, it must be viewed as an essential part of a goal-oriented process designed to control the disruptive behavior of individual employees while ensuring the overall efficiency, effectiveness, and productivity of the workforce. Employees who cannot measure up to reasonable performance standards or who refuse to toe the line in terms of their on-the-job behavior are legitimate targets of formal disciplinary action. They should be penalized in such a way that they learn to achieve acceptable performance standards and exhibit appropriate behavior. Employees who do not respond or who are incapable of making a substantive change become a liability to the department and must be removed from their job for the good of the service.

Fair and equitable disciplinary procedures are necessary to protect the integrity of the service and provide an adequate frame of reference for all police personnel. Police officers (like all other employees) have emotional job-related security needs that must be considered by management. As the first-line supervisor, the sergeant has the primary responsibility for satisfying a subordinate's:

1. Need to be treated as an individual with intrinsic value and the capacity to make a contribution to the organization.
2. Need to know exactly what management expects in terms of work performance and on-the-job conduct.
3. Need regular feedback from management concerning job performance (including praise as well as censure).
4. Need to be treated fairly and impartially by those in management.
5. Need to be judged by management based on facts and standards rather than on personal opinion or assumptions.

The failure to recognize and deal with employee needs in these very critical areas often leads to job dissatisfaction, interpersonal conflict, poor performance, disciplinary problems, and high employee turnover (Robbins & Judge, 2012). It represents a sergeant's dereliction of duty and the abdication of responsibility by management.

All seasoned first-line supervisors know that rationality is a prerequisite for effective disciplinary action in law enforcement. Good disciplinary systems do not materialize out of thin air; they are, in fact, crafted very carefully by management (Plunkett, 1992) and generally exhibit the following characteristics:

1. Proper assignment of personnel to jobs within the organization based on their interest, skill, utility, and specialized training.
2. Necessary and reasonable job-related policies, procedures, rules, and regulations formulated to govern behavior in the workplace, meet employee needs, and accomplish the department's mission, goals, and specified objectives.
3. Effective communication of information regarding expected performance and acceptable behavior to all employees, along with an explanation of the probable consequences of noncompliance.

4. Continuous review, evaluation, and appraisal of all personnel to assess strengths, detect weaknesses, and identify disciplinary problems that may require immediate attention.
5. Consistent, fair, and equitable enforcement of all policies, procedures, rules, and regulations within the organization.
6. Mutually acceptable, institutionalized disciplinary procedures based on a "due process" model that is in harmony with applicable civil service regulations and negotiated collective bargaining agreements.
7. A formal appeals procedure designed to ensure the fairness of all disciplinary actions and to serve as a check and balance on the imposition of punitive sanctions.

While no manager really likes the idea of being the disciplinarian, using disciplinary action is an unavoidable part of each first-line supervisor's job. No matter how alert or skillful the particular supervisor is, the imposition of discipline (in one form or another) is inevitable in virtually all work situations. Consequently, supervisors must face the fact that, in all likelihood, they will be called on to take disciplinary action against a subordinate. The imposition of punishment is normal and to be expected, although hopefully an infrequent aspect of the first-line supervisor's role in complex criminal justice organizations.

Inconsistency and favoritism in disciplining subordinates will have an adverse, potentially destructive effect on employee morale and productivity (Guthrie, 1996). The effective sergeant understands departmental policies, procedures, rules, and regulations; trains and guides immediate subordinates; and is both fair and impartial when dispensing discipline. From a pragmatic point of view, a sergeant's actions must be legal, reasonable, consistent, and timely. Employees react strongly and frequently challenge management prerogatives in court when they believe they have been treated unfairly due to the arbitrary denial of some "due process" right. As the first-line supervisor, it is the sergeant who is the central character in the drama to preserve management's authority to discipline errant, disruptive, or deviant subordinates.

The Use and Abuse of Discipline

Although punishment might produce some negative effects (such as resentment, interpersonal conflict, and lower morale), it must sometimes be used simply because there is no practical alternative. Some of the adverse reactions to punishment will be tempered, however, if the punishment is carried out in an intelligent, fair, and predictable manner and if the employee targeted for disciplinary action understands that it was necessary due to poor performance or misconduct, not because of someone else's behavior (Iannone & Iannone, 2013).

Lack of trust is another factor that must be taken into consideration. Police officers learn to fear, lose respect for, and distrust supervisors who become entrenched in company politics, make decisions too quickly or irrationally, and invoke disciplinary measures for the slightest infractions. Mature officers want their sergeants to be equitable and to act in good faith when disciplining. When their first-line supervisors fail to live up to these expectations, the dissonance created makes matters even worse.

Each sergeant's approach to the use of discipline indicates the sergeant's view of the administrative power inherent in the rank. If the sergeant has an authoritarian personality, misunderstands the nature of the job, or lacks rudimentary leadership skills, the potential for abuse of the disciplinary apparatus is great. There is a solution for this problem, however. All newly promoted first-line police supervisors should be required to successfully complete a supervisory/management training program designed to familiarize them with their new administrative duties, their role as a supervisor, and their authority vis-à-vis the formal disciplinary system. Sergeants, like their subordinates, need to know what is expected of them.

The imposition of disciplinary action within an organization has two distinct, yet interactive, objectives: (1) to reform the individual offender and (2) to deter others who may be influenced by what has happened. From this perspective, all imposed discipline has value in terms of correcting errant, disruptive, or deviant behavior, as well as for its future effect on the individuals involved as offenders or observers. In light of these objectives, each sergeant must determine which penalties are available, feasible, and appropriate for use in a particular set of circumstances. While evaluating the alternatives, both short-term and long-term effects that punishment is likely to have must be estimated. It is then up to the sergeant, in conjunction with superior officers, to select the most effective form of punishment. All other things being equal, the punishment should be adequate based on the offense. Excessive punishment is counterproductive and becomes a stressor in labor–management relations.

On the other side of the coin, first-line supervisors, as human beings, must avoid the pitfalls of subjectivity and continuously guard against making discipline-related decisions based on emotion. Based on "people orientation" in contemporary applied management theory (Peters & Waterman, 2004), it is safe to say that there is no place for anger, revenge, or retribution in the disciplinary process. It is illegal for supervisors to harass employees through the capricious exercise of power or to intentionally humiliate those who have been targeted for disciplinary action. Finally, there is absolutely no justification for the behavior of supervisors who displace aggression by scapegoating their employees. The proper goal of imposed discipline is to make the future more satisfactory, not to vent emotions or to fulfill some abstract sense of justice (see Figure 10.3).

MOTIVE/GOAL	LIKELY EFFECT
Legitimate Reform Deterrence	 Improved performance or conduct Prevent similar violations by others
Unacceptable Revenge Capriciousness Displaced aggression Humiliation Retribution	 Anger, provocation to more violations Fear, loss of respect, distrust Uncertainty, confusion, resentment Anxiety, personal conflict, hatred Frustration, accusations of legalism

FIGURE 10.3 Objectives of disciplinary action. *Source: Adapted from Aaron Q. Sartain and Alton W. Baker (1979). The Supervisor and his Job. New York: McGraw-Hill.*

Administering effective discipline is one of the most demanding aspects of any first-line supervisor's job. It is both complex and time-consuming. The accused employee is presumed innocent until proven guilty, and in establishing that guilt (as a justification for using disciplinary action in the workplace), the burden of proof is almost always on those involved in direct supervisory management (Steinmetz & Todd, 1986). Many courts have now ruled that an employer violates an implied contract if a subordinate is disciplined without sufficient and just cause.

In the public sector, just cause refers to a cause of action that is legally adequate to sustain a decision to inflict negative sanctions. At this point, "sufficient and just cause" clauses have been incorporated into virtually all civil service regulations and grievance procedures mandated by negotiated collective bargaining agreements. The imposition of disciplinary action without just cause is viewed by most Americans as an unconscionable and unacceptable abuse of authority. This type of unprofessional conduct undermines the individual supervisor's effectiveness and subjects management itself to ridicule, charges of unfair labor practices, political repercussions, and civil lawsuits. The misuse of power destroys the sergeant's credibility and diminishes legitimate authority over subordinates.

While most supervisory personnel do an adequate job, police work has its share of poor first-line supervisors. There are sergeants who are merely putting in time and trying to survive. They take disciplinary action against co-workers only when they are backed into a corner and do not want to rock the boat unless their own career is on the line. Other sergeants are simply inept. They do not have the sensitivity, judgment, knowledge, training, or human skills needed to deal effectively with recalcitrant employees. These men and women are shackled by their own inadequacy. Malfeasance, misfeasance, and nonfeasance interact synergistically to produce a dual impact: police professionalism is diminished and public safety is jeopardized. In the long run, it is American society that suffers the consequences of poor first-line supervision in law enforcement.

Saying that firm, fair, equitable, and lawful disciplinary action is an essential ingredient in effective supervision is one thing; achieving it in a complex criminal justice organization is another matter altogether. Guthrie (1996) has proposed an automated system to apply disciplinary action fairly. A computerized database of complaints, officer characteristics, and disciplinary actions over a five-year period was developed by the internal affairs unit of the Fresno, California, Police Department. The automated system allowed supervisors to review histories, department-wide complaint characteristics, and disciplinary actions taken for categorized employee misconduct. The system helped supervisors achieve more consistent and equitable disciplinary decision-making.

Keys to Effective Discipline

In order to make disciplinary action more effective, it should be proactive as well as reactive in that police sergeants must be prepared, based on their education, training, and job-related supervisory experience, to detect and correct discipline problems before they become malignant and spread throughout the organization. Good supervisors know the keys to effective discipline (Preston & Zimmerer, 1983) and apply them as conscientiously as possible.

1. *Don't Be a Discipline Ostrich.* First-line supervisors should not slip into a pattern of overlooking discipline problems. In fact, they have a duty to take immediate and appropriate action to correct the situation. Failure to act promptly and decisively tends to perpetuate the problem and sets the stage for more debilitating interpersonal conflict. In addition, other employees will begin to question the sergeant's ability and fairness if they see that disciplinary action is put off or avoided altogether. Under these circumstances, subordinates will assume that most, if not all, of the department's policies, procedures, rules, and regulations are worthless. Violations may become the rule rather than the exception. This anomie, or "normlessness," is inherently destructive.

2. *Become a "Caesar's Wife."* All of the sergeant's behavior must be above reproach. There can be absolutely no doubt in the subordinate's mind about the sergeant's loyalty to the organization or willingness to comply with departmental policies, procedures, rules, and regulations. Employees cannot be expected to practice self-control if their immediate supervisors are poor role models who fail to set an example worthy of emulation. Sergeants lead others by example. Seeing supervisory personnel bend or break rules promotes disruptive and deviant behavior by others in the workforce.

3. *Practice the "Hot Stove" Rule.* According to this basic concept, discipline (like touching a hot stove) should be immediate, based on known rules, consistent, and impersonal. While the abstract principle of the "hot stove" is easy to remember, it is much more difficult to translate into practice in complex criminal justice organizations. Under less than ideal conditions, effective discipline is largely a matter of chance.

4. *Never Lose Control.* First-line supervisors must remain calm and in control as they deal with various types of disciplinary problems. They are expected not to show emotion, fly off the handle, or touch their subordinates. Unless the sergeant's authority is challenged publicly, employees should be disciplined in private and with dignity (Whittenberg, 1995). An open display of anger or power is normally counterproductive. It leads to resentment, game-playing, and lower morale. The supervisor's failure to exercise self-control and behave in a consistent and mature manner will result in a loss of respect (for the person and the rank) and a further erosion of authority.

5. *Be Instructive.* Good first-line supervisors are also teachers and counselors (Mahoney, 1986). Whenever disciplinary action becomes necessary, the errant, disruptive, or deviant employee should be told why the discipline is being imposed and how it can be avoided in the future. As supervisory managers, sergeants function as culture carriers. They clarify and explain policies, procedures, rules, and regulations to their subordinates. When it comes to disciplinary action, the sergeant is obligated to advise subordinates of the "due process" options available to them should they choose to challenge the propriety of the disciplinary process or the punishment. Sergeants should never hide anything from the employee. Deception will come back to haunt the supervisor. Sergeants should be open and honest with their subordinates and impose discipline in an intelligent, reasonable, and mature manner.

6. *Be Firm but Fair.* The first-line supervisor must always be firm but fair in administering disciplinary action. If the police sergeant wants subordinates to believe that discipline is both firm and fair, the sergeant must be open, honest, reasonable, and direct. Attitude is the key. Effective supervisors never joke about discipline; they take their responsibility as disciplinarians very seriously. They know that discipline administered in a firm, fair, consistent, and impartial manner helps correct performance problems; deters errant, disruptive, or deviant behavior by others; and generates respect for both the supervisor and the authority inherent in the rank. However, ambiguity and inconsistency will destroy the sergeant's credibility and overall effectiveness as a disciplinarian.

7. *Stay Out of the Employee's Private Life.* All other things being equal, a subordinate's private life is just that—private. Unless the employee's personal beliefs or off-the-job behavior has a direct bearing on job performance, it should not be factored into the disciplinary process (Marmo, 1986). As first-line supervisors who are charged with delegating authority, sergeants are responsible for the work being done under their personal direction. It is imperative to avoid making assessments based on irrelevant data. Personal value judgments often lead to interpersonal conflict and covert as well as overt discrimination. The scope of provisions dealing with "conduct unbecoming an officer" has been narrowed considerably by the courts in a series of recent decisions. This is hazardous uncharted territory.

8. *State Rules/Regulations in a Positive Manner.* Effective sergeants avoid negativism and treat department policies, procedures, rules, and regulations as positive control mechanisms designed to promote order and facilitate work related to the organization's mission, goals, and objectives.

9. *Don't Be a Disciplinary Magician.* A good supervisor avoids becoming the type of person who makes rules as he or she goes along in an effort to trap subordinates. The key to success as a disciplinarian is to ensure that all employees know and fully understand the department's policies, procedures, rules, and regulations. The best advice is to be upfront with all employees; don't spring new rules or variations of the old rules on them after the fact. Effective supervisors give every employee ample opportunity to comply with performance standards and behavioral expectations.

10. *Be Precise.* As first-line supervisors and departmental disciplinarians, sergeants must (based on the civil liability inherent in their position) comply with labor laws, collective bargaining agreements, and civil service regulations. Because their actions are subject to both administrative and judicial review, sergeants must be precise in assessing job performance and taking formal disciplinary action. They must not deviate from prescribed procedures and should document all of their actions very carefully. Lack of precision lessens the sergeant's credibility, weakens the case, and increases the likelihood that there will be subsequent litigation of the issue(s) under civil law.

While there is really no way to avoid the use of negative discipline in complex criminal justice organizations, it can be made more effective and much less stressful if supervisory personnel use these keys to unlock the productive potential of their immediate subordinates.

Once again, the sergeant is in the catbird seat and, in the long run, will determine the effectiveness of the discipline and the overall credibility of the disciplinary system.

First-line supervisors must realize that any disciplinary action they take with a subordinate will result in a negative response from the subordinate. Whittenberg (1995) indicates that employees facing disciplinary action go through five stages: denial, anger, bargaining, depression, and acceptance. In order to provide dignity to the subordinate being disciplined, the supervisor must allow him or her to progress through these stages. The supervisor should give the employee the opportunity to vent feelings, display anger, and show some disrespectful emotion without taking the reaction personally. If the supervisor has followed the keys to effective discipline, the subordinate will go through the five stages rapidly and accept the disciplinary action without an adverse effect on the employee/supervisor relationship. In fact, it should strengthen the relationship.

The Hot Stove Revisited

Taking appropriate disciplinary action creates a dilemma for first-line supervisors. Police sergeants walk a tightrope between two seemingly incongruent roles. As noted earlier, they are expected to be "teachers," "helpers," and "leaders" who nurture their subordinates; however, they are the "disciplinarians" who punish them for their errant, disruptive, or deviant behavior. The trick is to balance these roles in such a way as to avoid creating interpersonal conflict or generating deep-seated resentment.

Douglas McGregor, a noted management theorist, provides us with a very useful analogy concerning disciplinary tasks and earned punishment. He called his idea the "hot stove" concept, comparing an organization's disciplinary system to a hot stove and the burn victim to an employee who has earned punishment (Plunkett, 1992). When you touch a hot stove, the discipline is immediate, predictable, consistent, and totally impersonal.

McGregor's hot stove analogy is used to illustrate the essential elements of a functional disciplinary policy. It points out that when you burn your hand as a result of your own stupidity, you become angry with yourself. While you might be mad at the stove, the anger cannot last long because you should have known the consequences of your act. According to the hot stove rule, you learn your lesson quickly and effectively because:

1. The burn is *immediate*, with no question as to cause and effect. The sooner the disciplinary action is taken, the more automatic it will be and the more closely it will be associated with the errant, disruptive, or deviant behavior. While speed is an essential ingredient in effective discipline, undue haste should be avoided because it could lead to carelessness and the imposition of unwarranted punishments.
2. You had *advance warning* and knew (because the stove was red hot) exactly what would happen if you touched it. Unexpected discipline is almost always considered unfair and usually creates a great deal of resentment. Consequently, employees must be given a clear warning that a particular offense or type of behavior will result in disciplinary action, coupled with a definite warning as to the nature and extent of the discipline to be invoked.

3. The discipline is *consistent* because everyone who touches the hot stove is burned. Consistency means that each and every time there is an infraction, appropriate disciplinary action is taken. This helps set internal as well as external limits in terms of what subordinates may or may not do. Consistency also means that the punishment inflicted should be no more or no less than expected for a particular offense. However, inconsistent disciplinary action leads to uncertainty and confusion. It destroys the integrity of the disciplinary process and erodes the sergeant's legitimate authority. Inconsistency produces anxiety, insecurity, interpersonal conflict, resentment, and poor morale.

4. The discipline is *impersonal* in that victims are burned for touching the red-hot stove regardless of their identity. They are on the receiving end of discipline not because they are "bad," but because of their errant, disruptive, or deviant behavior. This helps remove the personal "you are always out to get me" element of disciplinary action because the discipline is directed against an act or unacceptable behavior, not the individual. When discipline is automatic and impersonal, it reduces resentment and clears the way for subordinates to assume responsibility for their own performance or job-related conduct.

In addition to their other supervisory responsibilities, sergeants add the human element to McGregor's hot stove concept. They tend the stove to make sure that it operates efficiently and effectively. Under ideal circumstances, the hot stove not only serves as a deterrent against whom it is applied, but also serves as a form of conditioning or training that will orient other police employees to the types of performance or on-the-job behavior the organization cannot and will not accept. Telling employees what is expected of them and explaining the negative consequences they may face are absolute prerequisites for effective discipline in law enforcement (see Figure 10.4).

Inflicting punishment is a painful experience for both the employee and the first-line supervisor. In order to reduce the unpleasantness and stress associated with the use of discipline, sergeants should incorporate the hot stove concept into their management repertoire. The hot stove replaces subjectivity with a philosophy of firm, fair, and impartial discipline designed to correct and deter the errant, disruptive, or deviant behavior of subordinates (Plunkett, 1992).

1. Delineation of what is unacceptable
2. Reasonable negative sanctions
3. Advance warning of consequences
4. Certainty of punishment
5. Immediate disciplinary action
6. Consistent application of negative sanctions
7. Impersonal and goal-oriented discipline
8. Adequate due process
9. Appellate review of all disciplinary action

FIGURE 10.4 Discipline and the hot stove analogy in law enforcement.

Various states, such as Illinois (Local Government Uniform Peace Officer's Disciplinary Act; 50 I.L.C.S. 725), have adopted peace officer bill of rights laws that superimpose additional constraints on the disciplinary process. These laws often mandate the warnings to be given and procedures to be followed when certain types of disciplinary actions are anticipated. Supervisors need to know and comply with what is required if they are to prevail when it comes to the imposition of discipline (Redlich, 1994).

Another right afforded police officers involved in disciplinary proceedings is known as Garrity protection, under the doctrines set forth in *Garrity v. New Jersey* (385 U.S. 493, 1967). Garrity protection applies whenever an employee is required to answer questions in an internal investigation. Under Garrity, the employer cannot use information provided by the employee in a criminal procedure against the employee. For Garrity to apply, the employee must believe that the statements he or she provides are compelled under threat of substantial disciplinary action or dismissal from his or her job (McGuinness, 1999).

Firm but Fair Disciplinary Action

Sergeants are the keystone around which the police discipline system is built and, as such, exert a tremendous influence on the disciplinary process. Consequently, they are expected to be "firm but fair" when inflicting negative sanctions on their subordinates. "Fairness" means being able to say that the punishment was warranted, justified, and appropriate in terms of its goal. In order to be fair, the first-line supervisor must be sure that all employees in the workforce are familiar with and understand the reasoning behind the department's policies, procedures, rules, and regulations. If a subordinate's performance or job-related conduct is errant, disruptive, or deviant, that person must be investigated. The sergeant should conduct an objective inquiry into the situation and must never, under any circumstances, exceed his or her legitimate authority when punishing subordinates.

According to Steinmetz & Todd (1986), one way to ensure basic fairness is to ask certain questions concerning the need for discipline or negative sanctions in a particular situation. These questions might include the following:

1. Is the disciplinary action based on violation of a known policy, procedure, rule, or regulation? The bottom line is determining whether there has been a "statutory violation." In other words, is the policy, procedure, rule, or regulation clearly spelled out in an employee handbook? Has it been posted as a general order or is it otherwise known to all employees within the police department? Have employees received a copy? Is the material easily understood? Is the policy, procedure, rule, or regulation reasonable in terms of promoting efficiency and effectiveness within a safe and orderly environment? Is it legal in that it complies with labor laws, collective bargaining agreements, and civil service regulations? Are you sure, as the responsible first-line supervisor, that there are no extenuating circumstances that may have contributed to a misunderstanding or belief that a policy, procedure, rule, or regulation does not apply to the situation? If all of these questions can be answered in the affirmative, the sergeant is justified in taking action against the subordinate.

2. What has happened to others who have knowingly violated this policy, procedure, rule, or regulation? This question is designed to help sergeants explore and understand the nature, significance, and appropriate disciplinary response to errant, disruptive, or deviant behavior in the workplace. Assuming the employee knowingly violated a departmental policy, procedure, rule, or regulation, the next logical step is to determine the seriousness of the problem and chart a course of action to correct or deter it in the future. The sergeant must determine whether other employees have been disciplined under similar circumstances and ascertain the kind of disciplinary action that was taken. In order to make the punishment fit the offender, as well as the crime, the sergeant should study the subordinate's background relative to the particular offense or unacceptable conduct. The worse the record in relation to others, the more severe the disciplinary action should be. Progressively severe discipline is often required because habitual offenders tend to develop a chronic attitudinal problem in which they do not care whether departmental policies, procedures, rules, and regulations are followed.

3. What is the subordinate's record concerning this specific policy, procedure, rule, or regulation? The sergeant must determine exactly how the employee has violated the specific policy, procedure, rule, or regulation and whether there had been a prior warning about this type of behavior. If the subordinate had been formally warned or disciplined on previous occasions, the disciplinary action should be more severe than for those who have neither been warned nor disciplined. In theory, this employee should know the policies, procedures, rules, and regulations and should understand the consequences of errant, disruptive, or deviant on-the-job behavior.

4. Has the employee ever received a written "final warning" from the supervisor? If an errant, disruptive, or deviant employee had been given a written final warning previously, the case must be treated more severely. It is the sergeant's job to ascertain whether the employee understood both the seriousness and the consequences associated with the final warning before disciplinary action is taken. As a general rule, if the employee was given a final warning and still continues to violate the policy, procedure, rule, or regulation, termination should be seriously considered as the appropriate response. The health of the organization will suffer unless this type of action is taken.

5. What caused the poor performance or unacceptable conduct? Here again, it is the sergeant who must determine whether the errant, disruptive, or deviant behavior was intentional. Was it triggered by ignorance or by maliciousness? Was it deliberate or was it caused by an oversight by the employee? In a rational disciplinary system, punishment is always contingent on and measured in relation to the offender's motive. Consequently, it is the sergeant's primary responsibility to assess the seriousness of the problem and to determine (as accurately as possible) why the subordinate is behaving in an errant, disruptive, or deviant manner. This information must then be factored into the disciplinary process.

6. What evidence is there that the employee intentionally or maliciously violated a departmental policy, procedure, rule, or regulation? As noted before, the accused employee is presumed to be innocent until proven guilty. It is the sergeant's job to identify disciplinary problems, analyze all of the relevant factors, initiate or carry out

appropriate disciplinary action, ensure due process, and document the case for subsequent administrative or judicial review. The sergeant, like the prosecutor in a criminal case, builds a case designed to demonstrate the extent, seriousness, and deliberateness of the errant, disruptive, or deviant behavior. In addition to this prosecutorial role, the sergeant is expected to discover any extenuating or mitigating circumstances that might justify lessening the punishment.

7. Are the intended disciplinary measures appropriate for use in this particular situation? The question comes down to whether the discipline to be inflicted is commensurate with the seriousness of the errant, disruptive, or deviant behavior. Is it consistent with the employee's prior record? Sergeants should base their actions (and measure the appropriateness of the discipline) on how other subordinates have been treated in similar situations and how prior service to the department has been factored (positively or negatively) into the punishment. If the officer has an extensive prior record, has been on the job a long time, and has involved others in serious discipline problems, the punishment must be severe. If, however, the officer is relatively new, has had few problems, acted as an individual, and has exhibited a cooperative attitude, the punishment should be less severe. Progressively severe punishment is calculated to correct or deter disciplinary problems. Here again, the strategy is to use the right type and amount of punishment in a given situation to achieve the goals of the disciplinary system.

Firm but fair discipline is the ideal that each first-line supervisor should strive to achieve. Actually achieving this ideal in a complex criminal justice organization is another matter. Whether the discipline is firm and fair will depend, in the long run, on four critical factors: (1) the quality of the personnel being recruited by the department, (2) the effectiveness of the promotion system, (3) the training given to newly promoted sergeants, and (4) the support that first-line supervisors receive from their superiors.

Types of Disciplinary Actions

The decision to discipline a subordinate is not an easy one and should be made with a great deal of care. Sergeants are expected to know each employee; the employee's work record; and the nature, relative seriousness, and cause(s) of the particular offense. First-line supervisors must be aware of and understand the powers listed in their job description. In order to be effective, they must be familiar with the department's personnel policies (including applicable collective bargaining agreements or civil service regulations), as well as the basic policies, procedures, rules, and regulations that govern on-the-job behavior.

Once the decision to discipline has been made, the sergeant (in consultation with superiors) must select the appropriate type of punishment. As a general rule, the different types of punishment available to the first-line supervisor are spelled out in departmental manuals, civil service regulations, or labor contracts. This specificity is designed to eliminate ambiguity, ensure fair treatment, and protect police employees from impulsive, arbitrary, and unusually harsh punishments.

Most police departments have created discipline systems based on the idea of progressive discipline, which provides for an increase in punishment for each subsequent offense. Certain steps have become institutionalized as part of the disciplinary process. These steps have been incorporated into the process to ensure fundamental fairness and to demonstrate to trial boards, arbitrators, and the courts that the supervisor made a good faith effort to correct the errant, disruptive, or deviant behavior through some type of remediation or rehabilitation. The normal sequence of punishment with progressively severe discipline action is as follows: informal discussion, oral warning, written reprimand, final written warning, transfer, suspension, demotion, and discharge.

1. **Informal Discussion.** If the offense is relatively minor and the employee has not been disciplined for similar misconduct in the past, an informal, friendly discussion will often clear up the problem. During the discussion, the sergeant should determine the cause of the errant, disruptive, or deviant behavior; reaffirm the employee's responsibility for self-discipline; and make constructive suggestions for improvement. Should this approach fail to produce the desired result, the sergeant must be prepared to give the subordinate a more formal oral warning.

2. **Oral Warning.** The oral warning is probably the most common form of punishment inflicted on employees. When subordinates fail to meet prescribed performance standards and continue to violate policies, procedures, rules, or regulations, they must be put on "notice" that their behavior is unacceptable and that repetition will result in formal disciplinary action. They need to know, in no uncertain terms, that their misconduct will not be condoned and that future violations will produce more severe punishments. The effectiveness of an oral warning will generally depend on past experience, the strength of the supervisor–subordinate relationship, and the employee's desire to conform to shared group expectations. The spirit in which the warning is given is often more important than the oral warning itself. If the oral warning fails to correct the problem or deter an employee's errant, disruptive, or deviant behavior, the sergeant must be prepared to use a formal written reprimand.

3. **Written Reprimand.** As the term implies, the written reprimand is a formal warning issued to an errant, disruptive, or deviant employee by the immediate supervisor. For all practical purposes, it is the first official step in progressive discipline. No matter whether it is general or specific, the written reprimand is designed to spell out the problem, recommend corrective measures, and specify the probable consequences of further misconduct. Written reprimands must not exaggerate the problem or make idle threats. They should be used sparingly in an effort to accentuate their importance. As a general rule, written warnings should be fairly simple and to the point. The original letter should be given to the employee with a copy placed in the personnel file. When appropriate, a copy of the reprimand should be sent to civil service or the union. The written reprimand becomes part of the case file and can be used as evidence in a subsequent arbitration or civil action. If the written reprimand fails to correct the problem or deter further misconduct, the sergeant should issue a final written warning to the employee.

4. **Final Written Warning.** Because we live and work in a litigious environment in which employees frequently challenge management's authority, the sergeant must be able to prove (based on objective evidence) that progressively more severe disciplinary action was required to correct the problem or to deter further misconduct. Keeping written records is extremely important in complex criminal justice organizations. Written records help demonstrate that the employee was apprised of the seriousness of the situation and that notification had been given indicating that there would be a significant escalation in punishment for continued errant, disruptive, or deviant behavior. The final written warning becomes the bottom line, so to speak, and shifts all responsibility for compliance to the employee. If this strategy fails to resolve the problem, the sergeant has no alternative but to consider transferring or suspending the subordinate.

5. **Transfer.** Transferring an officer from one unit or assignment within the department to another as a form of punishment has long been used. However, transfers in and of themselves are merely punitive and generally do not correct the officer's behavior. In fact, the transferred officer may become disillusioned and become an even worse disciplinary problem. There are times when transfers for disciplinary action may be appropriate. For instance, officers who need more structured supervision may be transferred from a low supervision position to a more structured, highly supervised position. The transfer cannot be viewed solely as punitive, but must be constructive and for the good of the officer as well as the organization. Many police agencies do not use transfers as part of their progressive discipline policy.

6. **Suspension.** Suspension, or "disciplinary layoff" as it is called in the private sector, is the next step in progressively severe disciplinary action and is not uncommon in police work. The police officer who has not profited from informal discussions or a formal warning is suspended. Suspension may be with or without pay for a period ranging from a few days to one week or more. Under normal circumstances, the employee loses wages and fringe benefits based on those wages. Suspension is viewed as being severe in that it "hits the employee where it hurts most, in the pocketbook." In addition, suspensions usually become common knowledge and the focus of peer interest. While an ill-conceived suspension can aggravate the situation and may even make the employee's behavior worse, if used properly it can be one of the most effective disciplinary tools available to the supervisor. It might shock the errant, disruptive, or deviant officer back to a sense of responsibility. It shows that the department means business. If, however, there is no substantive change in the employee's work-related behavior, further disciplinary action must be taken. The suspension is merely a prelude to further disciplinary action in the form of a demotion or discharge.

7. **Demotion.** Due to the paramilitary structure of most police departments, demotion from a higher to a lower rank within the same department has persisted as an alternative form of disciplinary action. It is common in highly political situations. Many police administrators, however, are beginning to question the validity of demotion as a disciplinary measure. They contend that the negatives far outweigh the positives, and they prefer resocialization or retraining to demotion. Maintaining good morale is the issue. Demoted officers suffer loss of income, social status, and self-esteem. They tend to become resentful, discouraged, and

dissatisfied. Disgruntled personnel normally continue to challenge legitimate authority and sow the seeds of discontent. When all else fails, the errant, disruptive, or deviant employee must be terminated or discharged for the good of the police service.

8. **Discharge.** Discharging an employee is, without doubt, the most drastic form of disciplinary action and, as such, must be reserved for only the most serious offenses. In today's legalistic environment, the employee must be given every opportunity to change his or her behavior and conform to departmental policies, procedures, rules, and regulations. While it is possible under unusual circumstances, very few police officers are discharged without warning. Discharge is a costly, albeit necessary, type of discipline in some cases. The employee loses his or her income, seniority, and, in some cases, even employability. The department, however, loses an experienced and potentially valuable human resource. It also forfeits all that has been invested in that particular employee's professional development. In addition, costs are associated with recruiting, screening, training, and orienting a replacement. Because discharge is viewed by many as a form of industrial capital punishment, it often leads to lengthy, costly arbitrations or civil court cases. This does not mean that supervisors should not recommend that management discharge an employee in appropriate situations. There are times when the department must take a stand and notify all personnel that there are certain behaviors that simply cannot or will not be tolerated. Used sparingly and in a judicious manner, discharge is the ultimate disciplinary tool.

No matter what type of disciplinary action sergeants opt to use, they must be careful to observe all labor laws, collective bargaining agreements, and civil service regulations. In addition, the sergeant must pay close attention to procedural due process. Failure in either area will destroy the first-line supervisor's credibility and substantially undermine authority. Of primary importance is the first-line supervisor carefully documenting any and all discussions with the subordinate regarding behavior and discipline issues.

Modern management theory has rejected the imposition of negative sanctions for the sake of inflicting punishment. It views disciplinary action as being an essential ingredient in a goal-oriented intervention strategy designed to correct problems and deter future misconduct. Progressive discipline (see Figure 10.5) is based on the notion that the punishment should fit

1. Informal discussion
2. Oral warning
3. Written reprimand
4. Final written warning
5. Transfer
6. Suspension
7. Demotion
8. Discharge

FIGURE 10.5 Steps of progressive discipline.

the crime and that progressively more severe punishment will trigger a "hedonistic calcula-tion." The repetitively recalcitrant offender assesses the pleasure derived from the errant, dis-ruptive, or deviant behavior vis-à-vis the pain caused by the escalating punishments. All other things being equal, when the perceived pain outweighs the pleasure, there will be a substan-tive change in the employee's behavior. Progressive discipline is not a cure-all; it is a tool.

Progressive discipline may not work with indifferent, irrational, or socially maladjusted subordinates. When it becomes necessary to discharge an employee, progressive discipline is used. While the decision to fire an employee is the prerogative of management, it is almost always based on direct input from the first-line supervisor. Again, this awesome responsibility is part of the job and rests squarely on the sergeant's shoulders.

Progressive discipline may not be appropriate with serious infractions. Even if an officer has a spotless record, it may be necessary to provide a more severe sanction for misconduct. According to a CNN (2013) report, more than one-third of the entire police force on duty in Cleveland, Ohio, in 2012 was involved in a high-speed chase that resulted in the shooting deaths of two people. According to the CNN report, the two deceased individuals were shot by police in "a hail of 137 bullets." The incident began when officers pursued a vehicle in which a driver and his passenger refused to stop. Although officers reported seeing a gun in the car, no firearm was found. Disciplinary actions ranged from reprimand to termination for 74 officers.

Making the Disciplinary Action Stick

In what some managers consider to be the "good old days," employers hired their employees at will and could discipline or fire them for any reason or for no reason at all. Employees had no right to their jobs. Consequently, they had no legal standing to sue their superiors for arbi-trary or capricious disciplinary action. Needless to say, things have changed dramatically. Labor laws, collective bargaining agreements, and civil service regulations are now in place to protect workers in the public sector. In addition, the courts have begun to recognize that employees have (at least to some extent) a property right in their jobs (Schofield, 1997; Swanson, Territo, & Taylor, 2012). A property right or interest is an aggregate of rights that are guaranteed and protected by government. When an employee is hired by a public agency and the rules require discipline or termination only "for cause," the employee is said to have a property interest—an expectation of continued employment. Property interest for police officers generally takes effect after the initial probationary period. This swing in legal philosophy has ushered in a new era of judicial activism. Gone forever are the days when sergeants could talk tough, act on impulse, and inflict punishments on subordinates without careful administrative or judicial review.

Even with these constraints, however, it is still possible to use disciplinary action as a tool to promote efficiency, effectiveness, and productivity within the workplace. Police officers, in particular, are held to a higher standard of conduct than private employees (*Merrifield v. Illinois State Police Merit Board*, 691 N.E.2d 199, 1997). It is the sergeant (as the responsible first-line supervisor) who plays the pivotal role and, in large measure, determines whether the police department will face unfair labor practice charges, costly arbitrations, lengthy liti-gation, and more union activism. According to many labor relations specialists, reasonable disciplinary action can be made to stick if it is fair and if first-line supervisors learn to avoid the following mistakes:

1. **No Clear-Cut Misconduct or Violation.** Under normal circumstances, disciplinary action is considered to be a legitimate option only when it can be tied to a specific offense.
2. **Inadequate Warning.** Trial boards, civil service hearing officers, arbitrators, and the courts have held that police personnel are entitled to both direct and sufficient warning that their poor performance or misconduct will not be tolerated.
3. **Absence of Positive Evidence.** The absence of positive evidence to support the charge against the employee jeopardizes the case, subjects the sergeant's motives to question, and destroys confidence in the department's disciplinary system.
4. **Acting on Prejudice.** Real or imagined favoritism or discrimination has a debilitating effect on discipline, undermines legitimate authority, and creates poor morale.
5. **Inadequate Records.** The value of written records of warnings and reprimands cannot be overestimated because they are documentary evidence of the action taken to correct personnel problems and to deter further misconduct. It is recommended that the first-line supervisor keep a log or notebook documenting any and all discussions with subordinates regarding behavior and discipline. Such documentation should include not only the nature of the discussion, but the time, date, place, and any results observed from the discussions.
6. **Excessive Punishment.** Most civil service hearing officers, arbitrators, and judges subscribe to the concept of progressive discipline and look unfavorably on punishment that is too severe, especially for first-time offenders.
7. **Violation of Procedural Due Process.** A lack of concern for just cause and procedural due process taints the disciplinary action and pits the employee against the employer in a struggle for power (Bittel & Newstrom, 1990).

In order to make any disciplinary policy or procedure work effectively and remain within the legal guidelines, management and supervision must ensure that employees know (1) the expected standards of behavior and (2) what sanctions will be imposed if the standard is violated.

It is the responsibility of police managers and supervisors to communicate to each officer under their command or supervision these expected standards of behavior. Such communication may be in the form of training, through observation of desired behaviors (role models), and seeing disciplinary action applied to others. Above all, supervisors should carefully document all forms of communication regarding acceptable and unacceptable behavior with subordinates in the event an inquiry needs to be made later. Poorly prepared, carelessly investigated, and inadequately documented cases reflect negatively not only on the first-line supervisor who conducted the inquiry, but also on the police department that based disciplinary action on it. Consequently, the errant, disruptive, or deviant employee who should have been disciplined severely or even discharged for the good of the service often wins the case on appeal. More often than not, that employee returns to the job an embittered, marginal performer who attempts to contaminate others at every opportunity. Not only does the employee's morale suffer, but the morale of all those who work with that employee suffers as well. From a very practical point of view, greater harm may result when the undeserving subordinate is returned to duty because the disciplinary action was not sustained than if that particular employee had never been disciplined at all. It is the sergeant's responsibility to take appropriate disciplinary action and to make sure that it sticks.

Constructive Discharge

Many police officers facing severe disciplinary action may elect to resign from their position voluntarily rather than risk formal discharge. Typically, this is seen as a benefit to the employee, who would rather resign than face formal charges and termination. It is also a benefit for the organization in that formal charges do not have to be made and the matter can be closed. However, constructive discharge is a claim or legal finding that an employee who purportedly voluntarily resigned from a position should be treated as though the employee was actually discharged or fired by the employer. In other words, if the employee feels compelled to resign under threat of management pursuing termination, the resignation is actually a constructive discharge. Constructive discharge is much more beneficial to the employer than to the employee because time and money are saved by forcing the employee to resign. An employee who resigns voluntarily has little legal recourse against his or her employer. However, there are two situations in which an employee who resigned may obtain legal remedy against the employer. These issues are:

1. Was the employer attempting to avoid the legal protections due the employee?
2. Did the employer make the working situation intolerable for the employee?

In order for the employee to prevail in a legal case against the employer, the court must find that a reasonable person faced with similar unfair conditions would leave rather than continue to suffer such condition or treatment.

Results of Absent Discipline

The lack of self-control and the absence of meaningful disciplinary action in police organizations are antithetical to the common good. When they are compounded by benign neglect or deliberate indifference on the part of police supervisors and managers, they lower the quality of service provided by a given department and undermine the integrity of the entire profession.

We have argued that disciplinary action must be prompt, certain, reasonable, and fair if it is to deter misbehavior and help purge undesirables from police work. The absence of effective (positive as well as negative) discipline is the harbinger of systematic failure.

In a series of well-researched and very disturbing articles, *The Washington Post* (Flaherty & Harriston, 1994) chronicled such a failure in a large police department located in the mid-Atlantic region of the United States. The department hired nearly 1500 new police officers in a two-year period (1989–1990). For unfathomable reasons, the department was not effective in screening, selecting, appointing, training, and evaluating many of these new officers.

On-the-job supervision was lax and, in many cases, nonexistent. According to *The Washington Post*, inaction on the part of police supervisors and managers tacitly allowed incompetence, misconduct, and corruption to flourish.

While it is impossible to quantify incompetence or to assess the impact of minor misconduct as well as unreported misconduct, there is one chilling statistic in *The Washington Post* series that should give every professional police officer cause for concern. Since 1991, 256 of the police officers who were suspended or fired have had the adverse disciplinary actions overturned by the courts or labor arbitrators solely because the department took too long to initiate formal disciplinary action. The lack of prompt disciplinary action has permitted incompetents, malcontents, and criminals to remain on the public payroll in critically important positions.

The Washington Post series underscores the importance of self-control and formal discipline. Poor supervision and the lack of effective disciplinary mechanisms allow "loose cannons" who are in positions of power to abuse that power.

Personal and Vicarious Liability

Failure to sustain a disciplinary action against an employee puts the supervisor at risk for a subsequent civil suit. The suit may involve abuse of authority, discrimination, or defamation of character. Employers and supervisors also incur civil liability if they deprive a subordinate of a guaranteed due process right. As a general rule, police officers can go to either state or federal courts to seek monetary damages or injunctive relief against an employer or supervisor at any stage of the disciplinary process if it is determined that they may have been denied procedural due process.

Public employees have always been liable for their own negligent or wrongful acts. They are liable, in most situations, for compensatory as well as punitive damages. Until quite recently, however, public entities (units of state, county, and local government) were considered immune from civil liability resulting from the negligent or wrongful acts of their employees. Once again, things have changed rather drastically. While the individual employee is still liable, the courts, based on case law and recently enacted statutes, have held that public agencies are often liable for compensatory damages when the wrongful acts or omissions occur while employees are acting within the scope of their employment. Based on the fact that government is perceived as having "deep pockets" and a virtually inexhaustible source of revenue, vicarious liability suits have become commonplace. If the litigant can show by a preponderance of evidence that the police department failed to train, supervise, or discipline errant, disruptive, or deviant employees properly, the department may be held liable. It will pay for the misconduct of its personnel when that misconduct (violation of policies, procedures, rules, or regulations) causes injury to others. Recent monetary judgments have been enormous. Some local governments have been forced into bankruptcy. It is in the police department's best interest, then, to promote only competent employees to the rank of sergeant and to strengthen the internal disciplinary system (Iannone & Iannone, 2013).

References

Aragon, R. (1993). Positive organizational culture: A practical approach. *FBI Law Enforcement Bulletin, 62*(12).

Bittel, L. R., & Newstrom, J. W. (1990). *What every supervisor should know* (6th ed.). New York: McGraw-Hill Book Company.

Blanchard, K. (1989). A PRICE that makes sense. *Today's Office* (September).

CALEA, (2006). *Standards for law enforcement agencies.* Fairfax, VA: Commission on Accreditation for Law Enforcement Agencies, Inc.

Carnegie, D. (1992). *The Dale Carnegie course (syllabus).* New York: Dale Carnegie and Associates.

CNN. (2013). <www.cnn.com/2013/08/02/justice/Cleveland-police-shooting>.

Covey, S. R. (1992). *Principle-centered leadership.* New York: Simon & Schuster.

Flaherty, M. P., & Harriston, K. (1994). Law and disorder: The district's troubled police. *The Washington Post* Aug. 28–31, Section A.

Fyfe, J. J., Greene, J. R., Walsh, W. F., Wilson, O. W., & McLaren, R. (1997). *Police administration* (5th ed.). New York: McGraw-Hill Book Company.

Guthrie, M. (1996). Using automation to apply discipline fairly. *FBI Law Enforcement Bulletin, 65*(5).

Iannone, N. F., & Iannone, M. (2013). *Supervision of police personnel* (8th ed.). Englewood Cliffs, NJ: Prentice Hall, Inc.

LeBoeuf, M. (1985). *GMP: The greatest management principle in the world.* New York: Barkley Books.

Leonard, E. C. (2013). *Supervision: Concepts and practices of management* (8th ed.). Stamford, CT: Cengage Learning.

Mahoney, T. (1986). Problem employee or problem supervision? *Journal of California Law Enforcement, 20*(1).

Marmo, M. (1986). Off-duty behavior by police: Arbitration determines if on-the-job discipline is appropriate. *Journal of Police Science and Administration, 14*(2).

McGuinness, J. M. (1999). Point of law. *Police, 23*(9).

Peters, T. J., & Waterman, R. H., Jr. (2004). *In search of excellence: Lessons from America's best-run companies.* New York: Warner Books, Inc.

Plunkett, R. W. (1992). *Supervision: The direction of people at work* (6th ed.). Boston, MA: Allyn & Bacon, Inc.

Preston, P., & Zimmerer, T. W. (1983). *Management for supervisors* (2nd ed.). Englewood Cliffs, NJ: Prentice Hall, Inc.

Redlich, J. W. (1994). Disciplinary interrogations: Which warnings apply? and when? *The Police Chief, LXI*(6).

Robbins, S. P., & Judge, T. (2012). *Organizational behavior* (15th ed.). Englewood Cliffs, NJ: Prentice Hall, Inc.

Sartain, A. Q., & Baker, A. W. (1979). *The supervisor and his job, International 2nd Revised ed.* New York: McGraw-Hill Book Company.

Schofield, D. (1997). Constitutional issues in employee discipline. *Police Law Journal, 5,* 119–127. (May).

Sherman, M., & Lucia, A. (1992). Positive discipline and labor arbitration. *Arbitration Journal, 47*(2).

Steinmetz, L. L., & Todd, H. R., Jr. (1986). *First-line management: Approaching supervision effectively* (4th ed.). Plano, TX: Business Publications, Inc.

Swanson, C. R., Territo, L., & Taylor, R. W. (2012). *Police administration* (8th ed.). Englewood Cliffs, NJ: Prentice Hall, Inc.

Whisenand, P. M., & Rush, G. E. (2011). *Supervising police personnel* (7th ed.). Englewood Cliffs, NJ: Prentice Hall, Inc.

Whittenberg, P. (1995). Discipline with dignity: A positive approach for managers. *Federal Probation, 59*(3).

11 ⣿

Internal Discipline
A System of Accountability

CASE STUDY

Sergeant Hank Patterson

DEPARTMENT

The Waynesville Police Department is a small, 31-officer department located in a rural area of the southeast. The department has two criminal investigators and the rest are uniformed patrol officers. There is low turnover at the department due to the high pay officers receive and the benefits of the job. In fact, applications are always coming in from highly qualified persons seeking employment with Waynesville. Chief Pearson has been with the department for 32 years and there seems to be no retirement in the immediate future for him. The city council has always admired Chief Pearson and the officers of his department. The department is organized with the chief, one assistant chief, a captain in charge of both operations and staff functions, one lieutenant and one sergeant as criminal investigators, and three sergeants in charge of patrol shifts. Each patrol shift has seven patrol officers and usually a reserve officer or two.

CRIME

There is not much crime in Waynesville, but thefts and burglaries always seem to lead the crime statistics. In fact, the two criminal investigators spend the majority of their time working burglaries and larcenies. When a burglary or larceny call comes in, the department sends out a patrol officer to do a preliminary report and then calls in a detective if needed. Often, a report is only needed for insurance purposes and a detective is not actually called to the scene.

COMMUNITY

Waynesville enjoys a large tourist industry due to the number of outlet malls, a nearby Indian reservation with a gambling casino, and a federal park and forest area. Consequently, Waynesville has a substantial number of transients, and property values are quite high because it is a resort-type city. The tourist industry is the main reason for the high salaries and benefits that Waynesville city employees enjoy. Business and traffic are booming during the spring, summer, and early autumn months. Reserve officers with the police department receive pay during this period of high tourist traffic. Many residents live in Waynesville only during the "busy" months and have residences in other areas of the country. The cabin rental business is especially good, and there has been a steady increase in the number of cabin rental resorts developed in the Waynesville area. The city leaders were great visionaries. Ten years ago, they saw the potential for tourist development and annexed huge tracts of vacant land into the city. These tracts eventually became home to numerous outlet malls and rental resorts.

OFFICER

Sergeant Hank Patterson is a nine-year veteran of the Waynesville Police Department. During nights and weekend duty, Sergeant Patterson is in charge of the entire on-duty patrol force. During the day shift, he is fourth in command of all operations due to his senior status. Chief Pearson has recommended to the city council that Hank be promoted to the rank of lieutenant because he is over a lieutenant in CID most of the time. It would mean a $12,000 per year increase in salary. Sergeant Patterson is a highly ethical, moral individual who is proud to be a member of the department and proud of the job he is doing. Hank has lived here all of his life and knows almost all the "regular" residents by name.

PROBLEM

Two years ago, Waynesville hired a patrol officer by the name of Tim Payne. Officer Payne receives good evaluations and gets along well with other officers and the community. He is personable and well liked by nearly everyone. The criminal investigators say that Officer Payne does a great job on preliminary investigations at crime scenes. He has made the investigators' jobs easier by the detail and extra effort he puts in during preliminary investigations. Chief Pearson even suggested that Payne would be the next candidate for a criminal investigator position with the department.

Chief Pearson has just returned from a state chiefs association meeting and is fuming. The chief calls Sergeant Patterson in for a conference about Officer Payne. It seems Chief Pearson learned that Officer Payne was posting inappropriate material on Facebook and making comments regarding the department and the community on Twitter and other social media outlets. Chief Pearson learned of the postings from other chiefs attending the conference. "Hank, I don't do Facebook and I don't do the chirping thing. I expect you to find out what these young officers are up to and ride herd on them," Chief Pearson exclaims. "I don't do Facebook either, chief, and I believe it's called tweeting rather than chirping." "Well, whatever it is, it's wrong. He was posting obscene pictures with him and some girls drinking and partying, and now we're the laughing stock of the state. I want you to find out what he's up to and either stop it or fire him," Chief Pearson adds. "I don't think we have a policy on that, chief. Perhaps we should…" "We have a policy on conduct unbecoming an officer. And this is conduct unbecoming an officer," Chief Pearson retorts.

WHAT WOULD YOU DO?

If you were Sergeant Patterson, how would you deal with this situation? Does this type of incident fall under "freedom of speech?" If Officer Payne were posting inappropriate material on Facebook and Twitter, should he be fired or reprimanded? What role does the supervisor play in monitoring social media postings of officers? Is there legal authority to terminate an employee based on what they post on social media?

Police Work

Police work is an incredibly complex human enterprise. The assigned mission of the American police establishment is to serve and protect the community. While the "law enforcer" image has been made popular by the mass media, it is inaccurate and far too simplistic (Crank, 2004). According to one expert (Anderson, 1997), general assignment police personnel spend no more than 10 to 15 percent of their on-duty time actually enforcing criminal law. Most of their time is spent keeping the peace and providing essential nonpolice services. In carrying out their mission, police departments are expected to:

1. protect life and property
2. resolve interpersonal conflict and preserve the peace
3. maintain social order
4. prevent crime by proactive patrol and other measures
5. repress crime through effective law enforcement
6. create and perpetuate a sense of security
7. identify and apprehend those who have broken the law
8. regulate various types of noncriminal behavior
9. recognize and deal with police/public safety hazards
10. facilitate the movement of people and motor vehicles
11. provide essential emergency services
12. help individuals who cannot care for themselves
13. safeguard the legal and constitutional rights of citizens

The job is complex; it lacks clear-cut boundaries and is frequently underrated, unappreciated, and unpleasant. Even though policing is a rewarding career, it is often dull, monotonous, dirty, and dangerous.

Police officers work at the critical pressure point where law, human tragedy, and society's expectations (for safety and a sense of security) come together. The police represent the fine line that separates freedom from chaos, and legitimate social control from tyranny. American police officers are inundated with complexity and buffeted by change, ambiguity, stress, and radically different demands coming from various segments of the community. While they also come from the community, police officers are isolated from it in terms of their power, formal authority, occupational role, and distinct subcultural orientation. American police personnel exercise virtually unlimited discretion in low-visibility transactions with all sorts of people. They are constantly bombarded with reality as they grapple with uncontrolled passion, brutality, and the evil side of human nature. Men and women who wear the badge see crime, predatory violence, human degradation, insanity, corruption, and bizarre behavior on a daily basis. They are often confronted with grisly reminders of man's inhumanity and mortality. Mark Baker (1986) has observed that police officers are a composite of their unique experiences and a reflection of the people they police. Many police officers perceive themselves as society's "garbage men."

Because of their broad discretionary power, the inordinately complex nature of their work, and the type of clientele with whom they interact, police officers are particularly vulnerable to corruption and other forms of police deviance. Police deviance describes activities that are inconsistent with the officer's legal authority, organizational authority, or standards of ethical conduct. Corruption usually refers to the sale of legitimate authority for personal gain. Police occupational deviance includes not only corruption, but also the unlawful use of force, mistreatment of prisoners, discrimination, illegal search and seizure, perjury, planting of evidence, and other forms of misconduct that are committed under the color of police authority (Barker & Carter, 1994). For the purpose of analysis, occupational deviance can be broken down into three general categories:

1. **Nonfeasance.** Failure to take appropriate action as required by law or department policy.
2. **Misfeasance.** Performing a required and lawful task in an unacceptable, inappropriate, or unprofessional manner.
3. **Malfeasance.** Wrongdoing or illegal conduct that depends on or is related to the misuse of legitimate authority.

Police deviance is a persistent and inescapable reality that serves to spotlight incompetence and the seedy side of human nature.

Police personnel work in a complex, hazard-prone environment and, like all other human beings, are fallible. Some make errors, fail to perform assigned duties, abuse authority, misuse discretion, commit illegal acts, and engage in behavior "unbecoming an officer." Police administrators and first-line supervisors (i.e., sergeants) are responsible for policing the police.

No one can say with certainty just how much corruption, crime, and other forms of deviance exist in law enforcement because those who participate in it often have the power and know-how to cover it up. In addition, most police departments are simply not equipped to keep score. According to many of those who study this phenomenon, the nature of police crime, corruption, and occupational deviance makes it impossible to quantify. Consequently, when we try to estimate the extent of the problem, we are forced to deal with general impressions and isolated bits of information.

Due to the nature of their job, the clientele with whom they interact, and the wide variety of temptations they face every day, police officers represent an at-risk population in terms of illegal and other forms of inappropriate behavior. They find themselves with ample opportunity to commit crimes and to benefit from the largesse of those who seek to influence them. There are police officers who sell their professional souls for power, money, sex, and drugs. They mortgage the public interest for their own personal gain. Incompetent and corrupt police officers are a plague.

Police administrators are finally beginning to acknowledge that crime, corruption, and other forms of occupational deviance may be endemic to policing and accept the idea that many types of unlawful behavior exist in all police agencies (Kappeler, Sluder, & Alpert, 2000). Many now realize that corruption may be the oldest and most persistent problem in American policing (Katz, 2013). Policing the police is a paramount issue and a growing concern for all police managers.

Researchers have identified five basic problems in urban policing as institutional preconditions for police crime, corruption, and occupational deviance.

1. **Broad Discretion.** Discretion does not, in itself, make illegal police behavior inevitable, but it enables police officers to conceal their poor decisions and improper conduct. If used inappropriately, discretion fosters the belief that justice is a matter of personal judgment that should be auctioned to the highest bidder.

2. **Low Managerial Visibility.** Police officers, as a general rule, work on their own or with one partner. Due to the nature of police work, supervisors rarely observe line officers as they provide services, conduct investigations, make arrests, enforce criminal laws, or use discretion. Institutional controls on the use of police discretion are very weak (and almost always after the fact). Officers prefer to be left alone to do the job. Sergeants, however, often adopt the attitude that what they do not know will not hurt them.

3. **Low Public Visibility.** If police supervisors have little knowledge about the on-the-job behavior of their immediate subordinates, the public has even less knowledge. When they see the police in action, they rarely know what is going on. Low public visibility, like low managerial visibility, gives police officers the opportunity to conceal poor decisions, corruption, and criminal behavior.

4. **Peer Group Secrecy.** The person most likely to see a "blue coat" criminal or corrupt cop at work is another cop. In many, if not most, cases they do little or nothing about the illegal behavior. The socialization process in the police department may promote illegal behavior or encourage other officers to passively accept the crime and corruption of their colleagues. Loyalty, brotherhood, and an "us against them" attitude (a garrison mentality) help protect those who have become morally bankrupt.

5. **Managerial Secrecy.** Most police supervisors come from the ranks. They have been socialized by the system and have used it to enhance their status. They are reluctant to investigate and discipline police officers for criminal behavior unless they are forced to do so. Even today, proactive strategies against police crime and corruption (accessible complaint procedure, active investigation, imposition of effective sanctions, and an ongoing effort to stop wrongdoing before it starts) are not being used in all police departments. Police administrators often want to keep the problem within the department. Police supervisors are not immune from the effects of the "garrison mentality" (Crank, 2004; Johnston, 1982).

Low visibility, coupled with a vast amount of discretion, creates an environment in which police crime, corruption, and occupational deviance can germinate and flourish. Discretion, secrecy, and lack of supervision are three important factors that lead to police deviance.

The most effective means of fighting deviance and corruption within the police department is to build a strong supervisory structure in which sergeants have both the authority and the skills needed to regulate the behavior of their subordinates. As Chief Bill Sullivan (2004) notes: "Virtually every police scandal has at its core a lack of adequate first-line supervision." Supervisors and managers must make an upfront and proactive commitment to integrity. They must do everything they can to prevent deviance and corruption in the department. They must also be willing to do whatever it takes to separate undesirables from the police service.

While there is no doubt that individual police officers must be held accountable for unacceptable on-the-job performance or inappropriate behavior, police managers must establish realistic ethical and professional standards by which to judge their employees. The organizational response to occupational deviance should be tempered with an understanding of human nature and some appreciation for the milieu in which police work takes place.

Americans have traditionally had a love/hate relationship with the police establishment. While the police are generally acknowledged to be an essential element in the glue that holds our pluralistic society together, they are (at the same time) viewed with a great deal of suspicion. Power, authority, discretion, and the potential for abuse are indigenous to the police role. Trust in and fear of authority are deeply rooted in the American psyche and are wrapped in the persona of the individual police officer. We often cast police officers as superheroes who:

> *are expected to be knights errant, fearless in the face of danger, incorruptible in the midst of corruption, cool and knowledgeable in the determination of constitutional questions over which learned judges may reflect and wrangle and divide. They are supposed to be tough on criminals but tender regarding rights of individuals, minority groups, and the innocent generally. They are asked to be incessantly courteous, kind and cheerful, and to be ready to lay down their lives at any moment if need be in the defense of law and order. (Smith, 1969)*

No police officer can reasonably be expected to play each and every one of these roles simultaneously. There is far too much ambiguity; there are too many contradictions. It appears that the pathway to professional police work may have been booby-trapped with good intentions.

When police officers act appropriately and in accordance with the law, they are treated with deference and respect. If, however, an officer's job-related behavior falls short of culturally prescribed or group-shared expectations, there is likely to be a collective sense of betrayal. Under these particular circumstances, even petty violations tend to elicit very strong reactions from the community. Conflicting perceptions are formed and are used to vilify the police as a group and to scapegoat individual officers for the transgressions of their peers. The misconduct of one police officer frequently casts suspicion on the entire department, and police managers soon discover that the integrity of the police force cannot be restored by simply punishing the offending officer. Such discipline is usually viewed as being merely cosmetic. A managerial commitment to continuous monitoring (for accountability) is by far superior to an occasional witch hunt. It represents a genuine good-faith reaffirmation of the community's control over the police.

Strong internal discipline and a commitment to accountability are required in order to safeguard the organizational health of the police department. The integrity of police work and those who serve as police officers can be maintained only if there is an efficient, effective, and responsive discipline system. Public confidence will be restored and strengthened if there is a proactive effort to protect all citizens from police deviance. This can be accomplished by revising inadequate policies and procedures and correcting or separating from police service the individuals who have been found guilty of serious professional misconduct.

Controlling the Police

Police officers are government officials with a special duty to serve and protect the community. They are responsible for public safety and security. The concept of responsibility encompasses such notions as professional ethics, answerability, and accountability (Gaines & Kappeler, 2011). While these are noble ideals, they often degenerate into empty rhetoric. Ethical ambiguity permits the police to operate in a vacuum. Left uncontrolled, police officers may pursue their own ends by whatever means they choose. Under these circumstances, deviance (legal, moral, and ethical) often becomes the rule rather than the exception. Police occupational deviance represents an insidious threat to the democratic process.

The National Commission on Law Observance and Enforcement (1931), the President's Commission on Law Enforcement and the Administration of Justice (1967), the National Advisory Commission on Criminal Justice Standards and Goals (1973), and the American Bar Association's Task Force on the Urban Police Function (1973) came to the conclusion that public control over the police is a national imperative. In the words of the American Bar Association:

> *Since a principal function of police is the safeguarding of democratic processes, if police fail to conform their conduct to the requirements of law, they subvert the democratic process and frustrate the achievement of a principal police function. It is for this reason that high priority must be given for ensuring that the police are made fully accountable to the police administrator and to the public for their actions.*

Ethics, answerability, and accountability are essential ingredients in police professionalism and have, as guiding principles, been incorporated into police codes of conduct. It is the police manager's job to develop and implement the policies, procedures, rules, and regulations needed to translate ethics theory into practice. First-line supervisors, however, are the operating engineers who make sure that the internal discipline apparatus works properly.

Occupational deviance will occur in virtually all police departments over time. Allegations of personal and professional misconduct are commonplace. In fact, they are an occupational hazard. As long as police officers are empowered to restrict the activities of people, intervene when they commit criminal acts, and engage in authoritative control over their behavior in ways that cause inconvenience or resentment, complaints can be expected. It is imperative, then, that every police department establishes a fair and impartial mechanism designed to deal with these complaints. This will help ensure the integrity of the police department and the law enforcement process.

The chief executive officer of the police agency is ultimately responsible for the discipline and control of all subordinate personnel. In order to fulfill this responsibility, the chief should formulate policies, procedures, rules, and regulations that define occupational deviance and specify how complaints against police officers are to be received, processed, and adjudicated.

Policing the police is a volatile issue in contemporary American society. Good intentions are simply not enough to placate the community. Police administrators must now demonstrate, through policy statements and deeds, that they are willing to ferret out and deal decisively with all types of police misconduct (Los Angeles Police Commission, 1997). Anything less will fan the fires of social discontent and could rekindle the spark of violent civil disobedience that was so prevalent in the late 1960s and early 1970s. This phenomenon manifested itself again during the Lozano incident in Miami (1989), and throughout the Rodney King (1991) and O.J. Simpson (1995) occurrences in Los Angeles.

Personnel Complaint Investigation Policy

A forthright policy that defines, prohibits, and encourages the reporting of occupational deviance is in the public interest and represents yet another step on the road to accountability. Policies of this nature serve as a guide to thinking and decision-making within the police department. They reflect the purpose and philosophy of the organization and help convey that purpose and philosophy to all members. Policy creates realistic parameters that control the use of discretion in criminal justice organizations. The control of discretion is absolutely essential if the department is to:

1. Protect individual citizens from police misconduct.
2. Build community confidence in the police department.
3. Protect the integrity and reputation of the entire police force.
4. Protect the accused employee from unfounded or malicious allegations of occupational deviance.
5. Guarantee equal protection of the law and administrative due process to those accused of misbehavior.

In order to accomplish these critically important objectives, police managers must make a commitment to investigate all substantive complaints lodged against their personnel. In addition, they must become proactive in preventing police deviance. It is no longer sufficient to merely react to complaints initiated by those outside the organization (Arnold, 1999; Leonard & More, 2000).

Police officers must understand policies, procedures, rules, and regulations if they are to conform to them. Consequently, directives should be written clearly and concisely and distributed to those expected to obey them. According to the Commission on Accreditation for Law Enforcement Agencies (CALEA, 2006):

Accredited agencies must have a formal written directive system. The system can be in paper or electronic form. Components of the written directive system should be suited for the specific communications needs and capabilities of the agency. Clarity and rapid access to information are essential to effective implementation of agency written directives.

The agency's written directive system should evolve from its legal authority, core values, and mission statement. All agency personnel should have a clear understanding of their

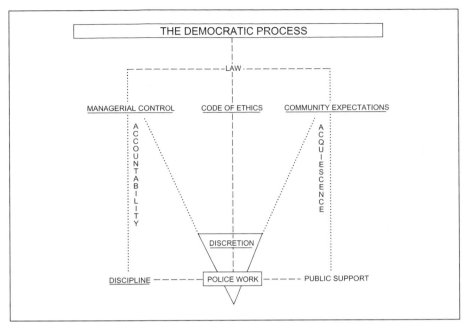

FIGURE 11.1 The synergistic balance.

individual discretionary powers in carrying out their duties in accordance with agency written policy, procedure, rules, and regulations (Standard 12). Additionally, CALEA Standard 52.1 (2006) stipulates:

> *A written directive requires all complaints against the agency or its employees be investigated, and specifies:*
> *a. the type of complaints to be investigated by line supervisors;*
> *b. the type of complaints that require investigation by the internal affairs function;* *and*
> *c. the type of complaints to be reviewed by the internal affairs function.*

While the police department's personnel complaint investigation policy cannot, and indeed should not, be written to cover every possible contingency, it is a valuable administrative tool that establishes a regularized approach to defining, detecting, and dealing with various forms of police misconduct. The written policy statement must be carefully crafted to strike a synergistic balance among managerial control, community expectations, professional ethics, and the discretionary flexibility needed to perform complex police work on the streets (see Figure 11.1). Ill-conceived, hastily prepared, and overly rigid policy statements are inherently counterproductive and tend to aggravate the problems they were designed to resolve.

Dealing with Police Occupational Deviance

As noted previously, the chief executive officer of the police department is responsible for the discipline and control of agency personnel. In medium- to large-sized police departments, occupational deviance occurs frequently enough to justify the creation of a specialized internal affairs unit. In small departments, the chief or chief's designee (often a patrol sergeant) conducts internal investigations. Most of the municipal police agencies in the United States are small. More than 80 percent of them have fewer than 20 sworn officers (Adams, 2013). Consequently, sergeants often take center stage in dealing with occupational deviance at the local level.

The procedures (or specific guidelines for action) involved in conducting internal personnel complaint investigations will differ somewhat depending on the origin, nature, and seriousness of the allegation. If, during the normal course of supervision, the sergeant observes a minor infraction, the situation should ordinarily be discussed with the employee, an on-the-spot warning may be issued, and the incident should be recorded for future reference or follow-up to determine what effect the intervention had on that individual officer. Procedures to be followed by a supervisor confronted with a serious complaint of misconduct coming from inside or outside the police department, however, will be more structured and much more formal. The seven basic steps involved in the investigation of serious personnel complaints are as follows:

1. The nature and extent of the alleged police occupational deviance must be determined.
2. An internal investigation must be conducted to ascertain the merit of the complaint and the extent to which the accused police officer is culpable if the allegation is, in fact, sustained.
3. Logical conclusions must be drawn based on evidence that is uncovered during the investigation.
4. Alternative courses of action must be evaluated and converted into recommendations concerning an appropriate disposition of the case.
5. If corrective disciplinary measures are required, they must be administered in an impartial, firm, fair, and timely manner.
6. Precautions must be taken to ensure administrative due process and equal protection under the law for those who are accused of serious misconduct.
7. Supervisors must perform a follow-up in order to assess the positive or negative effects of any disciplinary action that has been taken.

Department-specific policies, procedures, rules, and regulations will determine the investigative protocol to be used in police misconduct cases.

Social Media Concerns

Law enforcement agencies are increasingly implementing policies regarding employee use of social media. Many police agencies have been made aware of how social media affect their image in the community by the postings on Facebook, MySpace, and Twitter by police employees. Most law enforcement agencies have policies in place that deal with how employees are to conduct themselves while off duty. But many departments are now finding that postings on Twitter and Facebook may not be considered "conduct" by employees. In 2010, the International Association of Chiefs of Police (IACP) issued a model policy to guide police agencies in developing policies that deal with social media postings by officers (International Association of Chiefs of Police, 2010). The model policy states that sworn and non-sworn police employees "should be mindful that their speech becomes part of the worldwide electronic domain." The IACP (2010) further stated that what officers post online may reflect poorly on the police profession and department and "adherence to the department's code of conduct is required in the personal use of social media."

Two Washington police officers, one a state police officer in and the other an officer with Kennewick Police Department, were fired due to comments they posted on Facebook and blogs (Horton, 2009). The images and comments they posted were not illegal but cast them and their departments in a bad light with the community.

Police supervisors are always cautioned about developing close friendships with subordinates. Newly promoted supervisors know all too well how difficult it is to maintain a disconnect with subordinates that were formally close friends. Cara Donlon-Cotton (2010) warns that this disconnect from subordinates should also be applied to social media friendships. Some police supervisors do not see the harm in being a subordinate's "friend" on Facebook. However, Donlon-Cotton (2010) indicates that this is a dangerous practice for the supervisor. At what point during the "friendship" does the supervisor need to take action on posts he or she sees that may be inappropriate? A failure to take action on the supervisor's part could result in the supervisor being held responsible, even if the supervisor did not see the postings but is still a "friend" of the officer. The best recommendation is for supervisors to refrain from being friends with subordinates on social media sites.

Personnel Complaints

A personnel complaint is a formal accusation alleging that a particular employee is guilty of legal, moral, or professional misconduct. These complaints run the gamut from trivial to extremely serious. Trivial complaints should be filtered out immediately and disposed of through appropriate administrative action. Substantive personnel complaints, however, should be plugged into the internal investigations process and dealt with in a very straightforward manner. If there is any doubt as to how a specific complaint should be classified in terms of its validity or seriousness, it should be targeted for a thorough internal investigation. While discretion may be the better part of valor, the zealous pursuit of integrity is a prerequisite for police professionalism.

Misconduct complaints lodged against police officers come from two sources. Internal complaints originate within the organization. They are initiated by first-line supervisors or command officers who have witnessed occupational deviance firsthand and choose to deal with it. Unfortunately, some police managers tacitly condone unprofessional conduct rather than create bad publicity or risk employee hostility by aggressively pursuing cases of police misconduct. Internal personnel complaints also come from police officers who, based on their particular job in the department or their personal interaction with other employees, know or have reason to believe that another employee is guilty of misconduct. Mark Baker (1986) has noted that good cops often are more outraged by the misdeeds of their colleagues than are the general public, simply because these officers know that their reputation and character are being maligned because the "bad cops" wear the same uniform.

External complaints, however, come from outside the police department. These complaints come from lawyers, elected officials, pressure groups, relatives, and others who (for whatever reason) have chosen to focus their attention on police misconduct (real or imagined). Most of the complaints lodged against municipal police personnel come from external sources.

Due to the nature of their job, the power they wield, and the milieu within which they work, police officers are often targeted for criticism or allegations of wrongdoing. Some of these accusations are justifiable and serve as indicators of real occupational deviance or personal misconduct, whereas others are not. Unless personnel complaints are obviously frivolous, they should be investigated. Sergeants must also be concerned with due process. Perceptions are not always accurate, and complainants are not always truthful. In addition, there are those (criminals, political activists, and mentally ill individuals) who are inclined to fabricate stories designed to discredit the police or the entire criminal justice system. They will do anything to achieve their own personal, political, or social goals. The end justifies the means (distortion, lies, and false accusations). Sergeants often walk a tightrope between fact and fiction. They are the guardians of integrity and represent the bulwark of professional responsibility. Receiving, investigating, and resolving personnel complaints test the mettle of the men and women who are first-line supervisors in complex criminal justice organizations. It is the inglorious part of the job that many sergeants avoid.

Personnel complaints are a fact of life in modern police work. They are a permanent part of the occupational landscape and will not disappear just because they are cloaked in a "blue veil of secrecy" (Crank, 2004). While most personnel complaints prove to be unfounded (Alpert & Dunham, 1997), they still provide first-line supervisors and police managers with invaluable feedback. Complaints, whether they are substantiated or not, increase awareness of both actual and potential problems, help sharpen problem-solving skills, and provide yet another basis for the evaluation of the department's human resources. Consequently, every precaution must be taken to guard against artificial barriers that hinder or discourage the filing of legitimate personnel complaints. Without complaints, problems that could be resolved fester and poison the whole system. Inaction almost always makes the problem worse. Problems that are hidden or ignored are like a cancer. As the malignancy spreads, it eats away at the integrity of the police department and undermines community confidence in the police establishment. Thus, the purpose of police internal affairs is fivefold:

1. It ensures a professional image.
2. It fosters confidence and trust between the public and its police department.
3. It provides a mechanism for the public to seek redress for alleged acts of police misconduct.
4. It ensures that policies exist to provide guidelines for internal affairs investigations.
5. It ensures that members of the police agency know that a code of conduct exists and is enforced.

From a practical as well as a theoretical point of view, internal and external "whistle-blowing" should not be considered negative. In fact, it is one of the checks and balances built into the democratic process. The most effective way to prevent abuse of police power (occupational deviance) is through vigilance and the prompt use of disciplinary action when abuse is found.

Processing Personnel Complaints

Even though an overwhelming majority of the misconduct complaints filed against police personnel are proven to be unfounded, most police organizational and management theorists agree that all substantive complaints (from whatever the source) should be accepted and investigated thoroughly. This type of openness is the natural enemy of arbitrariness and an ally in the battle against occupational deviance (Kappeler et al., 2000). The Commission on Accreditation for Law Enforcement Agencies Standard 52 (2005) recommends that:

1. all complaints of misconduct against department members be accepted
2. any attempt to discourage, interfere with, or delay an individual from filing a complaint be prohibited
3. the process for filing a complaint should be professional, convenient, and prompt
4. the complainant need not physically come to the police department to lodge a complaint

Filing a complaint alleging police misconduct should be a quick and simple process. The public has the right to present reasonable grievances and to have them investigated properly. By ignoring negative feedback from citizens, police supervisors and managers insulate themselves improperly from those whom they are sworn to protect and serve (Kappeler et al., 2000).

Sergeants and command officers often share responsibility for receiving and processing personnel complaints in the nation's small police departments. They deal primarily with three types of complaints:

1. *Primary Complaints.* Complaints that are received directly from the alleged victim of the police misconduct.
2. *Secondary Complaints.* Complaints from persons who, while not victims themselves, complain about police misconduct on behalf of others.
3. *Anonymous Complaints.* Complaints of police occupational deviance coming from an unidentified source

Complaints from anonymous sources must be handled with the greatest care and utmost discretion because of the impact they might have on the morale of the employees involved. No police supervisor or manager, however, can afford to discount the validity of a personnel complaint solely because it comes from an unidentified source. Each complaint must be judged on its own merits.

It has been pointed out (Iannone & Iannone, 2013) that some of the most serious and bizarre cases of police misconduct have been brought to light by anonymous information. Once it is determined that a personnel complaint is not merely frivolous, it is preferable to deal openly and honestly with it in the public arena. Openness serves as an antidote to suspicion and distrust.

Commendable Action [ ]   Censurable Conduct [ ]

              Personnel Investigation _____ – _____

Officer(s) _____   Rank _____

            _____

Complainant _____   Telephone: Home _____

Address _____   Office _____

Incident: Date ____ / ___ / ___   Time: _____ Hours   Unknown [ ]

           Location _____

Summary of Incident: Department Complaint # (if any) _____

Witness No. 1 _____   Telephone: Home _____

Address_____   Office _____

Witness No. 2 _____   Telephone: Home _____

Address_____   Office _____

Violations(s): Section _____ Major _____ Minor _____

           Section _____ Major _____ Minor _____

           Section _____ Major _____ Minor _____

Assigned Investigating Officer

Date _____

FIGURE 11.2 Personnel incident report.

In order to initiate a formal inquiry, the complaint should be summarized on a personnel incident report form (see Figure 11.2), assigned an administrative control number, and processed according to department policies, procedures, rules, and regulations. The person filing the complaint should be given a copy of the report form as a receipt. This is tangible evidence that the personnel complaint is being taken seriously and that the police department is making a sincere effort to monitor the legal, moral, and professional conduct of its employees. It is in the best interests of the police service that all incidents of serious misconduct be discovered. Unless the public is convinced that the police department is truly receptive to complaints, it will not participate actively in this critically important process.

Personnel Complaint Investigations

There are more than 18,000 law enforcement agencies in the United States. While some of them (such as Chicago, Los Angeles, and New York) are huge bureaucracies, most police departments are small and not very sophisticated in terms of their organization/management structure. Under these circumstances, specialization is usually the exception rather than the rule. As generalist administrators in small organizations, sergeants play a variety of different and, at times, unconventional roles. Consequently, it is difficult to describe with precision the part that sergeants play in personnel complaint investigations.

Sergeants are usually the most visible and often the most approachable members of the police department's management team. They interact with police officers and civilians from all walks of life on a regular basis. Because they represent the first link in the chain of command, it is likely that many, if not most, of the allegations of personal or professional misconduct will be channeled through them to their superiors. Dealing with the corrupt side of human nature (inside and outside the department) goes with the territory. Streetwise supervisors know the score. As one sergeant put it, every cop has had a bad day (a hangover, a domestic squabble, a mistake at work, or a disagreement with the boss) and has taken it out on the people the officer has sworn to protect and serve. The officer may be rude, insulting, intimidating, or downright criminal in dealing with others.

According to Mark Baker (1986), many cops give in to temptation and misuse their discretionary power to gratify their own ego by tormenting a civilian, like a cat tormenting a mouse. As one cynical officer said, in any department 5 percent of the officers are hardworking and honest in all situations. They never do anything wrong. Five percent are always on the other side of the continuum. They have character flaws and would be ordinary criminals if they had not become police officers. The remaining 90 percent tend to go whichever way peer pressure goes. While this might be a gross overstatement, sergeants have an ethical obligation, as well as a functional obligation, to accept, investigate, and resolve all legitimate allegations of personal or professional misconduct lodged against their subordinates.

Sergeants, as first-line supervisors, are almost always given the power to receive and process personnel complaints. Based on the authority inherent in their rank, they monitor employee performance and serve as departmental disciplinarians. In minor cases involving police deviance, they bring charges, investigate, adjudicate, and (where appropriate) punish their subordinates. Summary action of this type is normally subject to administrative review and must be consistent with departmental policy, civil service regulations, collective bargaining agreements, and the law. In large police departments, specialization rather than rank determines who will conduct the investigation of serious personnel complaints. Corruption and other forms of serious occupational deviance are usually investigated by a special internal affairs unit. Internal affairs units report directly to the chief executive officer. In smaller departments, sergeants normally work in tandem with command officers and are frequently called on to help investigate serious allegations of police misconduct.

Investigating alleged police misconduct requires a great deal of skill. In order to be effective, the investigator (a sergeant, an internal affairs officer, or a police manager) must be specifically trained for the task and given constant guidance and administrative support. Because the internal investigation process must be swift, certain, fair, and lawful, only the most competent employees should be selected and trained to conduct personnel investigations. Few of the small police departments provide any, let alone sufficient, training for those involved in personnel complaint investigations. Police managers in smaller agencies do have several options when faced with an internal affairs investigation situation. The police manager may conduct the investigation him- or herself; assign the case to a supervisor; or, if the situation is serious enough, ask an outside police agency to investigate. There are advantages and disadvantages for each option. Whichever option is selected, the chief executive officer of the department must ensure that a high-quality, fair, and impartial investigation will be conducted (Courtney, 1996).

Once a formal personnel complaint enters the internal investigations process, official fact-finding begins. The tools and techniques used to investigate police misconduct should not differ substantially from those used in other types of investigations. The investigator must approach each complaint objectively and should avoid drawing any conclusions concerning the merits of the case until all the evidence has been collected and analyzed.

The first step in a personnel investigation is to interview the complainant. When accusations have been raised anonymously or by second parties, every effort should be made to contact the victim or whistle-blower directly. All other things being equal, direct evidence is the best evidence. The function of the interview is to:

1. Gather additional information concerning the personnel complaint.
2. Identify witnesses and investigative leads related to the alleged police misconduct.
3. Assess the complainant's credibility.
4. Determine the merits of the accusation.
5. Ascertain, if possible, the complainant's motive or motives for making the allegation.

The interview is a primary source of investigative data, and as such, its importance should not be underestimated.

Preparation is the key to conducting a successful investigative interview. The person assigned to conduct the internal investigation should review the personnel incident report carefully (filed by the complainant) in order to become familiar with the case and to make a preliminary determination as to the specific department policies, procedures, rules, and regulations that may have been violated by the accused. In addition, the investigator should develop a complainant profile. Based on a thorough records check, the profile should indicate whether the complainant has had previous encounters with the police, the nature of those incidents, and that individual's proclivity to file misconduct complaints against police personnel. Armed with this type of information, the internal investigator is in a position to assess the validity of the individual's complaint more accurately.

The interview itself must be handled discreetly and conducted in a skillful manner. Sergeants or other internal personnel complaint investigators should not editorialize or reveal information that could be misconstrued by the complainant. The interviewer should be careful not to:

1. Commit the police department to a particular course of action regarding the internal investigation, disposition of the complaint, or discipline to be imposed.
2. Indicate his or her personal professional opinion concerning the merits of the allegation, the culpability of the accused officer, or the officer's behavior in similar situations.
3. Prejudge the validity of the complaint or formulate subjective conclusions as to the complainant's veracity.

The interview gives direction to and provides a foundation for the internal investigation. It is, therefore, a critically important component in the personnel complaint investigation process.

Information acquired during the investigative interview should be put in writing as soon as possible. The official written account of the interview must be clear, concise, and accurate. Depending on the nature, seriousness, and complexity of the police deviance, it may be advisable to have the interview transcribed or tape-recorded. This is standard operating procedure in cases involving criminality, corruption, serious misconduct, and vicarious civil liability. As a general rule, the scope of the investigative interview and the precision with which the information is recorded should be proportional to the severity of the alleged misconduct (Redlich, 1994). It should also be noted that what starts out as fact-finding might well become documentary evidence in a subsequent criminal trial. In many states, it is illegal to make false reports to law enforcement authorities (Scoville, 1999). According to the Pennsylvania Consolidated Statutes (Title 18, Chapter 49a, Section 4906):

> *False Reports to Law Enforcement Authorities*
> *a. Falsely Incriminating Another. A person who knowingly gives false information to any law enforcement officer with the intent to implicate another commits a misdemeanor of the second degree.*
> *b. Fictitious Reports. A person commits a misdemeanor of the third degree if he:*
> *1. reports to law enforcement authorities an offense or other incident within their concern, knowing that it did not occur; or*
> *2. pretends to furnish such authorities with information relating to an offense or incident when he knows he has no information relating to such offense or incident.*

While recent court decisions have given sergeants and other internal personnel complaint investigators some leeway in dealing with police misconduct, they are still constrained by the due process provisions contained in administrative law, civil service regulations, and collective bargaining agreements. The rules governing procedural due process almost always require that police officers accused of serious misconduct be informed of their civil law and contract rights, notified as to the specific nature of the allegation, and advised when they are under investigation. Notice must be timely and in sufficient detail to permit the accused officer to prepare an adequate defense.

If the allegation of police deviance constitutes a violation of the criminal law, as well as a breach of agency policies, procedures, rules, and regulations, the officer involved should (with a few exceptions arising from his or her personal role as a government official) be allowed to exercise the constitutional rights accorded to all other citizens of the United States (see Figure 11.3). Consequently, first-line supervisors and other internal personnel complaint investigators must familiarize themselves with administrative and constitutional rules governing procedural due process in criminal justice organizations. Procedural due process protects innocent police officers and ensures that those who are guilty of legal, moral, and professional misconduct are treated fairly as they are brought before the bar of justice (Rothlein & Lober, 1996).

Dunham & Alpert (2009) argue that the use of administrative discipline should not be viewed as a substitute for, or an impediment to, criminal prosecution when serious police deviance is discovered. While justice can often be served by the administration of internal discipline, police managers must not resist or avoid criminal prosecution. The police service must not treat employees who break the law differently from other criminal offenders within the community.

Once the complainant has been interviewed and it is determined that there may be some substance to the accusation, the internal investigation should be expedited. Delays hamper the inquiry, lower employee morale, and erode public confidence in the police force. If first-line supervisors and police managers fail to put their house in order, someone from the outside (i.e., an interest group or civilian review board) will attempt to do it for them.

Some type of immediate intervention may be required in cases involving crime, corruption, or other kinds of serious misconduct. In the absence of departmental policy to the contrary, the sergeant should attempt to defuse the situation. Police officers who are temporarily unable to function due to alcohol or other drug abuse should be relieved of duty and taken home by the supervisor. Appropriate disciplinary action can be taken at a later time. Officers who are suspected of corruption or serious misconduct and pose a threat to the integrity of the department should, based on the authority of a command officer who has reviewed the evidence, be suspended from duty pending a thorough internal investigation. Any officer engaged in felonious crimes involving violence, moral turpitude, or theft should be suspended from the department, arrested, and booked. The decision to arrest a police officer must be approved by the chief executive officer of the department. Immediate and radical action of this type is usually unnecessary. Most criminal complaints against police officers may be processed normally through the district attorney's office.

As a condition of employment, police officers are required to cooperate with supervisors and others within the department who are investigating them for alleged legal, moral, or professional misconduct that is directly related to the performance of their assigned duties. Administrative law and recent court decisions give internal personnel investigators a great deal of latitude in dealing with police employees suspected of serious misconduct. The failure to cooperate subjects them to further disciplinary action and possible separation from the police service.

Given to_____

Officer _____ Date _____Time _____

Rank _____Badge No. _____

Unit of Assignment_____

The law provides that you are to be advised of the following:

1. Any admission made in the course of this hearing, interrogation, or examination may be used as evidence of misconduct or as the basis for charges seeking your suspension, removal, or discharge.

2. You have the right to counsel of your choosing to be present with you to advise you at this hearing, interrogation, or examination and you may consult with him or her as you desire. Your counsel may be present at any stage of this interrogation.

3. You may request counsel at any time before or during this interrogation. You have a right to be given a reasonable time and opportunity to obtain counsel of your own choosing.

4. You have no right to remain silent. You are ordered to truthfully answer questions put to you. You are advised that your statements or responses constitute an official police report.

5. If you refuse to answer questions put to you, you will be ordered by a superior officer to answer the question.

6. If you persist in your refusal after the order has been given to you, you are advised that such refusal constitutes a violation of the rules and regulations of the police department and will serve as a basis for which disciplinary action will be sought.

7. You are further advised that by law, any admission made by you during the course of this hearing, interrogation, or examination cannot be used against you in a subsequent criminal proceeding.

8. The law provides that you may not be subjected to interrogation without first being informed in writing of the nature of the investigation. The nature of this investigation is as follows:

The undersigned hereby acknowledges that he/she was informed of the above at:

_____ This _____ Day of _____

Year _____, Time _____

and that he/she received a copy of this document entitled Statement and Rights Prior to Interrogation.

Signature _____

Witnesses _____

_____

_____

FIGURE 11.3 Statement and rights prior to interrogation.

Legislatures and courts have generally supported the right of government agencies to protect themselves (and the public) against unethical or criminal employees. In many jurisdictions, supervisors and other personnel complaint investigators have been given the authority to:

1. Access the accused officer's personnel file, performance evaluations, merit ratings, attendance records, and other relevant information.
2. Deny the accused officer's request for legal representation during the investigatory interview.
3. Obtain a verbatim transcript or tape-recording of the investigatory interview.
4. Search, with or without a warrant, areas in the workplace where there is no reasonable expectation of privacy.
5. Require the accused officer to participate in a properly constituted and representative lineup.
6. Order the accused officer to take a polygraph examination (unless such an order is specifically prohibited by a collective bargaining agreement or state law).
7. Demand that the accused officer submit to physical testing (blood, urine, breath, etc.) designed to yield tangible evidence that can be used in disciplinary hearings.

This authority must be regulated carefully and should be codified in department-specific policies, procedures, rules, and regulations. According to Iannone & Iannone (2013), the law is clear—almost any "reasonable" order to an employee is administratively enforceable. The courts have been reluctant to interfere in employer/employee relations unless the employer's directives are arbitrary, capricious, or breach procedural due process requirements in established administrative law, civil service regulations, or labor contracts.

After all the relevant evidence has been gathered and evaluated, the sergeant, internal affairs officer, or police manager must attempt to reconstruct reality in such a way as to prove or disprove the allegation. The findings should be integrated into a comprehensive investigative report (keyed to who, what, where, when, why, and how) and used to formulate a recommendation concerning the best disposition of the case (see Figure 11.4). All of the material should be forwarded to the chief executive officer of the police department for appropriate administrative action.

The Adjudication of Personnel Complaints

The chief executive officer of the police department is responsible for the adjudication (or final disposition) of all internal discipline complaints. The person who conducted the investigation and prepared the investigative report, however, should have laid the foundation for the adjudication. If everything works properly, the chief executive's decisions should flow logically from the investigation, conclusions, and recommendations made by the internal complaint investigator. Steps must be taken to ensure the assumption of responsibility and to safeguard the

```
┌─────────────────────────────────────────────────────────────────────┐
│                                                                       │
│   Final Report Censurable Conduct          Personnel Investigation ___-___   │
│                                                                       │
│   Summary of Findings                                                 │
│                                                                       │
│                                                                       │
│   Attachments: Complainant Statement [ ], Witness Statement [ ], Officer │
│   Statement [ ], Other [ ] (explain) _____   │
│   Recommendation: Unfounded [ ] Exonerated [ ] Not Sustained [ ]      │
│   Sustained [ ]                                                        │
│   (State Section # charged)                                           │
│                                                                       │
│                                                                       │
│   Recommended Disciplinary Action (Refer to Manual Section 5-055/000) │
│                                                                       │
│                                                                       │
│                Investigator _____  │
│                Division Commander _____  │
│   Final Disposition:                                                  │
│   Concur [ ]                     Do Not Concur [ ]                     │
│   Reason _____        │
│   _____   │
│   _____   │
│   _____   │
│   Final Disposition:                                                  │
│   _____   │
│   _____   │
│   _____   │
│   Date _____ Chief of Police _____│
│                                                                       │
└─────────────────────────────────────────────────────────────────────┘
```

FIGURE 11.4 Personnel incident final report.

integrity of the decision-making process. According to the National Advisory Commission on Criminal Justice Standards and Goals (1973):

> *Every police agency immediately should ensure that provisions are established to allow the police chief ultimate executive authority in the adjudication of internal discipline complaints, subject only to appeal through the courts or established civil service bodies, and review by responsible legal and governmental entities (see Figure 11.5).*
>
> *1. A complaint disposition should be classified as sustained, not sustained, exonerated, unfounded, or misconduct not based on the original complaint.*

Civil Service [ ]   Noncivil Service [ ]

Employee _____ I.D. # _____

Position Classification _____

Personnel Investigation # _____ Dept. Complaint # _____

Date of This Statement _____

Person Making Personnel Complaint _____

Police Department Manual of Policy and Procedures—Section(s) Violated:

_____   _____

Personnel Rule(s) Violated (if applicable):

_____

Section Description:

Synopsis of Incident:

Findings:

Disciplinary Action Taken:

I have read and understand the charges filed against me and have received a copy of said charges. I also understand that I may appeal this finding within seven (7) calendar days from the date shown below to either the Civil Service Commission or the Department Personnel Officer depending upon my status as indicated on this form.

_____
Employee Signature   Date

_____
Officer Serving Charges   Date

FIGURE 11.5 Statement of charges.

2. Adjudication and, if warranted, disciplinary action should be based partially on recommendations of the involved employee's immediate supervisor. The penalty should be at least a suspension up to six months or, in severe cases, removal from duty.

3. An administrative fact-finding trial board should be available to all police agencies to assist in the adjudication phase. It should be activated when necessary in the interests of the police agency, the public, or the accused employee and should be available at the discretion of the chief executive or on the request of any employee who is to be penalized in any manner that exceeds verbal or written reprimand. The chief executive of the agency should review the recommendations of the trial board and decide on the penalty.

4. The accused employee should be entitled to representation equal to that afforded to the person representing the agency in the trial board proceeding.

5. Police employees should be allowed to appeal a chief executive's decision. The police agency should not provide the resources or fund the appeal.

6. The chief executive of every police agency should establish written policy on the retention of internal discipline investigation reports. Only the reports of sustained investigations and, if appealed, investigations that are upheld should become part of the accused employee's personnel folder. All disciplinary investigations should be kept confidential.

7. Administrative adjudication of internal discipline complaints involving a violation of law should neither depend on nor curtail criminal prosecution. Regardless of the administrative adjudication, every police agency should refer all complaints that involve violation of law to the prosecuting agency for the decision to prosecute criminally. Police employees should not be treated differently from other members of the community in cases involving violations of law. The complainant, witnesses, and accused employee should be encouraged to participate in the process that leads to a final disposition, even though that decision rests squarely on the shoulders of the police chief executive.

Regarding the classification of personnel complaint dispositions, the following general categories may be used to reflect adjudicatory findings:

1. **Sustained** indicates that, based on the facts obtained, the accused committed all or part of the alleged police misconduct.
2. **Not sustained** means that the investigation produced insufficient evidence to prove or disprove the allegation and that the matter is being resolved in favor of the employee.
3. **Exonerated** denotes that the alleged act or omission occurred, but was, in fact, legal, proper, and necessary.
4. **Unfounded** is used when the alleged police misconduct did not occur and the complaint was false.
5. **Misconduct not based on original complaint** means that while there was misconduct on the part of the police officer, it was separate and distinct from that alleged in the original complaint.
6. **Policy failure** means that the allegation was true, but the action of the agency or the officer was not inconsistent with agency policy.

In the event that someone other than the employee's immediate first-line supervisor conducted the internal personnel complaint investigation and prepared the comprehensive investigative report, the chief executive officer should contact the sergeant before making a final disposition in the case. All other things being equal, the sergeant is in the best overall position to assess the accused officer's job performance, professional conduct, and value as a human resource. The sergeant's input must be evaluated carefully in terms of its objectivity and consistency and should be considered a major factor in determining the final disposition and selecting the appropriate disciplinary action.

When an internal discipline complaint is sustained, the chief of police must select the most appropriate remedy available. Corrective measures may include reassignment, retraining, psychological counseling, or participation in a multipurpose employee assistance program. The most frequently used sanctions in serious misconduct cases, however, are separation from the police service, suspension, and loss of seniority in lieu of suspension.

If a serious personnel complaint is sustained by the evidence and the loss of time, a suspension, or a dismissal is considered an appropriate sanction, emphasis during the investigation should be placed on procedural due process. If accused officers are arbitrarily denied procedural due process, the courts will reverse on appeal and the police department may be civilly liable. Iannone & Iannone (2013) suggest that the safest way to avoid reversal and civil liability in cases involving serious legal, moral, or professional misconduct is to adhere to the minimum requirements of procedural due process as outlined by the U.S. Supreme Court in the 1972 case of *Morrissey v. Brewer*:

1. Written notice of the specific charge or charges filed against the officer.
2. Disclosure of the evidence that will be used against the officer during the disciplinary hearing.
3. The opportunity to appear in person and to present witnesses and evidence.
4. The right to confront and cross-examine adverse witnesses (unless the hearing board specifically finds good cause for not allowing the confrontation).
5. An impartial hearing before a "neutral and detached" administrative body.
6. A written statement by that body concerning the evidence it relied on and the reasons for its action.
7. Administrative and/or judicial review of adverse dispositions.

These provisions represent the concern for fairness and procedural due process in labor/management relations and should be incorporated into department policies, procedures, rules, and regulations.

Many police departments have adopted some form of trial board system. These trial boards are designed to help the police chief executive make sound decisions in internal discipline cases. They provide for a diversity of opinion and allow more direct participation in the adjudication of police misconduct cases by those who conducted the internal complaint investigation.

Under ideal circumstances, the administrative trial board should consist of five police officers from within the department. Four of the members should be appointed by the chief and one by the accused officer. Trial boards should not have any investigative authority and should handle only serious cases of police misconduct assigned to them by the chief of police or cases (regardless of their seriousness) in which accused officers specifically request a disciplinary hearing.

Trial boards are administrative proceedings in which a "neutral and detached" body hears the evidence and oral arguments and renders a decision concerning the appropriate action to be taken on a personnel complaint. Members of the trial board are expected to use rational, objective, and analytical reasoning in reaching that decision. The board is responsible for determining fact and making a recommendation to the chief executive.

Trial boards are quasi-judicial entities. Their hearings must be governed by the principle of fundamental fairness and need not comply with strict courtroom protocol. The board should, however, have a presiding officer who understands the adjudication process and is familiar with parliamentary procedure. Decisions (usually determined by majority vote) should be based on "a preponderance of evidence" and not "proof beyond a reasonable doubt." The rules of criminal procedure are simply not germane to administrative decision-making. According to Gaines, Southerland, & Angell (2012), the trial board should conclude its deliberations with a formal recommendation accompanied by a written summary of the evidence it relied on and the rationale behind its recommendation.

The recommendation of the trial board, however, is purely advisory. It is up to the police chief executive to institute proper corrective action. If the chief habitually ignores or modifies the trial board's suggestions, this noble experiment in what Mary Parker Follett (Fox & Urwick, 1977) or Stephen Covey (1992) might refer to as "participatory management" is bound to fail. Under these circumstances, the police are denied the right to police themselves and lose the key element needed to achieve professional status (Katz, 2013).

Unless it is monitored and managed carefully, the trial board apparatus can become defective and function as an impediment to good discipline. Instead of an objective "peer review" process, it may become self-serving by shifting to a cover-up modality situated in the morass of procedural due process. The Los Angeles Police Department has been criticized in this regard. Additionally, in Pittsburgh, the trial board system deteriorated to such a degree that the city had to seek state legislative relief to correct the problem. The union contract and state law that created the original system made it virtually impossible for police administrators to exercise management's right to discipline officers even in cases of serious occupational deviance.

In most police departments, only the internal personnel complaint investigations that are sustained are placed in the employee's personnel file. It is standard operating procedure in some agencies to remove investigative reports from personnel files after what is considered to be a reasonable length of time (from two to five years) if no other complaints are sustained. Keeping unproven and possibly false personnel complaints on file is a dangerous practice because they are subject to subpoena in subsequent civil litigation against the officer or the police department. Because introduction of this evidence could prejudice a jury, the benefit of keeping it must be weighed against the risk of incurring greater civil liability. In addition, it is inappropriate for police managers to use unsubstantiated allegations of police misconduct as a negative factor in performance evaluation or promotion considerations. Superfluous paperwork of this type should be disposed of on a regular basis.

The prompt adjudication of serious personnel complaints gives police chiefs an opportunity to make it clear, through the imposition of firm and fair disciplinary action, that they will not tolerate serious employee misconduct. In addition, when serious personnel complaints are not sustained, it allows them to go on record in support of the legal, moral, and professional conduct exhibited by the vast majority of the nation's police personnel.

The Civilian Review Movement

Many police departments have flirted with the concept of civilian control since the late 1950s. Direct review of police behavior is as popular with critics of the police as it is unpopular with police officers themselves. Most traditional civilian review boards, such as those established in New York, Philadelphia, Detroit, and Kansas City, were created in response to specific police–community relations problems. They were organized so that complaints about police occupational deviance could be channeled through a formally structured committee of citizens who would examine complaints and recommend remedial action. Unfortunately, the civilian review process did not resolve problems and, in many situations, made the problems worse. Consequently, most traditional civilian review boards have been abandoned (Johnson, 1998). Because police misconduct has not disappeared and the internal investigation process does not always work as well as it should, other alternatives are now being explored (U.S. Department of Justice, 2001).

The renewed interest in civilian oversight of government activity in the mid-1980s has produced a second generation of review strategies with interests far broader than law enforcement. The "accountability" movement is based on the fact that unless government is receptive and agrees to deal with citizen complaints, there will be more than the usual amount of fear and distrust (Walker & Kreisel, 1996). The ombudsman and the independent review panel are examples of this renewed emphasis on accountability. The ombudsman, or "citizen advocate," is a government official who acts as a grievance commissioner with the authority to investigate all complaints of administrative abuse. The ombudsman has discretion in determining which cases to probe. While ombudsmen usually have no power to discipline or prosecute government employees, they usher in openness, raise issues, and marshal public sentiment. The advantage of the ombudsman approach to accountability is that it does not single out one particular agency (like the police) but covers all government agencies (Johnson, Misner, & Brown, 1981; Walker & Kreisel, 1996).

However, some political subdivisions are establishing independent review panels to deal with citizen complaints. The panels accept complaints, conduct fact-finding inquiries, and make remedial recommendations to appropriate authorities. While some independent review panels have a great deal of authority, others are very limited in scope. The Baltimore police review board was recently accused of being irrelevant and ineffective. According to the *Baltimore Sun* (2013), "When the board was created more than a decade ago, boosters promised it would prove a crucial check on brutality and abusive language by police officers. Opponents called it an intrusion into departmental discipline. It proved to be neither, and members say the panel has become irrelevant, ineffective and disengaged from the public it's supposed to represent."

Not all civilian review boards are ineffective. The Chicago police review board analyzes police-involved shootings and posts their investigative reports online. The Washington DC police review board has a staff of more than 20 investigators that reviews allegations of police misconduct and makes policy recommendations to the police. The review process ensures that all public employees are treated in the same way, regardless of their job classification. Many police officers and public employee unions oppose outside review in any form. Only time will tell whether independent review will be any more successful than the first-generation civilian review boards and which model, if any, will survive (Alpert & Dunham, 1997).

Militarization of the Police

One complaint against the police that seems to be on the increase is the overuse of military-style tactics against the public. Traditionally, the police are supposed to keep the peace as citizens and not as a military force. Sir Robert Peel, the father of modern policing, stated that the police are the public and the public are the police. This supports the contention that it is every citizen's responsibility to see that the law is enforced and that a few citizens are set aside to help them do this in a professional manner, called the police. However, in the last few decades with political and racial riots, the war on drugs, and terrorist attacks, the police have turned more and more toward arming themselves against threats. Police forces have acquired the latest technology, equipment, tactical training, and military-style combat uniforms for specialized units commonly referred to as SWAT (Special Weapons and Tactics). And, while specialized units are necessary for hostage situations, armed robberies, school shootings, and serving warrants on known dangerous suspects, they seem to be used more frequently in seemingly more mundane and routine incidents. In the past decade, police have used SWAT teams to raid small-time household poker games, domestic violence calls, loud teen parties, license and ordinance enforcement, and other infractions that were once routinely handled by the patrol officer on the beat (Balko, 2013). According to Timothy Lynch at the Cato Institute, "the more police fail to defuse confrontations but instead help create them—be it with their equipment, tactics or demeanor—the more ties with community members are burned" (Baker, 2011). In many cases, it is the first-line supervisor at the scene that has the discretion to call in specialized units. Using more discretionary decision-making to use paramilitary operations may reduce the number of complaints against the police for being too overbearing in their tactics and create more trust with the community.

Forecasting and Dealing with Potential Disciplinary Problems

One approach to forecasting and dealing with potential disciplinary problems that is now being used in progressive police departments is known as the early warning system (EWS, see Chapter 12). The EWS is programmed, either manually or by computer, to keep track of all personnel complaints lodged with the department, whether they are substantiated or not

(Guthrie, 1996). The program tracks complaints in terms of type, seriousness, location, and other important variables. After a specified number of complaints have been filed against a particular officer, the proverbial red flag is raised and the officer's entire file is reviewed to assess potential problems (Walker, 2000). Even a number of unsubstantiated or relatively minor complaints, for example, trigger the review and interview process built into the EWS.

The sole function of the EWS is to alert internal affairs personnel and first-line supervisors that there may be potential disciplinary problems on the horizon. Because the EWS is a diagnostic tool, it need not be cloaked in the same procedural due process as an internal investigation or a formal disciplinary action (Katz, 2013).

The interview is a critical component in the EWS process. After meeting with the officer, it may become apparent that the concerns are unfounded. The officer might be assigned to a high-crime area and has been tough on both crime and alleged criminals. Complaints against the officer may be an orchestrated attempt to have the officer transferred from the area so that the criminal element can return to its old habits.

The same interview could produce a different result, however. Internal affairs personnel or the sergeant might realize that the officer's on-the-job behavior is being affected adversely by problems at home, alcohol abuse, emotional stress, or other factors. As a result, the investigator or sergeant (based on impetus from the EWS) can advise police managers that the officer is in need of help before the problem becomes too serious. Help may come in the form of coaching, counseling, professional care, or referral to the department's employee assistance program (EAP).

The Los Angeles Police Department has incorporated a number of policies in direct response to the Mark Fuhrman affair. In the context of the internal affairs investigation of Mark Fuhrman, five central issues surfaced: gender bias, racial discrimination, excessive force, code of silence, and discourtesy. In addition to addressing these issues through training and policy statements, the Los Angeles Police Department developed their own version of the EWS, known as TEAMS (Training Evaluation and Management System). TEAMS is an incident-based computerized database that allows a review of employee histories to better identify trends and patterns of employee behavior (Los Angeles Police Commission, 1997).

An early warning system, whether manual or computerized, is diagnostic and help oriented rather than punitive. It is part of the total quality management commitment to personnel development within the police department (Alpert & Dunham, 1997).

Discipline and the Employee Assistance Movement

Many progressive police administrators now realize that formal disciplinary action designed primarily to punish marginal employees or to separate them from police service may be objectionable and even counterproductive. Collective bargaining agreements and civil service regulations often stress intervention and remediation rather than termination of employment. Consequently, employee assistance programs have sprung up all over the country. These programs offer a wide range of diagnostic, counseling, and other remedial services to police officers whose on-the-job performance is affected adversely by physical, psychological, or social problems. Employee assistance programs are based on the assumption that it is more humane to treat (and hopefully to resolve) an employee's problems rather than to terminate that employee. It is also considered more cost-effective to invest in existing human resources than it is to recruit, screen, hire, orient, and train new employees.

Employee assistance programs give police managers the opportunity to use intervention and remediation strategies to keep discipline problems from developing. As first-line supervisors, sergeants are expected to know their personnel well enough to spot personal problems that could have a negative impact on performance. They act as referral agents. In some cases, police officers are given a choice. Participation in the EAP is strictly voluntary. At other times, it is mandatory and stipulated as a condition of continued employment.

The EAP may also be incorporated into the department's disciplinary process. Under these circumstances, officers being disciplined are required (by trial board or chief of police) to participate in counseling or other forms of remedial treatment in lieu of demotion, suspension, or termination. As in the case of probation, these negative sanctions will be held in abeyance, or not imposed at all, if the officer makes an honest effort to change his or her behavior. Employee assistance programs substitute intervention and treatment for punishment when remediation is in the best interests of the police department. Sergeants monitor the on-the-job performance of the officer during and after treatment. They must be willing to make an objective appraisal. Officers who do not respond to the treatment provided through the EAP must (based on the recommendation of their supervisor) be considered for termination. This is a great responsibility.

References

Adams, T. F. (2013). *Police field operations* (8th ed.). Englewood Cliffs, NJ: Prentice Hall, Inc.

Alpert, G. P., & Dunham, R. G. (1997). *Policing urban America* (3rd ed.). Prospect Heights, IL: Waveland Press, Inc.

American Bar Association, (1973). *Standards related to the urban police function*. Chicago, IL: American Bar Association.

Anderson, P. (1997). *Introduction to criminal justice* (6th ed.). New York: McGraw-Hill.

Arnold, J. (1999). Internal affairs investigation guidelines. *Law and Order, 47*(5).

Baker, A. (2011). When the police go military. *The New York Times* December 3

Baker, M. (1986). *Cops: Their lives in their own words*. New York: Pocket books/Simon & Schuster, Inc.

Balko, R. (2013). *Rise of the warrior cop: The militarization of America's police forces*. Jackson, TN: PublicAffairs Publishers.

Barker, T., & Carter, D. L. (1994). *Police deviance* (3rd ed.). Cincinnati, OH: Anderson Publishing Co.

CALEA, (2006). *Standards for law enforcement agencies*. Fairfax, VA: Commission on Accreditation for Law Enforcement Agencies, Inc.

Courtney, K. M. (1996). Internal affairs in the small agency. *FBI Law Enforcement Bulletin, 65*(9).

Covey, S. R. (1992). *Principle-centered leadership*. New York: Simon & Schuster, Inc.

Crank, J. P. (2004). *Understanding police culture* (2nd ed.). Newark, NJ: LexisNexis/Matthew Bender (Anderson Publishing).

Donlon-Cotton, C. (2010). Facebook: Risks for the supervisor. *Law & Order, 58*(11), 12.

Dunham, R. G., & Alpert, G. P. (2009). *Critical issues in policing* (6th ed.). Prospect Heights, IL: Waveland Press, Inc.

Fox, E., & Urwick, L. (Eds.). (1977). *Dynamic administration: The collected papers of Mary Parker Follett* (2nd ed.). New York: Hippocrene Books, Inc.

Gaines, L. K., & Kappeler, V. E. (2011). *Policing in America* (7th ed.). Boston: Elsevier (Anderson Publishing).

Gaines, L. K., Southerland, M. D., & Angell, J. E. (2012). *Police administration* (3rd ed.). New York: McGraw-Hill Book Company.

Guthrie, M. (1996). Using automation to apply discipline fairly. *FBI Law Enforcement Bulletin, 65*(5).

Horton, P. (2009). Two Washington officers fired over Facebook indiscretions. *The Tri-City Herald* January 19.

Iannone, N. F., & Iannone, M. (2013). *Supervision of police personnel* (8th ed.). Englewood Cliffs, NJ: Prentice Hall, Inc.

International Association of Chiefs of Police, (2010). *Social media model policy.* Alexandria, VA: International Association of Chiefs of Police.

Johnson, R. R. (1998). Citizen complaints: What the police should know. *FBI Law Enforcement Bulletin, 67*(12).

Johnson, T. A., Misner, G. E., & Brown, L. P. (1981). *The police and society.* Englewood Cliffs, NJ: Prentice Hall, Inc.

Johnston, M. (1982). *Political corruption and public policy in America.* Monterey, CA: Brooks-Cole Publishing Company.

Kappeler, V. E., Sluder, R. D., & Alpert, G. P. (2000). *Forces of deviance: Understanding the dark side of policing* (2nd ed.). Prospect Heights, IL: Waveland Press, Inc.

Katz, C. (2013). *The police in America* (8th ed.). New York: McGraw-Hill Book Publishers.

Leonard, V. A., & More, H. W. (2000). *Police organization and management* (9th ed.). New York: The Foundation Press, Inc.

Los Angeles Police Commission, (1997). *Mark Fuhrman task force: Executive summary.* Los Angeles, CA: Los Angeles Police Department.

National Advisory Commission on Criminal Justice Standards and Goals, (1973). *The police.* Washington, DC: U.S. Government Printing Office.

Pennsylvania Consolidated Statutes. (1993). Title 18, Chapter 49a, Section 4906—False Reports to Law Enforcement Authorities.

Redlich, J. W. (1994). Disciplinary interrogations: Which warnings apply? and when? *The Police Chief, LXI*(6).

Rothlein, S., & Lober, R. (1996). The ramifications of internal affairs investigations. *The Police Chief, LXIII*(5).

Scoville, D. (1999). Citizen complaints are part of the business. *Police, 23*(11).

Smith, R. L. (1969). *The tarnished badge.* New York: Thomas Y. Crowell Company.

Sullivan, B. (2004). Police supervision in the 21st century: Can traditional police work standards and the contemporary employee coexist? *The Police Chief, 71*(10).

U.S. Department of Justice, (2001). *Citizen review of police.* Rockville, MD: National Institute of Justice.

Walker, S. (2000). *Responding to the problem police officer: A national study of early warning systems.* Rockville, MD: National Institute of Justice.

Walker, S., & Kreisel, B. W. (1996). Varieties of citizen review: The implications of organizational features of complaint review procedures for accountability of the police. *American Journal of Police, 15*(3).

12

Supervising the Difficult Employee
Special Considerations

KEY TERMS

alcohol	indecisives
ambivalent employees	indifferent employees
ascendant employees	manipulators
Badge of Life critical-incident stress management	marginal performers
	millennials
	peer counseling
departmental values	post-traumatic stress disorder
defeatists	
divorce	problem employees
early warning systems	suicide
employee assistance program	task stressors
	tyrants
erudites	value statements
fitness-for-duty evaluations	work stressors

CASE STUDY
Officer Robert Clarke

DEPARTMENT

The Davenport Police Department is a small department with 32 sworn officers. It has a basic organizational structure with line and staff functions. The line function includes 24 patrol officers and four investigators. Staff functions include three records clerks and four secretarial staff. The department supplements the patrol force by using reserve officers on a frequent basis. Reserves must go through the same training as regular officers but they pay for the training, uniform, and most equipment. Reserves are required to work 16 hours per month. They are especially useful when the town has special events that require assistance with traffic control. However, the department is short-handed at times. If an officer calls in sick or is on vacation, the entire department is affected with increased workloads. Often, the chief himself fills in, answering calls on patrol. Because the department is small, officers consider themselves more like family than colleagues.

CRIME

Davenport enjoys a low crime rate. There has not been a homicide in seven years. Sexual assaults are rare or at least rarely reported. Assaults are typically domestic in nature, although there was one felonious assault at a Little League game between a father and an umpire last year. Burglaries and larcenies are within normal rates for a town of this size. Most of the burglaries and larcenies are committed by juveniles who live in the area. There is a high clearance rate for most crimes because almost everyone knows everyone else, and everyone else's business, in Davenport.

COMMUNITY

Davenport is an old historic community of 48,000 people. Most residents grew up in Davenport and have old family ties to the area. Many of the houses date back to the Victorian era or even earlier. Davenport is 26 miles from Evansville. Evansville is a larger city, which is where most of the residents of Davenport go to do their weekly shopping or to eat out at upscale restaurants. There are a few restaurants in Davenport but they are either fast-food chains or "mom and pop" diners. Davenport is known for one event: storytelling. One week a year, people from all over the country come to Davenport to the annual Storytelling Festival. Usually in July, when the weather is at its best, Davenport hosts nearly 3000 visitors.

OFFICER

Officer Robert Clarke has been a patrol officer with the Davenport Police Department for four years. He is well liked by other officers and has always performed outstandingly with the department. It has even been recommended that Clarke be considered for the sergeant's slot when Sergeant Anderson retires next year. Officer Clarke also serves with the interagency emergency response squad. The squad is referred to as the special operations squad (SOS) and is composed of local and state officers. Clarke was selected to serve based on his completion of the special training that was offered last year. Clarke made the squad and made his department proud. The SOS is used for hostage details, drug busts, and other situations that may require an assault team. For the last four years Officer Clarke's evaluations have been exemplary. He has never taken a sick day and is always prepared and willing to take on additional duties and responsibilities.

PROBLEM

Officer Clarke is young and unmarried. During the last four years, he has had a few girlfriends, but nothing serious. He dated a woman at the court clerk's office last year, but nothing came of it. He seems the type to be married to his job and not one to settle down. However, several months ago, he met a woman at an elementary school where he had given a lecture to some children. She was a teacher's aide and ready to graduate with her degree and teaching certificate. Peggy is an extremely beautiful girl. The other officers in the department thought she was a model when they saw her with Officer Clarke. Officer Clarke began to date Peggy frequently, and they became somewhat of a couple. But Peggy had a job waiting for her in Williamsville, a city about four hours from Davenport. Peggy had grown up in Williamsville and had gotten a job as a teacher in one of the elementary schools there. She was looking forward to the job, but Officer Clarke wasn't too excited about it.

When Peggy left for her new job, Officer Clarke was depressed and despondent. He was in love, and the separation from Peggy was almost more than he could bear. Over the next few months, he traveled to Williamsville as much as possible. In fact, he would sometimes get to work late because he had driven to see her the previous evening and would just be getting back. Officer Clarke's behavior on the job began to change for the worse. He started coming to work late or calling in sick and sometimes would not show up or call at all. When he did get to work, his uniform was wrinkled, he appeared as though he had not slept, he was sometimes unshaven, and he was becoming forgetful. He forgot to go to traffic court last week, and the judge dismissed all of the traffic citations he had written.

Sergeant Gregory, Clarke's supervisor, understood what was wrong with Clarke, but things were getting out of hand. The Storytelling Festival starts in a few weeks and the department will need everyone working. Clarke needs to straighten up.

WHAT WOULD YOU DO?

If you were Sergeant Gregory, how would you "straighten up" Officer Clarke? Can the problems Officer Clarke is experiencing be overcome with minimal effort or will it take more substantial action to correct his behavior?

Value Statements

Contemporary supervisors must set the tone, change the paradigms, and create a foundation that results in a truly supportive working environment. There is a need to change supervisory values and beliefs. They should be built on, or replaced with, new ones (Zook, 1994). This changing role presents not only a challenge to each supervisor, but also the concomitant possibility of creating apprehension and anxiety caused by the change. It demands the application of new skills and the modification of traditional guidelines and creeds. Imaginative leadership will be the key if consistent, high-quality performance is to be required of every employee. The supervisor plays a crucial role in managing a productive contemporary workplace. There is a need for a new accountability within police organizations, which strains the traditional way of dealing with employees. A transformation is necessary as organizations change, the workforce becomes increasingly diversified, and communities demand improved police services at lower costs. The first-line supervisor is the key if the new organization is to become a learning organization.

The psychological quality of a work environment should be such that employees feel at ease and new patterns of thinking are accepted. It is where officers are encouraged to improve themselves and where new ways of thinking about problem solving occur (Zook, 1994). In a positive working environment, supervisors tailor the supervisory techniques they use to fit the competence level of each employee. Some employees will need closer supervision than others. Some will respond to one motivational technique, whereas others will respond to a different technique.

Employees should be part of the decision-making process and should be responsible for results. This makes officers accountable and allows them the freedom to "buy in" to the situation. This results in the actual implementation of accountability (Cottringer, 1994). As an officer assumes responsibility and completes operations successfully, supervisors can increase officer responsibility. All of this leads to an improved quality of life in the workplace.

In recent years, value statements have set the tone for many organizations. Typical of these is the value statement of the Alexandria, Virginia, Police Department as it relates to the members of the organization (see Figure 12.1). Values are the basis for the beliefs and actions taken

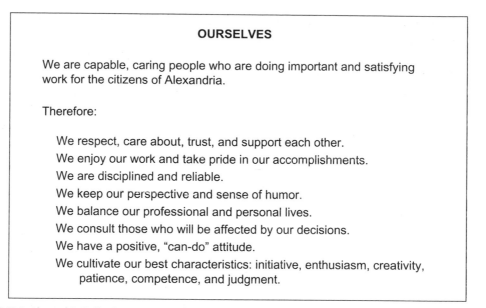

OURSELVES

We are capable, caring people who are doing important and satisfying work for the citizens of Alexandria.

Therefore:

We respect, care about, trust, and support each other.
We enjoy our work and take pride in our accomplishments.
We are disciplined and reliable.
We keep our perspective and sense of humor.
We balance our professional and personal lives.
We consult those who will be affected by our decisions.
We have a positive, "can-do" attitude.
We cultivate our best characteristics: initiative, enthusiasm, creativity, patience, competence, and judgment.

FIGURE 12.1 Alexandria Police Department values. *Source: Charles E. Samarra (1992). Alexandria Police: These Are Our Values. Alexandria, VA: Alexandria Police Department.*

by the department. The values guide the work and decisions of the department. They represent ideals and are the foundation for the policies, goals, and operations that affect employees. They are nonnegotiable and are never ignored for the sake of expediency or personal preference. Such values constantly remind supervisors and managers of the factors that contribute to a positive work environment (Samarra, 1992).

Employees as Individuals

Unfortunately, there are many "rocks in the roadway" that impede progress as change occurs. One of these is the problem employee. Dealing with problem employees occurs more often than most supervisors would like. We do not live in a perfect world, and employees are not perfect. Everyone is not equal, as is clearly evident in our society and the workplace. Some employees are more productive than others. Some are more analytical than others. Some have special skills that others do not have, such as writing, verbal, or physical skills. Others are more effective working with young people or with older people. Some officers function most effectively on undercover assignments, whereas others would never be selected for such a task.

Each officer is a distinct person with a personality, needs, and a personally unique lifestyle. A supervisor is also an individual with experiences, needs, and drives that may or may not be similar to those he or she supervises (Harvey, 2001). This presents a real challenge, especially if the value systems conflict. The police field is in a state of flux, and diversity is increasingly common in the workplace. As the work environment has undergone change, the role of the first-line supervisor has become increasingly important. The supervisor must develop or be knowledgeable about the skills of his or her subordinates and provide a supportive climate in which the common purposes of the organization become achievable (Kouzes & Posner, 2011). This presents the supervisor with a dilemma. When an employee becomes difficult to work with, tasks are not accomplished, or work is done with indifference, a supervisor must take corrective action. In some situations, unsuitable behavior can impair the effectiveness of the officer, whereas in other cases, unacceptable behavior can affect other organization members negatively. Inappropriate behavior can occur at any stage of an officer's employment, ranging from newly appointed individuals to those who are nearing retirement.

Types of Employees

One expert found three types of individuals in organizations: ascendant, indifferent, and ambivalent. The number of employees in each group varies from agency to agency, and this grouping of employees seems to be what supervisors actually find in an organization (Leonard & More, 2000). We acknowledge that it is not easy to categorize employees because of our limited knowledge of why people behave the way they do. Human beings are very complex, and individuals can and do change, depending on needs, aspirations, attitudes, and beliefs. With a change in departmental policies, some officers have shifted from one class to another. In other instances, officers who are either ascendant or ambivalent have "burned out" because of excessive stress. These generalized groupings can be used by the supervisor for viewing employee conduct that is similar to other employees. Also, the supervisor must deal with employees on an individual basis (Steinmetz & Todd, 1992). Figure 12.2 lists the attitudes that each of these groups has toward work.

Ascendant

Compared to the other two groups, there are few ascendant officers within an organization. In fact, if a supervisor had to manage a squad of ascendants, in all likelihood, it would prove disastrous for both the supervisor and the officers. The ascendant is a workaholic, an "organizational person," or someone on the "fast track." This group of employees is work oriented and perceives the job as being uppermost in life (More, Wegener, Vito, & Walsh, 2005). They are success driven and exhibit a high energy level. They focus on their assignment, as well as the needs of the department, and are self-starters. Recognition and promotion are the name of the game, and everything else is secondary. Ascendants believe in themselves and know that they can produce. They especially accept the challenge of the unknown and relish working on difficult assignments. They are loners and believe they are the only ones who can accomplish tasks quickly and effectively.

Ascendants are usually intolerant of others who fail to work rapidly and effectively. They usually take the position that if something is to be done, they would rather do it themselves. Goal orientation dominates their work style, and they ardently support the values and mission of the department. Ascendants actively seek advancement and do everything possible to

Ascendant
>   High achievement orientation
>   Identifies with the department
>   Strong work orientation
>   Works effectively under pressure
>   Receptive to feedback from superiors
>   Accepts rules and regulations readily
>   Can overcome failure by hard work

Indifferent
>   Works at a minimal level
>   Resists motivational efforts
>   Does not seek promotion
>   Gravitates toward off-the-job satisfaction
>   Reluctant to accept change
>   Identifies with the work group and police union
>   Will not seek added responsibilities

Ambivalent
>   Does not like to make decisions
>   Seeks approval and recognition
>   Superior work performer if tasks are challenging
>   Often creative and intelligent
>   Most likely to challenge departmental policies
>   Receptive to change
>   Tends to rise to a supervisory position

FIGURE 12.2 Officer attitudes toward work.

make themselves eligible for promotion. Whenever possible, they volunteer for special assignments, attend as many training programs as possible, and vigorously pursue advanced academic degrees. Their allegiance is usually to the profession rather than the department, and they actively pursue openings in other agencies. Others with similar views attract them, and they use information obtained from others to enhance their own position.

Supervisors usually work well with ascendants. This is because, unless they become excessively exuberant, they require little supervision. Because they are achievers, supervisors turn to them when time constraints are such that immediate completion of a project is essential. This is done with the full knowledge that the task will be accomplished swiftly and correctly. Ascendants accept and follow departmental rules readily and require limited supervision. This allows supervisors to spend more time with subordinates in the other groups (Steinmetz & Todd, 1992).

Indifferent

Some police departments have more indifferents than they would like to have, but most agencies usually have to deal with few such officers. They perform their duties at what they perceive is an acceptable level, which proves to be minimal. It does not take them long to determine what is an acceptable performance level, and they never exceed that level. Yet they make sure they never do so little that discipline, reprimand, or termination might occur. Their primary motivation is to earn enough money so they can concentrate on their family or nondepartmental activities. Indifferents have a strong affiliative drive and get along with almost everyone (Steinmetz & Greenridge, 1976). The department becomes just a place of work for this type of employee. Such an individual never volunteers or seeks promotion. The desirable operating mode is maintaining existing conditions—change is definitely undesirable. If change is personally inimical, the indifferent seeks protection from the work group or the union. This type of individual strengthens informal work groups and views peers as a primary support element. He or she will socialize with other officers and is prone to violate departmental rules. Even though policy might prohibit officers from leaving their beat, indifferents will leave the beat and join other officers at restaurants. When the union wants cooperation from officers during negotiations, these are the officers who will respond. They will enforce the letter of the law or engage in a slowdown. Then, for some reason, they will get the "blue flu" when appropriate.

When working with this group, supervisors find that motivational efforts have a short life span and that close supervision is the only way to ensure completion of tasks within a reasonable time. Indifferents, by their performance, require the supervisor to document their activities constantly. This is done to ensure compliance with departmental policy and their functioning at an acceptable work level. They are really "good old boys," but they can be a headache for a supervisor. These individuals just slide by, seldom make waves, and escape by daydreaming. They function at such a borderline level that discipline can occur only after an extensive paper trail. One needs to expend an exceptional amount of effort documenting an unacceptable performance level. Officers in this group have decided the pace at which they will work even if that work level is less than acceptable. Even at a slow pace, these employees accomplish a considerable amount of work (Steinmetz & Todd, 1992).

Ambivalent

Most officers in a police organization are ambivalent. They are often imaginative and intelligent. They spend a considerable amount of time becoming knowledgeable about critical areas, such as the use of deadly force, narcotics, and dangerous drugs. They also concentrate on such areas as surveillance, crime prevention, juvenile delinquency, and problem solving. Upon mastering a technique or procedure, they search for more interesting work. To the ambivalent, the routine task quickly becomes boring and is usually put off. Procrastination becomes the order of the day.

If the frustration level becomes excessive, these officers will become anxious about their work and become less decisive. As a result, poorer decisions will be made. Resistance to new rules is quite common and becomes a typical behavior pattern. Additionally, ambivalent officers will, over time, become less committed to the department. If work is dull and routine, this type of employee will become less productive. Many employees in this group do not aspire to higher ranks because of a general distrust of management. In fact, many officers in this group become antagonistic toward high levels of management. If appropriate, they will actively oppose policy changes that they perceive as detrimental (Leonard & More, 2000).

A challenging assignment is what this type of individual needs if performance is to remain high. The supervisor must spend considerable time finding new assignments, identifying new responsibilities, and recognizing solvable problems to motivate and challenge these employees. Similar to the ascendants, ambivalents respond to praise and commendation for work done well. They participate in professional development programs readily, and supervisors can recommend them for training as a motivational technique. They covet promotions at least to the level of first-line supervisor or promotion within rank. Sergeants can use this desire to increase their involvement, improve work habits, and change behavior (Steinmetz & Todd, 1992).

Supervisory expectations are critical to subordinate performance. No matter what group an employee might fall into, it is essential for the supervisor to express and act in such a way that every employee knows the acceptable level of job performance. High expectations are an essential ingredient of positive performance. The reason for this is that research supports the motivational aspects of the Pygmalion effect. Most employees in an organization perform as they are expected to perform. If a supervisor conveys to an officer that a task will probably not be completed up to standards, there is every reason to believe that the employee will respond accordingly. If one expects poor performance, that will be the result. If one expresses high expectations, the results are more likely to be positive (Steinmetz & Todd, 1992). A supervisor should never conduct himself or herself in such a way that negative expectations are part of the message received by those supervised.

As a supervisor, you will have to deal with a wide range of employee behavior. Like most supervisors, you will do your best to deal with officers fairly and competently when assessing their behavior. A simple way to rate yourself is to identify the most troublesome employee supervised. It should be someone you feel a little uncomfortable with and someone to whom you have difficulty giving negative feedback. List the beliefs, attitudes, and behavior of that individual that cause you difficulty. The goal is to describe what it is about the employee that distinguishes him or her from others. Next, create a second list that describes the employee with whom you are most comfortable. List that officer's behavior, characteristics, attitudes, and beliefs (Holton & Holton, 1992).

Compare the descriptions, and you will find that if you are like most supervisors, you are much more similar to the officer with whom you are comfortable. All of us are more comfortable around people who have similar beliefs, attitudes, and behaviors (Mann, 1993). You will judge those who are different from you more severely. You might want to use this information to rate how you deal with those you supervise.

Problem Employees

Supervisors spend a considerable amount of time dealing with conflict created by officers. These officers behave in a way that is unacceptable to the organization. One study pointed out that approximately 70 percent of behavior problems involve the organization itself, the immediate supervisor, and the employee (Orthmann & Hess, 2012). In many instances, the conflict affects performance negatively. When managing personnel, you must consider a minimum of three variables: the supervisor, the officer, and the officer's performance. Too often, one of these variables is no longer part of the equation.

The failure to perform effectively is conditioned by other variables. Each feature must be given careful consideration as modified by the situation. Performance problems require a supervisor to analyze the situation carefully and spend the time necessary to resolve the problem (Kottler, 1994).

Problem behavior seldom evolves from a personality conflict between a supervisor and an officer. Most often it is the result of the failure of one of the involved parties to accept tenets, behaviors, and views other than their own (Steinmetz & Todd, 1992). Whatever the cause of conflict, the supervisor must deal with conduct that is inimical to the organization. If unacceptable behavior occurs, the supervisor must respond. If ignored, it can negatively affect other employees as well as the organization itself (Jones, 1999; Mahoney, 1986; Orthmann & Hess, 2012). Problem employees can usually be placed in one of the following categories: erudites, tyrants, defeatists, manipulators, or indecisives. These categories are not mutually exclusive and provide the supervisor with a typology that can be useful when dealing with conflict (see Figure 12.3).

Erudites

Erudites have an opinion on just about everything. This is especially true if they have just completed a college course or a specialized training program. Officers in this group are seldom at a loss for words and pride themselves on their command of language. The more loquacious they can be, the better they like it. They see themselves as intellectuals, learned, and in a class by themselves. Their tolerance level is somewhat low, and acceptance of others usually comes with reluctance. This is especially true when there is a difference of opinion. They respect order and work comfortably within departmental regulations. These officers use their expertise as a power base for influencing decisions.

Supervisors can deal with this type of employee by using their own expertise, especially when facing the unknown or engaging in complex problem solving. The supervisor should

Erudites
Tyrants
Defeatists
Manipulators
Indecisives

FIGURE 12.3 Problem employees.

assimilate the knowledge of erudites in such a way that others do not take offense. The erudite should never be allowed to take over the leadership position. As a supervisor, you should acknowledge their contributions with appropriate praise.

Tyrants

Tyrants are control oriented and do not respect others. These officers respond explosively and do everything possible to intimidate anyone who stands in their way. If someone resists their ideas, the reaction of the tyrant is immediate. Denunciations and even personal attacks are used to maintain their position. Domination of the situation is the goal, and open warfare is the game. This type of officer wants to win and will not hesitate to use coercion or create a climate of fear. They also will use threats to get their way. Their technique of choice is that of overwhelming the opposition. They follow the principle of always attacking to keep those they oppose off balance. This behavior allows them to gain control over others.

Supervisors must deal with this type of behavior by responding at the same level. The supervisor should maintain control and rebuff aggressive behavior. It requires an authoritarian response, and the supervisor must convert a lose–lose situation to one that is win–lose. Rejection of aggressive behavior is essential, and supervisors should use every tool at their disposal. Confrontation may be necessary, and it should be done privately and as often as needed.

Defeatists

Defeatists are those who resist every new idea. Change is something of which to be skeptical, and enjoyment is only found in performing a cynical role. These officers never say anything good about anyone or anything. They are chronic "bitchers." They never have solutions, feel comfortable being disrupters, and are rigid (CareerTrack, 1995). The name of the game is that no one wins; everyone is a loser. Defeatists complain about administrators, politicians, citizens, the Supreme Court, and prosecuting attorneys. New policies are rejected out of hand, and new programs are viewed as worthless.

The way to deal with this type of employee is to confront him or her about an issue by asking for specifics, not generalities. Make the employee explain his or her position. Ask penetrating questions and address the core of the issue. When rules are in dispute, review a copy of the document and discuss it in depth. Everything possible should be done to clarify the situation and deal with the specific problem. It is not the supervisor's place to try to change the personality of the defeatist.

Manipulators

There are a few officers who fall into this group. Manipulators are fundamentally unethical and have no difficulty doing anything necessary to gain an advantage. Half-truths and innuendo are acceptable and part of the arsenal used to maintain or enhance their position. Knowledge is power, and manipulators gather and impart information that will lead to an advantageous position. They enjoy dividing and conquering and, when possible, play one person against another, or officers against managers. Manipulators are masters of deceit, and they strive to create conflict and an atmosphere in which they win and others lose (Jones, 1999). Supervisors must investigate every action taken by a manipulator and then provide feedback to reduce or neutralize the impact of this type of officer. The supervisor must learn to pass judgment based on facts and refute the manipulator objectively.

Indecisives

Indecisives are impervious to praise and punishment. Officers in this group will work diligently to avoid making a decision and are experts at procrastination. Their position is to delay until tomorrow what can be done today. They hide their attitudes and beliefs. They suppress their feelings and remain as neutral as possible. This makes it very difficult for the supervisor to judge their response. One never knows whether they support or disapprove of a decision. By never expressing support or rejection of anything, they become experts at neutrality. If indecisives do not respond negatively or positively, they are protected from others who pass judgment.

Supervisors must try to determine why the indecisive is stonewalling. What is the real reason he or she refuses to make a decision? One must listen carefully and then ask specific questions directed toward clarification and illumination. Ask indecisive officers to simplify their response and do not allow them to use platitudes, vagueness, or a nondefinitive posture. The supervisor should respond with specificity and decisiveness to every dubious answer.

The Marginal Performer

When officers perform marginally, they become a problem for a supervisor and can consume an inordinate amount of supervisory time. A minimally performing officer does just enough to get by, with the intent of avoiding reprimand or discipline. The marginal performer knows all of the work norms and consistently performs just below the acceptable level. Report writing takes longer than expected, fewer traffic citations are issued, and field interviews may be conducted, but with reduced frequency. Coffee and meal breaks are either taken more frequently or the time of each break is extended. In some instances, marginal performers accept the challenge of finding ways to barely get by. These officers take the position that there is no reason they should work any harder than necessary. Just getting by seems to be a badge of honor.

Some marginal performers are habitually late and absent themselves from duty as much as possible. They believe sick leave is a right, not a privilege (McNaught & Schofield, 1998). They never volunteer for any assignment and, if selected, beg off. Their general demeanor is such that they always look busy and highly involved, but this is not the case. Their complacency extends to every aspect of the job, and their primary interests are external to the department. Their overall behavior is passive, and they have a short-term perspective.

The marginal performer readily accepts a subordinate position and strives to never "rock the boat." Promotions are of little consequence. Opposition to change is part of an overall resistance format. They point out that there is nothing wrong with the way the organization is currently doing things. If the proposed change is important enough, they will vigorously oppose the change, but this is usually done through the informal structure of the department.

Beyond the problems generated by their supervisor, the police organization is seen as the real culprit. Top brass are viewed as being out of step with reality. Hiding behind their desks, marginal performers see policy makers performing in a vacuum. Blaming management for their problems is a means by which marginal employees excuse themselves from personal responsibility. They believe that if the supervisor and the "brass" are sources of the problem, there is little they can do to correct the situation.

Marginal employees seldom have clearly defined short- or long-range goals, and if this is true, the supervisor should sit down with the employee and formally set goals. A plan should be agreed upon that will help the employee achieve his or her goals. The supervisor should ensure that goals are compatible with departmental mission and value statements. If there is a question of formal authority, the supervisor should review what makes up the mutual working relationship. All employees must understand their status and place within the organization. The supervisor's task is to place responsibility where it belongs. Job descriptions should be reevaluated, and the supervisor should review the tasks that are the employee's responsibility (Brown, 1992).

The supervisor should praise marginal employees when they have performed effectively and should keep in mind the need for giving feedback as soon as possible after completion of a task or assignment. The supervisor should express confidence in the employee and voice the need for the employee to maintain acceptable performance standards and a positive attitude. The employee should be told about promotional opportunities and encouraged to attend special training programs as a means of improving his or her performance. The officer should be made aware of the importance of volunteering for new assignments. It is hoped that all of these will increase the officer's potential for promotion.

The supervisor should strive to deal with the employee on a positive level, displaying enthusiasm and a positive attitude. The employee should have every opportunity to improve performance and become a viable member of the organization. When performance exceeds recognized standards, the officer should be given better assignments. He or she should be supported for promotion and, at the very least, praised for a job well done. If the employee fails to follow performance standards, this should be documented and corrective action should be taken. See Chapter 11 for a discussion of internal discipline.

Millennial Generation

A study of 655 high school juniors in Fairfax County, Virginia, was conducted in 1999 by two generational researchers, Neil Howe & William Strauss (2000). They labeled this group of rising seniors as "the millennial generation." The millennials are those born between the years 1982 and 2002 and make up much of the younger, new-generation police officers. According to Henchey (2005), parents of millennial children were most often overly supportive and protective of them, with more permissiveness and a less structured social environment than that which previously existed in American society. Millennial children were taught in educational institutions that stressed trying rather than succeeding. In this "no one loses" environment, millennial children often developed high levels of self-esteem, a need for immediate gratification, and an entitlement mentality. Many of these millennial children did not enter the military and had no experience with military structure and supervision. Those that entered the police profession either had to adapt to the paramilitary structure of the organization or leave. In addition, turnover tends to be high with millennial-generation police officers. This is due in part to the relationship they have with their immediate supervisor (Sullivan, 2004). This is not to say that the millennial generation does not produce good police officers; it just indicates they have a different perspective of employment than older generations of police officers. Since they are most likely being supervised by an older-generation officer, the older supervisor may use a traditional supervision style that does not fare well with the younger officer.

Sullivan (2004) recommends that police supervisors of millennial-generation officers would be more effective if they made working conditions more attractive. The goal of supervision should be to provide opportunities for advancement, specialized training, exciting work assignments, and experience. This type of supervision may decrease the rate of turnover and prepare the millennial officer to move up the ranks.

Work Stressors

Organizational stress can have an effect not only on the organization, but also on the individual. From an organizational viewpoint, supervisors can see productivity slip and morale decline. They can also see delayed task completion, increased use of sick leave, and other signs of employee discontent. Figure 12.4 lists a number of personal and organizational effects of work stressors. For the individual, stress can result in numerous problems, ranging from alcohol abuse to suicide.

The police culture and work environment have a definite impact on police officers, and this interaction can result in an acute interruption of psychological or behavioral homeostasis. These reactions or disruptions, if prolonged, are believed to lead to a variety of illnesses. The most commonly researched job stress-related illnesses are hypertension, heart disease, alcoholism, and mental illness. Additionally, unrelieved stress can cause chronic headaches, sleep disorders, and gastric ulcers (Rajaratnam et al., 2011). Job stress can lead to severe depression, alcohol or other drug abuse, aggression, marital problems, and suicide. Other stressors that are endemic to police work include boredom, danger, shift work, lack of public support, unfavorable court decisions, unfair administrative policies, and poor supervision (More et al., 2005).

Everyone is affected by stress to one degree or another; in some instances it is positive, whereas in others it is negative. Of concern to the supervisor are the negative consequences of stress, which can affect officers' alertness, physical stamina, and their ability to work effectively (Goolkasian, Geddes, & DeJong, 1985). Stress can also lead to excessive absenteeism, disability, or early retirement; thus, stress can be costly to an organization. For example, in one state, courts have ruled that heart disease is occupationally related.

Personal

Alcohol abuse	Anxiety
Drug abuse	Psychosomatic diseases
Emotional instability	Eating disorders
Lack of self-control	Boredom
Fatigue	Mental illness
Marital problems	Suicide
Depression	Health breakdowns
Insomnia	Irresponsibility
Insecurity	Violence
Frustration	

Organizational

Accidents	Unpreparedness
Reduced productivity	Lack of creativity
High turnover	Increased sick leave
Increased errors	Premature retirement
Absenteeism	Job dissatisfaction
Damage and waste	Poor decision-making
Antagonistic group action	

FIGURE 12.4 Personal and organizational effects of work stress. *Source: Adapted from Lawrence R. Murphy & Theodore F. Schoenborn (eds.) (1987).* Stress Management in Work Settings. *Washington, DC: U.S. Government Printing Office.*

Task Stressors

Task stressors are wide ranging and include role conflict and ambiguity, control of work, use of excessive force, danger, boredom, and shift work. All of these complicate not only the officer's personal life, but also the officer's organizational life.

Danger. The possibility of an officer being seriously injured or killed when on duty is somewhat remote, but these events do occur. Unfortunately, attacks on police officers are happening with increasing frequency. When emergency calls come over the radio, the officer usually responds and energy is mobilized to deal with the contingency. In 2012, 47 officers were feloniously killed in the line of duty in the United States. Situations in which these killings occurred were disturbance calls, arrest situations (i.e., robberies and burglaries in progress), drug-related arrests, and attempting other arrests. It also included investigating suspicious persons/circumstances, ambush situations, traffic pursuits/stops, and mentally deranged individuals. Additionally, 45 officers were accidentally killed in the line of duty—the majority in automobile accidents. During 2011, 54,774 officers were assaulted and 26.6 percent of these were injured (U.S. Department of Justice, 2013). In recent years, soft body armor has been worn by more and more police officers, and it has saved numerous lives. Over a 20-year period ending in 1992, 1440 officers were "saved" from assaults and accidents. Of these, the top three circumstances were traffic pursuits/stops, investigating suspicious persons, and drug-related matters (Geller & Scott, 1992).

Boredom. One major stressor that is unique to the operational role of law enforcement is boredom. Patrolling a beat in a low-crime area can be less than challenging. Time can pass very slowly during the wee hours of the morning with little to do. Dealing with the same drunk time after time presents little challenge. The same applies to those who are mentally ill or live on the street. When enforcing traffic laws, officers soon find that in a short time they have heard every excuse possible for failure to comply with the law. However, an emergency can arise in which an officer must shift gears and respond to stressful and traumatic events. Confronting an armed suspect, entering a dark building, viewing the victim of a drive-by shooting, and comforting an abused child are all emotionally traumatizing events that can take their toll (Phillips & Schwartz, 1992).

Role Conflict and Ambiguity. These two factors are significant sources of stress for law enforcement personnel and the police organization. This is especially true with the move toward community policing and the emphasis on resolving community problems. How does this new approach balance out against the more traditional crime-control role? Which is more important, responding to calls for service or working with a neighborhood to reduce narcotics trafficking? These competing demands can result in role pressures that cause conflict. The greater the conflict, the greater the potential for the creation of negative stress.

Role ambiguity occurs when there is a lack of clarity about the way tasks should be carried out. This is especially true when managers create policies that leave line personnel hanging out to dry. This happens, for example, when a new policy is written so broadly that it makes interpretation difficult, such as a use-of-force policy in which the phrase "use force necessary and appropriate for the situation" is used. Without amplification, such a statement is open to conflicting interpretations (More et al., 2005).

Ambiguity includes lack of clarity about objectives associated with the work role, expectations concerning the work role, and the scope and responsibilities of the job (Murphy & Schoenborn, 1987). Employees who experience role ambiguity and conflict often have low self-confidence, higher job-related tension, and lower job satisfaction.

Control over Work. Evidence suggests that the amount of work is not as critical to the health of a worker as the worker's control over the pace of work and related work processes. In departments engaging in community policing, it is anticipated that the officer will have more control over the tasks he or she has to perform. Thus, it is hoped that there will be a reduction in stressors. One study found that workers with a heavy workload and low control have an increased risk of heart disease and high blood pressure, and smoke more than employees in jobs without these characteristics.

Shift Work. An additional job demand that affects the health of workers is shift work. Evidence shows that night shifts and rotating shifts can lead to gastrointestinal disorders, emotional disturbances, and an increased risk of on-the-job injury. A disruption of biological rhythms results in biochemical and physiological disturbances. The shift worker becomes sleep deprived for two reasons: (1) sleeping during the day conflicts with the biological clock, which says it is daytime, and (2) numerous interruptions occurring during a normal day

(Mahowald, 1994). The average day-shift worker gets eight hours more sleep weekly than the typical night-shift worker. Cumulative sleep deprivation causes the night-shift worker to be sleepier while on the job.

In a study of scheduling shift changes, the researcher recommended that shifts be changed in a clockwise direction. It was also suggested that officers spend three weeks on each shift and limit their work time to either a four- or five-day week. When comparing officers working under the new system to officers who worked under the old system, it was determined that:

1. The frequency of poor sleep decreased fourfold.
2. There was a decline of 25 percent in incidents of falling asleep on the night shift.
3. Officers had 40 percent fewer on-duty automobile accidents per mile compared to the previous two years.
4. When officers experienced sleep deprivation, they used alcohol and sleeping pills less often (*Law Enforcement News*, 1989).

Shift work causes officers to have impaired judgment, insight, and reasoning; as a consequence, it can create supervisory problems (Mahowald, 1994). Shift work is an essential ingredient of police work, and the supervisor should strive to create a work environment that provides for optimal functioning.

Use of Excessive Force. Civilian deaths caused by police in the United States average approximately 375 per year. The number of felons killed by police in justifiable homicides in 2010 was 387 (U.S. Department of Justice, 2013). Accurate data on the actual number of justifiable and unjustifiable killings of civilians by police simply do not exist. Official reports submitted to the FBI and information collected by coroners and medical examiners on death certificates may not reflect the true nature of the deaths.

Actually, police shootings are infrequent, and only one officer in 60 has killed someone during a 15-year period (Fyfe, 1982). In a study of the Los Angeles Police Department, it was determined that a significant number of officers repeatedly misused force and persistently ignored written policies. An assistant chief of the department pointed out that the department had failed miserably to hold supervisors accountable when officers under their command used excessive force (Independent Commission on the Los Angeles Police Department, 1991).

Officers who have been involved in excessive force situations can have severe legal, physical, and emotional problems (Neubauer, 1999). In one study, respondents to a survey indicated that involvement in a shooting incident was the most dangerous and traumatic experience that an officer could face during a career. Postshooting traumatic responses include a wide range of stressful reactions; these are listed in Figure 12.5.

Without question, an officer involved in a shooting is seldom prepared to cope with such a traumatic event, and the same is true of the officer's family, fellow officers, and supervisors. The supervisor should ensure that an officer involved in a shooting is referred to available employee assistance programs. In one survey, it was found that 79 percent of police psychologists counseled officers charged with excessive force (Scrivner, 1994).

1. Guilt
2. Anxiety
3. Fear
4. Nightmares
5. Flashbacks
6. Social withdrawal
7. Impaired memory
8. Inability to sleep
9. Sensory distortion
10. Grasping for life
11. Crying
12. A heightened sense of danger
13. Sorrow over depriving a person of life
14. Family problems
15. Alcohol abuse
16. Fear of being fired, criminally charged, or sued

FIGURE 12.5 Postshooting traumatic responses. *Source: Adapted from Harold E. Russell & Allan Biegel (1990).* Understanding Human Behavior for Effective Police Work, *Third Edition. New York: Basic Books; Roger M. Solomon & James M. Horn (1986). "Post-Shooting Traumatic Reactions: A Pilot Study." In James T. Reese and Harvey A. Goldstein (eds.),* Psychological Services for Law Enforcement. *Washington, DC: Federal Bureau of Investigation; and Bill Clede (1994). "Stress, Insidious or Traumatic, Is Treatable."* Law and Order, *Vol. 42, No. 6.*

Personal Problems

Information can come to the attention of the supervisor that could possibly require his or her intervention. In some instances, the supervisor intervenes directly, whereas in other cases an officer asks for help. Of all management levels, the close contact the supervisor has with line personnel will usually result in his or her becoming aware of inadequate or deteriorating work performance before other managers. In some situations, the supervisor can function as a counselor, whereas in others the officer can be referred to the appropriate employee assistance program. Symptoms of stress can lead to a wide variety of maladies; those that have been studied and found important to law enforcement officers are discussed next.

Suicide

Studies conducted from the 1930s through the 1960s concluded that police officers had a high suicide rate. These studies included officers from such diverse police departments as San Francisco, Chicago, and New York. In a Wyoming study, it was determined that the suicide rate for officers was the second highest among occupational groups studied. In Tennessee, a report published in 1975 found that police officers had the third highest suicide rate among occupational groups. In a study of Chicago police officers, it was found that 60 percent of the suicides were linked to alcoholism (Wagner & Brzeczek, 1983).

From 1950 to 1967, the suicide rate of officers in the New York City Police Department averaged 22 per 100,000 annually (Friedman, 1967), and in 1994 there were 29 per 100,000 (*Law Enforcement News*, 1994b). This contrasts with the general population rate of 12.2 per 100,000. In 1998 the suicide rate in the United States was 11.31 per 100,000 (U.S. Department of Justice, 2013).

Given the high numbers of police suicides, many police departments began peer support counseling and professional mental health programs in the mid-to late-1990s. Apparently, these programs may have helped. The Badge of Life (BOL) is an organization of active and retired police officers, medical professionals, and surviving families of suicides dedicated to helping bring support to police suffering from post-traumatic stress disorder (PTSD) and depression. The BOL conducted studies of police suicides in 2008, 2009, and 2012. According to their findings, police officers commit suicides at a rate of 18 per 100,000 compared to 12 per 100,000 for the United States population, 1.5 times more frequently (Clark & O'Hara, 2013). The rate of police suicides has dropped slightly, about 12 percent, in 2012 compared to the previous three years. According to the BOL, the demographic characteristics of an officer most at risk of committing suicide includes: 40–44 years of age, unmarried, male, with an average of 16 years on the job (Clark & O'Hara, 2013). There is no single reason for the suicide of police officers, but depression seems to be the most frequently cited. It is happening with such frequency that supervisors should not overlook the possibility of such an occurrence.

Alcohol Abuse

Studies by the federal government point out that one in 10 adults in the United States has a drinking problem. Nationally, 64 percent of the adult population drinks alcoholic beverages (U.S. Department of Justice, 2013). In 1992, the adult population consumed 37.4 gallons of alcohol per capita. A 1990 study showed that among people 26 years of age and older, 5.51 percent had five or more drinks in a single day during the two weeks before the study (Statistical Abstract of the United States, 1994). Additionally, in 1989 there were 374,437 adults in alcohol treatment programs. It has also been estimated that 200,000 individuals die annually of alcohol-related diseases (Autry, 1994). One estimate puts the number of alcoholics at 10 million, including individuals from every occupation and age level. Many use alcohol as their drug of choice to reduce discomfort and provide a degree of pleasure. It has been suggested that stress may be involved in the decision to use alcohol (Violanti, Marshall, & Howe, 1985). Whatever the reason for the consumption of alcohol, it can become a serious supervisory problem.

Alcohol as a drug of choice is extolled in advertisements suggesting that it leads to happiness and enjoyment. Based on advertising, one can hardly imagine having a party without alcoholic refreshments (Campbell & Graham, 1988). Police officers in many agencies find a subculture that supports heavy drinking (Farmer, 1990). Within the police field, the practice of "hoisting a few" is common and has become known as "choir practice." When officers drink to deal with problems, it can lead to a wide range of job behaviors.

Alcoholics Anonymous (1998) has defined alcoholism as follows:

Whether or not you are an alcoholic is not determined by where you drink, when you started drinking, how long you have been drinking...what, or even how much. The true test is the answer to this question: What has alcohol done to you? If it has affected your relationships; if it has influenced the way you schedule your days; if it has affected your health...if you are in any way preoccupied with alcohol—then the likelihood is that you have a problem.

As far back as 1955, the Chicago Police Department organized officers to help other officers with drinking problems. Another early program was the police stress program of the Boston Police Department. It initially focused on police officers with drinking problems and, in later years, expanded to include a wide range of stress-related difficulties (Goolkasian et al., 1985). Today, it is quite common to find departments that have their own counseling program for alcoholics or refer officers to other agencies or organizations (Alpert & Dunham, 1997). Treatment has proven to be effective as indicated by a program in the Philadelphia Police Department. Officers had a 38 percent reduction in sick days and a 62 percent annual reduction in injury days (Campbell & Graham, 1988).

Divorce

The incidence of divorce has increased considerably over the years. In 1970 the divorce rate was 4.3 million in the United States, which has increased to more than 17 million in 1996 (Statistical Abstract of the United States, 2000). Whatever the divorce rate, most observers agree that police work is especially demanding on the officer's personal life. Officers can become very involved in their work and often bring their problems home. Consequently, police work tends to become a 24-hour-a-day involvement that can strain the best of relationships. Shift changes are especially difficult for family members. It seems to some police officers that they are on a constant shift merry-go-round in which they hardly get accustomed to a shift and it is time to change. It interrupts the social life of the officer and his or her spouse. In many instances, officers socialize only with other officers and their spouses.

Early research reflected a high divorce rate. In three communities, the percentage of divorced officers ranged from 17 to 33.3 percent. This was in contrast to a 1983 study, which showed a divorce rate of 5 percent in the Los Angeles Police Department. Training programs for spouses describing the nature and problems of police work, support groups, and counseling have all contributed to stronger police families (Alpert & Dunham, 1997).

Spousal Concerns About Danger

Spouses are also in the position of being constantly concerned about the physical well-being of officers. Our society can be violent and police work can be a violent occupation. In 2011 there were 54,774 assaults on law enforcement officers, with 26.6 percent of those involving officer injury (U.S. Department of Justice, 2013). If other officers in the department are injured or killed, the spouse reacts by becoming increasingly concerned about his or her loved one. Peer counseling, spouse support groups, and police psychologists have been especially effective in dealing with this problem.

Early Warning Systems

The early warning system has been instituted in several departments as a means of monitoring officer conduct and alerting managers to inappropriate behavior. The development of these programs is still in its infancy. There is a clear-cut impetus and need for developing a system that deals with certain traits or behavior patterns. This system usually uses information based on the behaviors of officers who have been fired for disciplinary reasons and then identifies officers who have been recognized as having similar problems.

Using computer software, the department tracks and records incidents as they occur. It is a nondisciplinary management system and "flags" officers at risk. Behavioral activities are used to establish a pattern, even though a single activity may, in and of itself, prove to be of limited consequence. When combined with other activities, the early warning system may indicate a behavioral pattern that needs to be reviewed by management (Guthrie, 1996; Oliver, 1994). It allows managers to intervene before the occurrence of serious misconduct that could result in officers being arrested, fired, or sued (*Law Enforcement News*, 1994a).

Factors considered relevant vary considerably. One set of factors used to assess an officer's propensity to misuse force is listed in Figure 12.6. In Chicago, information used to identify behavior problems included such variables as race, sex, age, education, marital status, and frequency of sick days. It also includes traffic accidents and lost weapons or badges. This list of characteristics was derived from the analysis of information about 200 terminated officers (*Law Enforcement News*, 1994b). Of the police officers who were fired, a majority of the problems identified extended over a number of years. Treated as isolated incidents, they were not serious enough to warrant disciplinary action (Ehrenhalt, 1994).

---

1. Complaints
2. Discipline records
3. Commendations and evaluations
4. Assignments, including partners and supervisors
5. Rate of disorderly conduct charges filed against arrestees
6. Rate of charges against arrestees for resisting or assaulting the officer
7. Shooting incidents
8. Incidents resulting in injury

FIGURE 12.6 Factors used to assess an officer's propensity to misuse force. *Source: William A. Geller & Michael Scott (1992).* Deadly Force: What We Know. *Washington, DC: Police Executive Research Forum.*

Another list of elements, prepared by Will Oliver (1994), includes:

1. Loss of equipment
2. Vehicular accidents
3. Injured-on-duty reports
4. Discharge of firearms
   a. Accidental
   b. Duty related
5. Use of excessive force reports
6. Sick leave in excess of five days
7. A pattern of taking one or two days of sick leave over a long period
8. Complaints
9. Reprimands
10. Disciplinary action
11. Pursuits
12. Resisting-arrest reports
13. Performance reports
14. Financial difficulties
15. Frequent transfers

The early warning system should be monitored by supervisors or higher ranking management personnel. Those conducting such a review should remember that the process at this point is nondisciplinary. Database information should be analyzed in an attempt to discover the source of a problem. The goal is to intervene and prevent behavior from becoming a disciplinary problem. This is done by tailoring a response to the identified behavior. The response can include:

1. Counseling
2. Training
3. Referral to departmental resources, such as an employee assistance program
4. Psychological examination
5. Physical examination
6. Urinalysis (Oliver, 1994)

The response is predicated on a discussion with the officer during which the problem(s) is identified and treatment strategies are determined. The desire is to move the officer back into the departmental "mainstream." It is nondisciplinary, and the officer has the right to refuse to participate (*Law Enforcement News*, 1994a). In one department, treatment strategies are referred to the chief for approval before the implementation of corrective action. It is essential to monitor an officer's progress on a quarterly basis to see that the treatment strategies are effective (Oliver, 1994).

Employee Assistance Programs

The majority of organizations recognize that it is very costly to keep nonproductive employees who have personal or behavioral problems on the staff. However, managers know that it

Alcohol and other drug abuse	Job stress
Anxiety	Legal problems
Career development	Marital problems
Compulsive gambling	Monetary problems
Depression	Nutrition
Disciplinary action	Police shootings
Divorce	Retirement planning
Eating disorders	Smoking
Exercise	Spouse abuse
Grief	Termination
Job burnout	Weight control

FIGURE 12.7 Problems that can be dealt with by an employee assistance program. *Source: Adapted from John G. Stratton (1987). "Employee Assistance Programs—A Profitable Approach for Employees and Organizations." In Harry W. More and Peter C. Unsinger (eds.),* Police Managerial Use of Psychology and Psychologists. *Springfield, IL: Charles C. Thomas; and James M. Jenks & Brian L.P. Zevnik (1993).* Employee Benefits: Plain and Simple. *New York: Collier Books.*

is costly to lose well-trained, experienced officers. Consequently, agencies have created programs to provide structured assistance to employees. These programs have been part of businesses for many years and, more recently, part of public administration. One part of these programs, employee counseling, has been a fixture in law enforcement for a long time. In 1990, approximately 77 percent of municipal police agencies had a policy about this activity (Reaves, 1992). During the last decade, a wide range of assistance activities have been incorporated into what are called employee assistance programs (EAPs). Comprehensive programs use in-house and external specialists when providing assistance to employees. Employees are offered the same kind of assistance that is given to those who have physical illnesses (Plunkett, 1992). Today, EAPs cover a wide range of services to help employees deal with emotional, family, psychological, financial, and retirement matters. Figure 12.7 lists some of the problems addressed by employee assistance programs.

Critical-Incident Stress Management

Extreme violence and trauma do not occur on a daily basis in the lives of a majority of police officers. When they do occur, they can leave numerous psychological scars. It is not just the taking of a life. It can be involvement in a shooting or assisting at a disaster such as an earthquake, tornado, or flood. Other incidents that can cause significant emotional responses include vehicle and airplane crashes. Continued exposure to violence can result in post-traumatic stress disorder (PTSD), a psychological condition that is caused by one's inability to successfully manage an emotional response triggered by severe trauma (Paradise, 1992).

The symptoms of PTSD generally include:

1. When exposed to places and situations resembling the initial traumatic event, the officer reexperiences the traumatic event. The officer can have nightmares, flashbacks, or hallucinations.
2. Continual avoidance of any thought about the traumatic event.
3. A sense of detachment from others, including family members.
4. Insomnia.
5. Spontaneous outbursts of anger.
6. Preoccupation with thoughts of death or dying.
7. Inability to concentrate (Phillips & Schwartz, 1992).

If any of the aforementioned symptoms persists for more than one month, an officer is probably suffering from PTSD. Because they are exposed repeatedly to critical incidents, the daily pressure of police work can take a toll on officers. These officers will have marital problems, become chronically irritable, and may abuse alcohol or other drugs. They can also suffer from depression, use excessive force, or develop ulcers (Clede, 1994). All of these can impair the officers' usefulness—not only to the agency, but to themselves.

On December 14, 2012, seven Newtown, Connecticut, police officers were the first to respond to a shooting at Sandy Hook Elementary School. What they found upon arrival were dead and dying school staff and children. In the aftermath of the shooting, officers displayed symptoms of PTSD. Eric Brown, a union lawyer representing the Newtown police, estimated that 12 to 15 officers would suffer from PTSD as a result of the massacre (Manes, 2013).

Early intervention after a critical incident or identification of an officer who is having problems similar to those listed can help eliminate the propensity for the development of full-blown symptoms of PTSD (Paradise, 1992). As soon as possible after a critical incident, officers should participate in a debriefing session. Typical of these programs is the one used by the Drug Enforcement Administration (DEA). This organization requires agents involved in a shooting to attend a briefing session within 48 hours. During this session, it is stressed that the officer is human, and although a reaction may not have occurred yet, it can occur. Information about PTSD is discussed. As trauma occurs, the DEA utilizes trauma teams composed of trained agents who provide nonclinical supportive intervention (Paradise, 1992).

Peer Counseling

One of the first programs in peer counseling was started by the Boston Police Department. Its first program was limited to officers with alcohol problems. Peer counselors have several years of "street experience" in order to enjoy the trust and respect of fellow officers. One's credibility rating is high when one has "been there." Peer counselors can truly empathize with fellow officers who are experiencing problems created by the unique demands of police work. Officers trust other police officers and, if nonpolice personnel are used, they must first demonstrate their credibility.

Officers are often reluctant to seek help or admit that they have stress-related problems they are not coping with (Shearer, 1993). Professional psychologists have been used to train police peer counselors, serve as consultants, and function as referral sources (Stratton, 1987). Peer counselors have been highly successful in dealing with such problems as alcoholism, other drug abuse, terminal illness, deaths, on-the-job injuries, and retirement. The real advantage of peer counseling is that it provides officers and their family members with an opportunity to discuss personal and professional problems confidentially (Janik, 1995). Peers are equals, readily available, and have a greater ease of interaction than professionals. Some peer counseling programs are quite well developed, as illustrated by the Fort Worth Police Department program. It has a ratio of one peer to every 60 officers, allowing for an immediate response to critical incidents, including mass casualty situations (Greenstone, Dunn, & Leviton, 1995).

Fitness-for-Duty Evaluations

When an officer's behavior calls into question his or her judgment, stability, self-control, or emotional control in performing the duties of a police officer, a fitness-for-duty evaluation (FFDE) may be appropriate (IACP, 1998). Most states require emotional and psychological stability as a requirement for entry-level police officers. However, few police agencies require routine or periodic mental evaluations after employment. If a police officer begins to experience severe depression, anxiety, or problems in judgment or emotional control, the police agency may be liable for any improper or illegal actions the officer takes. According to IACP guidelines:

1. Fitness-for-duty evaluations are highly specialized activities within the police psychology discipline and should only be conducted by qualified mental health professionals.
2. An FFDE is not a substitute for supervision or modes of discipline.
3. No FFDE should be conducted without either the officer's informed consent or a reasonable alternative.
4. The client in an FFDE is the referring agency and not the officer being evaluated (IACP, 1998).

However, fitness-for-duty evaluations should not be used unless there is strong documentation from the officer's supervisor that the officer is mentally unstable and may be a hazard to himself or herself, other officers, or the organization itself.

References

Alcoholics Anonymous (1998). *The grapevine*. New York: Alcoholics Anonymous.

Alpert, G. P., & Dunham, R. G. (1997). *Policing urban America* (3rd ed.). Prospect Heights, IL: Waveland Press, Inc.

Autry, J. A. (1994). *Life and work*. New York: William Morrow and Company, Inc.

Brown, M. F. (1992). The Sergeant's role in a modern law enforcement agency. *The Police Chief, LIX*(5).

Campbell, D., & Graham, M. (1988). *Drugs and alcohol in the workplace*. New York: Facts on File Publications.

CareerTrack, (1995). *How to overcome negativity in the workplace*. Boulder, CO: CareerTrack.

Clark, R., & O'Hara, A. (2013). 2012 Police Suicides: The NSOPS Study. In *The badge of life police mental health foundation*. Jan. 4, p. 1.

Clede, B. (1994). Stress: Insidious or traumatic, is treatable. *Law and Order, 42*(6).

Cottringer, W. (1994). Managing: Creating quality work environments. *Security Management, 38*(6).

Ehrenhalt, A. (1994). Cops, computers and the concept of character. *Governing, 91*(10).

Farmer, R. (1990). Clinical and managerial implications of stress research on the police. *Journal of Police Science and Administration, 17*(4).

Friedman, P. (1967). Suicide among police. In E. Shneidman (Ed.), *Essays in self-destruction*. New York: Human Sciences Press.

Fyfe, J. J. (1982). *Readings on use of deadly force*. Washington, DC: Police Foundation.

Geller, W. A., & Scott, M. S. (1992). *Deadly force: What we know*. Washington, DC: Police Executive Research Forum.

Goolkasian, G. A., Geddes, R. W., & DeJong, W. (1985). *Coping with police stress*. Washington, DC: National Institute of Justice.

Greenstone, J. L., Dunn, J. M., & Leviton, S. C. (1995). Fort Worth's departmental peer counseling program. *The Police Chief, LXII*(1).

Guthrie, M. (1996). Using automation to apply discipline fairly. *FBI Law Enforcement Bulletin, 65*(5).

Harvey, T. R. (2001). *Checklist for change* (2nd ed.). Lanham, MA: Scarecrow Press Inc.

Henchey, J. P. (2005). Ready or not, here they come: The millennial generation enters the workforce. *The Police Chief, 72*(9).

Holton, B., & Holton, C. (1992). *The manager's short course*. New York: John Wiley and Sons, Inc.

Howe, N., & Strauss, W. (2000). *Millennials rising: The next generation*. New York: Knopf Doubleday Publishers.

IACP, (1998). Fitness-for-duty evaluation guidelines. *The Police Chief, LXV*(10).

Independent Commission on the Los Angeles Police Department, (1991). *Report of the Independent Commission on the Los Angeles Police Department*. Los Angeles, CA: Independent Commission on the Los Angeles Police Department.

Janik, J. (1995). Who needs peer support? *The Police Chief, LXII*(1).

Jenks, J. M., & Zevnik, B. L. P. (1993). *Employee benefits: Plain and simple*. New York: Collier Books.

Jones, T. L. (1999). Confronting the problem performer. *Law Enforcement Technology, 26*(10).

Kottler, J. (1994). Beyond blame: Resolving conflict at work. *Hemispheres* (April) 4, 1. Chicago, IL: Pace Communications, Inc.

Kouzes, J. M., & Posner, B. Z. (2011). *Credibility: How leaders gain and lose it, why people demand it, revised edition*. San Francisco, CA: Jossey-Bass Publishers.

Law Enforcement News (1989). Police study in Philadelphia finds benefits in revised shifts. October 15, XV, 300.

Law Enforcement News (1994a). Artificial intelligence tackles a very real problem—Police misconduct control. September 30, XX, 408.

Law Enforcement News (1994b). NYPD officials grope for answers to record-tying binge of cop suicides. October 31, XX, 410.

Leonard, V. A., & More, H. W. (2000). *Police organization and management* (9th ed.). New York: The Foundation Press, Inc.

Mahoney, T. (1986). Problem employee or problem supervision? *Journal of California Law Enforcement, 20*(1)

Mahowald, M. W. (1994). Sleep disorders and their effect on law enforcement. *The Police Chief, LXI*(6)

Manes, H. (2013). PTSD from Sandy Hook Horrors Haunt Newtown Police Force. <www.opposingviews.com> 29.01.13.

Mann, R. (1993). *Behavioral mismatch: How to manage problem employees whose actions don't match your expectations*. New York: AMACOM.

McNaught, M., & Schofield, D. (1998). Managing sick and injured employees. *FBI Law Enforcement Bulletin, 67*(1).

More, H. W., Wegener, W. F., Vito, G. F., & Walsh, W. F. (2005). *Behavioral police management* (2nd ed.). New York: Macmillan Publishing Co.

Murphy, L. R., & Schoenborn, T. F. (Eds.). (1987). *Stress management in work settings.* Washington, DC: Department of Health and Human Services.

Neubauer, R. S. (1999). Police use of force in America: An IACP update. *The Police Chief, 9*(2).

Oliver, W. (1994). The early warning system. *Law and Order, 42*(9).

Orthmann, C. H., & Hess, K. M. (2012). *Management and supervision in law enforcement* (6th ed.). Stamford, CT: Cengage Learning.

Paradise, P. R. (1992). The DEA trauma team. *Law and Order, 39*(6).

Phillips, W., & Schwartz, G. (1992). Post-traumatic Stress. *Sheriff, 44*(2).

Plunkett, W. R. (1992). *Supervision: The direction of people at work* (6th ed.). Boston, MA: Allyn & Bacon, Inc.

Rajaratnam, S. M., Barger, L. K., Lockley, S. W., Shea, S. A., Wang, W., Landrigan, C. P., et al. (2011). Sleep disorders, health, and safety in police officers. *The Journal of the American Medical Association, 306*(23), 2567–2578.

Reaves, B. A. (1992). *Law enforcement management and administrative statistics, 1990: Data for individual state and local agencies with 100 or more officers.* Washington, DC: Bureau of Justice Statistics.

Reese, J. T., & Goldstein, H. A. (1986). *Psychological services for law enforcement.* Washington, DC: Federal Bureau of Investigation.

Russell, H. E., & Biegel, A. (1990). *Understanding human behavior for effective police work* (3rd ed.). New York: Basic Books.

Samarra, C. (1992). *Alexandria police: These are our values.* Alexandria, VA: Alexandria Police Department.

Scrivner, E. M. (1994). *Controlling police use of excessive force: The role of the police psychologist.* Washington, DC: National Institute of Justice.

Shearer, R. W. (1993). Police officer stress: New approaches for handling tension. *The Police Chief, LX*(8).

Solomon, R. M., & Horn, J. M. (1986). Post-shooting traumatic reactions: A pilot study. In T. R. James & H. A. Goldstein (Eds.), *Psychological services for law enforcement.* Washington, DC: Federal Bureau of Investigation.

Statistical Abstract of the United States, (1994). *Statistical abstract of the United States* (114th ed.). Lanham, MD: Bernard Press.

Statistical Abstract of the United States, (2000). *Statistical abstract of the United States* (120th ed.). Washington, DC: U.S. Census Bureau.

Steinmetz, L. L., & Greenridge, C. D. (1976). Realities that shape managerial style: Participative philosophy won't always work. In L. S. Lawrence & C. D. Greenridge (Eds.), *Participative management: Concepts, theory and implementation.* Atlanta, GA: Georgia State University.

Steinmetz, L. L., & Todd, H. R., Jr. (1992). Supervision: First line management (5th ed.). Homewood, IL: Richard D. Irwin, Inc.

Stratton, J. G. (1987). Employee assistance programs—A profitable approach for employees and organizations. In W. M. Harry & P. C. Unsinger (Eds.), *Police managerial use of psychology and psychologists.* Springfield, IL: Charles C Thomas, Publisher.

Sullivan, B. (2004). Police supervision in the 21st century: Can traditional work standards and the contemporary employee coexist? *The Police Chief, 71*(10).

U.S. Department of Justice, (2013). *Crime in the United States.* Washington, DC: Federal Bureau of Investigation.

Violanti, J. M., Marshall, J. R., & Howe, B. (1985). Stress, coping, and alcohol use: The police connection. *Journal of Police Science and Administration, 13*(2).

Wagner, M., & Brzeczek, R. (1983). Alcoholism and suicide: A fatal connection. *FBI Law Enforcement Bulletin, 52*(8), 8–15.

Zook, F. B. (1994). Deming's ideas to live by: Not just empty buzzwords. *Pennsylvania Business Central, 3*(9).

13

Supervising Minorities
Respecting Individual and Cultural Differences

CASE STUDY
Sergeant Dan Ridgeway

DEPARTMENT

Lakeview Police Department is a small department located in a conservative region of the southeastern United States. The police department has a good reputation in the community and there is little turnover in the 61-officer department. In fact, the youngest officer is 34 years old. Only two officers have a college education, and they hold only associate's degrees in criminal justice from an online university. The department consists of all white males even though Lakeview has an African-American population of about 7 percent and a Hispanic population of about 3 percent. While the officers do not appear to be overtly biased or prejudiced against minorities, it is common knowledge that minorities are not hired by the police department.

There are three major divisions in the department: patrol, investigation, and support. Communications services are provided by the 911 office. The patrol division is augmented by an 18-member reserve force. The reserve force does have one female officer but she is the medical examiner for the county and the appointment was honorary. There is a walking beat in the downtown area but there are no bicycle or motorcycle patrols. The department does have one canine unit, but the dog is called more for demonstration duties at schools and scout meetings than for crime control. There is one school resource officer at the local high school.

CRIME

The Uniform Crime Report for Lakeview indicates that the city had 1688 Part 1 offenses reported this year. This was a 2.5 percent decrease from the previous year and more than a 19 percent decrease over the last five years. Last year, one homicide was reported, a domestic case in which a wife shot her abusive husband. Last year there were also three rapes reported, 23 robberies, and 61 assaults. Property crimes led with the highest number of crimes reported—261 residential burglaries, 89 commercial burglaries, 1010 larcenies, two motor vehicle thefts (joyriding), and one arson.

Recently, the city authorized the use of photo-enforced traffic devices on two stretches of well-traveled highways near the industrial complex. The speed and traffic cameras were met with some complaints from the community but provided enough revenue to significantly reduce city property taxes. Once city property owners saw the financial benefit, the complaints died down.

COMMUNITY

Lakeview is a quiet community of 62,000 people in a rural setting. The main industry is the auto manufacturing plant that assembles small trucks for a Japanese company. There is also a bookbinding plant and a glass plant. The surrounding area is composed mainly of farmland and woodlands. The favorite pastime of many residents is to go deer hunting in the fall season and fishing the rest of the time. There is a large freshwater lake bordering the city. Many of the city's more affluent population have homes on the lake.

The city has one residential area that is made up of mostly African-Americans. The Ridgedale community has always been recognized as the "black" part of town, and residents there rarely venture out to acquire homes in other areas of the city. After all, this is a conservative, old southern town. Other than the small Hispanic population, there are few other minorities in the city. Most are white Protestants who have grown up in the city and tend to remain there. About once a year, the city gets several transient migrant workers of Hispanic ethnicity coming into town. When the nearby strawberry farm needs to have produce gathered, they hire the migrant workers on a temporary basis. The younger residents either leave the area after graduating from high school or stay to work in one of the local industries.

OFFICER

Sergeant Dan Ridgeway is 46 years old. He has been with the Lakeview Police Department since he turned 21. Prior to his appointment with the police department, Dan worked as a shoe salesman at one of the downtown stores after graduating from high school. The chief hired Dan not because he would make a good cop but because of his high school football record. Dan was a star football player in high school and the community loved him. It took Dan several years to show that he could be a good cop and he was promoted to sergeant and shift supervisor 15 years ago when he was only 36. He is still the youngest sergeant on the force.

PROBLEM

Recently, the Lakeview Police Department was awarded enough money to hire two new police officers. This was a direct result of the income produced from the photo-enforced traffic devices. One requirement of the city council was an aggressive recruiting effort for minorities. Lakeview has always had an equal employment opportunity policy but no qualified minorities had ever applied. However, William Jackson, a former football player for the local high school, applied for one of the positions and passed the exams with exceptionally high scores. Jackson went to the state university on a football scholarship and obtained a bachelor's degree in criminal justice. Jackson will be assigned to Sergeant Ridgeway's shift after graduating from the police academy. The second applicant hired was Alina Martinez, a young Hispanic female. Alina had just graduated from the same university that Jackson did, but she had majored in political science. Alina speaks Spanish fluently and will be an asset in dealing with the Hispanic population in Lakeview. Alina will also be assigned to Sergeant Ridgeway's shift.

Sergeant Ridgeway is apprehensive about Jackson's and Martinez's employment. They have two strikes against them even before they report to duty. First, they will be the most educated officers on the force; second, they are minorities. Sergeant Ridgeway has already heard many snide remarks among the officers about the new "tokens" on the force. Sergeant Ridgeway is determined to try to make the transition for the two recruits as smooth as possible and to head off any attempts by his subordinates not to accept them on the force.

Sergeant Ridgeway researched all the materials he could find regarding discrimination, hiring practices, state and federal laws governing employment of minorities, and so on. He then held a shift meeting with his subordinates and advised them of the material he had researched and that he fully endorsed Jackson and Martinez. He went on to state that any officer not treating Jackson and Martinez in a professional manner would be disciplined severely.

WHAT WOULD YOU DO?

If you were Sergeant Ridgeway, do you think you used the right tactic in getting the officers to accept Jackson and Martinez? What other method would you use, if any, and why? Do you think Jackson and Martinez should have been at the meeting? Why or why not?

Coming to Grips with the Past

Until fairly recently, police work could easily have been described as a bastion for politically conservative white males. Police sergeants supervised other white men, like themselves, who came primarily from the working class. The typical police officer was a high school graduate with some military experience who had worked in blue-collar or lower level, white-collar occupations before joining the police department. Most of these men were attracted to police work for its job security and masculine camaraderie. In many areas of the country, a succession of ethnic groups (such as the Irish, Italians, and Jews) controlled police departments and used them as stepping stones to higher socioeconomic status.

Applicants who met the minimum qualifications were allowed to take a civil service examination, demonstrate their physical prowess in an agility test, and spar with inquisitors on an oral board examination. If the applicant passed a background investigation, his final score was calculated and placed in its proper order on the certified list of candidates. Candidates with the highest score were evaluated by the chief of police (based on the "rule of three"), and an appointment was made. Appointment as a probationary patrol officer offered young men a career with job security, prestige, a chance to exercise authority, and a bit of glamor. It represented a rite of passage and an induction into the "old boy network."

Newly sworn rookie police officers were issued a uniform, a badge, a service revolver, and other symbols of their new status. They were normally given a few words of advice, such as "Use your common sense," or "When you're in doubt, ask!" and put to work with little or no formal training. In most departments, police academy training (if there was any) came later. Rookie police officers learned on the job from the old-timers, who served as their mentors. The new men internalized the norms and values of their teachers. They learned quickly that in order to get ahead in the bureaucratic world, they had to play smart politics and "work the system." If they learned well enough, promotions came along at fairly regular intervals (Broderick, 1987).

Police ranks were filled by men recruited not necessarily because of their ability or potential, but because of their ability to fit into the police mold. They were hired to maintain the status quo, not to rock the boat. Rookie police officers were taught that criminals, liberals, civil rights activists, and feminists were all part of a diabolical conspiracy to undermine law and order. Cynicism and a unique occupational paranoia became part of the police culture. Perplexed and disillusioned by rapid sociopolitical change, all but the most resilient retreated to the security of "the womb" (the police subculture) that the late William H. Parker called the "shell of Minorityism" (Turner, 1968). The police considered themselves to be outsiders who functioned as instruments of civil society and resented it when that role was challenged as racist.

Police work has changed during the past 40 years, and so has the composition of the workforce. Sergeants are now called on to supervise more minority, female, and other nontraditional police employees. In order to do the job properly, they must respect the individual and cultural differences of their subordinates. The same holds true for nontraditional employees who are going to be hired and promoted in far greater numbers in the future.

Women have been disadvantaged and discriminated against based on the cultural myth that police work is "men's work." The opposition to blacks, Hispanics, and other racial minorities is simply the result of bigotry. The police establishment has always resisted the assimilation of these nontraditional employees because it would mean sharing the power associated with the police function. This problem is exacerbated by the mentality of some white males. They have a deep-seated belief that they have a calling and are ordained to control the police profession (Holden, 1993). Their lock on power is self-evident.

In only a few major cities in the United States does the percentage of nonwhites in blue approximate the proportion of nonwhites in the overall community. National surveys reveal that the percentage of African-American and Hispanic officers, previously reported to be about 50 percent in some of America's 50 largest cities, has been increasing steadily and that there has been a significant increase in minority police officers hired in a number of metropolitan areas (Katz, 2013). As political power begins to shift toward minorities in some of the nation's cities, we can anticipate even more emphasis on African-American and Hispanic employment.

However, even the selection of African-American or Hispanic mayors may not precipitate radical changes in the composition of police departments. Political power is a crucial factor. In many large cities, the police are able to muster the political power needed to protect their turf from encroachment by those considered "outsiders," even if those outsiders are elected officials (Cole, Gertz, & Bunger, 2003).

The importance of attracting women and minority officers cannot be overestimated. It is not the question of providing them with economically desirable government jobs that is important. Effective policing is the issue. It is very difficult for minorities who feel discriminated against to view law enforcement as being responsive to their needs, unbiased, and generally interested in justice if they do not see members of their group represented on the department's roster. According to Cole et al. (2003), the ethnic character of American society makes it absolutely essential that participants in the administration of criminal justice reflect the ethnic character of the whole community.

Discrimination based on race and sex has been and continues to be a persistent human relations problem in our pluralistic society. It was, in fact, institutionalized by law (de jure) and through customary interpersonal relationships (de facto) until the mid-1960s. Propelled by deep-seated prejudices, discrimination permeated virtually every facet of American life. White Anglo-Saxon Protestant (WASP) values set the moral tone and ensured that almost all substantive political power remained in the hands of white males. Municipal police departments (as instruments of the white political establishment) were composed of white males whose major function was to "protect and serve" the white community while preserving the status quo. The constitutional guarantees of due process and equal protection of law contained in the Bill of Rights and the antislavery amendments took a back seat to reality. The Constitution became little more than an abstract statement of human values unrelated to the treatment of racial minorities and women.

According to Johns (2000), "prejudgment" is normal human behavior. People make all sorts of judgments based on previously acquired knowledge and experience to bring some order into their lives. The mind assimilates as much as it can and then arranges the information in categories by which it prejudges a person or event. This saves time and effort. Such a mechanism, however, at times tends to produce irrational categories. This is where prejudice, stereotyping, and discrimination come in. These terms can be defined as follows:

1. **Prejudice** is a negative attitude toward a particular group considered different and inferior. The opinion is based partially on observation and partially on ignorance, ethnocentrism, and xenophobia. These erroneous generalizations are applied to all members of the group, regardless of individual differences.
2. **Stereotypes** are standardized mental images held by members of one group regarding the characteristics or traits of another group. A stereotype is a set of group-shared and generally negative attitudes based on tradition, limited interaction, or ignorance, which assigns similar undesirable attributes to all members of the "out" group.
3. **Discrimination** refers to the negative and unfavorable treatment of people based on their membership in a minority group. Discriminatory practices involve an act or omission that puts one person at a disadvantage in order to satisfy some prejudice.

Prejudice, stereotyping, and discrimination against minority groups are normally by-products of uncontrolled ethnocentrism or xenophobia. A minority group is one that has subordinate status and is the object of discrimination. Ethnocentrism is the natural tendency of human beings to view their own culture and customs as right and superior and to judge all others by those standards (Zastrow, 2000). Xenophobia, however, refers to the irrational fear or hatred of strangers and other foreigners. Minorities, especially racial minorities, are often viewed as strangers in their own land.

Prodded into action by racial unrest, social activism, antisegregation rulings (such as *Brown v. Board of Education*), Kennedy's "Camelot," and the Johnson administration's desire to create a discrimination-free "Great Society," Congress reassessed its stand on the need for civil rights legislation to protect blacks and other minorities. One of the most important anti-discrimination bills in American history was enacted into law in 1964. The Civil Rights Act of 1964 prohibited discrimination based on national origin, ethnic group, sex, creed, age, or race. According to Title VII of the Act (42 United States Code A4 2000e-2[a][1]):

> *It shall be an unlawful employment practice for an employer (1) to fail or refuse to hire, or discharge any individual or otherwise to discriminate against any individual with respect to his compensation, terms, conditions, or privileges of employment, because of such individual's race, color, religion, sex, or national origin; (2) to limit, segregate, or classify his employees or applicants for employment in any way which would deprive or tend to deprive any individual of employment opportunity or otherwise adversely affect his status as an employee because of such individual's race, color, religion, sex, or national origin.*

Title VII prohibits employers and unions from discriminating against their employees in the following areas:

1. Hiring Employees
2. Compensating Employees
3. Terms of Employment
4. Conditions of Employment
5. Privileges of Employment
6. Classifying Personnel
7. Assigning Personnel
8. Promoting Personnel
9. Disciplining Personnel
10. Demoting Employees
11. Providing Facilities
12. Assigning Facilities
13. Training Employees
14. Retraining Employees
15. Providing Apprenticeships

In an abrupt departure from past practices, Congress issued a call for justice and equality in the workplace. The Civil Rights Act of 1964 was a major battle in the revolution of rising expectations (Leonard, 2013).

Under the authority of Title VII as amended in 1966, the Equal Employment Opportunity Commission (EEOC) was created as a regulatory agency. It was authorized to set standards and establish guidelines for compliance with the requirements of the Civil Rights Act. The commission issued a set of comprehensive guidelines on employee selection procedures in 1970.

In 1972, Congress extended the coverage of Title VII to include all state and local government operations with more than 15 employees. The amendment, known as the Equal Employment Opportunity Act of 1972, gave the EEOC more authority to formulate policies, procedures, rules, and regulations designed to ensure compliance with the law. Many of the complaints filed with the EEOC and cases that ended up in court arose from personnel practices involving the employment or supervision of police officers and firefighters (Thibault, Lynch, & McBride, 2010). These complaints and court cases ushered in a new era of affirmative action.

While the number of women and other minorities employed in state and local government increased, there really was no dramatic shift in the makeup of the public service. White males got most of the jobs and held on to them by virtue of their civil service status or seniority. In addition, nontraditional employees were not (for a variety of reasons) being promoted into the higher ranks as rapidly as had been originally anticipated. As a result, the EEOC adopted a proactive affirmative action strategy. Affirmative action required employers to take positive steps to overcome "present and past discrimination" in an effort to achieve equal employment opportunity. The affirmative action guidelines adopted by the commission were designed to promote activism without creating the type of "reverse discrimination" prohibited by the Civil Rights Act. Section 703(j) provides:

Nothing contained in this title shall be interpreted to require any employer…subject to this title to grant preferential treatment to any individual or to any group because of the race, color, religion, sex, or national origin of such individuals or group on account of an imbalance which may exist, with respect to the total number or percentage of persons of any race, color, religion, sex, or national origin employed by any employer…in comparison with the total number or percentage of persons of any race, color, religion, sex, or national origin in any community, state, section, or other area, or in the available workforce in any community, state, section, or other area.

Affirmative action stressed the need for "goals," "timetables," and "actions" designed to deal with discrimination. The process involved four basic steps:

1. An analysis of all major job categories to ascertain whether women and other minorities were being underutilized.
2. Development of goals, timetables, and affirmative actions designed to correct identifiable deficiencies.

3. Maintenance of a comprehensive database for use in determining whether the goals were being accomplished.
4. Continuous assessment of utilization patterns to prevent the reintroduction of discriminatory practices.

Although goals, timetables, and actions were (under appropriate circumstances) a proper means for implementing equal employment opportunity, the concept of "quotas" and "preferential treatment" based on race, color, national origin, and sex were contrary to the law. In fact, the federal government issued the following policy statement:

Under a system of goals, therefore, an employer is never required to hire a person who does not have the qualifications needed to perform the job successfully; and an employer is never required to hire such an unqualified person in preference to another applicant who is qualified; nor is an employer required to hire a less qualified person in preference to a better qualified person, provided that the qualifications used to make such relative judgment realistically measure the person's ability to do the job in question, or other jobs to which he is likely to progress. The terms "less qualified" and "better qualified" as used in this memorandum are not intended to distinguish among persons who are substantially equally qualified in terms of being able to perform the job successfully. Unlike quotas, therefore, which may call for a preference for the unqualified over the qualified, or for the less qualified over the better qualified to meet the numerical requirements, a goal recognizes that persons are to be judged on individual ability, and therefore is consistent with the principle of merit hiring. (Equal Employment Opportunity Coordinating Council, 1973)

Some courts held that a statistical imbalance between minorities represented in the police department and to those residing in the community constituted prima facie evidence of discrimination and imposed quotas. In Alabama, for example, the court ordered the state Department of Public Safety to hire one African-American trooper for each white trooper hired until 25 percent of all troopers were African-American (*NAACP v. Allen*, 1972). The central thrust became to gauge equal employment opportunity not by the methods used, but solely by the results achieved in the organization's workforce (Stahl, 1983).

Most police departments used some type of written examination and a physical agility test to screen prospective personnel. The written examinations often had a built-in cultural bias that discriminated against racial minorities (Sauls, 1995). Physical agility tests, however, almost always discriminated against women (Sass & Troyer, 1999). In order to ensure that protected classes (African-Americans, women, and other nontraditional employees) were not tested out of equal employment opportunity, the Supreme Court ruled that screening devices such as those just discussed had to be valid, reliable, job related, and based on bona fide occupational qualifications (*Richmond v. Croson Co.*, 1989). These terms are best defined in the following manner:

1. **Validity** simply means that the test measures what it is supposed to measure.
2. **Reliability** is the consistency with which any test yields accurate measurements.

3. **Job relatedness** means that the knowledge or skill being measured by the screening device is directly related to the actual job to be performed.
4. **Bona fide occupational qualification** is an attribute or skill that is actually required in order to do a particular job.

In 1971, the U.S. Supreme Court held in *Griggs v. Duke Power Company* that standardized testing requirements prevented a disproportionate number of African-American employees from being hired. The company's requirement that employees have a high school diploma and pass aptitude tests did not measure an employee's ability to learn or perform a particular job or category of jobs within the company. The court concluded that the subtle, illegal purpose of these requirements was to safeguard Duke Power's longstanding policy of giving job preferences to white employees. The *Griggs* decision set a standard protecting prospective employees from arbitrary and discriminatory screening. Police personnel administrators took the *Griggs* decision seriously and immediately began to modify their testing procedures. A great deal of time and energy was invested to make sure that examinations were job related, valid, reliable, and nondiscriminatory. A number of standardized entry-level and promotional tests were developed and are currently being marketed by groups such as the International City Management Association and the International Association of Chiefs of Police (IACP).

In the time since the *Griggs* decision, employers and courts have attempted to define and evaluate a wide range of employment and promotional practices. Certain factors have emerged as keys to assessing the legality of employment and promotional practices that create disparity. According to Sauls (1995), these factors include:

1. The degree of disparity created by use of the standard.
2. The demonstrated factual relationship between achieving the employment standard and successful performance of the job in question.
3. Whether achievement of the employment standard is determined by a "neutral" entity external to the employer.
4. Whether the employment standard focuses on innate, unalterable characteristics of candidates.
5. Whether the job in question has a direct impact on public safety.
6. The availability of effective alternative standards that create a lesser disparity.

Some police departments have moved away from using a comprehensive written test and now use the "assessment center" method to select personnel for entry-level positions or promotions. An assessment center is a multiple assessment strategy that involves using various techniques (job-related simulations, structured interviews, psychological evaluations, etc.) to screen candidates. "Behavioral samples" are obtained and submitted to a standardized evaluation based on multiple inputs by trained observers. Judgments are pooled by the observers at an evaluation meeting during which all relevant assessment data are reported and discussed. A final assessment is drafted, and a recommendation is submitted to the hiring authority (Swanson, Territo, & Taylor, 2012). Assessment centers have proven to be far less discriminatory than many other pre-employment screening procedures.

While the assessment center approach is certainly superior to the standardized test, it is a fairly sophisticated process and requires a great deal of skill. It also costs more. Consequently, many medium-sized and small police departments are simply not able to make the switch.

There is no doubt that Equal Employment Opportunity and Affirmative Action (EEO/AA) were designed to deal with and remediate a very serious problem. The ideal of social justice was corrupted, however, when affirmative action goals became quotas and the noble end began to justify unscrupulous means in the hands of relatively unsophisticated police administrators. While EEO/AA opened the door for more African-Americans, women, and other nontraditional employees, they also created deep wounds that have yet to heal. Many white police officers believe (rightly or wrongly) that they were victimized by reverse discrimination. They harbor a great deal of resentment and hide their true feelings. White police officers cheered when the Supreme Court ruled in the *Bakke* case (1978) that it was wrong for employers to use quotas designed to accommodate African-Americans and women in such a manner as to withhold gainful employment from eligible white males. The recent de-emphasis of EEO/AA has reduced anxiety somewhat, and there is an uneasy truce between white male police officers and new nontraditional police officers.

Police sergeants find themselves in a very difficult spot. Regardless of their ethnicity, race, or sex, they must work with and help bridge the gap between the white male majority and various minority groups within the police department. It is a job that has been added to and yet transcends their other duties. If they perform this human relations function well, there will be a cooperative effort to accomplish the department's mission, goals, and objectives. Failure, however, could serve to reignite the virulent racism and sexism of the past.

The Changing Face of America

It is estimated that there are 300.2 million people in the United States. A little more than one-half of them are females. While the overwhelming majority of all Americans are white, 13 percent are African-American and another 12.5 percent are Hispanic. Growing three times faster than the United States total, Hispanics may account for one-quarter of the nation's growth over the next 20 years. The Census Bureau indicates a nearly doubling of the Hispanic population since the last census in 1990 (U.S. Census Bureau, 2003). Even without immigration (legal or illegal) for the next 100 years, the Hispanic population will increase at twice the national rate. Asian and Native Americans round out the picture and contribute to the ethnic diversity of modern American society.

It is clear that minorities and women remain underrepresented in virtually all specialties and at all ranks in law enforcement, despite the aggressive EEO/AA programs of the past (see Figures 13.1, 13.2, and 13.3). In 1975, only 6.5 percent of all police officers were African-American, even though African-Americans represented 11 percent of the total population. While females constituted a little more than one-half of the population, somewhere between 2 and 4 percent of the sworn officers were women (Katz, 2013). The situation did not change much over the next two decades. While the number of female police officers has increased dramatically over the past 10 years, they still only comprise approximately 11 percent of all sworn police personnel. African-Americans now constitute approximately 12 percent of all sworn police personnel, and Hispanics account for about 10 percent of sworn police personnel (U.S. Department of Justice, 2010).

Gender of full-time sworn personnel in local police departments, by size of population served, 2007

Population served	Percent of full-time sworn personnel	
	Male	Female
All sizes	88.1%	11.9%
1,000,000 or more	82.1,%	17.9%
500,000–999,999	84.5	15.5
250,000–499,999	85.7	14.3
100,000–249,999	87.2	12.8
50,000–99,999	90.6	9.4
25,000–49,999	91.8	8.2
10,000–24,999	92.1	7.9
2,500–9,999	92.5	7.5
Under 2,500	94.4	5.6

FIGURE 13.1 Gender of full-time sworn personnel in local police departments, by size of population served, 2007. *Source: U.S. Department of Justice, Bureau of Justice Statistics,* Local Police Departments 2007. *Washington, DC: U.S. Department of Justice, 2010, p. 14, Table 10.*

Every precaution must be taken to protect the gains that African-Americans, Hispanics, women, and other nontraditional employees have made in the past and to ensure equal employment opportunity for everyone in the future. With the assistance of supervisory personnel, police managers should work diligently to comply with the expectations of the Commission on Accreditation for Law Enforcement Agencies (CALEA, 2006). According to CALEA Standard 31:

The recruitment standards of the law enforcement accreditation process have embraced several important philosophical concepts in this chapter. The first concept is the expectation that an accredited agency will be an equal opportunity employer. EEO understands equal opportunity as the removal of barriers that prevent people from being treated fairly for employment purposes.

The second concept is the expectation that the agency's sworn workforce will be representative of the available workforce in the agency's service community relative to its ethnic and gender composition. If any group is underrepresented, the recruitment plan will include proactive steps to encourage members of that group to seek employment opportunities.

Under the accreditation program, the recruitment plan does not mandate hard quotas, such as hiring one female for every two males hired, nor is an agency expected to lower legitimate job-related hiring standards or criteria. Agencies are never expected to hire an individual who is not qualified to perform the duties of the job involved.

Full-time Law Enforcement Employees
by Population Group
Percent Male and Female, 2011

Population group	Total law enforcement employees	Percent law enforcement employees		Total officers	Percent officers		Total Civilians	Percent civilians		Number of agencies	2011 estimated population
		Male	Female		Male	Female		Male	Female		
TOTAL AGENCIES:	**1,001,984**	**73.4**	**26.6**	**698,460**	**88.2**	**11.8**	**303,524**	**39.2**	**60.8**	**14,633**	**293,058,940**
TOTAL CITIES	**568,786**	**75.7**	**24.3**	**442,931**	**88.1**	**11.9**	**125,855**	**31.8**	**68.2**	**11,234**	**197,246,457**
GROUP I (250,000 and over)	199,012	72.0	28.0	153,550	83.4	16.6	45,462	33.8	66.2	75	56,398,148
1,000,000 and over (Group I subset)	107,522	70.6	29.4	81,805	82.0	18.0	25,717	34.1	65.9	10	25,247,146
500,000 to 999,999 (Group I subset)	54,212	74.8	25.2	42,633	84.9	15.1	11,579	37.3	62.7	25	17,298,847
250,000 to 499,999 (Group I subset)	37,278	72.4	27.6	29,112	84.9	15.1	8,166	27.8	72.2	40	13,852,155
GROUP II (100,000 to 249,999)	67,506	73.4	26.6	51,553	88.0	12.0	15,953	26.2	73.8	196	29,447,050
GROUP III (50,000 to 99,999)	63,556	76.5	23.5	49,229	90.4	9.6	14,327	28.6	71.4	428	29,634,590
GROUP IV (25,000 to 49,999)	62,758	78.1	21.9	49,876	91.2	8.8	12,882	27.2	72.8	828	28,652,012
GROUP V (10,000 to 24,999)	67,544	79.6	20.4	54,462	92.3	7.7	13,082	26.8	73.2	1,834	29,005,261
GROUP VI (under 10,000)	108,410	79.4	20.6	84,261	91.1	8.9	24,149	38.7	61.3	7,873	24,109,396
METROPOLITAN COUNTIES	300,568	69.5	30.5	177,406	86.4	13.6	123,162	45.2	54.8	1,285	68,238,191
NONMETROPOLITAN COUNTIES	132,630	72.1	27.9	78,123	92.7	7.3	54,507	42.6	57.4	2,114	27,574,292
SUBURBAN AREAS[1]	465,194	72.9	27.1	306,562	88.4	11.6	158,632	43.0	57.0	7,630	125,240,573

[1] Suburban areas include law enforcement agencies in cities with less than 50,000 inhabitants and county law enforcement agencies that are within a Metropolitan Statistical Area (see Data Declaration). Suburban areas exclude all metropolitan agencies associated with a principal city. The agencies associated with suburban areas also appear in other groups within this table.

FIGURE 13.2 Full-time law enforcement employees by population group, percent male and female, 2011. *Source: U.S. Department of Justice, Federal Bureau of Investigation (2011). Crime in the United States. Washington, DC: U.S. Government Printing Office, Table 74.*

Race and ethnicity of full-time sworn personnel in local police departments, by size of population served, 2007

	Percent of full-time sworn personnel who are—					
Population served	White	Black/ African American	Hispanic/ Latino	Asian/Pacific Islander	American Indian/ Alaska Native	Multi-race
All sizes	74.7%	11.9%	10.3%	2.0%	0.7%	0.3%
1,000,000 or more	56.0%	17.6%	22.9%	3.2%	0.3%	0.0%
500,000–999,999	60.6	24.1	9.3	4.1	0.4	1.6
250,000–499,999	69.5	16.5	11.2	2.0	0.6	0.1
100,000–249,999	73.7	13.4	9.1	2.6	0.9	0.3
50,000–99,999	83.6	7.0	7.5	1.4	0.3	0.3
25,000–49,999	88.2	5.0	5.1	0.9	0.6	0.2
10,000–24,999	87.5	5.6	5.1	0.6	1.0	0.2
2,500–9,999	87.9	5.1	4.4	0.6	1.8	0.1
Under 2,500	88.3	5.8	3.0	0.1	2.3	0.5

FIGURE 13.3 Race and ethnicity of full-time sworn personnel in local police departments, by size of population served, 2007. *Source: U.S. Department of Justice, Bureau of Justice Statistics,* Local Police Departments 2007. *Washington, DC: U.S. Department of Justice, 2010, p. 14, Table 9.*

The employment of African-Americans, women, and other nontraditional employees (Hispanics, Native Americans, older workers, college graduates, etc.) should be a recruitment goal, not a quota governing the hiring of police personnel. The composition of the community should serve as a guide for recruitment policy, not discriminatory affirmative action. According to Leonard & More (2000), primary consideration should be given to employing the best qualified candidates available, regardless of ethnicity or sex. While members of minority groups and women have been and continue to be underrepresented in virtually all aspects of modern police work, we should not lose sight of the fact that a great deal of progress has already been made. Police personnel administrators have intensified their efforts to recruit, train, and retrain qualified human resources from all segments of the community (Swank & Conser, 1983). As a result, the number of nontraditional employees in the workforce has increased appreciably. This is especially true of agencies seeking accreditation through CALEA. As CALEA (2006) Standard 31.2 stipulates:

The agency has ethnic and gender composition in the sworn law enforcement ranks in approximate proportion to the makeup of the available workforce in the law enforcement agency's service community, or a recruitment plan pursuant to standard 31.2.2. Recruitment steps should be directed toward the goal of approximating within the sworn ranks the demographic composition of the community that it serves. Statistics on the composition of the workforce in the agency's service community are available from a variety of sources, including the U.S. Department of Labor's Bureau of Labor Statistics. For the purposes of this standard, the agency may also expand its recruitment efforts beyond the immediate service community.

Progressive police administrators are committed to ensuring equal employment opportunity. They favor an aggressive, proactive approach to recruitment. Their recruiters use a variety of innovative techniques to target specific ethnic and racial groups in a genuine effort to increase the number of nontraditional applicants and enrich the pool of qualified candidates.

Recruitment is a multidimensional process designed to encourage people to seek careers in police work and to select individuals who are qualified to do the job. Researchers note that successful recruitment programs exhibit similar characteristics:

1. An internal commitment to equal employment opportunity.
2. A strong, well-managed minority recruitment component.
3. Utilization of minority police officers in recruitment.
4. Targeted recruitment of especially promising applicants.
5. Screening based on valid, reliable, and fair procedures.
6. Appointment contingent on qualifications, not politics.
7. Promotion based on interest and on-the-job performance (Swanson et al., 2012).

Police recruit classes today are far different from those of the past. Based on pressure from minorities, changes in the law, and our national commitment to social equality, the composition of the workforce is slowly but surely being transformed into a mirror image of the community at large.

Supervising Minorities

With an increased emphasis on recruiting, hiring, and nurturing nontraditional employees, first-line supervisors are more likely than ever to have supervisory responsibility for African-Americans, Hispanics, and women. These employees, like all other employees, expect to be given a chance to succeed. They want to carry their own weight and be appreciated for their potential contribution to the police department. Women and other minorities do not want to be patronized. They want and need to be respected as human beings. Due to the debilitating effects of past discrimination, they may need extra care, training, and coaching to help them adjust to their new environment. This is where the knowledge and human skills of first-line supervisors come into play.

The supervisor, according to Lawrence A. Johnson (1969), is a "major key" to the minority worker's success or failure. A supervisor who wishes to change the status quo and improve human relations within the workplace must be prepared not only to avoid discrimination, but also to actively help everyone overcome it. The bottom line is very clear. It is the supervisor's primary responsibility to create and maintain an environment in which all employees are able to satisfy some of their needs while working cooperatively with others to accomplish the mission, goals, and objectives of the department.

White male sergeants must begin to understand that many of their nontraditional employees have been conditioned to expect the worst. African-Americans, Hispanics, and women assume they will face varying degrees of and be forced to deal with:

- prejudice
- discrimination

- resentment
- rejection
- hostility
- isolation
- scapegoating

They may use selective perception to confirm these suspicions. Women and other minorities are often very sensitive to incidents, actions, or events that nonminority workers brush aside. They are considered insults or personal attacks. In a longitudinal study of African-American police officers in the Washington, DC Metropolitan Police Department, more than 65 percent reported that they trusted few or no white officers. These data were drawn from 947 (90 percent) of the African-American police officers in the District. Nearly 84 percent of the respondents were patrol officers, and 80 percent believed that African-Americans were discriminated against in hiring, job assignments, enforcement of rules and regulations, and job performance ratings (Thibault et al., 2010). Until all subordinates believe they are being treated as valued persons, there will always be a measure of discontent. It is hoped that as more minority police officers achieve rank in management positions within the department, discontent will fade (see Figure 13.4).

Unfortunately, there will always be a few police officers who, regardless of their ethnic background or sex, will try to take advantage of their supervisors. Some will be looking for special privileges. They may use their sex or minority status to gain favored treatment. This ploy, while understandable, must be prevented. The supervisor's success in working with other employees will be undercut if favoritism and privilege are allowed to flourish. Impartiality and fairness are absolutely essential in effective supervision.

The National Center for Women in Policing honored Assistant Commissioner for Field Operations Bonni Tischler, while Assistant Commissioner for Investigations, with its Lifetime Achievement Award at its annual March conference in Baltimore, Maryland. The award is given to female law enforcement officers with exceptional service and career achievement who have helped other women in law enforcement as mentors and role models.

"It was a very exciting moment, and I was extremely pleased," says Tischler, who has been in law enforcement for almost 29 years. "I thought that it was a real compliment, not only to me, but to all the women who are in law enforcement in the federal sector."

The trail-blazing Tischler, one of the very top women in federal law enforcement, will be similarly honored at the annual Women in Federal Law Enforcement conference in July, in Washington, D.C.

Breaking the glass . . .
In 1971, when President Nixon signed the executive order granting women equal status in the federal law enforcement community, it was necessary

---

FIGURE 13.4 Bonni Tischler earns top cop award. *Source: U.S. Customs Today, Vol. 36, No. 6 (June 2000).*

for a few pioneering women to open the doors and eventually break the glass ceiling. Tischler helped do that.

When "women in federal law enforcement" was very nearly an oxymoron, Tischler became a Customs Sky Marshal, eventually joining the ranks of Customs Special Agents in 1977.

As a special agent, she pioneered an oversight function, which would act as a clearinghouse for various problems facing women in the federal law enforcement community.

As Tischler sees it, the job of law enforcement demands an enormous sense of humor: "You must be able to laugh at your mistakes while learning an intense lesson from them. You must learn to tell a good war story and make fun of yourself. You must laugh. You must employ humor if you are to succeed."

She received her first big break in 1980 when she became the only female agent assigned to the newly formed taskforce in Miami known as Operation Greenback, which became the first major federal investigation into drug money laundering.

When detailed to the Office of the Federal Women's Program at the Office of Personnel Management, she recruited other interested individuals and developed what is now known as the Women in Federal Law Enforcement Interagency Committee (WIFLE). She co-chaired the committee in 1984 and became the first recipient of the Julie Y. Cross Memorial Award in recognition of her outstanding achievements in law enforcement.

Her expertise in money laundering investigations, coupled with successful undercover assignments, landed Tischler in Washington where she became the Director of the Financial Investigations Division, which later became Smuggling Investigations when narcotics and marine interdiction were added to its duties in 1986.

In 1987, she was promoted to Special Agent in Charge of the Tampa office where she supervised agents investigating money laundering at the Bank of Credit and Commerce International (BCCI) in what was to become one of the largest money laundering cases ever prosecuted.

In 1995, Tischler returned to her home turf as Special Agent in Charge for Miami to supervise customs' biggest and most active group of 360 agents and investigative personnel. In 1997, she was summoned to Washington where she was selected to become customs' first female Assistant Commissioner for the Office of Investigations.

On June 19, 2000, Tischler was appointed Assistant Commissioner for Field Operations, effective July 1. She is the first woman to hold this post with responsibility for all cargo and passenger processing of the customs service. She will oversee approximately 13,000 customs employees at more than 300 ports of entry, customs management centers, and field laboratories.

Tischler has combined her expertise, poise, and confidence to become a highly visible and popular representative of the Customs Service both in the media and on Capitol Hill where she regularly testifies on behalf of the agency.

FIGURE 13.4 (Continued)

Effective supervision always begins with an awareness of the individual and cultural differences among employees. These differences affect performance and must be accepted as fact (Longenecker & Pringle, 1984). Knowing their subordinates and basing decisions on that knowledge helps supervisors avoid unreasonable expectations and provides a valid basis for understanding job-related behavior. Converting facts into performance-related information allows the supervisor to match the talents of the employee with the job to be done. If this approach is to be successful, supervisors must:

1. Be knowledgeable, approachable, and empathetic when dealing with subordinates.
2. Learn to listen to and really understand the minority employee's point of view.
3. Communicate openly and honestly with their subordinates in all matters pertaining to the job.
4. Expect a considerable amount of testing and probing by minorities concerning the department's philosophy on human relations and the supervisor's attitude, sincerity, and commitment regarding equal employment opportunity.
5. Practice introspection and be aware of their own possible reactions to probable situations involving on-the-job relationships with minority employees (Plunkett, 1992).

The effectiveness of supervision can almost always be measured by the empathetic quality of the relationship between a good supervisor and receptive subordinates. Empathy (the capacity to participate in and appreciate another person's feelings or ideas) provides the foundation for positive human relations.

Sergeants must make a special effort to motivate nontraditional employees. Consequently, they should analyze the situation and develop an action plan to:

1. **Make the work interesting.** Sergeants should examine each job in terms of how it could be enriched and made more challenging. There is a limit to the extent that employees will be satisfied performing repetitive or routine tasks.
2. **Relate rewards to performance.** While they may be limited by civil service regulations or collective bargaining agreements, sergeants should, whenever practical, try to relate rewards (special projects, recommendations for promotion, pay increases, etc.) to performance. The cost of failing to relate rewards to performance is high. Low performers will not be motivated to do a better job, and top performers may be motivated to do less.
3. **Provide valued rewards.** Supervisors should do their best to determine the type of rewards that are valued most by employees. The most important thing is for supervisors to know what rewards they have at their disposal and exactly what employees find most valuable.
4. **Treat employees as individuals.** As noted earlier in this chapter, different people have very different needs and want different things from their job. Individualized attention enhances self-esteem and makes the police officer feel like a valuable member of the organization. It also tends to produce more frequent and candid interaction between supervisors and minority employees.

5. **Encourage participation and cooperation.** It is natural for people to commit themselves to decisions that they help make. Unfortunately, many supervisors do little to encourage active participation. They have not learned the value of sharing power with, rather than exercising power over, their employees.

6. **Explain why the action is being taken.** Police officers are usually more supportive and tend to perform better if they know why they have been asked to do something. Blind obedience to authority is passé in complex criminal justice agencies.

7. **Provide accurate and timely feedback.** A lack of feedback generally frustrates employees and has a negative impact on performance. Providing meaningful feedback is a normal part of supervision. People do not like to be left in the dark as far as their on-the-job performance is concerned. They want to know where they stand and resent being taken for granted. In fact, a negative performance evaluation may be better than no evaluation at all (Martin, 1987).

Nontraditional employees need competent and supportive supervisors who exercise good judgment and make reasonable decisions concerning them. In order to do the job right, police sergeants need a bag of tricks filled with technical, human, administrative, and problem-solving skills.

Many municipal police departments that have actively recruited and hired nontraditional personnel did so because of federal EEO/AA initiatives, state human relations commission regulations, court rulings, voluntary consent decrees (court-supervised agreements hammered out and implemented in order to avoid future litigation), or a personal commitment to equal employment opportunity on the part of the chief police executive. Unfortunately, none of these decision-making processes does much to build mid-management or supervisory support for African-Americans, Hispanics, women, or other minorities. According to Territo & Vetter (1981), minority police officers are a very special breed. They are subjected not only to the normal stressors of police work, but also to the additional stress of skepticism and rejection by their own kind. In addition, minority police officers are not likely to be fully accepted into the police culture (which is a source of support, camaraderie, and occupational identity). A female officer is subject to other unique stressors. These include: (1) her own feeling of competence; (2) her perception of her peers' views of her competence, particularly those of male officers; (3) reluctant acceptance into the male-dominated police culture; (4) unfavorable stereotypical reactions by some citizens; and (5) sexual harassment.

Sergeants must be trained not to place a value judgment on cultural differences. These differences must be understood and respected. A disregard for individual and cultural differences erodes productivity and may even be discriminatory (Schroeder, 1996). Minority police officers may become disillusioned, resentful, bitter, and resistant to supervision. Fulmer & Franklin (1982) argue that supervisors who behave responsibly toward their subordinates know and consider them individually and personally. They cultivate sincere, honest, open, accepting, and trusting relationships designed to instill self-confidence and a desire to achieve personal satisfaction through work. Competent sergeants are firm, fair, and impartial. They possess a certain amount of charisma and the ability to focus their attention on the growth and development of their subordinates. This is particularly true in the case of minorities. The sergeant who takes this responsibility seriously may find the following guidelines helpful:

1. Consider minorities as individuals and important human beings at all times. Respect them and accept their individual and cultural differences. Know something about the "person" the police officer is when off duty.

2. Represent the interests and concerns of your employees to top management with understanding and candor. Listen carefully to minorities as individuals and members of a group. Organize and communicate what you have heard so that police managers get the same message.

3. Make every effort to interpret and explain department policy accurately to nontraditional employees. Clarity is essential to compliance. Never withhold information that they need to know. Explain why policies have been adopted and the contribution the employee will make in achieving the department's mission, goals, and objectives.

4. Be a role model for women, African-Americans, Hispanics, and others. Forthrightness and fair play are critical variables in positive relationships. Keep a sense of humor, and be prepared to laugh at yourself from time to time.

5. Reprimand minorities when necessary; remember to praise them for a job that is well done. Follow the golden rule: "praise in public and reprimand in private."

6. Let nontraditional workers know that they will be given every opportunity to develop and improve their skills and earnings. Always encourage questions and reply in a concise and straightforward manner. Share what you know with minority employees. Allow them to assist with work that may be routine but will teach them new and useful skills through active learning.

7. Evaluate performance and potential very carefully and objectively. Never permit individual personalities or prejudices to cloud objective opinions about any minority employee. Judgments must be based only on the aspects of personality that directly affect an employee's on-the-job performance.

8. Try to improve the minority worker's confidence by being considerate, firm, fair, and impartial in dealing with all employees under your supervision. Never play favorites, and never allow personality or cultural differences to cause you to abuse a subordinate.

9. Place minority workers in a job according to their skill, ability, attitude, and civil service or bargaining agreement classification. Do not break probationary minority officers in by putting them on the toughest assignment. Whenever possible, do not assign nontraditional employees to jobs for which they are overqualified. They will feel bored and unchallenged.

10. Never "pass the buck" if something goes wrong. Always assume responsibility for the actions of minority employees when appropriate. This will encourage nontraditional employees to take responsibility for themselves. The final responsibility for the operation and on-site management of a work unit cannot be shifted to others by the first-line supervisor.

11. Learn as much as possible about how your minority workers relate to their occupational role. Develop an empathetic appreciation of their individual interests, likes, and dislikes. Find out what nontraditional employees really enjoy about their job. Try to discover what frustrates them the most. Be on the lookout for small changes that might make a big difference in how minority workers view their job.

12. Always take time to give proper and adequate instructions to new nontraditional employees. Make them feel at home through proper job orientation. Be patient. Use counseling, coaching, and on-the-job training to help minority employees overcome their anxieties.

13. Always stress the importance of safety. Be mindful of the fact that all people have a need for safety and security. A lack of attention to these needs will produce poor morale and a sense of alienation. Encourage employees to share their suggestions on how to make the job safer.

14. Assume responsibility for communicating, as accurately as possible, the feelings and attitudes of all line personnel to your superiors (middle-level managers). Police managers, however, expect (and sergeants should try to build) team spirit, high morale, job satisfaction, and harmony among all police employees regardless of race, color, creed, sex, or national origin.

15. Set the moral and ethical tone for human relations within the police department with an absolute and unconditional commitment to equal employment opportunity. Anything less is an abdication of leadership and will serve to confirm the perception of a racist, sexist, and ethnocentric criminal justice system.

These are awesome responsibilities that require a great deal of sensitivity, talent, knowledge, skill, training, and courage. Sergeants are "change agents" and, as such, must take risks in order to do their job. Unfortunately, many sergeants are ill-equipped to carry out these duties. They do not have the experience or training needed to fulfill their role in personnel development. Far too many sergeants are, in fact, little more than promoted patrol officers.

Sergeants, of course, cannot (even if they are competent) do the job alone. Managers at all levels of complex criminal justice organizations must make a commitment to social justice through equal employment opportunity. It is up to the police chief executive to set the stage for change. The chief must formulate a no-nonsense policy in support of equal employment opportunity and be prepared to use all available resources to accomplish that policy. Continuous reinforcement is absolutely essential. The chief should be prepared to take immediate and appropriate action against any manager or supervisor who fails to support and carry out the department's policies in the area of human relations.

When all is said and done, however, it is the police sergeant who translates equal opportunity theory into practice within the police department. Without a genuine commitment on the sergeant's part, EEO/AA becomes ritualistic mumbo-jumbo designed to placate supposedly naive minorities while perpetuating the status quo. Sergeants are in a position to activate and guide equal opportunity or turn it into a social placebo.

Dealing with Employees in a Protected Class

The phrase protected class has a special meaning when it comes to supervising employees who belong to certain minority groups. A protected class is composed of individuals who have been unfairly or illegally discriminated against in the past or who are believed to be entitled to preferential consideration due to past or present aspects of their life situation. Protected class is currently used as a classification for individual employees based on their:

1. racial or ethnic origin
2. sex (gender or preference)
3. age (over 40)
4. physical status (disabilities)
5. religion

Members of other groups, such as veterans, have also been granted protected status based primarily on political grounds.

As more women join the ranks of police officers, the possibility of employee pregnancy must be considered. Many women choose to have both a family and a career, and policies should be in place to accommodate both. In 1978, Congress amended Title VII of the Civil Rights Act of 1964 to provide protection against pregnancy discrimination. The legislation, known as the Pregnancy Discrimination Act, expanded the existing prohibition against discrimination "because of sex" or "on the basis of sex" also to include "because of or on the basis of pregnancy, childbirth or related medical condition."

The identification of individuals who are accorded special legal consideration when it comes to employment arises from federal civil rights legislation, equal employment opportunity regulations, and court decisions. As a manager of human resources, it is in the sergeant's best interest to become familiar with groups that have been granted "minority" status and to develop an understanding of why they are classified as such.

Irrespective of their social perspectives or personal biases, sergeants, as first-line supervisors who interact with a diverse workforce on a daily basis, must be sensitive when it comes to potentially illegal discriminatory practices. They must also adjust their supervisory methods in a concerted effort to avoid these practices. The OUCH test is one effective strategy that applies to the supervision of employees who are members of a protected class (Leonard, 2013).

Being aware of and understanding the OUCH test helps remind supervisors that all of their actions as first-line managers must be:

O—Objective
U—Uniform in application
C—Consistently applied
H—Have job relatedness

While it is straightforward as well as simple, the OUCH acronym provides practical guidance for ethical, nondiscriminatory supervision in the context of modern police work.

From the OUCH perspective, a supervisor's action is objective when it addresses the employee's job-related behavior without being distorted by personal feelings. It is uniform in application when it is applied consistently to all employees. The action is consistent in effect when it has the same proportional impact on members of protected classes as it does on others in the workforce. Finally, the action has job relatedness if it can be shown to deal with behavior that is necessary to perform the job.

The OUCH test should be viewed as much more than a statement of one's personal philosophy, however. It represents criteria that management and the courts use to determine whether real discrimination has occurred. By adopting the OUCH perspective as it relates to human resources management, sergeants may well avoid allegations of discrimination and the lengthy administrative or legal entanglements that go along with them. Once again, the old adage may be correct: An ounce of prevention is worth a pound of cure.

Handling Sexual Harassment in the Workplace

Studies indicate that there have been some positive changes in the status of women in police work. The percentage of women in the workforce is up and continues to increase each year. Nearly 20 percent of the current applicant pool and recruits are female. This clearly indicates that there is no longer any systematic discrimination against women in the application process. On the downside, women police officers have much higher turnover rates than their male counterparts. Consequently, more women must be recruited and processed just to maintain the current sex ratio (Swanson et al., 2012).

One cause of the high turnover rate for female police officers is sexual harassment. Sergeants are in a strategic position when it comes to dealing with this type of harassment in the workplace. As first-line supervisors and representatives of management, they are expected to be proactive rather than reactive in this regard.

Sexual harassment in the workplace is a major problem facing both public and private sector employers in the United States. This is particularly true in male-dominated occupations. Twenty years of research have provided overwhelming evidence indicating that unwelcome and offensive sexual conduct is both pandemic and problematic in many organizations. Conservative estimates suggest that about 40 percent of working women and 5 to 10 percent of their male counterparts have experienced some type of sexual harassment in the workplace (Thomann, Strickland, & Gibbons, 1989).

In a study involving 81 of 122 female police officers in a metropolitan police department, 62 percent of the respondents reported that they had been subjected to sexual harassment by their male colleagues. Of these, one-third confronted the offender, 6 percent talked to their supervisors, and a few contacted the Equal Employment Opportunity Commission; however, 21 percent took no action at all. Very few took strong measures to deal with the problem (Daum & Johns, 1994). Many female officers feel intimidated. Consequently, many of them make a conscious decision to not "rock the boat" (Brown & Heidensohn, 2000).

Sexual harassment is prohibited by the Civil Rights Act of 1964. The act specifies that it is unlawful for an employer to discriminate against any individual with respect to his or her compensation, terms, conditions, or privileges of employment because of such individual's race, color, religion, sex, or national origin (42 U.S.C. 2000e-2[a][1]). Sexual harassment can take one of two forms:

1. **Quid pro quo sexual harassment.** An individual is forced to grant sexual favors in order to obtain, maintain, or improve employment status.
2. **Hostile work environment sexual harassment.** Individual employees are subjected to suggestive comments, photographs, jokes, obscene gestures, or unwanted physical contact. This type of harassment has the following four elements:
   a. The conduct is unwelcome.
   b. The conduct is sufficiently severe or pervasive to alter the conditions of the victim's employment and create an abusive work environment.
   c. The conduct is perceived by the victim as hostile or abusive.
   d. The conduct creates an environment that a reasonable person would find hostile or abusive.

Victims of sexual harassment report that they suffer from various physical and psychological maladies, diminished morale, and a loss of productivity. Studies indicate that direct and indirect costs associated with sexual harassment are great. The federal government, for example, estimates that sexual harassment cost it $267 million between 1985 and 1987—$204 million in lost productivity, $37 million to replace federal workers who left their jobs, and $26 million in medical leaves due to stress induced by sexual harassment (U.S. Merit Systems Protection Board, 1987).

Litigation focusing on sexual harassment has also been very costly to an increasing number of public and private organizations. Some have been required to pay judgments and legal fees exceeding six figures (Thomann & Serritella, 1994). The array of compensatory and punitive damages awarded in sexual harassment cases has been truly mind-boggling.

Under normal circumstances, sexual harassment between co-workers does not produce employer liability under Title VII of the Civil Rights Act because it is not considered an action of the employer. In addition, management will ordinarily not be held liable if it has taken "immediate" and "effective" steps to remedy sexual harassment that occurs in the workplace. An exculpatory response includes a formal policy prohibiting sexual harassment, a user-friendly and effective complaint procedure, and appropriate disciplinary action in cases of sexual misconduct. As a general rule, when management acts "in good faith" to deal with known sexual harassment and management itself has clean hands, all liability is shifted to those engaged in the harassment. In addition, a comprehensive sexual harassment educational program for employees serves a dual purpose. It is not only the first step toward prevention, but it is also a vital element of any defense to sexual harassment litigation (Heckeroth & Barker, 1997).

Title VII provides a remedy for discrimination when there is an indication of employer responsibility in sexual harassment cases. Employers act through their supervisory agents. As a result, the police department (and the governmental entity of which it is a part) can be held liable if one of its supervisors actively participates in the harassment of one of its employees.

It can also be held liable if its supervisors are responsible for, actively participate in, or otherwise encourage the creation of, a hostile work environment. Civil liability may also arise when first-line supervisors ignore open harassment, fail to assist subordinates who are seeking a remedy, or otherwise attempt to subvert a remedy (IACP National Law Enforcement Policy Center, 1991).

Sergeants are key players in the ongoing battle against sexual harassment in police work. No police department can maintain a workplace that is free of harassment without the cooperation and support of its first-line supervisors. Apathetic, hostile, or openly chauvinistic supervisors can quickly subvert an otherwise effective antiharassment policy due to their actions or inactions regarding that particular policy. However, supportive and proactive supervisors are in a strategic position to assist other police managers to identify, stop, and prevent sexual harassment.

According to the IACP Policy Center, supervisors play a unique role in preventing as well as dealing with sexual harassment:

1. Supervisors, based on their own actions and words, function as role models for their subordinates. They help set the moral tone. Consequently, they must never initiate or participate in sexual harassment. On the contrary, supervisors must be prepared to stop the behavior of others that can be perceived as harassment and to take immediate steps to prevent further occurrences. Even the tacit acceptance of sexually inappropriate behavior on the part of employees sends the message that sexual harassment will be tolerated, regardless of formal department policy.

2. Supervisors have an affirmative duty to deal effectively with and to report all known or reported cases of sexual harassment to the unit responsible for investigating employee misconduct. Failure to take appropriate action or failure to report incidents of harassment as required by department policy is normally grounds for disciplinary action. This is essential if management wants to ensure the integrity of the antiharassment effort at all levels of the process.

3. Each supervisor has a responsibility to reinforce the department's antiharassment training and behavior modification efforts by actively counseling subordinates on the topic of sexual harassment in the workplace. Supervisors must make themselves accessible to victims and ensure that their complaints will be handled in a proactive, yet discreet and confidential manner. In situations in which allegations of sexual harassment have been lodged, confirmed, and resolved, the supervisor should continue to interact with the parties in order to ensure that the offensive behavior does not resume. The supervisor should also work with the victim to find ways of making the workplace more comfortable for all of the parties concerned.

Once again, these are awesome responsibilities that have been thrust upon first-line supervisors in the ever-changing social and cultural environment of modern police work. Being a successful police supervisor in the twenty-first century requires more commitment, knowledge, and human skills than it has at any time in our history.

Supervising Gay and Lesbian Police Officers

A great deal has been written about the police subculture. It has been described as male dominated, isolationist, elitist, and authoritarian. Primarily a workplace phenomenon, the police subculture is the sum of the beliefs, values, and norms shared by those within the law enforcement organization that communicates both formally and informally what is expected from members of the work group (Orthmann & Hess, 2012).

While the police subculture has traditionally been homophobic, this situation is changing rather rapidly in some areas of the country and more slowly in others. Change, however, is the rule rather than the exception in regard to sexual diversity in the workforce.

Many police departments have tacitly adopted a "don't ask, don't tell" philosophy regarding the sexual preferences of applicants and employees. Others actively recruit gay and lesbian police officers. These agencies do all they can to create a positive workplace culture and hospitable environment for their homosexual employees. After a statewide study, the California Commission on Peace Officer Standards and Training (1983) singled out the gay community as a "key" pool for recruiting new police officers by police departments trying to bolster their sagging recruitment efforts. On the national level, the IACP rescinded its decades-old policy opposing the hiring of homosexual police officers (*Law Enforcement News*, 1990).

It is clear that barriers blocking the employment as well as effective utilization of gay police officers are slowly but surely coming down (Cherney, 1999). In their role as first-line supervisors, most sergeants will very likely be responsible for supervising either discreet or openly gay police personnel at some point in their careers. It is incumbent upon management to help them prepare for this task. It is also up to individual first-line supervisors to prepare themselves.

Interviews with dozens of police officers and gay advocates indicate that the New York Police Department is successfully integrating gay and lesbian officers into virtually every policing function. According to one openly gay supervisor, "We are everywhere." In fact, the city's Gay Officers Action League (GOAL) claims to have a membership of nearly 800 police officers. GOAL recently opened chapters in Denver; Springfield, Massachusetts; San Francisco; Seattle; Chicago; and Marlboro, Maryland. It also has affiliates in London and Amsterdam (Blumenthal, 1993). Additionally, Law Enforcement Gays and Lesbians International has membership worldwide.

While no one should underestimate the homophobic hostility that remains in police work, change is on the horizon. First-line supervisors are in a position to help facilitate a meaningful change in human relations by embracing diversity rather than opposing it.

As supervisors, ranking officers must be open and accepting when it comes to gay personnel. While homosexual officers may have a radically different lifestyle, they are nonetheless human beings with distinctly human aspirations for a personally rewarding and successful career in their chosen field. Empathy is the key to understanding and using the talents of these individuals. The supervisor's strategy for dealing with homosexual employees must conform to the OUCH test, in that his or her actions regarding gay subordinates must be objective, uniform in application, consistently applied, and have specific job relatedness.

As leaders who set the ethical tone for their subordinates, supervisors have a professional obligation to act as role models for other police personnel. As part of the management team, they have an affirmative responsibility to assist top management in facilitating meaningful change within the organization. These are critically important as well as awesome responsibilities that go with the turf.

A subcultural transformation such as the employment of gay and lesbian police officers requires changes in the hearts and minds of heterosexual personnel. This means that those in management and first-line supervisory positions have to live the new culture and become the embodiment of it. They also must have their antennae up so that they can identify and reinforce other people whose behavior exemplifies the new values and norms they wish to inculcate in members of the workforce.

In order to achieve these objectives, managers and supervisors need to adopt a viable personal strategy for facilitating changes in the workplace culture. The key elements in such a strategy are as follows:

1. Supervisors must really understand the old culture. They cannot chart a new course until they know exactly where they are at the present time.
2. Supervisors should familiarize themselves with the new culture and hold it up as an example from which others can learn. A genuine commitment is an essential element in the acceptance process.
3. Supervisors should encourage police officers willing to discard the old culture and adopt the new one. Reinforcement is the key if new behaviors are to be adopted, internalized, and retained by members of the work group.
4. Supervisors should not attack the tenets of the old culture head on. As leaders, they should allow their subordinates to find new cultural perspectives for themselves and have faith that substantive change will follow.
5. Supervisors should not count on vision to work miracles. At best, vision acts only as a guiding principle for meaningful cultural change.
6. Supervisors should understand that they are in it for the long haul. It takes anywhere from five to 10 years for substantive cultural change to become institutionalized.
7. Supervisors must learn to live the culture they advocate. As always, actions speak much louder than words (Dumaine, 1990).

Supervisors are change agents. Based on their rank and authority within the police department, they are also culture carriers. Without their commitment and support, both substantive and durable change will be very difficult to achieve. By becoming proactive, they can help chart a new, more open, and accepting course for the police subculture.

Managing a More Educated Workforce

Police supervisors are being called upon to manage an increasingly more educated workforce. The educational level of American police officers has risen significantly since the mid-1980s. While the vast majority of police agencies require only a high school diploma, about 60 percent of all sworn officers have more than two years of college education (Carter, Sapp, & Stephens, 1989; Fulton, 1999). This represents a dramatic departure from the past, when a high school education was considered sufficient preparation for a career in law enforcement.

Based on a comprehensive study commissioned by the Police Executive Research Forum (PERF), researchers were able to identify what they consider to be advantages of a college education. College-educated men and women tend to have:

1. Greater knowledge of procedures, functions, and principles related to their present and future assignments.
2. Better understanding of their professional role and its importance in the criminal justice system and in society at large.
3. More desirable psychological makeup (including alertness, empathy, flexibility, initiative, and intelligence).
4. Greater interpersonal skills—focusing on the ability to communicate, to respond to the needs of others, and to exercise compassionate leadership.
5. Greater ability to analyze situations, exercise discretion, and resolve problems through appropriate decision-making.
6. Stronger moral character, as reflected in a sense of conscience and qualities, such as honesty, reliability, and tolerance.
7. More desirable system of personal values that is consistent with police work in a democratic society (Sapp & Carter, 1992).

On the downside, college-educated police officers seem to experience more stress than their less-educated colleagues. This is due, in part, to the animosity demonstrated by "streetwise" police officers, the unrealistic expectations of family and friends, misconceptions about advancement on the job, lack of input into policy formulation and decision-making, and boredom (Swanson et al., 2012). According to Molden (1999), police administrators report that college-educated police officers are more likely to question orders, request more frequent reassignment, have lower morale and more absenteeism, and become frustrated more easily by bureaucratic procedures. Stress-induced productivity problems and high turnover rates are not uncommon. However, the advantages of advanced education appear to outweigh the disadvantages. PERF has recommended that all entry-level law enforcement officers should complete a four-year degree (Molden, 1999).

First-line supervisors are granted the power to perform specific tasks in concert with and through the efforts of others. In order to work more collaboratively with their subordinates (especially college-educated men and women), sergeants must cast aside the traditional "overseer" mentality common in police work and accept the fact that their job is no longer one of supervision per se, but one of sharing power and providing leadership.

The supervisor who chooses to share power with subordinates automatically expands his or her influence as a leader. By empowering others, the supervisor is in a much better position to accomplish assigned tasks. Delegation is the sharing of power. The sharing of power, coupled with meaningful participation in the decision-making process, leads to empowerment. Empowerment means that employees experience ownership in their job and accept 100 percent of the responsibility for doing it right. For all practical purposes, effective supervision is effective delegation (Whisenand & Rush, 2011).

Effective delegation does not just happen. It takes a great deal of thought and preparation. As Whisenand and Rush (2011) point out:

1. Recipients of the delegation must be well trained to perform their job.
2. Training must be relevant, reliable, and ongoing.
3. Supervisors should set high performance standards for themselves as well as for their subordinates.
4. Supervisors should understand the needs and values of each of their employees.
5. There must be pertinent, open, and frank communication between supervisors and their subordinates.
6. Those who fulfill their delegated responsibilities at an acceptable level should be rewarded.
7. Those who do not perform their delegated responsibilities at an acceptable level should be reprimanded.
8. There must be meaningful feedback systems in place to ensure the success of the delegation process.

The success or failure of this empowerment strategy will depend on the commitment and human skills possessed by those seeking to implement it.

Four parties benefit from increased employee participation and effective delegation power—the community, the police department, first-line supervisors, and employees (Whisenand & Rush, 2011).

The local community benefits from the empowerment process. Empowered employees are ordinarily more skillful and dedicated to their job. Consequently, they tend to provide better and less costly police services. Better individual performance is likely to generate more respect and community support for the police department.

The police department benefits from the empowerment process. Employee participation, input into the decision-making process, and acceptance of responsibility create an environment in which everyone is encouraged to pursue excellence. This strengthens the organization as it seeks to accomplish its mission, goals, and objectives.

Supervisors benefit from the empowerment process. Supervisors benefit in that they are:

1. Instilling a commitment for getting the job done.
2. Strengthening mutual trust between themselves and their subordinates.
3. Enhancing their officers' knowledge and job skills.
4. Encouraging and reinforcing the feeling of job ownership.
5. Utilizing the power of leadership to provide quality police services through the efforts of their employees.

By empowering subordinates, supervisors empower themselves as effective leaders. Rank-and-file police officers benefit from the empowerment process. Empowerment and its accompanying collegial status benefit employees in that they become much more:

1. Positive in terms of commitment to their work.
2. Trusting, trustworthy, and openly participatory.

3. Self-confident.
4. Competent.
5. Professional in their orientation.
6. Capable of working alone or with others to perform top-notch police work.

The empowerment of police personnel is essential if governments are to attract, field, and retain college-educated officers.

Empowerment substitutes self-supervision for traditional organizational control mechanisms. An empowered organization is one in which individual police officers have the knowledge, skill, desire, and opportunity to personally succeed in a way that leads to collective organizational success. Helpful systems and structures, win–win situations, self-supervision, and personal accountability are at the heart of the empowerment process (Covey, 1992).

Once again, sergeants are key players in the empowerment process. In order to succeed in this role, they must truly believe that people are their greatest asset. They must be trusting and willing to take risks by delegating power to individual police officers while holding them and themselves accountable. Sergeants must be prepared to accept the mantle of leadership as they consciously reject the supervisor's traditional role as an overseer of "employees" in the workplace.

Training for the New Supervisor

As noted earlier, as first-line supervisors, sergeants are in a strategic position to determine whether equal employment opportunity becomes a reality or remains a figment of our collective imagination. Even if they are committed to fairness and decency, sergeants cannot learn the information and human skills they need to play their staff development role through osmosis. Whether they are traditional or nontraditional employees, sergeants must be trained for their new duties. They should also be given the opportunity to apply supervisory theory to real-life situations as part of an extended training process. Once they are on the job, new sergeants should be evaluated for competency and coached by a certified trainer. Without extensive supervisory training and on-the-job coaching, there is little chance that new police sergeants will be able to cope with the human relations challenges of the twenty-first century. The California Commission on Peace Officer Standards and Training (1996) has developed an extensive supervisor development course of study consisting of 16 areas of competency for general supervision (see Figure 13.5). Within each competency area there are skills or knowledge areas that the student trainer must master before moving to the next skill or knowledge area. For example, Figure 13.6 depicts competency area number 5.0 (employee relations) with seven subareas of skills and knowledge areas that must be evaluated by a supervisor trainer.

Municipal governments are reluctant to spend money on supervisory training. Part of the problem is that training itself has taken a back seat to economic reality. Many police departments now receive minimum budgetary allocations. The abandonment of training for economic reasons borders on the absurd and will cost much more in the long run. Without adequate supervisory training, police departments run the risk of more vicarious liability suits and face potentially disruptive behavior by nontraditional employees in response to inadequate supervision. Proactive police managers know that the only way to guard against these problems is to strengthen the rank of sergeant through selective promotion, upgraded supervisory training, and unequivocal support.

1.0 ROLE IDENTIFICATION
a. Management's expectations
b. Subordinate's expectations
c. First-line supervisor's role
d. External expectations (i.e., community, media, family)
e. Results-oriented approach to job (i.e., human relations skills)
f. Peer expectations

2.0 VALUES, ETHICS, AND PRINCIPLES
a. Definitions
b. Different value systems
c. Commitment to ethics, values, and principles
d. Supervisor's role/responsibilities
e. Applying ethics and integrity to decision-making
f. Ethical resources

3.0 COMMUNICATION
a. Verbal and nonverbal communication skills
b. Benefits of active listening
c. Communication skills in conflict resolution
d. Rumor control responsibilities
e. Must develop good public speaking skills
f. Understands effective communications techniques when dealing with the media
g. Understands agency's policy on dissemination of information

4.0 LEADERSHIP
a. What is a leader?
b. Difference between leaders and managers
c. Characteristics of effective leaders
d. What motivates others
e. Show respect for subordinates
f. Demonstrate responsibility for subordinates
g. Maintain productive and positive relations
h. Recognize and reward good performance
i. Identify poor performance and take appropriate steps
j. Properly delegate work to subordinates
k. Resolve issues/problems through negotiations
l. Apply proactive leadership

FIGURE 13.5 General supervision competency areas.

5.0 EMPLOYEE RELATIONS

a. Employee bargaining agreements
b. Agency's affirmative action policy and program
c. Agency's sexual harassment policy and program
d. EEOC/FEPC guidelines and how they apply to the agency
e. Applicable laws
f. Supervisor's role in conflict resolution
g. Grievance process and supervisor's role in handling and resolving grievances

6.0 STRESS

a. The fight-or-flight syndrome
b. Recognize the signs of stress
c. Practice stress management techniques
d. Referral policy and procedure for the agency

7.0 COUNSELING

a. Types of counseling sessions
b. Goals of counseling session
c. Preparation for counseling session
d. Examples of special counseling issues
e. Examples of barriers to successful counseling
f. Examples of contemporary counseling issues
g. Documentation

8.0 EMPLOYEE PERFORMANCE APPRAISAL

a. Agency's performance appraisal policy and procedures
b. Reasons for evaluation
c. Performance/accountability
d. Agency's acceptable standards of performance
e. Common problems and errors of supervisors
f. Common problems with appraisals
g. Sources of information on performance
h. Preparation for evaluation
i. Presentation of evaluation to employee
j. Follow-up on performance deficiencies

9.0 LIABILITY ISSUES

a. Issues and agency policies
b. Potential liability to the supervisor

10.0 DISCIPLINE

a. Agency's process to ensure that performance standards are adhered to by its members
b. Factors that may contribute to misconduct
c. Supervisor's actions (legal, reasonable, consistent, appropriate, timely)
d. Supervisor's role in the disciplinary process
e. Agency's policies and procedures related to investigations
f. Recognition of substandard, standard, and exceptional job performance
g. Application of Peace Officer Bill of Rights, MOU/MOA, and other constitutional protections

FIGURE 13.5 (Continued)

h.   Civil ramifications of violating subordinate's rights
i.   Due process and Skelly Conference procedures
j.   Legal parameters related to administrative records and files

11.0 ADMINISTRATIVE SUPPORT

a.   Use of statistical data (i.e., deployment of personnel, crime trends, employee productivity)
b.   Fiscal issues related to agency operation
c.   Supervisor's role in fiscal management
d.   Agency's protocol for completed staff work assignments
e.   Audits and controls
f.   Personnel deployment and scheduling

12.0 PLANNING AND ORGANIZING

a.   What is planning?
b.   What is organizing?
c.   Planning and organizing are routinely done by everyone
d.   Benefits of planning and organizing
e.   Hurdles to planning and organizing
f.   Understands the planning process (scientific model)

13.0 TRAINING

a.   Training is a primary responsibility
b.   Importance of initial and ongoing training
c.   Techniques of instruction
d.   Supervisor accountability for training received by subordinates
e.   Documentation of training provided by the supervisor
f.   Safety considerations

14.0 REPORT REVIEW

a.   Review and approval of written documents produced by subordinates
b.   Some causes of report-writing problems
c.   Ethical considerations (i.e., invented probable cause, misreporting of event chronology, misquoting of statements, intentional omissions)

15.0 INVESTIGATIONS

a.   Agency investigative policy and procedures related to police shootings, employee injuries, property damage, traffic accidents, use of force, complaints, and internal investigations

16.0 THE TRANSITION

a.   Difference between doing the work and getting it done through others
b.   Potential problem areas (i.e., supervising friends, problem employees, unreasonable expectations)
c.   Personal integrity

FIGURE 13.5 (Continued)

SUPERVISOR DEVELOPMENT GUIDE

GENERAL SUPERVISION

5.0 CA EMPLOYEE RELATIONS

The student supervisor will understand the supervisor's roles and responsibilities related to employer–employee relationships within the workplace.

q   A. EMPLOYEE BARGAINING AGREEMENTS
        Both sworn and nonsworn personnel
q   B. AGENCY'S AFFIRMATIVE ACTION POLICY AND PROGRAM
q   C. AGENCY'S SEXUAL HARASSMENT POLICY AND PROGRAM
q   D. EEOC/FEPC GUIDELINES AND HOW THEY APPLY TO THE AGENCY
q   E. APPLICABLE LAWS

        Brown Act (54950 CGC)
        Meyers-Mileas-Brown Act (3500 CGC)
        Ralph C. Dills Act (3512 CGC)
        Fair Labor Standards Act (Garcia v. San Antonio)
        Local ordinances

q   F. SUPERVISOR'S ROLE IN CONFLICT RESOLUTION
        Loyalty: must support department and policy
q   G. GRIEVANCE PROCESS AND SUPERVISOR'S ROLE IN HANDLING
        AND RESOLVING GRIEVANCES

I have explained and/or demonstrated the above critical tasks and feel that my student supervisor can perform these tasks in a competent manner.

Trainer_____Date_____
The above tasks have been explained and/or demonstrated to me and I feel I can perform these tasks in a competent manner.
Student Supervisor_____Date_____

Check box indicates task has been completed

FIGURE 13.6 General supervision—employee relations. *Source: California Commission on Peace Officer Standards and Training (1996). Supervisor Development Program and Guide. Sacramento, CA: California POST*

References

Blumenthal, R. (1993). Gay, lesbian cops gaining acceptance in New York. *The Denver Post* March 7: 33A.

"Bonni Tischler earns top cop award". U.S. Customs Today, June 2000, p. 1.

Broderick, J. J. (1987). *Police in a time of change* (2nd ed.). Prospect Heights, IL: Waveland.

Brown, J., & Heidensohn, F. (2000). *Gender and policing: Comparative perspectives*. New York: Macmillan.

CALEA, (2006). *Standards for law enforcement agencies.* Fairfax, VA: Commission on Accreditation for Law Enforcement Agencies, Inc.

California Commission on Peace Officer Standards and Training, (1983). *Supervisory training guide.* North Highlands, CA: California POST.

California Commission on Peace Officer Standards and Training, (1996). *Supervisor development program and guide.* Sacramento, CA: California POST.

Carter, D. L., Sapp, A. D., & Stephens, D. W. (1989). *The state of police education: Policy direction for the twenty-first century.* Washington, DC: Police Executive Research Forum.

Cherney, A. (1999). Gay and lesbian issues in policing. *Current Issues in Criminal Justice, 11*(1).

Civil Rights Act of 1964. Title VII. 42 United States Code A4 2000e-2(a)(1).

Cole, G. F., Gertz, M., & Bunger, A. (2003). *Criminal justice system: Politics and policies* (9th ed.). Boston, MA: Wadsworth Publishing Co.

Covey, S. R. (1992). *Principle-centered leadership.* New York: Simon and Schuster.

Daum, J. M., & Johns, C. M. (1994). Police work from a woman's perspective. *The Police Chief, LXI*(9).

Dumaine, B. (1990). Creating a new company culture. *Fortune, 121*(1).

Equal Employment Opportunity Coordinating Council, (1973). *Federal policy on remedies concerning equal employment opportunity in state and local government personnel systems.* Washington, DC: U.S. Government Printing Office.

Fulmer, R. M., & Franklin, S. G. (1982). *Supervision.* New York: Macmillan.

Fulton, R. (1999). Do supervisors need degrees? *Law Enforcement Technology, 26*(3).

Griggs v. Duke Power Co.(1971). 401 U.S. 431.

Heckeroth, S. E., & Barker, A. M. (1997). Police department efforts to deter sexual harassment. *USA Today* (July): A2.

Holden, R. N. (1993). *Modern police management* (2nd ed.). Englewood Cliffs, NJ: Prentice Hall.

IACP National Law Enforcement Policy Center, (1991). Harassment in the workplace: A proactive approach. *The Police Chief, LVIII*(12).

Johns, G. (2000). Organizational behavior: Understanding life at work: *5th ed..* Englewood Cliffs, NJ: Prentice Hall.

Johnson, L. A. (1969). *Employing the hard-core unemployed.* New York: American Management Association.

Katz, C. (2013). *The police in America* (8th ed.). New York: Humanities and Social Sciences.

Law Enforcement News. (1990). LAPD Gays' hope: Mainstream acceptance. XVII, 321.

Leonard, E. C. (2013). Supervision: Concepts and practices of management: *12th ed..* Stamford, CT: Cengage Learning.

Leonard, V. A., & More, H. W. (2000). *Police organization and management* (9th ed.). New York: The Foundation Press.

Longenecker, J. G., & Pringle, C. D. (1984). *Management.* Columbus, OH: Charles E. Merrill Publishing Co.

Martin, R. (1987). *Personnel and supervision in criminal justice.* Indiana, PA: Kinko Professor Publishing.

Molden, J. (1999). College degrees for police applicants. *Law and Order, 47*(1).

NAACP v. Allen, 340 F. Supp. 703 (M.D. Ala. 1972).

Orthmann, C. H., & Hess, K. M. (2012). *Management and supervision in law enforcement* (6th ed.). Stamford, CT: Cengage Learning.

Plunkett, W. R. (1992). *Supervision: The direction of people at work* (6th ed.). Boston, MA: Allyn & Bacon.

Richmond v. Croson Co., 109 S. Ct. 706 (1989).

Sapp, A. D., & Carter, D. L. (1992). Should all policemen be college trained? *The Police Chief, 38*(12).

Sass, T., & Troyer, J. (1999). Affirmative action, political representation, unions, and female police employment. *Journal of Labor Research*, *20*(4).

Sauls, J. (1995). Proving business necessity: The disparate impact challenge. *FBI Law Enforcement Bulletin*, *64*(4).

Schroeder, T. (1996). Avoiding and defending employment discrimination charges. Police Law Journal (February).

Stahl, O. G. (1983). *Public personnel administration*. New York: Harper and Row.

Swank, C. J., & Conser, J. A. (1983). *The police personnel system*. New York: John Wiley & Sons.

Swanson, C. R., Territo, L., & Taylor, R. W. (2012). *Police administration: structures, processes and behavior* (8th ed.). New York: Macmillan.

Territo, L., & Vetter, H. J. (1981). *Stress and police personnel*. Boston, MA: Allyn & Bacon.

Thibault, E. A., Lynch, L. M., & McBride, R. B. (2010). *Proactive police management* (8th ed.). Englewood Cliffs, NJ: Prentice Hall.

Thomann, D. A., & Serritella, T. M. (1994). Preventing sexual harassment in law enforcement agencies. *The Police Chief, LXI*(9).

Thomann, D. A., Strickland, D. E., & Gibbons, J. L. (1989). An organizational development approach to preventing sexual harassment: Developing shared commitment through awareness training. *College and University Personnel Association Journal*, *40*(1).

Turner, W. W. (1968). *The police establishment*. New York: G.P. Putnam's Sons.

U.S. Census Bureau, (2003). *Resident population estimates of the United States by sex, race and hispanic origin*. Washington, DC: U.S. Census Bureau.

U.S. Department of Justice, (2010). *Local police departments 2007*. Washington, DC: Bureau of Justice Statistics.

U.S. Department of Justice, Federal Bureau of Investigation, (2011). *Crime in the United States*. Washington, DC: U.S. Government Printing Office.

U.S. Merit Systems Protection Board, (1987). *Sexual harassment of federal workers: An update*. Washington, DC: U.S. Government Printing Office.

Whisenand, P. M., & Rush, G. E. (2011). *Supervising police personnel* (7th ed.). Englewood Cliffs, NJ: Prentice Hall.

Zastrow, C. (2000). *Social problems* (5th ed.). Stamford, CT: Wadsworth.

14

Tactical Operations
Critical Incident Deployment

critical incident	post-traumatic stress
Critical Incident Stress	disorder
Management	special weapons and
emotional debriefing	tactics
Federal Emergency	strike team
Management Agency	tactical debriefing
Incident Command	tactical operation
System	taskforce

CASE STUDY

Sergeant Bill Bass

DEPARTMENT

Bill Bass has been with the Henderson County Sheriff's Office for 11 years. The sheriff's office has 88 sworn officers, 32 detention officers, four court bailiffs, four courthouse security officers, and 27 civilians. The sheriff's office manages the county jail, which is rated for 150 inmates but exceeds that number frequently. In addition, the sheriff's office operates a patrol division, a criminal investigation division, and an administrative division. The patrol division is the largest, with 64 sworn officers. The patrol division is subdivided into three units: patrol, process servers, and school resource officers. Twenty-one reserve deputies are required to work a minimum of 16 hours per month. Reserve officers are used for patrol, courthouse security, prisoner transport, and special events. The criminal investigation division houses 11 detectives with two assigned to work juvenile cases and child sexual abuse cases on a full-time basis. The administrative division consists of 13 officers, one of which is the sheriff. The remaining 12 are chief deputies, majors, and command staff for operations and staff functions. With the exception of reserve officers, detention officers, and courthouse security officers, all sworn officers are state POST certified and trained. Most of the officers have basic training with no specialized training certifications (such as traffic accident reconstructionists). A few officers have specialized training and/or certifications as crime scene investigators, child sexual abuse investigators, and domestic violence specialists.

CRIME

Henderson County, being a rural area, has a fairly low crime rate compared to surrounding counties in the state. Last year, the county answered a little more than 3000 calls for emergency service, mostly traffic related. Index crimes are down from last year by nearly 3 percent. There was only one homicide reported last year. Arson increased over the last few years mainly due to a volunteer firefighter who was burning barns and vacant buildings in the county before being apprehended. Larceny and burglary are the highest index crimes reported in the county. There were two rapes, 22 felonious assaults, and one robbery reported last year.

COMMUNITY

Henderson County is a southeastern rural county with a county-only population of 112,000 people. There are two incorporated municipalities within the county, Henderson City and Market City. Both Henderson City and Market City have their own police departments. Henderson City is the county seat and is a small town with a population of 14,000 people. Market City, however, has a population of 92,000 people. Over the past 10 years, Market City has annexed a number of new subdivisions located in the county, which has decreased the amount of patrol coverage for the sheriff. The sheriff's office is still responsible for serving warrants and other court processes in both Henderson City and Market City.

Henderson County is typical of many southeastern rural areas—friendly and laid back. The sheriff has been reelected five times and is well liked and respected by the community. While there are many open fields and much farmland in the county, there has been an increase in population growth and subdivision development over the past few years. A number of new industries have located to Henderson County due to the low tax rate and the accessibility to interstate highways and the railroad system. In fact, Henderson City is home to the main line office for the Southeastern Railway Company and serves a number of area businesses in transporting goods and materials. There are 14 main railway lines crossing through the county and cities, one of which splits Market City in half. When a train goes through, all traffic is held up on both sides of the city. This has been a particular headache for city planners in developing ways to get emergency vehicles through intersections during emergencies while a train is going through the city. While the rest of the county has not had that particular problem, there are numerous railroad crossings on county highways, some of which have no safety systems.

OFFICER

Sergeant Bill Bass was promoted to sergeant two years ago. He is a local, having been born and raised in Market City. Bill went to Market City High School and took a job with the railroad after graduation. He married his high school girlfriend and they had one child before he applied to the Henderson County Sheriff's Office (HSCO). Bill had always liked law enforcement as a career choice, and when the advertisement ran in the paper that the HCSO was hiring, he immediately applied. Bill started working in the jail and quickly moved into the patrol division after demonstrating his ability. Bill began work on his college degree at a community college in the next county. When Bill was promoted to sergeant, he and his wife began planning their second child. Bill's wife, Anne, obtained a job with the county board of education as an elementary school teacher at Meadow View Elementary School. Bill and Anne have no further ambitions, both wanting to stay in Henderson County and raise their two children. Both Bill's and Anne's families live here so there is good family support and, of course, built-in babysitters with the grandparents.

PROBLEM

It has been three weeks since the accident and everyone still seems numbed by the experience. A county school bus was attempting to cross a railroad track when it was struck by an oncoming train. The deaths and injuries sustained in the crash made national news. Fourteen elementary school children were killed, along with the driver of the bus. Nineteen children were injured. The children ranged in age from seven to 12, mostly first grade through sixth grade, and all attended Meadow View Elementary School. Some of the children were or are Anne Bass's students. The crash is still under investigation and some, including the district attorney, are calling for an indictment of the train driver and engineer. However, investigators for both the state police and the railroad have yet to determine the exact cause of the accident or whether anyone was negligent. The accident occurred on a county road with no railroad warning devices other than the traditional signs. Some say the driver of the bus was trying to beat the train and was at fault. Others are saying the train was coming through the intersection too fast. Nevertheless, the railroad, state police, and federal transportation authorities are investigating the crash.

Bill and his six subordinates were the first on the scene after the report came in to the 911 office. It is an image that Bill will never forget—the bus, laying on its side, crumpled from the impact of the train. Children's bodies were strewn across the road, and the injured and frightened children were all crying. The deputies did what they were trained to do—maintain control of the area, cordon off traffic flows, and help medical personnel. One of Bill's officers, John Scott, was very emotional at the scene. Scott knew some of the dead and injured children and their families. At one point, the incident commander, state police Sergeant Welch, mentioned to Bill that Deputy Scott seemed to be "losing it" and should be removed. When Bill tried to comfort Scott and have him return to headquarters, Scott refused and wanted to help with the incident.

After three weeks, Bill has noticed not only a change in his subordinates but in himself as well. He is quick to anger and has little patience with those he interacts with, including his own subordinates. His subordinates, especially Scott, show signs of depression and anger.

WHAT WOULD YOU DO?

If you were Sergeant Bill Bass, how would you deal with your own emotional problems relating to this incident? How would you deal with the officers under your supervision? Are there any resources available to you or your officers to deal with this type of emotional depression? Do you think this is a temporary condition or will it affect you and your officers for a long time?

Critical Incidents

Whatever their size, every police and sheriff's department will answer critical incident calls requiring rapid deployment of officers, equipment, and other emergency personnel. Some departments may answer such calls on a daily basis, others only sporadically. One thing is clear—there is no warning and action must be taken immediately and effectively. Such calls may range from locating lost children to handling a major disaster such as a storm or terrorist attack. Generally, these types of calls can be divided into the following three major categories.

1. Man-made or natural disasters
   a. Fires, both structural and woodland
   b. Weather (hurricanes, tornadoes, floods, earthquakes, etc.)

2. Safety and rescue
   a. Lost children and missing persons
   b. Toxic spills, evacuations, and disease outbreaks
   c. Major accidents (roadway, railway, workplace)
3. Criminal or threat incidents
   a. School or workplace shootings
   b. Barricaded suspects and hostage taking
   c. Civil disorder, riot, and crowd control
   d. Bomb threats, explosions, and other terrorist threats

While police departments have dealt with such calls for decades, recent incidents have indicated the need for better planning and operational tactics training for law enforcement officers. Unfortunately, it sometimes takes a disastrous event to occur to trigger new tactics for dealing with such incidents.

In 1966, Charles Whitman positioned himself in the tower of the University of Texas at Austin and shot and killed 15 and wounded 31 before being killed by two patrol officers and one armed civilian. This incident has been cited as demonstrating the need for special weapons and tactics (SWAT) teams to handle such calls. More recently, in 1999, first responding officers waited for SWAT to arrive at the Columbine High School shooting before taking action. Officers at the Columbine incident were criticized for waiting outside the school while active shooters were still in the building. This incident resulted in a call for first responder rapid deployment tactics. While the effectiveness of rapid deployment in such incidents is arguable, it does illustrate how a disastrous event can trigger policy changes for police operations (Fairburn, 2004).

Other recent incidents have indicated a need for preplanning of events that are difficult to even conceive. The September 11, 2001, attacks may have been thwarted or the devastating results lessened had intelligence information been acted upon earlier through planning. However, it was not envisioned at the time that such an attack would or could occur. Hurricane Katrina, which nearly destroyed New Orleans in August 2005, had been conceived but never properly planned for. Even with emergency plans in place, mistakes do and will happen. The law enforcement community must be able to learn from these mistakes in order to lessen death, injury, and destruction in future similar incidents. The media are quick to point out mistakes and to criticize the efforts of law enforcement but slow to commend actions based on good planning.

Boltz (2001) and Solis (2002) point to the need for precrisis intelligence gathering by law enforcement personnel. Questions must be asked during the precrisis intelligence gathering and planning phase, such as "What are we likely to encounter in the way of critical incidents?" Both Solis and Boltz point out that information can be gathered about schools, workplaces, hospitals, and other locations that are possible targets during the precrisis planning phase. Pregathered information about contact persons, floor plans, and schedules are invaluable during the chaotic moments of a critical incident. Police line supervisors are in a particularly good position to gather such precrisis information. Because they are familiar with their assigned work zone, they can readily determine potential targets, locations for command posts, alternate traffic routing, evacuation routes and procedures, contact persons in workplaces and schools, and so on.

As Standard 46.1.2 of the Commission on Accreditation for Law Enforcement Agencies (CALEA, 2006) states:

> *Thorough planning is a fundamental requirement in responding to natural and man-made disasters as well as civil disturbances and other unusual occurrences. Of particular importance is the unified command of personnel from other agencies responding to the unusual occurrence.*

In 2005, the Department of Homeland Security issued a mandate for state and local governments to comply with the National Incident Management System (NIMS). The NIMS is designed to provide a consistent nationwide approach for federal, state, and local governments to work effectively and efficiently together to prepare for, prevent, respond to, and recover from domestic incidents, regardless of cause, size, or complexity. One of the requirements for implementing NIMS at the state and local levels is for police agencies to institutionalize the Incident Command System (ICS).

Incident Command System

The ICS is, by definition, a standard, on-scene, all-hazard incident management system. The Federal Emergency Management Agency (FEMA) has used this model for more than two decades and has demonstrated effectiveness when used properly. Standard 46.1.11 of the Commission on Accreditation for Law Enforcement Agencies (CALEA, 2006) states:

> *The expanding scope and sophistication of emergency operations, along with increased possibilities of acts of terrorism, require law enforcement agencies to quickly act to stabilize and control emergency situations. Increasingly, law enforcement agencies must deal with large catastrophes with little or no notice. Immediate and decisive action is required to minimize loss of life, reduce property damage, and permit involved authorities to fulfill their responsibilities.*

Even for small police agencies where CALEA accreditation is beyond their reach financially, implementing an ICS is an essential element of complying with the NIMS.

There are three basic elements of the ICS: common terminology, communications, and accountability. The incorporation of these three elements is what makes ICS effective regardless of the nature or scope of the critical incident.

Common Terminology

The use of plain English without the use of agency-specific codes or jargon is a necessity for the ICS. Local law enforcement must be able to communicate not only within their own agency during a critical incident, but also with other local agencies, such as emergency medical personnel, firefighting personnel, public utilities, and others as the need arises. Standard uniform titles for facilities and positions within the organization avoid confusion and enhance interoperability. For example, only the incident commander is called commander, and there is only one incident commander per incident. Facilities are addressed using common terminology to help clarify the activities that take place at a specific facility and identify which members of the organization can be found there.

Communications

A hard lesson was learned during the September 11, 2001, attacks on the World Trade Center. The inability of police and fire personnel to communicate directly with each other, along with radios that had difficulty transmitting from within the buildings, hampered rescue efforts. For the ICS to work properly, an integrated communications network must be established, including the necessary hardware to transfer information and a process by which information can be transmitted internally and externally.

Accountability

Effective accountability at all jurisdictional levels and within individual functional areas during a critical incident is essential. The ICS requires that there be an orderly chain of command and line of authority within the organization. All responders, regardless of agency affiliation, must adhere to a "check-in" procedure. In addition, each individual involved in a critical incident response must be assigned to only one supervisor.

Role of the First-Line Supervisor in Critical Incidents

Many critical incident calls for service can be handled effectively by the first responding officer and/or supervisor on the scene. However, any critical incident, regardless of how minor or routine, can quickly escalate into a major incident if not handled properly and in a timely manner. The first-line supervisor on the scene of a critical incident has two main priorities: (1) to act and (2) to communicate.

A failure to act promptly in a critical incident can result in unnecessary death or injury to citizens. Consider the 1982 incident in Torrington, Connecticut, in which Tracy Thurman was brutally attacked by her ex-husband and barely survived. Police were called to the Thurman residence on a domestic violence call. The police did not take the call seriously and were not timely in responding. When they did finally arrive, they failed to take the suspect into custody and were present when he attacked Ms. Thurman again while she was being placed into an ambulance. The result of this "routine" critical incident call was a civil suit costing the city hundreds of thousands of dollars in damages and a national call for reform of police policies dealing with domestic violence.

A failure to communicate can be equally disastrous for a police agency. While the first officer on any scene has the responsibility to aid the injured, take custody of perpetrators, and secure the scene, the first supervisor on the scene of a critical incident must communicate promptly to headquarters the nature of the situation once a quick assessment has been made (Solis, 2002). As information becomes available, the supervisor must be able to communicate the following information, if applicable:

1. Nature and scope of incident: The exact nature of the incident, such as a fire, hostage situation, hazardous material spill, suspicious packages, and so on, must be described in as much detail as possible to headquarters. The scope of the incident includes the extent of the damage or potential damage, location and geographic description, need for evacuation or containment, and so on.
2. Perimeter security needs: If geographic areas need to be evacuated or contained, the supervisor is in the best position to direct responding officers to locations for redirecting traffic flows and to keep routes open for other emergency service vehicles. Establishing the "hot zone" or staging area and selecting locations for command posts must also be communicated if the situation calls for it.
3. Need for specialized personnel: The first supervisor on the scene must communicate quickly the need for firefighting personnel, bomb technicians, tactical teams, negotiators, and medical and rescue services. Public utility services may also be needed to cut off gas lines, electrical power, or reestablish services to an area.

Patrol supervisors are generally the first supervisory officers on the scene of a critical incident. It is necessary that the supervisor and his or her subordinates understand the role and nature of the ICS. The information that the supervisor dispatches will be vitally important for responding emergency personnel. Mattoon (1996) indicates a number of complaints that responding SWAT and tactical teams had regarding the information provided to them by patrol personnel:

1. The crisis site was contained improperly.
2. They had not been told what kind of an incident was in progress other than barricaded individual with a gun, nor did they know what he was armed with.
3. They did not have a clear description of the crisis site (color, address, etc.).
4. They had not been told the safest approach route (out of suspect's sight and line of fire).
5. They were not informed of any special hazards or equipment needed.
6. They were not briefed on the current state of containment.
7. If at night, they did not know the current lighting conditions in area.
8. Several times, various departments did not know the site officer in charge or his call sign.

The information the first supervisor on the scene provides to headquarters usually dictates how the critical incident is to be handled. If the incident is deemed to be critical, an incident commander should take the primary leadership role to direct activities of all responding units. The incident commander must be the primary director of all operations in a critical incident deployment. There is no relationship between ranks under normal circumstances. In other words, someone who serves as a chief every day may not hold that title when deployed under an ICS organization.

Critical Incident Management

First-line supervisors deployed under an ICS must understand that they are part of a team designed for one special operation. An organizational structure that is different from the one under which they routinely function may be in place. The team may also have multijurisdictional components. For instance, one ICS incident may involve a police department, a sheriff's office, tribal police, or another agency within the jurisdiction. There are five major management functions of an ICS. These functions apply whether the department is handling a routine emergency or managing a response to a major disaster. A supervisor may be deployed under any of these functions, depending on the nature of the incident and his or her training. These functions are as follows:

1. **Incident Command:** Sets the incident objectives, strategies, and priorities and has overall responsibility at the incident or event.
2. **Operations:** Conducts tactical operations to carry out the plan. Develops the tactical objectives and organization and directs all tactical resources.
3. **Planning:** Prepares and documents the incident action plan to accomplish the objectives, collects and evaluates information, maintains resource status, and maintains documentation for incident records.
4. **Logistics:** Provides support, resources, and all other services needed to meet the operational objectives.
5. **Finance/Administration:** Monitors costs related to the incident. Provides accounting, procurement, time recording, and cost analyses (FEMA, 2006).

In small, routine emergencies, the incident commander may accomplish all five management functions. Large critical incidents require that these functions be established as separate sections within the ICS organization. Figure 14.1 depicts an organizational chart showing the relationship of these functions to the operation.

As Figure 14.1 illustrates, the incident commander has direct lines of communication to the four other functions (operations, planning, logistics, and finance/administration) and to three additional personnel depending on the nature and size of the incident:

> **Public information officer**—serves as a conduit of information to the media or other organizations seeking information directly from the incident scene.
> **Safety officer**—monitors safety conditions and develops measures to assure the safety of assigned personnel.
> **Liaison officer**—serves as the primary contact for supporting agencies assisting at an incident.

The operations function is where tactical tasks are performed and most resources are assigned. This is often where the most hazardous activities are carried out by the police agency. Unless operations is established as a separate section, the incident commander has direct control of tactical resources. If the need arises to establish operations as a separate section, the incident commander will assign an individual as the operations section chief.

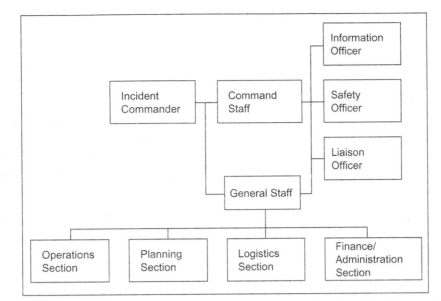

FIGURE 14.1 Organization of ICS general and command staff. *Source: FEMA (2006).* Incident Command System Training. *Washington, DC: U.S. Government Printing Office.*

The operations section chief is normally a person with the greatest technical and tactical expertise in dealing with the situation at hand.

Supervisory Span of Control

A basic feature of the ICS involves the supervisory structure of the organization. Maintaining an effective span of control is important where safety and accountability are priorities in critical incidents. While the span of control may vary from three to seven, FEMA (2006) recommends a ratio of one supervisor to five reporting officers. If the number of reporting officers falls outside these ranges, expansion or collapsing of the ICS organization may be necessary. There may be exceptions where there is low risk or where resources are in close proximity to each other. If additional supervisory levels are needed to manage the span of control, FEMA (2006) recommends adding the following levels to the operations function:

Divisions: used to divide an incident geographically.
Groups: used to describe functional areas of operation.
Branches: used when the number of divisions or groups exceeds the span of control (can be either geographical or functional).

Figure 14.2 depicts the organizational chart for these span-of-control efforts. Officers in charge of divisions and groups are designated as supervisors, while those directing the efforts of a branch are designated as directors or deputies. Branches may be subdivided into another group, usually referred to as divisions. It is important to remember that the operations

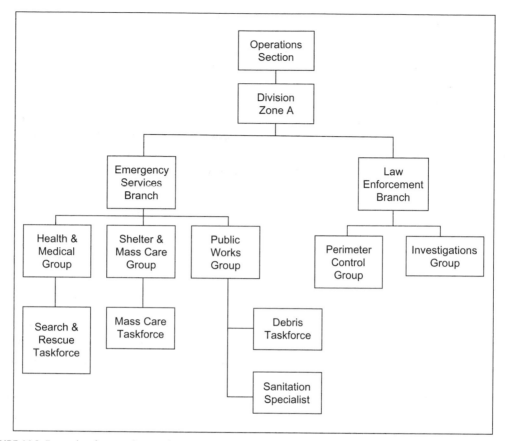

FIGURE 14.2 Example of span of control organization under ICS. *Source: FEMA (2006).* Incident Command System Training. *Washington, DC: U.S. Government Printing Office.*

section develops from the bottom up—expanding only when additional levels of supervision are needed and more resources are deployed. For example, the use of specialists, taskforces, strike teams, and single resources may be established depending on the nature of the critical incident.

Specialists: individual supervisors who may not be affiliated with the law enforcement agency who have special knowledge of plans of operation, tactics, and procedures necessary to attain the objectives of the ICS problem.

Taskforce: a combination of mixed resources with common communications operating under the direct supervision of a leader. The combining of resources into taskforces allows for several resource elements to be managed under one individual's supervision.

Strike Team: a set number of resources of the same kind and type with common communications operating under the direct supervision of a strike team leader.

Single Resources: may be individuals, equipment, crews, or teams with an identified supervisor that can be used at a critical incident.

Tactical Teams

As most law enforcement agencies do not have a standing tactical team awaiting deployment, most teams are made up of patrol officers who respond when a critical incident arises. As a result, tactical team members are primarily recruited and selected based on supervisor evaluations. Applicants for a tactical team unit should be assessed based on their immediate supervisor's evaluations and recommendations. Supervisors should be questioned about the applicant's level of common sense, emotional stability, and self-confidence (MacKenna & Stevens, 1989; McMains & Mullins, 2014). Additionally, applicants should be in excellent physical condition and should have outstanding supervisory evaluations, excellent communication skills, and a demeanor and bearing that would be conducive to being a team member (McMains & Mullins, 2014). A failure of the immediate supervisor to properly evaluate an applicant's ability to become a tactical team member could result in a disastrous event. Also, team supervisors must understand that they are supervising a team rather than individuals. Tactical teams are deployed as a unit and are supervised as a unit.

A tactical team is generally composed of three structures: perimeter control, assault team, and sniper/observer. Perimeter control teams are responsible for maintaining inner and outer perimeters. The perimeter team may be supervising other law enforcement personnel for this task and arranging for manpower to be posted in proper locations. The assault team usually consists of officers who make undetected approaches to the prime location, plan and prepare for release of hostages, and make assaults if necessary. The sniper/observer team has two primary responsibilities: intelligence and sniper fire. Intelligence gathering through observation is the primary responsibility in all critical incidents. Information regarding the physical layout of buildings and people in the area is vital for the incident commander. In hostage situations, this team would be responsible for sniper fire if the situation called for it.

Critical Incident Debriefing

As soon as possible after a critical incident, debriefings should be conducted with all officers involved. The debriefings have two major purposes: tactical and emotional. Tactical debriefings allow officers to critique actions and procedures and to identify mistakes and areas that need improvement in future incidents. Emotional debriefings attempt to minimize the potentially negative psychological effects of traumatic incidents on officers' psychological well-being.

Tactical Debriefing

Mattoon (1996) recommends that the following questions be addressed as soon as possible after a critical incident operation:

1. Was this the best response to the crisis incident?
2. If not, would it be best for a different incident?
3. What was the response time of the crisis team? Were there any notification problems?

4. How much time was required to put the command post in operation?
5. How long was it before all communication channels were functioning?
6. What communications problems were encountered?
7. What was the response time for other outside agencies responding?
8. How quickly were intelligence-gathering personnel and systems in place?
9. What problems were experienced by tactical teams, and how can they be minimized?
10. What problems were experienced by the negotiators, and how can they be minimized?
11. What problems were experienced by containment units?
12. Did the command post and subordinates use available intelligence and information as effectively as possible?
13. Were "think-tanks" initiated? If so, were they utilized properly?
14. Were chronological log, event journal, and other after-action reports submitted and correct?
15. Did the negotiators follow proper procedure?
16. Was any needed outside liaison effective?
17. Were facilities provided for media? Were there problems with the media?
18. What weapons and equipment needed were not available?
19. What other personnel and equipment were needed?
20. Were physical evidence and the crime scene handled correctly?
21. Were medical units requested and deployed properly?

Emotional Debriefing

Critical incidents are unexpected, tense events that fall outside the range of ordinary human experiences. Because they occur so abruptly, they can have a strong psychological and emotional impact on even the most experienced and well-trained officer (Kureczka, 1996). Fowler (1986) defines a critical incident as any situation in which a police officer's expectations of personal infallibility suddenly become tempered by imperfection and crude reality. A critical incident, however, may affect some officers emotionally and not others. For instance, a school bus accident where several children are killed may have a strong emotional impact on an officer who has young children, while the same incident may not have the same effect on an officer who has no children. And, as Kureczka points out, the circumstances of the incident, the officer's personality, the way the department handled the incident, the way the media portrayed officer's actions, and the officer's family all affect how an individual officer will react to the incident emotionally.

Pierson (1989) states that up to 87 percent of all emergency service workers will be affected by critical incident stress at least once in their careers. Symptoms vary according to the individual but generally are the same as for depression (withdrawal, numbing, sleep disturbances, anxiety, flashbacks, etc.). Police supervisors should be aware of these symptoms and watch subordinates for signs of stress after a critical incident (Figure 14.3). Blak (1991) indicates that it is natural for most people to exhibit these symptoms temporarily after a critical incident. However, if the symptoms persist for more than 30 days, the officer may be suffering from

Physical Reactions
Headaches
Muscle aches
Sleep disturbances
Changed appetite
Decreased/increased interest in sexual activity
Impotence

Emotional Reactions
Anxiety
Fear
Guilt
Sadness
Anger
Irritability
Feeling lost and unappreciated
Withdrawal

Cognitive Reactions
Debilitating flashbacks
Repeated visions of the incident
Nightmares
Slowed thinking
Difficulty making decisions/solving problems
Disorientation
Lack of concentration
Memory lapses

FIGURE 14.3 Common reactions to critical incident stress. *Source: Adapted from Kureczka (1996). "Critical Incident Stress in Law Enforcement."* FBI Law Enforcement Bulletin, *Vol. 65: 10–16.*

post-traumatic stress disorder (PTSD). Blak further notes that 4 to 10 percent of individuals who experience a critical incident will develop PTSD.

There are numerous approaches to critical incident stress debriefing. Mitchell (1983) describes a seven-phase method using critical incident stress management teams that provides psychological support to police officers and other emergency personnel following exposure to critical incidents (Figure 14.4). While the literature suggests that such debriefings are beneficial, police officers frequently see such counseling as showing weakness (Malcolm, Seaton, Perera, Sheehan, & Van Hasselt, 2005; Reese, 1991). Some experts suggest that such debriefings should be mandatory for police officers and other emergency personnel following a severe critical incident (Bohl, 1991; Reese, 1991).

Two of the more frequently reported reasons for police officer resignations are departmental policies and procedures and quality of supervision (Evans & Coman, 1988). These internal work-related stressors may exacerbate symptoms associated with critical incident stress, and officers may need to address these issues during debriefing as well. Additionally, officers may need to discuss life events that may affect symptoms associated with critical incidents, such as

First Stage	Introduction	Process description, rules (i.e., confidentiality), expectations.
Second Stage	Fact Phase	Officers asked to introduce themselves and their role in the incident.
Third Stage	Thought Phase	Officers share their first thoughts after the incident.
Fourth Stage	Reaction Phase	Explores the personal reactions surrounding the event.
Fifth Stage	Symptom Phase	Signs and symptoms of critical incident stress are discussed and normalized.
Sixth Stage	Teaching Phase	Officers are taught different ways of dealing with critical incident stress in their lives.
Seventh Stage	Reentry Phase	Officers are encouraged to discuss any other issues and ask questions. Focus is on returning the officer to duty.

FIGURE 14.4 Seven stages of critical incident stress management. *Adapted from A.S. Malcolm et al. (2005). "Critical Incident Stress Debriefing and Law Enforcement: An Evaluative Review."* Journal of Brief Treatment and Crisis Intervention, *Vol. 5: 261–278.*

thinking about their own family. Understanding the nature and culture of the police profession is a necessary foundation for any mental health professional taking on the task of critical incident stress debriefing; in some instances, peer officers are trained to conduct these debriefings (Malcolm et al., 2005).

In addition to being vigilant for signs and symptoms of postcritical incident stress in subordinates, the police supervisor should be supportive of any program designed for critical incident stress debriefing. The supervisor should encourage officers to accept these debriefings, not as a sign of weakness on their part, but as a sign of strength and stability.

SWAT—Special Weapons and Tactics

In the late 1960s, local law enforcement officers were faced with increasingly well-armed criminals who were willing to engage in armed confrontation with the police. The Los Angeles Police Department began using a military-style response to armed confrontation, hostage taking, drug arrests, and other potentially deadly encounters. Known as special weapons and tactics, or SWAT, the idea was to prevent needless gunfire in an encounter by using high-energy tactics to take down suspects quickly without endangering the general population. SWAT has evolved into the management of barricaded suspect situations, serving high-risk warrants and raids, dignitary protection, and hostage rescue.

A report by the California Attorney General's Commission on Special Weapons and Tactics in 2002 indicated the need for a number of changes and improvements in the way SWAT teams operated in California. The Commission (2002) indicated that:

> *...the clearest issue to emerge was the need for a set of standards in all aspects of SWAT operations. The lack of clear standards in training, tactics, and policy can and must be addressed.*

The National Tactical Officers Association (NTOA) has published SWAT Best Practices (2002) as a guide for local law enforcement agencies developing a tactical team. NTOA suggests written policy statements be developed for the department, including:

1. A written statement describing the mission of the SWAT team that also addresses the need and rationale for staffing the team.
2. A written description of the composition and structure of the team. This should include an organizational chart.
3. A written statement describing a clear incident command and control structure that delineates chain of command and lines of communication/notification, both within the team and in the context of the parent organization.
4. A written process for activation of the team. This should include a clear rationale justifying the standards for activation.
5. A written statement on the use of deadly force consistent with department policy.
6. A written description of the selection process for all ranks within the team. The description should include clearly defined and validated selection criteria that are specific to the tasks to be performed. If the selection process has not been formally validated, it should conform to Equal Employment Opportunity Commission guidelines.
7. A written description of standards regarding qualification and subsequent periodic requalification for all team members.
8. A written standard for a minimum number of hours of tactical training per month for all members and positions. The NTOA recommends a minimum of two days each month for a part-time team and 25 percent of on-duty time for a full-time team.
9. A written standard for safety equipment, including, but not limited to, helmets, eyewear, hearing protection, body armor, equipment-bearing vests, chemical agent mask and/or belts, and footwear.
10. A written statement of the need and rationale for all weapons, ammunition, diversion devices, chemical agents, forced-entry tools, less-than-lethal devices, and explosives.
11. A written standard detailing use of a complete and formatted operation plan that is written/documented and retained for a prescribed length of time after the operation. The plan should be designed to fit all predictable uses of the team.
12. A written standard detailing the development and use of team incident reports for activation and implementation phases of all callouts and operations.

13. A written standard detailing development and use of an after-action critique format to be completed and retained for a prescribed length of time following all team callouts, operations, and significant training events.
14. A written standard detailing the timeline and conditions for periodic review and updating of all applicable policies.
15. A written policy statement ensuring that standards adopted meet local and state requirements and are approved by the agency head.
16. A written policy statement regarding the option chosen for the incorporation and use of tactical emergency medical support.
17. A written policy statement defining mutual aid agreements with federal, state, and local agencies, including a clear incident command structure during mutual aid.

In addition to written policy statements and standards, NTOA recommends that standard operational deployment procedures should be developed. Issues such as containment, immediate action, deliberate action, suspect/hostage control measures, negotiations, and liaison with command are all part of the procedures that should be addressed in standard operational procedures. According to the NTOA (2002), things to consider in such deployment procedures are as follows:

1. Establishing priorities of life by understanding how the lives of hostages, officers, and suspects are balanced against each other.
2. Callout (activation) procedures, which facilitate a timely and prepared response by the team.
3. Minimum staffing levels for response to certain types of critical incidents.
4. Mutual aid/assistance protocols.
5. SWAT response to "suicide-by-cop" incidents.
6. Barricaded suspect response.
7. Hostage-barricade situation response should direct specific actions and activities for various elements of the team and address procedures of containment, immediate action, deliberate action, and coordinated initiation of negotiations.
8. Sniper incident response should delineate team response to a situation where a suspect is actively engaging targets from a fixed or mobile position.
9. High-risk warrant service should include practices and procedures to be used in planning and conducting the service of warrants. Consideration should also be given to categorizing warrants by degree of risk to determine which unit should serve them, that is, SWAT or narcotics.
10. Active shooter response should consider that the first officers on scene must respond within their capabilities to an active shooter at a school or public building as soon as possible and not await arrival of a SWAT team. The SWAT team will play an important role in the resolution should the situation transition to a barricade incident or the suspect's location is unknown.
11. VIP/dignitary protection duties and protocols.

12. A clearly defined ICS containing command and supervisory responsibilities, tactical intelligence gathering, operational procedures, and integration of crisis/hostage negotiation team operations.
13. Establishing a written procedure as to who can authorize the use of chemical agents, diversionary devices, explosives, and other special equipment, including equipment provided by outside sources.
14. Establish minimum numbers of personnel required to carry out high-risk preplanned or emergency operations.

In recent years, the use of SWAT and tactical teams has received criticism based on the military-style operation of the units, the increasing number of deployments of teams, and incidents of mistaken identity (Baker, 2011; Balko, 2013). The California Commission (2002) noted some considerations regarding the use of tactical units to ensure that serious mistakes do not occur:

1. Does the team have a lawful right to be where it is and to do what is proposed?
2. Do the circumstances justify the use of a SWAT team?
3. Has every step been taken to ensure that the team is at the correct location?
4. Can the situation be resolved safely through negotiations?
5. Do the circumstances warrant a crisis entry?
6. Do the circumstances warrant the immediate use of deadly force to neutralize the suspect?
7. Does the team have adequate information about the suspect (i.e., violent history, mental state, previous acts, military experience)?
8. Have the consequences of the tactical mission been considered (i.e., other options, evacuations, use of chemical agents, proximity to schools)?
9. Is the risk versus benefit decision-making process an ongoing process involving the incident commander, SWAT commander, negotiation team, and supervisors?
10. Has relief for team members been considered (i.e., fatigue, hunger, exposure to elements)?

The California Commission (2002) concluded that there are occasions when immediate and decisive action must be taken in a crisis. However, the need to take action must, at times, be suppressed, as protracted negotiations may be the best course of action. But whatever course of action is taken, deployment of tactical teams in critical incidents is an "extremely high-stakes situation, and our actions will be closely scrutinized" (California Commission, Appendix C).

References

Baker, A. (2011). When the police go military. *The New York Times* December 3.

Balko, R. (2013). *Rise of the warrior cop: The militarization of America's police forces.* Jackson, TN: PublicAffairs Publishers.

Blak, R. A. (1991). Critical incident debriefing for law enforcement personnel: A model. In J. T. Reese, J. M. Horn, & C. Dunning (Eds.), *Critical incidents in policing.* Washington, DC: U.S. Government Printing Office.

Bohl, N. (1991). The effectiveness of brief psychological interventions in police officers after critical incidents. In J. T. Reese, J. M. Horn, & C. Dunning (Eds.), *Critical Incidents in policing.* Washington, DC: U.S. Government Printing Office.

Boltz, F. A., Jr. (2001). Intelligence requirements in hostage situations. *Journal of Police Crisis Negotiations, 1,* 61–68.

CALEA (2006). *Standards for law enforcement agencies.* Fairfax, VA: Commission on Accreditation for Law Enforcement Agencies, Inc.

Commission on Special Weapons and Tactics (2002). *Final report.* Sacramento, CA: California Attorney General's Office.

Evans, B. J., & Coman, G. J. (1988). The worst part of the job. *Police Review, 96,* 968–969.

Fairburn, R. (2004). Rapid deployment research project. *The Tactical Edge, Spring,* 24–26.

FEMA (2006). *Incident command system training.* Washington, DC: U.S. Government Printing Office.

Fowler, W. (1986). Post-critical incident counseling: An example of emotional first-aid in a police crisis. In J. Reese & H. Goldstein (Eds.), *Psychological services for law enforcement.* Washington, DC: U.S. Government Printing Office.

Kureczka, A. W. (1996). Critical incident stress in law enforcement. *FBI Law Enforcement Bulletin, 65,* 10–16.

MacKenna, D., & Stevens, J. (1989). Selecting and training police tactical officers. *The Police Chief, 56,* 12–15.

Malcolm, A. S., Seaton, J., Perera, A., Sheehan, D. C., & Van Hasselt, V. B. (2005). Critical incident stress debriefing and law enforcement: An evaluative review. *Journal of Brief Treatment and Crisis Intervention, 5,* 261–278.

Mattoon, S. (1996). *SWAT/SRT instructional manual.* Washington, DC: Defense Technology Corporation of America.

McMains, M. J., & Mullins, W. C. (2014). *Crisis negotiations* (5th ed.). Boston: Elsevier (Anderson Publishing).

Mitchell, J. T. (1983). When disaster strikes: The critical incident stress debriefing process. *Journal of Emergency Medical Services, 1,* 36–39.

National Tactical Officers Association (2002). *Suggested SWAT best practices.* In Commission on Special Weapons and Tactics, California Attorney General's Office, Appendix.

Pierson, T. (1989). Critical incident stress: A serious law enforcement problem. *The Police Chief, 56*(2), 32–33. (February).

Reese, J. T. (1991). Justifications for mandating critical incident aftercare. In J. T. Reese, J. M. Horn, & C. Dunning (Eds.), *Critical incidents in policing.* Washington, DC: U.S. Government Printing Office.

Solis, L. F. (2002). Critical incident intelligence gathering, coordination and analysis. *Journal of Police Crisis Negotiations, 2,* 91–98.

15

Labor Relations
Problem Solving through Constructive Conflict

KEY TERMS

balance through
  constructive conflict
bargaining in good faith
choosing a bargaining
  agent
collective bargaining
compulsory binding
  arbitration (CBA)
designated rights
exclusive bargaining
  agent
grievance
impasse resolution
  techniques
management rights/
  union responsibility
negotiating a CBA or
  contract
noneconomic issues

participatory
  management by
  contracts
reserved rights
role conflict and its
  impact on morale
scope of bargaining
sergeants as contract
  administrators
sergeants as
  disciplinarians
"traditional" versus
  "innovative" bargaining
unionism—the hidden
  revolution
union security measures
wages, hours, and
  conditions of
  employment

CASE STUDY
Sergeant Tom Scott

DEPARTMENT

The Edwardsville Police Department is a medium-sized department with 312 sworn officers. The local chapter of the Fraternal Order of Police (FOP) established a collective bargaining unit nearly 15 years ago. Since that time, the collective bargaining unit has worked fairly smoothly in getting a number of much-needed changes in the police department.

Edwardsville Police Department has a long history that can be traced back to 1866 when it was first incorporated. In fact, the first chief of police was a highly decorated union colonel of the civil war. Having lost a leg at Gettysburg, he was affectionately called Peg-Leg by residents of the new city. The police department has gone through many changes since then, and Peg-Leg would hardly recognize the department now. The city has never recruited an outsider to fill the role of chief of police, opting instead to allow officers to move up through the ranks and selecting from within.

The police department is traditionally organized along line and staff operations and contracts with the county sheriff's office for detention of prisoners. There is a juvenile detention center located in the city operated by a private corrections company. The police department has its own certified training academy for basic and specialized training. And while there are plans to seek accreditation through the Commission on Accreditation of Law Enforcement Agencies (CALEA), the cost of doing so is not within the budget in the foreseeable future.

CRIME

Edwardsville police responded to more than 231,000 calls for service last year. Most of these calls were domestic violence, public intoxication, fighting, lost children, prowlers, road hazards and accidents, and driving under the influence. According to last year's Uniform Crime Report filed by the police, the city had 10,647 Part 1 offenses, an increase of nearly 3 percent over the previous year. Violent crimes had decreased, however, by nearly 8 percent over the previous year. Property crimes increased, especially burglary and larceny, by just over 15 percent.

According to the police crime analysis statistician, police officers had a reduction in the number of citations for moving traffic and parking violations in the city. This trend began about the same time the city started to have financial problems. Police managers were instructed by the city leaders to pick up the pace on citations because that was a valuable source of revenue for the city. The managers in turn instructed supervisors to be sure officers were not lax in their efforts to issue more citations.

COMMUNITY

Edwardsville has a population of 216,000 and is growing at a rate of approximately 2 percent per year. It is a popular location for retired individuals due to numerous housing areas near golf courses and lakes. Edwardsville has long been an industry town with three major manufacturing industries in paper, chemicals, and fabrics. The industries have attracted a number of new employees over the past several years. However, these new residents have elected to move into subdivisions that have been developed in neighboring incorporated towns with a lower tax rate than Edwardsville. And because the neighboring cities are incorporated, Edwardsville has not been able to annex more areas to increase the tax base. In an effort to attract more residents to the city, Edwardsville entered into a number of bond packages to develop more attractive facilities for potential residents. The city developed two golf courses and built a multimillion dollar performing arts center that resulted in the loss of several million dollars. Given the serious financial situation, city leaders decided they needed to cut back on expenditures in order to stay afloat.

OFFICER

Sergeant Tom Scott has been with the Edwardsville Police Department for more than 22 years. He was promoted to sergeant after having worked as a patrol officer for seven years. He has passed up opportunities for promotion to lieutenant because he likes his role as a supervisor in patrol. Scott sees himself as more of a street cop than a "paper pusher." It was this perspective that gained him the respect and admiration of his subordinates. He was the only sergeant selected on the newly formed negotiating team for the collective bargaining unit. Over the years, many of the officers on the negotiating team have been promoted to sergeant, and a couple have been promoted to lieutenant. Although the lieutenants are not now part of the negotiating team, the team has six sergeants and nine officers. Scott has enjoyed his role on the team and is perceived by management as a fair negotiator. Scott believes he is able to see both sides of a situation and can compromise if warranted.

PROBLEM

Over the past several months, many officers have filed grievances and morale has been low due to the city's financial strains. Much of the problem has been the obvious violation of contract agreements by the city. The city took away several benefits the collective bargaining team had negotiated, including overtime pay, educational tuition payments and leave time, maternity leave for female officers, and even reduced insurance benefits for all city employees. The city claims they are in a serious financial crunch and that they are invoking the exigent circumstances clause in the collective bargaining agreement. The exigent circumstances clause allows the city to override the negotiated agreement in the best interests of the city. In a few months, a new collective bargaining contract will be negotiated, and there is talk among the city leaders that these reductions in benefits will be permanently installed with the new contract. This has created quite a stir among the officers, and there is a call for a new slate of negotiating team members. One of the major controversies is the presence of sergeants on the negotiating team. Many of the officers claim that the sergeants are condescending to management's side, resulting in contracts that are not truly good faith agreements. They also point out that many of the negotiating team members have been promoted as a reward for helping management in these contract agreements. The FOP has petitioned the State Labor Relations Board to hold a hearing on the merits of having sergeants on the negotiating team. The FOP claims that sergeants are more policy-making managers than first-line supervisors and should be excluded from any bargaining unit.

As the senior supervisor on the collective bargaining unit, Sergeant Scott has been asked by the FOP and the chief of police to testify at the State Labor Relations Board hearing on the matter.

WHAT WOULD YOU DO?

If you were Sergeant Scott, what issues would you address at the hearing? What kinds of information would you need to present at the hearing? Should sergeants and first-line supervisors be allowed to serve on bargaining teams? Why or why not? Should there be a limit on how many supervisors can serve on a collective bargaining team?

Sowing the Seeds of Unionism

European-style unionism never caught on in the United States. As a matter of fact, labor unions were banned in this country until the mid-1930s. It took the economic upheaval of the Great Depression to change public policy concerning collective bargaining. The legalization of collective bargaining ushered in a new and very different era.

The Wagner Act was signed into law by President Franklin D. Roosevelt in 1935. Officially known as the National Labor Relations Act, it permitted workers in private industry to form labor unions and actually encouraged them to bargain with their employers concerning "wages, hours, and working conditions." While the National Labor Relations Act is often referred to as organized labor's Magna Carta, it was never intended to cover everyone in the workforce. Government employees, for example, were specifically excluded from participation in the collective bargaining process.

After the initial surge of organizing activity in traditional blue-collar industries, union membership stabilized and then began to decline. In 1945, union membership reached an all-time high of 35.5 percent of the workforce (Foulkes & Livernash, 1989). By the late 1970s, however, less than one-quarter of the nation's workers were still unionized (Dressler, 1979). It is now estimated that only 16.1 percent of all American workers are represented by unions (World Almanac, 1993). The face of organized labor has changed, and the future of the labor movement is uncertain.

Public employees at all levels of government resented the fact that they were excluded from collective bargaining and rejected this prohibition as an unwarranted intrusion on their First Amendment right to freedom of association. As their influence and purchasing power lagged behind that of other workers, they became much more militant in their demands for equality under the law (Stahl, 1983). Union organizers seized on this widespread discontent. It gave them a chance to fan the fire of collectivism among government employees. Unionism was actively promoted as a viable alternative to the managerial despotism of the past. By working together, public employees and unions delivered a classic one-two punch, and the legal barriers to collective bargaining in the public sector began to erode slowly.

The Boston police strike of 1919, viewed by many unionists as one of the most important events in American police history, was the cause célèbre that gave the nation its first real exposure to labor problems in municipal government. The basic issue involved the right of the police, as public employees, to form a union and to affiliate with the American Federation of Labor. The strike shocked the national conscience and solidified political opposition to all forms of collective bargaining. The response was both swift and decisive. The Boston police had to be kept in their place irrespective of the cost. According to Shafritz, Rosenbloom, Riccucci, Naff, and Hyde (2001), it was political power and not strict rationality that determined the rules of play and the winner of the game. While the unionization of public employees is now legal in most states, there is a distinct undercurrent of antiunion sentiment that can be traced directly to the Boston police strike of 1919.

In 1919, Boston police officers earned $1400 a year and had not received a pay raise in nearly 20 years. They worked an average of 87 hours per week under deplorable conditions. The cost of living had skyrocketed (by 86 percent), and promotions were based solely on political considerations. The situation was truly grim. Morale hit an all-time low. When the police officers' demand for a $200-a-year pay raise was rejected, they voted to convert their social club into a bona fide labor union and join the American Federation of Labor. The city's police commissioner reacted immediately. He suspended the leaders of the new organization. Tension mounted. All attempts at mediation failed and a strike seemed to be inevitable. On September 9, 1919, 1117 Boston police officers went on strike in the first publicly proclaimed "job action" against a municipal government in the United States. Only 427 policemen remained on the job (Walker, 1999).

Violence, disorder, and crime erupted as Boston reverted to a Hobbesian "state of nature." Looting was commonplace. Lawlessness and mob action became the rule rather than the exception. Declaring a state of emergency, the mayor asked the governor to help restore law and order in the city. On the third day of the strike, more than 7000 fully armed members of the state militia took control of the city. In defending the state's action, Governor Calvin Coolidge made the famous statement that now serves as a rallying cry against unionism in the public sector saying, "There is no right to strike against the public safety by anybody, anywhere, at any time." All of the strikers were fired, and antiunion sentiment spread like wildfire throughout the nation.

While the Boston police strike failed to achieve its objectives, it sent reverberations throughout the American political establishment. Maintaining control over public employees became a national obsession. In what amounted to a knee-jerk reaction, state legislatures enacted very repressive legislation prohibiting the unionization of state and local government employees. The courts, responding to social and political pressure to maintain the status quo, consistently ruled that public employees per se had absolutely no statutory or constitutional right to organize for the purpose of collective bargaining with their employers. In most states it was illegal for any government unit to engage in collective bargaining with its employees. The gerrymandering of public employees out of the National Labor Relations Act was by no means accidental. The die was cast in Boston. Public employees were to be excluded from the collective bargaining process for the next 40 years.

Public sector labor–management relations deteriorated during World War II. Poor pay, rampant inflation, and a generalized sense of exploitation took its toll on police morale. Perceiving strength in numbers, the police flirted with unionism once again. While they had absolutely no legal standing, beginning in 1943 these unions experienced some limited success in negotiating with their employers. The informal collective bargaining process seemed to be working. Within a few years, however, these fledgling unions were crushed by even more restrictive legislation, unfavorable court decisions, firm opposition from police administrators, and the refusal of local politicians to alter the existing balance of power in any way, vis-à-vis meaningful collective bargaining with their employees. No one was willing to compromise. The battle lines were drawn.

Government employees did not give up on the idea of collective bargaining. They formed union-like professional associations and continued to push for substantive changes in the law. These groups lobbied legislators, agitated for social change, and, on occasion, took illegal job actions to press their demands. As the number of state and local government employees mushroomed, these groups flexed their muscles and were able to exercise more clout in the political arena. Everything seemed to come together in 1959. In that year, Wisconsin became the first state in the nation to grant public employees a limited right to bargain with their employers concerning typical union items such as wages, hours, and working conditions. Wisconsin's public employees were specifically prohibited from using the strike as a tool for impasse resolution. Public employees found the door open and were prepared to seize the opportunity to solve their problems through constructive conflict.

Things have changed dramatically since 1959. More than 80 percent of states have now adopted legislation that permits public employees to participate in the collective bargaining process. In some states, public employees (with the exception of fire and police personnel) are allowed to strike. Ohio's 1984 public bargaining law is a classic example. It gives all employees, except public safety personnel, the right to strike (after a mandatory 10-day advance notice). By 1985, 24 states had opted to provide public employees with some type of arbitration as an alternative to a strike. Figure 15.1 is an analysis of Pennsylvania's Act 111 (Commonwealth

In May 1968, Governor Raymond Shaffer appointed a commission to review the Pennsylvania Public Employee Act of 1947. The commission was to be known as the Heckman Commission, taking the name of its chairman, Leon E. Heckman. Governor Shaffer directed this commission to "review the whole area of public relations dealing with public employees and public employers and to make recommendations to him for the establishment of orderly, fair and workable procedures governing those relations; including legislation, if the commission deems it appropriate."

After several months of intensive review, the commission stated that the Public Employee Act of 1947 had at least three major weaknesses in its basic structure.

1. The act does not require public employers to bargain collectively with their employees. This has led to a near-breakdown in communication, where the public employer has not chosen to recognize the right of its employees to bargain collectively. This inability to bargain collectively has created more ill-will and led to more friction and strikes than any other cause.

2. The act forbids any and all strikes by public employees. Twenty years of experience have taught us that such a policy is unreasonable and unenforceable, particularly when coupled with ineffective or nonexistent collective bargaining. It is based upon a philosophy that one may not strike against the sovereign. However, today's sovereign is engaged not only in government, but in a great variety of other activities. The consequences of a strike by a police officer are very different from those of a gardener in a public park.

3. The mandatory penalties of the 1947 act are self-defeating. Forbidding a public employer to give normal pay increases for three years to one who has struck and has been reemployed simply reduces the value of such position to that employee and drives him or her to seek other work.

The commission made the following recommendations:

A. The Public Employee Act of 1947 should be replaced by an entirely new law governing relationships between public employees and employer.

    1. The commission forged a single statute for all public instrumentalities and their employees in order to ensure a uniform policy for all agencies of government.

B. The new law should recognize the right of all public employees, including police and firefighters, to bargain collectively subject to enumerated safeguards.

    1. The bargaining unit should be determined in each instance by the Pennsylvania Labor Relations Board pursuant to statutory guidelines.

    2. The bargaining agent should be determined only by elections supervised by the labor board.

    3. Bargaining should be permitted with respect to wages, hours, and conditions of employment, appropriately qualified by a recognition of existing laws dealing with aspects of the same subject matter and by a carefully defined reservation of managerial rights.

FIGURE 15.1 Public Employee Act.

4. Employees should be protected from an obligation to become members of an employee organization as a condition of employment, but the right to collect dues from members of the employee organization should be recognized as a bargainable issue under appropriate safeguards.

C. The law should require both parties to bargain in good faith through the following steps:

1. Face-to-face collective bargaining between the parties, with the final agreement to be reduced to writing and signed by representatives of all parties.

2. Use of the state mediation service in the event collective bargaining is not successful without it.

3. Fact-finding, recommendations, and publication thereof by a tribunal of three experienced arbitrators appointed by the labor board.

4. In disputes involving police officers and firefighters, if collective bargaining and mediation do not resolve the dispute, mandatory binding arbitration.

D. Except for police officers and firefighters, a limited right to strike should be recognized, subject to these safeguards:

1. No strike should be permitted for any reason whatsoever until all of the collective bargaining procedures outlined above have been fully complied with.

2. No strike should be permitted to begin or continue where health, safety, or welfare of the general public is in danger.

3. Unlawful strikes should be subject to injunctions and violations thereof enforced by penalties that will be effective against the bargaining agent or individual employees or both.

The Heckman Commission favored a single statute for all public instrumentalities, but Pennsylvania now has two laws providing for collective bargaining for public employees. These two laws are indeed a strange contrast, particularly because they were passed by essentially the same legislature and signed by the same governor.

As a result of a constitutional change in 1967, Act 111 of June 24, 1968, provided for collective bargaining of police officers and firefighters of public jurisdiction in the Commonwealth. It designates binding arbitration for impasses in lieu of the right to strike. Act 111 was rushed through the legislative process in four days without staff work, publicity, or public hearings.

It took a little more than two years to complete Public Employee Relations Act 195 from commission to operation. Members of the commission wrote the act, public hearings were held, interest and viewpoints of opposing parties were solicited, and the act received widespread publicity. As passed by the general assembly, Act 195 permits strikes by public employees in nonsafety categories, such as teachers, health care providers, social services personnel, and so forth. Act 195 is completely silent on the salient issue of binding arbitration.

FIGURE 15.1 (Continued)

of Pennsylvania, Revised Statutes, 1987). While compulsory binding arbitration was initially intended only for those involved in critical services, there has been some movement to broaden the scope of coverage to include other types of public employees as well (Swanson, Territo, & Taylor, 2007).

While Act 111 has been modified somewhat, its basic thrust remains unchanged. Pennsylvania labor law encourages collective bargaining between local governments and certified employee organizations authorized to represent police personnel. Act 111 has served as the prototype for collective bargaining statutes throughout the United States.

According to O. Glenn Stahl (1983), most state and local government employees are now represented by labor unions. The American Federation of State, County, and Municipal Employees (AFSCME) is one of the largest and most powerful unions in America. AFSCME has more than 3000 locals and more than 1,280,000 members. It is affiliated with the American Federation of Labor and Congress of Industrial Organizations. In addition to AFSCME, there are scores of smaller labor organizations (such as the American Federation of Teachers, Fraternal Order of Police, International Association of Fire Fighters, Service Employees International Union) engaged in collective bargaining on behalf of public employees. Independent and unaffiliated local unions have sprung up to represent the unique interests of specialized government personnel. Teachers, firefighters, and municipal police officers are the most heavily unionized groups in the public sector.

The public sector is a natural habitat for labor unions. They serve two masters, by providing gains for workers and political support for legislators, as well as government managers. Given this situation, it is conceivable that the upper limit of public sector unionization may reach nearly 100 percent at some time in the future (Bellante & Porter, 1992).

The dramatic rise of membership in police unions can, in large measure, be attributed to one or more of the following factors:

1. Job dissatisfaction (especially with regard to wages and working conditions).
2. The perception that other public employees are improving their situation through the collective bargaining process.
3. A deep-seated belief that the public is unsympathetic or even hostile to the personal and professional needs of police officers.
4. An influx of younger police officers who hold a far less traditional view of authority and bureaucratic regimentation.
5. A strong recruiting effort by organized labor to make up for a decline in membership caused by the shift from an industrial to a service-based economy.

Today, nearly three-quarters of all American police officers are dues-paying members of labor unions (Cole & Smith, 2008). In fact, law enforcement membership in unions is one of the fastest growing labor groups in the nation (Stone, 1998).

Many of the existing police unions evolved from social or fraternal organizations. Local police benevolent associations and the national Fraternal Order of Police are excellent examples of this phenomenon. Due to the decentralization of municipal government (with more than 17,000 separate police departments), unions were forced to focus on local issues rather than national concerns. Consequently, there is no national labor organization that can legitimately claim to represent the interests of all police personnel in the United States. Juris and Feuille (1973) argue very convincingly that it is the local character of the employment relationship that helps explain why the relatively centralized national police organizations have not attracted large numbers of rank-and-file police officers as members.

While they do not represent the interests of all police officers, national labor organizations such as the AFSCME, Fraternal Order of Police, International Brotherhood of Police Officers, International Conference of Police Associations, International Union of Police Associations, and the Teamsters wield a substantial amount of political power and have the ability to influence public policy making at all levels of government. Unionism and collective bargaining have now become permanent fixtures in public sector labor relations (Stone, 1998).

Unionism and collective bargaining by police officers represent what Samuel Walker has referred to as "the hidden revolution" in contemporary police administration. According to Walker (1999), there has been a fundamental shift in the balance of power as far as management and labor are concerned. Unilateral decision-making by supervisors and managers is a thing of the past. Participatory, bilateral management is a fait accompli. Collective bargaining is a vehicle for problem solving through constructive conflict (Carter & Sapp, 1993).

One of the most important issues in labor relations relates to the scope of bargaining. What should or should not be determined at the bargaining table? Management has not, for a variety of reasons, been particularly successful in limiting the scope of negotiations. An analysis of various police collective bargaining agreements shows that most of them do not have the strongest management rights clauses. This would suggest that police administrators have been less than vigorous in preserving their prerogatives. They have failed to regulate the input of organized labor in the decision-making process (Rynecki, Cairns, & Carnes, 1984). Consequently, police unions have had a profound influence on such matters as:

1. Salaries, supplemental pay, and benefits
2. Hours and working conditions
3. Manpower allocation
4. Job assignments
5. Occupational safety
6. Discipline and procedural due process
7. Evaluation and promotion procedures
8. Resource allocation
9. Law enforcement policy
10. Police–community relations
11. Training and professional development

Balanced power is the key to success in collective bargaining. In some unionized departments, however, there is an unhealthy shift of administrative power from the chief executive officer to the union. This is unfortunate. An organization needs someone to take charge and provide a sense of direction. The leader must have the managerial skill and legitimate authority to keep the organization operating as a goal-oriented system of coordinated and cooperative effort. The function of the police executive is to mobilize the human and economic resources necessary to accomplish the police department's mission, goals, and objectives (Barnard, 1976).

Many first-line supervisors, managers, elected officials, and police theorists have not come to grips with unionism. They do not fully appreciate the magnitude of the hidden revolution that has taken place since the early 1980s. Many practitioners seem content to muddle their way through life and are unconcerned with the legacy they will leave to the next generation of managers. Some police theorists, however, are in a state of denial. Some new textbooks on police management and supervision fail to mention labor relations, unions, collective bargaining, or contract administration. This ignorance and denial could transform the hidden revolution into degenerative conflict between organized labor and management.

Management Rights

Management rights refer to decisions that govern the conditions of employment over which management claims to have exclusive jurisdiction. Because almost every management right can be and has been challenged by unions, the ultimate determination will depend on the relative bargaining power of the two sides. Union concessions and cooperation have a price tag. Under these circumstances, time-honored management rights are often negotiable.

There are two basic ways to approach the management rights issue. One is the reserved rights concept. The other is referred to as the designated rights concept. They are based on different sets of assumptions. The reserved rights approach presumes that management authority is supreme in all matters except those it has expressly conceded in the collective bargaining agreement or when its authority is restricted by law. Consequently, little or nothing is said about management rights in the contract. The designated rights approach, however, is specifically intended to clarify and reinforce the rights claimed by management. A management rights clause is made part of the bargaining agreement in an effort to reduce confusion and misunderstanding. A strong management rights clause sets very clear boundaries designed to help both parties understand the ground rules for future negotiations (Bohlander, Snell, & Sherman, 2013).

The lack of attention to the issue of management rights has had a far-reaching effect on police organization and management. In a national survey of police administrators, almost 50 percent of the respondents stated that their managerial prerogatives related to improving the police service had been "lost" as a result of collective bargaining (Sapp, Carter, & Stephens, 1990).

Understanding Labor Relations

Collective bargaining is built on the assumption that a certain amount of controlled conflict is healthy. It promotes organizational growth and development. If police officers are going to benefit fully from their association with one another (in labor unions), they and their managers should be willing to differ, to push self-interests, and to accept the idea that there is inherent value in conflict. If employees and managers do not oppose each other enough, their relationships tend to become static or counterproductive. If they oppose each other too much, conflict may get out of hand and could upset even routine operations in the police department. Here again, balance is the key to success in labor relations. Mutually acceptable collective bargaining procedures and sound judgment help ensure that differences and conflict will remain within reasonable limits. Integrity, goodwill, and procedural regularity are essential elements in an ethical collective bargaining process. While tension may be a catalyst for mutual problem solving and coordinated action, there is nothing to be gained from the intraorganizational conflict created by petty feuding, malice, or self-destructive behavior. Management prerogatives, employee rights, and organizational needs might best be viewed as a three-legged stool. If one of the legs is weakened, the stool will collapse. No matter how strong the other legs are, they cannot, in and of themselves, keep the stool in an upright position. When the stool collapses, the community is the loser. It is the community that ends up paying (in higher taxes and fewer services) when the collective bargaining process breaks down (Ewing, 1983).

As peripheral members of the management team, sergeants interact most directly with the line personnel who do the actual work of the police department. They deal with unionized employees on a daily basis. In order to do their job properly, sergeants need to have a fairly comprehensive understanding of human behavior, work, workers, unions, and the collective bargaining process. In addition, they must prepare themselves for a unique role in labor contract administration.

Selecting a Bargaining Agent

Police officers, as public employees, are not covered by the National Labor Relations Act of 1935. As noted previously, more than 80 percent of the states have passed legislation specifically authorizing collective bargaining by public employees. No two bargaining statutes are exactly the same. Some public employee bargaining laws are fairly permissive (even allowing strikes under certain circumstances), whereas others are more detailed, specific, and much more restrictive. In most states, the State Labor Relations Board (SLRB) administers the law and regulates the collective bargaining process. Almost all administrative and regulatory decisions made by these boards are reviewable in the courts.

An employee, a group of employees, a union, or an employer can petition the SLRB for a representation election. The purpose of the election is to determine whether the employees want to select an exclusive bargaining agent. In most cases, a petition must be supported by a show of interest on the part of a specified percentage of the workforce. The federal standard of 30 percent has been adopted in a large number of states.

Once a petition for a representation election has been accepted, it is up to the SLRB to determine (based on job descriptions) who should and should not be in the proposed bargaining unit. In determining the exact composition of the unit, the SLRB looks for a commonality of interest based on factors such as:

1. Similarity of duties, skills, wages, and working conditions.
2. Pertinent collective bargaining history of those involved.

3. Nature and extent of union organization that is already in place.
4. Employees' wishes in the matter (when they are consistent with other factors).
5. Appropriateness of the proposed unit in relation to the organizational structure of the department.

Unions should represent employees whose jobs are similar and who also share a common interest. Unfortunately, labor relations theory is not always translated into practice. Bargaining unit determination in law enforcement has been a mixed bag. In Pittsburgh, for example, the FOP represents all police officers up to the rank of captain. In Toledo and Detroit, the union represents only the employees at the rank of police officer. Toledo has a separate Command Officers' Association that represents sergeants, lieutenants, and captains. Civilian personnel are often represented by AFSCME. It is not uncommon for a local government to deal with three or four separate unions representing employees in the same police department.

From a practical point of view, it is far better for management personnel to be in the same bargaining unit with other managers who have similar duties, responsibilities, and interests. This is also true when it comes to sergeants. They are much more likely to support management initiatives and function as effective first-line managers if they consider themselves to be a real part of the management team (Ayres & Coble, 1987). Unfortunately, there has been little consistency in this area, and many existing bargaining unit configurations simply cannot be justified in logical terms.

Assuming that there are no problems in determining the composition of the proposed bargaining unit and that no other group has been certified as the exclusive bargaining agent for the employees, the SLRB is obligated by law to conduct a representation election. If everyone agrees, the staff of the SLRB will conduct what is called a consent election. In the event that there is any disagreement, an election will be authorized after a formal hearing has been held and an official finding is made by the board. The time and date of the election will be set in an effort to ensure that most of the eligible employees on all shifts will have the opportunity to vote. All parties to the election are expected to adhere to the pre-election campaign guidelines set by the SLRB. Both labor and management have the right to appoint a number of observers to act as poll watchers, checkers, challengers, and tabulators. Everything must be done to ensure the fairness of the election and the validity of each ballot.

If no objections are filed or if those that are filed are rejected, the board has the legal authority to certify the results. There are two basic types of certification:

1. **Certification of Representation.** Attesting to the fact that a majority of those in the bargaining unit voted for the union.
2. **Certification of Election Results.** Attesting to the fact that employees in the bargaining unit voted against union representation.

Certification of representation makes the union the sole bargaining agent for all members of the bargaining unit. It also gives the union authority to enter into legally binding negotiations with the state or local government (Anderson, 1975).

A certified police union is a force to be reckoned with. It is, by law, the exclusive bargaining agent for all members of the bargaining unit, whether they belong to the union or not.

Management is not permitted to negotiate directly with individual police officers or other groups within the police department. There are other benefits to certification as well. For example:

1. The employer (state or local government) must bargain in good faith with a certified union and usually is required to meet and discuss items of mutual concern on a timely basis.
2. The employer (state or local government) is obligated to seek a collective bargaining agreement or contract with the certified union representing bargaining unit employees.
3. Certified unions may be authorized to file policy grievances, to strike, or (if strikes are prohibited) to seek binding arbitration in an effort to enforce the collective bargaining agreement, depending on how the public employee bargaining law is written.
4. Rival unions are not permitted to engage in striking or picketing for recognition under the collective bargaining statute if there is a certified labor organization already in place.
5. Even if the parties cannot reach a collective bargaining agreement, rival unions are normally prohibited from filing a petition for a new representation election within 12 months of the original certification election.
6. An existing contract (for a definite term of up to three years) is usually considered a bar to a new election while it is in force.

In the event that union members become dissatisfied with its performance, they can petition for "decertification" of the union as their collective bargaining agent. A petition for an election to decertify a union can be filed by another union, a group of disaffected members, or an individual member of the bargaining unit. If, after review, the SLRB accepts the petition, it has an obligation to conduct a fair and impartial decertification election. While decertification efforts are usually unsuccessful, the process serves as a check and balance. It helps ensure that the union's leadership continues to be responsive to the needs of its members (Myers & Twomey, 1975).

Most state public employee bargaining laws ban certain unfair labor practices. The prohibition against unfair labor practices is designed to keep labor and management coequal for purposes of collective bargaining. According to Sloane and Witney (2009), it is usually considered an unfair labor practice for management to:

1. Interfere with, restrain, or coerce employees in the exercise of their rights to organize, bargain collectively, and participate in other activities for their mutual aid or protection.
2. Dominate or interfere with the formation or administration of any labor union or contribute financial or other support to it.
3. Encourage or discourage membership in any labor union organization by discrimination with regard to hiring or tenure or conditions of employment (with the exception of a valid union-security agreement).
4. Discharge or otherwise discriminate against an employee because he or she filed unfair labor practice charges against the employer.
5. Refuse to bargain collectively and in good faith with the employees' bargaining agent.

However, it is considered to be an unfair labor practice when unions do any of the following:

1. Restrain or coerce employees in exercising their rights under the law.
2. Restrain or coerce an employer in selection of a bargaining agent or grievance representative.
3. Cause or attempt to cause an employer to discriminate against an employee based on the person's membership or nonmembership in a labor organization.
4. Refuse to bargain collectively and in good faith with an employer if the union has been designated a bargaining agent by a majority of the employees.

There is an assumption that collective bargaining is the product of independence and strength. The strong are inclined to bargain. The weak cave in. Weakness undermines the bargaining process.

Once the ground rules have been accepted and the union is in place, collective bargaining is set to begin. The initial bargaining session is a prelude to participatory management in police work.

Collective Bargaining

Collective bargaining is the process by which a labor contract is negotiated and enforced between the employees' exclusive bargaining agent (the union) and the state or local government responsible for operation of the police department. Labor and management have a mutual obligation to meet at reasonable times and to confer in good faith with respect to wages, hours, and other terms and conditions of employment. While there is an affirmative duty to bargain, neither side is required to accept a proposal or make a concession. Most labor negotiations do, however, result in a formal written agreement that both sides can live with until the next regularly scheduled round of contract talks (Bittel & Newstrom, 1992).

The Bargaining Team

One of the first steps in the actual bargaining process is for each side (union and management) to select a competent negotiating team. This is an extremely important and, at times, difficult task. Most bargaining teams are fairly small. They normally consist of a chief negotiator, a recording secretary, and three or four members who have conducted research in areas of special interest to management or the union. The knowledge, skill, and dedication of the negotiators will determine the quality of the collective bargaining agreement and set the moral or ethical tone for all future labor relations. Selectivity is a prerequisite for success.

While there are no hard-and-fast rules concerning the composition of the union's bargaining team, there are a few general principles that should be kept in mind. The union president (or a designee) almost always serves, along with other members of the bargaining unit, as part of the core team. The chief negotiator, who is usually not a police officer, leads the team and coordinates the bargaining effort. By bringing in an outside labor relations specialist as its chief negotiator, the union strengthens its position with regard to management and gains practical advantages from that person's experience, expertise, and objectivity. The chemistry of the team usually determines the quality of the contract.

The chief of police, however, seldom, if ever, serves as an official member of the management bargaining team. The chief's designee (or designees) represents the department's interest during the negotiations. This is an attempt to separate the politics of negotiation from the science of contract administration (Fyfe, Greene, & Walsh, 1997). Other department heads (legal, personnel, finance, etc.) are often pressed into service as members of the core team. In most jurisdictions, the director of labor relations serves as chief negotiator for the state or local government. Here again, the composition of the team and the way members of the team work together become critical factors in the outcome of the negotiations.

A major problem in many jurisdictions is that either police management has no representation at the bargaining table or its representation is inadequate to deal with the task at hand. Civilian managers normally represent the municipality. While these people may know a great deal about public administration and the budgetary process, they often know little or nothing about the needs of police managers. Consequently, they frequently bargain away management rights for concessions in the economic package. This leaves police managers who are accountable for achieving the department's mission, goals, and objectives without the necessary authority to do the job (Ayres & Coble, 1987).

Once the bargaining teams have been formed, they must try to reach a consensus on the appropriate scope of the bargaining. In other words, what issues are to be discussed? While it is in management's interest to limit the scope of collective bargaining, organized labor normally wants everything placed on the table for discussion.

Scope of the Bargaining

Most public employee bargaining laws are patterned after federal statutes and, as such, attempt to identify subjects that are either appropriate or inappropriate for collective bargaining. There are three types of bargaining proposals that merit further attention:

1. **Mandatory subjects.** These subjects (such as disability pay, occupational safety, and minimum staffing requirements) clearly fall within the category of wages, hours, and other terms and conditions of employment.
2. **Voluntary subjects.** These topics (such as health club memberships, volume discounts based on group purchases, and new benefits for retirees) clearly fall outside the mandatory category but are placed on the table for voluntary consideration and agreement. The other party is not required to bargain on them or to agree to include them in the new contract.
3. **Illegal subjects.** These subjects (such as union shop agreements, binding arbitration, and the right to strike) have been specifically prohibited by the public employee bargaining law.

Negotiating the first contract requires a great deal of preparation and skill. Issues related to the mandatory subjects of wages, hours, and conditions of employment become mind-boggling in complex criminal justice organizations.

While both union and management want to negotiate a contract that gives them the greatest control over decision-making, parameters must be established to give some focus to the collective bargaining process. "Rights and responsibilities" clauses are usually built in as an integral component of the collective bargaining agreement. These clauses are specifically designed to limit the scope of bargaining and delineate areas of mutual concern.

According to the Police Executive Research Forum (1978), the goal of management is to obtain contract language that gives it maximum discretion and flexibility in running the police department. The power that management retains is ordinarily spelled out in a management rights clause. A strong management rights clause gives the police administration a great deal of control over the operation of the department. A weak management rights clause gives away too much power. The National League of Cities (Rynecki et al., 1984) has recommended that a management rights clause be inserted in all municipal collective bargaining agreements. Such a clause could be stated as follows:

> *It is agreed that the department possesses all of the rights, powers, privileges, and authority it had prior to the execution of this agreement. Nothing in this agreement shall be construed to limit the department or the operation of the police enterprise, except as it may have been specifically relinquished or modified herein by an express provision of the collective bargaining agreement itself.*

In simple terms, this contract language states that management retains certain rights that may not be challenged by the union, no matter how infrequently they are used (Thibault, Lynch, & McBride, 2010).

Swank and Conser (1983) argue that a strong management rights clause is probably the most important part of any contract or negotiation with an employee organization. A strong management rights clause and a mutually acceptable no-strike impasse resolution process are essential components of an effective management strategy. A good management rights clause should contain, but not be limited to, the following items:

1. Determining occupational qualifications and hiring human resources.
2. Directing the workforce through the formulation of departmental policies, procedures, rules, and regulations.
3. Establishing work schedules and regulating overtime in a manner that is most advantageous to the employer.
4. Determining the method, process, and manner used to perform police work.
5. Disciplining, suspending, demoting, and discharging police personnel for reasonable and just cause.
6. Relieving and/or laying off police officers due to a lack of work, lack of funding, or for disciplinary reasons.
7. Assigning, transferring, and promoting police officers to positions within the department.
8. Consolidating and reorganizing operations of the police department.
9. Taking action in emergency situations to ensure proper operation of the police department.

While the enumeration of management rights may prove to be a stumbling block in negotiations, specificity is critically important. Managers need to know what is expected of them. They must be free to exercise legitimate authority.

Management rights clauses are usually negotiated in tandem with an employee responsibility clause. The first union responsibility clause in Detroit was very specific. According to the Contract between the City of Detroit and the Detroit Police Officers' Association (1973):

1. Recognizing the crucial role of law enforcement in the preservation of public health, safety, and welfare of a free society, the union agrees that it will take all reasonable steps to cause the employees covered by this agreement, individually and collectively, to perform all police duties, rendering loyal and efficient service to the very best of their ability.
2. The union, therefore, agrees that there shall be no interruption of these services for any cause whatsoever by the employees it represents nor shall they absent themselves from their work or abstain, in whole or in part, from the full, faithful, and proper performance of all the duties of their employment.
3. The union further agrees that it shall not encourage any strikes, sit-downs, stay-ins, slow-downs, stoppages of work, malingering, or any acts that interfere in any manner or to any degree with the continuity of police services.

Management rights and union responsibility become the starting point for all future negotiations.

The rights and responsibilities just discussed are fairly easy to understand. They are also subject to change. Management's right to make policy, for example, can be weakened or lost entirely as the result of negotiation, arbitration awards, court challenges, or substantive changes in the collective bargaining statute. The only inherent rights of management are those that labor does not bargain away from it (Bouza, 1990). Unions, however, have been known to abdicate their responsibility to the public when they try to win policy concessions from their employers through intimidation rather than constructive conflict. It takes a great deal of time and effort on the part of labor and management to make the collective bargaining process work the way it was designed to work.

The Bargaining Table

The basic purpose of bargaining is to reach a mutually acceptable agreement on the issues raised at the table. The first meeting is ordinarily devoted to establishing the bargaining authority of each team, determining the ground rules for the negotiations, and adopting a schedule. If the parties have not distributed their formal proposals previously, they may be distributed and clarified at this time. This gives the other side some indication as to why particular proposals are being made, how much thought has gone into them, and the amount of support they have. The first session almost always sets the tone for subsequent meetings and may eventually determine the success or failure of the collective bargaining process.

Labor contract negotiations take on the characteristics of a poker game in which each side attempts to determine the opponent's hand without revealing its own (Bohlander et al., 2013). The parties try to avoid disclosing the relative importance they attach to each proposal. They do not want to pay a higher price than is necessary to achieve the proposals that are of the greatest importance to them. Proposals can generally be divided into four basic categories:

1. Nonnegotiable. Those the team believes it must have.
2. Negotiable. Those the team would like to have, but on which it is willing to compromise.
3. Trade-off. Those the team should submit for trading purposes.
4. Expendable. Those the team is willing to give up.

All proposals should be realistic. Unrealistic proposals serve only to irritate the opponent and can, if taken seriously, create an impasse. It has been noted that unrealistic bargaining proposals have an unpleasant way of becoming real issues.

In order for a bargaining issue to be resolved satisfactorily, the point at which an agreement is possible must fall within limits that both the union team and the management team are willing to concede. This is called the zone of acceptance. In some situations, proposals to the negotiations made by one party clearly exceed the tolerance limit of the other party. If this is the case, the solution is outside the zone of acceptance. If the party refuses to modify its demands enough (through compromises or trade-offs) to bring them within the zone of acceptance or if the opposing party will not extend its tolerance limit (based on some other form of compensation) to accommodate those demands, an impasse will result. The key to successful collective bargaining is to ascertain the parameters of the opponent's zone of acceptance and to compromise in such a way that all proposals fall within those parameters. This requires a great deal of skill.

The proposals submitted by each side must, regardless of the importance attached to them, be dealt with at the table if there is to be a collective bargaining agreement. Once a particular issue, clause, or proposal is placed on the table, the other team is obligated to respond to it. There are four basic responses:

1. Accepted
2. Accepted with minor modification
3. Rejected
4. Rejected with counterproposal

An opponent cannot reject an issue, clause, or proposal without an explanation. This would not be considered bargaining in good faith. A reason for the rejection must be given and that reason must, in and of itself, be reasonable. Having been informed of the opposing team's position, the bargaining begins. Also, as noted earlier, the bargaining process involves a great deal of give and take. It is designed to move opposing teams closer to a mutually acceptable middle ground within the tolerance limits of both labor and management. From this perspective, collective bargaining is an applied art rather than an exact science.

Union Goals

The union always enters the collective bargaining process with a preset agenda. It wants to share power with the top police executive through bilateral negotiations and to have a meaningful say in the day-to-day operations of the police department. Anything less is unacceptable and would be considered a sellout by the membership. The union bargaining team's big-ticket items usually fall into seven basic categories:

1. Wages and working conditions
2. Union security measures
3. Impasse resolution techniques
4. Meet-and-discuss provisions
5. Grievance procedures
6. Procedural due process
7. Job security and seniority

Two additional bargaining categories have emerged as priority items for police officers in recent contract negotiations. One deals with issues surrounding officer safety in terms of personnel deployment, workplace security, and equipment. The other focus is on adequate insurance coverage and the maintenance of fully paid health care benefits for officers who have been injured on or retire from the job.

Concerns about wages, hours, and other terms and conditions of employment are traditional items that serve as a catalyst for unionization. One study indicated that 96.5 percent of the officers surveyed were concerned primarily about their compensation (Leonard & More, 2000). Union security measures, impasse resolution techniques, and "meet-and-discuss" mechanisms are designed specifically to ensure the stability of the union, whereas the grievance procedure, due process, job security, and seniority deal with the noneconomic issues that are considered most important to the membership.

Union bargaining teams place a high priority on negotiating very strong union security measures. These measures, such as dues checkoff, maintenance of membership, and compulsory participation, give unions stability and enhance their clout in dealing with management. Basic union security measures can be summarized as follows:

1. **Dues Checkoff.** Management agrees to deduct union dues directly from the pay of its employees and to deliver funds to the union on a regularly scheduled basis.
2. **Maintenance of Membership.** Management agrees that voluntary membership in a union cannot (as a condition of continued employment) be terminated by an employee while the negotiated contract is still in force.
3. **Compulsory Participation.** Management agrees that as a condition of employment, newly hired employees will join the union (union shop) or pay a "service fee" in the form of union dues to the employee organization (agency shop).

Whether union or agency shop agreements can be negotiated as part of a labor contract depend on the state's collective bargaining statute. In many southern and western states with so-called "right-to-work" statutes on the books, most union security measures are outlawed. It is a different story in the northeastern states, however. The Pennsylvania General Assembly narrowly defeated a very comprehensive agency shop bill for public employees during its 1987 legislative session. The agency shop bill was endorsed by Governor Robert Casey in 1987 and later enacted into law as Act 84 of 1988.

There are trying times when, due to the nature of the collective bargaining process, negotiations become deadlocked and something must be done to resolve the impasse if there is to be a mutually acceptable accord. The best way to prevent police strikes (and other job actions) is to provide for some combination of methods that will diffuse conflict and help implement the impasse resolution process (Holden, 1993). The most common impasse resolution techniques used in police work today (mediation, fact-finding, final best offer arbitration, and binding arbitration) have been borrowed from private sector labor relations. Impasse resolution techniques are generally categorized as being either "nonbinding" or "binding" and may best be described in the following manner:

1. **Mediation** is a nonbinding impasse resolution technique in which an authoritative third party attempts to help the disputants reach a mutually acceptable agreement. Mediators facilitate communication and clarify issues. Their value lies in their ability to review the dispute from an objective perspective, inject fresh ideas into the negotiations, recommend solutions, and, when appropriate, extricate the parties from difficult or untenable positions. Professional mediation services are available from various state and federal agencies. While mediation is certainly not a panacea, evidence suggests that it has worked in more than 50 percent of documented cases.

2. **Fact-Finding** is a nonbinding impasse resolution technique in which a fact finder or panel of fact finders gathers, interprets, and assigns relative weight to data related to an issue in dispute. The process involves quasi-judicial hearings, compilation of an investigative report, and formulation of very specific recommendations for resolving the impasse. An old study found that 89 percent of disputes submitted to fact-finding were resolved (Stern, 1967). More recent data suggest that a success rate of 60 to 70 percent would probably be more accurate.

3. **Final Best Offer Arbitration** is a binding impasse resolution technique in which each side submits a "final" offer to the arbitrator chosen to decide the issue. The arbitrator has absolutely no power to compromise and must select one of the final offers submitted by the two parties. It is up to the arbitrator to choose the offer that is, on the whole, the most reasonable and fair. This plan encourages all parties to make concessions, as the arbitrator's "award" is most likely to go to the party that has moved closest to a reasonable middle-ground position.

4. **Binding Arbitration** is an impasse resolution technique in which the disputants elect (voluntary) or are required (compulsory) to submit impasses to a neutral and mutually acceptable third party who is empowered to decide the issue. The decision is legally binding and enforceable in the courts. Most collective bargaining agreements now require that certain, if not all, labor disputes be submitted to binding arbitration for resolution (Myers & Twomey, 1975). A list of qualified and experienced arbitrators is available from the American Arbitration Association.

The most popular approach to impasse resolution in police work appears to be binding arbitration. The power that makes the arbitration binding may be found in the collective bargaining agreement, state law, a local ordinance, jurisdictional policy, and court decisions (Sapp & Carter, 1991).

Whether these impasse resolution techniques work will depend, in large measure, on the importance of the issue, the intensity of the conflict, and the good faith bargaining of the disputants. Although some elected government officials attempt to renege on arbitration awards and openly challenge the legitimacy of the arbitration process as an unlawful encroachment on their legislative or administrative power, the courts have generally upheld the use of binding arbitration in the public sector. Many state and local governments have been forced, through the judicial process, to fund expensive, as well as very unpopular, police arbitration awards.

Communication is the lifeblood of the collective bargaining process and is an absolutely essential ingredient in successful conflict management. Regularly scheduled (and contractually mandated) meet-and-discuss sessions are designed to bring union representatives and managers together in an effort to promote communication, resolve issues, and guarantee joint administration of the contract. Meet-and-discuss sessions provide a vehicle for participatory management in criminal justice organizations.

Dealing with Grievances

A grievance is a complaint arising out of the interpretation, application, or compliance with provisions of a collective bargaining agreement. Grievance procedures and due process safeguards are built into virtually every labor contract. According to CALEA (2006), Standard 25 stipulates:

> *Unless there is controlling construct language, a written directive establishes a grievance procedure, which includes the following:*
> a. *Identification of matters that are grievable (scope) and the levels in the agency or government to which the grievance may be filed and/or appealed.*
> b. *Establishment of time limitations for filing or appealing the grievance to the next level.*
> c. *A description of the type of information to be submitted when filing a grievance.*
> d. *Establishment of procedural steps and time limitations at each level in responding to grievances or appeals.*
> e. *Establishment of criteria for employee representation.*
> *A written directive identifies a position responsible for coordination of grievance procedures and for the maintenance and control of grievance records.*
> *A written directive requires an annual analysis of grievances.*

A multistep grievance process is the norm in police work. In most cases,

1. There is a specific time limit within which a grievance must be filed once the police officer becomes aware that there is, or appears to be, a violation of the contract.
2. The officer is expected to discuss the alleged grievance informally with the immediate supervisor in an effort to resolve the problem.

3. If the grievance cannot be resolved informally and the employee wishes to pursue it further, a formal grievance is filed with the appropriate command officer.
4. The command officer processes the formal grievance and holds hearings at which the employee (and the union) presents oral and written statements.
5. The command officer, based on the evidence, determines the merit of the grievance and notifies the grievant of the decision.
6. If the grievance is not resolved satisfactorily at the command level, it is sent to the chief executive officer for a final in-house disposition.
7. In many states (depending on the language of the public employee bargaining statute), an unresolved grievance goes to the political executive, Civil Service Commission, State Labor Relations Board, or an arbitrator for final disposition.

If the grievant and the police union are dissatisfied with the final disposition of the grievance, they may (under most state laws) go to court for judicial review or injunctive relief. Winning the grievance is very important to both of them. A victory in each case is considered a victory for the union and for the organized labor movement as a whole.

Procedural due process is near and dear to the heart of every unionist. It has long been the rallying cry for union activism in police departments. Unions and their members want to protect themselves from the arbitrary and capricious behavior of their employers. From their perspective, a "police officers' bill of rights" and due process standards for discipline are indispensable in a good contract. Procedural due process is considered sacrosanct and nonnegotiable by virtually all rank-and-file police officers.

According to the Bureau of National Affairs (2001), more than 90 percent of all union contracts emphasize the importance of worker seniority. Police work is no exception. In some cases, seniority has (based on negotiated collective bargaining agreements) become an overriding factor in the promotion, scheduling, and assignment of personnel. In Pittsburgh, Pennsylvania, for example, police officers select their shifts, patrol zones, and partners based on the seniority principle (Contract between the City of Pittsburgh and the Fraternal Order of Police, 1992). The city can bypass a uniformed police officer for an open vehicle assignment on a particular shift only if it believes in good faith that because of incompatibility, the officer will not be effective in that assignment on that shift. Under these circumstances, it is not uncommon to find two rookie police officers patrolling high-crime areas together on a midnight shift. While seniority should be considered, it is often antithetical to merit and often unduly limits management's ability to use its human resources in an efficient, effective, and productive manner.

Impasse Resolution Through Job Actions

Most police union goals are attained at the bargaining table or through very skillful political manipulation. Police unions have usually been able to deliver the goods to their members with a minimum amount of hassle. Tangling with the union is often considered to be political suicide. Consequently, most unions have been content to walk softly and carry a big stick.

When a police union is unable to obtain its goals through constructive conflict in collective bargaining and all of the normal impasse-resolution techniques have failed, it may be forced to use a coercive strategy. While union leaders tend to oppose the tactical use of job actions, they know that job actions (whether they are legal or not) are a necessary part of the bargaining process. Without job actions to back them up, police unions believe they may lack the wherewithal to pressure the employer into making necessary concessions. A job action is, and should always be, the impasse resolution of last resort.

A job action is defined as a calculated disruption in normally assigned duties. The term can be used to describe any of several different types of activities that police officers engage in to show their dissatisfaction with a particular person, event, condition, or situation. A job action can also be used in an effort to influence the deliberations of policy makers. Job actions send out a clear signal that there has been an unhealthy escalation in conflict and that the collective bargaining process has broken down.

Even though almost all states legally prohibit job actions by police personnel, the law has not proven to be an effective deterrent to poor labor relations. In 1979 alone, there were 52 police strikes throughout the United States (U.S. Department of Labor, 1981). While there were actually fewer job actions by police personnel in the 1980s and 1990s, no one should be lulled into a false sense of security. The Johnstown, Pennsylvania, police strike of 1987 is a clear demonstration that if they believe it is necessary, union members will attempt to resolve a bargaining impasse through some type of job action. Because of public safety considerations (directly related to the strike), the Pennsylvania State Police assumed jurisdiction over and provided law enforcement services for the city of more than 37,000. Prohibition of police walkouts without a viable alternative to resolve a labor–management impasse is, in reality, no prohibition at all.

Job actions short of actual strikes or other work stoppages are much more common in today's labor relations environment. In New York City, where police officers were protesting an impasse in contract negotiations, the union—the Police Benevolent Association—tacitly supported a well-orchestrated work slowdown to demonstrate its displeasure with city government. As a result, the number of traffic tickets and summonses issued by 21,000 rank-and-file police personnel declined by more than 60 percent. This resulted in $1.5 million in lost revenue that the cash-starved city could ill afford to lose. Needless to say, the conflict was resolved rather quickly and in favor of the police. The power of organized labor should not be underestimated (Swanson et al., 2007).

Four basic types of job actions are used in law enforcement. Swanson and colleagues (2007) describe these job actions in the following way:

1. **No-Confidence Votes.** In a no-confidence vote, rank-and-file union members formally signal their dissatisfaction with administrative policies or an administrator through a public and often highly publicized statement that, while it has no legal standing, can lead to the person's removal, resignation, or early retirement. Even though no-confidence votes have played an important role in the departure of some police chief executives, such as the removal of Robert Digrazia in Montgomery County, Maryland, and the retirement of Harold Bastrup in Anaheim, California, they have not always accomplished the union's goal and have, in fact, been interpreted as a positive sign that needed reforms are taking place.

2. **Work Slowdowns.** In work slowdowns, while the police continue to provide all essential law enforcement services, police officers use less initiative and do their work at a measured pace so that each unit of work takes longer to complete. This causes a steep drop in productivity. Work begins to accumulate, and benefits (in terms of public safety, a sense of security, and revenues generated) are reduced. Pressure increases as more and more people perceive the loss in benefits and take affirmative action to reestablish the normal state of affairs. The effectiveness of the slowdown has been demonstrated in writing traffic tickets (California Highway Patrol), conducting criminal investigations (Phoenix, Arizona), and making arrests (Long Beach, California).

3. **Work Speedups.** In work speedups, there is intentional acceleration in one or more types of police services, designed to create anxiety and disruption through calculated overproduction. Speedups produce social stress and usually precipitate demands for acquiescence to the union. Work speedups have been used very successfully in New York City (transit authority smoking and littering violations), Chicago (moving violation "ticket blizzards"), and Holyoke, Massachusetts (parking tickets). Speedups alter the normal pace of life and generate public demands for a return to the status quo.

4. **Work Stoppage.** Work stoppages involve the total withholding of production in one or more areas of service. The ultimate work stoppage—the strike—represents the total withholding of all services by union members. Described in picturesque terms such as "blue flu" and the "blue-bonic plague," mass resignations, "sick outs," and strikes have been used to protest economic conditions, judicial leniency, inadequate safety measures, staffing patterns, and so forth. While police strikes are illegal in almost all states, they usually accomplish their overall objective, and few, if any, result in reprisals against the strikers or their union.

Job actions are one of the most controversial aspects of police unionism. While they may achieve the union's objectives, they also create anxiety, fear, resentment, and a debilitating sense of betrayal within the community.

While it is easy to overemphasize the negative aspects of job actions, the relations between police unions and management are normally constructive. Despite all the attention they receive, job actions are relatively infrequent events. The elimination of federal revenue sharing, erosion in state and local tax revenues, and an unstable national economy have caused unions to reassess their demands. Most union effort is now designed to avoid cutbacks (retrenchment) or reductions in existing benefits (givebacks), strengthen job security clauses in existing collective bargaining agreements, and gain more input into the policy formulation process. Labor-management conflict is more and more symbolic and is played out on the bargaining table. Unions are attempting to achieve their objectives through accommodation and cooperation with management.

Union–Management Relations

Leonard and More (2000) contend that unionization of the police can usually be traced to the inadequacies of management. In most cases in which unionization has occurred, officers had been frustrated by intolerable working conditions and were unable to obtain corrective action from indifferent state or local government officials. Trying to identify the impetus for unionization and to demonstrate that unions (based on inherent conservatism) generally have a negative effect on the development of professionalism may be counterproductive. Most of the nation's more than 800,000 sworn police officers (U.S. Department of Justice, 2001) are union members. Police administrators and elected officials have little or no choice except to work with the representatives of their employees. Trying to recapture the past through antiunion activity is a bit like closing a barn door after the horses have escaped. The National Advisory Commission on Criminal Justice Standards and Goals (1973) came to the conclusion that the nation's police executives should recognize that police employees have a legal right, subject to certain reasonable limitations, to engage in activities protected by the First Amendment. They should acknowledge the right of their employees to join (or not join) employee organizations that represent their employment interests and give appropriate recognition to these organizations.

The commission went on to emphasize the importance of the collective bargaining process in contemporary American society. The CALEA reemphasized the importance of collective bargaining (CALEA, 2006). CALEA Standard 24 stipulates:

> *If there are represented employees in the agency, a written directive describes the role of the agency in the collective bargaining process, and includes:*
>   *a. Establishment of a collective bargaining team for the agency with one person designated as the principal negotiator.*
>   *b. Identification of the bargaining unit or units representing an agency's employees with which it will negotiate.*
>   *c. A commitment by the agency to participate in "good faith" bargaining with the duly recognized bargaining units representing its members.*
>   *d. A commitment to abide by the ground rules for collective bargaining that arise out of the collective bargaining process or labor arbitration.*
>   *e. A commitment to abide, in both letter and spirit, by the negotiated labor agreement that has been signed by management and labor representatives and ratified by the bargaining unit.*
> *When a negotiated labor agreement is ratified by all parties, the agency's CEO or designee will:*
>   *a. obtain a written, signed copy of the labor agreement;*
>   *b. review and amend, if necessary, all written directives and procedures to coincide with the terms of the labor agreement; and*
>   *c. disseminate information relative to a new labor agreement, including modifications to existing agreements, to managers and supervisors of bargaining unit employees.*

The Commonwealth of Pennsylvania could be described as avant garde when it comes to promoting positive labor–management relations through the collective bargaining process. Pennsylvania's Collective Bargaining and Compulsory Arbitration Act for Police and Fire

(Act 111) was enacted into law in 1968. It authorizes collective bargaining by police officers and firefighters and imposes binding arbitration as the final means of impasse resolution. An employee organization with more than 50 percent of the department's sworn personnel may be certified as the exclusive bargaining agent for all rank-and-file officers. The union helps formulate, implement, and administer a collective bargaining agreement. In the event that there is an impasse, a three-person arbitration panel is appointed. Management chooses one member, labor another, and the third is selected by mutual agreement. If the parties cannot decide on a mutually acceptable third member, an arbitrator must be chosen from a roster of names provided by the American Arbitration Association. The panel studies the issues and makes a final award that is binding on all parties. Act 111 has worked well most of the time.

Contract Administration

Signing a contract guarantees continuation of the collective bargaining relationship for the duration of the agreement. One of the most important aspects of contract administration involves dissemination of information to all members of the department concerning the policies, programs, equipment, and resources that are to be affected by the new agreement. It also requires labor and management to reach a consensus concerning the nature and extent of the participatory management to be allowed within the police department.

A police labor contract is a living document that is applied to a variety of very different issues in an ever-changing socioeconomic environment. In order to make it work, the parties must be prepared to spend a great deal of time and effort interpreting contract language, working out the bugs, making necessary adjustments, resolving problems through the formal grievance process, and reaching ethical compromises that promote the interests of the employee, the department, and the community at large.

Role of the Sergeant in Collective Bargaining

In small police departments, sergeants may be considered managers and assigned to play a significant role in the collective bargaining process. In most situations, however, the sergeant's role is limited to contract implementation or administration.

As first-line supervisors in police departments, sergeants are responsible for both people and production. They occupy an often-ambiguous position between management and labor. Based on prevailing police organization/management theory, sergeants represent labor to management and management to labor. They are expected to identify minor problems and deal with them before they become major issues. Sergeants have an obligation to help their subordinates as well as to apprise their superiors of potential problems. The police sergeant is a linchpin in effective labor relations. Even perfect labor relations policies will fail unless they are translated into practice by the sergeant (Walsh & Donovan, 1990). This is challenging and demands very specific skills.

The importance of sergeants in labor relations is underscored by their role in recommending or taking disciplinary action against their subordinates. Despite the many different types of issues that can be or are actually filed as grievances, nearly 90 percent of those taken to arbitration involve discipline against sworn police personnel. Because sergeants are departmental disciplinarians, they and their actions often become the focus of personnel as well as policy grievances. One study of arbitrated grievances disclosed that the officers involved were assigned to the uniformed patrol division in 84 percent of the cases and that the union won the arbitration award in more than 75 percent of the grievances (Lavan & Carley, 1985). Sergeants also play a very important role in resolving grievances. They are normally the first representative of management authorized to receive and settle grievances. Most truly effective grievance procedures formalize the sergeant's role by requiring grievants to seek an informal resolution of the case before it can be taken to the command level for a review and disposition. This emphasis on the sergeant corresponds to the principle that the best management decisions come from those directly involved in or that are most familiar with the situation under review.

The sergeant's position is often very frustrating and is complicated by the conflicting demands made by fellow police officers and management. If management pushes too hard, sergeants may be forced to align themselves with labor. Under these circumstances, police managers become their own enemy, and sergeants revert to the role of a promoted patrol officer. Ineffective supervision reduces productivity and has a deleterious influence on the overall quality of police service.

Unions have had both positive and negative effects on modern-day police work. On the plus side, they help shield police personnel from inept, autocratic, and morally bankrupt managers and supervisors. However, they have also been known to protect less-than-competent police officers, to make the taking of appropriate disciplinary action very difficult, and to block the reforms needed to professionalize police service. Ineffective sergeants use the specter of unionization as an excuse to avoid the legitimate process of observing on-the-job performance, collecting information, documenting deviant behavior, and knowing departmental policies, procedures, rules, and regulations well enough to carry out their job-related supervisor responsibilities. It is much easier to blame the union (the union steward or grievance committee) than to acknowledge one's own shortcomings as a first-line supervisor.

Inadequate supervisory personnel react to crisis situations. They lack the skills required to manage them. Poor supervisors have not, as a general rule, formulated a workable set of principles to guide their actions. They are neither thorough nor consistent and do only what is absolutely essential to guarantee their survival. Poor supervisors are usually not conscientious enough to put in the hard work that is required to represent their supervisees to management or to carry out the management responsibilities assigned to them by their superiors (Trojanowicz, 1980). Poor first-line supervision, coupled with dynamic unionism, creates an unhealthy climate for constructive conflict. It sets the stage for a dramatic deterioration in public sector labor relations.

If they are going to be good first-line supervisors, sergeants need to understand contemporary labor relations and appreciate the value of constructive conflict in the collective bargaining process. They also need to develop a sound working relationship with the local union president (or "shop steward" in larger organizations). While sergeants and union representatives may be adversaries under certain circumstances, they should not be enemies.

SERGEANT	REPRESENTATIVE
1. Accept collective bargaining.	1. Accept collective bargaining.
2. Know the contract.	2. Know the contract.
3. Enforce the agreement.	3. Enforce the agreement.
4. Look out for the welfare of all subordinates.	4. Look out for the welfare of all constituents.
5. Be a spokesperson for both management and employees.	5. Be a spokesperson for both union and constituents.
6. Settle grievances fairly (in line with management's interpretation of the contract).	6. Settle grievances fairly (in line with the union's interpretation of the contract).
7. Keep abreast of grievance solutions and changes in contract interpretation.	7. Keep abreast of grievance solutions and changes in contract interpretation.
8. Be firm, fair, and impartial when dealing with the union.	8. Be firm, fair, and impartial when dealing with management.
9. Maintain a good working relationship with the steward.	9. Maintain a good working relationship with the sergeant.
10. Keep the union representative informed of management decisions and sources of trouble.	10. Keep the sergeant informed as to the union's position and sources of trouble.
11. Protect management rights.	11. Protect labor rights.

FIGURE 15.2 Labor relations roles played by the police. *Source: Adapted from W. Richard Plunkett (1992). Supervision: The Direction of People at Work, Sixth Edition. Boston, MA: Allyn & Bacon.*

The sergeant should keep in mind that the union representative is an employee and a "worker." That person has been selected by his or her peers to do an important job and is often given "release time" by the police department to see that the contract is implemented and administered fairly. The union representative has a legal responsibility and an absolute ethical obligation to fight for the contractual rights of all bargaining unit employees covered by the collective bargaining agreement. This symbolic conflict, no matter how intense it becomes, should never be allowed to degenerate into destructive personal animosity.

Competent first-line supervisors accept the fact that the union exists and, because they are powerless to change the situation, opt for constructive coexistence with, rather than open hostility to, the union representative. Figure 15.2 sets forth labor relations duties of the police sergeant and his or her counterpart, the union president, or shop steward. Based on a comparative analysis of their duties, it is clear that there are far more similarities than differences.

Sergeants play a pivotal role in contract implementation and contract administration. Once again, the success or failure of the police department's labor relations effort will depend on the intelligence, knowledge, skill, and dedication of the men and women who are selected to serve as first-line supervisors in these criminal justice agencies.

Many sergeants have experienced role conflict. They find it very difficult to perform well in all the roles assigned to them by virtue of their rank. Some are frustrated because they are not treated as managers or as patrol officers. They believe that they have little or no meaningful input into departmental policy and do not see themselves as part of the management team. However, management expects them to maintain a social as well as professional distance from their subordinates, who do the actual work of the organization, in order to preserve their objectivity and authority. This causes a dilemma for sergeants. Because of this role conflict and sense of frustration, sergeants in larger police departments have begun forming their own labor unions.

Sergeants often bemoan the fact that they find themselves "in the middle"—between labor and management. Some use this ambiguity as a rationale for inactivity and perpetuation of the status quo. Others see it as an opportunity for personal growth and development. They strive to carve out a niche in which they can satisfy their professional needs while making a meaningful contribution to law enforcement.

In healthy police organizations, sergeants are assimilated into the management team. Progressive managers know that police departments function much like military units. Commanders give orders. Sergeants, as first-line supervisors, see that rank-and-file police officers carry them out. Successful police work requires communication, cooperation, and coordination. Under ideal conditions, sergeants facilitate communication, elicit voluntary cooperation, and provide absolutely essential coordination. In other words, they energize and guide personnel in an effort to accomplish the organization's mission, goals, and objectives. Sergeants are expected to be advocates, leaders, problem solvers, disciplinarians, labor relations specialists, and contract administrators. They play a demanding role that requires a great deal of knowledge and interpersonal skill.

Many newly promoted sergeants are ill-equipped to handle the multidimensional role thrust upon them. Many are still promoted on the basis of political affiliation or some paper-and-pencil test, are given little training in supervisory skills, and are largely left to fend for themselves in a hostile environment. New sergeants adopt survival strategies keyed to the dangers they face. Some cave in to union demands and become "promoted patrol officers" who use the extra income to salve their conscience. Others attach their star to management and exude a hard-line, antiunion bias. Based on current legal and philosophical support for public sector collective bargaining, neither approach is productive. Both will lead to a sense of frustration and failure.

The occupational landscape has changed dramatically, as has the role of the sergeant in a paramilitary police organization. In order to fulfill this new role, sergeants must shed their paranoia and unshackle themselves from the past. They must learn to establish empathetic, goal-oriented relationships with their subordinates. Gamesmanship must be replaced with an honest, open, and participative approach to the resolution of common problems. Sergeants themselves must be prepared to face tough issues. They cannot afford to allow contract disputes or grievances to go unattended. Unresolved issues fester. They destroy unity of purpose and undermine the common interest. Tomorrow's first-line supervisor must understand the human dynamics involved in collective bargaining, have the ability to motivate subordinates, and be capable of forging a consensus about what needs to be accomplished and how it is to be done. Leadership will be the prerequisite for successful supervision in the future.

If sergeants are going to perform managerial duties related to supervision, discipline, evaluation, and labor relations, we can no longer afford to debate the issue of their status within the police department. While they are supervisors, they are also involved in directing, planning, leading, controlling, and coaching the activities of others. These are management functions (Steinmetz & Todd, 1992). Consequently, police sergeants are de facto managers and should be considered part of the department's management team.

Interest-Based Bargaining Process

As collective bargaining has become institutionalized in modern police work, there are signs that a subtle shift in its emphasis is beginning to take place. In 1981 the Police Executive Research Forum and the National League of Cities jointly sponsored a comprehensive comparative analysis of critical clauses in police collective bargaining agreements. In an attempt to expand on this research, Carter and Sapp (1993) surveyed 328 police collective bargaining agreements held by federal, state, and local law enforcement agencies. According to their survey, most police management–labor differences have moved closer to a homeostatic relationship. Management rights clauses have moved toward more comprehensive statements of such rights and away from provisions that make management decisions and actions subject to grievance and arbitration processes. Management's position at the bargaining table is increasingly one of true negotiation rather than reaction.

Because both management and unions desire to enhance, rather than destroy, their relationship, they are beginning to look for a process that minimizes confrontation and facilitates open and candid discussion of what are perceived as mutually significant issues. The movement away from traditional (position-based) negotiations to innovative (win–win) negotiations is buoyed when two strong institutions (union and management) respect each other and decide to work together cooperatively in an effort to achieve their mutual interests whenever possible. This interest-based bargaining approach may well become the rule rather than the exception in the future.

The win–win negotiation concept was originally developed by the U.S. Department of Labor and was used to reach collective bargaining agreements with its own personnel. The focus is on mutual interests rather than preconceived positions.

With reference to the negotiation sessions themselves, there are two absolutely critical objectives:

1. Dynamic interaction among team members unencumbered by formal environmental arrangements or occupational status considerations.
2. Open and candid discussion of mutual interests or concerns with respect to a particular issue.

Once the salient issue or issues have been identified, the parties working together collectively as a team develop a variety of alternatives designed to deal with them and satisfy their mutual interests. All team members are encouraged to participate actively in this brainstorming process. The alternatives or options are recorded without evaluation or judgment. Team members take turns serving as facilitators and recorders. Information is shared openly to ensure that everyone is actively involved in the negotiations.

After the alternatives have been developed, team members formulate a set of standards or criteria for use in evaluating the overall acceptability of the options. They use brainstorming techniques to compile an initial list of criteria and pare it down through candid discussion (designed to eliminate duplicative, vague, or unmeasurable standards) until there is a genuine consensus. A final list of decision-making criteria might well include the following:

1. Legality
2. Constituent acceptability
3. Effectiveness
4. Efficiency
5. Workability
6. Cost-effectiveness
7. Adequacy of representation

These standards are then applied through open discussion designed to determine the options on which members can reach agreement. Once the best option is selected, union and management negotiators work together to draft contract language and a brief history of the bargaining process. The proposed agreement is forwarded to management and the union for final review and adoption.

As the collaborative relationship between management and unions matures to the degree discussed earlier, more police departments are likely to engage in interest-based bargaining. It is the collegial alternative to traditional position bargaining designed to empower both parties as they jointly seek to achieve consensus on items of mutual interest. The differences in the two processes are reflected in Figure 15.3.

While there is no way to predict whether interest-based bargaining will become a widespread phenomenon in modern police work, it has the potential to revolutionize the way in which we currently approach labor relations. Success or failure will be determined by key factors such as those listed here:

1. *Commitment to the Process.* Management and labor must be committed to bringing about a cultural change in which they listen to each other, understand each other's needs and interests, and seek collaborative solutions designed to strengthen each side in pursuit of the department's mission, goals, and objectives.

BARGAINING PROCESS

Traditional Negotiations	Interest-Based Negotiations
Positions developed separately by each side	Emphasis on issues of mutual importance to both sides
Arguments made in an adversarial environment	Mutual interests are discussed candidly in a collegial atmosphere
Power/competition determines who wins or who loses	Joint development of mutually acceptable options
Eventual outcome: WIN–LOSE LOSE–LOSE	Consensus concerning criteria to be used when evaluating proposed options
	Selection of the best option designed to satisfy the mutual interests of both sides
	Collaborative development of contract language for the collective bargaining agreement
	Sign-off by both management and the union
	Eventual outcome: WIN–WIN

FIGURE 15.3 Two types of bargaining strategies. *Adapted from Larry K. Goodwin (1993). "Win-Win Negotiations: A Model for Cooperative Labor Relations."* The Public Manager, *Vol. 10, Summer.*

2. *Information Sharing and Trust.* Meaningful interaction and absolute candor are essential to building mutual trust. Neither side should be surprised by the other, and privileged or private conversations must remain confidential.

3. *Model Behavior.* At all stages of negotiations and during day-to-day contract administration, police managers and union leaders need to model collaborative behavior. Leaders on both sides must set the tone and exhibit behavior that is expected from all other members of the organization.

4. *Time to Prepare.* Members of the bargaining team must have a sense of trust in and commitment to the process so that they are willing to take risks, share vital information, and model collaborative behavior. It takes time to create an interactive environment based on rapport and trust between key players. From a practical point of view, most of the groundwork must be done before anyone sits down at the bargaining table.

5. *Isolate the Problems.* Management and the union need to understand and accept the fact that some of their people simply will not buy interest-based bargaining in lieu of the traditional collective bargaining process. Managers and union leaders need to isolate these

individuals, if possible, and concentrate on the vast majority of their constituents, who prefer the cooperative model of labor relations.

6. *Contract is Only Paper.* The key to success in interest-based bargaining is understanding that the conclusion of negotiations represents nothing more than the beginning of a long-term partnership between management and the union to implement the contract and market this new collaborative approach to labor relations in the public sector. Traditional perspectives and organizational culture cannot be changed by issuing a new contract to everyone. Both sides must work together to develop a strategy for change over the life of the current collective bargaining agreement and beyond. (Goodwin, 1993)

References

Anderson, H. J. (1975). *Primer of labor relations.* Washington, DC: Bureau of National Affairs, Inc.

Ayres, R. M., & Coble, P. R. (1987). *Safeguarding management's rights.* Dubuque, IA: Kendall/Hunt Publishing Company.

Barnard, C. I. (1976). *The functions of the executive.* Cambridge, MA. Harvard University Press.

Bellante, D., & Porter, P. K. (1992). Agency costs, property rights, and the evolution of labor unions. *Journal of Labor Research, 11*(3).

Bittel, L. R., & Newstrom, J. W. (1992). *What every supervisor should know* (6th ed.). New York: McGraw-Hill.

Bohlander, G. W., Snell, S. A., & Sherman, A. W., Jr. (2013). *Managing human resources* (16th ed.). Mason, OH: Cengage Publishing.

Bouza, A. V. (1990). *The police mystique.* New York: Plenum Press.

Bureau of National Affairs (2001). *Collective bargaining agreements database.* Washington, DC: BNA, Inc.

CALEA (2006). *Standards for law enforcement agencies.* Fairfax, VA: Commission on Accreditation for Law Enforcement Agencies, Inc.

Carter, D., & Sapp, A. (1993). A comparative analysis of clauses in police collective bargaining agreements as indicators of change in labor relations. *American Journal of Police, 12*(2).

Cole, G. F., & Smith, C. (2008). The American system of criminal justice (12th ed.). Belmont, CA: Wadsworth.

Commonwealth of Pennsylvania, Revised Statutes (1987). Act 111 of 1968. Compulsory collective bargaining and contract arbitration for police and fire. Harrisburg, PA.

Contract between the City of Detroit and the Detroit Police Officers' Association (1973).

Contract between the City of Pittsburgh and the Fraternal Order of Police (1992).

Dressler, G. (1979). *Management fundamentals.* Reston, VA: Reston Publishing Company.

Ewing, D. W. (1983). *Do it my way or you're fired.* New York: John Wiley & Sons.

Foulkes, F., & Livernash, E. R. (1989). *Human resources management* (2nd ed.). Englewood Cliffs, NJ: Prentice Hall.

Fyfe, J. J., Greene, J. R., & Walsh, W. F. (1997). *Police administration* (5th ed.). New York: McGraw-Hill.

Goodwin, L. K. (1993). Win–win negotiations: A model for cooperative labor relations. *The Public Manager, 10*(2).

Holden, R. N. (1993). *Modern police management.* Englewood Cliffs, NJ: Prentice Hall.

Juris, H. A., & Feuille, P. (1973). *Police unionism.* Lexington, MA: Lexington Books.

Lavan, H., & Carley, C. (1985). Analysis of arbitrated employee grievance cases in police departments. *Journal of Collective Negotiation in the Public Sector, 14*(3).

Leonard, V. A., & More, H. W. (2000). *Police organization and management* (9th ed.). New York: The Foundation Press.

Myers, A. H., & Twomey, D. P. (1975). *Labor law and legislation.* Cincinnati, OH: South-Western.

National Advisory Commission on Criminal Justice Standards and Goals (1973), & U.S. Department of Justice (1973). *The police.* Washington, DC: U.S. Government Printing Office.

Plunkett, W. R. (1992). *Supervision: The direction of people at work* (6th ed.). Boston, MA: Allyn & Bacon.

Police Executive Research Forum (1978). *Police collective bargaining agreements: A national management survey.* Washington, DC: Police Executive Research Forum.

Rynecki, S., Cairns, D. A., & Carnes, D. J. (1984). *Police collective bargaining agreements.* Washington, DC: National League of Cities.

Sapp, A. D., & Carter, D. L. (1991). Conflict and conflict resolution in police collective bargaining. *The Police Forum, 1*(1).

Sapp, A. D., Carter, D. L., & Stephens, D. W. (1990). *Police labor relations: Critical findings.* Washington, DC: Police Executive Research Forum.

Shafritz, J. M., Rosenbloom, D., Riccucci, N., Naff, K., & Hyde, A. (2001). *Personnel management in government* (5th ed.). New York: Marcel Dekker, Inc..

Sloane, A. A., & Witney, F. (2009). *Labor relations* (13th ed.). Englewood Cliffs, NJ: Prentice Hall.

Stahl, O. G. (1983). *Public personnel administration.* New York: Harper and Row.

Steinmetz, L. L., & Todd, H. R., Jr. (1992). *Supervision: First-line management* (5th ed.). Boston, MA: Richard D. Irwin, Inc..

Stern, J. L. (1967). The Wisconsin public employee fact-finding procedure. *Industrial Labor Relations Review, 20*(10).

Stone, R. (1998). Police unions marks 20 years, adds members. *Police, 22*(6).

Swank, C. J., & Conser, J. A. (1983). *The police personnel system.* New York: John Wiley & Sons.

Swanson, C. R., Territo, L., & Taylor, R. W. (2007). *Police administration* (7th ed.). Englewood Cliffs, NJ: Prentice Hall.

Thibault, E. A., Lynch, L. M., & McBride, R. B. (2010). *Pro-active police management* (8th ed.). Englewood Cliffs, NJ: Prentice Hall.

Trojanowicz, R. C. (1980). *The environment of the first-line police supervisor.* Englewood Cliffs, NJ: Prentice Hall.

U.S. Department of Justice, Bureau of Justice Statistics (2001). *Sourcebook of criminal justice statistics.* Washington, DC: U.S. Government Printing Office.

U.S. Department of Labor, Bureau of Labor Statistics (1981). *Work stoppage in government, 1979.* Washington, DC: U.S. Government Printing Office.

Walker, S. (1999). *The police in America* (3rd ed.). New York: McGraw-Hill.

Walsh, W. F., & Donovan, E. J. (1990). *The supervision of police personnel: A performance-based approach.* Dubuque, IA: Kendall/Hunt Publishing Company.

World Almanac, The. (1993). Pittsburgh, PA: The Pittsburgh Press/Pharos Books.

16

Homeland Security and Terrorism
A Changing Role

KEY TERMS

Domestic terrorism
Foreign terrorism
Earth Liberation Front
Department of
   Homeland Security
Infrastructure
National Infrastructure
   Protection Plan
Counterterrorism
   Watch
Fusion centers

HazMat
Nationwide SAR
   Initiative
Information Sharing
   Environment
Suspicious Activity
   Reporting
National Crime
   Information Center
Terrorist Screening
   Center

CASE STUDY

Sergeant Rhonda Fleming

DEPARTMENT

The Riverdale Police Department is a medium-sized department with 156 sworn officers. The department has 118 uniformed officers in patrol division and 32 plain-clothes investigators in the criminal investigations division. The remaining six officers are administrators and internal affairs officers. Patrol is divided into three main shifts (7 am–3 pm, 3 pm–11 pm, 11 pm–7 am) with a fourth overlapping shift (4 pm–12 midnight). Each shift has between 25 and 35 officers on patrol at any given time. The department also has a reserve officer program, which has 36 sworn officers. While they are not allowed to drive police vehicles, they do have the same authority as regular officers. Reserve officers generally work special events and support regular officers with security details, traffic control, crowd control, and in emergencies. The department is Commission on Accreditation of Law Enforcement Agencies accredited and is slated to be reaccredited next year. Riverdale does not have a city jail but contracts with the McMinn County Sheriff's Office to keep city prisoners at the county detention center also located in Riverdale. All regular sworn officers in Riverdale are Peace Officers Standards and Training certified and trained. Some have advanced training in traffic crash reconstruction, crime scene investigation, K-9 handling, and explosives. All reserves must go through a state-mandated training academy and firearms training program. The department does not have

---

a helicopter but relies on the state police helicopter, which is stationed at a regional airport just a few miles from Riverdale. The department has also relied on the regional hospital's Wings medical helicopters on a few occasions for aerial views of traffic and spotting assisted police with suspect pursuits.

CRIME

Riverdale has a reasonably low crime rate as compared to similar sized cities in the state. There have been substantial increases in property crime, domestic violence, and alcohol-related traffic accidents in the last two years, most likely due to the poor economy. Crimes against persons were only slightly higher this year than in previous years with seven homicides, 35 felonious assaults, 12 sexual assaults, four armed robberies, and 113 misdemeanor assaults. Crimes cleared by arrest have increased significantly this year as compared to recent years. Crimes against persons have a clearance rate of nearly 92 percent, and crimes against property have a clearance rate of 56 percent.

COMMUNITY

Riverdale is the largest city and county seat of McMinn County. It has a population of slightly more than 100,000 and is located in a conservative region of the Midwest. Riverdale has three major industries all located near a major railroad hub. Sutton Chemicals employs over 3000 people and is the largest industry in Riverdale. Madison Pharmaceuticals and Randolph Paper are the other two major industries in Riverdale. Employment has slackened off substantially in recent years due to the economy, but the city has not been seriously hurt by the recession. Riverdale is the informal headquarters of the Tea Party Movement for the state. This is not surprising given the conservative nature of the community. There have been several "town hall" meetings in Riverdale over the past 24 months with few or no disorderly incidents.

OFFICER

Sergeant Rhonda Fleming is a seven-year veteran of the Riverdale Police Department. She was promoted to sergeant two years ago and supervises a platoon of seven patrol officers. She is currently in charge of one of four platoons on the 7 am–3 pm shift. Rhonda has always loved patrol work. She obtained her bachelor's degree in criminal justice from the state university and did an internship with the Riverdale police prior to her being hired. She was offered a position with criminal investigations last year but turned it down in favor of staying with patrol. Rhonda is not married but, according to her Facebook profile, is "in a relationship." She has an excellent working relationship with her colleagues and subordinates. This is somewhat surprising since she is the only female in her platoon.

PROBLEM

Railway safety inspectors were making a routine check of an outbound train from the railway yard when they found two propane tanks attached to the bottom of a tanker car filled with chlorine. The propane tanks had what looked to be timing devices and wiring attached to them. They immediately called the railroad police and the Riverdale Police Department. This set up a series of emergency notifications to HazMat, the fire department, emergency medical personnel, the state police, Department of Homeland Security (DHS) personnel, and the Bureau of Alcohol, Tobacco, Firearms, & Explosives (BATFE). Riverdale police and fire units were first to respond and quickly set up a command center. Sergeant Fleming's officers were deployed to direct incoming emergency units and to help establish a perimeter around the rail tanker cars. Captain Jon Murdock with the Riverdale police and Lieutenant Stan Whitman with the state police began operationalizing the command center.

As emergency units rolled into position and bomb technicians were suiting up to inspect the tanker cars, Rhonda could not help but feel impressed with how smoothly the operation was proceeding. "Nothing like good planning," she thought to herself as she recalled all the DHS planning sessions she attended to prepare for just this sort of thing. Emergency units from as far away as Carson County were now arriving on the scene. Riverdale reserve police officers were assisting with making evacuations of citizens surrounding the railroad yard. If the tanks were to explode, it would send deadly chlorine gas into the air for several thousand yards. HazMat agents had instructed all emergency workers who did not have personal protective equipment to remain on the outside perimeter of the scene in case of a blast.

Rhonda noted that BATFE agents had come on the scene very quickly. She decided to strike up a conversation with one of the agents who was standing near her position. When asked how the Feds had gotten to the scene so quickly, the agent replied that they had information that something like this was going to happen in Riverdale. The agent further stated that they had originally thought the attack would be at a "town-hall" meeting Senator Stevens was having that afternoon. Rhonda now remembered that a town-hall meeting with Senator Stevens was scheduled for 2:00 pm that afternoon at the Riverdale Civic Auditorium. The auditorium is located on the other side of the city from the railroad yard. The agent also mentioned that the timing devices on the propane tanks were set to go off at 2:49 pm, the exact time when the train would be passing by the civic auditorium on the way out of town. "Have to give 'em credit for a well-planned bomb attempt," the agent stated. "Who is 'them'?" Rhonda asked the agent. "Uh, not allowed to discuss that…sorry," the agent replied as he walked away.

Unsettled by the agent's comments, Rhonda asked her lieutenant what detail is working the town-hall meeting, noting that almost every law enforcement officer and emergency response unit within a 30-mile radius were all at the railroad yard. Lieutenant Franklin explained that Sergeant Wayne Speer and 15 Riverdale reserve officers were at the auditorium to take care of that detail. She further inquired if Riverdale police had been given any information by the Feds regarding a possible bomb threat at the town-hall meeting, to which the lieutenant replied, "No, I haven't gotten any information about that."

WHAT WOULD YOU DO?
If you were Sergeant Rhonda Fleming, how would you respond to the lieutenant? A well-planned terrorist attack might include using a diversionary tactic to lure emergency personnel away from the intended target. How could plans be made to consider the possibility of a diversion or even a multiple-target attack? If your lieutenant ordered you and your officers to proceed to the town-hall meeting, what would you do when you got there? It is now 1:45 pm.

The Nature of Terrorism

Terrorists attempt to disrupt a community and create fear in order to advance a religious, social, or political agenda. Terrorism is generally defined as "the unlawful use of force or violence against persons or property to intimidate or coerce a government, the civilian population, or any segment thereof in furtherance of political or social objectives (U.S. Department of Justice, 1993). While the term terrorism is relatively new, acts of terrorism date back as far as the human race first began to form communities. And, as the term is defined today, many

Type of Terrorism	Incidents	Fatalities
Domestic terrorism		
White racist/rightist	31.2	51.6
Revolutionary left	21.2	2.0
Black militants	14.7	25.0
Antiabortion	6.2	0.9
Jewish	3.6	0.8
Other/unknown	2.8	8.1
Foreign		
Cuban émigré	5.2	1.5
Puerto Rican	11.9	4.3
Islamic	1.1	1.7
Other	2.1	4.1
Total number of incidents and fatalities	3228	661

FIGURE 16.1 Terrorist incidents and fatalities by those responsible, 1954–2000 (%). *Source: Christopher Hewitt (2003). Understanding Terrorism in America. New York: Routledge, p. 15.*

historical events that we may consider to be patriotic would be defined as terrorism, an example of which is the American Revolution. Terrorism generally falls into two categories: domestic and foreign. Domestic terrorism is carried out by persons who are citizens of the country against whom their attacks are targeted. Foreign terrorism is carried out by citizens of another country who target other countries.

Domestic Terrorism

Domestic terrorism is, by far, the most common form of terrorism in the United States (Hewitt, 2003). In a study of terrorist incidents in the United States from 1954 through 2000, Hewitt (2003) noted that domestic terrorism accounted for approximately 80 percent of terrorist incidents prior to September 11, 2001 (see Figure 16.1). Also, most of these incidents involved hate groups such as white racists and black militants or antiwar political activists in the 1960s. However, since the 1960s, domestic terrorism has increased in technology, frequency, and diversity (Dyson, 2012). Advances in weapons, communication, and transportation technology have made it easier for domestic terrorists to wreak havoc on great masses of the population. In addition, other groups besides hate groups have increasingly organized and used terrorist tactics to further a political or moral agenda. The bomb that destroyed the Murrah Federal Building in Oklahoma City in 1995 was delivered by Timothy McVeigh, a member of the Michigan Militia group. The large rental truck McVeigh used was filled with 400 pounds of chemical fertilizer commonly available to the general public. In 1998, the Army of God bombed an abortion clinic in Birmingham, Alabama, resulting in one of the longest manhunts for a domestic terrorist suspect, Eric Rudolph. And, more recently in 2009, Dr. George Tiller, a late-term abortion doctor, was shot dead in a Wichita, Kansas, church by Scott Roeder, an antiabortion activist. Other single-issue terrorist groups include animal rights activists and environmentalists. While many people may have sympathies with these issues, it is those that use extreme violence that create the terrorist threat. In England, animal rights activists virtually brought the fur industry to a halt by setting animals free, burning stores that sold furs, and attacking those wearing furs (Dyson, 2012). In the United States, the Earth Liberation Front, an environmental terrorist group, credits itself with causing $55 million dollars in damage to sport utility vehicles and the destruction of $7 million dollars worth of luxury homes (Ohtake, 2008).

Organized domestic terrorist groups may be radicals on the political right or left and may be religious fanatics. Some of the more "famous" organized domestic terrorist groups include the following:

The Ku Klux Klan (KKK)—From the end of the Civil War to the end of the civil rights movement, the KKK remained one of the most active domestic terrorist groups in the United States.

The Weathermen—A radical-left organization active between 1969 and 1975, the group referred to themselves as the "revolutionary organization of communist women and men." Their mission was simply to overthrow the United States government and change the policy in Vietnam. The group was responsible for several bombings, including the Pentagon. The group ended shortly after the end of the Vietnam War.

The Jewish Defense League (JDL)—Formed in 1969 by Rabbi Meir Kahane in New York, its mission is to protect Jews from harassment and anti-Semitism. Between 1980 and 1985, the JDL attempted 15 terrorist attacks inside the United States.

The Symbionese Liberation Army (SLA)—A radical-left urban guerilla warfare group that considered itself a revolutionary vanguard army, the SLA robbed banks, and committed two murders and various other forms of violence between 1973 and 1975. Their most noted act was the kidnapping of Patricia Hearst.

The Army of God—A loose network of individuals and other groups opposed to abortion. During the mid-1990s when antiabortion violence was increasing, Eric Rudolph bombed two abortion clinics, a gay nightclub, and the 1996 Olympics in Atlanta.

The Animal Liberation Front—A group committed to liberating animals from laboratories and fur farms. While the group is not known to have caused harm to human life, the group is classified by the DHS as a terrorist organization.

The Black Liberation Army (BLA)—A splinter group made up of the more radical members of the Black Panther Party, the BLA was most active between 1970 and 1981. Its mission was to overthrow the United States government. The BLA is credited with the murders of 13 police officers and more than 60 acts of violence.

The Aryan Nations—Loosely organized in Idaho during the 1980s, they have committed bank robberies through a splinter group, the Aryan Republican Army, to finance domestic terrorist acts. They are connected to other hate groups such as The Order and Christian Identity.

Some religious-based hate groups have aligned themselves with other groups having a shared enemy. The most obvious of these alliances has been the Aryan Nations and Islamic Jihadists. Both groups have targeted the Jews in terrorist activities and share a common enemy. As Borgeson and Valeri (2009) point out:

> *In response to the dying Christian Identity movement in America, Aryan Nations members began to develop a camaraderie with those who they felt had more "spine"—namely, Islamic Jihadists. As the Aryan Nations began to branch out in its religious denominations, members began to see that they shared similar group characteristics: analogous moral values, perceived media persecution, and hatred for the United States government (p. 79).*

Domestic terrorism did not receive much attention from the public until the Oklahoma City Murrah Federal Building bombing. The bombing was the deadliest terrorist attack on American soil perpetuated by an American citizen. While some security measures were taken as a result, the interest in domestic terrorism died until the 9/11 attacks. With the 9/11 attack, increased focus on immigrants and foreigners resulted in the Patriot Act and the Homeland Security Act of 2002. Domestic terrorism is still not perceived as a major threat by many Americans (Costanza, Kilburn, & Helms, 2009).

Foreign Terrorism

Foreign terrorist attacks on the United States have generally been religious based. Middle Eastern extremists are usually driven by both religion and politics. Their view of the United States as an immoral and evil country, and their extremist religious viewpoint that it is their duty to kill or convert "infidels" gives them their reason to use terrorist tactics against Americans. The two worst attacks of foreign terrorism on American soil were the World Trade Center bombing in 1993 and the coordinated aircraft hijackings that resulted in the attacks of September 11, 2001. Since September 11, 2001, there have been several thwarted attempts by foreign extremists to commit terrorist acts on American soil. The recent Fort Hood, Texas, shootings by an American United States army major may have been supported and encouraged by foreign Islamic extremists (Youssef, 2010).

The FBI (Freeh, 2001) divides the foreign terrorist threat into three categories:

1. Foreign sponsors of international terrorism. Currently, there are seven countries that sponsor, support, and/or fund terrorist groups and extremists. Iran, Iraq, Syria, Sudan, Libya, Cuba, and North Korea fund, organize, network, and provide support to formal terrorist groups.
2. Formalized terrorist groups. These are terrorist groups that have an organized infrastructure, training facilities, and financial backing. The Taliban, al Qaeda, Hezbollah, Al-Gama's Al-Islamiyya, and HAMAS are examples of formalized terrorist groups.

3. Loosely affiliated international radical extremists. These may be unorganized groups or even individuals who take it upon themselves to make a terrorist attack. An example would be those who bombed the World Trade Center in 1993. A more recent example is Umar Farouk Abdulmutallab who attempted to ignite an explosive device on a Northwest Airlines plane on Christmas Day in 2009. While Abdulmutallab was known to have ties to terrorist groups, there was no evidence of his being formally trained by al Qaeda.

Loosely affiliated terrorist groups and individuals may pose the most serious threat to the United States due to the difficulty of law enforcement intelligence to identify these individuals. The Internet is being used increasingly to recruit and train home-grown terrorists (Weimann, 2006). While these "lone wolfs" may not inflict as much damage as the well-planned September 11 attacks, they are effective in creating chaos and fear. A Philadelphia woman, Colleen Renee LaRose, assumed the name Jihad Jane on the Internet and tried to recruit radicalized individuals to stage attacks in the United States and other countries in an effort to help Muslims. Also, there is mounting evidence that formalized terrorist groups from overseas are recruiting United States citizens as operatives. A failed bomb attempt on Times Square in New York City in the spring of 2010 was executed by Faisal Shahzad, a naturalized American citizen who was working for al Qaeda. Furthermore, formalized terrorist organizations tend to cooperate with each other. Hezbollah is known to maintain close ties with al Qaeda. There is also a growing concern that terrorists may use biological, neurological, and even nuclear weapons in an attack against the United States.

American Response to Terrorism

Traditionally, only federal law enforcement agencies, mainly the Federal Bureau of Investigation (FBI), took on the responsibility of investigating terrorist activities (Freeh, 2001). Local and state law enforcement were generally "kept out of the loop" in terms of intelligence gathering and sharing of information. Likewise, local and state law enforcement sometimes refused to share information regarding terrorist group activities with each other and with federal law enforcement. The terrorist attacks of September 11, 2001 made both local and federal authorities keenly aware of the need for sharing information and intelligence on terrorist group activities.

In response to September 11, 2001, the Department of Homeland Security was established by President George Bush as a cabinet-level department. The DHS is responsible for coordinating some 22 previously separate agencies to protect the United States against terrorist attacks. It is the largest cabinet-level department in the federal government, with over 180,000 employees (Department of Homeland Security, 2010). A number of agencies originally under the U.S. Treasury department were moved under the DHS. These included the Federal Law Enforcement Training Center; Customs, Border Patrol, Immigration and Naturalization; Secret Service; and Coast Guard (see Figure 16.2, organizational chart of the DHS). The movement of these agencies from Treasury to DHS created many organizational and administrative difficulties. Foremost among these difficulties was the restatement of agency goals, responsibilities,

U.S. DEPARTMENT OF HOMELAND SECURITY

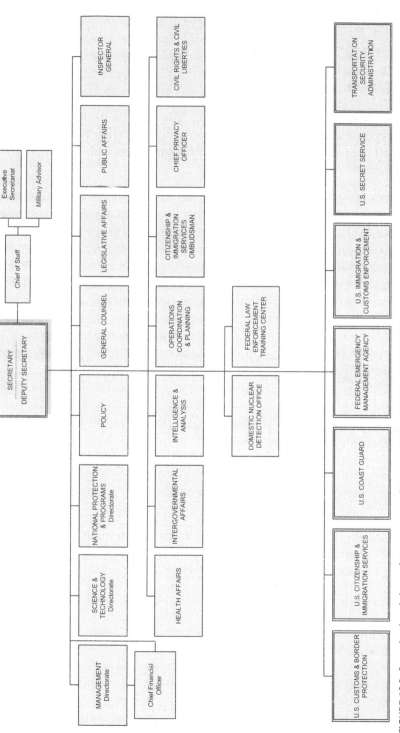

FIGURE 16.2 Organizational chart of Department of Homeland Security (April 10, 2013).

and operational procedures (Perrow, 2006). In addition, the integration of newly formed agencies, such as the Transportation Security Administration under the DHS, has made the development of common goals and objectives a slowly evolving process.

The major responsibility of the DHS is to coordinate the efforts of federal, state, and local law enforcement and emergency response agencies to prevent and respond to terrorist and natural disaster incidents. To address this effort, the DHS established the National Infrastructure Protection Plan (NIPP) in 2002. The NIPP is designed to coordinate terrorist threat and response efforts among federal, state, and local authorities. The plan consists of six steps designed to protect physical, cyber, and human assets within the nation's infrastructure and key resources:

1. Establish security goals or performance targets that constitute a protective posture.
2. Identify assets, systems, networks, and functions within and outside the United States that require a level of protection.
3. Assess risks in terms of a direct or indirect attack on particular assets and the probability that a target will be attacked.
4. Establish priorities in terms of risk and levels of current protection and mitigation systems.
5. Implement protective programs for those high priority assets, especially those that currently have low levels of protection.
6. Measure effectiveness in terms of progress toward hardening assets and preventing attacks (Department of Homeland Security, 2009, p. 30).

In order to facilitate and implement the six-step plan of the NIPP, the federal government, under the Bush administration, provided billions of dollars to pay for the operation. The plan provided $3.5 billion dollars to first responders, such as law enforcement, firefighters, and emergency medical personnel for training, equipment, and local counterterrorism training. Approximately $11 billion dollars were dedicated to enhanced border security, and $6 billion dollars were devoted to defending the country against bioterrorism threats. Nearly $1 billion dollars were provided to improve the federal government's ability to gather and share intelligence with other federal, state, and local agencies (Department of Homeland Security, 2010).

The FBI also made significant changes to responding to terrorism following 9/11. The bureau created the Office of Intelligence to focus on increasing intelligence and analysis related to terrorism. It also created the Counterterrorism Watch (CT Watch) to help prevent terrorist attacks. The CT Watch is a global command center that constantly reviews and analyzes potential terrorist threats. It also provides daily reports to the president and other national security policy makers (Federal Bureau of Investigation, 2010).

Local Response to Terrorism

Local police are typically the first responders to a terrorist attack. Clearly, a primary goal of the DHS and the FBI is to help train, equip, provide intelligence, and support local law enforcement in preventing and responding to terrorist attacks. Also, local law enforcement may be the first to receive information from citizens regarding potential terrorist threats. A study conducted in Phoenix, Arizona, reported that 95 percent of residents were likely to report suspected terrorist activity to local police (Schnebly, Ballance, & Katz, 2006). However, another study by the National Crime Prevention Council (2002) indicates that a majority of local law enforcement agencies have made little or no changes in preparation for a terrorist attack. The National Crime Prevention Council survey further found that the biggest barrier for local police to become more effective in their response to terrorism was politics and turf battles with state and federal agencies.

September 11, 2001 served as a wake-up call to the nation's law enforcement community. No longer was foreign terrorism a federal law enforcement problem. Immediately following 9/11, there were shifts in responsibilities and organizational structures in the law enforcement community. New roles for state and local law enforcement emerged, including:

1. Coordinating homeland security at state and local levels.
2. Collecting, analyzing, and sharing critical information and intelligence.
3. Protecting critical infrastructure and key assets.
4. Securing the nation's borders, air, and sea ports.
5. Collaborating with federal, state, and local law enforcement agencies on taskforces.
6. Preparing for new response equipment, tactics, systems, and training (U.S. Department of Justice, 2005).

There has long been a tradition of turf disputes between local police and federal law enforcement. Local police resent it when they do all the work on a case only to have it taken over by federal law enforcement, which receives the credit for the investigation. Understandably, local police are wary of cooperating with and sharing information with federal authorities in cases involving potential terrorist threats. But this, too, is changing for local law enforcement. According to the 9/11 Commission Report, "the concern with the FBI is that it has long favored its criminal justice mission over its national security mission" (National Commission on Terrorist Attacks, 2005, p. 390). In 2002, the FBI reorganized and reshaped its missions to reflect a new number one priority, "protecting the United States from terrorist attacks" (Federal Bureau of Investigation, 2003). The FBI has now become more selective in what criminal cases it becomes involved in, leaving state and local law enforcement a greater role in investigating and prosecuting financial crimes, bank robbery, drug trafficking, and organized crime (U.S. Department of Justice, 2005).

Many police administrators complain that federal law enforcement, and the DHS in particular, do not share vital intelligence information with local police. Local police claim that they need intelligence from federal authorities in order to ensure the safety of residents and to be effective as first responders to a terrorist attack. Federal authorities fear that sharing high-level intelligence with local police might lead to misuse or leaks to the public (Block, 2006).

There is some debate whether terrorist intelligence gathering should be a function of federal law enforcement or one of local law enforcement (Thacher, 2005). Logically, it should be a function of both. Many larger local police departments have increased their intelligence-gathering capabilities to meet the terrorist threat. Many of these larger departments already had intelligence-gathering mechanisms in place dealing with organized crime, narcotics, gangs, and hate groups. It is well known that many terrorist groups obtain funding through illegal narcotics trafficking (Kleiman, 2004; McCaffrey & Basso, 2003). It would be reasonable that local police could enhance their intelligence-gathering capabilities to include terrorist threats. This would require expanding community-based efforts to educate and rely more on citizens to keep a watchful eye out for possible terrorist activities and to report such activities to the police. Such an expansion would complement community-based policing and crime prevention efforts already in place in most local police agencies.

Information Versus Intelligence

There may be some confusion over the use of the terms "information" and "intelligence" (Figure 16.3). Intelligence is sometimes viewed erroneously as pieces of information about people, places, and events that can be used to provide insight about criminal threats. Pieces of information gathered from diverse sources (i.e., wiretaps, informants, surveillance) are simply raw data, which frequently have limited inherent meaning (Carter, 2004). Intelligence is when a wide array of raw information is assessed for validity, reliability, and materiality to the issues in question and subjected to inductive and deductive reasoning. In other words, intelligence is the product of an analysis process that provides an integrative perspective to disparate

Information	Intelligence
Criminal histories, driving records	Conclusions drawn about a person's criminality
Offense and incident reports	Crime and terrorist trends, characteristics of offenders, probable targets
Statements from informants, witnesses, suspects	Using past experiences to draw conclusions and make forecasts on criminal and terrorist activities
Motor vehicle registrations, boat and aircraft records	Estimates of income from crime and terrorist activities based on market and trafficking analysis
Leases, rentals of motor vehicles	
License applications, vehicles, professional services	
Information from surveillance sites	
Banking, credit, financial information	
Travel information, names, dates, destinations	

FIGURE 16.3 Comparative examples of information and intelligence. *Source: Adapted from Carter, D. (2004).*

Traditional Law Enforcement Data	Nontraditional Law Enforcement Data
Calls for service	Financial/credit records
Offense reports	Pawn information
Modus operandi information	Census information
Arrest reports	Student truancy data
Property	Tax and license information
Field interview information	Home ownership information
Citations	Public housing
Accidents	Drug court information
Traffic stops	Liquor licenses
Domestic violence	Geographic data (aerial, floor plans, utilities)
Hate crimes	
Citizen tips	
Confidential informant information	

FIGURE 16.4 Data types to assist in examining potential terrorist threats. *Source: U.S. Department of Justice (2002b). Local Law Enforcement Responds to Terrorism. Washington, DC: Office of Community Oriented Policing Services, p. 4.*

information about crime, crime trends, security threats, and conditions associated with criminality. The International Association of Chiefs of Police (2002) defines intelligence as "the combination of credible information with quality analysis-information that has been evaluated and from which conclusions have been drawn" (p. v).

Several local law enforcement agencies have initiated a data analysis system in which both traditional and nontraditional law enforcement data are used for a more in-depth analysis of crime problems (U.S. Department of Justice, 2002b). These data are collected and used for both incident level and aggregate level analyses. Incident level analysis is important as it can be analyzed at different levels of geographic locations (i.e., address, patrol zone, census tract, reporting district, and city). Nontraditional law enforcement data may be combined with traditional police data analysis systems to provide a higher level of terrorist threat analysis (see Figure 16.4). For example, a police department may include in its data analysis system tax and license information on pharmaceutical, farm supply, chemical, and other local businesses that may be targeted for theft or sabotage by a terrorist group or individual. Purchases of hazardous materials as well as thefts may be tracked using this combined system.

The need for local police to educate citizens and encourage reporting of suspicious activities has always been a part of crime prevention and community-based policing efforts. Expanding these efforts to potential terrorist attacks could lead to fruitful intelligence and even prevent a terrorist incident. For example, it was a clerk in a photography store that alerted police to the planned attack by terrorists on Fort Dix, New Jersey, in 2007. The clerk had received a video tape to copy onto DVD. When the clerk noticed that the video contained footage of terrorists training for their attack, the clerk notified police and FBI, resulting in the prevention of the attack and arrest of the terrorists.

Several local and state law enforcement agencies have partnered with the FBI to form terrorist early warning teams called fusion centers (Sullivan, 2006). Fusion centers provide for collaboration and coordination of all emergency response departments within a given metropolitan area. Intelligence information from both federal and local law enforcement is collected and analyzed at the fusion center and disseminated to those emergency personnel involved in first response to a terrorist attack.

Many local police departments are now equipped with mobile computer terminals in police vehicles. These mobile terminals can link directly to the National Crime Information Center (NCIC) and with the Terrorist Screening Center (TSC). The TSC maintains a database of "sensitive" but "unclassified" information that is available to local law enforcement during on-scene traffic stops. If a local police officer makes a traffic stop of a suspect, the officer enters the suspect's information into the mobile terminal to NCIC. If a "hit" is made on a suspected terrorist, the officer is advised to approach with caution and phone the TSC immediately. Once the officer phones the TSC, the officer is directed to arrest, detain for questioning, or obtain information from the suspect. Through the Terrorist Screening Operations Unit, local officers also have access to a wide range of information sources from the federal government, including "no-fly" lists, passport and visa information, and border inspection data.

Identifying Potential Terrorist Targets

One of the major functions of local law enforcement is to identify potential targets of a terrorist attack. This involves not only identifying critical infrastructure assets, such as industrial areas, dams, shopping malls, medical facilities, schools, and mass transportation centers, but also transient targets. Transient targets would include any function that may attract large crowds of people on a temporary basis, such as sporting events, festivals, fairs, and carnivals. Once identified, plans can be developed for each location in the event of a terrorist attack. In addition, identifying these potential targets allows for increased surveillance through employees, camera monitoring, and private security personnel. Terrorist attacks are generally not random but are planned events with reconnaissance activities being conducted by the terrorists days and weeks before the actual attack. Surveillance of potential targets may help identify these reconnaissance activities and prevent an attack. Suspicious activity around potential target areas should also be reported to state and local fusion centers so that the activity can be documented, shared, and analyzed. Such information may be included in the Information Sharing Environment and Suspicious Activity Reporting (SAR) system. The Nationwide SAR Initiative (NSI) is an outgrowth of several separate but related intelligence-gathering activities designed to coordinate all SAR-related activities into a unified national SAR capability. The NSI strategy is to develop, evaluate, and implement common processes and policies of gathering, documenting, processing, analyzing, and sharing information about terrorist-related suspicious activities. It allows for the adoption of consistent policies and procedures for sharing of information between law enforcement agencies while ensuring that privacy and civil liberties are protected (U.S. Department of Justice, 2010).

Developing contingency plans is a critical aspect of homeland defense (Pelfrey, 2005). However, many local police departments do not have adequate plans in place in the event of a terrorist attack. Those that do have plans may not have adequate plans. As Donahue and Tuohy (2006) point out, plans may fail due to uncoordinated leadership, lack of communication between responding agencies, and lack of resources. Also, local police may fail to coordinate efforts with private security personnel at potential target locations (Ohlhausen Research, Inc., 2004). Private security personnel at shopping malls, industries, schools, and medical facilities should be included in any contingency planning efforts by local police (Gaines & Kappeler, 2011).

Police Supervisor's Role

The first-line police supervisor has three primary responsibilities to deal with the terrorist threat: safety, information, and effective first response. The first responsibility of the police supervisor is safety of the public and subordinate officers. Calls for service that involve suspicious persons, vehicles, and packages cannot be taken lightly, particularly in areas that have been identified as possible terrorist targets or in areas where large numbers of people are gathered. The supervisor should also be aware of potential terrorist threats in seemingly routine police calls for service. Garrett (2002) notes there are five types of situations in which police officers may be vulnerable to terrorist attack:

1. Routine traffic stops. A police officer may unknowingly stop a radicalized terrorist for a moving violation or suspicious activity.
2. Routine domestic disturbance and residence calls. Officers may respond unknowingly to a terrorist's residence and find themselves faced with heavily armed and dangerous individuals.
3. Public rallies and marches. While the danger may not come from the organization holding an event, protestors and radicals may incite violence and attack officers present.
4. Confrontations and standoffs. These may be the result of any of the previously mentioned threats, but can also be a hostage situation (U.S. Department of Justice, 2002a).
5. Revenge and retaliation. A terrorist may target a police department headquarters, government offices, financial institutions, or individuals. In February 2010, Joseph Stack flew his single-engine plane into the Internal Revenue Service building in Austin, Texas. Stack's motivation for the attack was revenge and retaliation.

The police supervisor should stress the importance of observation and caution to subordinate officers when responding to seemingly routine calls for service.

Police patrol officers and first-line supervisors are likely to be the first recipients of potentially important information regarding terrorist activities. The information may come from astute citizens, public utility workers, postal workers, delivery companies, retail business clerks, or others who may notice something out of the ordinary. For example, a hardware store clerk may report the purchase of large quantities of drain clog removal chemicals, bleach, and other chemical cleaning items that could be used to make bombs. The information should not be dismissed as mischievous teenagers making backyard explosives. In the hands of a terrorist, these types of explosives could create panic and trampling deaths in crowded locations. The police supervisor should stress to subordinates that information is crucial to preventing terrorist attacks. It is also the supervisor's responsibility to pass on information to superiors and other agencies as departmental policy dictates.

In the event of a terrorist attack, the police will be among the first responders to the scene. Other emergency personnel will include firefighters, emergency medical personnel, and other disaster response agencies. It will most likely be the police's responsibility to coordinate the efforts of these other emergency responders. Proper coordination would depend on the nature of the attack. An explosion would require the immediate presence of hazardous materials personnel (HazMat) and firefighting personnel, whereas a biological threat may require specialized medical personnel for immediate response. Again, planning for a possible terrorist attack is crucial for an effective police response. The Federal Emergency Management Agency has provided some training and guidelines for local law enforcement response to a terrorist attack:

1. Secure the scene and establish a perimeter.
2. Assist with establishment of a command center.
3. Assist with placement of emergency vehicles and personnel upon arrival at the scene.
4. Evaluate the scene safety and identify any secondary threats.
5. Detain witnesses and obtain statements.
6. Identify resources needed and make appropriate notifications.
7. Control traffic and initiate evacuation procedures if needed.
8. Use appropriate self-protection gear.
9. Assist with the removal of the injured and with the location of injured persons.
10. Work as a team with other law enforcement agencies, medical personnel, firefighting personnel, public utilities, and other emergency agencies (U.S. Department of Justice, 1999).

In addition, the Office of Domestic Preparedness (U.S. Department of Justice, 2002a) has prepared guidelines for police, firefighters, emergency medical personnel, public works personnel, HazMat personnel, and emergency management personnel on first responder responsibilities at the awareness, performance, and planning/management levels (see Figure 16.5). The success of this type of awareness was evidenced in 2010 in New York City when a Times Square bomb attempt failed due to the observance and vigilance of street vendors and a mounted NYPD officer.

I. **Recognize hazardous materials incidents.** The law enforcement officer should

   a.   Understand what hazardous materials are, as well as the risks associated with these materials in an emergency incident or event.

   b.   Identify if hazardous materials are present in an emergency incident or event.

   c.   Know how to use the *North American Emergency Response Guidebook* (NAERG) published by the U.S. Department of Transportation.

   d.   Use the NAERG (or other available resources) to identify the hazardous material.

   e.   Understand the potential outcomes or consequences of an emergency due to the presence of hazardous materials.

II. **Know the protocols used to detect the potential presence of weapons of mass destruction (WMD) agents or materials.** The law enforcement officer should:

   a.   Understand what WMD agents or materials are and the risks associated with these materials in an emergency incident or event.

   b.   Know the indicators and effects of WMD on individuals and property. Be able to recognize signs and symptoms common to initial victims of a WMD-related incident or event. Know the physical characteristics or properties of WMD agents or materials that could be reported by victims or other persons at the scene.

   c.   Be familiar with the potential use and means of delivery of WMD agents or materials.

   d.   Know locations or properties that could become targets for persons using WMD agents or materials.

   e.   Recognize unusual trends or characteristics that might indicate an incident or event involving WMD agents or materials.

III. **Know and follow self-protection measures for WMD events and hazardous materials events.** The law enforcement officer should:

   a.   Understand the hazards and risks to individuals and property associated with WMD agents and hazardous materials. Recognize the signs and symptoms of exposure to WMD agents and hazardous materials.

   b.   Know how to use, inspect, and properly maintain the personal protective equipment issued to the officer. Understand the limitations of this equipment in protecting someone exposed to WMD agents or hazardous materials.

   c.   Understand that ambulatory victims should move upwind and upgrade from the area. Know that potentially contaminated victims should be isolated from others. These victims should be advised about appropriate actions to take and that they may need to be decontaminated. Minimize contamination of adjacent areas.

FIGURE 16.5 Awareness level guidelines for law enforcement officers.

d. Understand the role of the first responder as well as other levels of response in the department's emergency response plan.

e. Be familiar with his/her agency's emergency response plan and procedures. Understand the individual officers' role in those procedures.

f. Know what defensive measures to take during a WMD or hazardous materials incident or event to help ensure personal and community safety. These measures may include maximizing the distance between the officer and hot zone, using shielding such as solid walls for protection, minimizing personal exposure time to agents or materials that might be found in the warm zone or within the plume, and moving upgrade and upwind.

IV. **Know procedures for protecting a potential crime scene.** The law enforcement officer should:

a. Understand and implement procedures for protecting evidence and minimizing disturbance of the potential crime scene while protecting others. Understand the roles, responsibilities, and jurisdictions of federal agencies related to a WMD event or incident.

b. Recognize the importance of crime scene preservation and initiate measures to secure the scene.

c. Protect physical evidence such as footprints, relevant containers, or wrapping paper.

d. Advise witnesses and bystanders who may have information to remain at the scene in a safe location until they have been interviewed and released. Be aware of people arriving or departing the scene. Note license plate numbers or other relevant data. Question the caller, witness(es), or victim(s) to obtain critical information regarding the incident or event. Such questions include "Where is the package, and what does it contain?" "Does the package have an unusual odor or smell?" "Has the package been disturbed?" "Have there been any threats received before receipt of the package" "Does the package contain a written threat, and if so, what does it say?"

FIGURE 16.5 (Continued)

References

Block, R. (2006). Big-city police chiefs assail homeland security's secrecy. *Wall Street Journal Online*, B1. (June 30).

Borgeson, K., & Valeri, R. (2009). *Enemy of my enemy*. In K. Borgeson & R. Valeri (Eds.), *Terrorism in America*. Boston, MA: Jones and Bartlett.

Carter, D. (2004). *Law enforcement intelligence: A guide for state, local, and tribal law enforcement agencies.* Washington, DC: Office of Community Oriented Policing Services.

Costanza, S. E., Kilburn, J. C., & Helms, R. (2009). "Counterterrorism". In K. Borgeson & R. Valeri (Eds.), *Terrorism in America*. Boston, MA: Jones and Bartlett.

Department of Homeland Security (2009). *National infrastructure protection plan*. Washington, DC: DHS.

Department of Homeland Security (2010). <http://www.dhs.gov/index.shtm>, April 22, 2010.

Donahue, A., & Tuohy, R. (2006). Lessons we don't learn: A study of the lessons of disasters, why we repeat them, and how we can learn from them. *Homeland Security Affairs, 2*(2), 1–28.

Dyson, W. E. (2012). *Terrorism: An investigator's handbook* (4th ed.). Boston: Elsevier (Anderson Publishing).

Federal Bureau of Investigation (2003). Facts and figures available at: <http://www.fbi.gov/priorities>.

Federal Bureau of Investigation (2010). <http://www.fbi.gov/terrorinfo/counterrorism/waronterrorhome.htm>.

Freeh, L. (2001). Threat of terrorism on the United States. In Testimony of Louis J. Freeh, Director, FBI, before the United States Senate, Committees on Appropriations, Armed Services, and Select Committee on Intelligence. May 10, 2001.

Gaines, L., & Kappeler, V. (2011). *Policing in America*. Boston: Elsevier (Anderson Publishing).

Garrett, K. (2002). Terrorism on the homefront. *Law Enforcement Technology*, 22–26. (July).

Hewitt, C. (2003). *Understanding terrorism in America*. New York: Routledge.

International Association of Chiefs of Police, (2002). *Criminal intelligence sharing: A national plan for intelligence-led policing at the federal, state and local levels*. Alexandria, VA: IACP.

Kleiman, M. (2004). *Illicit drugs and the terrorist threat: Causal links and implications for domestic drug control policy*. Washington, DC: Congressional Research Service.

McCaffrey, B., & Basso, J. (2003). Narcotics, terrorism, and international crime: The convergence phenomenon. In R. Howard & R. Sawyer (Eds.), *Terrorism and counterterrorism: Understanding the new security environment*. Guilford, CT: Dushkin.

National Commission on Terrorist Attacks (2005). *The 9-11 commission report*. Washington, DC: U.S. Government Printing Office.

National Crime Prevention Council (2002). *Building the homeland security network: What will it take?* Washington, DC: National Crime Prevention Council.

Ohlhausen Research, Inc. (2004). *Private security/public policing: Vital issues and policy recommendations*. Alexandria, VA: International Association of Chiefs of Police.

Ohtake, M. (2008). From green to black. *Newsweek* March 6.

Pelfrey, W. V., Sr. (2005). The cycle of preparedness: Establishing a framework to prepare for terrorist threats. *Journal of Homeland Security and Emergency Management, 2*(1), 1–21.

Perrow, C. (2006). The disaster after 9/11: The Department of Homeland Security and the intelligence reorganization. *Homeland Security Affairs, 2*(1), 1–32.

Schnebly, S., Ballance, S., & Katz, C. (2006). *Data sharing between the police and the public: Citizens' needs for information on neighborhood crime, terrorism, and public emergency planning and response*. Phoenix: Arizona State University.

Sullivan, J. (2006). Terrorism early warning groups: Regional intelligence to combat terrorism. In R. Howard, J. Forest, & J. Moore (Eds.), *Homeland security and terrorism*. New York: McGraw-Hill.

Thacher, D. (2005). The local role in homeland security. *Law & Society Review, 39*, 635–676.

U.S. Department of Justice (1993). *Terrorism in the United States, 1982–1992*. Washington, DC: Federal Bureau of Investigation.

U.S. Department of Justice (1999). *Emergency response to terrorism: Self-study*. Washington, DC: Federal Emergency Management Agency.

U.S. Department of Justice (2002a). *Emergency response guidelines*. Washington, DC: Office of Domestic Preparedness.

U.S. Department of Justice (2002b). *Local law enforcement responds to terrorism*. Washington, DC: Office of Community Oriented Policing Services.

U.S. Department of Justice (2005). *The impact of terrorism on state law enforcement.* Washington, DC: National Institute of Justice.

U.S. Department of Justice (2010). *Final report: Information Sharing Environment (ISE)—Suspicious Activity Reporting (SAR) evaluation environment.* Washington, DC: Bureau of Justice Assistance.

Weimann, G. (2006). *Terror on the Internet: The New Arena, the new challenges.* Dulles, VA: Potomac Books, Inc.

Youssef, N. (2010). Fort Hood shooting probe slams Pentagon policies. *The Kansas City Star*, April 15.

Name Index

Note: Page numbers followed by *"f"* refers to figures.

Subject Index

Note: Page numbers followed by *"f"* and *"b"* refers to figures and boxes, respectively.